REPORT OF THE COMMISSION ON GOVERNMENT SECURITY

A Da Capo Press Reprint Series

CIVIL LIBERTIES IN AMERICAN HISTORY

GENERAL EDITOR: LEONARD W. LEVY
Claremont Graduate School

REPORT OF THE COMMISSION ON GOVERNMENT SECURITY

DA CAPO PRESS • NEW YORK • 1971

A Da Capo Press Reprint Edition

This Da Capo Press edition of
Report of the Commission on Government Security
is an unabridged republication of the 1957
edition published by the Government Printing
Office, Washington, D.C.

Library of Congress Catalog Card Number 79-152788

SBN 306-70146-4

Published by Da Capo Press, Inc.
A Subsidiary of Plenum Publishing Corporation
227 West 17th Street, New York, N.Y. 10011

Manufactured in the United States of America

REPORT OF THE COMMISSION ON GOVERNMENT SECURITY

REPORT

of the

COMMISSION ON GOVERNMENT SECURITY

PURSUANT TO PUBLIC LAW 304
84TH CONGRESS, AS AMENDED

Commission on Government Security

Loyd Wright, *California, Chairman*
John Stennis, *Mississippi, Vice Chairman*

Norris Cotton, *New Hampshire*
F. Moran McConihe, *Maryland*
William M. McCulloch, *Ohio*
James P. McGranery, *Pennsylvania*
Edwin L. Mechem, *New Mexico*

Franklin D. Murphy, *Kansas*
James L. Noel, Jr., *Texas*
Susan B. Riley, *Tennessee*
Louis S. Rothschild, *Missouri*
Francis H. Walter, *Pennsylvania*

STAFF

D. Milton Ladd
Administrative Director

Richard A. Edwards
Research Director

L. Dale Coffman
Chief Consultant

Douglas R. Price
Executive Secretary

Samuel H. Liberman
General Counsel

Stanley J. Tracy
Project Surveys

CONSULTANTS

Lawrence G. Blochman
Richard E. Combs

John Stewart Newlin
Harry B. Reese

On Loan From Other Government Agencies

John C. Herberg
Office of the Legislative Counsel, U. S. Senate

Arthur A. Sharp
Government Printing Office

ii

Appointments to the Commission

By the President of the United States

The Honorable F. MORAN McCONIHE,[1] Rockville, Md.
Commissioner, Public Buildings Service
General Services Administration

DR. FRANKLIN D. MURPHY, Lawrence, Kans.
Chancellor, University of Kansas

The Honorable LOUIS S. ROTHSCHILD, Kansas City, Mo.
Under Secretary, Department of Commerce

The Honorable JAMES P. McGRANERY, Philadelphia, Pa., and
Washington, D. C.
Attorney at Law

By the President of the Senate

The Honorable NORRIS COTTON, Lebanon, N. H.
United States Senator

DR. SUSAN B. RILEY, Nashville, Tenn.
Professor of English, George Peabody College for Teachers

The Honorable JOHN STENNIS, DeKalb, Miss.
United States Senator

The Honorable LOYD WRIGHT, Los Angeles, Calif.
Attorney at Law

By the Speaker of the House of Representatives

The Honorable WILLIAM M. McCULLOCH, Piqua, Ohio
Member, U. S. House of Representatives

The Honorable JAMES L. NOEL, JR., Houston, Tex.
Attorney at Law

The Honorable FRANCIS E. WALTER, Easton, Pa.
Member, U. S. House of Representatives

The Honorable EDWIN L. MECHEM, Sante Fe, N. Mex.
Governor of New Mexico

---

[1] Appointed by the President on February 1, 1957, to complete the unexpired term
of office of Carter L. Burgess, former Assistant Secretary of the Department of Defense,

Subcommittees of the Commission

At its meeting on June 18, 1956, the Commission formed four subcommittees, which were to become operative in October 1956.

The purpose in creating subcommittees was to provide an opportunity for each of the Commissioners to give special attention and study to specific segments of the Commission responsibility, thereby expediting the preparation of recommendations to the President and the Congress.

Subcommittee I, on Personnel and Military Security, originally consisted of Congressman Walter, as chairman, and Dr. Murphy and Secretary Burgess, as members. Commissioner McConihe succeeded Secretary Burgess as a member of the Commission and of the subcommittee on February 1, 1957.

Subcommittee II, on Industrial Security and Atomic Security, consisted of Governor Mechem, as chairman, and Dr. Riley and Mr. Noel, as members.

Subcommittee III, on Legislation and Classification of Documents, consisted of General McGranery, as chairman, and Senators Cotton and Stennis, as members.

Subcommittee IV, on Immigration, Passports, International Organizations, Airport Security, and Port Security, consisted of Secretary Rothschild, as chairman, and Dr. Riley and Congressman McCulloch, as members.

The chairman of the Commission was ex officio a member of each subcommittee.

Within the resident staff of the Commission, each of the four subcommittees formed its own staff consisting of a chairman and one representative each from the survey division, research division, and the office of the general counsel. All materials submitted to the Commissioners were provided through the appropriate subcommttee staff, which in each instance suggested alternative courses of action for the supervisory staff, composed of the executive director, the general counsel, the director of the survey division, the director of the research division, and the chief consultant. The supervisory staff submitted its recommendations to the several subcommittees mentioned above.

The subcommittees met at intervals of 4 to 8 weeks for the purpose of adopting, rejecting, or modifying the supervisory staff recommendations. Subcommittee recommendations were then submitted to meetings of the full Commission, convening when necessary to dispose of the previous subcommittee actions.

Citizens Advisory Committee

As the work of the Commission progressed, it became increasingly apparent that an enormous benefit would be derived from the views of private citizens who had attained positions of eminence in their respective fields of activity, and who were experienced in many of the problems that confronted the Commission.

Invitations were accordingly extended to a distinguished group of men and women to serve as members of a citizens advisory committee to the Commission. Many outstanding Americans accepted the invitation and, despite heavy schedules, agreed to serve on the advisory committee and to give the Commission the benefit of their views and advice.

The membership of the committee was drawn from all parts of the Nation, and comprised prominent educators, industrialists, clergymen, scientists, newspapermen, State officials, attorneys, jurists, and representatives from both labor and management.

A joint meeting of the Citizens Advisory Committee and the Commission on Government Security was held in Washington on May 20, 21, and 22, 1957. During each of the several sessions many aspects of the Commission's conclusions and recommendations were discussed. These conferences provided views that emanated from fresh, new perspectives, and contributed to the solution of many complex and challenging problems.

The Commission is grateful for the expert assistance and gracious cooperation of these distinguished Americans who so ably and conscientiously assisted the Commission out of a deep sense of public duty.

Members of the Citizens Advisory Committee were:

Mr. Frank R. Ahlgren
Editor
The Commercial Appeal
Memphis 1, Tenn.

Mrs. Olive Ann Beech*
President
Beech Aircraft Corporation
Wichita 1, Kans.

Dr. Helen D. Bragdon
General Director
American Association of University
    Women
1634 Eye Street, N. W.
Washington 6, D. C.

Hon. Carter L. Burgess*
President
Trans World Airlines, Inc.
380 Madison Avenue
New York 17, N. Y.

Mr. James P. Carey*
President
International Union of Electrical
    Radio and Machine Workers
1126 Sixteenth Street, N.W.
Washington 6, D. C.

Mr. Henry L. Clark
Regent of Loyola University
10940 Bellagio Road
Los Angeles 24, Calif.

* Prevented from attending by emergency matters.

MISS JACQUELINE COCHRAN
Aviatrix
Cochran-Odlum Ranch
Indio, Calif.

MR. W. C. DANIEL
National Commander of the
American Legion
Danville, Va.

DR. LEE A. DuBRIDGE
President
California Institute of Technology
Pasadena, Calif.

MR. ARTHUR ECKMAN
General Counsel
Christian Science Church Office
107 Falmouth Street
Boston 15, Mass.

IRVING FERMAN, Esq.
American Civil Liberties Union
412 Fifth Street, N. W.
Washington, D. C.

MR. LUIS A. FERRE
Vice President
Puerto Rican Iron Works
Ponce, Puerto Rico

MR. E. K. GAYLORD
Publisher
The Daily Oklahoman-Oklahoma
City Times
Oklahoma City, Okla.

RABBI NORMAN GERSTENFELD
Washington Hebrew Congregation
2329 California Street, N. W.
Washington, D. C.

MR. PAUL HANSEN
American Society for Industrial
Security
2500 South Third Street
Louisville 1, Ky.

DR. BEN HILBUN
President
Mississippi State College
State College, Miss.

MR. COOPER T. HOLT
Commander-in-Chief
Veterans of Foreign Wars of the
United States
Care of Mr. Julian Dickenson
V. F. W. Building, Broadway at
34th St.
Kansas City 11, Mo.

MR. EDWARD F. HOLTER
Lecturer of the National Grange
744 Jackson Place, N. W.
Washington, D. C.

NICHOLAS KELLEY, Esq.
Attorney
Kelley, Drye, Newhall and
Maginnes
70 Broadway
New York, N. Y.

MRS. JOHN G. LEE
President
League of Women Voters
1026 - 17th Street, N. W.
Washington 6, D. C.

ARTHUR C. LOGAN, M. D.
1865 Amsterdam Avenue
New York 31, N. Y.

MR. GEORGE MEANY †
President
AFL-CIO
815 - 16th Street, N. W.
Washington, D. C.

HON. J. L. MORRILL
President
University of Minnesota
Minneapolis 14, Minn.

DR. JOHN H. MORROW
Chairman, Department of Romance
Languages
North Carolina College
Durham, N. C.

DR. JOHN B. PHELPS
Physics Department
Sloane Laboratory
Yale University
217 Prospect Street
New Haven 11, Conn.

DEAN ROSCOE POUND
Law School of Harvard University
Langdell Hall
Cambridge 38, Mass.

MR. M. C. SCHINNERER
Superintendent of Schools
Board of Education
Cleveland, Ohio

MR. HAROLD V. SELL
Co-Publisher and Editor
The Register-Herald Company
111 East Israel Street
Eaton, Ohio

† Referred Commission to testimony previously given congressional committees.

Letter of Transmittal

COMMISSION ON GOVERNMENT SECURITY
WASHINGTON 25, D. C.

JUNE 21, 1957.

DEAR SIRS:

In conformity with the requirements of Public Law 304, 84th Congress, as amended by Public Law 786, 84th Congress, I have the honor to submit to the President and to the Congress the Report of the Commission on Government Security.

The report proposes such legislative enactments and administrative actions as, in the judgment of the Commission, are necessary to carry out its recommendations.

Respectfully,

Chairman.

The Honorable
The President of the United States
The Honorable
The President of the Senate
The Honorable
The Speaker of the House of Representatives

Foreword

The Commission on Government Security was established by Congress in 1955 to fill an urgent need for an objective, nonpolitical, and independent study of the innumerable laws, Executive orders, regulations, programs, practices, and procedures intended for the protection of the national security; to establish fair, uniform, effective, and realistic measures to safeguard both the national security and the rights of individuals; to obtain to the greatest practical uniformity; and to restore full public confidence in the Government's program to protect the national security. This was the mandate under which the Commission labored.

While the United States was militarily allied with the Soviet Union during World War II, the Kremlin rulers succeeded in creating the impression, unfortunately accepted by too many Americans, that they were our friends when in fact they still regarded the United States as an enemy, even while they were accepting our sacrifice of blood and treasure. The emotional involvements of the war, and the propaganda of the Soviets combined to retard our awakening to their implacable hostility, with the result that there was a tendency to react to isolated incidents and situations rather than to the unchanging, basic facts.

Between 1947 and 1955, there grew up a vast, intricate, confusing and costly complex of temporary, inadequate, uncoordinated programs and measures designed to protect secrets and installations vital to the defense of the Nation against agents of Soviet imperialism. The ceaseless campaign of the Soviet Union and international communism to infiltrate our Government, industry, and other vital areas and to subvert our citizenry for purposes of espionage and sabotage not only was threatening our military and industrial strength but was intended to impair our national economy.

As a result of congressional subcommittee hearings, which thoroughly reviewed and studied all phases of our security and loyalty programs, the Congress unanimously provided in Public Law 304, 84th Congress, as follows:

SECTION 1. It is vital to the welfare and safety of the United States that there be adequate protection of the national security, including the safeguarding of all national defense secrets and public and private defense installations, against loss or compromise arising from espionage, sabotage, disloyalty, subversive activities, or unauthorized disclosures.

It is therefore, the policy of the Congress that there shall exist a sound Government program—

(*a*) establishing procedures for security investigation, evaluation, and, where necessary, adjudication of Government employees, and also appropriate security requirements with respect to persons privately employed or occupied on work requiring access to national defense secrets or work affording significant opportunity for injury to the national security;

(*b*) for vigorous enforcement of effective and realistic security laws and regulations; and

(*c*) for a careful, consistent, and efficient administration of this policy in a manner which will protect the national security and preserve basic American rights.

.   .   .   .

Sec. 6. The Commission [on Government Security] shall study and investigate the entire Government Security Program, including the various statutes, Presidential orders, and administrative regulations and directives under which the Government seeks to protect the national security, national defense secrets, and public and private defense installations, against loss or injury arising from espionage, disloyalty, subversive activity, sabotage, or unauthorized disclosures, together with the actual manner in which such statutes, Presidential orders, administrative regulations, and directives have been and are being administered and implemented, with a view to determining whether existing requirements, practices, and procedures are in accordance with the policies set forth in the first section of this joint resolution, and to recommending such changes as it may determine are necessary or desirable. The Commission shall also consider and submit reports and recommendations on the adequacy or deficiencies of existing statutes, Presidential orders, administrative regulations, and directives, and the administration of such statutes, orders, regulations, and directives, from the standpoints of internal consistency of the overall security program and effective protection and maintenance of the national security.

After passage and approval of Public Law 304, on November 10, 1955, six persons from each of the two major political parties were selected by the President of the United States, the President of the Senate, and the Speaker of the House of Representatives to constitute a bipartisan Commission on Government Security.

At its first meeting, on December 14, 1955, the Commission elected Mr. Loyd Wright, a former president of the American Bar Association, Chairman, and the Honorable John Stennis, United States Senator from Mississippi, Vice Chairman. The Commission was sworn in on January 9, 1956.

After acquiring office space in the General Accounting Office building, the Commission began recruiting a staff for its challenging task. The chairman, with the approval of the Commission, selected the supervisory staff, consisting of an administrative director, a director of project surveys, a director of research, a general counsel, a chief consultant and an executive secretary.

The entire staff, carefully selected on a basis of personal integrity, unquestionable loyalty, and discretion, combined with appropriate experience and a record of devotion to duty in responsible positions, worked under the personal direction of the Chairman.

To avoid entanglement in public controversies, to maintain an objective and impartial approach to its work, the Commission held no public hearings and made no press releases or public statements reflecting its views or describing its activities.

The Commission, aided by Executive directive, was fortunate in obtaining a maximum of cooperation from all departments and agencies of the Government and is believed to have been the first organization of its kind to have direct access to confidential files and documents without reservation.

Hundreds of persons outside the Government also contributed freely and graciously of their time, skill, and knowledge, to the great benefit of the work.

Pursuant to the letter from the President of the United States to the heads of all executive departments and agencies, dated March 6, 1956, directing them to give the Commission every assistance possible within statutory limitations, each department and agency designated a member of its staff to act as a liaison officer to the Commission. Through them, a tremendous volume of useful information was obtained, including agency regulations, security instructions, case histories, statistics, and responses to hundreds of questions.

Some 1,500 letters were written to individuals and to labor, industrial, and other organizations having special interest in the Federal security programs soliciting information, advice, and suggestions. Representatives of the Commission conferred with officers of organized labor on the very complex problems in the area of industrial security seeking their views, suggestions, and recommendations. The Small Business Administration, asked to ascertain the opinions of small-business concerns throughout the Nation, sent a questionnaire to the 650 businessmen who act as advisers to its field offices and are able to speak for colleagues in their areas. The United States Chamber of Commerce, at the request of the Commission, obtained advice and suggestions from its large membership. The National Security Industrial Association, the American Society for Industrial Security, the Aircraft Industries Association, the Automobile Manufacturers Association, the Associated Industries of Massachusetts, and the Small Defense Industries Association, representing a total of 2,052 companies, furnished detailed reports and valuable conclusions concerning the industrial security programs and desirable changes. The New York City Bar Association and the American Jewish Congress made long and detailed recommendations. Hundreds of interviews were conducted throughout the country with persons in and out of the Federal Government who could furnish information and suggestions. Reports and transcripts of hearings prepared by congressional committees and subcommittees yielded a mass of invaluable data.

Full evaluation of past and present Federal loyalty-security programs by the Commission would have entailed the analysis of thousands of individual personnel actions covering at least 10 years. Such a study would have occupied the entire time of a large staff. Fortunately, the Civil Service Commission had been engaged in just such a task for some three and one-half years and by furnishing the complete results of its work saved the Commission on Government Security much tedious and unnecessary duplication and the taxpayers many thousands of dollars.

The staff of the Commission was functionally organized in three divisions. The survey division collected information, suggestions, and advice. To the research division was entrusted the task of analyzing the available material and preparing detailed papers for Commission consideration. All legal questions requiring interpretation of statutes, Executive orders, regulations, or court decisions were submitted to the office of the general counsel, the third staff division.

When subcommittees of the Commission were established, as detailed elsewhere in this report, representatives of each division were assigned to them.

In sifting, analyzing, correlating, and evaluating the tremendous volume of information, emphasis was placed upon original sources rather than on secondary literature, and the record, reliability, and firsthand experience of each source was considered.

At every step of collecting and digesting the data upon which this report is based, there was an awareness of the need for objectivity, of the importance of protecting both the national security and the rights and interests of individuals, and of the grave significance of the work delegated to the Commission by Congress. From the outset, the Commission and the staff were guided by the directives and policy formulated by Congress in Public Law 304, 84th Congress, as to the scope of their activities, their approach to the problems involved, and their recommendations for improvement.

The Commission wishes to express its deep appreciation to the thousands of public-spirited persons throughout the country, in and out of the Government, who, by their gracious cooperation, made possible the completion of its appointed task. The Commission is gratefully aware of the competent participation of all the anonymous employees who helped assemble the necessary information and statistics.

The report which follows concludes the first complete and detailed study of the subject matter ever undertaken in the history of the Nation.

In the firm knowledge that Americans are loyal and devoted to their country, the Commission has striven at every point to emphasize the protection and safeguarding of their rights and liberties equally with the need of protecting our national security from the disloyal few, even though it recognizes that the disloyal are dangerous and the Communist threat is both real and formidable.

Summary of Recommendations

The Commission's recommendations, if put into effect, would enhance the protection afforded national security while substantially increasing the protection of the individual.

The Commission recommends retention, with fundamental revisions, of the programs affecting Federal civilian and military personnel, industrial security, port security, employees of international organizations, the classification of documents, passport regulations, and the control of aliens. In addition, the Commission recommends an entirely new program to safeguard national security in the vital operations of our civil air transport system.

At the core of the Commission's plan for a uniform, comprehensive, and practical security mechanism is its recommendation for a Central Security Office to provide a continuous study of security needs and measures, conduct loyalty and security hearings, and furnish advisory decisions to heads of government departments and agencies.

And at the very basis of the Commission's thinking lies the separation of the loyalty problem from that of suitability and security. All loyalty cases are security cases, but the converse is not true. A man who talks too freely when in his cups, or a pervert who is vulnerable to blackmail, may both be security risks although both may be loyal Americans. The Commission recommends that as far as possible such cases be considered on a basis of suitability to safeguard the individual from an unjust stigma of disloyalty.

Some problems, such as the maintenance and use of the Attorney General's List, the right to subpena witnesses, and the extent to which the principle of confrontation is applicable in security cases, cut across the entire field of loyalty and security problems and are subjects of special recommendations.

CENTRAL SECURITY OFFICE.—The Commission recommends an independent Central Security Office in the executive branch of the Government. One of the principal deficiencies of past loyalty and security programs has been a shortage of trained, qualified personnel to administer them. Hence, the first duty of the director of the proposed central office would be to select eminently qualified personnel, including hearing examiners to conduct loyalty hearings under the Federal civilian employe program and security hearings under the industrial, atomic energy, port and civil air transport programs. The Central Security Office would also assist the various agencies, through consultations and conferences, in training screening and other security personnel. A Central Review Board would review cases, on the record, as appealed from adverse decisions of the heads of agencies. Decisions of both hearing examiners and the Central Review Board would be advisory only to agency heads. The various loyalty and security programs of the Government would be reviewed and inspected to insure uniformity of rules, regulations and procedures; however, the Central Security Office would not have authority to review secret or other files of any agency. Complaints from industry relating to the various industrial security programs would be received and, through conferences with industry and the interested Government agencies, inconsistencies and duplications would be corrected.

ATTORNEY GENERAL'S LIST.—The Commission believes that the Attorney General's list of proscribed organizations, or something similar to it, is essential to the administration of the Federal loyalty and security programs. While it therefore recommends continuance of the list, the Commission also recommends a number of major changes to minimize possible abuses. The Commission recommends a statutory basis for the list and that future listings be authorized only after FBI investigation and an opportunity for the organization to be heard by examiners of the Central Security Office, with the right of appeal to the Central Review Board. Decisions of the examiners and the Central Review Board would be advisory to the Attorney General.

SUBPENA POWER.—In the past, neither the Government nor any person involved in loyalty or security cases could compel attendance of witnesses at hearings. The Commission would give the hearing examiners the power of subpena, with wide discretionary latitude to prevent excessive costs, unnecessary delays, and obstructive tactics. Witnesses would be allowed travel and per diem expenses. The Government would pay witness costs only for an individual who was cleared by the hearing.

CONFRONTATION.—The Commission recommends that confrontation and cross-examination be extended to persons subject to loyalty investigations whenever it can be done without endangering the national security. Those whose livelihood and reputation may be affected by such loyalty investigations are entitled to fair hearings and to decisions which are neither capricious nor arbitrary. It is the prime duty of Government to preserve itself, and in the carrying out of this duty it has the indisputable obligation to avail itself of all information obtainable, including information from confidential sources. Full confrontation, therefore, would be obviously impossible without exposing the Government's counterintelligence operations and personnel with resulting paralysis of the Government's efforts to protect the national security. The Commission recommends that, where loyalty charges are involved, no derogatory information, except that supplied by a regularly established confidential informant engaged in intelligence work for the Government whose identity may not be disclosed without compromising the national security, shall be considered over the objection of the individual involved unless such individual is given the opportunity to cross-examine under oath the person supplying such derogatory information. Where the informant is not available for process by reason of incompetence, death or other cause, the derogatory information may be considered, but due regard must be given to the absence of opportunity to cross-examine.

FEDERAL CIVILIAN EMPLOYEES.—The program recommended for civilian Government employees consists of a loyalty program applicable to all positions and a suitability program within the framework of civil service regulations. In the executive branch, the Commission would exclude the Central Intelligence Agency and the National Security Agency from the program. The Commission recommends changes in civil service regulations to allow the transfer of "loyal security risks" to nonsensitive positions or their dismissal under normal civil service procedures. The Commission recommends equal treatment on loyalty and suitability grounds for veterans and nonveterans in Federal employ. The Commission has also strongly urged that all departments of Government be treated alike and therefore the legislative and judicial branches should develop loyalty and security programs.

MILITARY PERSONNEL.—The Commission recommends that the standard and criteria for separation, for denial of enlistment, induction, appointment, or recall to active duty in the Armed Forces, including the Coast Guard, should be that on all the available information there is a reasonable doubt as to loyalty. The Commission recommends that the opportunity for a hearing presently afforded inductees rejected for security reasons be extended to enlistees who are rejected on loyalty grounds, if requested. The cost of such hearings should be borne by the Government and military counsel should be assigned, if requested. The recommendations in other programs for subpena and confrontation would also apply in the military personnel program. The Commission also recommends that in loyalty separations, the type of discharge given a serviceman should depend solely upon the conduct of such serviceman during the term of his military service, including the period of membership in the active or inactive reserve, and that, except to the extent that there has been falsification of his official papers, preservice conduct should not be considered in determining the type of discharge to be given.

DOCUMENT CLASSIFICATION.—The changes recommended by the Commission in the present program for classification of documents and other material are of major importance. The most important change is that the Confidential classification be abolished. The Commission is convinced that retention of this classification serves no useful purpose which could not be covered by the Top Secret or Secret classification. Since the recommendation is not retroactive, it eliminates the immediate task of declassifying material now classified Confidential. The Commission also recommends abolition of the requirement for a personnel security check for access to documents or material classified Confidential. The danger inherent in such access is not significant and the present clearance requirements afford no real security-clearance check.

The report of the Commission stresses the dangers to national security that arise out of overclassification of information which retards scientific and technological progress, and thus tend to deprive the country of the lead time that results from the free exchange of ideas and information.

ATOMIC ENERGY.—The Atomic Energy Commission is an employer of Federal civilian workers and also operates an industrial security program. In general, the Commission's recommendations are designed to bring both AEC's Federal civilian employee and its industrial security programs in line with the comprehensive programs planned for general application throughout the Government.

INDUSTRIAL SECURITY.—Uniformity of regulations, of procedures and their application, and of administration appeared as the needed goal of any reform of the present industrial security program. Therefore, the Commission recommends the establishment of a Central Security Office in the executive branch of the Government, as previously noted. With this arrangement, the hazards of consolidation of all industrial security programs into a single agency are avoided, but the benefits of a unified program will be available by means of a monitoring system exercised through such a central office. The Director of the Central Security Office will advise with the heads of the various government agencies as to issuance of uniform regulations, the interchangeability and transference of clearances from one agency to another, the adoption and use of uniform forms for applicants for clearance, and the provision for hearing officers to preside over hearings afforded applicants for clearance whose clearance has been denied or revoked.

To insure uniformity within the armed services with respect to the Department of Defense Industrial Security Programs, the Commission recommends establishment of an Office of Security within the Office of the Secretary of Defense. This office would integrate, control, and supervise the industrial security programs of the three services, thus eliminating duplicate clearances, investigations, fingerprinting and repetitious execution of clearance applicant and related forms, and accomplishing a streamlined administrative pattern eliminating delay resulting from use of chain-of-command communications regarding security matters. Classification guides would be issued by such office, and close scrutiny maintained on the classification of materials contracted for by the services. Downgrading and declassification programs would be monitored from this office, as well as disposition of classified material upon completion of contracts.

Confrontation and subpena powers are recommended as discussed in the Commission's general recommendations on that subject.

Replacement of the present security standard by a more practical and positively worded one is recommended, namely, that clearance for access to classified material should be denied or revoked if it is determined on the basis of all available information that "access to classified information and materials will endanger the common defense and security." Also, ambiguous criteria relative to associations are omitted in the Commission's recommendation, and the test of refusal to testify at an authorized inquiry has been added.

PORT SECURITY.—The Commission's study revealed defects in the regulations and the operation of the port security program. The Commission therefore recommends that the Commandant of the Coast Guard be vested with full jurisdiction to administer the program with the exception that designated Army and Navy installations continue to be administered by the cognizant military authority. The Commission further recommends that clearances for port workers by the Coast Guard, Army, and Navy be interchangeable.

The Commission emphasizes the importance of administration by recommending that personnel of the Coast Guard assigned to duties in the security program be thoroughly trained in security matters and be assigned to duty in the program on a full-time basis.

One of the problems which has arisen in the administration of the security program by the Coast Guard has been the failure to give an applicant for clearance adequate notice of the reasons for a denial of clearance. The Commission recommends that in the future the applicant be given specific and detailed notice to the extent that the interests of national security permit. The Commission recommends that standards and criteria for clearance in the Coast Guard be uniform with the standards in other major security programs. The Commission also recommends that hearings heretofore conducted by the Coast Guard be the responsibility in the future, of the Central Security Office. Compliance with this recommendation will promote uniformity in standards and procedure throughout the Government.

AIR TRANSPORT SECURITY.—The Commission recommendations for a security program in civil air transport recognizes the need for initial Federal action at the industrywide level in this important field. At present, only the employees of CAA, CAB, or other Federal agencies involved in air transport are subject to the formal program, required under Executive Order 10450. The Commission has recommended, however, that only those employees actually in a position to do substantial damage should be included in the program.

The recommendation that CAB have final authority as to admission to "restricted" facilities under its jurisdiction reflects the opinion of the Commission that, when such authority is divided among CAA, CAB, and military agencies sharing civil air transport facilities, there is strong likelihood that overall national security interest cannot be adequately protected. The agency which has the responsibility for such protection should have sole authority for implementing measures for that protection. The Commission, however, recognizes the important dual interests of CAA and CAB in national security in civil air transport and recommends that, subject to other recommendations, the Secretary of Commerce and the CAB should have joint responsibility for airport security.

INTERNATIONAL ORGANIZATIONS.—The existing loyalty program for United States nationals employed by international organizations should be continued, but the standard should be broadened to include those who are security risks for reasons other than doubtful loyalty. The standard should be whether or not, on all the information, there is reasonable doubt as to the loyalty of the person to the Government of the United States or reasonable ground for believing the person might engage in subversive activities against the United States.

The Commission is recommending amplification of the criteria, reconstitution of the International Organizations Employees Loyalty Board and streamlining of its operations to minimize delays, and the rights of subpena and confrontation applicable to other programs.

PASSPORT SECURITY.—In the passport field, Congress should enact legislation defining the standards and criteria for a permanent passport security program. The procedures would continue to be defined by regulation.

Proposed amendments to the criminal statutes would make it unlawful for a United States citizen to travel to any country for which his passport is declared invalid, and would penalize willful refusal to surrender a passport lawfully revoked.

The Commission also recommends that the legal adviser of the Department of State determine the legal sufficiency of all passport denial cases before final action by the Secretary.

In the operational phase, the Commission recommends that, at all levels, there be strict compliance with the provision of the regulations that notice in writing and the reasons for decisions shall be stated as specifically as security considerations permit. An applicant would also be required to state whether, as the result of any security investigation or proceedings, he has been advised of an adverse finding. The Commission also proposes that a single fingerprint be required on the application and on the passport itself.

The Commission believes also that qualifications should be specified for Passport Office employees charged with responsibility for security decisions and that there should be a training program for such employees.

IMMIGRATION AND NATIONALITY.—The Commission recommends in the field of immigration and nationality that the functions of visa control, except for diplomatic and official visas, be transferred from the Department of State to the Department of Justice and that the Attorney General be authorized by law to maintain personnel abroad to carry out these functions.

The Commission also found that the admission to the United States of any large group of aliens en masse creates a serious security problem. It, accordingly, recommends (1) that the parole provision of the Immigration and Nationality Act of 1952 be amended to clarify with greater specificity the intent of Congress relative to its use, (2) that the status of refugees admitted under such emergency conditions not be changed until all have been adequately screened, and (3) that the Government sponsor an Americanization program for all refugees ultimately granted permanent status.

Overhauling of the deportation provisions of the Immigration and Nationality Act is also recommended to provide:

(1) suspension of the issuance of all but diplomatic and official visas and of the use of bonded transit by nationals of any country which refuses to accept a deportee who is a national, citizen, or subject of such country;

(2) detention at this discretion of the Attorney General of any alien against whom a final order of deportation is outstanding more than 6 months, if required to protect national security or public safety;

(3) greater specificity in the conditions under which deportable aliens will be subject to supervision; and

(4) authorization for the Attorney General to order a deportable alien to refrain from subversive activities or associations.

The Commission also recommends that, if the visa control function is shifted to the Department of Justice, the Immigration Service fix a definite date by which all alien crewmen will be required to have individual visas.

The Commission also urges that the provisions of the Act for fingerprinting and registration of aliens remain in force, and that an adequate training program be conducted for personnel engaged in the discharge of visa functions.

NEW LEGISLATION.—Two new substantive laws are recommended.

The first would penalize unlawful disclosures of classified information with knowledge of their classified character by persons outside as well as within the Government. In the past, only disclosures by Government employees have been punishable.

The second recommended legislation would make admissible in a court of law evidence of subversion obtained by wiretapping by authorized Government investigative agencies. Wiretapping would be permissible only by specific authorization of the Attorney General, and only in investigations of particular crimes affecting the security of the Nation.

Note.—The foregoing Summary of Recommendations is necessarily a brief and concise statement of conclusions. However, for a better understanding of the report, please note respective chapters which set forth a full discussion and rationale of each program briefed.

Contents

Federal Civilian Loyalty Program

Federal Civilian Loyalty Security Program—Continued

International Organizations Program

Passport Security Program

Separate Statements of Commissioners

Proposed Legislation and Executive Orders

Biographical Sketch of Commissioners and Staff

Federal Civilian Loyalty Program

Introduction

The concept that the Government should employ no disloyal citizen has been universally accepted, but the methods and standards used by the Government to rid itself of these persons have raised one of the most controversial issues of our times. The criticisms have been vehement, both that the Government has been too harsh and that it has been too lenient; that loyal citizens have been branded as traitors and that disloyal persons have been permitted to remain in strategic positions where they continue to undermine our form of government.

Congressional committees have conducted innumerable hearings and rendered voluminous reports stressing both sides of the question. Universities, individuals, patriotic and civic societies, bar associations, veterans organizations, and commissions have made intensive studies of the problem and released a mass of written findings based on their research. Some of these reports emphasized the damage that has been inflicted to our national security and others have portrayed the loss of our inherent civil liberties through these same loyalty-security programs of the Government.

During World War II, the standard and procedures of the Government were not uniform in the conduct of the loyalty program. President Truman, in 1946, appointed a temporary commission to make a study of the problem and, as a result of this commission's report, issued Executive Order 9835 (March 1947), which formalized the loyalty program for the entire executive branch of the Government, and provided uniform investigation, standards and procedures for the treatment of applicants and employees. The 81st Congress passed Public Law 733, which gave to certain agency heads the authority to summarily suspend employees and to terminate their employment in the interest of the national security. This law made permanent authority primarily granted by other acts and by riders attached to appropriation bills. Meanwhile, the criticism continued unabated, some in good faith, some inspired by the undercover propaganda of the Communist Party, and some motivated by political reasons.

President Eisenhower issued Executive Order 10450 on April 27, 1953. This order abolished the loyalty program of Executive Order 9835, placed all departments and agencies under the provisions of Public Law 733, and made each department and agency head responsible for seeing "that the employment and retention in employment of any civilian officer or employee within the department or agency is clearly consistent with the interests of the national security." This program was hailed as correcting two alleged main defects in the old system so that (1) dismissed persons would no longer be stigmatized as disloyal, and (2) the Government could remove employees, although loyal, who had character defects or associations that constituted a security risk to the Government. The new security program was in effect only 6 months when the criticisms began to mount. Charges were leveled that Federal employees were being dismissed and branded as security risks on flimsy and unsupported evidence, and that there was no uniformity of decisions among the departments and agencies. As these criticisms increased, the Congress reviewed the situation and, during the 1st session of the 84th Congress, passed Public Law 304 (approved August 9, 1955), stating it was the policy of the Congress "that there shall exist a sound Government program—

(a) establishing procedures for security investigation, evaluation, and, where necessary, adjudication of Government employees, and also appropriate security requirements with respect to persons privately employed or occupied on work requiring access to national defense secrets or work affording significant opportunity for injury to the national security;

(b) for vigorous enforcement of effective and realistic security laws and regulations; and

(c) for a careful, consistent, and efficient administration of this policy in a manner which will protect the national security and preserve basic American rights.

Federal employment is a high privilege and one which should be extended only to those who are fully qualified in every way.

In these hazardous times when there is such grave danger that freedom may be banished from the face of the earth, the security of the Nation must not be needlessly exposed to compromise or injury.

A realistic approach to the problems of national security compels recognition of the fact that there is a controlling difference in the nature of the dangers presented by disloyal employees from those posed by loyal but unreliable personnel. The first interest of the Government is to preserve itself; the primary interest of the disloyal is the destruction of the Government. They are intent upon weakening, undermining, compromising, and destroying our security and can find opportunities to carry out their purpose in any position in the Government.

This conclusion is reinforced by a consideration of personnel policy not related to security and is the principle that disloyalty should not be rewarded by the prestige and emoluments of public employment.

Proceedings for screening out, transferring, or discharging employees necessary to the maintenance of national security are not judicial, or adversary in character. They do not establish guilt or mete out punishment. They merely determine suitability from a security viewpoint.

In the interests of justice and fairness, however, the proceedings must be such as will insure, so far as it is humanly possible, that decisions are reached which are in accord with the facts and that there be no arbitrary, ill-founded, or capricious denials of employment, transfers, or discharges in the name of security.

HISTORY

Although the history of the civilian employees loyalty-security program is generally considered to have begun with the act of August 2, 1939 (the Hatch Act, 53 Stat., 1148; 5 U. S. C., 118j), executive and legislative concern with the problem of loyalty in Government actually dates back to the Civil War.

Civil service investigations prior to 1939, however, were limited to questions of character and general suitability; questions of political beliefs were considered outside the legal competence of the Civil Service Commission. President McKinley's Executive Order 101 of 1897 laid down the rules for dismissal from Federal civil service which became the basis for the Lloyd-La Follette Act of 1912. That act provides that an employee cannot be suspended or removed except for such cause as will promote the efficiency of the service, that employees be notified of the charges against them, that they be given reasonable time to answer in writing, and that no hearing or examination of witnesses be required except at the discretion of the dismissing officer.

During World War I the Civil Service Commission sent President Wilson a letter dated April 5, 1917, which suggested "the desirability of an order intended to safeguard the public interest in the present national crisis by excluding from the government any person of whose loyalty to the government there is reasonable doubt." The President then issued a confidential Executive order authorizing the heads of departments and agencies to remove any employee believed to be "inimical to the public welfare by reason of his conduct, sympathies, or utterances, or because of other reasons growing out of the war."

Following the end of World War I, the loyalty issue became dormant until the 1930's, a period of international lawlessness, of the rise of totalitarianism abroad, and of severe strains on the social and economic system of the United States. Then in 1939 the Hatch Act was passed, section 9A of which prohibited Federal employees from "membership in any political party or organization which advocates the overthrow of our constitutional form of government in the United States." The act further ordered the immediate removal of any person violating this provision and prohibited the appropriation of funds to pay him.

At this time application for Government employment was made on form 8, which contained no reference to affiliation with parties or organizations, but in February 1940, a question was added which embodied the language of the Hatch Act. The following year the question specifically named Communist and German Bund organizations. In 1942, form 8 was replaced with form 57, which phrased the question as follows: "Do you advocate or have you ever advocated, or are you now or have you ever been a member of any organization that advocates the overthrow of the Government of the

5

United States by force or violence?" This question went through several other changes until 1947, when, in addition to the general question, two other questions specifically mentioning Communist and Fascist organizations were inserted.

President Roosevelt's Executive Order 8781 of June 12, 1941, required the fingerprinting of every employee in the executive civil service whose prints were not already on file in the Federal Bureau of Investigation or in his own agency. The order further charged the FBI to establish a permanent classification and filing system of these fingerprints and to check them for possible criminal records.

By this time the fingerprinting of Federal employees had become an accepted practice. Since July 1931 the Commission has been provided with funds for fingerprinting all persons appointed under the civil service act and rules.

Eight months after issuing Executive Order 8781, President Roosevelt ordered the issuance of War Service Regulation II, which disqualified for civil service examination or appointment any person whose loyalty to the United States Government was in reasonable doubt. (Executive Order 9063, which established this regulation was revoked on February 4, 1946, by Executive Order 9691.)

In 1940 and again in 1942 the Secretaries of War and Navy and the Coast Guard were given "summary removal" powers against employees deemed risks to national security. The Department of State received similar authority from the 79th Congress in 1946, and the authority was later extended to the Secretaries of Defense and the Air Force.

Since July 1941, Congress has added to appropriation bills the proviso that no part of any appropriation could be used to pay the salary or wages of any person advocating the overthrow of the Government of the United States by force or violence.

Under War Service Regulation II, the Civil Service Commission refused employment to people actively associated with Nazi, Fascist, and Japanese groups, or who were members of the Communist Party. The Commission conducted preappointment investigations of applicants for classified civil service employment, and if derogatory information resulted, the applicant was called to the regional civil service office and confronted with the information, at which time he could answer or explain his activities. His complete file would then be sent to a rating unit in the central offices of the Civil Service Commission, which had taken no part in the investigation. Any adverse decision by the rating unit would be forwarded through channels to the Commission for approval. If the Commission upheld the adverse decision, the applicant and the agency were so notified and either or both could appeal to the Commission's Board of Review.

In the spring of 1944, the Civil Service Commission created a full-time Loyalty Rating Board to which cases of derogatory information involving loyalty were referred by the regional offices. After analyzing the evidence, the Board sent the applicant a questionnaire to which he could reply in writing and under oath. He also was permitted to appear in person before the Loyalty Rating Board if he wished.

During this same period the Civil Service Commission began compiling a security index and general information file. The index lists all persons who had been investigated by the Federal Government. The information file contains the names of persons allegedly associated with subversive activities or organizations. The names in this file come from various sources, mainly Communist Party publications, congressional hearings, and the files of the Un-American Activities Committee.

Congress in 1941 voted $100,000 for the Department of Justice to investigate disloyalty complaints against such employees, and report its findings to Congress and the heads of the departments and agencies involved. At this time the Attorney General advised the FBI that membership in the Communist Party, the German-American Bund, or in any of seven other organizations would constitute questionable loyalty within the intent of Congress. In April 1942, the Attorney General created an Interdepartmental Committee on Investigations, which President Roosevelt replaced a year later with the Interdepartmental Committee on Employee Investigations. By this time the Attorney General's list of questionable organizations had grown to 47.

The interdepartmental committee did not feel it had jurisdiction to class as subversive the organizations listed by the Attorney General. However, the committee did forward the list to the departments and agencies with the statement that it "does not purport to be a complete report on the organizations named. It is intended only to acquaint you . . . with the nature of the evidence which has appeared to warrant an investigation of charges of participation. It is assumed that each employee's case will be decided on all the facts presented in the report of the FBI where a hearing is ordered."

The committee also forwarded a general memorandum No. 6 advising that applicable legislation was to be construed literally and administered with a view to protect the Government yet dealing fairly and impartially with accused employees. The memorandum further stated that dismissal or action looking toward dismissal was not recommended by the committee except on the basis of credible evidence of membership in an organization which had been authoritatively held to be subversive; i. e., one which advocates the overthrow of the United States Government by force or violence. The memorandum also indicated that past membership or past subversive advocacy (unless casual and remote in time) constituted a case which could not be dropped without evidence that membership or advocacy had been discontinued completely and sufficiently prior to the inception of the case. Advocacy was defined as consisting of spoken words, conduct, or actions which lead to the conclusion that the employee singly or in consort with others sought to . . . overthrow the Government of the United States by force or violence.

7

Thus it was that in 1943 there were two different standards of loyalty for Federal employees: The Civil Service Commission's general standard of "reasonable doubt" and the interdepartmental committee's standard, keyed to membership in organizations adjudged subversive by statute.

On January 18, 1945, the House of Representatives authorized the House Civil Service Committee to investigate policies and practices pertaining to Federal employment. A subcommittee was consequently created consisting of J. M. Combs, Texas, chairman; George M. Fallon, Maryland, and Edward H. Rees, Kansas. The subcommittee's report, issued on July 20, 1946, pointed out that the existence of two sets of standards was causing trouble and recommended that ". . . a consistent and uniform policy among the agencies of the Federal Government with respect to investigating and removing employees who are known to be disloyal should be placed into effect as soon as possible," and "that techniques and procedures must be devised that will prevent persons rejected by one agency on loyalty grounds from being accepted in another."

Mr. Rees, who did not feel the subcommittee's recommendations were sufficient to deal with the serious problem involved, issued a minority report calling for a thorough housecleaning of all those of doubtful loyalty. While advocating complete fairness, he felt that a reasonable doubt of loyalty must at all times be resolved in favor of the Government, and recommended further hearings and investigation leading to legislation or other means "of eliminating without delay employees in every department or agency of Government where there is reasonable doubt concerning their loyalty."

President Truman's Executive Order 9806 on November 25, 1946, established a Temporary Commission on Loyalty. The President's commission was composed of one representative each of the Departments of Justice, State, Treasury, War and Navy, and of the Civil Service Commission.

The President's commission was authorized to study standards and procedures of investigation and dismissal or disqualification of Government employees and applicants for Federal jobs. The order directed the commission to "give consideration to the findings and recommendations of the Subcommittee of the Civil Service Committee of the House of Representatives. . . ."

The President's temporary commission reported that while it believed the employment of disloyal persons presented more than a speculative threat to our system of government, it was unable to state on the basis of facts presented just how far reaching the threat was. The commission found that the Canadian exposé, the Communist Party-line activities of some leaders and members of a Government-employee organization, and current disclosures of employee disloyalty constituted convincing evidence that the threat did exist.

The temporary commission further reported a wide disparity in standards for judgment of employee loyalty, in procedures to determine loyalty prior to employment, in procedures designed to effect removal from service, and of opinion as to the character and scope of desirable administrative or legislative remedies. It found that the agencies normally rely on civil service investigation to determine the loyalty of a prospective employee, and that as the Civil Service Commission can investigate only a limited number of applicants, "the agencies have relied almost exclusively on the veracity attributed to the oath of office and affidavit executed by the new appointee, and signature to these two instruments is taken as prima facie evidence of loyalty. . . . Several agencies in their replies stated that they had no established procedure designed to substantiate allegations of disloyalty."

The temporary commission, in addition to analyzing information from the intelligence service and from Government agencies, also heard testimony from Attorney General Tom C. Clark; Mr. D. Milton Ladd, Assistant Director of the FBI; and Mr. Herbert A. Gaston, Chairman of the Interdepartmental Committee on Employee Investigations. Representative Edward R. Rees, of Kansas, chairman of the House Civil Service Committee, also appeared, as did Representative J. M. Combs, of Texas, former chairman.

The views of Mr. Gaston, although not published at the time of the Commission's report, were submitted in 1955 to the Hennings Subcommittee on Constitutional Rights of the Senate Judiciary Committee. Mr. Gaston declared that all who hold the responsibility of selecting loyal employees and excluding all others "must be alert to screen out the subversive, the dishonest, the incompetent, and the unambitious. Examinations and investigations intended to exclude advocates of violent revolution from employment by a Government they would overthrow are essential, but they need to be conducted with extreme care and wisdom lest they should have the effect of setting up bars against the employment of those who conscientiously advocate constitutional and peaceful changes in forms and methods of government."

Mr. Gaston found that to give to "a screening agency power to refuse candidates or to an investigating agency power to exclude from Federal service those who merely hold political views not consonant with those of the examiners and investigators would be to set up an intolerable tyranny comparable to that of the systems of government which we, as advocates of democracy and liberty, most strongly condemn. No screening or selecting agency should ever be given the power to bar citizens from service to their Government because of their political ideas. This is the way to totalitarianism and despotism." Mr. Gaston added that his views were wholly apart from the reasonable freedom that naturally belongs to the executive and to the heads of governmental departments and agencies to select employees sympathetic to and zealous for the government ideals and plans of the existing administration.

The temporary commission's report was dated March 22, 1947, although Executive Order 9835, which embodies substantially all the commission's recommendations, was announced one day earlier. The standard for refusal of employment in the executive departments or agencies on grounds relating to loyalty was that ". . . on all the evidence reasonable grounds exist for the belief that the person involved is disloyal to the Government of the United States."

Executive Order 9835 made a loyalty investigation mandatory for any person entering the civilian employ of any department or agency. When necessary, the investigation could be made after a person had entered service, but must have been completed within 18 months of a person's entry on duty or the mandatory condition would expire.

Incumbent employees were also made subject to loyalty investigation. The right to administrative hearing and appeal to the head of a department or agency was established, and a Loyalty Review Board set up within the Civil Service Commission.

Because Executive Order 9835 was limited by statutory authority to proof of actual disloyalty, President Truman amended it on April 28, 1951, to read as follows:

The standard for the refusal of employment or the removal from employment in an executive department or agency on grounds relating to loyalty shall be that on all the evidence, there is reasonable doubt as to the loyalty of the person involved.

On July 14, 1951, less than 3 months after he had made the amendment by Executive order, President Truman wrote to Mr. James S. Lay, Jr., executive secretary of the National Security Council, as follows:

DEAR MR. LAY: I have become seriously concerned by a number of reports I have heard recently concerning the administration of the provisions of existing law which authorize the heads of the various departments and agencies to discharge government employees, or to refuse Government employment to applicants, on the ground that they are poor security risks.

If these provisions of law are to achieve their purpose of protecting the security of the Government without unduly infringing on the rights of individuals, they must be administered with the utmost wisdom and courage. We must never forget that the fundamental purpose of our Government is to protect the rights of individual citizens and one of the highest obligations of the Government is to see that those rights are protected in its own operations.

The present situation does not make for good administration. There are no uniform standards or procedures to be followed in the different departments and agencies concerned. Neither is there any provision for review at a central point as there is in the case of the Government employee loyalty program. This is a problem that falls within the scope of the work which I have asked to have undertaken by the Commission on Internal Security and Individual Rights. However, the work of that Commission has been delayed because of the failure of the Senate Committee on the Judiciary to report legislation which would exempt the members and staff of the Commission from the conflict-of-interest statutes.

I believe that the present problems involved in the administration of the Government employee security program are so acute that they should be given at least preliminary consideration without waiting further for the Commission on Internal Security and Individual Rights. Consequently, I should like the National Security Council, utilizing its Interdepartmental Committee on Internal Security, and with the participation of the Civil Service Commission, to make an investigation of the way this program is being administered, and to advise me what changes are believed to be required. In particular, I should like consideration given to whether provision should be made for uniform standards and procedures and for central review of the decisions made in the various departments and agencies.

When the Commission on Internal Security and Individual Rights is able to resume its work, it would, of course, have the benefit of the work done pursuant to this request.

I am asking each of the departments and agencies concerned to cooperate fully in this study.

Sincerely yours,

HARRY S. TRUMAN.

Pursuant to the President's request, the Interdepartmental Committee on Internal Security (ICIS) of the National Security Council, with the participation of the Civil Service Commission, prepared a report on the Government employee security program and forwarded it to the President on April 29, 1952. The ICIS report indicated that its recommendations were unanimous, except for certain changes which the Department of Defense desired. The Department of Defense disagreed with the standard which the ICIS report recommended. The ICIS standard was worded as follows:

The standard for the denial of employment, or the removal from employment, in an executive department or agency on security grounds shall be that, on all the evidence, there is reason to believe that the employment or retention of the individual in a sensitive position would be prejudicial to the national security.

The Department of Defense requested that the word "particular" be inserted before the phrase, "sensitive position," arguing that security determinations should be made on the basis of the fitness of the person to hold a specific position. Also, that recognition be given to the fact that access to classified information varied with the degree of sensitivity of the information, and that it was unrealistic to insist that all employees be cleared for the highest classification.

The dissent by the Department of Defense pointed out that the criteria recommended by the ICIS report were phrased in too general terms, and probably would not bring about the desired Government-wide uniformity in the administration of security programs.

The Department of Defense suggested instead that three categories of criteria be adopted as follows:

(a) Criteria which would create a prima facie case of reason to believe that the employment or retention of the individual in a particular sensitive position would be prejudicial to the national security;

(b) Criteria which would not create a prima facie case but which might properly be considered in making the contemplated security consideration; and

(c) Those personal characteristics which, while they might indicate that the individual's employment in a particular sensitive position might be dangerous, would normally justify removal on grounds of character or suitabiliy and not on grounds of security.

The other departments represented on ICIS and the Civil Service Commission did not agree with the dissent by the Department of Defense, but forwarded the dissent as an appendix to their report to the President on April 29, 1952.

11

The report pointed out that there were several Federal statutes which authorized the removal, or prohibited the employment of persons because they are so-called security risks. ". . . Some of the statutes give direct authority to agency heads to remove employees in the interest of national security. Other statutes prohibit access by employees to information or property unless they are determined to be of unquestionable reliability for security purposes. Still other statutes prohibit the continued employment or hiring of persons unless there has been an FBI investigation and an evaluation of the information contained as a result of such investigation."

The report declared that the one general statute authorizing suspensions and removals of security risks was Public Law 733, 81st Congress, specifically applicable to 11 Federal departments and agencies.

The agencies within the scope of 733 have authority to remove employees in the interests of national security, and yet the employee has the additional right of a written statement of charges, a hearing, and in the event of an adverse decision, a review of his case by the agency head or official designated by him. Further, it gives him the right to go to the Civil Service Commission to determine his eligblity for employment in other agencies of the Government . . .

"Furthermore," the report continues, "even in those departments and agencies which have need of an employee security program, not all positions . . . will necessarily be concerned with the national security, and therefore not all employees will be in a position to compromise or endanger the national security. The program must be applicable only with respect to those positions which may be designated as 'sensitive positions,' whose incumbents might be in a position to endanger the national security . . .

"The committee believes that those agencies which have need of an employee security program should each have the same basic legal authority upon which to establish such a program . . . to insure such uniformity in the administration of the programs as may be desirable."

The report considered creating a new appellate body to review appeals in security cases, but concluded "that the Civil Service Commission would be the most logical body to accept employee appeals from removal actions on security grounds for the following reasons":

(a) Public Law 733 provides that termination of employment shall not affect the right of an officer or employee to seek or accept employment in any other department or agency of the Government. It further provides that the Civil Service Commission shall have the authority to determine whether such person is eligible for employment by any other department or agency . . . It is therefore contemplated by Public Law 733 that in cases in which individuals have been removed under that law for security reasons the Commission will review the case and determine whether the affected employee may be employed elsewhere in the Government. Such determination cannot be made by any other department, agency, or body, and it is prerequisite to employment of any such individual by any other department or agency.

(b) Some departments and agencies operating under Public Law 733 are now processing loyalty cases simultaneously as both loyalty and security cases. The charges given the individual are under both Public Law 733 and Executive Order 9835, as amended,

12

and the hearing is joint, serving both for adjudication of loyalty and security. Separate determinations are made with respect to loyalty and security. There is, however, a right of appeal from an adverse loyalty finding to the Loyalty Review Board of the Civil Service Commission. It would therefore seem unwise to provide a new and different body to which an appeal could be taken from an adverse security finding, thereby multiplying the avenues of appeal. It would seem more logical to afford an employee an appeal from an adverse finding on security simultaneously with his appeal from an adverse finding on loyalty; or, where there is no adverse finding on loyalty, to the same body which would handle a loyalty appeal. In this manner, where both loyalty and security are involved, each of these matters could be disposed of in one appeal, and, in addition, a finding could be made as to the individual's eligibility for other Federal employment.

.   .   .   .

The committee recommended that ". . . Decision to take any adverse action should be reached only after there has been a judicious evaluation of all available information, favorable as well as unfavorable, by a responsible official or officials of the department or agency. Investigations which form the basis for any such action should be made by competent investigators and should include all pertinent facts, favorable as well as unfavorable, together with information on which to base a decision as to the credibility of confidential informants. The fullest practicable use should be made of supplemental investigations, including interviews with the employee when appropriate, in order to clear up doubtful points which are material and thus avoid the stigma of formal charges based upon an incomplete record."

Lastly, the committee stated that, "In no event should any official make a commitment or a promise of employment to an applicant for a sensitive position, subject to completion of the required investigation. When it is considered that an applicant's services are so urgently needed as to make it desirable that he be given such commitment or promise, the head of the department or agency concerned should provide for his actual appointment to the position in question, subject to the necessary investigation and with the employee being fully informed of the limited nature of such appointment. Such appointment will assure him all of the procedural and other rights accorded an employee and, at the same time, will not serve to modify or change established minimum requirements for access to classified security information."

Following the receipt of the ICIS report, President Truman wrote a letter to the Honorable Robert Ramspeck, Chairman of the Civil Service Commission. This letter, dated August 8, 1952, said in part:

I have given considerable thought to the recommendations contained in this report. I have concluded that the most desirable action at this time would be to merge the loyalty, security, and suitability programs, thus eliminating the overlapping, duplication, and confusion which apparently now exist. *It is my understanding that the status of the incumbent employees loyalty program is now so advanced that there would be little or no obstacle in accomplishing this from the standpoint of the future needs of that phase of the loyalty program.* Accordingly, I should like for the Civil Service Commission to take the necessary steps to provide me with a plan for combining the

13

three existing programs into one at the earliest practicable date. To achieve this end, I am directing all executive departments and agencies to cooperate fully with the Commission and to furnish the Commission with such personnel and other assistance as it may require.

Pending action to merge the existing three programs, it does not seem advisable to issue an Executive order establishing uniform standards and procedures comprising an overall Government employee security program, with provision for Civil Service Commission review of agency decisions. Such an Executive order would presumably have only temporary effect, since it would be superseded shortly by the new program I am requesting the Commission to prepare. I believe we can utilize our efforts most effectively by going straight to what we regard as the best solution. [Emphasis added.]

A committee was established to study the possibility of combining the three existing programs into one. The members of that committee were as follows:

1. L. V. Meloy represented the Commission and was chairman of the committee.

2. Leon Wheeless and David T. Stanley were designated as member and alternate, respectively, for the Secretary of Defense.

3. Col. George W. Hanson was designated as a member representing the Interdepartmental Committee on Internal Security, with Col. Joseph Alverson as alternate.

4. Clive W. Palmer was designated as a member representing the Office of the Attorney General.

5. E. B. Jackson, Chief Clerk and Director of Personnel, was designated as a member representing the Office of the Postmaster General.

6. W. Davidson Teeney, of the State Department, was designated as a member with Arch K. Jean as his alternate.

This committee organized on October 9, 1952, and met regularly. It disbanded in February 1953, its work unfinished, because of the change in administration. The committee did, however, draft a proposed Executive order which might be considered for a one-package, loyalty-security-suitability program.

The seventh paragraph of the preamble stated that it was ". . . desirable in the interest of efficient, economical, and equitable administration to establish a single standard against which to measure the fitness of persons for employment in the Federal service and to provide a common basic procedure within the framework of the various statutes pertaining to the denial of employment or the removal from employment in the Federal service."

The standard recommended in the proposed Executive order was that the denial of employment, or the removal from employment, should be on the grounds of fitness or suitability to promote the efficiency of the service, and it was to be based upon a finding that on all the information there was reasonable doubt regarding the fitness of the person involved for employment in the Government of the United States.

14

Factors upon which the proposed Executive order would have determined ineligibility on grounds of fitness or suitability included, but were not necessarily limited to, the following:

(1) Failure to meet and maintain established qualifications for fitness standards of the position applied for or occupied.

(2) Inadequate performance in employment.

(3) Delinquency, misconduct, insubordination, or other conduct which interferes with the efficiency of the service.

(4) Physical or mental unfitness for the position applied for or occupied.

(5) Criminal, infamous, dishonest, immoral, or notoriously disgraceful conduct, habitual use of intoxicants to excess, drug addiction, or sexual perversion.

(6) False statements made with the intent to deceive, or material misstatements, misrepresentations, or omissions of a material fact.

(7) Refusal to furnish testimony as required by section 5.3 of the Civil Service Commission's regulations, or to furnish similar information or testimony, as required, to duly constituted agency officials in the performance of their proper duties in the application of this standard.

(8) Intentional, unauthorized disclosure to any person of official documents or information of a nonpublic character.

(9) Prior conviction of sabotage, espionage, treason or sedition; or

(10) Advocacy of treason, sedition, or the overthrow of our constitutional form of government; or

(11) Attempts or preparations for sabotage or espionage; or intentional disclosure to any unauthorized person of classified security information; or

(12) Knowingly associating with spies or saboteurs.

(13) Performing or attempting to perform his duties, or otherwise acting, so as to serve the interests of another government in preference to the interests of the United States.

(14) Activities or associations which establish a reason to believe that the individual may be subject to influence or pressure which may cause him to act contrary to the best interests of our constitutional form of government.

(15) Lack of adherence to our constitutional form of government of the United States as evidenced by personal advocacy or activities and associations or by past or present membership in, affiliation with, or sympathetic association with, any foreign or domestic organization, association, movement, group, or combination of persons designated by the Attorney General, as totalitarian, Fascist, Communist, or subversive, or as having adopted a policy

15

of advocating or approving the commission of acts of force or violence to deny other persons their rights under the Constitution of the United States, or as seeking to alter the form of government of the United States by unconstitutional means.

(16) Activities or associations which establish a reason to believe the individual is not reliable or trustworthy.

On April 27, 1953, Executive Order 10450 was promulgated establishing the present security program which in effect combines loyalty, suitability, and security considerations. Its development will be discussed in the section of this report covering the present program. A backward glance at the historical record is necessary, however, at this point.

It will be recalled that the preamble to Executive Order 9835 stated that it was to become effective immediately, but compliance with such of its provisions as required the expenditure of funds should be deferred pending the appropriation of such funds. Before appropriations were made, however, Congressman Rees convened the Subcommittee of the House Committee on Post Office and Civil Service in June 1947, to discuss H. R. 3588, which provided for a proposed Federal Employees Loyalty Act of 1947.

The main features of H. R. 3588 were indicated as:

(1) All applicants for Federal positions and all Federal employees are to be investigated to determine whether they are loyal to the Government of the United States.

(2) A preliminary investigation of each applicant and employee will be conducted by the Civil Service Commission.

(3) If this investigation results in revealing any derogatory matter regarding the loyalty of the person under investigation, the Civil Service Commission will terminate its investigation and turn the investigation over to the Federal Bureau of Investigation.

(4) The bill provides for the establishment of a Loyalty Review Board within the Civil Service Commission which will consider all reports of loyalty investigations conducted by the FBI.

(5) The Loyalty Review Board will be composed of 5 members, not more than 3 of whom shall have been employees of the Civil Service Commission.

(6) *The Loyalty Review Board will have the power and authority to enforce its adverse decisions. That is, the department or agency heads will be compelled either to discharge or to refuse employment to persons about whom the loyalty board finds some reasonable doubt regarding their loyalty.* [Emphasis added.]

(7) Adequate provision is made to protect the civil rights of persons under investigation.

H. R. 3588 was not enacted into legislation, but a substitute bill, H. R. 3813, was reported out. " . . . The principal reason for the substitute bill was that in the opinion of the Attorney General and the Civil Service

Commission the previous bill, H. R. 3588, might be considered unconstitutional because it provided that the loyalty board could compel the heads of departments and agencies to remove disloyal employees."

H. R. 3813 passed the House of Representatives, but died in the Senate following adverse reports from the Army, Navy, and Air Force.

The military services were anxious for permanent legislation similar to the war service legislation they had been granted in Public Law 808. On July 2, 1947, the Department of Defense submitted a draft bill to the Senate, which was discussed in the Senate Armed Services Committee. The bill, S. 1561, passed the Senate on June 1, 1948, and was referred to the House Committee on Post Office and Civil Service on June 8, 1948. No action was taken before the end of the session of the 80th Congress and the bill died on the calendar.

On February 21, 1950, a proposed draft of legislation was again submitted to the Senate by the Department of Defense. On February 27, 1950, the chairman of the House Committee on Post Office and Civil Service introduced the proposed draft as H. R. 7439, which ultimately became Public Law 733, 81st Congress.

During the hearings on H. R. 7439, it became clear that the Department of Defense preferred to handle its dismissals under the legislative authority of Public Law 808, to avoid the necessity of any appeal going outside to the Loyalty Review Board under Executive Order 9835.

There is evidence to indicate that some members of the Senate Armed Services Committee wanted the provisions of Public Law 733 to be extended to apply to all departments and agencies. A rollcall vote was necessary to indicate decisively the wishes of the committee. The request to extend the application of the provisions of Public Law 733 to other departments and agencies failed to carry. Public Law 733 does, however, carry a provision that the Act can apply to such other departments and agencies of the Government as the President may, from time to time, deem necessary in the best interests of the national security.

President Eisenhower extended Public Law 733 to all departments and agencies with the promulgation of Executive Order 10450.

The history of the civilian employees loyalty-security program reached its present stage on August 9, 1955. On that date Congress passed Public Law 330 which replaced section 9A of the Hatch Act by legislation of similar intent. On that day also Public Law 304 was passed establishing the present Commission on Government Security.

More recent developments are summarized under Present Program.

17

LEGAL BASIS

Introduction

The present loyalty-security program for civilian employees of the executive branch of the Federal Government is based upon Public Law 733,, Eighty-first Congress,[1] and Executive Order 10450.[2] This statute and the implementing Executive order expressly authorize the program.

For an adequate understanding of the legal framework of the program, however, it is necessary to consider the respective areas of authority of the executive branch and the Congress with respect to the appointment and removal of Federal employees.

Constitutional Background

THE POWER TO APPOINT.—Congress has the power to create the office—United States Constitution, article I, section 8, clause 18 ("necessary and proper clause") ; and the power to vest the appointment of inferior officers in the President alone, in the courts of law, or in the heads of departments (art. II, sec. 2, clause 2). As a concomitant of these powers, the Congress has the authority to legislate with respect to the qualifications and manner of choice of applicants for those offices created by the Congress and for those inferior offices as to which the Congress has acted by vesting the power of appointment in the President, courts, or heads of departments.[3]

The President, and the heads of departments (when the Congress has vested them with the power of appointment), have the power to appoint civilian employees in the executive branch (art. II, sec. 2, clause 2). As a concomitant of this power, the President and the heads of departments may, in their discretion, determine what persons shall be appointed to office, subject only to the power of Congress described in (1) above to limit and regulate appointments to certain offices.

THE POWER TO REMOVE.—The President and the heads of the departments and agencies of the Federal Government may summarily dismiss an employee of the executive branch without notice and without advising the employee of the reason for such action, except to the extent that Congress has exercised its constitutional power [4] to pass laws limiting the President's removal power,[5] and to the extent that the due process clause of the Constitution may limit this power.[6]

---

[1] 5 U. S. C. 22–1, et seq. (1950).

[2] 18 F. R. 2489 (1953).

[3] *Roth* v. *Brownell*, 215 F. 2d 500 (1954) (C. A. D. C.).

[4] Based upon art. II, sec. 2, clause 2—the power to vest the appointment of inferior officers in the President alone, in the courts of law, or in the heads of departments.

[5] *Bailey* v. *Richardson*, 183 F. 2d 46 (1950) (C. A. D. C.). (The Supreme Court affirmed by an equally divided court, with no opinion. 341 U. S. 918 (1951).)

[6] *Wieman et al.* v. *Updegraff et al.*, 344 U. S. 183 (1952) ; *Slochower* v. *The Board of Higher Education of the City of New York*, 350 U. S. 551 (1956).

Under the *Myers* and *Humphreys* cases,[7] the Congress can *not* constitutionally limit the President's removal power with respect to those officers of the executive branch who are or were appointed by the President or his predecessors with the advice and consent of the Senate, if the positions occupied by such officers are not quasi-legislative or quasi-judicial in nature; in this area the President has an "illimitable" removal power. This area of Presidential authority is not large, however, for the major part of all offices in the executive branch of the Government are inferior offices, and the Congress has usually vested the power of appointment thereto in the heads of departments.

General Provisions

APPOINTMENT.—The act of March 3, 1871, the Civil Service Act of 1883, as amended, and the Veterans' Preference Act of 1944, as amended, constitute the major expression of the Congress' power to specify the qualifications of appointees in the executive branch of the Government. (5 U. S. C. 631, 5 U. S. C. 632, et seq., and 5 U. S. C. Cum. Supp. 851, et seq.)

The act of 1871 authorizes the President to prescribe such regulations for the admission of persons into the civil service of the United States as may best promote the efficiency thereof and ascertain the fitness of each candidate. The Civil Service Act establishes the merit system, and provides for competitive examinations and for the making of appointments to the competitive civil service from among those graded highest in the examinations. The Veterans' Preference Act gives veterans of the Armed Forces preference in appointments to all civilian positions in the Federal Government, whether in the competitive civil service or not.

Unless an executive branch civilian position is specifically excepted by Congress or by action of the Civil Service Commission, it is in the competitive civil service and subject to civil service rules. (Sec. 01.2, rules of the Civil Service Commission.) Today, approximately 85 percent of all positions in the Federal Government are included in the competitive civil service. Excepted positions are not, generally, covered by the provisions of the Civil Service Act or the rules and regulations of the Civil Service Commission.[8]

INVESTIGATIONS.—(*a*) Section 05.2 of the civil service rules provides that the Commission is authorized to make appropriate investigations, including investigation of the qualifications and suitability of applicants for positions in the competitive service.

(*b*) Section 2.107 of the civil service regulations provides that all types of appointments under the regulations, with a few exceptions, shall be subject to investigation by the Commission to establish the appointee's qualifications

---

[7] *Myers* v. *United States*, 272 U. S. 52 (1926); *Humphrey* v. *United States*, 295 U. S. 602 (1935).

[8] The Role of the Civil Service Commission in Federal Employment—U. S. Civil Service Commission pamphlet No. 52, January 1955.

19

and suitability for employment in the competitive service. Rule V, section 05.2, of the civil service rules authorizes the Commission to require appointments to be made subject to investigation to enable the Commission to determine, after appointment, that the requirements of law or the civil service rules and regulations have been met.

CRITERIA FOR APPOINTMENT.—Section 2.106 of the civil service regulations provides that an applicant may be denied examination and an eligible may be denied appointment for any 1 of 8 reasons:

(1) Dismissal from employment for delinquency or misconduct;

(2) Physical or mental unfitness for the position for which applied;

(3) Criminal, infamous, dishonest, immoral, or notoriously disgraceful conduct;

(4) Intentional false statements or deception or fraud in examination or appointment;

(5) Refusal to furnish testimony as required by section 05.3 of rule V of the civil service rules.

(6) Habitual use of intoxicating beverages to excess;

(7) Reasonable doubt as to the loyalty of the person involved to the Government of the United States; or

(8) Any legal or other disqualification which makes the applicant unfit for the service.

TENURE AND DISCHARGE.—As set forth in the power to appoint, above, the President and the heads of departments may summarily dismiss an employee of the executive branch without notice and without advising the employee of the reason for such action, except to the extent that Congress has exercised its constitutional power to pass laws limiting the removal power of the President and the heads of departments, and to the extent that the due process clause of the Constitution may limit this power.

The Congress has exercised this power by passing two principal statutes—the Lloyd-LaFollette Act of 1912, as amended, and the Veterans' Preference Act of 1944, as amended.

The Lloyd-LaFollette Act of 1912, as amended (5 U. S. C. 652), restricts the discretionary power of the superior officers in the executive branch in matters of removal by establishing procedures which must be followed in suspending or dismissing employees in the competitive civil service. These procedures have been restated in the civil service regulations, part 9:

(a) Under these procedures permanent employees in the competitive civil service who have completed their probationary or trial period can be removed or suspended without pay only under the following conditions:

(1) The removal or suspension without pay must be for such cause as will promote the efficiency of the service. The grounds for disqualification of an applicant for examination (set forth in criteria for appointment, above), are included among those constituting sufficient cause for removal of an employee.

20

(2) The employee must be notified in writing of the proposed removal or suspension without pay and the specific reasons for it.

(3) He must be given a reasonable time to reply in writing.

(4) His reply must be considered by the agency.

(5) He must be given a written decision containing the reasons for the action and its effective date.

(6) There is a right of appeal to the Civil Service Commission on the basis of a claim that the procedure for suspension or removal prescribed by the Commission was not followed or a claim that the suspension or removal was made for political reasons, except as may be required by law, or because of marital status.

(7) The Commission can direct the appointing officer of the department or agency to take corrective action, if such is called for.

(8) There is no right to examine witnesses, or to have any trial or hearing, except in the discretion of the agency.

(b) Under the rules and the regulations of the Civil Service Commission (rule V, sec. 05.2 and sec. 2.107 (c), respectively), the Commission may, for a period of 18 months after the appointment of an employee made subject to investigation (see investigations (b), above), instruct an agency to remove the said employee, or to suspend him pending an appeal from the Commission's finding, if the investigation discloses that the employee is disqualified for any of the reasons set forth in criteria for appointment above. Section 9.102 of the Civil Service Commission regulations provides that the procedural requirements of part 9 of the said regulations shall not apply to any employee who is removed pursuant to instructions of the Commission.

(c) Under these procedures, employees serving their probationary or trial period of 1 year may be removed merely upon written notice giving the reasons therefor, with no right of appeal. Employees having purely temporary appointments (or occupying excepted positions) may be removed merely upon written notice without being given the reasons, and with no right of appeal.

(d) Under the civil service regulations, part 9, an employee who has received a notice of proposed action under this section is retained in an active-duty status during the period of notice of such proposed action, except that the employee may be placed on annual leave without his consent where the administrative officer does not consider it advisable to retain him in an active-duty status during the advance notice period. Where the employee is not placed on annual leave and the circumstances are such that his retention in an active-duty status may result in damage to Government property, or may be detrimental to the interests of the Government, or injurious to the employee, his fellow workers, or the general public, he may be temporarily assigned to duties in which these conditions would not exist or placed on leave without pay with his consent. In emergency cases requiring prompt suspension

21

of an employee, the employing agency may require the employee to answer the charges and submit affidavits within such a time as under the circumstances would be reasonable, but not less than 24 hours.

The Veterans' Preference Act of 1944 provides the veteran with certain additional rights:

(*a*) The notice of proposed removal must be given at least 30 days in advance.

(*b*) The notice of the final decision must inform the employee that he is entitled to appeal the removal to the Civil Service Commission.

(*c*) The permitted appeal to the Civil Service Commission covers sufficiency of the reasons for dismissal, as well as the prescribed procedure.

(*d*) Veterans in excepted positions who have had 1 year or more of continuous service receive all of the rights of a nonveteran in a competitive civil service position insofar as removal is concerned.

The Loyalty-Security Program

APPOINTMENT.—The procedures for the appointment of civilian employees of the Federal Government are generally unchanged by the loyalty-security program. Executive Order 10450 issued by virtue of authority vested in the President by the act of March 3, 1871, the Civil Service Act of 1883, the Hatch Act, sec. 9–A, of 1939, and the act of August 26, 1950 (Public Law 733), requires the heads of departments and agencies to insure that the employment of any civilian officer or employee (whether or not in the competitive civil service) is clearly consistent with the interest of the national security, and provides that each appointment shall be made subject to investigation by the Civil Service Commission or the department or agency doing the hiring, as the case may be. The order also sets forth the security criteria to be used:

(*a*) Unsuitability and pressure risk.

(*b*) Sabotage, espionage, treason, etc.

(*c*) Sympathetic association with subversive individuals.

(*d*) Advocacy of force or unconstitutional means to overthrow the Government of the United States.

(*e*) Membership or sympathetic association with subversive groups.

(*f*) Violation of security regulations.

(*g*) Disloyalty.

(*h*) Claim of privilege against self-incrimination.

Some departments and agencies are specifically required by law, independent of Executive Order 10450, to have appointees investigated prior to employment. The Atomic Energy Commission is one such agency. (42 U. S. C. 2165 (b).)

Public Law 733 of 1950. (*a*) This law authorizes the heads of certain specified departments and agencies to summarily suspend without pay and to terminate employment "when deemed necessary in the interest of national security," and further provides that its provisions shall apply to such other departments and agencies as the President may deem necessary in the best interests of national security. The determination of the agency head is conclusive and final. The Supreme Court in 1956, held that Public Law 733 applied only to positions affected with the "national security," as that term was used in the act (i. e., "sensitive" positions).[9]

(*b*) This law is an exception to and acts as a limitation of the Lloyd-LaFollette and Veterans' Preference Acts.

(1) One major new feature of this law is its provision for summary suspension without pay. Under the civil service regulations, certain definite procedures must be followed before suspension can take place, except that the department or agency head may place the employee on annual leave with pay, leave without pay if the employee consents, or reassign him. Under Public Law 733, immediate suspension is authorized, without any procedural prerequisites.

(2) A second major new feature of this law is its elimination of any appeal to the Civil Service Commission, under either the Lloyd-LaFollette or Veterans' Preference Acts in security cases.

(3) The standard to be used in determining when an employee shall be suspended or removed from office ("interest of national security") is also a major change, of course.

(*c*) Public Law 733 does provide for certain procedures to be followed subsequent to suspension. These procedures supplemented in the "Sample Security Regulations" issued by the Department of Justice pursuant to the authority contained in the act and in Executive Order 10450; these regulations have been adopted, with some modifications, by the various departments and agencies of the Government.

Executive Order 10450 of 1953. (*a*) This order, which also is an exception to and acts as a limitation of the Lloyd-LaFollette and Veterans' Preference Acts, requires the heads of departments and agencies "to insure that the employment and retention in employment of any civilian officer or employee within the department or agency *is clearly consistent with the interests of the national security.*" [Emphasis added.]

(*b*) The order requires the head of each department and agency to review the cases of all civilian officers and employees with respect to whom there has previously been conducted a full field investigation under Executive Order 9835, and to thereupon readjudicate, in accordance with Public Law 733, those cases which had not been adjudicated under a similar security standard to that of Executive Order 10450 (sec. 4).

(*c*) The order requires the head of each department or agency to review, and readjudicate, where necessary, the case of any officer or employee with

---

[9] *Cole* v. *Young*, 351 U. S. 536 (1956).

respect to whom there is received information indicating that his retention in employment may not be clearly consistent with the interests of the national security (sec. 5).

(d) The order requires the head of a department or agency to immediately suspend the employment of any officer or employee with respect to whom any information is received indicating that his employment may not be clearly consistent with the interests of the national security, if the head of the department or agency deems such suspension necessary in the interests of national security (sec. 6).

(e) Finally, the head of the department or agency is required to terminate the employment of such suspended officer or employee if he shall determine such termination necessary or advisable in the interests of the national security (sec. 6).

OTHER LAWS.—(a) At various times, particular departments or agencies have been specifically authorized by law to summarily dismiss officers or employees of their department or agency, independent of Public Law 733 or any other law. The Central Intelligence Agency is currently so authorized. (50 U. S. C. 403 (c).) The Atomic Energy Commission operates a personnel security program for its own employees based upon the Atomic Energy Act of 1954 (42 U. S. C. 2011, et seq.), which is independent of the program provided for by Public Law 733 and Executive Order 10450.

(b) It is unlawful for any person to accept or hold office in the Government of the United States who advocates the overthrow of our constitutional form of government or is a member of an organization that advocates the overthrow of our constitutional form of government, knowing that such organization so advocates. Any person who violates this section shall be guilty of a felony, and shall be fined not more than $1,000 or imprisoned no more than one year. (Public Law 330, Act of August 9, 1955, 5 U. S. C. Cum. Supp. 118 (p)–(r).)

(c) 50 U. S. C. 784 (a) (1) provides it shall be unlawful for any member of an organization which is registered as a Communist organization, with knowledge that such organization is so registered, to hold any nonelective office under the United States.

SUMMARY.—The present loyalty-security program is expressly authorized by statute and Executive order, and the statute and Executive order are founded upon adequate constitutional authorization to the Congress and the President, respectively.

PRESENT PROGRAM

Statutory Authority

Testifying before the Senate Committee on Armed Services, 81st Congress, 2d session, in its 1950 hearings on the bill which became Public Law 733,

General Counsel Felix Larkin, of the Office of the Secretary of Defense, repeated again and again that security risks are not necessarily disloyal and therefore the procedure of Executive Order 9835 relative to loyalty cases were often ineffective in removing employees who were a potential danger to the national security. Alcoholics, people with unsatisfactory associations, persons subject to blackmail, and those who were simply overly loquacious, he pointed out, very well might endanger the security of the United States, but could not necessarily be proved disloyal. On the other hand, he said, those who are disloyal are of course security risks.

Public Law 733, which is the statutory basis for Executive Order 10450, applied only to 11 departments and agencies: The Departments of State, Commerce, Treasury, Justice, Defense, Army, Navy, and Air Force; the Coast Guard, Atomic Energy Commission, the National Advisory Committee for Aeronautics, and the National Security Resources Board (the functions of which were transferred to the Office of Defense Mobilization by Executive order in 1953). Executive Order 10237 of April 26, 1951, made the act applicable to the Panama Canal and the Panama Railroad Company.

The first official announcement of an impending overall security program to study the existing loyalty program of the previous administration was in President Eisenhower's state of the Union message of February 2, 1953, when he told members of the Eighty-third Congress:

The safety of America and the trust of the people, alike, demand that the personnel of the Federal Government be loyal in their motives and reliable in the discharge of their duties . . . Only a combination of both loyalty and reliability promises genuine security.

The President further declared:

The heads of all executive departments and agencies have been instructed to initiate at once effective programs of security with respect to their personnel.

A representative of the Department of Justice in February 1953 was designated by Attorney General Brownell to chair an ad hoc committee to develop the details of the new program requested by President Eisenhower. The committee was composed of representatives of each Cabinet department and of other agencies which were included because of their size or their natural interest in the program, such as the Civil Service Commission and the Veterans' Administration.

The committee drafted a program which resulted in Executive Order 10450. While the loyalty program set up by Executive Order 9835 permitted the appeal of unfavorable decisions from the regional loyalty boards of the Civil Service Commission and the loyalty boards of department and agencies to the Loyalty Review Board under Executive Order 10450 the final decisions of departmental and agency heads are not subject to appeal. The committee felt that Public Law 733 of the 81st Congress offered a sound basis for an Executive order, even though the law made no provision for an appeal from a departmental or agency decision. Executive Order 10450 was therefore worded to comply with this statute.

25

The question of final determination actually goes to the heart of the issue in deciding between a loyalty program and a security program. Under the loyalty program if it was found that there were reasonable grounds for belief that an employee was disloyal or that there was a reasonable doubt of his loyalty, he could not be reemployed in the Federal service for a period of 3 years.[10] Under the security program as presently laid down by Executive Order 10450 although an employee can be discharged by decision of the agency head without appeal, in accordance with the provisions of section 7, he may be reemployed in the same department or agency in another position or in another department or agency, although in the latter instance the Civil Service Commission must make a determination that he is eligible for such employment.[11]

Extension of Statutory Authority

As previously noted, the President promulgated Executive Order 10450 April 27, 1953, establishing a governmentwide employee security program, based on the authority and the approach set forth by Congress in Public Law 733, and abolished the old loyalty program. By the terms of the Executive order, the provisions of Public Law 733 were made applicable to all other departments and agencies of the Government.[12] This made the head of each department and agency responsible for establishing and maintaining "an effective program to insure that the employment and retention in employment of any civilian officer or employee within the department or agency is clearly consistent with the interests of national security."[13]

Mechanics of the Program

Section 3 of Executive Order 10450 requires that all appointments to Government positions shall be subject to investigation. The scope of the investigation will vary according to the degree of adverse effect upon the national security which could be brought about by the incumbent of a particular position. In no case will this be less than what is called a national agency check and inquiry. This involves a check of name and finger-

---

[10] On April 20, 1950, the Civil Service Commission added to part 5 of its rules, sec. 5.101 (a), which provides (15 F. R. 2239): "Persons disqualified for any of the reasons stated under civil service rule II, sec. 2.104 (a), (1) through (8) of this chapter, may, in the discretion of the Commission, be denied examination, or be denied any of the types of appointments listed in civil service rule II, sec. 2.112 (a), (1) through (6), namely, original probational, reappointment, reinstatement, temporary appointment, interagency transfer, and conversion from excepted, war service indefinite or temporary indefinite appointment to competitive appointment, for a period of not more than 3 years from the date of the determination of such disqualification."

[11] Sec. 7, Executive Order 10450, April 27, 1953.

[12] Ibid., sec. 1.

[13] Ibid., sec. 2.

print files of the FBI and the files of the Civil Service Commission, the House Committee on Un-American Activities, and the military intelligence agencies. It also involves written inquiries to appropriate local law enforcement agencies, former employers and supervisors, persons given as references, and schools attended. If at any stage of the investigation information indicates that the employment of an individual may not be clearly consistent with the interests of national security, a full field investigation is required, or such less investigation as the head of the department or agency may direct.

Subsection 3 (b) requires heads of agencies to define as sensitive positions those jobs within their agencies the incumbents of which could, by virtue of their position, bring about a material adverse effect on the national security. Agencies are not declared sensitive, but rather the positions within an agency, and it is up to the head of the agency to make the ruling.

In subsection 3 (a) there is a proviso that upon request by the head of the department or agency concerned, the Civil Service Commission may in its discretion authorize such lesser investigation as may meet the requirements of the national security with respect to per diem, intermittent, temporary, or seasonal employment of aliens employed outside the United States. The Civil Service Commission does, by agreement with the head of a department or agency, authorize a lesser investigation than that set up in the order for certain per diem and seasonal employees.

As far as pending adjudication throughout the Government as a whole is concerned, the job is completed, and this is now a program dealing with new applicants and appointees for the Federal service.[14] The normal monthly enrollment of new employees is approximately 27,000 a month. Some 55,000 full field investigations were made by the Civil Service Commission, Federal Bureau of Investigation, and other Government agencies during fiscal year 1956 under the order.

Section 4 provides for review of all cases where full field investigation was made under the old loyalty program, and a readjudication of cases not measured against the broader concept of security. This program is completed.

Section 5 provides for consideration by the agency head of new information which may be obtained regarding the case of an employee under his jurisdiction, together with investigation and readjudication of the employee's case where necessary.

Section 6 authorizes an agency head to immediately suspend an employee if at any stage of investigation information indicates that the employee's retention may not be clearly consistent with the national security. The head of the agency may also, upon appropriate investigation and review, terminate the employment of the suspended employee.

The Attorney General has interpreted Public Law 733 the statutory basis of the Executive order as making suspension mandatory prior to termina-

---

[14] P. 400, hearings before a Subcommittee of the Committee on Post Office and Civil Service, United States Senate, 84th Cong., 1st sess., pursuant to S. Res. 20, pt. I, May 26 through September 28, 1955.

tion. On November 6, 1953, the Department of Justice suggested to the Securities and Exchange Commission that it could amend its personnel security regulations to permit acceptance of a signed statement from an employee in lieu of full satisfaction of the procedural rights accorded him by the act of August 26, 1950.[15] Subsequently, however, the Attorney General advised the SEC:

This waiver procedure has been reconsidered by the Department, and the Attorney General is of the opinion that its exercise would interfere with the effective operation of the personnel security program of the Government. Accordingly, it is now the view of the Department that the provisions of your regulations providing an alternative to suspension should be rescinded.[16]

Section 7 sets up appropriate safeguards against the reemployment of a suspended or terminated employee in the same agency or in another agency, making specific provisions for a determination by the Civil Service Commission before any employee in this category may be employed by any other agency. Only one agency of the 45 departments and agencies queried concerning their practice on this score indicated that it had employed a person after suspension or termination under Executive Order 10450 by another agency. The one accepted was so employed only after the Civil Service Commission had certified his acceptability for Federal employment.

Section 8 (a) 1–8 sets forth the factors to be investigated to determine whether a person should be employed or retained in the Federal service in relation to the national security.

Subsection 8 (a) 1 reads as follows:

Depending on the relation of the Government employment to the national security:
(i) Any behavior, activities, or associations which tend to show that the individual is not reliable or trustworthy.
(ii) Any deliberate misrepresentations, falsifications, or, omissions of material facts.
(iii) Any criminal, infamous, dishonest, immoral, or notoriously disgraceful conduct, habitual use of intoxicants to excess, drug addiction, or sexual perversion.
(iv) Any illness, including any mental condition, of a nature which in the opinion of competent medical authority may cause significant defect in the judgment or reliability of the employee, with due regard to the transient or continuing effect of the illness and the medical findings in such case.
(v) Any facts which furnish reason to believe that the individual may be subjected to coercion, influence, or pressure which may cause him to act contrary to the best interests of the national security.

Sections 8 (a) 2–8 include: Sabotage, espionage, associating with saboteurs, traitors, seditionists, anarchists, revolutionists, spies or other secret foreign agents, or persons advocating the overthrow of the United States Government by force or violence; advocacy of force or violence to overthrow the Government; membership in Communist, Fascist, totalitarian, or other subversive groups; disclosure of classified information or violation of security regulations; acting in the interests of another government and

---

[15] Letter of Robert W. Minor, Acting Deputy Attorney General, to Hon. Ralph H. Demmler, Chairman, Securities and Exchange Commission, dated November 6, 1953.
[16] Letter of William P. Rogers, Deputy Attorney General, to Ralph H. Demmler, Chairman, Securities and Exchange Commission, dated January 8, 1954.

contrary to those of the United States Government; refusal to testify before a congressional committee on the grounds of possible self-incrimination. The factors noted in section 8 (a) are not exclusive.

It should be noted section 8 (a) 1 includes many traditional suitability elements to be considered along with other security tests. Actually, the vast majority of so-called security dismissals were on suitability grounds under civil service and related procedures.

Section 8 (b) of Executive Order 10450 provides that the investigation of persons entering employment in the competitive service shall primarily be the responsibility of the Civil Service Commission except where the head of an agency assumes the same. Sections 8 (b), (c), and (d) assign investigative responsibilities under the order to the Civil Service Commission, the employing agencies, and the FBI, with the provision that where information is developed pertaining to sections 8 (a) 2–8 or that an individual may have been subjected to coercion, influence, or pressure to act contrary to the interests of national security, the FBI shall make a full field investigation.

The Civil Service Commission is the central personnel investigative agency today, by virtue of Public Law 298, 82d Congress, 2d session,[17] which transferred considerable applicant investigations to it from the FBI and Executive Order 10450. Today, other agencies can make their own investigations by agreement with the Civil Service Commission. When Executive Order 10450 was promulgated, the Civil Service Commission actually could not handle all of the investigations and the Commission urged those agencies with investigative staffs to conduct their own inquiries. These agencies were the Department of Defense, Department of Justice, Treasury Department, Post Office Department, Department of State, Department of Agriculture, and the Central Intelligence Agency. Since then the Civil Service Commission has taken over the major responsibility of investigating civilian employees and applicants of the Department of Defense, including the Department of the Army, and the Department of Agriculture.

Under Executive Order 9835 all investigations were referred to the FBI if there was any shadow of doubt concerning an employee. As a result, some questionable information was often sent to loyalty boards. Now the Civil Service Commission has a system for screening cases before they are referred to the FBI.

During fiscal year 1956 the Civil Service Commission investigated approximately 42,000 cases. The estimate for fiscal year 1957 is 48,000, and the estimate for fiscal year 1958 is 44,000. The great bulk of these cases involve applicants for positions with the Atomic Energy Commission and with AEC contractors. The estimate for 1957 for the AEC is 35,572, and for 1958, 30,633. The actual figure for 1956 was slightly less. The other agencies with the largest number of cases are the Department of the Army, United States Information Agency, and International Cooperation Administration.

---

[17] Public Law 298, 82d Cong., 2d sess., April 5, 1952, "An act to provide for certain investigations by the Civil Service Commission in lieu of the Federal Bureau of Investigation, and for other purposes."

The Civil Service Commission now has approximately 1,000 investigators to handle some 50,000 cases per year. Each man handles about one case per week, and each case involves checks in 6 or 7 different parts of the country in addition to the regular national agency checks.

The Civil Service Commission promises full field investigations within 60 days, and actually concludes most cases in slightly over 40 days. The Commission in each case plans 1 week from the time the case is received from the agency until it gets to the field, 21 days to complete the field work, and about 4 days to prepare the report and return it to Washington, D. C.

A national agency check in connection with a sensitive job takes about 8 days. Such a national agency check includes a check not only of the individual but of any family references in the Commission's own files. A national agency check and inquiry, which takes about 60 days, is conducted for all nonsensitive positions. The delay is caused by waiting for the inquiry answers.

The Civil Service Commission reports include all information received, including favorable information in the form of positive data and not merely a conclusion that the information was favorable. The report identifies all informants except other agencies from whom it has received classified information under the "third party rule." The Commission investigators are under instructions to include evaluations or qualifications of testimony as, for example, that the witness was intoxicated when interviewed or apparently prejudiced.

Sections 9 (a) and (b) require the Civil Service Commission to maintain a security-investigation index covering all persons who have been investigated under Executive Order 10450. Department and agency heads must furnish the Commission with pertinent information for this index file, including the name of each person investigated together with adequate identifying information, reference to each department and agency which has investigated him, or which has suspended or dismissed him under the authority granted them or in accordance with Public Law 733.

The security-investigations index contains more than 5½ million card records on personnel investigations made in the Federal service since 1947. Prior to October 1947, a similar file was maintained in the central office of the Civil Service Commission. The master index also contains appropriate bars and flags providing immediate notice of previous derogatory information when checking names received for investigation.

During the war years many agencies of Government made personnel investigations. There was much justifiable complaint of duplication simply because one agency did not know that another agency had previously investigated the same individual. It was to eliminate this complaint that the master index file was formally established in 1947 by Executive Order 9835.

Subsection 9 (c) provides that information developed pursuant to any statute, order, or program described in section 7 of Executive Order 10450 must remain confidential. Such information remains the property of the investigating agency, but may be retained by the department or agency concerned if it is desirable and consistent with the national security.

Section 10 provides that Executive Order 10450 shall not eliminate or modify any requirements for any investigation or any determination as to security which may be required by law.

Section 11 provides for the disposition of cases under the old loyalty program. It requires, generally, that appeals and agency determinations pending before the Loyalty Review Board or the Civil Service Commission's regional loyalty boards, be processed to completion or, when hearings were not yet initiated, that they be referred to the appropriate department or agency for processing.

Section 12 revoked Executive Order 9835, but provided that the Loyalty Review Board and the Civil Service Commission's regional loyalty boards would continue to function for 120 days after the effective date of Executive Order 10450.

Section 13 requested the Attorney General to give the department and agency heads such advice as would be necessary to enable them to set up and maintain an appropriate employee-security program.

The Attorney General's part of the program has consisted of making full field investigations through the Federal Bureau of Investigation, maintaining a list of totalitarian, Fascist, Communist, or subversive organizations, and giving agencies advice in establishing and maintaining their security programs. The Attorney General also supplied to the agencies sample regulations for establishing minimum standards for implementing the security program.

Section 14, as amended, makes the Civil Service Commission responsible for a continuing study of the employee security program to assure that adequate employee security programs are established and operating in each department and agency and that employees are receiving fair, impartial, and equitable treatment. It further requires the Commission to report the results of its study to the National Security Council at least semiannually, and to inform the National Security Council immediately of any deficiency which is deemed to be of major importance.[18]

The Department of Justice has dealt with the basic subject matter of the Executive order and the law, rather than with the establishment and operation of the program. The Civil Service Commission set up a security appraisal unit within itself, and facilities for making such appraisals of other agencies. The appraisal reports are used as a basis for a letter from the Civil Service Commission, usually to the head of the department or agency, pointing out what the Commission might regard as deficiencies or making suggestions as to how the program might be improved. They were also used as the primary basis for the semiannual reports which the Commission made to the National Security Council.[19]

---

[18] Executive Order 10550, dated August 5, 1954.

[19] Hearings before a subcommittee of the Committee on Post Office and Civil Service, U. S. Senate, 84th Cong., 1st sess., pursuant to S. Res. 20, May 26 through September 28, 1955, p. 685.

Since the fifth semiannual report, December 21, 1956, the Civil Service Commission has not furnished copies of its semiannual report to the Council.

Philip Young, Chairman, Civil Service Commission, in letter dated January 7, 1957, to the Chairman of the Commission on Government Security stated:

> As you are aware, section 14 provided that the Civil Service Commission would submit periodic reports to the National Security Council as a result of its appraisal of the employee security program. I believe that you are also aware that this reporting procedure was subsequently changed to provide that the Commission would report directly to the President through the Cabinet. The technical provision of Executive Order 10450 for reporting to the National Security Council has not yet been officially amended, as it was considered that would be accomplished at a time when other provisions of Executive Order 10450 were amended, in order for it to be consistent with the decision in *Cole* v. *Young*.
>
> The sixth report under the provisions of section 14 of Executive Order 10450, which technically was due as of June 30, 1956, has not yet been submitted due to the basic changes in the program caused by the Cole decision. The effects of this decision have been under study by the Attorney General and the Civil Service Commission, as well as by the departments and agencies, since last June, and it is the intent of the Civil Service Commission to file its section 14 report after the study has been completed and the present program clarified. At the appropriate time, this report will be transmitted directly to the President, through the Cabinet in accordance with the revised procedure.

The Sample Security Regulations

At the time the President issued Executive Order 10450, he noted in an accompanying memorandum to all department and agency heads that the Attorney General would issue sample regulations designed to establish minimum standards for the operation of the security program.

The sample regulations define a sensitive position as any position which by its very nature would permit the occupant of it to bring about a material adverse effect on the national security.[20] These positions include those giving access to security information or to other classified material, as well as those jobs where the employee may have an opportunity to commit acts affecting the national security adversely.

The sample regulations define the procedures for handling a specific case in more detail than Public Law 733. In cases of suspension, for example, the employee is to be notified in writing with the reasons being as specific as security consideration will permit, and is given at least thirty days to answer the charges, including submission of affidavits or statements.

If the employee is a citizen of the United States, has a probational or indefinite appointment, and has completed his probationary or trial period, the employee may also be given a hearing before a board composed of at least three impartial and disinterested persons furnished from the roster

---

[20] Subsec. 1 (b).

32

which the Commission maintains.[21] The employee may participate in the hearings, be represented by counsel of his choice, present witnesses, and offer other evidence in his own behalf and may cross-examine witnesses offered in support of the charges against the employee. A copy of the written decision of the board is to be furnished the employee.

The regulations of some departments however, differ from the sample regulations in the matter of the written decision. For instance, Navy civilian personnel instructions, commonly termed NCPI 29, as amended September 13, 1955, section 29.4–14 (a) (6) provides that under no circumstances will the decision of the security hearing board be given the employee or his representative. This is repeated in section 29.4–14 (c) (9) with the provision added: "or memorandum of reasons prepared by a Security Hearing Board." Section 11N of the Department of Justice security regulations provides: "the employee shall not be advised of the decision of the Board (Security Hearing Board) or of the dissenting opinion of its members."

Summary of Agency Head Responsibilities Under the Employees Security Program

The head of each agency is responsible for establishing and maintaining within his agency a program to insure that the employment and retention of his civilian employees is clearly consistent with the interests of national security.

In carrying out these responsibilities the agency head must designate which of the positions in his agency are sensitive, cause the proper investigations to be made, reopen any cases that were decided under a lower security standard after a full field investigation, readjudicate any cases on which new information is received, and suspend or terminate any employee whose employment is not clearly consistent with the interests of the national security.

The agency head is also responsible for keeping investigative reports confidential, for furnishing the Civil Service Commission with information for use in maintaining the security investigations index, for cooperating with the Civil Service Commission in its work of studyng the administraton of the program, and for designating persons of integrity, ability, and good judgment for servce as members of security hearing boards of other agencies.

Subsequent Developments

On January 7, 1955, Thomas J. Donegan, special assistant to the Attorney General, was authorized by Cabinet action to advise department heads on diffi-

---

[21] In compliance with request made by the President at the time Executive Order 10450 was issued, the Civil Service Commission established rosters of employees who serve on these boards. The names were furnished the Commission by the heads of the various departments and agencies. They sit only on boards which hear cases involving other than their own employing department or agency.

cult security cases requiring coordination. Later Mr. Donegan recommended to the Attorney General the formation of a "personnel security coordination committee" to be composed of representatives of certain of the larger agencies and departments. The Attorney General agreed and the first meeting was held on January 19, 1955. Shortly thereafter the name was changed to "Personnel Security Advisory Committee," because it exercised advisory authority only. On March 23, 1956, its jurisdiction was extended when the Cabinet, on the recommendation of the Attorney General, agreed that PSAC would also have the responsibility of coordinating matters of concern within the executive branch relative to the work of the Commission on Government Security. This committee had no formal legal basis, no definite tenure, and no definite official identification. The functions of the PSAC have now been taken over by the Internal Security Division of the Department of Justice.[22]

Under date of March 4, 1955, the Attorney General in a letter to the President made certain recommendations for all agencies and departments relative to the handling of cases under Executive Order 10450. The President had charged the Attorney General specifically with studying and suggesting revisions in the content and subject matter of the program.

The Attorney General suggested seven procedural improvements. In the interest of protecting the rights of employees as well as the national security, he recommended that charges should be drawn "as specifically as possible, consistent with the requirements of protecting the national security," and that in all cases the agency's top legal officer should be consulted on the drafting of the statement of charges so that "the charges are specific enough to be meaningful to the employee." He recommended "meticulous care" in suspending employees, and suggested that in most cases a previous personal interview would be helpful. After securing the opinion of the agency's highest legal officer, the final decision to suspend should not be delegated below the Assistant Secretary level. It was urged that a legal officer be present at security board hearings to advise the board and also the employee if unrepresented by counsel; that greater efforts should be made, particularly through periodical personal review by the agency head, to secure high caliber men for the hearing boards, men possessing "the highest degree of integrity, ability, and good judgment." When an agency decides to make an adverse finding concerning a person who had previously been cleared by another agency head, the Attorney General recommended consultation between them to avoid conflicting evaluations not based on a difference in the sensitivity of the jobs. He urged that the hearing boards make every effort to produce witnesses at the hearings to testify in behalf of the Government so that such witnesses may be confronted and subjected to cross-examination, consistent, of course, with the requirements of national security. It was also suggested that all violations of law as disclosed in investigations or

---

[22] P. 875, Hearings before a subcommittee of the Committee on Post Office and Civil Service, U. S. Senate, 84th Cong., 1st sess., pursuant to S. Res. 20, May 26 through Sept. 28, 1955.

proceedings should be reported immediately to the Division of Internal Security of the Department of Justice.

The President promptly approved all of these recommendations and the letter was transmitted to the heads of all departments and agencies for their information.

The Program Today

The United States Supreme Court in the case of *Cole* v. *Young* [23] ruled that Public Law 733 applies only to officers and employees in "sensitive" jobs, and that the act was not intended to cover all Government activities. The Court held that the statute related only to activities directly concerned with the Nation's safety as distinguished from the general welfare. The Court thought it was "virtually conclusive" that had Congress intended to use the term "national security" in a sense broad enough to include all Government activities, it would have granted the power of summary dismissal to all agencies.[24] "Indeed," said Justice Harlan, "in view of the stigma attached to persons dismissed on loyalty grounds, the need for procedural safeguards seems even greater than in other cases, and we will not lightly assume that Congress intended to take away those safeguards in the absence of some overriding necessity, such as exists in the case of employees handling defense secrets." [25]

According to a Department of Justice press release of June 15, 1956 issued as a result of the Courts holding:

Attorney General Herbert Brownell, Jr., announced today that all departments and agencies of the Federal Government have been advised that any employee holding a nonsensitive position and presently under suspension in pending civilian employee security proceedings should be restored to duty immediately. There were 17 such employees.

They were advised to do this, the Attorney General said, in order that the executive branch complies fully with the opinion of the Supreme Court in the case of *Cole* v. *Young*.

Additionally, the agencies were advised that, pending further study of the effect of the opinion upon the Federal employee security program, no removal proceedings should be commenced against any employee in a nonsensitive position under Executive Order 10450.

Shortly after the Court's decision, bills were introduced during the Eighty-fourth Congress to extend the application of Public Law 733 to all positions, sensitive and nonsensitive, and to broaden the meaning of "national security" as used in the act.

---

[23] 351 U. S. 536, *Kendrick M. Cole* v. *Philip Young et al.*, decided June 11, 1956.

[24] "Congress specified 11 named agencies to which the act should apply, the character of which reveals, without doubt, a purpose to single out those agencies which are directly concerned with the national defense and which might endanger the country's security, the so-called 'sensitive' agencies. Thus of the 11 named agencies, 8 are concerned with military operations or weapons development, and the other 3 with international relations, internal security, and the stockpiling of strategic materials." 351 U. S. 536, 544.

[25] 351 U. S. 536, 546.

In the House, Congressman Francis E. Walter introduced H. R. 11721, a bill "to protect the national security of the United States by permitting the summary suspension of employment and dismissal of civilian officers and employees of the Government, and for other purposes." Congressman Edward H. Rees introduced H. R. 11841, a bill "to protect the security of the United States by preventing the employment by the United States of persons found to be disloyal to the United States." Both bills failed to pass.

At the hearings before the House Committee on Post Office and Civil Service, July 6, 1956, the Honorable Tom Murray, chairman of the Committee stated:

These bills have been introduced on account of the decision of the Supreme Court in the case of *Cole* v. *Young*. . . . As I understand the decision, it holds it was the intent of the Congress to apply the provisions of Public Law 733 of the 81st Congress only to sensitive positions.

I might say I am the author of the legislation, H. R. 7439, which subsequently became Public Law 733, and it certainly was not my intent or my understanding that this committee, in reporting the bill out, or Congress, in enacting it, ever intended that it should apply only to sensitive positions.

Section 3 of the law provides:

1. The provisions of this act shall apply to such other departments and agencies of the Government as the President may, from time to time, deem necessary in the best interests of national security.

.   .   .   .

The minority opinion in the *Cole* v. *Young* case, which was concurred in by Mr. Justice Clark, Mr. Justice Reed, and Mr. Justice Minton, stated in part:

We believe the Court's order has stricken down the most effective weapon against subversive activity available to the Government. It is not realistic to say that the Government can be protected merely by applying the act to sensitive jobs. One never knows just which job is sensitive. The janitor might prove to be in as important a spot securitywise as the top employee in the building. The Congress decided that the most effective way to protect the Government was through the procedures laid down in the act. The President implemented its purposes by requiring that Government employment be 'clearly consistent' with the national security. The President's standard is 'complete and unswerving loyalty' not only in sensitive places but throughout the Government. The President requires, and every employee should give no less.

Herbert Brownell, Jr., Attorney General, sent the following letter dated July 5, 1956, to the House Committee on Post Office and Civil Service:

This is in reply to your letter of recent date, requesting my views with respect to the pending bills designed to amend the Act of August 26, 1950 (Ch. 803, 64 Stat. 476). As you know, the recent decision of the Supreme Court in *Cole* v. *Young* construes the 1950 act as requiring a determination by the agency head that the position from which the Government employee is suspended affects the national security. The Court held that it was not the intent of Congress to extend that act to what the Court referred to as nonsensitive positions.

If the Congress wishes to make it clear that a law such as the 1950 act may cover any position of Federal employment, it has that power as recognized by the Court's decision. I favor the enactment of H. R. 11721 which would grant authority for ex-

36

tension of the employee security program to all employees. As you know, Congress has established the Wright Commission to review the security program, including the question of coverage. I believe it should be understood that any new legislation adopted now would be primarily for the interim period until the Wright Commission reports and would be subject to review at that time.

I also recommend that any new legislation should include an amendment so that suspension would not be mandatory but permissive, and the head of the department or agency could exercise discretion and yet adequately provide for the security of the country as I have previously recommended.

The same congressional committee received a report from the Civil Service Commission which was placed in the hearing records. In this report, the Commission endorsed the bill introduced by Congressman Francis E. Walter of Pennsylvania (H. R. 11721), with one amendment, and stated:

The Cole decision limits drastically the operation of the present security program. This program can no longer be applied to the approximately 80 percent of the 21,000 persons entering the Federal Service monthly in nonsensitive positions. This decision will require corrective action in many of the cases which are being processed under the present program and will also nullify many actions heretofore taken during the past 3 years in the interests of national security.

For example, at the time of the decision there were 17 cases in which employees had been suspended pending adjudication. These 17 individuals have been restored to duty and their cases must now be processed under some authority other than the act and Executive Order 10450.

The two cases cited below are illustrative of the type of cases involved among these 17 cases:

CASE A. A member of the Communist Party in 1945 and press director of the Paul Robeson Club of the Communist Party. An active supporter of a Communist Party member who ran for a State office and was subsequently indicated under the Smith Act and given a sentence of 5 years and fined $5,000. Subject has been a close associate of known members of the Communist Party.

CASE B. From approximately 1930 to 1934 was a member of the Young Communist League and subsequent to 1934 attended mass meetings and parties of the Young Communist League and of the Communist Party. Subject's wife and his brother were members of the Young Communist League and subject has been a close associate of Communist sympathizers.

In addition to these 17 cases, we estimate that there are some 280 cases involving individuals who have been removed under the program and who will be seeking restoration and back pay as a result of the decision. All those cases must be reviewed to determine whether further action will be necessary.

.   .   .   .   .   .

The impact of the Court's decision on the present program will be strongest perhaps in the area of new appointments.

.   .   .   .   .

The Civil Service Commission urges the enactment of H. R. 11721. In addition, we suggest the desirability of incorporating in the bill the proposal sent to the Congress on April 16 of this year which is contained in H. R. 10667. This can be accomplished by adding at the end of section 1 of the act of August 26, 1950, amended by H. R. 11721, the following proviso: *"Provided further,* That nothing in this section shall be deemed to require the suspension of any civilian officer or employee prior to hearing or termination."* We have been advised by the Bureau of the Budget that there is no objection to the submission of this report.

Following the earlier announcements that the administration would comply fully with the Supreme Court's decision in *Cole* v. *Young*, the Attorney General formulated a policy that reinstatement and back pay claims by Federal employees in nonsensitive positions who had been fired as security risks should be granted, unless there was a lapse of more than 18 months "from the date of the dismissal to (1) the filing of court action, or (2) a claim for reinstatement after the decision in *Cole* v. *Young*." [26]

A letter of January 8, 1957, from the Personnel Security Advisory Committee to the Commission on Government Security contained the following table showing the status of claimant cases as of January 8, 1957:

Agency	Total	Restored from Termination	Restored from Suspension	Restored and terminated[1]
Post Office	46	31	13	2
Veterans' Administration	12	6	4	2
Navy	9	4	2	[2] 3
Civil Service Commission	2	2	......	....
Securities and Exchange Commission	1	1	......	....
Health, Education, and Welfare	4	3	......	1
Treasury	2	2	......	....
Interior	2	2	......	....
Army	4	2	2	....
Agriculture	2	2	......	....
Air Force	2	1	......	1
Housing and Home Finance Agency	1	......	......	1
Total	87	56	21	10

[1] Resignations.
[2] One of these employees separated by reduction in force.

As a result of the Supreme Court decision in *Cole* v. *Young*, and upon advice of the Department of Justice, no further action was taken against employees occupying nonsensitive positions under Executive Order 10450. The legal effect of the *Cole* case was to terminate any pending proceedings of cases under Executive Order 10450 when the occupant was in a nonsensitive position. The Cole decision does not affect any new action which may be appropriate under the Lloyd-LaFollette Act [27] or the Veterans' Preference Act. [28] The Commission has been informed, however, that no action has been taken to date under either of these two Acts against any of the individuals thus restored.

During the first 6 months of 1956 the Atomic Energy Commission revised its criteria and administrative review procedures for determining the eligibility for security clearance in the atomic energy program or entering it. The Commission announced the revision on May 10, 1956, and published the regulation the same day in the *Federal Register* to take effect

---

[26] Memorandum to the heads of all departments and agencies, Office of the Attorney General, Washington, D. C., Aug. 1, 1956, Subject: Claims for reinstatement by former employees dismissed under Executive Order 10450.

[27] Sec. 6, 37 Stat. 555 as amended, 5 U. S. C. sec. 652.

[28] Sec. 14, 58 Stat. 390, as amended, 5 U. S. C. sec. 863.

immediately.[29]   According to the Commission, the differences between the new regulation and the previous standards and procedures are as follows:

1. The previous section on "Criteria for Determining Eligibility for Security Clearance" has been clarified by the new regulation, particularly in the area of associations.

2. The new regulation provides for appointment to hearing boards of counsel whose function will be to develop all information, favorable and unfavorable, bearing upon an individual's eligibility for clearance.

3. The new regulation recognizes the use of informal interviews to determine, where possible, the eligibility of an individual for security clearance.

4. The new regulation provides that when a hearing board determines the presence of a witness is important to the resolution of material issues, the board shall request the appropriate Commission officials to arrange, if possible, for the witness to appear, and be subject to examination and cross-examination. If such a witness is unavailable, his unavailability and the reasons therefor will be considered by the hearing board in making its determination. Because of the confidential nature of sources of some information, confrontation of witnesses may not always be possible. In such cases, the hearing board may request the Commission to arrange for such a witness to testify privately and be subject to questioning by the board.[30]

The Attorney General was requested to furnish the Commission on Government Security with a formal statement concerning the operation and effectiveness of the civilian employees security program. Under date of December 11, 1956, the Attorney General responded in part as follows:

In addition to extending the "security" test and the power of suspension to all departments and agencies of the executive branch, there have been two other major accomplishments under Executive Order 10450 which should not be overlooked. Executive Order 10450 established a uniform policy and procedure to be used by those agencies specifically enumerated in Public Law 733, thus affording a greater protection of the rights of employees proceeded against. Furthermore, by requiring a review of old loyalty cases under the "security" test and compelling investigation of all employees in positions deemed sensitive, Executive Order 10450 permitted an effective analysis of the personnel picture in Government from the standpoint of security. This review of the old loyalty cases was a tremendous undertaking on the part of the Administration but, in view of the inadequacy of the "loyalty" test, one that was deemed absolutely unavoidable. Concerning these review cases, I am pleased to state that the Civil Service Commission advised as of May 15, 1956, that approximately 18 out of an original total of approximately 12,500 employees on Government rolls remained to be readjudicated under the present criteria.

It is most significant to note that the great majority of cases which became the subject of controversy were review cases, many of which resulted in suspension and hearing. Experience has shown that current cases do not present the adjudication problems found in the old loyalty cases, which usually related to activities taking place when Communist-inspired or Communist-influenced functions and organizations were quite prevalent. With the adjudication of the review cases now virtually completed, the incident of hearing cases is sharply reduced.

In the early period of Executive Order 10450 the combination of the workload and the newness of the program resulted in an unexpected delay in some departments and agencies with the result that, while those who were suspended were entitled to back pay if finally cleared, some suspended employees underwent obvious financial hardships pending a final determination of their status. In view of this, by letter dated April

---

[29] P. 117, 20th Semiannual Report of the Atomic Energy Commission, S. Doc. 130, 84th Cong., 2d sess.
[30] P. 118, 20th Semiannual Report of the Atomic Energy Commission, S. Doc. 130, 84th Cong. 2d sess.

16, 1956, I recommended to Congress that mandatory suspension under Public Law 733 is not necessary in all proceedings and that the interests of the national security could still be protected if the decision to suspend were placed within the discretionary authority of the heads of the departments and agencies. Such an amendment to Public Law 733 would facilitate administration of the program to meet individual cases.

There are some who feel that any employee security program should have provisions for appeal of an unfavorable decision to higher authority. As I have already pointed out, the head of the department or agency is responsible for the protection of Government affairs entrusted to his jurisdiction. Being responsible, he should be able to choose those with whom he must share his responsibility. Also, in practical operation, the head of the department or agency is in a far better position to judge his security needs than any outside authority. The matter of appeal was considered fully by Congress in passing Public Law 733, but it was concluded that no outside agency should be in a position to impose its judgment upon the head of the department or agency. Instead, Congress in Public Law 733 provided that a dismissed employee could be hired by other departments or agencies if the Civil Service Commission and the hiring agency concluded that the employee would not jeopardize security interests in the new position.

Another popular misconception concerning this program is that it is ineffective because it has caused no communists to be prosecuted. The primary concern of Public Law 733 and Executive Order 10450 is not to secure criminal prosecutions, but to guard against employment of individuals who may be unreliable because of matters relating to their loyalty, background, or personal conduct. Just as much damage to our national interest may be caused by such noncriminal factors as irresponsibility and lack of due care, as by one possessing criminal intent. It is not a crime to be unsuitable at this time for Federal employment and the Government should not be compelled to wait until someone violates one of the laws relating to security which we have discussed before he may be discharged. By then it will be too late. I would like to remind the Commission, however, that an employee security investigation played a role in the recent Petersen espionage prosecution,[31] and individuals who have sworn falsely in security matters arising from the operation of the security program have been prosecuted under the law.[32]

RECOMMENDATIONS

NECESSITY

The executive branch must maintain a program for screening civilian personnel as well as applicants for employment.

The necessity of screening civilian employees as well as applicants for employment to insure that they are loyal to the United States and that their employment is otherwise compatible with the national security has not been seriously controverted.

---

[31] The case of Joseph Sidney Petersen, Jr., *U. S.* v. *Petersen*, Indictment No. 3049, U. S. District Court of the Eastern District of Virginia (Alexandria division), October 20, 1954, violation title 50, U. S. C. sec. 31 (1946 ed.); title 18, U. S. C. sec. 2071. (Footnote added.)

[32] False statement on the form 57 (application for Federal employment) is punishable by law (U. S. C., title 18, sec. 1001). (Footnote added.)

Congressional committees have previously traced the evolution of the Communist conspiracy and analyzed its methods of subversion, including the penetration of Government.[33] That infamous, and now well established, story of design and deceit will not be repeated here. Suffice to say that for many years the executive and legislative branches of the Government have been aware of the national threat through subverted Federal workers, conspiratorial or otherwise, and have taken certain measures to terminate or prevent their employment.[34]

The Congress in Public Law 304, 84th Congress, the instrument creating the Commission on Government Security, recognized the present danger and declared it to be the policy of the Congress—

. . . that there shall exist a sound Government program (a) establishing procedures for security investigation, evaluation, and, where necessary, adjudication of Government employees, . . .

The question at issue, therefore, is not the need for a personnel screening program, but the type of program which can most effectively safeguard the Nation's security with the minimum intrusion on the rights and privileges of Federal employees.

Senator Hubert H. Humphrey in opening the hearings on S. J. Res. 21, "A Joint Resolution to Establish a Commission on Government Security." [35] put the matter in proper focus when, in commenting on the Federal security program as a whole, he stated:

All devoted Americans must be concerned with assuring that our Nation's security is adequate to protect against the Soviet conspiracy, the most monstrous conspiracy against freedom in the history of men. They must also be concerned with the protection and preservation of our basic democratic freedom. *The most crucial problem of our day is to find the formula for obtaining the maximum degree of security with the minimum sacrifice of our great national traditions.* (Italic supplied.)

This section of the report will address itself to the attempted resolution of this problem in the civilian employees area.

STANDARD

The loyalty standard for the denial of employment or the removal from employment in an executive department or agency should be that, on all the information there is reasonable doubt as to the loyalty of the individual to the Government of the United States.[36]

---

[33] See, e. g., "Interlocking Subversion in Government Departments," Internal Security Subcommittee to the Committee on the Judiciary, U. S. Senate, 83d Cong., 1st sess., July 30, 1953.

[34] See History, p. 5, et seq.

[35] Hearings before a subcommittee on reorganization of the Committee on Government Operations, U. S. Senate, 84th Cong., 1st sess., Mar. 1955, p. 3.

[36] To the extent the Commission's recommendations are inconsistent with Public Law 733, the statutory basis of the present program (Act of Aug. 26, 1950, 64 Stat. 476, 5 U. S. § 21–1, 22–2, 22–3, 81st Cong., 2d sess.) or any other legislation, such conflicting legislation should be repealed. Where legislation or Executive orders are believed mandatory or desirable for the implementation of Commission recommendations, suggested drafts are set forth on p. 693, et seq. of this report.

The formulation of a standard for a personnel screening program is more than an exercise in semantics. The standard should keynote the entire program and clearly reflect its governing philosophy and objectives.

The Commission recommends that the denial of employment or removal from employment (for reasons other than nonsuitability) be predicated on reasonable doubt of loyalty. It has further recommended that the standard of the suitability program be such cause as will promote the "efficiency of the service," i. e., personal nonsuitability.[37] Each of these standards complements the other and in the Commission's considered judgment, together they constitute an adequate basis for the development of a program which will provide full protection against those who would intentionally harm our interests as well as against those who, because of personal defects, abnormal habits, or related reasons, may also constitute a danger to the national security.

The heart of the Commission's recommended program, however, is the reestablishment of a loyalty standard applicable to all employees and all applicants for employment. Before arriving at this position, the Commission studied and weighed the comparative merits of the security standard for Federal civilian employment presently in effect, as well as the standards of other loyalty and security programs past and present.

From this analysis it became clear that in selecting a standard we had two general alternatives:

(a) An *absolute* standard which can be applied by examining an individual's case history in itself without regard to the relationship of his job to the national security, i. e., a loyalty standard.

(b) A *relative* standard which can be applied only by weighing an individual's case history in the light of the relationship, if any, of his job to the national security, i. e., a security standard.

Both of these types of standards have advantages and, under certain circumstances, disadvantages. Both have been tried in the Federal service, so we are in a position to judge their comparative effectiveness.

As long ago as the middle of the last century, the Government had a policy of dismissing employees deemed disloyal.[38] Since 1940,[39] loyalty has been a factor for consideration in the civil service rules governing the selection of appointees to the Federal service.

During the period March 1947, to May 1953, the entire Federal service was subject to a loyalty standard. Executive Order 9835, promulgated by President Truman on March 21, 1947, provided that the standard for refusal of employment was that ". . . on all the evidence, reasonable grounds exist for the belief that the person involved is *disloyal* to the Government of the United States." (Italic supplied.) This standard was amended on April 28, 1951, to substitute the wording "on all the evidence there is reasonable

[37] For the Commission's recommendations concerning the suitability standard and program generally, see p. 82.

[38] Attorney General's statement to Commission, Dec. 11, 1956.

[39] Pursuant to Executive Order 8423, May 28, 1940.

42

doubt as to the *loyalty* of the person involved to the Government of the United States." [40]   (Italic supplied.)   On April 27, 1953, President Eisenhower, through Executive Order 10450 effective 30 days thereafter, revoked Executive Order 9835, as amended, and instituted the present government-wide security program, wherein an employee or applicant must demonstrate that his employment is "clearly consistent with the interests of the national security."

The major issue the Commission pondered, therefore, was whether the present security program should be continued or amended or whether it should be replaced with a program based on loyalty.   It is the profound conviction of the Commission that the cornerstone of the civilian program must be a standard related to the loyalty of the employee.   It is fundamental that there is no place in the Federal service for a disloyal person.   Whether his loyalty is pledged to the Communist Party or to some new and equally evil movement, where his interests are irreconcilably in conflict with the interests of the United States, he must be barred from employment.

The Commission further believes that a loyalty program is the only test of employment which, when the national security is involved, can satisfactorily protect the rights and interests of both the Government and the individual.

This is recognized even under the current program.   While Executive Order 10450 ostensibly functions under a security standard, it does not abandon the fundamental concept that Federal employment at a minimum demands individual loyalty.   Thus, the preamble of the Executive order refers to the "complete and unswerving loyalty to the United States," a phrase transferred bodily from Executive Order 9835.   Again, seven of the eight major criteria or categories of facts which may be considered in the evaluation of a specific case deal with loyalty type information, the majority of which were contained in similar or identical language in Executive Order 9835.[41]   The Supreme Court in the historic case of *Cole* v. *Young* [42] put the matter in clear perspective stating:

Executive Order 9835 . . . as amended by Executive Order 10241 . . . had established the loyalty program under which all employees, regardless of their position, were made subject to discharge if there was a "reasonable doubt" as to their loyalty.   That order was expressly revoked by § 12 of the present Executive order.   *There is no indication, however, that it was intended thereby to limit the scope of the persons subject to a loyalty standard.*   And any such implication is negatived by the remarkable similarity in the preambles to the two orders and in the kinds of information considered to be relevant to the ultimate determinations.   In short, *all* employees were still to be subject to at least a minimum loyalty standard, though under new procedures which do not afford a right to appeal to the Civil Service Commission.   (First emphasis supplied.)

The fusion of normal suitability factors with loyalty factors in the name of security in the current program has led to anomalous results.   Although

---

[40] Executive Order 10241.

[41] Secs. 8 (a) 2–8. Sec. 8 (a) 1 on the other hand embodies four subcategories directly related to personal suitability and only one, the so-called "pressure risk" category, which may properly be called a true security criterion.

[42] 351 U. S. 536, 1956.

there are no absolute, definitive statistics, the best evidence available to the Commission indicates that, since the beginning of the program, the vast majority of removals which have been reported as security removals have, in fact, been suitability removals handled under the normal civil service or related procedures. In the comparatively few remaining cases where loyalty was involved, only a loyalty and not a security finding was required. Thus the Supreme Court stated in *Cole* v. *Young*:

> We therefore interpret the Executive Order as meaning that when "loyalty" charges are involved an employee may be dismissed regardless of the character of his position in the Government service, and that the agency head need make no evaluation as to the effect which continuance of his employment might have upon the "national security."

In short, therefore, while the current program has been labeled and justified as a security program, it has in practice been an unnatural blend of suitability, loyalty, and security programs. The hybrid product has been neither fish nor fowl, resulting in inconclusive adjudications, bewildered security personnel, employee fear and unrest, and general public criticism.

The return to a loyalty program complemented by the suitability program will clear away the haze of doubt and confusion and place the matter of denial of employment or removal from employment upon the basis of personal responsibility. Pure suitability cases will be treated as such. Persons removed from their jobs because of personal aberrations or unfortunate associations where loyalty is not in issue, will not be branded as security risks. Persons charged with alleged disloyalty will be given the fullest opportunity to try the issue. Final determinations will be based upon personal accountability and not upon a nebulous relationship of conduct to employee to position to national security.

The principal reason for recommending a loyalty standard, however, is the belief that, in the final analysis, with rare exceptions, the real danger to the nation from this source lies with that small coterie of individuals who are now or may later be disloyal to the United States. A careful review of our record of infamy to date—the Hiss, Remington, Greenglass, Rosenberg, Gold, White, and Silvermaster cases, and many others—makes it clear that their perfidy can be traced to a fundamental allegiance to another cause, principally communism, and a deep-seated disloyalty, or lack of loyalty, to the United States. David Greenglass, confessed spy, in testifying before a congressional subcommittee, recounted the following personal rationalization by Julius Rosenberg of why he was serving the Soviet Union:

> He said that he was a Communist and that he wanted to see communism triumph throughout the world, and he was going to do it in the best way he knew how, and the best way he was fitted to do it, because of his technical skill, and, of course, another thing he did not list: his complete—his willingness to use anybody to gain his ends. He would do anything in his power to bring about the hegemony of the Soviet Union.[43]

---

[43] Hearings before the subcommittee to Investigate the Administration of the Internal Security Act and Other Internal Security Laws of the Committee on the Judiciary, U. S. Senate, 84th Cong., 2d sess., pt. 21, p. 1110.

The report of the Royal Commission on Espionage of the Commonwealth of Australia issued in August 1955, in reviewing the assistance given the Soviet agents by Australian citizens, stated in part:

Above all, the Soviet has in Australia, as in other Western countries, an auxiliary force composed of Communists and like-minded persons, some of whom are ready and willing to further the Soviet cause, some even to the point of the destruction of Australian sovereignty. The Communist Party supplies the fundamental organization for this force.[44]

Again,

Quite apart from the known Party member, the auxiliary force comprises some persons whose role it is to conceal their Communist affiliations and sympathies and to operate in the guise of ordinary loyal Australian citizens. This class provides the most dangerous pool of helpers in fifth-column and espionage work, and it is amongst this class that the Moscow Centre usually looks for aid.[45]

Later,

All the persons whose acts were directly or indirectly connected with espionage *were either members* of the Communist Party or ex-members or pretending *ex-members thereof or sympathizers with communism*, and some of them were high-ranking functionaries of the Party.[46]

and finally,

We have stressed these matters in this part of our Report because it is clear to us that *without the element of Communism Australia would be barren soil in which Soviet espionage could not even take root*, let alone flourish.[47] (Emphasis supplied.)

The Commission recognizes that the operation of a program founded on a loyalty standard presents certain dangers and difficulties. The principal criticism made is that a finding of disloyalty or doubt of loyalty requires a finding of state of mind, i. e., scienter. Contrary to some views, however, this is not an insurmountable obstacle. Judges as well as juries composed of men and women of average intelligence make thousands of analogous decisions daily in civil and criminal court cases. While neither unanimity nor perfection of judgment is attained, the results have been eminently satisfactory and fully consonant with our democratic concepts. The same can be said of the conduct of a loyalty program.

Having once decided that it must be founded upon a system of personal accountability, however, it remains for us to gird the program with as many procedural safeguards as possible so that the loyalty issue may be fairly and reasonably tested with parallel regard for the national security and individual rights. This the Commission has done, first by the selection of a workable, understandable, and equitable standard,[48] and secondly, by developing an elaborate code of rights and privileges [49] far greater than those accorded

---

[44] Sec. 308, p. 99.
[45] Sec. 310, p. 99.
[46] Sec. 315 (1), p. 100.
[47] Sec. 317, p. 101.
[48] For a discussion of suggested principles to be followed in the application of the loyalty standard and criteria, see Criteria and Principles of Application, p. 46 et seq.
[49] Set forth in subsequent recommendations.

Federal employees in the past, including a right of appeal to a Central Security Office.

In recommending a loyalty standard and a suitability standard as the twin bases for denial of Federal employment or removal from employment, the Commission also recognizes that certain positions in Government are so identified with the national security interest, i. e., sensitive positions,[50] that special precautions must be exercised in the selection of personnel. Many persons, though not disqualified for service generally because of personal unsuitability or disloyalty, nevertheless may be considered unsuitable to hold a sensitive position. Therefore, the Commission has also recommended in connection with the suitability program that where the head of the employing agency believes the national security can be adequately protected by transferring the employee to another position for which he is qualified and suitable, every effort should be made to do so.[51]

The Commission feels that, on balance, this correlated power afforded the Government will provide adequate protection for our Nation's security while not jeopardizing the fundamental concepts of the removal program.

CRITERIA AND PRINCIPLES OF APPLICATION

Criteria

Activities and associations of an applicant or employee which may be considered in connection with the determination of the existence of a reasonable doubt as to his loyalty may include one or more of the following:

1. Sabotage, espionage, or attempts or preparations therefor, or knowingly associating with spies or saboteurs;

2. Treason or sedition or advocacy thereof;

3. Advocacy of revolution or force or violence to alter the constitutional form of Government of the United States;

4. Intentional, unauthorized disclosure to any person, under circumstances which may indicate disloyalty to the United States, of documents or information of a confidential or nonpublic character;

5. Performing or attempting to perform his duties, or otherwise acting, so as to serve the interests of another government in preference to the interests of the United States;

6. Membership in, or affiliation or sympathetic association, with any party or association which the Congress of the United

---

[50] For the Commission's recommended definition of a sensitive position, see p. 54.
[51] See Suitability Program, p. 81.

46

States, or any agency or officer of the United States duly authorized by the Congress for that purpose, finds:

(*a*) Seeks to alter the form of Government of the United States by force or violence, or other unconstitutional means; or,

(*b*) Is organized or utilized for the purpose of advancing the aims and objectives of the Communist movement; or,

(*c*) Is organized or utilized for the purpose of establishing any form of dictatorship in the United States or any form of international dictatorship; or,

(*d*) Is organized or utilized by any foreign government, or by any foreign party, group or association acting in the interest of such foreign government for the purpose of (*a*) espionage, or (*b*) sabotage, or (*c*) obtaining information relating to the defense of the United States or the protection of the national security, or (*d*) hampering, hindering, or delaying the production of defense materials; or,

(*e*) Is affiliated with, or acts in concert with, or is dominated or controlled by, any party, group, or association of the character described in (*a*) or (*b*) or (*c*) or (*d*) above.

7. Membership in or affiliation with any organization which the Congress of the United States, or any agency or officer of the United States duly authorized by the Congress for that purposce, finds has adopted a policy of advocating or approving the commission of acts of force and violence to deny others their rights under the Constitution of the United States.

8. Refusal to testify upon the ground of self-incrimination in any authorized inquiry relating to subversive activities conducted by a congressional committee, Federal court, Federal grand jury, or any other duly authorized Federal agency, as to questions relating to subversive activities of the individual involved or others, unless the individual, after opportunity to do so, satisfactorily explains his refusal to testify.

9. The foregoing enumeration should not be deemed to exclude any other factors tending to establish reasonable doubt as to loyalty.

As indicated, the Commission recommends the foregoing specific criteria in full recognition of the fact that they are not, and could not be, all-inclusive. They are set forth merely as guidelines for the assistance of security officers, screening officers, agency heads, hearing examiners, members of the Central Review Board, and others concerned with the loyalty program, in carrying out their responsibilities. The wording of each criterion has been formulated after consideration of criteria established for other programs, past and present, and with particular consideration to its application to current conditions. The language used is purposely broad and general to obviate the necessity of amending it when less than major changes occur in the present danger. Each case must be resolved in the light of its particular facts and in the best judgment of those responsible for its adjudication.

It is believed that the recommended wording in the main is self-explanatory. The following differences from the wording of Executive Order 10450 should be noted, however:

1. The suitability criteria set forth in section 8 (a) 1 of the Executive order, including the so-called "pressure risk" criterion,[52] have not been included here but are contained substantially in the Commission's recommended suitability criteria.[53] The Commission is convinced that all cases falling in these categories can and should be handled under suitability procedures, thereby avoiding erroneously and unjustly stigmatizing nonsuitable individuals as security risks or disloyal.

2. The types of memberships, affiliations, and associations which should be examined have been more finely delineated. In this connection reference should be made to the Commission's recommendations concerning the appropriate function of the Attorney General in identifying certain organizations.[54]

3. The criterion relating to the use of the privilege against self-incrimination has been expanded to include refusal to testify not only before a congressional committee, but before other authorized United States agencies. Further, such action does not become a factor for consideration if the individual involved "after opportunity to do so, satisfactorily explains his refusal to testify." For a fuller treatment of the problem posed by the fifth amendment generally and further rationale for its inclusion in the loyalty criteria, see the special paper entitled "Privilege against self-incrimination" set forth on page 675.

Principles of Application

In the application of the loyalty standard and the criteria, the Commission further recommends that consideration be given to the following principles of definition, construction, and application.

1. The term "national security" relates to the protection and preservation of the military, economic, and productive strength of the United States, including the security of the Government in domestic and foreign affairs against or from espionage, sabotage

---

[52] Sec. 8 (a) 1 (v).
[53] See Suitability Program, criteria, p. 82.
[54] See p. 96.

and subversion, and all other illegal acts designed to weaken or destroy the United States.

2. Where a reasonable doubt as to loyalty exists, no person should be retained in Government service, no matter how valuable his contribution might be.

3. Past Communist membership or associations are factors which must be considered, but they should not be applied mechanically or automatically. Efforts should be made to determine the degree to which the person concerned has broken with these past contacts. One's associates, past and present, as well as one's conduct, may properly be considered in determining fitness and loyalty. The greatest care must be taken to avoid misinterpretation of affiliation. The affiliation should be viewed in the light of the member's knowledge of the purposes of the organization, or the extent to which such organizational purposes had been publicized at the time the individual joined the organization or retained membership therein. The character and history of an organization must be closely examined with the realization that loyal persons may have been persuaded to join for innocent reasons. Hence, the need for a full-time hearing examiner who can become a student of the subject, and a central board to review the findings of membership and inferences drawn therefrom.

4. The normal relationships with the family do not create a reasonable doubt as to loyalty unless they fall within the prescribed type of close, continuing, or sympathetic association, and unless such association with members of the family is of such a nature as to indicate sympathetic association with an organization of the type described in Criteria, pages 46–7.

5. The standard "that on all the information, a reasonable doubt as to loyalty exists" requires that an adverse determination must be based upon information that the hearing examiner, or the agency head charged with final decision, regards as reliable and trustworthy, for obviously a doubt not based upon such information would be arbitrary or fanciful as distinguished from reasonable.

(a) Since the charging agency must present to the hearing examiner information which is reliable and trustworthy, there will be no basis for any claim that the burden of proof is upon the employee.

(b) Since the proceeding is administrative in character and for the purpose of ascertaining the truth, the burden of proof should not rest either upon the government or the employee, but the decision should be reached upon the evaluation of all the information, favorable as well as unfavorable.

6. In the application of the standard, the hearing examiner should consider the entire file, including the favorable information

on the employee, as well as the derogatory information, such as (1) his reputation as to veracity, integrity, and strength of character among his friends, associates, and employers, and (2) his demonstrated appreciation of the need for protection of the national security against enemies, foreign and domestic.

7. Where there is convincing evidence that a former member of the Communist Party has recanted and no longer subscribes to its objectives, such evidence should be considered in determining whether there is reasonable doubt as to his loyalty. The Commission believes that a policy which would allow the employment or retention in employment of a former Communist who has genuinely recanted, and provides convincing evidence to that effect, would be in the best interests of the Government.

8. In the absence of new evidence there should be no reinvestigation or readjudication of old security or loyalty cases in the event that a new standard is adopted.

The recommended loyalty criteria are not perfect or inflexible. In every case their application in the light of the standard demands the maximum in understanding, common sense, and moral perspective. The Commission commends the above principles to agency heads and all security personnel in the discharge of that responsibility.

SCOPE OF PROGRAM

General

The loyalty program should extend uniformly to all employees and applicants for employment in all departments and agencies with the exception of the Central Intelligence Agency and the National Security Agency.

The Commission recommends a program under which all employees, including employees of wholly owned Government corporations and all applicants for employment must meet certain standards of loyalty and general suitability. The specific standards, as well as the implementary criteria and certain principles and procedures proposed for each phase, are delineated in other recommendations.[55]

The recommended loyalty program should extend with equal application to all employees, veterans and nonveterans alike, in all departments and

---

[55] See Standard, p. 41; Criteria and Principles of Application, p. 46; and Suitability Program, p. 81 et seq.

agencies.   It should also extend to applicants and probationary employees in all executive departments and agencies.[56]

The Commission, however, in formulating its recommendations has consciously endeavored to provide the very fullest measure of procedural protection to the employee or applicant against whom a doubt as to loyalty has arisen.   At the same time it has not relinquished any part of the protection presently accorded the Government.   In so doing it has struck a fine balance which, it submits, should not be disturbed except in those instances where the national security interests are so great and the consequences of error could be so devastating, that extraordinary authority and powers must be given to the agencies involved.

From its review of the mandates, responsibilities, and operations of the executive departments and agencies, the Commission has concluded that the exceptional authority to depart from the procedures of the loyalty program should extend only to the Central Intelligence Agency and the National Security Agency.[57]   It is recognized, of course, that Congress in its wisdom may see fit to grant further exceptions to other agencies on the showing of new facts or the intervention of emergency conditions not now foreseen by the Commission.   In no instance should the standards and criteria be less than those applicable to other departments and agencies in the executive branch.

Applicants

It is recognized that no person has a right to employment in the Government, but as a matter of policy and fairness, an applicant for such employment should be accorded the protection hereinafter described: [58]

Where one of the reasons given for rejecting an application is reasonable doubt as to the applicant's loyalty, the applicant should be given the opportunity to explain his answer to the charges in an informal interview with an officer of the employing agency, as well as an opportunity to supply affidavits or other information deemed relevant.

---

[56] By executive departments and agencies the Commission would include all departments and independent agencies, commissions, boards, authorities, and other agencies listed on the chart "Organization of Federal Executive Departments and Agencies" published by the U. S. Senate Committee on Government Operations, dated Jan. 1, 1957.

[57] The Atomic Energy Commission presently functions under a separate standard and separate procedures by virtue of its basic Act (42 U. S. C. 2165) and implementing regulations. The Commission believes that the Atomic Energy Commission employees should be subject to the proposed loyalty program. For the Commission's specific recommendations in this regard see Atomic Energy program, p. 214.

[58] For the Commission's recommendations concerning the nature and extent of investigations on applicants, see Investigations, p. 55.

No applicant for employment in the competitive service of the Federal Government should have his name removed from the Civil Service Commission register, where the sole cited basis or one of the cited bases for such removal is reasonable doubt as to his loyalty, without such applicant being accorded an opportunity for hearing before a Central Security Office hearing examiner as provided for employee loyalty cases.[59]

Where an application for the noncompetitive service of the Federal Government is denied and one of the grounds cited for such denial is reasonable doubt as to the applicant's loyalty, the applicant should be accorded an opportunity for a hearing before a hearing examiner.

In each situation, the same procedures should be followed as in employee loyalty cases.

Hearings on loyalty or security matters have been routinely provided for applicants under the present program only by the Atomic Energy Commission.[60] In some cases the Air Force has granted hearings. There appears to be no question of the moral soundness and equity of giving applicants rejected on the grounds of loyalty a chance to explain. The Commission has elsewhere taken notice of the fact that employee interviews often can resolve a loyalty issue even before it proceeds to hearing and has recommended that such interviews be mandatory.[61] The Nation has lost much valuable manpower because otherwise qualified individuals have not been permitted to present their side of the case. Once rejected by one agency an applicant is in a disadvantageous position in applying for other Federal employment.

The principal arguments against providing hearings for applicants appear to be the administrative burden and costs.

The Commission feels that the same principles which ordain the necessity of hearings and appeals in employee cases should apply to applicants as well.

Probationary Employees

1. Probationary employees should be accorded the protection hereinafter described:

(a) Where one of the reasons given for dismissing a probationary employee is reasonable doubt as to his loyalty, the employee should be given the opportunity to explain his answer

---

[59] See Hearings, p. 61.

[60] The Civil Service Commission does not provide hearings in loyalty cases to applicants for nonsensitive positions in the competitive service, but does give them the opportunity to answer written interrogatories when the investigation develops loyalty information.

[61] See Screening; Charges, p. 57.

to the charges in an informal interview with an officer of the employing agency, as well as an opportunity to supply affidavits or other information deemed relevant.

(*b*) Where a probationary employee of the Federal Government is dismissed and one of the grounds cited for such dismissal is reasonable doubt as to the employee's loyalty, the head of the employing agency should refer the file to the director of the Central Security Office for assignment to a hearing examiner, and the same procedures are to be followed as in employee loyalty cases.[62]

2. These procedural rights do not apply to seasonal or temporary employees.

Under Public Law 733,[63] the statutory basis for Executive Order 10450, only United States citizens holding permanent or indefinite appointments who have completed their trial or probationary period are entitled to a statement of the charges against them, an opportunity to answer the charges, a hearing upon request, a review of the case by the agency head or his designee, and a written statement of the decision of the agency head. Other employees are entitled only to a statement of the reasons for their suspension and an opportunity to submit statements or affidavits to show why they should be reinstated. Since the Supreme Court decision in *Cole* v. *Young* [64] the Civil Service Commission has the responsibility of processing loyalty cases involving conditional appointees to nonsensitive positions in the competitive services. As in the case of applicants, hearings are not held, but written interrogatories requiring written replies may be transmitted to the employee.

The arguments which prevail for providing hearings and other procedural safeguards to applicants apply a fortiori to probationary employees. Further, both the individual and the Government have an investment in his service which should not be lost without benefit of the full loyalty procedures.

Veterans and Nonveterans

Uniform rights and privileges should be afforded to veterans and nonveterans.

The rights and privileges which the Commission has recommended be afforded to employees and applicants under the loyalty program, including the right of appeal to the Central Security Office, are unparalleled in current practice or in the history of Federal employment. The reasons which

---

[62] See Hearings, p. 61.
[63] 64 Stat. 476, 5 U. S. C. 22–1 (1950).
[64] 351 U. S. 536, 1956.

53

have caused the Commission to recommend the individual procedures are of such importance that they should apply uniformly to all employees, veterans and nonveterans.

There is no right of appeal from the decision of the agency head under Public Law 733 (64 Stat. 476, 5 U. S. C. 22-1, 1950) or Executive Order 10450, for nonveterans or veterans. Preference eligible veterans, unlike nonveterans, are given a right to appeal suitability removals to the Civil Service Commission under section 14 of the Veterans' Preference Act of 1944, 58 Stat. 390, as amended, 61 Stat. 723 (1947), 5 U. S. C. 863. The Commission on Government Security has recommended that section 14 be repealed except as applying to employees of the District of Columbia.[65]

Definition of Sensitive Position

The head of any department or agency should designate, or cause to be designated, as sensitive any position within his department or agency the occupant of which could bring about, by virtue of the nature of his position, a material adverse effect on the national security.

Under the loyalty-suitability program recommended by the Commission, removals from the service will not be related to the designation of an employee's position as sensitive or nonsensitive. The executive branch should continue, however, to identify those positions the functions of which are so related to the national security that the occupants are in a position to cause damage. As indicated elsewhere,[66] an employee otherwise suitable for Federal service and whose loyalty is not in question, may be unsuitable for a sensitive position, necessitating an administrative transfer by the agency head. Sensitive positions should also be identified in order to determine the scope of necessary investigation.

The Commission analyzed definitions of a sensitive position previously used or proposed and has concluded that its recommended definition, which is identical with that embodied in Executive Order 10450, is the most appropriate. The task of identifying sensitive and nonsensitive positions of course will vary from agency to agency depending upon the nature of the business transacted by that agency and other conditions. The final decision in each case is one that should be made by the agency head or his designated representative who has full knowledge of agency conditions. The Commission feels that the recommended definition while sufficiently clear as to general policy, gives the agency head adequate freedom in carrying out this responsibility.

---

[65] See Suitability Program, equal treatment for veterans and nonveterans, p. 86.
[66] See Suitability Program, criteria, p. 82.

INVESTIGATIONS

The nature and scope of loyalty investigations should be as follows:

1. There should be a loyalty investigation of every person entering the civilian employment of any department or agency of the executive branch of the Federal Government.

(a) Investigations of persons entering the competitive service should be conducted by the Civil Service Commission, except in such cases as are governed by special agreement between the Commission and any given department or agency.

(b) Investigations of persons other than those entering the competitive service should be conducted by the employing department or agency. Departments and agencies without investigative organizations should utilize the investigative facilities of the Civil Service Commission.

2. The investigations of persons entering the employ of the executive branch may be conducted after any such person enters upon actual employment therein only in emergencies, but in any such case the appointment of such persons should be conditioned upon a favorable determination with respect to his loyalty.

3. An investigation of all applicants should be made. A national agency check with written inquiry is required for non-sensitive positions and a full field investigation for sensitive positions. In either case, if derogatory subversive information is developed, the investigation should be referred to the Federal Bureau of Investigation for a full field investigation.

4. A full field investigation should be made at all available pertinent sources of information and should include reference to:

(a) Federal Bureau of Investigation files;

(b) Civil Service Commission files;

(c) Army, Navy, and Air Force intelligence files;

(d) The files of any other appropriate Government investigative or intelligence agencies;

(e) House Committee on Un-American Activities files;

(f) Local law enforcement files at the places of residence and employment of the applicant, including municipal, county, and State law enforcement files;

(g) Schools and colleges attended by applicant;

(h) Former and present employers of applicant;

(i) References given by applicant;

(j) Any other appropriate source.

5. Where the employment is not to exceed three months and the position is nonsensitive the employee should undergo a national agency check. In the case of a sensitive position, the employee should undergo a full field investigation even though the employment is seasonal or temporary in character.

6. Both favorable and unfavorable information should be included in all investigative reports.

7. Investigative agencies should continue not to evaluate information collected.

8. In the event that an employee is transferred from a nonsensitive to a sensitive position, the applicable investigative standards should be the same as those for applicants for sensitive positions.

The Commission's recommendations retain without substantial changes, the practice under the loyalty program established by Executive Order 9835 and the security program initiated by Executive Order 10450. They reaffirm the basic principles effective since the issuance of Executive Order 9835 in March 1947, that every employee should be subject to investigation—that the scope of investigation should depend upon the relationship to the national security of the position applied for, or to which an employee is being transferred.

At a minimum, for nonsensitive positions, there should be a national agency check supplemented by written inquiry to local law enforcement agencies, former and present employers and supervisors, schools, and references.[67]

For sensitive positions [68] a full field investigation should be conducted. As is the current practice, the Civil Service Commission will conduct all investigations in the absence of special agreement between the Commission and any given department or agency.[69]   In any case where derogatory loyalty information is developed the investigation shall be referred to the Federal Bureau of Investigation.[70]

The Commission has found little fault with the investigative standards, methods, or personnel of the executive branch. The competency and fairness of the Federal Bureau of Investigation's trained force in investigating and reporting on Federal personnel loyalty and security matters has not been seriously questioned except by the perennial critics of all security measures and by the uninformed.

---

[67] For employment not to exceed three months in a nonsensitive position a national agency check is sufficient.

[68] For the Commission's recommendation as to sensitive position see Definition of Sensitive Position, p. 54.

[69] Such agreements are now in effect between the Commission and the Departments of the Navy, Air Force, State, Justice, Treasury, and Post Office, all of which have their own investigative staffs.

[70] The Commission has recommended that in the absence of new evidence there should be no reinvestigation or readjudication of old security or loyalty cases in the event new standard of employment is adopted. See Criteria and Principles of Application, p. 46 et seq.

56

The Civil Service Commission has developed its own career investigative force with basic qualification prerequisites, training courses, and rigid rules and regulations.

The loyalty program can be only as effective as the quality of the loyalty investigations. The most competent administrators cannot operate without recourse to the full and accurate facts of each case. An inescapable corollary of the Commission's recommendation that every person entering the civilian service be investigated is the continuance of an adequate staff of professional investigative employees capable of carrying the heavy annual work load.

During the fiscal year 1956 more than 50,000 full field investigations were made under the provisions of Executive Order 10450 by the Civil Service Commission, the Federal Bureau of Investigation, and other agencies. Over 300,000 national agency checks were made. Since the establishment of the loyalty program by Executive Order 9835 it has been Federal experience that each year some 3,000 or more cases must be processed where loyalty information is developed.

SCREENING—CHARGES

1. The evaluation of derogatory information relating to loyalty should be conducted by such officer as the head of the employing department or agency shall designate for that purpose. Such officer should perform the screening function.

2. It is the responsibility of the screening officer to determine whether there is substantial information justifying the issuance of a letter of charges and bringing the case to a hearing.

3. In the discharge of such responsibility, the screening officer should grant the individual involved an opportunity for an interview, at which he may offer his explanation of the derogatory information, prior to the issuance of a letter of charges.

4. If the interview discloses the need for additional investigation, the screening officer may request the investigative agency to conduct such investigation.

5. The letter of charges should be as specific and detailed as the interests of national security permit and should include pertinent information such as name, dates and places, in such detail as to permit reasonable answer thereto; the hearing should be confined to the matters contained in the letter of charges.

The screening process is highly important and should be assigned to competent personnel.

Under Executive Order 10450 [71] the agency head had the responsibility of screening information indicating wherever an employee's retention may not be clearly consistent with the interests of the national security. The Department of Justice, with the approval of the President, suggested to all departments and agencies that the general counsel or other top legal officer should be consulted "as to the sufficiency of information justifying suspension" and on the drafting of the letter of charges, and that the final decision as to suspension should not be delegated below the assistant secretary level.[72]

There have been many provocative arguments advanced to the Commission that the screening responsibility should rest in whole or in part with some central body.

The Commission rejects this contention, however, on the ground that the agency head has the ultimate responsibility for the disposition of each case and the decision whether to issue loyalty charges must be his. Further, the Commission has elsewhere recommended that whenever proper, removal proceedings should be founded upon suitability rather than loyalty grounds.[73] It is at the agency level that this initial decision can best be made.

The agency screening officer, however, need not operate in an isolation booth. When a loyalty issue exists the Commission has recommended that the loyalty standard and criteria be applied according to the principles of definition, construction and application set forth in Criteria and Principles of Application, page 46.

The Commission recommends further that the Central Security Office should promulgate regulations embodying interpretative guides for screening officers in loyalty cases. In any doubtful case appropriate officials of the Central Security Office will be available for consultation. The responsibility will properly remain, however, with the employing agency.

Perhaps the Commission's major recommendation in this area is that in loyalty cases it should be mandatory that employees and applicants be given an interview and opportunity to explain such derogatory information as the investigation has developed.

Under present practice there is no requirement that an employee be interviewed prior to suspension or issuance of charges, although the Attorney General has suggested that a personal interview prior to suspension is helpful in most instances.[74] The Atomic Energy Commission regulations issued May 10, 1956, provide that the director, Division of Security, may authorize the granting of security clearance on the basis of the existing record, "or *may* authorize the conduct of an interview with the individual" and on the basis of such interview and such other investigation as he deems appropriate, may authorize the granting of security clearance." [75] (Emphasis added.)

[71] Sec. 6.
[72] See letter of Herbert Brownell, Jr., Attorney General, to the President, dated Mar. 4, 1955; under Pub. Law 733, 64 Stat. 476, 5 U. S. C., 22–1 (1950) the statutory basis for Executive Order 10450, suspension is a condition precedent to removal. See Suspension, p. 59.
[73] See Suitability Program, p. 81.
[74] Attorney General's letter to the President dated Mar. 4, 1955.
[75] Sec. 4.10 (C).

The Commission's survey has indicated that many cases would never have reached the hearing stage, with consequent hardship to the individuals and needless administrative effort and cost to the Government, if opportunity had been given for employees to explain certain information in the investigative reports. Precharge interviews are not a panacea for all procedural ills but not unlike the informal pretrial examination in Federal court practice, they should so simplify each case that the genuine loyalty issues, if any, can be tested in the hearing.

When the position has been finally taken that charges should be preferred against an employee, they must be as specific and detailed as the national security interests permit and the hearing shall be confined to those charges.

SUSPENSION

The circumstances under which, and the bases upon which, an employee should be suspended or transferred, should be as follows:

1. Where there is derogatory information indicating the existence of reasonable doubt as to the loyalty of an employee, and the character of such information and the weight attached thereto are such as to require the removal of the employee from the position he then occupies in order to protect the national security, the head of the department or agency should:

(a) Transfer such employee to another position where there is no opportunity adversely to affect the national security; or

(b) If there is no such other position available for which the employee is qualified, suspend the employee with pay.

(c) If a letter of charges has been issued and the case has been referred to the hearing examiner and if, after receipt of the report of the hearing examiner, the decision of the head of the agency is adverse to the suspended employee, he should not continue to draw pay pending an appeal to the central review board and pending final determination by the head of the agency after receipt of the report of the central review board. Should the final decision after receipt of such report be favorable to the suspended employee, he should be reimbursed for the loss of earnings during such suspension subject to reduction by his earnings from other sources in the interim.

2. The decision to transfer or suspend under such circumstances should be made by an officer of the department or agency not inferior in rank to that of an Assistant Secretary or the equivalent thereof.

3. At the time of transfer or suspension or as soon as practicable thereafter, the employee should be advised in writing of the reasons for the transfer or suspension.

4. Priority should be given to investigations or hearings, as the case may be, in transfer or suspension cases.

Public Law 733,[76] the statutory basis for Executive Order 10450, has been construed as requiring suspension without pay where derogatory information is developed before an employee can be granted a hearing. The Commission's recommendations would eliminate this requirement.[77]

The Commission believes that removal from a position, pending further investigation or pending final determination, if a letter of charges has been issued, may be necessary in order to adequately protect the national security.

Where derogatory information indicating reasonable doubt as to the loyalty of an occupant of such a position is grave and serious in character, and where the responsible evaluating officer reaches the conclusion that the information is apparently reliable, the retention of the employee in such a position pending the opportunity to make further investigation, if further investigation is required, and pending an initial determination if a letter of charges has been issued, may constitute a substantial threat to the national security.

Under such circumstances temporary removal from such a position should be required unless the employee's present or continuing contribution to the national security warrants retention.

Temporary removal should, wherever possible, be effectuated through the transfer of such employee, if he has the requisite qualifications, to a position where he would not have the opportunity to damage the national security. If no such position is available, suspension is the only means whereby national security can be adequately protected.[78]

The Commission has recommended that, where such suspension occurs, the employee should continue to draw his salary until the head of the responsible agency has received the report of the hearing examiner and made his initial determination as to removal from the service. If the decision of the head of the agency after receipt of the hearing examiner's report is adverse to the employee, he should not continue to receive his pay

---

[76] 64 Stat. 476, 5 U. S. C. 22–1, 2, 3 (1950).

[77] The Attorney General has also recommended to the Congress in the 84th and 85th sess. of the Congress that the exercise of suspension prior to hearing or termination be made discretionary. Under the present program large numbers of employees who were suspended in compliance with the statute were eventually reinstated.

[78] The Supreme Court in *Cole* v. *Young*, 351 U. S. 536, June 11, 1956, in interpreting Pub. Law 733 recognized that "summary suspension powers" provided in the Act should be sharply limited, stating "There is obvious justification for the summary suspension power where the employee occupies a 'sensitive' position in which he could cause serious damage to the national security during the delay incident to an investigation and the preparation of charges . . . in the absence of an immediate threat of harm to the 'national security' the normal dismissal procedures seem fully adequate and the justification for summary powers, disappears." For the Commission's recommended definition of a sensitive position and discussion thereunder see p. 54.

pending his appeal to the central review board, and pending the final decision of the head of the agency after receipt of the report of the central review board.

The Commission has made this recommendation because of its belief that it would be unfair and work an undue hardship upon the employee to stop his pay pending a further investigation by the Government if further· investigation is required, or pending an initial determination by the head of the agency after he has had an opportunity to weigh the recommendations of the hearing examiner.

The Commission believes that the facts to be weighed in determining that a transfer or suspension is necessary are of such a nature as to require that the person charged with making the decision be a highly responsible officer of the agency. Accordingly, it has been provided that such person must occupy a rank not inferior to that of assistant secretary or its equivalent.[79]

It believes that this requirement will do much to insure that the transfer or suspension procedures herein recommended will be utilized only when necessary.

The provision requiring that priority be given to investigations or hearings in transfer or suspension cases will result in a prompt and expeditious consideration and disposition of such cases.

HEARINGS

Hearing Examiners

1. In all loyalty cases the initial hearing on the letter of charges should be conducted by a hearing examiner in accordance with rules and regulations to be promulgated by the Central Security Office.[80]

2· The hearing examiners should be appointed by the director of the Central Security Office from an appropriate civil service register created for the purpose.

3. Hearing examiners should be full-time governmental employees adequate in number to hear civilian employee loyalty cases throughout the country.[81]

---

[79] The Attorney General made a similar suggestion relative to suspension for all departments and agencies in his letter of Mar. 4, 1955, to the President stating: "Meticulous care should be exercised in the matter of suspension of employees against whom derogatory information has been received. It is suggested that a personal interview with the employee prior to suspension is helpful in most instances. The general counsel of the department or agency should be consulted and his opinion should be secured as to the sufficiency of the information justifying suspension. The final decision as to suspension should not be delegated below the assistant secretary level." The Commission has recommended that a personal interview be mandatory prior to issuance of a letter of charges. See Screening; Charges, p. 57.

[80] For the Commission's recommendation concerning the proposed Central Security Office, see p. 81 et seq.

[81] Hearing examiners would also be available to hear cases involving clearances under the port security, air transport security, and industrial security programs, as well as cases of organizations designated by the Attorney General. See Central Security Office, p. 89, and separate recommendations concerning these programs.

4. The qualifications of a hearing examiner should be fixed by the Civil Service Commission after consultation with the head of the Central Security Office.

5. The hearing examiners' experience should include legal practice or technical work performed in a field appropriate to the Government's loyalty and security programs. The Civil Service Commission should prepare an appropriate job description sheet and requisite qualifications after consultation with the director of the Central Security Office.

6. There should be an appropriate initial training program and periodic in-training service which, in addition to appropriate technical subjects, would make provision for indoctrination in constitutional and related matters affecting Federal employment.

7. The decisions of the hearing examiners should be advisory to the head of the employing agency whose decision shall be final.

The Commission considered the comparative advantages of having loyalty cases heard by hearing boards or single hearing examiners. Hearing boards were utilized under the loyalty program established by Executive Order 9835, as amended, as well as the security program established by Executive Order 10450 as amended. Under the former program cases involving applicants for, and conditional appointees to, the classified civil service were heard by regional loyalty boards composed of non-Government personnel appointed by the Civil Service Commission under its general mandate to establish rules governing appointment to the competitive service. Cases involving all other employees were heard by agency loyalty boards composed of Government personnel appointed by the agency heads.[82] No special qualifications were prescribed for the board members. All appeals were to the Loyalty Review Board established in the Civil Service Commission whose opinions (except in the case of veterans) [83] were advisory to the head of the employing department or agency.[84]

Under Executive Order 10450, as amended, the Civil Service Commission has the responsibility of maintaining a roster of Government employees available to serve on security hearing boards of not less than three persons. More than 1,800 persons are presently listed on the roster, all of whom were nominated by their employing agencies. The only requirements for nomination to the roster announced by the President are that they be "competent and disinterested Government employees from outside the department or

---

[82] Executive Order 9835, pt. II, par. 2.

[83] By virtue of sec. 14 of the Veterans' Preference Act of 1944, 58 Stat. 390, as amended, 61 Stat. 723 (1947), 5 U. S. C. 863, the decision was mandatory on the head of the agency. See also suitability program, equal treatment for veterans and nonveterans, p. 86.

[84] Executive Order 9835, pt. III, par. 1.

agency concerned" and "persons possessing the highest degree of integrity, ability, and good judgment." [85] The Department of Justice enlarged on these general concepts stating each designee must have been the subject of a full field investigation and shall be a person "of responsibility, unquestioned integrity and sound judgment," and his designation determined to be "clearly consistent with the national security." [86] There are no special qualifications as to training or experience, although many of the employees designated had some previous hearing experience under the loyalty program established by Executive Order 9835. The persons named to the roster are on call, available only when consonant with their other regular duties.

The Commission's sampling survey of cases heard under both the 9835 and the 10450 programs, as well as competent opinion in and out of Government, has led it to the definite conclusion that hearings of loyalty or security cases can more effectively be conducted by single examiners armed with sufficient training, experience, and supervision to insure that the interests of both the Government and the individual are adequately protected. It has carefully examined the "jury of peers" concept of the board system and found it wanting.

Whoever presides at a loyalty hearing sits not as a jury alone, nor as a judge alone, but to the degree that the taking of evidence is involved, as a combination of both, determining the facts and weighing their meaning in the light of the prevailing standard of employment.

The hearing of a loyalty issue is a grave and often complex matter. The task of sifting the evidence (some from confidential undisclosed sources); of evaluating the significance of past activities and associations, much of it relative in nature; of getting into the record all germane evidence without breaching the national security; of separating truth from falsehood; of determining the existence or nonexistence of reasonable doubt of loyalty—is a responsibility that should be entrusted only to specially selected, qualified, trained, full-time examiners. Establishing specific qualifications for hearing examiners is of course no guarantee they will be competent—to advocate no formal qualifications at all is to avoid the issue. The experience with hearing examiners under the Administrative Procedure Act and of Federal and State courts in assigning complicated issues to special masters to take testimony, is abundant proof of the advantages of the special examiner principle.

The above recommendations are self-explanatory. In brief they provide for the establishment of a selected and limited group of hearing examiners available to hear cases not only under the civilian employee loyalty program, but under the port security, air transport security, and industrial security

---

[85] See the President's memorandum of Apr. 27, 1953, to the heads of all departments and agencies accompanying the text of Executive Order 10450.

[86] Sample security regulations prepared by the Department of Justice and issued concurrently with Executive Order 10450, sec. 8 (e).

programs, as well as cases of organizations designated as subversive by the Attorney General. The use of hearing examiners is an integral part of the major recommendation of the Commission that a Central Security Office be created.[87]

The use of qualified examiners should insure more intelligently conducted hearings and less chance of injustice to Government or employee. The advisory nature of the examiners properly leaves the final responsibility for each case with the agency head; the supervision of the Central Security Office and provision for appeal [88] will provide for uniformity of procedure and evaluation. The use of examiners in several programs should insure uniformity, lessen hearing costs, and expedite hearing procedures.

Role of Agency at Hearing

1. Sufficiently in advance of the hearing to permit study by the hearing examiner, the agency should submit to the examiner the complete file on the individual and all pertinent supporting documents, plus a résumé of any administrative action and reasons therefor. At the hearing itself, the agency representative should be present to answer the questions of the hearing examiner and to assist the hearing examiner in any other appropriate way. He should not act as a prosecutor.

2. The agency head should have the authority to designate the person or persons to represent the agency at the hearing, and such representative(s) should not participate in the formulation of the hearing examiner's decision.

3. The agency representatives need not be licensed attorneys.

The loyalty hearing is an administrative one. It is not a trial or in any sense an adversary proceeding. As previously recommended,[89] there is no burden of proof on either the Government or the employee, but the decision should be reached upon the evaluation of all the information, favorable as well as unfavorable. The role of the hearing examiner is to determine the facts and to weigh them in the light of the loyalty standard, criteria and applicable principles. The role of the agency representative is impartially to assist the examiner in this task.

Under present practice the Attorney General has suggested to all departments and agencies that a legal officer should be present at security-hearing

---

[87] For a full discussion of the Commission's considerations which led to the recommendation that a Central Security Office be created including the use of hearing examiners, see p. 633.

[88] Hearings, Appeals, p. 72.

[89] See Criteria and Principles of Application, p. 46 et seq.

boards to act as adviser to the board as to procedural matters and to the employee, ". . . *if he is not represented by counsel . . .*" [90]

Under the Commission's recommendation the agency need not have an attorney present—a qualification not believed necessary in view of the presence of a trained hearing examiner who will have sole responsibility for the conduct of the hearing subject to the safeguards that his decision is only advisory to the agency head and can be appealed by the employee to the Central Review Board.[91]

It should be noted that investigative reports in the first instance will go to the employing agency (or the Civil Service Commission) and not the Central Security Office. Further, the "complete file" and related documents, including classified investigative reports, will be retained by the hearing examiner only until he has rendered his advisory decision, at which time it will be returned to the employing agency. The hearing examiners and the Central Review Board will service executive departments and agencies and the Central Security Office will not become a repository for such files or information.

Employee Counsel

The employee (applicant) should be entitled to counsel of his own choice at his own expense.[91a]

Under present practice the employee may select counsel of his own choosing at his own expense. The Commission believes the employee (applicant) should have counsel as a matter of right. It further believes that this is a matter for his decision alone and any expenses incidental thereto should be his as well. Under the procedures recommended for the loyalty program, including the mandatory personal interview,[92] before charges are issued a case will not go to hearing until a serious loyalty issue has developed which cannot otherwise be resolved. Under such circumstances it is not believed that the Government has any responsibility for providing counsel. Under certain conditions, however, when an employee is cleared the Government will pay for the travel and per diem costs of witnesses subpenaed for the employee.[93]

Counsel prerogatives during a hearing, including the extent of permissible cross examination of witnesses,[94] should be delimited in the rules and regulations for hearings promulgated by the Central Security Office.

---

[90] Attorney General's letter to the President, Mar. 4, 1955.
[91] To be established in the Central Security Office. See Appeals, p. 72, and Central Security Office, p. 89.
[91a] Commissioners Cotton, Noel and McGranery dissent as to method of payment only.
[92] See Screening; Charges, p. 57.
[93] See Hearings, Subpena, p. 69.
[94] On the question of witnesses generally see also Hearings, Confrontation and Subpena pp. 61, 66, 69.

Hearing Attendance Restricted

Loyalty hearings should not be open to the public because the informality of private hearings is more conducive to impartiality.

The mishandling by the Government of a few loyalty and security cases in the past and the consequent unwarranted deluge of unfavorable publicity for loyalty-security procedures generally has led some individuals to propose that hearings should be open to the public. The situation has been confused under the present practice. While in most agencies hearings are deemed private, neither Executive Order 10450 nor the sample regulations issued concurrently with the order by the Attorney General, nor the supplementary recommendation released by the Attorney General in his widely quoted letter to the President,[95] took a position in the matter.

Employee hearings should not be open to the public. They are administrative proceedings designed to establish the truth in matters of extreme importance to an employee and his Government, and the information developed therein is not in the public domain. Further, only through hearings, restricted in attendance to necessary participants, is it possible to arrive at a just and balanced resolution of the loyalty issue. In short, the informal atmosphere of private hearings is more conducive to an impartial determination of the facts. Further, to hold otherwise would tend to discourage the appearance of witnesses and thus restrict confrontation even further than necessary [96] and would subject the employee to additional unfavorable publicity which might do unwarranted violence to him and his reputation. Finally, in some cases open hearings would not only be undesirable, but impossible where classified information must be considered.

Whatever advantages open hearings might offer in protecting employee rights have been adequately provided for in the many procedural safeguards afforded employees under the proposed loyalty program, including the right of appeal to a Central Review Board.

Confrontation [97]

Confrontation of persons who have supplied derogatory information should be allowed to the maximum extent consistent with the protection of the national security and as provided below:

1. Confrontation of regularly established confidential informants engaged in obtaining intelligence and internal security information for the Government should not be allowed

---

[95] Dated Mar. 4, 1955.

[96] For the Commission's recommendation on confrontation, see Hearings; Confrontation, p. 66.

[97] See also Subpena, p. 69; Commissioner McGranery dissenting.

where the head of the investigative agency determines that the disclosure of the identity of such informants will prejudice the national security. In such cases the report supplied by the investigative agency should contain as much of the information supplied by the informant as may be disclosed without revealing the identity of the informant and without otherwise endangering the national security.

(a) If confrontation is not permitted under paragraph 1, the hearing examiner should furnish the individual involved with the substance of the information obtained from such informant to the extent that such information is material to the consideration of the issues involved; and should read into the record the substance of such information and the evaluation as to reliability placed upon such confidential informant in the investigative report.

(b) If the individual involved questions the accuracy or completeness of the information furnished pursuant to paragraph 1a above, he may file with the hearing examiner a written statement setting forth in detail so much of the information challenged by him as to accuracy or completeness. If the hearing examiner is of the opinion that the additional investigation as to the specific matters challenged is required in the interest of ascertaining the facts, he should request the investigative agency to make such additional investigation. Information obtained as a result of the additional investigation should be treated in the same manner as provided for in the original investigation.

2. (a) Derogatory information supplied by confidential informants other than those described in paragraph 1 should not be considered, over the objection of the individual involved, by any hearing examiner in arriving at his determination, or by any officer charged with the responsibility for making a final decision as to retention of an employee or as to clearance, unless such informants consent to the disclosure of their identity so as to enable the individual involved to obtain their testimony through the issuance of a subpena or by dispositions, orally or on written interrogatories.

(b) Derogatory information supplied by identified persons should not be considered, over the objection of the individual involved, by any hearing examiner in arriving at his determination, or by any officer charged with the responsibility for making a final decision as to the retention of an employee or as to clearance, unless the individual involved is given the opportunity to obtain the testimony of such identified persons

67

through the issuance of a subpena, or by depositions, orally or on written interrogatories; if the individual involved is given the opportunity to obtain the testimony of such identified persons through the issuance of a subpena, or by depositions, orally or on written interrogatories, such derogatory information supplied by identified persons should be considered. Where an identified informant gives a statement on the condition that he will not be called upon to testify or otherwise be subject to subpena, the hearing examiner should have no authority to issue a subpena for, or require depositions from, such individual. If the identified person supplying the derogatory information is unavailable for service of subpena or the taking of his deposition, orally or on written interrogatories because of death, incompetency, or other reason, such derogatory information may be considered by the hearing examiner with due regard for the lack of opportunity for cross-examination.

[It is not intended that the foregoing requirements of paragraphs 2*a* and 2*b* apply to preliminary interviews preceding issuance of letters of charges.] [98]

Nothing herein contained should be construed to require the investigating agency to exclude from its report any information derived from any source, but all information obtained should continue to be included in the report to be submitted to the appropriate agency.

The balance to be ever observed between protection of the national security and the safeguarding of individual rights stands out in sharper relief in the problem of confrontation than elsewhere in the loyalty program.

The Commission has studied the range of views, legal, constitutional and moral, running from providing a full confrontation in all cases to permitting ex parte dismissals with no hearings or privilege to refute charges. The solution lies somewhere between these opposite poles.

The sample regulations issued by the Department of Justice concurrently with the promulgation of Executive Order 10450 provide: [99]

Hearing boards shall conduct the hearing proceedings in such manner as to protect from disclosure information affecting the national security or tending to disclose or compromise investigative sources or methods.

Again,

If the employee is, or may be, handicapped by the nondisclosure to him of confidential information or by lack of opportunity to cross-examine confidential informants, the hearing board shall take that fact into consideration.[100]

---

[98] See Screening; Charges, p. 57.
[99] Sec. 9 (i).
[100] Sec. 9 (e).

And finally,

The board, in making its determination, shall take into consideration the inability of the employee to meet charges of which he has not been advised, because of security reasons, specifically or in detail, or to attack the credibility of witnesses who do not appear.[101]

Nowhere, however, are there any ground rules to guide hearing boards in the actual application of these general precepts. This the Commission has endeavored to do. It believes that under its recommendations maximum confrontation is allowed consonant with security requirements; that while not emasculating our confidential investigative sources, they provide for an employee, under definite understandable rules, the opportunity to obtain sufficient information to intelligently present his defense.

For a fuller exposition of the problems raised by the confrontation issue and further delineation of the considerations which led to the Commission's recommended position, see page 657.

Subpena [101a]

The power of subpena to compel the attendance of witnesses at loyalty hearings should be authorized as provided below: [102]

1. Either the Government or the employee should be permitted to apply to the hearing examiner to issue subpenas, except as to confidential informants and identified informants who have given their information on the condition that they will not be called as witnesses. Such application should state the name and address of such witness, as well as the substance of the testimony to be presented by the witness. If the hearing examiner deems the evidence relevant and not merely cumulative, he may issue the subpena. Under the same limitations, the hearing examiner may, on his own motion, subpena a witness.

2. In the exercise of his discretion to issue subpenas, the hearing examiner should consider such factors as the time and expense involved by reason of the travel required.

3. The witness should be compensated for travel expense and per diem, but where the cost is substantial, the hearing examined may in his discretion require the parties to use deposition procedures.

4. The Government should bear the cost of Government witnesses, but the hearing examiner should not subpena a witness for the employee until the employee deposits with the Government sufficient funds to pay the travel and per diem costs of

[101] Sec. 9 (k).
[101a] Commissioner McGranery dissenting.
[102] See also Confrontation, p. 66.

such witness.   In the event that the employee is not cleared, the funds deposited by the employee should be used to pay for the employee's witness expenses.   If, however, the employee is cleared, the funds deposited by the employee shall be returned to him and the Government should bear the travel and per diem costs of the employee's witness.

5. The right of subpena should be applicable where there is a right of confrontation, but this does not preclude the employee, or applicant for employment, from furnishing affidavits or the testimony of witnesses he wishes to present and who are willing to appear voluntarily.

There is no question that the power of subpena should be authorized for both the Government and the employee (applicant) to the fullest extent possible consonant with the materiality of the evidence sought, financial burden, and the degree of confrontation herein provided.[103]

There is no precedent for granting subpena power in loyalty or security hearings.   The Attorney General recommended to all departments and agencies:

> Even though the statute does not provide subpena power for witnesses, every effort should be made to produce witnesses at security-board hearings to testify in behalf of the Government so that such witnesses may be confronted and cross-examined by the employee, so long as the production of such witnesses would not jeopardize the national security.[104]

Providing this authority, under reasonable restrictions, is a natural corollary of the Commission's proposals for confrontation of witnesses with minimum exception, as well as other procedural rights for employees and applicants.

As in any other type of hearing, judicial or administrative, subpena power should be available if the production of witnesses in this manner will assist in arriving at the truth.[105]

Subpena authority without provision for witnesses expenses of course is abortive.   Under the Commission's recommendation the Government would bear these costs if the employee (applicant) is cleared.

Hearing Examiners Report; Transcript of Hearing

1. The hearing examiner should submit a written report to the head of the Central Security Office for transmittal to the head of the employing agency.

2. The report should contain the hearing examiner's finding of fact, advisory decision and statement of reasons for the decision.

---

[103] See Hearings, Confrontation, p. 66.

[104] Attorney General's letter to the President dated Mar. 4, 1955.

[105] For a fuller treatment of the background of the subpena problem see Subpena Power on p. 73.

3. The hearing examiner should have prepared a verbatim transcript of the hearing.

4. The employee (applicant) should be furnished a copy of the report and a copy of the transcript, following receipt by the Central Security Office of notice of appeal.

Under present practice a hearing board is required to prepare a "memorandum of reasons" and a "decision". The Civil Service Commission guides to hearing boards relative to the memorandum of reasons state in part:

> It is expected that the Board will make a finding with respect to each charge, and in some instances it will be necessary or desirable to explain the Board's reasoning and conclusion concerning each charge.[106]

The Commission believes, however, that findings of fact as well as a statement of reasons should be mandatory, analogous to the practice under the Administrative Procedure Act.[107]

The Commission has elsewhere recommended that the hearing should be confined to the matters contained in the letter of charges.[108] Requiring that the hearing examiner prepare findings of fact will insure that the examiner has actually based his decision on the facts.

Under present practice a complete verbatim stenographic transcript is made of employee security hearings and the transcript constitutes a permanent part of the record.[109]

Under the sample regulations [110] a copy of the decision is to be sent to the individual concerned. It should be noted that the Civil Service Commission specifies that the decision "will not contain the reasons upon which the board based its conclusion." [111]

In practice, with rare exception, only the bare decision, as to whether his employment has been found clearly consistent with the national security, is given the employee. This is actually the decision of the agency head which usually will refer to the decision of the board. This is, of course, consistent with Public Law 733 [112] which provides that an employee who has completed his probationary or trial period shall be given "a written statement of the decision of the agency head."

Regarding the transcript, the sample regulations provide that upon request the employee or his counsel shall be furnished a copy at reasonable cost.[113] The practice is not uniform. Thus some agencies furnish a copy on request; some automatically; some require payment; and some require none.

---

[106] Civil service handbook IN-203 (guides for members of security hearing board under Executive Order 10450).
[107] 5 U. S. C. 1007B.
[108] See Screening; Charges, p. 57.
[109] Civil service handbook IN-203. Department of Justice sample regulations, sec. 9 (J).
[110] Sec. 9K.
[111] Civil service handbook IN-203.
[112] 64 Stat. 476, U. S. C. 22-1 et seq. (1950).
[113] Sec. 9J.

The Commission believes that fair play demands the employee be furnished without charge a copy of the transcript and the hearing examiner's report which will contain the findings of fact, advisory decision, and statement of reasons for the decision. This should be done, however, only when a notice of appeal has been filed at the Central Security Office. It is believed that this condition will obviate unnecessary requests and keep reproduction costs at a minimum.

Appeals

An adverse decision by the head of the employing agency may be appealed on the record to the Central Review Board at the request of the employee within the time and subject to procedures to be prescribed by the Central Security Office.

In this recommendation the Commission sharply departs from one of the basic tenets of the present program. Under the loyalty program established by Executive Order 9835 an adverse decision of an agency head was appealable to the Loyalty Review Board located in the Civil Service Commission which was empowered in turn to make an *advisory* recommendation to the agency head.[114] Adverse decisions of the Commission's regional loyalty boards authorized to hear cases of applicants for (and conditional appointees to) the competitive service were also appealable.

Executive Order 10450, however, contains no such provision. In a statement specifically prepared for the Commission on Government Security concerning the current program, the Attorney General had this to say on the subject of appeals:

There are some who feel that any employee security program should have provisions for appeal of an unfavorable decision to higher authority. As I have already pointed out, the head of the department or agency is responsible for the protection of Government affairs entrusted to his jurisdiction. Being responsible, he should be able to choose those with whom he must share his responsibility. Also, in practical operation, the head of the department or agency is in a far better position to judge *his security needs* than any outside authority. The matter of appeal was considered fully by Congress in passing P. L. 733 *but it was concluded that no outside agency should be in a position to impose its judgment upon the head of the department or agency.* Instead, Congress in P. L. 733 provided that a dismissed employee could be hired by other departments or agencies if the Civil Service Commission and the hiring agency concluded that the employee would not jeopardize security interests in the new position." (Emphasis supplied.)

The Commission submits that this statement while a cogent summary of the governing philosophy of the present security program, at the same time clearly portrays its underlying weakness. Under the existing security standard the final decision in any case is at best a relative judgment. Job retention is related not only to an employee's personal conduct, but to the

---

[114] Pt. II 3 and pt. III 1.

relation of his position to the national security. Under such circumstances an appeal to a review body may well be merely an unnecessary and burdensome administrative step. The Commission has, in essence, recognized this and recommended that the majority of cases now being processed as security matters are in effect suitability situations and should be properly processed under the suitability program with no appeal on the merits from the decision of the agency head to the Civil Service Commission.[115]

The Commission has also recommended that in cases which involve the national security an absolute loyalty standard should be adopted for removals under which personal accountability alone and not the degree of job sensitivity is the governing factor.[116]

It has coupled this with a recommendation that where the head of the employing agency believes the national security can be protected by transferring the employee whose loyalty is not in doubt, to another position, for which he is qualified and suitable, every effort should be made to effect such transfer rather than to seek his removal from the service.

At the same time the Commission has endeavored to clothe the loyalty removal program with the maximum safeguards for the employee consonant with national security. Paramount among these is the right to appeal from an initial adverse agency head decision to the Central Review Board.

In so recommending, the Commission recognizes at once the seriousness and complexity of loyalty cases as well as the ultimate responsibility of the agency heads for their adjudication.

The Central Review Board will not "impose its judgment upon the head of the department or agency." It will review on the record the evidence brought out at the hearing below and give the agency head the advantage of its objective and considered review. The Commission believes that a tempered review of cases in which adverse decisions have been rendered will assist in determining the truth and effecting justice. The decision of the Central Review Board, however, as in the case of the decision of the hearing examiner, is only advisory and the final responsibility for deciding an individual case will revert to the agency head.

For a summary of the Commission's recommendations concerning the function of the proposed Central Security Office and the organizational position of the proposed Central Review Board, see Central Security Office, p. 89 et seq.

Final Determination

The final determination of a loyalty case shall be the responsibility of the employing agency and the agency head should make such determination. In the event of the incapacity or necessary absence

---

[115] See Suitability Program, p. 81.
[116] See Standard, p. 41.

of the agency head, the individual acting in his stead may make the final determination.

The Commission recognizes that the final responsibility for the removal of employees should rest with the agency head. This proposition has long been a basic tenet of Federal personnel policy [117] and was not seriously challenged until the passage of section 14 of the Veterans Preference Act of 1944 [118] which in addition to providing for appeals to the Civil Service Commission, has made the Commission's decision mandatory on the employing agency. The Commission on Government Security has recommended the repeal of section 14 in its entirety as administratively unsound.[119]

The gravity of each loyalty decision is such that this responsibility should not be delegated to, or in fact even exercised by a subordinate, barring the agency head's incapacity or necessary and prolonged absence.

Concurrent with this recommendation the Commission has recommended a Central Security Office which will assist departments and agencies in the processing of loyalty cases and through hearing examiners as well as a Central Review Board, furnish advisory opinions to agency heads. The operations of the Central Security Office are complementary to the final authority of the agency head and not in derogation of it.

When an employee has been charged with reasonable doubt as to his loyalty, after a hearing and final determination by the agency head as to the employee's loyalty such determination should be final and binding upon the heads of other departments and agencies, as well as the determining agency head and his successors, in the absence of new information justifying readjudication of the issue.

The decision of the head of the agency as to what constitutes "new information" within the meaning of the foregoing paragraph is final, but such decision should be made only after consultation with the appropriate legal officer of the agency.

A loyalty case can never be res adjudicata in the usual sense. A disloyal employee by definition has no place in the Federal service even though he may have emerged clean and clear from a score of investigations and as many hearings.

On the other hand, in the interest of employee morale and a constant personnel policy, the line must be drawn somewhere and the Commission has attempted to do so in this recommendation.

---

[117] Under Executive Order 10450 (sec. 2) the final responsibility lies with the agency head. Under Executive Order 9835 the decisions of the Loyalty Review Board were advisory to the agency head only, except in the case of veterans. For a review of the court decisions concerning the fundamental principle that the power of removal is incidental to the power of appointment, see Legal Basis, p. 18 et seq.

[118] 58 Stat. 390, as amended, 61 Stat. 723 (1947), 5 U. S. C. 863.

[119] See Suitability Program, equal treatment for veterans and nonveterans, p. 86.

The possibilities of successive differing determinations is immeasurably increased in a program functioning under a relative security standard such as the "clearly consistent with the interests of the national security" formula of Executive Order 10450.

The nadir of the present program to date was reached in the case of Wolf I. Ladejinsky who was in turn cleared, denied clearance, and cleared by three different agencies.[120]

In the heat of public bewilderment and criticism over such a spectacle of official uncertainty, the executive branch created the Personnel Security Advisory Committee, under the direction of Thomas J. Donegan, special assistant to the Attorney General, to coordinate cases involving conflicts between agencies in security evaluations.[121] The Commission's survey received considerable evidence that the Personnel Security Advisory Committee had been very effective in its task, indicating the definite need for inter-agency coordination.[122]

The Commission's proposed loyalty standard [123] will provide a more absolute measuring rule of employee conduct and should obviate in large part the possibility of differing successive determinations. Where two agencies may have conflicting views or an agency head may consider a case in a different light than his predecessor, recourse can be had to the Central Security Office [124] for consultation and assistance.

The ultimate decision, however, in any given case will remain with the head of the employing agency.

This is not to encourage agency autocracy. Under the Commission's recommendations, prior favorable loyalty decisions following hearings should not be reopened in the absence of new information "justifying" readjudication of the issue. While the Commission will not attempt to state what the nature of such new information should be, leaving this to the agency head, it is submitted that such decisions should be viewed with equal seriousness as original decisions to proceed against employees in loyalty cases. Where, even after consultation with the appropriate legal officer, the issue is not resolved, recourse should be made to the Central Security Office for assistance in the light of its wider experience.

When an agency receives an inquiry from outside the Federal service concerning the record and/or reason for separation from service of a former employee on loyalty or suitability grounds, the agency should furnish the dates of employment and the fact that

---

[120] See hearings before a subcommittee of the Committee on Post Office and Civil Service, U. S. Senate, 84th Cong., 1st sess., especially pp. 640, 742, 736, 712.

[121] *Ibid.*, p. 875.

[122] For a fuller discussion of the functions and composition of the Personnel Security Advisory Committee see the Present Program, p. 33.

[123] See p. 41.

[124] See Central Security Office, p. 89.

the employee was dismissed, resigned voluntarily, or transferred. No other derogatory information should be provided.

Personnel matters are confidential. Access to personnel files and particularly loyalty or security case files or the information they contain should be restricted to a minimum number of authorized governmental officials.

The Commission's survey reflected that a wide disparity of policy and practice exists on the issue of what information may properly be revealed to outside individuals or organizations concerning the facts of an employee's separation from service. It is the Commission's considered judgment that the executive branch should adopt a rigid, constant policy both for the protection of its employees and the absolute guidance of its administrative personnel.

Separation from the Federal service is an administrative action made in the good judgment of responsible officials. Only the results of that action should be the subject of public disclosure. It is recommended, therefore, that inquiries from unauthorized sources be answered as indicated and then only after a showing of reasonable justification for obtaining such information has been made.

Summary Recapitulation of Certain Advantages Under Recommended Civilian Employees Loyalty Program

Without reference to the constitutional or legal aspects of the problem, the Commission believes that when an individual is faced with the charge that a reasonable doubt exists as to his loyalty, he should be afforded the maximum opportunity consistent with national security to defend himself against such a charge. The proposed recommendations will provide such opportunity in the following ways:

1. By granting a larger measure of confrontation than exists in the present program;

2. By providing subpena power to implement the confrontation recommendation;

3. By providing a right to a hearing with trained hearing officers;

4. By providing a right of appeal to a central review board;

5. By defining standards and criteria with greater clarity than in the existing program;

6. By providing for assistance of counsel;

7. By providing that the Government shall bear the travel and per diem witness expenses incurred by an employee in the event that the employee is cleared;

8. By providing that the letter of charges shall be as specific and detailed as the interests of national security permit;

9. By providing that the hearing shall be confined to matters contained in the letter of charges;

76

10. By requiring that the employee be given an opportunity for an interview so that he may explain his answer to the charges prior to the issuance of a formal letter of charges; and

11. By providing that applicants shall have the same protection as employees where there is a charge of reasonable doubt as to their loyalty.

In addition the Government will have the benefit of a number of economies in the following respects:

1. The standard of "loyalty" as distinguished from "security" will result in fewer hearings.

2. The program will operate under standardized regulations, criteria, and interpretative guides, in lieu of the 60 various sets now prevailing.

3. The program will be administered by trained qualified personnel.

4. Unnecessary delays will be eliminated.

5. Centralization of responsibility in the Director of the Central Security Office will provide the opportunity for a continuing audit of the costs of the loyalty program, a function not now performed by any agency under the present program.

ADMINISTRATION [125]

Program Statistics

1. The Central Security Office should keep complete and comprehensive records which accurately reflect the operations of the loyalty program including the following:

(a) The number of individuals removed from federal service on the ground that there was reasonable doubt of their loyalty to the Government of the United States;

(b) The number of persons who resigned after receiving advice from the Government that there is derogatory information indicating reasonable doubt as to loyalty;

(c) The number of applicants who have had hearings on loyalty grounds and the results thereof;

(d) The number of cases in which the advisory recommendations of the hearing examiners have been accepted;

(e) The number of cases in which the advisory recommendations of the hearing examiners have been rejected;

(f) The number of cases which have been appealed to the central review board and the results of such appeals;

---

[125] The overall coordinative administration of the civilian employees loyalty program and certain security programs will rest with the recommended Central Security Office. The functions of the Office as they apply to the loyalty program have been set out individually in this report. For the Commission's recommendations concerning the Central Security Office, see p. 89.

(g) The number of cases in which the head of the agency has accepted the recommendation of the central review board;

(h) The number of cases in which the head of the agency has rejected the recommendation of the central review board;

(i) The number of cases in which there has been readjudication of the loyalty issue;

(j) The number of investigations resulting from National Agency checks, with written inquiry, which disclose derogatory subversive information requiring the referral thereof to the Federal Bureau of Investigation for a full field investigation.

2. Such statistics should be maintained for the information of the director of the Central Security Office, the President, and the Congress, and they should be included in the annual report of the director of the Central Security Office.

It is not believed necessary to review in detail the experience under the present program in the collection, correlation and publication of statistics concerning its operation. The flood of congressional and other criticism has publicly inundated the subject. Further, since the Supreme Court decision in Cole v. Young [126] holding that Public Law 733 [127] applies only to sensitive positions, the statistical reporting program has ceased. Mention should be made, however, of the organization of the program and the general criticisms that have been made concerning it.

The responsibility for maintaining statistics has been vested in the Civil Service Commission. There is nothing in Executive Order 10450 which requires the Commission to make a statistical analysis of operations under the program. The Commission originally compiled some overall figures at the request of the National Security Council.[128]

Beginning in December 1953, the Commission began the general collection of statistics using as a vehicle its standard form 77. The original form called for certain information relative to the handling of employee cases, applicant cases, and reemployments. The form was revised in October 1954, dropping the applicant cases category and adding a new category called, "types of information involved in removals and resignations."

The greatest concern was expressed over the publication of so-called "security risk" removals inasmuch as the statistics included not only removals through the summary removal or security procedures of Public Law 733 and Executive Order 10450, but removals under civil service and related suitability procedures as well. Until the form was revised in October 1954, they were in fact lumped together.

---

[126] 351 U. S. 536 (1956).

[127] 64 Stat. 476; 5 U. S. C. 22–I (1950) ; the statutory basis of Executive Order 10450.

[128] Testimony of former Civil Service Commission chairman Philip Young, hearing before a subcommittee of the Committee on Post Office and Civil Service, U. S. Senate, 84th Cong., 1st sess., pursuant to S. Res. 20, pt. I, p. 985.

The December 1953 form in the instructions for reporting termination stated:

ITEM 6.—Report here all terminations effected because of information coming to the agency's attention which falls within the purview of section 8(a) of Executive Order 10450, *regardless of whether the termination was effected under Public Law 733 or by other procedures.* Report separately the terminations in which a hearing was held and terminations in which no hearing was held. Do not report terminations specifically directed by the Civil Service Commission. (Emphasis supplied.)

Section 8 (a) of the order set out the criteria for consideration and includes not only loyalty type factors [129] but traditional suitability factors as well.[130]

The revised October 1954 form called for a breakdown between removals effected under Executive Order 10450 and under civil service procedures. The instructions as well were revised to read:

ITEM 6.—Report here all removals effected because of a determination that retention in employment was found not to be clearly consistent with the interests of the national security. Removals because of derogatory information of the type listed in section 8 (a) (2) through (8) of Executive Order 10450 shall be considered as security removals regardless of the relation of the position to the national security. *Whether removals effected because of derogatory information of the type listed in section 8 (a) (1) of Executive Order 10450 should be so considered will depend on the relation of the position to the national security.* Report under a (1) removals under Executive Order 10450 in which a hearing was held, and under a (2) such removals in which no hearing was held. *Removals effected under regular civil-service procedures shall be reported under b and should be included only when the removal is a direct result of an adverse security determination.* Do not report removals directed by the Civil Service Commission or removals effected solely because the individual was not a suitable employee. (Emphasis supplied.)

The anomalous situation which developed then is clear: While Public Law 733 as extended by Executive Order 10450 established an elaborate system for identifying and removing persons whose employment is not in the national security interest, even to the extent of making suspension mandatory prior to termination,[131] statistics were accumulated and publicly released labelling as security removals large numbers of terminations where the principal ground was suitability and the issue of security had not been processed under the established security procedure. While no definitive figures are available, particularly for the period prior to October 1954, when the standard form 77 was revised, evidence studied by the Commission indicates that the vast majority of all such removals were under normal suitability procedures. This uncritical blending of loyalty, suitability and security was one of the major factors which prompted the Commission's recommendation that a loyalty-suitability program be used as the basis for employee removals.[132]

The resulting confusion is well known, leading to a parade of Government officials to Capitol Hill to try to explain and re-explain to multiple con-

---

[129] Sec. 8 (a) 2.–8.
[130] Sec. 8 (a) 1.
[131] See Suspension, p. 59.
[132] See Loyalty Standard, and Suitability Program, p. 41–81.

79

gressional committees the meaning of the statistics, the meaning of "security risk", and, in fact, the basis of the entire security program. While the record is known, it is not clear; and the Commission feels that no useful purpose can be served by endeavoring to analyze once again the merits and demerits of the charges and countercharges. One conclusion, however, can and should be drawn. Any program which indiscriminately commingles loyalty, suitability, and security removals will be publicly pilloried. The fault lies not in the statistics themselves but in the very nature of the basic program.

To recount the experience of the past, however, is not to say that the collection, correlation and publication of statistics is an unnecessary or unsound practice. They are in fact one of the principal means of judging the operation and effectiveness of any administrative program. The Commission therefore submits the above recommendations related only to essential matters on which the Government must be informed in the conduct of the recommended loyalty program.

Security Personnel

1. The Civil Service Commission job description requirements for personnel security officers should be adopted by all agencies.
2. Security officers in excepted services or positions should meet at least the minimum qualifications of the competitive service.
3. The Central Security Office should arrange for periodic conferences at which all security officers may receive instruction and discuss problems of mutual concern.

The necessity of selecting competent personnel security officers under the recommended loyalty program is evident. While the final responsibility remains with the agency head to adjudicate each contested case, the preliminary processing must be delegated in large part to security officers. The personal and formal qualifications, the experience and the training of persons selected for these positions is therefore of basic importance. The Civil Service Commission has developed qualification standards for personnel security officers in the competitive service which appear to be adequate. Approximately one-half of the security officers, however, are in the excepted service and not required to meet these standards although the employing agencies are urged to comply with them. While many agencies have highly qualified personnel in excepted security officer positions, it is equally true that some agencies have entrusted such responsibilities to persons with little experience, particularly in the evaluation phases of the loyalty-security field.

The security field generally, of course, has a very short history. The professional level of security officers has steadily risen despite the confusion heretofore mentioned. The Commission feels that one gaping rent in the picture can be closed by all agencies concerned by providing that personnel security officers in the excepted service meet at least the minimum qualification standards for their grades and positions established by the Civil Service Commission.

In addition to careful selection, on-the-job training is essential. Under the present program there is no firm practice in this area. Following the promulgation of Executive Order 10450, conferences were instituted by the Department of Justice for security officers of the larger departments and agencies,[133] but they have long since been abandoned. The Personnel Security Advisory Committee [134] while composed of higher level officials, has had some security officers attend meetings on an ad hoc basis. The Department of Justice has now formally taken over the responsibilities of the Personnel Security Advisory Committee, and on May 16, 1957, advised the Commission that the permanent members would be representatives of the Departments of State, Defense, Army, Navy, Air Force, and Treasury; Civil Service and Atomic Energy Commissions, and the Veterans Administration.

There has been, however, no governmentwide training program, formal or informal. Under the Commission's recommendations, all personnel security officers would have the opportunity to attend periodic conferences at the Central Security Office for the purpose of receiving instruction and the discussion of current mutual problems. The regularization of such conferences should help in increasing the competency of our security personnel with consequent reflection in the level of the entire loyalty program.

The Commission's recommendations, of course, provide for a minimum program only.

SUITABILITY PROGRAM

Standard [134a]

The suitability standard for the denial of employment or the removal from employment in an executive department or agency should be "such cause as will promote the efficiency of the service."

The "efficiency of the service" or "suitability" standard is the standard established by the Lloyd-LaFollette Act of 1912 as amended,[135] and applicable, per se, only to the classified civil service. For 45 years the Act and the standard have proven a satisfactory basis for specific civil service

---

[133] Attorney General Brownell's letter to the President, Mar. 4, 1955.
[134] See Present Program, p. 24 et seq.
[134a] Commissioner McGranery abstains.
[135] Title 5, U. S. C. sec. 652.

81

regulations embodying grounds for disqualification of applicants and removal of employees in the competitive service. These regulations while not binding upon the non-competitive service have been followed to a large extent.

In another section of this report the Commission has recommended that in situations involving possible disloyalty, the denial of employment be predicated on the basis of reasonable doubt of loyalty [136] implemented by appropriate criteria and principles of application.[137] The Commission believes, however, that the loyalty program thereby established must be complemented by an adequate suitability program to provide protection not only against those individuals whose loyalty has been found wanting, but also against those who because of personal aberrations, or other reasons of conduct or peculiar personal circumstances, may also constitute a threat to the national security.

The Commission further believes that to accomplish this the current civil service regulations must be enlarged, and some of them amended, to cover certain security-type situations of a nonloyalty nature which, while not of a traditional suitability nature, nevertheless should disqualify an individual for Federal employment.[138]

Criteria

The existing civil service suitability regulations [139] should be amended as follows:

1. **Delete regulation 2.106 (7):**
   "Reasonable doubt as to the loyalty of the person involved to the Government of the United States."

2. **Amend:**

   (a) Current regulation:
   "Physical or mental unfitness for the position for which applied."

   Recommended revision:
   "Physical or mental unfitness for the position for which applied including any physical or mental unfitness of a nature which in the opinion of competent medical authority may cause significant defect in the judgment or reliability of the employee with

---

[136] See Standard, p. 41.
[137] See Criteria and Principles of Application, p. 46.
[138] See Suitability Program, criteria, p. 81.
[139] See sec. 2–106, disqualifications of applicants and sec. 9.101 agency responsibility for separation or demotion of employees, Federal Personnel Manual as amended, Jan. 23, 1955.

due regard to the transient or continuing effect of the illness and the medical findings in such case."

(*b*) Current regulation:
"Criminal, infamous, dishonest, immoral, or notoriously disgraceful conduct; habitual use of intoxicating beverages to excess."

Recommended revision:
"Any criminal, infamous, dishonest, immoral, or notoriously disgraceful conduct, habitual use of intoxicants to excess, drug addiction, or sexual perversion."

(*c*) Current regulation:
"Intentional false statements or deception or fraud in examination or appointment."

Recommended revision:
"Any deliberate misrepresentations, falsifications, or omissions of material facts."

3. Add:
(*a*) Any behavior, activities, or associations which tend to show that the individual is not reliable or trustworthy.
(*b*) Any facts, other than those tending to establish reasonable doubt as to loyalty, which furnish reason to believe that the individual may be subjected to coercion, influence, or pressure which may cause him to act contrary to the best interest of national security.
(*c*) Recurrent and serious, although unintentional, disclosure to any person of documents or information of a confidential or nonpublic character.
(*d*) Refusal to testify upon the ground of self-incrimination in any authorized inquiry conducted by a congressional committee, Federal court, Federal grand jury, or any other duly authorized agency, unless the individual, after opportunity to do so, satisfactorily explains his refusal to testify.

4. Retain unchanged:
(*a*) "Dismissal from employment for delinquency or misconduct."
(*b*) "Any legal or other disqualification which makes the applicant unfit for the service."

The foregoing regulations or criteria, as in the case of the loyalty program criteria, are of course not exclusive and are submitted as guide lines only, to be tempered with common sense as dictated by the facts of each case.

Existing suitability procedure as presently embodied in Civil Service regulations in the Commission's judgment requires the additions and clarifications embodied in the preceding recommendations. With the addition of these clarifications and additions, it is believed that suitability grounds will be sufficient in scope to take care of all types of security risks other than those predicated upon reasonable doubt as to loyalty.

It will be noted that the wording for certain of the amended and additional regulations has been taken directly from section 8 (a) 1 of Executive Order 10450 in the belief that the factors for consideration involved therein are more appropriately a part of the suitability program. It is suggested that the following changes be noted particularly:

1. Regulation 2.106 (7) dealing with reasonable doubt of loyalty is deleted as unnecessary in the suitability regulations in view of the Commission's recommendation for the establishment of a Government-wide loyalty program.[140]

2. Regulations 3 (a) and (b) as recommended are now substantially contained in section 8 (a) (1) of Executive Order 10450. Number 3 (a) is identical with the wording of section 8 (a) 1 (i) of the order. Number 3 (b) is identical except for the addition of the qualifying clause "other than those tending to establish reasonable doubt as to loyalty." Where loyalty is the controlling issue, the procedure of the recommended loyalty program should be followed. The Commission believes that 3 (a) and 3 (b) are properly included within the suitability regulations and while necessarily broad to protect the interests of the Government, they may be applied when required, without branding the individual involved as a security risk or disloyal.

3. Regulation 3 (c) as recommended is new, not having been contained in either the civil service regulations or Executive Order 10450. A similar criterion has been included in the loyalty criteria where the disclosure is under such circumstances as may indicate disloyalty to the United States.[141] The Commission believes, however, that where there is no indication of disloyalty but the disclosure has been recurrent as well as serious, the suitability of an individual comes into question.

4. Regulation 3 (d) as recommended would make refusal to testify under claim of constitutional privilege a criterion for consideration unless the individual, after opportunity to do so, satisfactorily explains his refusal to testify.

The Commission has no quarrel with the validity of the privilege. Federal employment, however, is not a matter of right. The plea of self-

---

[140] See Standard, p. 41.
[141] See Criteria, p. 46.

incrimination implies possible criminal implication which may make an individual unsuitable for such employment, particularly in the light of recommended regulation 2 (b). Where, after the opportunity to do so, he fails to satisfactorily explain the circumstances of his refusal to testify, these facts should be considered.

As recommended previously,[142] if the refusal is in an authorized inquiry relating to subversive activities, it should be a criterion for consideration under the loyalty program.

For a fuller look at the problems raised in this general area, see page 675 of this report.

The decision whether in a given case to proceed under the loyalty program may be a difficult one. As general guidance the Commission recommends:

Where suitability grounds and procedures are adequate to effectuate removal they should be followed.

Although there are no absolute definitive statistics, the best evidence available to the Commission indicates that since the beginning of the current security program established by Executive Order 10450, the vast majority of so-called "security removals" have in fact been suitability removals, handled under normal civil service or related procedures. There is no reason to doubt that this practice, particularly under the Commission's recommended expanded regulations, can be continued. Where there is a choice of procedures, the suitability procedures should be followed. Where, however, the basis indisputably is loyalty, the loyalty procedures should be faithfully followed.

It is further recommended that where the head of the employing agency believes the national security can be adequately protected by transferring the employee to another position for which he is qualified and suitable, every effort should be made to effect such transfer. While such transfer may in some instances require the consent of the transferee, the Commission believes that it affords an opportunity whereby a person otherwise suitable for employment in the Federal service may remain in the service in a position in which he no longer has the opportunity to adversely affect the national security.

The purpose of this recommendation is plain. There are certain positions in Government which are so identified with the national security

142 See Criteria, p. 46.

interest [143] that even though an incumbent employee may not be disloyal or unsuitable for employment generally under the recommended regulations, nevertheless his background may be such that he is unsuitable for a particular position. Under these circumstances the employee should not necessarily be removed but if suitable, should be transferred to a position where he would have no opportunity to affect adversely the national security.

Equal Treatment for Veterans and Nonveterans

Veterans and nonveterans should be afforded equality of treatment. Section 14 of the Veterans Preference Act should be repealed.[144]

The interrelation of the suitability program with the recommended loyalty program [145] led the Commission to examine the special privileges accorded certain veterans under section 14 of the Veterans Preference Act of 1944.[146] In the Commission's judgment the suitability procedures for removing employees from the Federal civilian service as fixed by the Lloyd-LaFollette Act, as amended,[147] and implemented by the civil service regulations, expanded as recommended,[148] are adequate for an efficient public service and should apply uniformly to veterans and nonveterans.

The Lloyd-LaFollette Act is applicable only to persons in the classified service. It prohibits suspension or removal except for such cause as will promote the efficiency of the service. It requires advance written notice with reasons for removal, a reasonable time for written answer, and a written decision by the employing agency on such answer. No examination of witnesses or hearing is required except in the discretion of the officer or employee directing the removal or suspension without pay. Under the Civil Service Commission's rules [149] the employee may appeal to the Commission where the employee establishes a prima facie case that his removal or suspension was not in accordance with prescribed procedures, was made for political reasons, or resulted from discrimination because of marital status or physical handicap. The Commission will not otherwise investigate or review the sufficiency of the reasons for removal or suspension, i. e., *there is no appeal on the merits.*

[143] For the Commission's recommended definition of a "sensitive position" see p. 54.
[144] Commissioner Stennis voted "No" on this recommendation; the recommendation does not apply to the District of Columbia.
[145] See p. 41.
[146] 58 Stat. 390, as amended, 61 Stat. 723 (1947), 5 U. S. C. 863.
[147] 37 Stat. 555, as amended (1912), 62 Stat. 354 (1948), 5 U. S. C. 652.
[148] See Suitability Program, criteria, p. 82.
[149] Section 9.106, Federal Personnel Manual as amended Jan. 23, 1955.

Under section 14 of the Veterans Preference Act of 1944 as amended, applicable to the classified and unclassified service, certain procedural benefits are accorded to all permanent and indefinite preference eligibles who have completed their probationary or trial period, which are not available to nonveterans under the Lloyd-LaFollette Act. Thus, they are entitled to written notice of charges at least 30 days in advance of a proposed suspension or removal, and to answer the charges "personally and in writing".[150] The statute also provides for an appeal to and personal appearance before the Civil Service Commission. During the appeal both procedural and substantive matters are reviewed. Finally, the decision of the Commission is made mandatory on the employing department or agency.

The Commission on Government Security believes that these special privileges accorded veterans under section 14 of the Act are violative of sound personnel management practice and should be abolished.

The Commission feels strongly that the authority to remove or suspend employees should rest with the head of the employing agency. This principle prevails throughout its recommendations. Even under the proposed loyalty program, where an appeal is provided to the Central Review Board from an adverse agency opinion, the final authority for adjudication would remain with the agency head.[151] The Act's provisions for overriding the employing agency abrogate that authority in suitability matters and make the decisions of agency heads vacuous and ineffectual.

On the issue of appeals under section 14 generally, the task force report on personnel and civil service of the Commission on Organization of the Executive Branch of the Government (Hoover Commission), dated February 1955, had this to say: [152]

An analysis of appeals under section 14 reveals that its requirements are far too elaborate to be consistent with efficient public management. It tends to make a judicial-criminal proceeding of an action which traditionally and necessarily has been one of the exercise of sound management judgment. It creates serious problems for management, unduly hampers operations, and burdens the Civil Service Commission with consideration of individual appeals cases to the detriment of other necessary personnel functions.

A judicial proceeding such as an appeal under section 14 leads to the worst kind of supervisory-employee relations because it requires the building of a written record and the accumulation of formal evidence sufficient to stand up as a support for the supervisor's action. It relieves the employee of any necessity for demonstrating his competence and usefulness to his department, and in effect, guarantees him a job unless his supervisor can prove in a formal proceeding that he is incompetent. This leads to working situations which are intolerable.

If the supervisor acts on his best judgment, he normally disciplines or separates an employee as soon as the misconduct occurs or the incompetence is evident. But, if

---

[150] The meaning of this phrase is unsettled. The Court of Appeals for the District of Columbia has construed this phrase to mean that the employee "shall personally answer the charges in writing;" that it does not mean he shall have a "minimal" hearing at the agency level, *Washington* v. *Summerfield*, 228 F. (2d) 452, 454 (1955). The Court of Claims in *Washington* v. *U. S.*, No. 44–56, decided Jan. 16, 1957, found, on the other hand, that Congress intended what it said and a veteran is given the right to answer the charges against him at the agency level "personally if he so chooses, or in writing or both."

[151] See Appeals, p. 72.

[152] P. 96.

he does so, he may be unable to substantiate his action judicially because he has not waited to accumulate documentary evidence. In other words, there now tends to be a fairly long series of events leading up to a final action by a supervisor. The requirements of section 14 emphasize the need to build a record to "get" someone rather than encourage good employer-employee relationships. The 1944 act creates a spectacle for others in the same organization who watch to see whether the supervisor or the employee will triumph. This sort of a struggle does not help the organization, the employee, or the supervisor.

The report of the parent Hoover Commission to Congress on personnel and civil service, also dated February 1955, accepted this analysis by its task force on the impact of section 14, adding this general comment:

Obviously, the granting of special employment privileges to any group runs counter to the basic principle of the Federal merit system, namely, open competition and equal treatment for all on the basis of their ability to serve the public as employees.[153]

The Hoover Commission then recommended that the veteran's special right to appeal be limited to the first 5 years after appointment to the service [154] on the ground that veterans should be given preference in Federal employment during the early years of their readjustment to civilian life. It added its own trenchant analysis of the effect of the appeal privilege, however, stating:

We are just as firm in believing that able-bodied veterans do not need or want special employment privileges after a reasonable period of readjustment, especially when the administration of those privileges complicates Federal personnel management and causes operational inefficiency, insecurity and an incalculable waste of money.[155]

The Commission on Government Security can add little to these appraisals of the appeals procedure created by section 14 of the Veterans Preference Act.

There is no question of the intolerable damage it does to the Federal service. The only question remaining is whether it is a necessary burden which must be further endured as a protection to our servicemen. The Commission submits that there are no administrative nor moral reasons necessitating the continuance of section 14 nor even requiring its application for a five-year period after a veteran's appointment to the service.

In today's Federal population of more than 2,000,000 employees, over 50 percent are veterans and the percentage is steadily increasing.[156] The procedures established by the Lloyd-LaFollette Act as implemented by the civil service regulations not only leave the conduct of agency affairs with the agency head where it properly belongs, but are eminently fair to the Federal employee. The Act and regulations were in fact designed for the very purpose of insuring that public officials do not abuse their power to remove employees—that there be equal treatment for all consonant only

---

[153] Pp. 68–69.
[154] Pp. 69–70.
[155] P. 69.
[156] Federal employment statistics bulletin, U. S. Civil Service Commission, Jan. 1957.

with the exercise of reasonable freedom in ridding the service of unsuitable personnel. For almost 50 years they have functioned as a sound vehicle of Government administration. To nullify their full application to the majority of all employees is to undercut the basic Federal personnel system and to deny the validity of its premises and policies for all other personnel.

It has been urged that the alternative to repealing section 14 is to provide its benefits to all personnel. This the Commission rejects as contrary to sound principle and at best an expedient compromise.

The Commission does not quarrel with the proposition that veterans are entitled to some special preferences in obtaining Federal employment and it does not advocate the repeal of other Sections of the Act. Once these pre-employment advantages have been provided, however, there should be equality of treatment for all employees. To hold otherwise not only casts a pall on the morale and effectiveness of all other personnel, but weakens the very tenets on which our administration of Government is based.

The Commission, therefore, recommends that section 14 of the Veterans Preference Act be repealed [157] and the implementary regulations of the civil service rescinded.

CENTRAL SECURITY OFFICE

The Commission recommends the creation of a Central Security Office in the executive branch independent of any existing department or agency.[158]

Composition and Organization

The general composition and organization of the office should be as follows:

1. There should be a director, appointed by the President with the advice and consent of the Senate, for a term of 6 years.

2. There should be a Central Review Board in Washington, D. C., to hear appeals on the record from the decisions of the hearing examiners. The Central Review Board should be composed initially of three members to be appointed by the President with the advice and consent of the Senate for 6-year terms. The initial appointments, only, should be for terms of 2, 4, and 6 years, respectively.

---

[157] See draft of suggested legislation on p. 693.

[158] Commissioner Cotton and Commissioner Noel abstained from the vote on this recommendation. Commissioner McGranery voted against this recommendation.

3. Hearing examiners:

(*a*) The number of hearing examiners should be determined by the director.

(*b*) The hearing examiners should be appointed by the director from an appropriate civil service register created for that purpose.

(*c*) The Civil Service Commission should prepare an appropriate job description sheet and requisite qualifications for hearing examiners after consultation with the director.

(*d*) Experience of hearing examiners should include legal practice or technical work performed in a field allied to the Government's loyalty and security programs.

(*e*) There should be an appropriate initial training program and periodic in-service training for hearing examiners, which in addition to technical subjects, would make provision for indoctrination in constitutional and related matters affecting Federal employment.

(*f*) Hearing examiners should be full-time governmental employees with a sufficient number throughout the country to hear cases involving:

(1) Government employees, applicants, and probationary employees whose loyalty is questioned under the civilian employees loyalty program;

(2) Individuals whose qualifications for clearance for access to classified information and materials are questioned under the industrial security program;

(3) Seamen and waterfront workers whose qualifications for clearance are questioned under the port security program;

(4) Crewmen and other persons requiring access to restricted airport facilities, whose qualifications for clearance are questioned under the proposed civil air transport security program;

(5) Organizations contesting designation on the Attorney General's list.

4. Administrative staff:

The number of administrative staff members should be determined by the director, and they should be appointed from the appropriate Civil Service Commission register.

5. General:

All officers and employees of the Office should be subject to a full field investigation.

Staff Duties and Responsibilities

1. The director should:

(*a*) Provide an appropriate initial training program and periodic in-training service for employees of the Central Security Office which, in addition to appropriate technical subjects, would make provision for indoctrination in constitutional and related matters affecting Federal employment.

(*b*) Assist department and agency screening officers and other security personnel in the performance of their responsibilities by holding periodic conferences for the purposes of instruction and discussion of current problems of mutual concern.

(*c*) Allocate the hearing examiners workload to minimize delay in adjudication.

(*d*) Promulgate rules and regulations governing hearing and review procedures, designed to bring about uniformity, to minimize delays, and implement the Commission's recommendations made throughout the various programs.

(*e*) Maintain a continuing critical review of security manuals issued by the Department of Defense and other departments and agencies having industrial security programs. Assist departments and agencies, simplify and make uniform, insofar as practicable, the language in the industrial security manuals, personnel security questionnaire forms, and facility clearance forms, through consultation with the Office of the Secretary of Defense and other departments and agencies having industrial security programs.

(*f*) Consult with and assist the various departments and agencies in the conduct of industrial security training programs.

(*g*) Issue interpretative regulations for security personnel of the various Government departments and agencies in connection with screening cases of Government employees, applicants, and probationary employees, to promote uniformity in the operations of the screening processes.

(*h*) Maintain the necessary statistics concerning the Government's civilian employees loyalty program, the industrial security program, the port security program, the civil air transport security program, and the Attorney General's list hearings, to make possible a continuing and constructive review of the operations of the various programs.

(*i*) Prepare and submit, at least annually and at such more frequent intervals as he deems necessary, a report and recommendations to the President.

(*j*) Undertake such other duties and responsibilities as the President may from time to time assign to him.

2. The Central Review Board should:

(*a*) Hear all cases properly appealed from the decision of the head of the respective agency. The opinion of the Board should be *advisory* only to the head of the agency.

(*b*) Confine its review to the record and not take any new evidence.

3. The hearing examiners should:

(*a*) Conduct hearings on letters of charges in accordance with rules and regulations promulgated by the director of the Central Security Office. The opinions of the hearing examiners should be *advisory* to the head of the employing agency, or the Attorney General, whose decision shall be final.

4. The administrative staff should:

(*a*) Review and evaluate procedures, practices and related manuals in the civilian employees loyalty program, the industrial security program, the civil air transport, and port security programs for the purpose of achieving as much uniformity as possible throughout the programs.

(The inspection authority of the Central Security Office should be limited to the examination and evaluation of such loyalty-security procedures and practices of executive departments and agencies for the purpose of determining whether they are in accord with existing governing acts of Congress, Executive Orders, and current rules and regulations promulgated by the Central Security Office. The Central Security Office should not have authority to examine other documents or files of any agency or department.)

(*b*) Receive and review complaints from industry concerning the operations of the industrial security program including that phase managed by the Atomic Energy Commission. Through conferences with representatives of industry and Government, and by means of continuing inspection (as delimited above) the Office should endeavor to correct inconsistencies, coordinate the various programs, eliminate unnecessary duplications of responsibility, and establish greater uniformity in the overall operations of such programs.

(*c*) Inspect, review, and make recommendations for the improvement of the document classification program, including such matters as the document classification and declassification guides, and department and agency rules and regulations. This function should involve the determination that all agencies have a definite program of declassification. Classification procedures should be reviewed in order to eliminate abuses arising from the de facto authority to classify exercised by employees who have de jure authority to *recommend* classification only.

The Commission vigorously and urgently recommends the establishment of a Central Security Office as an indispensable adjunct to its recommendations concerning the civilian employees loyalty program, the industrial' security program, the civil air transport security program, the Attorney General's list, the port security program and document classification.

Many correctable weaknesses in existing programs were disclosed by the Commission's study. Among the more serious were the following: A lack of uniformity in rules and regulations; a wide dispersion of responsibility among departments and agencies with little coordination of action; frequent inadequate selection, training, and direction of loyalty-security personnel. These shortcomings have resulted in inefficient, and in large part, ineffective and unsatisfactory programs.

To correct these and other deficiencies and weaknesses noted, the Commission has made a number of recommendations as set forth in the appropriate sections of this report. Perhaps its recommendation of greatest substantive, as well as administrative, consequence is that a Central Security Office be created.

A brief description of some phases of the operations of the current programs makes clear the need for such a central body.[159] Under the present civilian employees' security program, hearings are held within the employing agency by a board of three members, drawn from agencies other than the employing agency. The Civil Service Commission has a panel of over 1,800 employees available for service as part-time hearing board members. There are no full-time hearing officers and neither training nor experience is required. There is no provision for appeal. Each department or agency issues its own rules and regulations, and although many are informally approved by the Department of Justice, there have been wide differences among them as well as inconsistencies. Although both the Department of Justice and the Civil Service Commission exercise some degree of coordinative control, there is no single agency responsible for the supervision, control, or even coordination of the program. The result has been lack of uniformity, unnecessary duplications and expense, and, at times, severe inequities to employees.

Other programs suffer from similar defects. Under the present industrial security program, each principal department and agency of Government concerned issues its own rules and regulations and provides its own procedures for clearance for access to classified information. A plant having contracts with more than one department or agency of the Government may have to complete a separate series of forms and obtain separate clearances for its personnel from each department or agency. It may operate under three or

---

159 For a fuller discussion of some of the considerations which the Commission took into account, see p. 633.

more different regulations and as many interpretations of them. The Department of Defense has three hearing boards which sit in panels of three to hear cases of individuals denied access to classified information or materials. One board is located in New York, one in Chicago, and one in San Francisco. In San Francisco, there is a full-time permanent chairman of the board, with eight part-time members. In Chicago, an executive secretary serves as full-time chairman of the board with six part-time members. In New York, the board has ten part-time members.

Still different procedures are observed under the atomic energy program and under the port security program administered by the U. S. Coast Guard. There is at present no organized air transport security program. The Commission has recommended that such a program be instituted.[160]

At stake under these programs are the interests of citizens numbered in the millions. An adverse security determination in the present civilian employees security program carries with it serious economic and other consequences; an adverse determination on loyalty or security grounds in the case of a seaman in the port security program destroys his means of livelihood; an adverse determination on loyalty or security grounds in the industrial security program cripples the earning power of the worker and subjects him to stigma and suspicion. Also at stake is the security of the nation.

For years, public confidence in the handling of loyalty-security matters has been sorely tried. It is a fact that our loyalty-security programs have a comparatively short history. It is also true, however, that we have had sufficient time and experience to recognize the errors of the past and to put our programs on a sound, efficient, workable and fair basis capable of achieving the necessary balance between public protection and individual liberties.

Recognition of its responsibility in this area of human relationships intertwined with defense of constitutional government and the national security has led the Commission to recommend many procedures such as subpena powers, extension of the right to confront witnesses, payment of witnesses' expenses when an employee is cleared, and others, which should immeasurably add to the preservation of basic civil rights and at the same time strengthen the protection afforded the nation.

A study of some of the cases mishandled under present and past programs, with consequent individual injustices, indicates that they resulted in large part from indiscriminate, inept application of standards and criteria to the facts of particular cases. Decisions which too frequently may destroy the reputation of an individual, as well as that of his family, have been made by part-time, inexperienced hearing boards. The fault lies, however, not so much with those who have administered the program as with the programs themselves.

The issues with which security personnel must deal in determining whether a government employee lacks the requisite degree of loyalty to serve his

---

160 See p. 498.

country, whether a mariner lacks the requisite degree of loyalty or reliability to pursue his livelihood, whether a worker in an industry, be he a technician or a scientist of great renown, may be entrusted with classified information, equal in importance—if indeed they do not transcend—the issues which a court must face in dealing with rights of property, of liberty, or even of life.

The first essential in any program designed to protect the individual is to assure that the person who hears the facts and draws the inferences upon which an adverse determination of such grave consequence can be predicated, is qualified to discharge the commensurate responsibility involved. The Commission's proposal, calling as it does for qualified, adequately trained, full-time hearing examiners and appeal or review board, both in an independent office removed from the climate in a particular agency or a particular era, will provide such assurance.

The promulgation of rules and regulations governing hearings and other security procedures; the provision for instructional conferences of security personnel; the review and evaluation of procedures and practices as well as the other recommended coordinative functions of the Central Security Office—all of these should go far to achieve uniformity where needed, lessen delays and in sum, provide greater justice to the individuals concerned and greater protection to the national security.

A program involving protection of the national security cannot, of course, be measured in dollars. Millions of dollars are spent annually for external defense. If there is a serious need for improving our defense against internal enemies, we must meet the cost. The Commission believes, however, that the increased level of efficiency under the recommended Central Security Office, limited as indicated, will not increase costs but will actually result in considerable saving.[161] Further, there is no suggestion that the Office intrude on the rightful powers of agency heads. The decisions of hearing examiners and of the review board will be advisory only; the conferences for security personnel will be informal; there will be no authority for the Office to examine documents or files of any agency other than those manuals containing current rules and regulations and procedures. In summary, the Central Security Office will operate only as a service and recommendatory body to other departments and agencies concerned. The agency head authority will continue, aided and buttressed, however, by the coordinated and experienced assistance provided through the Central Security Office.

The Commission recognizes that the establishment of the Central Security Office represents a major step in the administrative machinery of our Government. The decision to so recommend is submitted in the considered judgment of the Commission that it will provide the necessary catalyst to immeasurably strengthen the potential good to flow from its other recommendations for improvements and to eliminate many of the general serious deficiencies of the present programs.

---

161 For a further discussion of cost factors, see Central Security Office, p. 633.

The Commission recommends:

1. The Attorney General's list should be retained with the modifications enumerated below.

2. The standard for inclusion of organizations on the List should be as follows: Any party, group, or association which the Congress of the United States, or an agency or officer of the United States duly authorized by the Congress for that purpose, finds:

(a) Seeks to alter the form of Government of the United States by force or violence, or other unconstitutional means; or

(b) Is organized or utilized for the purpose of advancing the aims and objectives of the Communist movement; or

(c) Is organized or utilized for the purpose of establishing any form of dictatorship in the United States or any form of international dictatorship; or,

(d) Is organized or utilized by any foreign government, or by any foreign party, group or association acting in the interest of such foreign government for the purpose of (a) espionage, or (b) sabotage, or (c) obtaining information relating to the defense of the United States or the protection of the national security, or (d) hampering, hindering or delaying the production of defense materials; or

(e) Has adopted a policy of advocating or approving the commission of acts of force and violence to deny others their rights under the Constitution of the United States; or

(f) Is affiliated with, or acts in concert with, or is dominated or controlled by, any party, group, or association of the character described in (a) or (b) or (c) or (d) above.

3. The designation of an organization should be accompanied by a statement showing:

(a) The date when the organization became of a character described above and the date when it ceased to be of such character, if such cessation has occurred.

(b) A description of the origin, history, aims and purposes of such organization.

---

[162] For a discussion of the history of the Attorney General's list, p. 645.

(c) If such an organization ceases to exist, it should be retained on the List, but with the date of its dissolution or other termination and relevant circumstances pertaining thereto.

4. No organization should be designated by the Attorney General unless prior thereto there has been a Federal Bureau of Investigation investigation of such organization.

5. Whenever the Attorney General, after appropriate investigation, proposes to designate an organization, notice of such proposed designation should be sent by registered mail to such organization at its last known address. Such notice should set forth the nature of the charges with such particularity as to permit the organization to answer and defend. If the registered notice is delivered, the organization, within such time as the Attorney General may by regulation prescribe, may file with the Attorney General a written notice that it desires to contest such designation. If the notice of proposed designation is not delivered and is returned by the Post Office Department, the Attorney General should cause such notice to be published in the *Federal Register*, supplemented by such additional notice as the Attorney General may deem appropriate. Within such time as the Attorney General may by regulation prescribe following such publication in the *Federal Register*, such organization may file with the Attorney General a written notice that it desires to contest such designation. Failure to file a notice of contest within the prescribed period should be deemed an acquiescence in such proposed action, and the Attorney General may thereupon, after appropriate determination, designate such organization and publish such designation in the *Federal Register*. The notice of contest should be signed by the executive officers (or persons performing the ordinary and usual duties of executive officers) of the organization which desires to contest such designation or proposed designation. Within such time as the Attorney General may by regulation prescribe following receipt of a notice of contest, the Attorney General should cause to be forwarded to the organization by Registered Mail a statement of the grounds upon which the designation was or is proposed to be made and written interrogatories with respect thereto. The organization, within such time as the Attorney General may by regulation prescribe, following receipt of such statement and interrogatories, may file a verified reply which should be signed by the executive officers (or persons performing the ordinary and usual duties of executive officers) of such organization. The reply should answer each interrogatory completely and

97

with particularity and should be limited to statements of fact. The organization may also submit supporting affidavits with its reply. Failure to answer any interrogatory or any part thereof should be deemed an admission of the truth of the facts to which such interrogatory or part thereof refers. The submission of an evasive reply to any interrogatory or any part thereof should likewise be deemed an admission of the facts to which such interrogatory or part thereof refers. Failure of the organization to file a reply, within such time as the Attorney General may by regulation prescribe, should constitute an acquiescence in designation. Any organization filing a reply may accompany its reply with a written request for a hearing. In the absence of such request, the Attorney General should determine the matter on the basis of the information available to him and the reply of such organization.

6. Upon receipt of a written request for a hearing, the Attorney General should transmit to the Central Security Office the complete file including the investigative reports, a copy of the proposed designation, a copy of the notice of intent to contest such designation, and any affidavits or interrogatories filed by the Attorney General or the organization. The Central Security Office should assign the matter to a hearing examiner who should fix a time and place for a hearing thereon and should promptly by registered mail notify the Attorney General and the organization thereof. When an organization declines or fails to appear at any scheduled hearing, the hearing examiner should without further proceedings make a recommendation to the Attorney General on the basis of the file.

7. The hearing should be conducted by a hearing examiner and he should prepare a record consisting of findings of fact, statement of reasons, and a decision which should be advisory to the Attorney General. If such recommendation is adverse to the organization, and the Attorney General accepts such recommendation, the organization may appeal, within such time as the Attorney General may by regulation prescribe, to the review board of the Central Security Office which should confine its review to the record prepared by the hearing examiner and should make an advisory recommendation to the Attorney General. The Attorney General may accept or reject the recommendation of the board. This decision should be final and not subject to review.

8. (*a*) If upon the basis of the statement, interrogatories, reply and affidavits (if any) submitted as hereinbefore provided it appears to the hearing examiner

98

that a determination may appropriately be made without the taking of evidence, the proceeding may be conducted without the taking of such evidence.

(*b*) The Attorney General, at his election, may rely upon the statement of grounds upon which the designation was or is proposed to be made, or may introduce evidence in support thereof or supplemental thereto, or in rebuttal of any evidence received on behalf of the organization.

(*c*) Hearings should be informal and should be conducted in an orderly and impartial manner.

(*d*) An organization should be entitled to appear by counsel or other representative of its own choice.

(*e*) Testimony should be given under oath or affirmation.

(*f*) The ordinary rules of evidence need not be adhered to at the hearings but reasonable bounds should be maintained as to relevancy, competency and materiality. Both the Attorney General, and the organization may introduce such evidence as the hearing examiner may deem proper in the particular case. In the discretion of the hearing examiner, the affidavit of any witness may be received in lieu of his oral testimony.

(*g*) Whenever, in the judgment of the hearing examiner, the proposed testimony of any witness appears to be irrelevant, immaterial, cumulative, or repetitious, the hearing examiner may refuse to receive such testimony.

(*h*) All objections to the admission or exclusion of evidence or other rulings of the hearing examiner should be limited to a concise statement of the reasons therefor and should be made part of the record. Argument upon such objections may be limited in the discretion of the hearing examiner.

(*i*) The hearing examiner should be authorized to receive as evidence on behalf of the Attorney General information or documentary material, in summary form or otherwise, without requiring disclosure of classified security information or the identity of confidential informants.

(*j*) The principles of confrontation set forth in hearings, confrontation, above, should apply in the conduct of such hearings.

99

9. Upon an adequate showing that the character of the organization has changed, the Attorney General in his sole discretion may cancel the designation of such organization.

10. There should be a statutory basis for the Attorney General's list.

11. The above recommendations are for future listings only, but it should be pointed out that all organizations now on the List have been tendered an opportunity for a hearing.

12. While the evaluation and effect of membership in, or affiliation with, any party, group or organization is governed by criteria and considerations elsewhere stated in the recommendations, the designation by the Attorney General as to the character of any party, group or organization heretofore designated by him, and hereafter designated by him in accordance with the procedures herein set out, should be conclusive in any inquiry relating to the eligibility of any individual for employment or retention in employment in the Federal Government, or for clearance by the Federal Government in programs requiring such clearance.

The Commission's recommendations concerning the Attorney General's list have been formulated for the benefit of Federal administrators in the exercise of their loyalty-security responsibilities.

The creation and use of the list is a part of the investigative process. For the sake of uniformity and to avoid a different list in each department and agency, it is important to retain a single list prepared by the Attorney General. Were such a list not available, the Attorney General would still be obligated to advise the various departments and agencies as to the subversive character of organizations to which employees or applicants for employment within such department or agency belong or have belonged. The discharge of such responsibility without the use of an official list would be more prejudicial to national security and freedom of association than the present system.

The mere fact that an employee or applicant for clearance is a member of an organization appearing on the Attorney General's list should not be interpreted as conclusive evidence of the employee's or applicant's unfitness for employment. The greatest care must be taken to avoid misinterpretation of affiliation. The affiliation should be viewed in the light of the member's knowledge of the purposes of the organization, or the extent to which such organizational purposes had been publicized at the time the individual joined the organization or retained membership therein. The character and history of an organization must be closely examined, with the realization that loyal persons, ignorant of its true purpose, may have been persuaded to join for innocent reasons. Hence, the need for a full-time hearing examiner who can become a student of the subject, and a central review board to review the findings of membership and inferences drawn therefrom.

Fairness to any organization requires a hearing prior to the listing of such organization by the Attorney General. The foregoing recommendations provide for such a hearing, as well as an opportunity to appeal from the Attorney General's acceptance of an adverse recommendation by the hearing examiner.

THE LEGISLATIVE BRANCH

The legislative branch of the Government should take effective steps to insure that its employees are loyal and otherwise suitable from the standpoint of national security.

The Commission believes that the necessity for an employee screening program in the Legislative Branch is incontrovertible. Since March 1947, when Executive Order 9835 was issued, it has been a cardinal tenet of executive branch personnel policy that every employee should be subject to investigation.[163] No comparable principle or practice exists in the legislative or judicial branches.[164]

The legislative branch has been the target of Communist and Soviet attack. The Senate Subcommittee to Investigate the Administration of the Internal Security Act and Other Internal Security Laws in reviewing Communist penetration of Government, noted:

They colonized key Committees of Congress . . . They help write laws, conduct Congressional hearings, and write Congressional reports . . ." [165]

The Committee on Un-American Activities of the U. S. House of Representatives made a similar finding, stating:

The Committee obtained evidence during the past year that 10 Communist cells, never before publicly identified, have operated within the executive *and legislative* branches of the Government. Members of these cells were without exception employees of the Government . . . Continued investigation eventually produced positive information regarding a total of not less than nine Communist cells which operated at different times within various departments of the executive branch of our Government and another which had operated *within the staff of a committee of the United States Senate.* (Emphasis supplied.) [166]

Senator William E. Jenner, then Chairman of the Senate Subcommittee to Investigate the Administration of the Internal Security Act and Other In-

---

[163] Running from a national agency to a full field investigation, depending upon the relation of the employee's position to the national security.

[164] For the Commission's recommendation relative to the judicial branch see p. 106.

[165] Subcommittee of the Committee on the Judiciary, report dated July 30, 1953, p. 20, 83d Cong., 1st sess.

[166] Annual report—1955, H. Rept. No. 1648, 84th Cong., 2d sess.

ternal Security Laws, delineated Communist activity directed toward the Congress in a speech on the Senate floor as follows:

The Communist attack on the membership of the American Congress is a three-pronged attack.

They work unceasingly in primaries and in the elections, to destroy the patriotic and the strong, and to elect the weak, the venal, and the noncontroversial.

Then when Congress is in session, they also work to spread confusion, doubt, and factionalism among the moderates who wish there was no controversy. How many time have I heard that?

The Communist attack on Congress includes also penetration of congressional committees.

In 1935, Alger Hiss, an unknown young lawyer in the Agriculture Department, was named general counsel for the Nye munitions investigating committee, a part of whose work was to smear American industry.

Hiss was suggested for this job by Lee Pressman, chief counsel of the CIO and an admitted party member.

I am speaking about a committee of the Senate.

Charles Kramer, also a party member, was counsel for Senator Wagner's Senate labor committee, and practically wrote the Wagner Act, which changed American free trade unionism into a centralized collectivist, state-directed unionism, until the Taft-Hartley Act reversed the trend.

The House Committee on Interstate Migration employed Henry H. Collins, Frederick Palmer Weber, and Charles Flato, as staff members.

Flato has told us how he falsely took the oath to uphold the American Constitution 14 times.

This committee cleverly built up documentary evidence about the "okies" and other migrants whom the Communists had adopted as exhibits of the decay of American capitalism.

The Senate Subcommittee on Civil Liberties of the Education and Labor Committee, had as staff members, John Abt, Allan Rosenberg, Charles Kramer, and Charles Flato.

Senator LaFollette publicly disclosed the infiltration of congressional committees, and the vast powers which hidden Communists could exercise from such a vantage point.

Secret Communists on the staffs gave valuable publicity to friendly witnesses, smeared or smothered unfriendly witnesses, slanted research activities, leaked information to friendly members of the press, slanted the documentary material on proposed legislation, and provided propaganda materials and a forum, for or against legislation, depending on which served the Communist Party. That went on here.

They made changes in the fine print of a bill which might completely alter its character.

They helped to slant congressional policies to fit Communist desires on China policy, German military government, United Nations, demobilization, heavy spending.

They had a perfect spot for espionage through access to confidential documents on military police, foreign policy, and atomic energy.[167]

While the Commission has neither the authority nor the means to verify the extent of the Communist attack upon, or infiltration of the Congress,

_____

[167] Congressional Record, Nov. 15, 1954, p. 4889.

it would appear indisputable not only from the statements above, the methods and goals of the Communist conspiracy generally,[168] and from the application of common sense, that the legislative branch is a target of the Soviet and the Communist Party and an adequate screening program for its employees is not only in order, but urgently imperative.

Today there is no general screening program in effect for the employees of the legislative branch, nor indeed for the members of Congress them-. selves for access to classified information or material.

In the United States Senate, S. Res. 16, a resolution "to provide for loyalty checks on Senate employees", was agreed to on March 6, 1953,[169] The resolution provides as follows:

Resolved, That hereafter when any person is appointed as an employee of any committee of the Senate, of any Senator, or of any office of the Senate the committee, Senator, or officer having authority to make such appointment shall transmit the name of such person to the Federal Bureau of Investigation, together with a request that such committee, Senator, or officer be informed as to any derogatory and rebutting information in the possession of such agency concerning the loyalty and reliability for security purposes of such person, and in any case in which such derogatory information is revealed such committee, Senator, or officer shall make or cause to be made such further investigation as shall have been considered necessary to determine the loyalty and reliability for security purposes of such person.

Every such committee, Senator, and officer shall promptly transmit to the Federal Bureau of Investigation a list of the names of the incumbent employees of such committee, Senator, or officer together with a request that such committee, Senator, or officer be informed of any derogatory and rebutting information contained in the files of such agency concerning the loyalty and reliability for security purposes of such employee.

The Committee on Rules and Administration reporting the Resolution on March 2, 1953 stated in part:

This resolution provides in modified form the same check for Senate employees as to loyalty that now applies to the employees in the executive departments. It does not, however, specifically require any form of clearance in advance of Senate employment, nor does it make that clearance a condition of continued employment. *Full field or background investigations of anyone, such as are reserved in the executive agencies for employees appointed to sensitive positions, are not contemplated by this resolution nor believed necessary.*

Under its terms, name checks for employees and prospective employees of the Senate shall be made with the Federal Bureau of Investigation by the employing Senator, committee, or officer of the Senate. If this name check shows information derogatory to the loyalty of the individual concerned, then the appointing officer shall take any additional steps he considers necessary to clarify the loyalty of that person. The extent of this clarification is not stipulated and, for that reason, shall be left to the discretion of the Senator, committee, or officer of the Senate.

In the case of an employee already on the payroll, this resolution also specifies that only a name check shall be made. Where such check develops adverse information, it will still be up to the Senator, committee, or officer of the Senate to take additional steps of further investigation and action. (Emphasis supplied.) [170]

---

[168] See footnote 33.

[169] Dated Jan. 7, 1953; reported favorably with amendments by the Committee on Rules and Administration on Mar. 2, 1953, and considered, amended and agreed to on Mar. 6, 1953. (83d Cong., 1st sess.)

[170] S. Cal. No. 46, rept. No. 50, 83d Cong., 1st sess.

S. Res. 16, however, was never implemented. The Department of Justice has taken no action through the Federal Bureau of Investigation to comply with requests received for transmittal of derogatory information concerning Senate employees.

The Commission inquired of the Department of Justice as to the reasons for this failure to comply and was advised by its Internal Security Division as follows:

1. Even if the Department was in sympathy with the Resolution, certain features of it would adversely affect the work of the FBI.

2. The Resolution failed to provide necessary safeguards for the protection of information in FBI files which would be made available to members of the Senate.

3. There was no resolution providing funds necessary for the FBI to conduct the investigation contemplated.

The Commission was later informed by the Department's Internal Security Division that the Attorney General personally had supplemented this brief statement of position with the following recapitulation:

Even if there had been an appropriation, we would not implement this Resolution because of *separation of powers*." (Emphasis supplied.)

For reasons not known to the Commission, the Department of Justice has not elaborated any further than indicated above on the reasons behind its refusal to carry out the provisions of S. Res. 16. It is not known whether its decision not to implement S. Res. 16 is directed at the Resolution alone or is indicative of a more general policy to deny information to the Congress involving loyalty or security matters.

The Commission will not review the long struggle, in and out of the courts, on the question of the relative powers of the legislative and executive branches—nor will it attempt to analyze the series of cases wherein information possessed by the executive branch was denied the legislative branch. It should comment, however, that S. Res. 16 is so broadly worded its implementation could conceivably create difficulties to the Department of Justice and the FBI in the exercise of their responsibilities to protect security information from unauthorized or widespread disclosure. Further, it would require the FBI to make a decision as to what information is derogatory, an evaluation function it does not now exercise, nor should ever exercise.

The Commission would be derelict, however, if it failed to point up the dilemma which results if the executive branch does not cooperate in some manner with the legislative branch in instituting and maintaining a screening program for all of its employees.

The Department of Justice, through the Federal Bureau of Investigation, has jurisdiction over violations of espionage, sabotage, treason, and other matters pertaining to the internal security of the United States. The FBI's files are the Government's central repository for information of such nature—developed through investigations and other sources. While the Congress, through independent investigations by its Senate Subcommittee to Investigate the Administration of the Internal Security Act and Other

104

Internal Security Laws and its House Committee on Un-American Activities, has collected information relating to subversive activities, the information in the committee files is plainly inadequate as the basis of an effective employee screening program. If, therefore, the executive branch, under reasonable ground rules providing for the protection of the FBI files and sources of information, can cooperate with the Congress on a matter of such grave significance and yet refuses to do so, the incongruous intra-Government result is not only clear but a tragic commentary on the entire Federal loyalty-security system.

In the United States House of Representatives, there is no counterpart for S. Res. 16 and no general loyalty or security program. There are, however, certain Legislative bodies which do screen their employees. Thus, staff members of the Joint Committee on Atomic Energy are subject to a full field investigation by the FBI under the authority of section 205 of the Atomic Energy Act [171] providing that:

> The Joint Committee is authorized to utilize the services, information, facilities, and personnel of the departments and establishments of the Government.

The results of the investigation are evaluated by the chairman of the Committee. This is consonant with the practice whereby employees of the Atomic Energy Commission itself are also subject to investigation by the FBI.

The Government Printing Office, the General Accounting Office, and the Library of Congress all voluntarily comply with the security standard for employment and the procedures of Executive Order 10450 applying to the executive branch. Actually all three of these agencies are in the legislative branch, although the first two mentioned have for years been considered as subject to the basic civil service removal statutes and the regulations of the Civil Service Commission. The Civil Service Commission and the Department of Justice cooperate with these agencies and full field investigations are conducted by the Commission and the FBI. All adjudications are made as in the executive branch by the head of each agency.

While these programs are undoubtedly effective within their limited spheres, they are the result of individual arrangements. The majority of legislative branch employees are not subject to any loyalty check.

Therefore, the Commission recommends that the legislative branch and the executive branch endeavor to work out a program under which adequate investigation or screening can be provided for all legislative employees. It recognizes, as indicated previously, that care must be taken to ensure that security information and the identity of some sources of information in FBI files are adequately protected. The need for such a program is urgent, however, and the Commission hopes that some reasonable plan will be negotiated providing for restricted use of security and loyalty data under which the security of the executive branch will not be jeopardized and the principle of separation of powers will not be violated.

[171] Pub. Law 703, 83d Cong., 2d sess., 42 U. S. C. 2165.

THE JUDICIAL BRANCH

The judicial branch of the Government should take effective steps to insure that its employees are loyal and otherwise suitable from the standpoint of national security.

The Commission believes that as a general principle all employees of the Government should be subject to at least a minimum investigation to insure that they are loyal and otherwise suitable from the standpoint of national security.

This principle has been an accepted tenet of personnel administration in the executive branch since the establishment of a loyalty program by Executive Order 9835 in March 1947.[172] The Commission has recommended that the legislative branch also take steps to institute a screening program for all employees.[173]

There is no general screening program for employees of the judicial branch who, for administrative matters, are subject to the supervision of the administrative office of the United States courts.[174] United States probation officers receive a full field investigation conducted by the Federal Bureau of Investigation. This is essentially a character or suitability type of investigation.

The U. S. Court of Military Appeals has a somewhat anomalous nature. While its functions are judicial, it is organizationally within the Office of the Secretary of Defense [175] and its employees are subject to the provisions of Executive Order 10450 with clearances granted or denied by the Department of Defense. The Tax Court of the United States, on the other hand, is an independent executive agency created by statute [176] and its employees are subject to Executive Order 10450.

It is fundamental that there should be no reasonable doubt concerning the loyalty of any Federal employee in any of the three branches of the Government. In the judicial branch, the possibilities of disloyal employees causing damage to the national security are ever present. As an example, Federal judges, busy with the ever-crowded court calendars, must rely upon assistants to prepare briefing papers for them. False or biased information inadvertently reflected in court opinions in crucial security, constitutional, governmental or social issues of national importance could cause severe effects to the Nation's security and to our Federal loyalty-security system generally.

---

[172] See Investigations, p. 55.

[173] See the Legislative Branch, p. 101.

[174] Created by Act of Congress approved Aug. 7, 1939, 53 Stat. 1223–25; 28 U. S. C. 601.

[175] See chart organization of Federal executive departments and agencies published by the U. S. Committee on Government Operations, dated Jan. 1, 1957.

[176] Formerly called the U. S. Board of Tax Appeals it was created by the Revenue Act of 1924 (43 Stat. 336). The change in name was made by the Revenue Act of 1942 (56 Stat. 957.)

There appears to be no valid reason why an employee of the judicial branch should not be screened, at least as to his basic loyalty to the United States. Certainly the judiciary proper and the public generally should have the assurance that the men and women who carry the administrative responsibilities of the courts or assist in the preparation of decisions are loyal, dependable Americans.

The Commission therefore recommends, as in the case of the legislative branch, that the judicial branch and the executive branch endeavor to work out a program under which adequate investigation or screening can be provided for all judicial employees.

Military Personnel Program

Introduction

The military personnel security program has as its objective the rejection or separation of persons whose membership in the Armed Forces does not meet the requirements of national security as expressed in directives of the Department of Defense. The operation of the program is carried out by the Departments of the Army, Navy, and Air Force under their separate regulations. These regulations, however, must conform to the standards, policies, and procedures outlined by the Department of Defense. The military program parallels in significant features the civilian program, but its authority rests neither on Executive order nor congressional enactment. The basis for the program is the inherent power of command exercised by the President as Commander in Chief under the Constitution. The military context is distinguished by a high degree of personnel control and a compelling necessity for loyalty and obedience. In the number of persons affected the military program ranks with the largest. As of September 30, 1956, the estimated number of Armed Forces personnel on active duty, including officer candidates, was 2,797,221; that of reservists not on active duty was 3,926,859. The approximate overall total is thus 6.7 millions.

HISTORY

The military security program, as a unified overall program, was essentially initiated by the joint agreement of the Secretaries of the Armed Forces on "The Disposition of Commissioned and Enlisted Personnel of the Armed Forces of Doubtful Loyalty," issued on October 26, 1948. The joint agreement was issued following the promulgation of Executive Order 9835 on March 25, 1947.

The joint agreement stated:

1. Conduct or associations which may be considered as establishing reasonable grounds for separation of personnel of the Armed Forces and the rejection of persons seeking to be enlisted or appointed in a service shall include, but not be limited to, one or more of the following:

(a) Sabotage, espionage, or attempts or preparations therefor, or intimate and sympathetic association with or voluntary assistance to persons who the subject of the investigation has reasonable cause to believe may be spies or saboteurs.

111

(*b*) Treason, sedition, or writings and acts which can reasonably be considered as intended to encourage seditious or treasonable opinions or actions.

(*c*) Advocacy of revolution or by force or violence to alter the existing constitutional form of government of the United States; advocacy of revolution or by force or violence to bring about economic, political, or social change.

(*d*) Intentional unauthorized disclosure to any person under circumstances which may indicate disloyalty to the United States, of documents or information of a classified or nonpublic character.

(*e*) Acting, attempting to act, or knowingly failing to act when such conduct is calculated to serve the interests of another government in preference to the interests of the United States of America.

(*f*) Membership in, affiliation or sympathetic association with any foreign or domestic organization, association, movement, group, or combination of persons,

(1) Which practices, seeks to practice or advocates:

(*a*) Denial, by force, violence, or intimidation, to any person, group of persons, or class of persons within the United States or territory subject to its jurisdiction, of any right or rights which the Federal Constitution guarantees or protects against encroachment by either or both Federal and State government.

(*b*) Alteration, through or with the aid of force, violence, or intimidation, of the existing form of government of the United States or Territory subject to its jurisdiction or of the existing economic, social, or political order within it.

(2) Which (regardless of practice, advocacy, or nonadvocacy of any of the tenets set forth in (1) (*a*) and (*b*) above), is disclosed by investigation or designated by the Attorney General to be totalitarian, Fascist, Communist, or subversive or as having adopted a policy of advocating or approving the commission of acts of force or violence to deny persons their rights under the Constitution of the United States by unconstitutional means.

2. The respective Secretaries of the departments of the Armed Forces shall immediately and concurrently publish to their respective departments the standards outlined above. Publication shall be of unrestricted classification and given wide dissemination.

3. It shall be the duty of every member of the Armed Forces to report to his commanding officer or intelligence officer any information coming to his attention concerning disloyal or subversive activities by any member of the service.

4. No person who admits or who is otherwise believed to have engaged in disloyal or subversive activities shall be appointed or enlisted in any of the armed services of the United States without the specific approval of the departments concerned.

5. Administration.

(*a*) The action to be taken in each case shall be determined by the department concerned. No action shall be taken to apprise any individual that he is under suspicion prior to consultation with the proper intelligence agency. Investigation shall be conducted as directed by the respective departments.

(*b*) Court-martial proceedings may and normally will be instituted against disloyal personnel who have committed triable offenses.

(*c*) Administrative procedures may and normally will be instituted against disloyal personnel who have committed offenses in the categories above not covered by existing law or where for other reasons court-martial proceedings are impracticable or deemed inadvisable.

(1) The basic standard for actions taken under this regulation shall be that, on all the evidence, reasonable grounds exist for belief that the individual involved is disloyal to the Government of the United States. No action shall be initiated

with a view toward possible separation from the armed services by reason of doubtful loyalty, unless tangible proof of concrete facts evidencing disloyalty shall have been developed by thorough and painstaking investigation. The standard to be used in any specific case to determine whether separation procedure be initiated shall be: Has the investigation thus far conducted so established detailed concrete facts that, were this an offense triable before a general court-martial, legally valid charges and specifications could be drafted and a prima facie case established in proof of such charges and specifications.

(2) Sufficient information shall be obtained about informants whose identities are not disclosed to permit adequate evaluation to be made of the information furnished by them.

(3) Careful judgment shall be exercised in weighing derogatory information, considering its recency, relative seriousness, attendant circumstances, whether the information was given under oath, whether it is relevant to the charges specified, whether the individual has had an adequate opportunity to rebut it, and whether there is similar or supporting evidence.

(4) Evidence of membership alone in a prescribed organization is not to be considered of itself as conclusively establishing disloyalty. Despite such membership it may properly be found, upon consideration of the entire record, that the individual in question is not disloyal. Membership is a fact to be considered but a determination of disloyalty must be made upon the entire record in the case. However, if it is firmly established that a suspect is currently a member in good standing in a prescribed active organization, a prima facie case of disloyalty shall be considered as having been established, which must be rebutted by evidence other than simple denial by the suspect.

6. The procedures given in paragraph 5 (c) above, issused to the field, shall be restricted to the using agencies and not become public information.

7. (a) When administrative procedures for discharge are instituted which require appearance before a board the individual concerned shall—

(1) Be given reasonable advance notice of the hearing.

(2) Be advised that he will be furnished military counsel, may select such counsel if available, or may introduce civilian counsel at his own expense.

(3) Be notified of the allegations and facts as indicated by the preliminary investigation. However, should any records include evidence of information, the disclosure of which might prejudice the safety or interest of the Government or the sources from which the evidence was obtained, the exact nature of such information or evidence and the methods by or sources from which it was obtained shall not be disclosed. Consideration shall be given to the fact that the individual may have been handicapped in his defense by the nondisclosure to him of confidential information or by the lack of opportunity to cross examine persons constituting such source of information.

(b) Strict legal rules of evidence shall not be applied in administrative hearings but reasonable bounds shall be maintained as to competency, relevancy, and materiality.

(c) Board proceedings shall be reviewed and final determination made as directed by the respective departments.

On November 15, 1949, a memorandum,[1] approved by the personnel policy board, was issued indicating that uniform standards of loyalty adopted by each service for enlisted and appointed personnel be similarly applied to inducted personnel.

---

[1] Office of the Secretary of Defense memorandum to department secretaries, Subject: Policy with respect to loyalty examination of inducted persons and disposition of inducted persons determined to be or suspected of being disloyal, dated Nov. 15, 1949.

Uniform loyalty forms were to be executed as soon as possible after induction and any inductee who refused to execute a loyalty certificate was to be suspected of disloyalty, and retained in the service pending investigation. Falsification or misrepresentation in executing a loyalty certificate was to be made the subject of disciplinary action.

The final disposition of each inducted person whose disloyalty was established or whose loyalty was suspect, was to be made as directed by the Secretaries of the respective services as follow:

> (1) Trial by court-martial for offenses committed subsequent to induction;
>
> (2) Administrative discharge; or
>
> (3) Retention in the service.

In cases not resolved by courts-martial, action would be—

1. *Now, and during peacetime*:

> (*a*) *Discharge*, under other than honorable conditions, men who are determined by the respective Secretaries to be presently disloyal.
>
> (*b*) *Retain in service*, men who are suspected of disloyalty, including those who refuse to execute loyalty certificates, and place them under surveillance and do not employ them in sensitive duties (duties where they might have access to classified matter or material) pending further investigation.
>
> (*c*) *Discharge under honorable conditions*, men who, after investigation, are not determined by the respective Secretaries to be disloyal, but as to whom, on all available evidence, there is reasonable ground to doubt the wisdom and desirability of their retention in the service. This shall include, among others, men who have not—
>
>> (1) Subsequent to induction, engaged in conduct or association in contravention of secretarial loyalty standards;
>>
>> (2) Willfully concealed or failed to divulge any material detail relative to conduct or association in contravention of secretarial loyalty standards occurring either prior or subsequent to induction.

2. In the future, in the event of national emergency, war, or mobilization—

> (*a*) *Discharge*, under other than honorable conditions, and deliver for appropriate disposition to an authorized Federal agency those persons who are determined by the respective Secretaries to be disloyal.
>
> (*b*) *Retain in service*, men who are suspected of disloyalty, including those who refuse to execute loyalty certificates, and place them under surveillance and do not employ them in sensitive duties (duties where they might have access to classified matter or material) pending further investigation. In the discretion of the respective Secretaries such "suspects" may be assigned to special organizations or specifically designated areas pending the outcome of the investigation and the determined disposition.

On February 19, 1951, a supplement [2] to the earlier announcements of policy was made. This announcement stated:

> In order to protect the national interest and preserve the security of the Department of Defense, appropriate restrictions upon assignments and access to classified matter will be imposed during the period when a suspect is under an investigation (other than routine background) by an intelligence agency for the purpose of determining whether disloyal or subversive tendencies exist.
>
> Where investigation of an individual reveals insufficient evidence to justify his separation from the service, but such individual is judged to be a potential military security risk, great care will be taken to insure restrictions upon assignment and access to classified matter in accordance with military necessity. Where practicable, the investigative agency concerned in the case should be consulted prior to any such restrictions or reassignment.

A major change in the development of the military personnel security program was occasioned by the promulgation of Executive Order 10450 in April 1953, subsequent to which a new interservice committee was convened to study the problem. As a result of the recommendations of this committee, Department of Defense directive 5210.9 of April 7, 1954, was issued.[3]

The refinements of Department of Defense directive 5210.9 and its operation will be discussed in the section of this report entitled "The Present Program."

LEGAL BASIS

The present military personnel security program is based on Department of Defense directive 5210.9, as amended through June 19, 1956. The purpose of this directive is "to establish uniform procedures and provide policy guidance pertaining to the acceptance, rejection or separation of persons whose membership in the armed forces would not be clearly consistent with the interests of national security in order to assure that the effectiveness of the armed forces of the United States will not be jeopardized by subversive elements within their ranks". Congress has never passed specific legislation to provide for such a program. Therefore, ascertaining the legal basis for the establishment of a military personnel security program involves a study of underlying constitutional and statutory authority.

The position taken by the Department of Defense concerning the legality of the program is that the President's authority over the armed services, which may be exercised in person or through his principal assistants, the Secretary of Defense and the Secretaries of the Military Departments, derives

---

[2] Office of the Secretary of Defense memorandum to department secretaries, Subject: Policy concerning military personnel who are considered security risks (M–11B–50), Feb. 19, 1951.

[3] DOD directive 5210.9 rescinded the earlier policy documents, i. e., Joint Agreement of the Secretaries of the Armed Forces, 26 Oct. 1948; Office of the Secretary of Defense memorandum, 15 Nov. 1949, and Office of the Secretary of Defense memorandum, 19 Feb. 1951.

from his position under Article II, Section 2 of the Constitution as Commander-in-Chief of the Army and Navy. Military regulations are promulgated by the Secretary of Defense and the Secretaries of the Military Departments acting for the President and have the force and effect of law when not inconsistent with statute. Therefore, concludes the Defense Department, "despite the fact the Congress has never passed specific legislation to provide a security program for military personnel, the President's authority with respect to the armed services and his responsibility to maintain loyalty, good order and discipline in the military establishment, constitute the basis for the promulgation and implementation of a military personnel security program by the Secretary of Defense and the heads of the Military Departments." [4]

The Defense Department in its letter noted, however, that Congress has also acted to give wide authority in general terms to the Secretary of Defense for the purpose of administering his department.

The Constitution empowers Congress, in article I, section 8, to raise and support armies and to make rules for the government and regulation of the land and naval forces. These powers authorize Congress to enact legislation concerning the acceptance of individuals into the military service (and as a consequence, their rejection) and the discharge and separation from the service.

As an example of congressional action in this field, the Universal Military Training and Service Act provides that no one shall be inducted into the Armed Forces "until his acceptability in all respects, including his physical and mental fitness, has been satisfactorily determined under standards prescribed by the Secretary of Defense."

Another section of this Act provides that a person inducted into the Armed Forces shall serve on active duty for 24 months, "unless sooner released, transferred or discharged in accordance with procedures prescribed by the Secretary of Defense. . . ."

Title 10 of the United States Code includes sections which set up certain qualifications for the entry of officers and enlisted men into the Army and Air Force. Also included in the appropriate sections is the prerequisite that such persons will only be acceptable if they are "otherwise qualified under regulations to be prescribed" by the Secretary of the department concerned.[5] Enlisted men or inductees in the Army and Air Force may be

---

[4] Letter dated Nov. 9, 1956, from Mr. Leonard Niederlehner, deputy general counsel, Department of Defense, to Mr. Loyd Wright, chairman, Commission on Government Security.

An illustration of the exercise of the President's inherent authority and responsibility to maintain loyalty and good order in the military establishment is found in part IV, sec. 4, of Executive Order 9835, which directed the Secretaries of War and Navy "to continue to enforce and maintain the highest standards of loyalty within the armed services. . . ." Mr. Niederlehner's letter advises that the Department of Defense interprets this language to be, in addition to a specific direction, a recognition that the power to maintain and enforce the highest standards of loyalty in the armed services existed in the past.

[5] E. g., 10 U. S. C. secs. 3254, 3285, 8254, and 8285.

discharged prior to the expiration of their term of service pursuant to procedures "prescribed by the Secretary" of the department concerned.

Where Congress has not acted on the question of separation and discharge, the courts have consistently recognized the discretionary authority of the President, acting through the heads of the military departments, to discharge members of the Military Establishment at will, in the absence of statutory restriction.[6]

As noted by the letter from the Department of Defense referred to earlier, Congress has acted to give wide authority in general terms to the head of each executive department for the purposes of administering his department. Section 161 of the Revised Statutes (5 U. S. C. 22) states that "the head of each department is authorized to prescribe regulations, not inconsistent with the law, for the government of his department. . . ."

The National Security Act of 1947 states in section 2 thereof that "In enacting this legislation, it is the intent of Congress to provide a comprehensive program for the future security of the United States; to provide for the establishment of integrated policies and procedures for the departments, agencies and functions of the Government relating to the national security. . . ."[7]

Section 202(a) of this act may be considered as clothing the Secretary of Defense with authority to set up a military security program. A portion of this section provides that "the Secretary of Defense shall be the principal assistant to the President in all matters relating to the national security. Under the direction of the President . . . he shall perform the following duties:

1. Establish general policies and programs for the National Military Establishment and for all of the departments and agencies therein;

2. Exercise general direction, authority, and control over such departments and agencies; . . . ."

Concerning the contention that the President, through his Secretary of Defense, is authorized to promulgate a military personnel security program by virtue of the constitutional authority vested in him as Commander in Chief in article II, section 2, prolonged discussion is unnecessary to recognize that the President is empowered to act in this sphere. In the administration of the Armed Forces, the President acts in two capacities. The first is as Chief Executive, whose duty is to carry into execution the laws passed by Congress, and the second is as Commander in Chief.

As Commander in Chief, the President is empowered to prescribe rules to maintain order and discipline in the Armed Forces. This is a natural and inherent prerogative lodged in any military commander. As has been aptly

---

[6] See *Harmon* v. *Brucker*, U. S. D. C., D. C., C. A. No. 1972–55 (1956), and *Schustack* v. *Herren*, U. S. C. A., 2d circuit, No. 23951 (1956).

[7] Act of July 26, 1947, 61 Stat. 495.

stated, ". . . where Congress has failed to make rules for the discipline of the Army, the power of command lodged in the President carries with it authority in him to issue an order absolutely necessary to the discipline of the Army." [8]

While the extent of the authority of the President as Commander in Chief has been subject to varied interpretations, it is submitted that his authority to act concerning a military security program in the absence of specific legislation ought not to be subject to substantial dispute.

On the question of separation and discharge, the courts have consistently recognized the discretionary authority of the President to discharge members of the Military Establishment at will, in the absence of statutory restriction. One such restriction appears in title 10, United States Code, section 3784.[9] Under the provisions of this section, the Secretary of the Army may remove a Regular Army officer with more than 3 years' service from the active list for cause, only if removal is recommended by a board of review. Separation of necessity is an important aspect of any security program. Members of the Armed Forces currently are separated for security reasons pursuant to court-martial proceedings whenever possible,[10] or administratively, under appropriate authority.

As to the question of character of discharge (e. g., honorable, general, or undesirable) it has been held that courts lack authority "to review, control, or compel the granting of particular types of military service discharge certificates." [11] While the courts are concerned where there appears to have been a denial of due process, they generally have upheld the principle that . . . "judges are not given the task of running the Army." [12]

In sum, the following conclusions would appear to follow:

1. The operation of the military personnel security program pursuant to DOD directive 5210.9, while not based on specific statutory enactment, has a legal basis which can be sustained, viz, the President's authority under article II of the Constitution, complemented by certain statutes enacted by Congress under authority of article I, section 8.

2. It must be acknowledged that the line of demarcation separating the powers of the Congress and the functions of the President in this field as set forth in the Constitution is not precise and distinct. New specific legislation designed to formalize the legal basis for the military personnel security program and the authority of the Secretary of Defense to act thereunder may be desirable in the interests of better administration.

---

[8] Corwin, *The President, Office and Powers* (2d ed.) p. 196 (1941).

[9] See 10 U. S. C. 1162 and 1193 for a somewhat similar provision applicable to Reserve commissioned officers of the Armed Forces; and sec. 8784, referring to Regular Air Force officers.

[10] DOD directive 5210.9, as amended through June 19, 1956, sec. VIII–C(3), separation under other appropriate directives or regulations; and sec. IX–G(1), separation of members.

[11] *Harmon* v. *Brucker*, U. S. D. C., D. C., C. A. No. 1972–55 (1956).

[12] *Orloff* v. *Willoughby*, 345 U. S. 83 (1953).

PRESENT PROGRAM

The present military personnel security program is governed by the Department of Defense directive 5210.9. This directive was first issued in April 1954, was revised three times, and finally reissued in present form June 19, 1956. The purpose of the DOD directive was to establish uniform procedures, binding on the military Departments of Army, Navy, and Air, and to provide policy guidance pertaining to the acceptance, rejection, or separation of persons "whose membership in the Armed Forces would not be clearly consistent with the interests of national security . . . ." (Sec. I).

Security Standard and Security Criteria

A. STANDARD.—The DOD directive uses the same standard as the civilian personnel security program; that is, appointment, enlistment or retention in the Armed Forces must be "clearly consistent with the interests of national security." (DOD directive, VIII.A.) However, the Army, until recently, used a lower standard of acceptance for inductees. An inductee was not normally discharged as a security risk unless his retention was inconsistent with national security; i. e., "inconsistent" even if placed on specially controlled duties. (AR 604–10, par. 3b.) The Army used this lower standard only for inductees to meet as far as possible the requirements of obligatory service under the Universal Military Training Act. The latest DOD directive 5210.9 of June 19, 1956, ended this "inconsistent" standard for inductees, and now the standard is "clearly consistent" in line with the rest of the program. Nevertheless, the Army still employs a double standard as to inductees, since it may accept a doubtful inductee on the condition that his papers are stamped "not eligible for security clearance."

B. CRITERIA.—The criteria used in the military program are generally identical with those of the civilian program embodied in Executive Order 10450. (See sec. VIII.C, DOD directive 5210.9, June 19, 1956.) The DOD directive, however, adds several criteria to those in the Executive order.

Generally these additional criteria are aimed at either the sympathetic association with individuals who are themselves subversive, or the knowledgeable "participation" (as opposed to "membership" or "association") in the activities of organizations which are subversive or infiltrated by subversives.

The DOD directive also repeats the "suitability" language of section 8 (a) (1) of Executive Order 10450 including the catch-all provision "all other behavior, activities, or associations which tend to show that the member is not reliable or trustworthy." This section is directed at conduct which could be described as military unfitness. These latter criteria are not to be used as a basis for a security separation unless the true security criteria

119

are also involved, to the degree that "national security is the primary consideration." (Sec. VIII.C.3.)

The departmental regulations of the Army, Navy, and Air Force repeat the DOD criteria. The Army adds parenthetically that sympathetic association with subversive individuals will not ordinarily "include chance or occasonal meetings, or contacts limited to normal business or official relations." (AR 604–10, par. 13b (10).)

Organizations on the Attorney General's list are presumed to be of a subversive character "until the contrary be established." (DOD, VIII.C.2.d)

Scope

The DOD directive 5210.9 "applies to all members and prospective members of the Armed Forces and their reserve components, including the Coast Guard when the Coast Guard is operating as a part of the Department of the Navy." (Sec. II.B.) The Coast Guard operates as part of the Navy only during wartime; however, its regulations closely follow those of the Navy.

The standards, criteria, and policies of the DOD program are directed toward:

(1) the separation of military members from the Armed Forces or its reserve components for security reasons, and

(2) the rejection of applicants for appointment or enlistment, or of persons who would otherwise be inducted or ordered into active military service, when the acceptance of such persons would not be clearly consistent with national security. (Sec. II.A.)

Separation From Military Service

A. Court-Martial and Nonsecurity Separation Action.—The DOD directive states that unless security criteria are involved in a given case to the degree that national security is the primary consideration, and unless action under other regulations of the military departments or the Uniform Code of Military Justice is inappropriate, action to separate a member under the security program shall not be taken. Furthermore, "cases susceptible to resolution under court-martial procedure shall normally be so processed." (Secs. VIII.C.3 and IX.G.1.)

All three military departments have suitability and unfitness regulations. Typically, the military unfitness regulations provide for administrative hearing and review, and administrative discharge.

Court-martial procedure is very rarely used in a security case. Since 1948, of approximately 800 security separations from the Army, only 1 involved a punitive discharge following court-martial.

120

B. Security Separations—The Type of Discharge.—Upon the separation of a member from military service, a certificate of discharge is required by law. There are three types of discharge which may be given by administrative action. These are:

(1) Honorable.

(2) General (under honorable conditions, but conduct is not sufficient for an honorable discharge).

(3) Undesirable (not under honorable conditions).

The bad-conduct and dishonorable discharges may be given pursuant to courts-martial decree only.

All three administrative discharges listed above are used in the military security program. The single exception concerns regular commissioned officers with more than 3 years' active service. Only a court-martial can give such officers a discharge under other than honorable conditions.

The DOD directive requires the character of the discharge in a security separation to be "predicated upon a careful consideration of all pertinent factors including the gravity of substantiated derogatory information and the character of service performed." (Sec. IX.G.5.) The phrase "gravity of substantiated derogatory information" means that civilian activity, if "derogatory," may be taken into account in determining the type of discharge the military security risk would get. The possibility that civilian activity may be taken into account in deciding the type of discharge is a unique feature of the military security separation. Nonsecurity separations, whether administrative or pursuant to court-martial, are based on a character of service criterion.

To appreciate the characterization of discharge in military security separations, a page of history is necessary. The first DOD directive 5210.9 of April 7, 1954, stated that "the character of the separation shall be predicated upon the gravity of the reasonably substantiated information in derogation." (Sec. VIII.F.5.) This language would seem to exclude "character of service" considerations. Thus the serviceman who was separated for security reasons might receive an undesirable discharge based on civilian activity alone. This language was in effect from April 7, 1954, to November 16, 1955, when it was changed to the present language which bases the discharge on both substantiated derogatory information and character of service rendered. (See above.) As to inductees, the first DOD directive 5210.9 of April 7, 1954, required their separation on security grounds to be "under other than honorable conditions" (sec. VIII.E.2) which means the undesirable discharge. On June 9, 1954, this requirement was modified to allow a discharge based on character of service for those inductees who, on their loyalty forms or otherwise, made disclosure of derogatory security information. The inductee who claimed the privilege against self-incrimination

121

(fifth amendment or art. 31, UCMJ), however, continued to receive an undesirable discharge if he was separated for security reasons.

At present less-than-honorable discharges are no longer required. All members who are separated for security reasons prior to the expiration of their active service are given discharges based both on substantiated derogatory information (which may, of course, include civilian activity) and character of service performed. Inductees are now screened prior to induction (discussed below), and those who are accepted after screening and who complete their obligated active service are separated with the discharge based on character of service performed.

"Character of service performed" is defined by the Army as including "those factors normally taken into account in determining the character of separation where no adverse security finding has been made, as well as any reasonably substantiated derogatory information concerning subversive activities occurring during the period of service, and falsification, in connection with security matters, occurring during the period of service or pertaining to entry into the service." (AR 604–10, C.2, par. 19 (4), June 12, 1956.) In the earlier stages of the DOD program the argument was made that less-than-honorable discharges based on derogatory information of civilian activity were in effect based on "character of service performed" since the subversive or security-risk serviceman had limited his usefulness to the military by virtue of being a risk. The Army definition above, which is based on a Secretary of Defense memorandum of January 11, 1956, abandons this theory.

"Factors normally taken into account in determining the character of separation" are generally the efficiency and conduct rating of the serviceman and any court-martial history.

Rejection From Military Service

A. GENERAL POLICIES.—The DOD directive states: "In no case will any person, reasonably believed to have at any time engaged in any of the activities listed [referring to the security criteria] be appointed, enlisted, or inducted into any of the Armed Forces without the approval of the Secretary of the military department concerned." (Sec. III.B.) Administratively this language applies to—

(1) Applicants (volunteers) for appointment or enlistment.
(2) Reservists, including retired personnel, recalled voluntarily or involuntarily.
(3) Inductees, including doctors and dentists subject to the draft. (DOD, sec. IX.B–F.)

The DOD directive further provides that "known Communists will not be inducted into the Armed Forces." (Sec. IX.F.1.) The Army regulations define a "known Communist" as "any person who claims to be a current member of the Communist Party and/or any person against whom credible derogatory information exists establishing such current membership." (AR 604–10, par. 2.f.) "Credible derogatory information" is defined as "information received from any source, which evaluated in the light of all other available information, both favorable and unfavorable, indicates that retention within the Army Establishment of the member concerned may not be, or is not, warranted under the standards and criteria prescribed by these regulations." (AR 604–10, par. 2.e.) The Navy refers to "known Communists" or any person "reasonably suspected" by any member of the Navy or Marine Corps to be a Communist. (SECNAVINST 5521.6, par. 17a.)

B. THE DD FORM 98—ARMED FORCES SECURITY QUESTIONNAIRE AND INDUCTEE SCREENING.—Section IX.A of the DOD directive 5210.9 requires a "certification as to nonaffiliation with certain organizations" by the following persons:

(1) Each applicant for initial appointment or initial enlistment prior to his appointment or enlistment.

(2) Each registrant prior to induction.

(3) Each Reservist entering upon active duty immediately upon reporting for such duty.

(4) Reserve personnel not on active duty, as determined by the Secretary of the military department concerned.

(5) Retired members of the Armed Forces when recalled to active military service.

The DD form 98 reproduces the Attorney General's list of subversive organizations. The signer of the form is advised that he cannot be compelled to furnish any statements which he reasonably believes may lead to his prosecution for a crime. It is pointed out that claiming the fifth amendment will not by itself constitute sufficient grounds for exemption from military service for reasons of security. The form refers to title 18, U. S. Code, section 1001, and advises that any false or fraudulent response to the questions on the form may give rise to criminal liability under this statute.

The questions on the form 98 are directed at any association with organizations on the Attorney General's list, including membership, attendance at gatherings, contributions of money or services, and subscription to publications. There are also questions directed at membership in the Communist Party of any foreign country. In addition, there is a catch-all question aimed at membership in any organization, association, movement, or group of persons not on the Attorney General's list which advocates the violent overthrow of our constitutional form of government. If there is any qualification of a negative answer to any of the questions on the form, a full explanation is required in a space provided. The signer of the form makes a certification as to the truth of his response. The form is also signed by a witness.

The DD form 98 plays an important part in the military personnel security program, especially in the Army, which is the only branch at present concerned with inducted personnel. The DOD directive 5210.9 provides in section IX.F.2 for the investigation and possible rejection of registrants with the draft who, in accomplishing the form, either refuse to answer certain questions or disclose derogatory security information about themselves. In such cases, the induction process is postponed pending a thorough investigation. The DOD directive states: "The initial determination concerning acceptance or rejection for induction shall be made by an Interservice committee which will be established and supervised by the Secretary of the Army as the executive agent for selective service . . . . In the event the registrant is rejected, an opportunity to be heard will be granted, if the registrant so requests." (Sec. IX.F.2.) This hearing is before a board of officers convened under the instructions of the Secretary of the Army.

The DOD directive 5210.9 under "application of criteria" lists the "intentional failure or refusal to sign the DD form 98," or "refusal to completely answer questions contained" in DD form 98. Thus any qualification of the form 98 may later be the basis of a security allegation against the serviceman responsible. This possibility, however, is not noted in the explanations on the face of the form. If the signer of the form fails to disclose thereon any derogatory information of the type requested, and a subsequent discovery of this is made, the question may arise of his falsifying his response, and he may be court-martialed.

It should be noted that the DD form 98 does not compel disclosure of kinship or sympathetic association with individuals who are subversive. Kinship with subversive persons, however, could be revealed by filling out DD form 398, which is a statement of personal history. On this form, certain close relatives must be listed. DD form 398 is not required of all members of the Armed Forces, or of inductees. It is filled out by all officers, upon appointment, or by personnel who must be cleared for access to classified material.

C. REJECTION OF PERSONS OTHER THAN INDUCTEES—(1) *Applicants for appointment or enlistment.*—The DOD directive denies enlistment or appointment to persons who refuse "to accomplish the DD form 98 in its entirety." This would exclude all those who plead the fifth amendment, for example. But if the DD form 98 is completed with entries indicating a security problem, the appointment or enlistment is held up pending a decision by the military department concerned. (Sec. IX.B–C.)

(2) *Reservists.*—The DOD directive provides that members of Reserve components who either refuse to fill out DD form 98 or who make qualifying entries thereon, will have security separation procedure initiated against them by the appropriate military department. (Sec. IX.D.)

(3) *Retired members of the Armed Forces.*—The DOD directive provides that if any retired member is voluntarily or involuntarily entering on active duty, and refuses to complete DD form 98 or makes qualifying entries

124

thereon, action with a view toward separation will be initiated by the Secretary of the appropriate military department. (Sec. IX.E.)

(4) *Doctor and dentist applicants for commission who are subject to induction.*—(a) Those who fail or refuse to fill out DD form 98 in its entirety are not appointed to a commission. Their induction is then handled under the usual screening procedure for inductees (described above). (DOD, sec. IX.F.3.)

(b) Those who qualify their form 98 with entries indicating a security problem are not appointed or inducted pending a decision by the military department concerned. The applicant is given an opportunity to be heard. Before hearing, however, the case is reviewed by a screening board, which makes appropriate recommendations to the Secretary, and if the case then goes to the hearing board, it too makes recommendations to the Secretary, either to tender a commission, or to induct in an enlisted capacity, or to be rejected outright for service in any capacity. (DOD, sec. IX.F.3.b.)

(5) *Students.*—The Army has added a provision (June 12, 1956) to its security regulations applicable specifically to ROTC, Officers Candidate Schools, "and other students pursuing courses of instruction at Army approved schools which lead to appointment" which brings these persons within the usual security procedures of investigation, postponement of appointment or induction, screening and hearing before a field board. The Secretary of the Army makes the final decision. (AR 604–10, par. 38.)

(6) *National Guard.*—The Army security regulations "apply to all military members of the Army Establishment including members of the National Guard of the United States on active duty and not on active duty . . . . The Chief, National Guard Bureau, will issue appropriate implementing instructions governing the National Guard of the United States not on active duty." (AR 604–10, par. 1b.)

Prehearing Board Procedures

A. INVESTIGATIONS—(1) *Reporting requirement.*—The DOD directive states "It shall be the duty of every member of the Armed Forces to report to his commanding officer any information coming to his attention which indicates that retention of any members of the Armed Services may not be clearly consistent with the interests of national security." (Sec. VI.) Inactive Air National Guard personnel and inactive Army National Guard personnel report to the Chief, National Guard Bureau, Washington, D. C. (AR 604–10, par. 4; AFR 35–62, par. 3; SECNAVINST 5521.6, par. 9.)

(2) *Investigative procedure.*—The DOD directive requires the departmental investigative agencies, when conducting security investigations, to develop "all relevant facts with special emphasis being given to that information which supports or refutes an allegation stemming from the (security criteria)." (Sec. VII.A.) There is further provision for a

125

national agency check to be conducted prior to the appointing or commissioning of any individual as an officer or warrant officer. (Sec. VII.B.)

When derogatory security information is received, the departmental regulations typically provide for routing through intelligence channels. In the Army the case would be referred to G–2 by the major command; in the Navy, to naval intelligence; in the Air Force, to the Office of Special Investigations (OSI). The three services conduct their own investigations (in the Army, the counterintelligence corps is the investigative arm of G–2) with appropriate reference to the national agency check and the FBI.

B. PROCEDURES THROUGH THE DRAWING OF ALLEGATIONS—(1) *The Navy.*—"The responsibility for implementation of the military personnel security program for members of the Navy has been vested in the Chief of Naval Personnel by the Secretary of the Navy. Likewise, the investigative responsibilities in the Navy are vested in the Director of Naval Intelligence. The Director of Naval Intelligence is responsible, among other things, for keeping the Chief of Naval Personnel informed of derogatory information concerning members of the Navy. As a corollary to these functions, the Director of Naval Intelligence is responsible for the preparation of the unclassified narrative statement of facts and interrogatory, when requested by the Chief of Naval Personnel, and for concurrence in the administrative processing of the individual using this material to avoid compromising impending prosecutions or investigations.

"In line with the above responsibilities, all information of a security nature involving naval personnel is forwarded by the Director of Naval Intelligence to the Chief of Naval Personnel. At times, of course, derogatory information of a security nature is received from commanding officers, commandants, and other sources, but the information is always checked by responsible agencies under the Director of Naval Intelligence. The investigative jacket transmitted by the Director of Naval Intelligence is routed to the Military Personnel Security Division, Bureau of Naval Personnel, for reviewing. If the information relates the subject member to acts of espionage, sabotage, or subversion, and falls within the criteria listed in SECNAV instruction 5521.6, the case is referred to a bureau security screening board for recommendation.

"After a thorough study of the investigative record, the Security Screening Board makes one of the following recommendations to the Chief of Naval Personnel:

"a. That further investigation be undertaken.

"b. That sufficient evidence is available to initiate action under the Uniform Code of Military Justice.

"c. That administrative action looking toward separation of the member be undertaken (refer to a local security board).

"d. That an applicant be accepted or rejected.

"e. That the case be closed without prejudice to the individual on the grounds that further processing under this instruction is unwarranted.

126

"f. That the case be referred to the Judge Advocate General for consideration or referral to appropriate federal or state civil authority.

"g. That specified other administrative action be undertaken.

"This other action may relate to promotion; retirement; separation from active duty; the granting, denial, or revocation of clearances; the restriction or removal of restriction on duty assignments; termination of temporary appointments, etc.

"The recommendations of the Security Screening Board are reviewed by the Chief of Naval Personnel. If the decision is to initiate processing for possible separation of the member, the Chief of Naval Personnel requests the Director of Naval Intelligence to prepare and forward an unclassified narrative statement of facts and interrogatory.

"Upon receipt of the narrative statement of facts and interrogatory from the Director of Naval Intelligence, the Chief of Naval Personnel transmits them to a command having general court-martial convening authority (the district commandant in this discussion) with a request that he proceed under the terms of the security instruction.

"The commandant transmits the narrative statement of facts and interrogatory to the respondent requesting that he reply to the interrogatory, and inform the commandant of his desire for a hearing, within 5 days of constructive date of receipt." [13]

2. *The Air Force.*—"The commander, upon receipt of sufficient information upon which to base a substantial and reasonable judgment, takes one of two actions. If in the judgment of the commander there is not a reasonable doubt as to whether the individual should be retained, the commander may recommend closing the case by forwarding to the Office of Special Investigations, Headquarters, United States Air Force, his statement and reasoning that no action is deemed appropriate. If the commander feels that possible discharge action is appropriate he will forward the case with his recommendation, through channels, to the Director of Special Investigations, Inspector General, Headquarters, USAF. In either type of recommendation by the commander, the case is forwarded to Headquarters, USAF. This is to maintain adjudicative consistency within the overall program and allow the Inspector General to evaluate the trends of subversive activity, if any, within the Air Force.

"The case is then reviewed by the Office of Special Investigations and a summary is prepared and forwarded to the Director of Military Personnel, with a recommendation concerning further action. Incidentally, OSI interviews every subject under oath and the results of such comprehensive interview are made a part of the forwarded file. The case is reviewed by the Military Personnel Security Committee which recommends appropriate action as previously stated. The Deputy Chief of Staff, Per-

[13] Quoted from written memorandum of briefing by naval security personnel of the Commission's representatives, May 11, 1956.

sonnel, approves or disapproves the committee's recommendation. If the case is determined to be 'no action,' the Security Branch then notifies the commander to consider the case closed and the individual follows a normal Air Force career.

"In 'action' cases, after the 'statement of reasons' is prepared and witnesses selected, the case is forwarded to the Deputy for Security Programs, Assistant Secretary of the Air Force, who approves or disapproves the issuance of the statement of reasons. The Secretary of the Air Force general counsel then reviews the statement of reasons for legal sufficiency. After the statement of reasons is thus approved, it is forwarded to the Office of Special Investigations for coordination and determination that techniques of investigation and sources of confidential information have not been compromised. After this coordination, the case is prepared by the Security Branch and forwarded to the major commander who is responsible for affording the individual an opportunity for a hearing board." [14]

3. *The Army.*—Upon completion of the investigation the major command evaluates it. The case may be closed favorably at this stage, with a review of favorable action by the Assistant Chief of Staff, Intelligence (ASCI). If not closed favorably, the case is forwarded to ASCI with appropriate recommendations.

ASCI further reviews the case, and may close it favorably. If not, it is forwarded to the Judge Advocate General (JAG) for review, and preparation of proposed allegations. ASCI prepares the summary of information for use of the subject. This is a précis of the derogatory information in the investigative file.

The case then goes to the Army Security Screening Board. This Board may close the case favorably. If not, it forwards the case to the Deputy Chief of Staff for Personnel (DCS/P). It is reviewed again, and if a hearing is decided upon, DCS/P directs the major command to convene a field board of inquiry (hearing board). The major command then transmits to the subject the letter of allegations, the summary of information, and the subject at this point may request a hearing.

4. *General provisions.*—The military services conduct interviews under oath with the subject, during the prehearing board stage. This is an informal affair, but the subject may have counsel.

At all stages of screening the case, further investigation may be requested of the investigative branch.

The great majority of cases are closed favorably at some point prior to hearing.

Pending the final outcome of a case all the services employ "flagging action" on the personnel file of the subject, to prevent reassignment, promotion, etc. The subject may be placed on specially controlled duties.

---

[14] Quoted from Air Force booklet entitled "Security Program," prepared pursuant to a June 1956 briefing of the Commission's representatives, pp. 64–65.

A. HEARING BOARD PROCEDURES.—The DOD directive requires that in any administrative security separation of a member of the Armed Forces, "such member will be afforded an opportunity upon request to present evidence in his behalf as to why he should not be separated. Reasonable time will be afforded the member to present this case; however, a period in excess of 15 days may be granted only when [justified]." (Sec. IX.G.3.)

The DOD directive further states that the hearings "shall not be trials or adjudications, but shall be directed to the end of obtaining factual findings and unbiased opinions by boards of officers." (Sec. IX.G.4.)

The details of hearing board procedure are left to implementing departmental regulations. The boards may summon witnesses on motion; although no power of subpena exists, it must be remembered that military personnel who are witnesses may be ordered to appear. However, although efforts are made to persuade witnesses to appear, if such witnesses wish to remain confidential, the wish is respected. Provision is made for the questioning of witnesses privately by the boards. Undercover informants are never called. Their identities are usually not disclosed even to the board, which would have their statements before it in the confidential investigation dossier.

The Army and Air Force have recently adopted the technique of having attorney-advisers guide the proceedings. This office is an impartial one; the attorney-advisers are charged with the duty of bringing out all the evidence, favorable and unfavorable. They also perform the useful function of apprising the board of the latest policy directives in the security field. Attorney-advisers do not participate in the final deliberations of the board.

Military counsel will be provided the subject, if he requests. Civilian counsel, if desired, must be retained independently.

No exclusionary rules of evidence apply, beyond a general one of relevance.

The subject is furnished a transcript of the record.

In general, the findings and recommendations of the board must be at least responsive to each allegation made in the letter of allegations. The Army and the Air Force require the board to take into consideration the lack of opportunity to cross-examine or rebut undisclosed classified information. Dissenting opinions by Board members may be submitted. The board's decision is *advisory*, not final. It may advise clearance, or discharge. It must specify the type of discharge.

The findings and recommendations of the board are not disclosed to the subject. The Army, at one time, allowed the subject to learn the board's recommendation, but this procedure has been abandoned.

B. FINAL REVIEW.—The review function in all three services, after board hearing, is performed at departmental headquarters in Washington. In the Army, the Security Review Board receives the field board's recommendations. In the Navy, this office is performed by the Chief of Naval Personnel. In the Air Force, the Secretary of the Air Force Personnel Council makes a final recommendation to the Secretary. In the Army, the major commander transmits the field board's recommendations with further recommendations of his own.

The review boards may require further investigation, or more detailed reasoning by the hearing boards.

The review boards may request the subject to appear. He has no right to do so, although he may submit to the review boards further evidence in his behalf. Thus there is no "appeal" in any judicial sense of the word. In the Navy and Air Force the final decision is made by the respective Secretaries. In the Army, the final decision is made by the Army Security Review Board, except in unfavorable decisions concerning officers, which go to the Secretary of the Army for final action.

The DOD directive provides that any member of the armed services who is separated for security reasons, shall not be accepted in any of the Armed Forces at a later date "without the approval of the Secretary of the military department concerned." (Sec. III.B.)

RECOMMENDATIONS

STANDARD AND CRITERIA

The Commission recommends that the standard for separation from, or denial of enlistment, induction, appointment, or recall to active duty in the Armed Forces, including the Coast Guard, should be, that on all the available information there is reasonable doubt as to loyalty.

The Armed Forces of the United States are the bulwark of the Nation's defense. Any individual whose interests are irreconcilably in conflict with the interests of the Government of the United States by reason of his adherence to or sympathy with an organization, movement, ideology, or foreign government hostile to the Government of the United States, should not be accepted or retained in the Armed Forces. A reasonable doubt as to loyalty must be universal in its application. There can be no distinction between sensitive and nonsensitive assignments, nor between classes of personnel. The need for strict and unswerving loyalty has been vividly brought out by Secretary of Defense Charles E. Wilson during his testimony concerning the Doctor Draft Act amendments in 1954. Secretary Wilson stated: [15]

Officers' commissions granted by the President of the United States contain the following time-honored language:

. . . reposing special trust and confidence in the patriotism, valor, fidelity, and abilities.

Every enlisted man is likewise expected to devote his unswerving loyalty to his country's cause against all enemies, foreign and domestic. Patriotism and fidelity are basic requirements for membership in the armed services. Conflicting loyalties cannot and will not be tolerated by the Department of Defense. There is no substitute for complete and undivided loyalty to the United States.

The Armed Forces in operating their military security programs have changed the standard used from time to time so as to maintain consistency with the expressed policy in the laws and Executive orders, relating to the Government's civilian loyalty and security programs.

The recommended standard, which follows the basic concept in the standard recommended for the civilian employees' loyalty program, is meant to strike directly at the heart of the problem; namely, to remove and deny entrance of those individuals whose loyalty can reasonably be doubted.

In those cases where an individual's conduct or background is such as to reflect unfavorably on his reliability or trustworthiness but does not cast doubt on his loyalty, rejection or separation on grounds other than for loyalty reasons should be made under applicable service directives relating to suitability.

The Commission recommends that the following criteria be used in the military personnel loyalty program.

Activities and associations of the Armed Forces personnel which may be considered in connection with the determination of the existence of a reasonable doubt as to loyalty may include one or more of the following:

1. Sabotage, espionage, or attempts or preparations therefor, or knowingly associating with spies or saboteurs;

2. Treason or sedition or advocacy thereof;

3. Advocacy of revolution or force or violence to alter the constitutional form of government of the United States;

4. Intentional, unauthorized disclosure, to any person, under circumstances which may indicate disloyalty to the United States, of documents or information of a confidential or nonpublic character;

5. Performing or attempting to perform his duties, or otherwise acting so as to serve the interests of another government in preference to the interests of the United States;

---

[15] Hearings before the Committee on Armed Services, U. S. Senate, 83d Cong., 2d sess., on S. 3096, p. 3.

6. Membership in, affiliation, or sympathetic association with any party, group, or association which the Congress of the United States, or any agency or officer of the United States duly authorized by the Congress for that purpose, finds:

(*a*) Seeks to alter the form of Government of the United States by force or violence, or other unconstitutional means; or,

(*b*) Is organized or utilized for the purpose of advancing the aims and objectives of the Communist movement; or

(*c*) Is organized or utilized for the purpose of establishing any form of dictatorship in the United States or any form of international dictatorship; or

(*d*) Is organized or utilized by any foreign government, or by any foreign party, group or association acting in the interest of such foreign government for the purpose of (i) espionage, or (ii) sabotage, or (iii) obtaining information relating to the defense of the United States or the protection of the national security, or (iv) hampering, hindering, or delaying the production of defense materials; or

(*e*) Is affiliated with, or acts in concert with, or is dominated or controlled by any party, group, or association of the character described in (*a*), (*b*), (*c*), or (*d*) above.

7. Membership in or affiliation with any organization which the Congress of the United States, or any agency or officer of the United States duly authorized by the Congress for that purpose, finds has adopted a policy of advocating or approving the commission of acts of force and violence to deny others their rights under the Constitution of the United States.

8. Refusal to testify upon the grounds of self-incrimination, in any authorized inquiry relating to subversive activities conducted by a congressional committee, Federal court, Federal grand jury, or any other duly authorized Federal agency, as to questions relating to subversive activities of the individual involved or others, unless the individual, after opportunity to do so, satisfactorily explains his refusal to testify.

9. The foregoing enumeration should not be deemed to exclude any other factors tending to establish reasonable doubt as to loyalty.

The criteria for the military personnel loyalty program follows that recommended for the civilian employees' loyalty program. The similarities of the two programs lend themselves to the use of like criteria. The

Armed Forces in the past have been guided by criteria used in the civilian employees' loyalty and security programs. The factors of definition, construction, and application of the standard and criteria to achieve an optimum balance between national security and individual rights as set forth in the recommended civilian employees loyalty program should also be considered in the military personnel loyalty program.

ACCEPTANCE AND REJECTION

The Commission recommends that the DD Form 98 (Armed Forces security questionnaire) should continue to be executed at the time of preinduction processing.

The present Department of Defense Directive 5210.9, dated June 19, 1956, provides that each registrant, prior to induction, shall execute a DD Form 98. Consideration has been given by the Commission to the possibility of having the DD Form 98 executed by the registrant for induction at the time of registration under the Selective Service Act, rather than at the preinduction processing, in order to expedite processing if entries made on the form require investigation. The Commission, however, feels that local selective service boards are inexperienced in the processing of such forms and are not in a position to fully advise registrants concerning the information requested or the consequences of qualifying the form. The usual length of time between registration and induction would probably necessitate reexecution of the form during the induction process. The investigation required when the form is qualified is the function of the military, which would not have jurisdiction to investigate until preinduction processing takes place. The Commission believes that the present system serves the purpose best.

The Commission recommends that the certification of nonaffiliation with subversive organizations, which is presently made on the DD Form 98, should not be confined to those organizations on the Attorney General's list, but should include any party, group, or association which the Congress of the United States, or any agency or officer of the United States duly authorized by the Congress for that purpose, finds:
> **(a) Seeks to alter the form of government of the United States by force or violence, or other unconstitutional means; or**
> **(b) Is organized or utilized for the purpose of advancing the aims and objectives of the Communist movement; or**
> **(c) Is organized or utilized for the purpose of establishing**

any form of dictatorship in the United States or any form of international dictatorship; or

(*d*) Is organized or utilized by any foreign government, or by any foreign party, group, or association acting in the interest of such foreign government for the purpose of (1) espionage, or (2) sabotage, or (3) obtaining information relating to the defense of the United States or the protection of the national security, or (4) hampering, hindering or delaying the production of defense materials; or

(*e*) Has adopted a policy of advocating or approving the commission of acts of force and violence to deny others their rights under the Constitution of the United States; or

(*f*) Is affiliated with, or acts in concert with, or is dominated or controlled by, any party, group, or association of the character described in (*a*), (*b*), (*c*), or (*d*) above.

The form should list not only those organizations found to be of the above character by the Attorney General, but also those found to be of such character by the Congress or any other duly authorized agency.

The execution of the certification of nonaffiliation with subversive organizations is the source of basic information upon which acceptance is made or rejection action is initiated in connection with a loyalty determination. All possible information should be supplied to the individual executing the form in order that he may be in a position fully to advise the military service of his associations and affiliations, and to allow him ample opportunity to offer explanations which may prevent the necessity of later hearing board action.

The Commission recommends that instructions appearing on the DD Form 98 should include a warning to the signer thereof that failure to answer completely the questions or pleading the privilege against self-incrimination may be used as an allegation against the individual in loyalty proceedings.

Information has been presented during the course of congressional hearings disclosing that charges made against individuals in the Armed Forces have included refusal to sign DD Form 98 and the claiming of the privilege against self-incrimination.[16]

The Commission recommends that in order to insure proper execution of DD Form 98, in addition to the instructions accom-

---

[16] Hearings before the Subcommittee on Constitutional Rights of the Senate Judiciary Committee, 84th Cong., 2d sess., S. Res. 94, pt. 1, Nov. 14–29, 1955, pp. 516–518.

panying the form, the inductee or enlistee should be orally advised by an appropriate official of the significance of the form, and particularly the consequences of failure to answer questions in whole or in part, or of answering them falsely.

The Armed Forces require that prospective members in executing the DD Form 98 shall read and/or have explained to them the criteria for the application of the standard.[17]

Instances have been brought to the Commission's attention indicating that this requirement is not being closely followed by some officials charged with the responsibility of handling preinduction processing. There have been cases reported where the prospective inductee was asked a general question by a service representative as to whether or not he was a Communist or a member of a subversive organization. When answering in the negative, the individual was asked to sign the back page of DD Form 98 without being afforded the opportunity of reading the organizations listed on the form. While there is no information that this is a common practice, the awareness of such specific examples indicates a definite need for close supervision of those charged with effectively carrying out the processing system.

The Commission recommends that where denial of enlistment is based on grounds of reasonable doubt as to loyalty, the individual involved should be furnished a letter of charges with such specificity as will permit him to prepare for a hearing, though not including information the disclosure of which would prejudice national security, and be given an opportunity for a hearing within the appropriate military service. In such a hearing, the individual involved should be entitled to rights of confrontation and subpena in accordance with the Commission's recommendations on those subjects.

The Department of Defense Directive 5210.9, dated June 19, 1956, states that, if an applicant for enlistment fails or refuses to execute the DD Form 98 in its entirety, his enlistment will be denied; or, if the DD Form 98 is completed and entries made thereon provide reason for belief that his enlistment may not be clearly consistent with the interests of national security, such enlistment will be held in abeyance pending decision of the military department concerned. The directive does not provide for a hearing for rejected enlistees.

Some of the Armed Forces do provide for a hearing for this class of individuals as noted in the Department of Navy SECNAV instruction 5521.6A, dated January 31, 1957, which states that no applicant will be rejected primarily on the grounds that his service would be not clearly

---

[17] Army Regulations 604–10, dated July 29, 1955.

consistent with the interests of national security without being afforded the opportunity for a hearing.

The Commission believes that in any case where action is taken concerning any individual based on loyalty information, the individual should be afforded a proper opportunity to offer any explanation or refutation concerning the allegations.

The Commission recommends that if an enlistee or inductee is rejected during preservice screening, on the basis of reasonable doubt as to loyalty, he may request and be granted a hearing, without any cost to him. It is also recommended that if a hearing is requested, the enlistee or inductee may request and have provided without any cost to him, counsel furnished by the military service. If the enlistee or inductee does not request a hearing, he should be furnished with a statement of reasons.

The Department of Defense Directive 5210.9, dated June 19, 1956, provides that in the event a registrant for induction is rejected, an opportunity to be heard will be granted if the registrant so requests. The initial determination concerning rejection is made by an interservice committee which is established and supervised by the Secretary of the Army as the executive agent for selective service. If the rejected registrant fails to request a hearing within a reasonable period, the initial determination of the interservice committee shall be final.

The Commission, after carefully considering the matter of affording hearings to individuals who are rejected during preservice screening, believes that equal opportunities in this regard should be provided for enlistees and inductees. The inductee is being called by the Government to serve in the Armed Forces. He is in a different position from the applicant, taken in the strictest sense, who is seeking entrance into Government service. Although a prospective enlistee is applying or seeking entrance into the service, the Commission feels that his status is very similar to that of the inductee. It is a commonly accepted fact that many of the individuals who are seeking enlistment are doing so because of the imminence of induction.

The fact cannot be disregarded that the majority of individuals who are being inducted or enlisted are in the late teens or early twenties. This is a group which, generally speaking, does not have much financial reserve, or experience in establishing a suitable defense against charges. The Commission is of the opinion that in order to allow the enlistee or inductee, rejected on reasonable doubt as to loyalty, adequate opportunity to refute allegations, the Government should assume the expense involved in affording these individuals hearings and provide the facilities which the military service has available for assistance of those who are in the Armed Forces.

In those cases where the individual does not request a hearing and is rejected from service, in all fairness and justice to the individual he should be furnished with the reasons for final rejection. These reasons should be set forth in as specific detail as the interests of national security shall permit.

The Commission recommends against the use of inductees, who would otherwise be rejected on loyalty grounds, in some semi-military status analogous to the policy toward conscientious objectors.

During a period of national emergency when it is necessary for the adequate protection of the national security, it is of the utmost importance for the Armed Forces to make use of all possible manpower and personnel. The Commission in reviewing this matter considered the possibility of using inductees, who would otherwise be rejected from regular military service on loyalty grounds, on assignments which would enable them to provide services of a semimilitary nature. The Commission, after careful consideration, decided that such a procedure would not be practicable. The Armed Forces require the complete devotion to duty and unswerving loyalty of each member irrespective of any particular duty or assignment. Basically and unequivocably, disloyal individuals should not be in the Armed Forces.

On this particular point, Secretary of Defense Charles E. Wilson in 1954 stated his opposition to the suggestion of setting up work camps for security risks and thus segregate them from loyal citizens.[18]

INVESTIGATIONS

The Commission recommends that in processing incoming personnel the use of the national agency check should be limited to individuals who qualify the DD Form 98 and should not be used for all incoming personnel.

Aware of the great necessity of preventing individuals concerning whom there is reasonable doubt as to loyalty from entering the Armed Forces, the Commission concerned itself with the possibility of having a national agency check conducted on each individual being considered for induction or enlistment. It was decided that to conduct such a check concerning the many thousands of individuals annually inducted or enlisted into the Armed Forces would be a very time-consuming and expensive procedure. The amount of information that would be uncovered would not justify the cost involved. The Department of Defense directive 5210.9,

---

[18] Hearings before Committee on Armed Forces, U. S. Senate, 83d Cong., 2d sess., on S. 3096, Doctor Draft Act amendments, Mar., Apr., 1954, p. 43.

dated June 19, 1956, provides that an investigation be conducted concerning those individuals who qualify their DD Form 98. This directive also provides that a national agency check be conducted prior to the appointment or commissioning of any individual as an officer or warrant officer in the Armed Forces. The Commission feels that the present use of the national agency check is adequate and should be continued.

The Commission recommends that each of the military services continue to conduct their own investigations in the military personnel loyalty program.

The military services presently conduct their own security investigations in the military security program. The Commission considered the advisability of centralizing military personnel security investigatons into a single security office within the Department of Defense. However, as each military service has its own security responsibility, it appears that the present procedure is practical and workable.

The present policy of close liaison between the military and nonmilitary investigative agencies for the exchange of security information is essential and should be continued.

The Commission recommends that the military services should continue their present policy of interviewing the individual who is being investigated.

The present policy of the military services is to conduct an interview with the subject during the course of the investigation. The Commission heartily endorses this policy. A properly conducted interview is a very important element of any investigation and can be the means for obtaining information from the individual which may serve as a basis for a prompt favorable determination of the case.

PREHEARING BOARD PROCEDURES

The Commission recommends that the present triservice screening procedure for inductees be retained and that each of the military services continue to screen cases involving their respective members.

The Department of Defense Directive 5210.9 of June 19, 1956, established a triservice procedure for inductee screening prior to induction.

138

The registrants for military service under the Selective Service Act are a manpower pool for all three services, although at present used only by the Army; therefore a triservice screening approach is useful.

The separation of a member of the Army, Navy, or Air Force, however, is a function of command and the present system of three separate screening boards is essential for the military services operation.

The Commission recommends that a prima facie case be made out prior to initiating hearing board action and that it be the responsibility of the screening officer to determine whether there is substantial information justifying the issuance of a letter of charges and bringing the case to a hearing.

The initiation of hearing board action is very important and has serious impact on the life of the individual involved. It commences an action which is time consuming and expensive both to the individual and the agency involved. Very careful consideration must be given during the screening phase to insure that a sound basis for proceeding has been established. It should be definitely ascertained that proceeding under the loyalty standard is proper and that the case could not be more readily handled under suitability regulations or court-martial procedures. Every action must be initiated on solid facts and must not be a "fishing expedition."

The Commission recommends that the current procedures be retained as to authority to make a final favorable determination.

At the present time within the Armed Forces if a case is not recommended for a hearing, the final favorable decision may be made within the Air Force by the Deputy Chief of Staff, Personnel; within the Army by the Assistant Chief of Staff, Intelligence; and within the Navy by the Chief of Naval Personnel or the Commandant of the Marine Corps. After hearing, the final favorable decision may be made by the respective Secretaries of the Air Force and Navy, and in the Army by the Army Security Review Board, except that in cases of regular officers with over three years of active duty, the final decision rests with the Secretary.

The Commission recommends that the letter of allegations be as specific and detailed as the interests of national security shall permit and should include pertinent information such as names, dates, and places in such detail as to permit reasonable answer thereto.

Great care must be taken in stating as specifically as possible events, incidents, or circumstances which are the reasons to cast doubt on an individual's

139

loyalty. It is important that sufficient information and detail be furnished which will permit the individual to prepare an adequate defense against any and all allegations.

HEARING BOARDS AND HEARING PROCEDURES

The Commission recommends that hearing boards should continue to be maintained in each of the military services.

The Commission believes that the present procedure of each of the military services maintaining hearing boards is useful. The recommendations made by the hearing boards in each case should continue to be advisory to the head of the appropriate military agency.

There is a continued need for having a central overall policy for guidance in the operation of the Armed Forces within the Department of Defense. The Office of the Secretary of Defense should see that the standard and criteria proposed for this program are applied to all three services. The Office of the Secretary of Defense should also issue appropriate regulations in line with those promulgated by the Director of the Central Security Office and issue instructions to the three services to standardize hearing and review procedures.

The Commission recommends that hearings be closed to all but the individual, his counsel, and those having an official capacity in the case.

The present Armed Forces regulations provide that no persons other than those having official capacity in the case will be present during any of the proceedings.

The Commission believes that public hearings would tend to discourage the appearance of witnesses, and would subject the employee to additional unfavorable publicity. The informal atmosphere of private hearings is more conducive to an impartial determination of the facts. Furthermore, open hearings would sometimes be inappropriate due to the necessity of considering classified information therein.

The Commission recommends that an individual should be entitled to confrontation and subpena to the following extent in the military personnel loyalty program:
    A. Where denial of enlistment, induction, appointment, or recall to active duty in the Armed Forces, including the Coast Guard, is based upon any ground other than

reasonable doubt as to loyalty, the individual involved should be advised that such denial is based upon the then current suitability grounds, and in such cases, no hearing should be required.

B. Where the separation or denial of enlistment, induction, appointment, or recall to active duty in the Armed Forces, including the Coast Guard, is based on grounds of reasonable doubt as to loyalty, the individual involved should be given an opportunity for a hearing within the appropriate military service. In such a hearing, the individual involved should be entitled to rights of confrontation and subpena to the following extent:

1. Confrontation of persons who have supplied derogatory information should be allowed to the maximum extent consistent with the protection of the national security.

2. Confrontation of regularly established confidential informants engaged in obtaining intelligence and internal security information for the Government should not be allowed where the head of the investigative agency determines that the disclosure of the identity of such informants will prejudice the national security. In such cases the report supplied by the investigative agency should contain as much of the information supplied by the informant as may be disclosed without revealing the identity of the informant and without otherwise endangering the national security.

(a) If confrontation is not permitted under paragraph 2, the hearing board should furnish the individual involved with the substance of the information obtained from such informant to the extent that such information is material to the consideration of issues involved; and should read into the record the substance of such information and the evaluation as to reliability placed upon such confidential informant in the investigative report.

(b) If the individual involved questions the accuracy or completeness of the information furnished pursuant to paragraph 2 (a) above, he may file with the hearing board a written statement setting forth in detail so much of the information challenged by him as to accuracy or completeness. If the hearing board is of the opinion that the additional investigation as to the specific matters challenged is required in the interests of ascertaining the facts, it should request the investigating agency to make such additional investigation. Information obtained as a result of the additional investigation should be treated in the same manner as provided for in the original investigation.

3. (a) Derogatory information supplied by confidential informants other than those described in paragraph 2 should not be considered, over the objection of the individual involved, by any hearing board in arriving at its determination, or by any officer charged with the responsibility for making a final decision as to retention of the individual involved or as to clearance, unless such informants consent to the disclosure of their identity so as to enable the individual involved to obtain their testimony through the issuance of subpena or by depositions, orally or on written interrogatories.

(b) Derogatory information supplied by identified persons should not be considered, over the objection of the individual involved, by any hearing board in arriving at its determination, or by any officer charged with the responsibility for making a final decision as to the retention of the individual involved or as to clearance, unless the individual involved is given the opportunity to obtain the testimony of such identified persons through the issuance of a subpena, or by depositions, orally or on written interrogatories; if the individual involved is given the opportunity to obtain the testimony of such identified persons through the issuance of a subpena, or by depositions, orally or on written interrogatories, such derogatory information supplied by identified persons shall be considered. Where an identified informant gives a statement on the condition that he will not be called upon to testify or otherwise be subject to subpena, the hearing board should have no authority to issue a subpena for, or require depositions from, such individual. If the identified person supplying the derogatory information is unavailable for service of subpena or the taking of his deposition, orally or on written interrogatories because of death, incompetency, or other reason, such derogatory information may be considered by the hearing board with due regard for the lack of opportunity for cross-examination. (It is not intended that the foregoing requirements of pars. 3 (a) and 3 (b) apply to preliminary interviews preceding issuance of letters of charges.)

Nothing herein contained should be construed so as to require the investigating agency to exclude from its report any information derived from any source but all information obtained should continue to be included in the report to be submitted to the appropriate agency.

C. The Commission believes that the right of subpena should be applicable where there is a right of confrontation, but this does not preclude the individual involved from furnishing affidavits or the testimony of witnesses he wishes to present and who are willing to appear voluntarily. If the individual involved presents an affidavit, and the Government has reason to doubt the affiant's veracity, the Government may subpena the affiant.

1. Either the Government or the individual should be permitted to apply to the hearing board to issue subpenas, except as to confidential informants and identified informants who have given their information on the condition that they will not be called as witnesses. Such application should state the name and address of such witness, as well as the substance of the testimony to be presented by the witness. If the hearing board deems the evidence relevant and not merely cumulative, it may issue the subpena.

2. Before issuing subpenas, the hearing board should consider such factors as the time and expense involved by reason of the travel required.

3. The witness should be compensated for travel expense and per diem, but where such costs are substantial, the hearing board may in its discretion require the parties to use deposition procedures.

4. The Government should bear the cost of Government witnesses, but the hearing board should not subpena a witness for the individual until the individual deposits with the Government sufficient funds to pay the travel and per diem costs of civilian witnesses. In the event that the individual is not cleared, the funds deposited by the individual should be used to pay for the individual's witness expenses. If, however, the individual is cleared, the funds deposited by the individual should be returned to him and the Government should bear the travel and per diem costs of the individual's witness. (The requirements of paragraph C4 should not be applicable to enlistees or inductees who are rejected at preservice screen-

143

ing on the grounds of reasonable doubt as to loyalty. The Commission has recommended that the cost of hearings for these individuals should be assumed by the Government.)

Where an individual is denied entrance into the Armed Forces upon charges which reflect upon his loyalty, the consequences are much more serious than is the case where such denial is based upon grounds reflecting upon his suitability.

Where an adverse determination is predicated upon loyalty factors, the person involved should be given the fullest opportunity, consistent with the protection of the national security, to defend himself.

The Commission, therefore, recommends that where the criteria relating to loyalty are included in the charges in the areas above set out, the recommendations heretofore made in respect to confrontation and subpena be applicable.

The Commission recommends that if the individual wishes to employ civilian counsel, the Government should not pay for such counsel.

The Commission's recommendation in the civilian employees loyalty program that the individual involved shall be entitled to counsel of his own choice, but that the Government should not pay the fees of such counsel, should apply equally to the military personnel loyalty program when civilian counsel is engaged.

REVIEW

The Commission recommends that each of the Armed Forces should continue to maintain separate boards for review of its own cases following board hearings.

The review functions in all three military services has been described in the section of this report which sets forth the present military security program.

Consideration has been given to possible merits of a central review board within the Department of Defense for this program, rather than separate review boards in each of the services. However, the Commission believes that the present review procedures are useful.

144

SEPARATIONS

The Commission recommends that in loyalty separations the type of discharge given a serviceman should depend solely upon the conduct of such serviceman during the term of his military service, including the period of membership in the active or inactive reserve, whether or not the reservist is on active duty, and that, except to the extent that there has been falsification of his official papers, preservice conduct should not be considered in determining the type of discharge to be given.

The present military security program has as its purpose the establishment of uniform procedures and the providing of—

Policy guidance pertaining to the . . . separation of persons whose membership in the Armed Forces would not be clearly consistent with the interests of national security in order to assure that the effectiveness of the Armed Forces of the United States may not be jeopardized by subversive elements within their ranks.[19]

The Department of Defense, in carrying out this purpose, considers the individual's civilian activity and associations prior to entering the Armed Forces. In determining the character of the discharge to be awarded, the Department of Defense directs that—

When, after a review of the findings and opinions of boards or officers, the decision is that the continued service of a member of the Armed Forces is not clearly consistent with the interests of national security, he shall be separated and the character of the separation shall be predicated upon a careful consideration of all pertinent factors including the gravity of substantiated derogatory information and the character of service performed.

The problem of the type of discharge given in separations from the Armed Forces for security reasons has been reduced by the Department of Defense adoption of a security screening procedure for registrants in the draft prior to their induction.

With regard to inductees accepted after screening procedure, the Department of Defense, on January 11, 1956, directed as follows:

[Any inductee accepted after screening procedures] shall, after completion of his term of service, be awarded a separation predicated on the character of service rendered. Character of service should be interpreted to include those factors normally taken into account in determining the character of separation where no adverse security finding has been made as well as any reasonably substantiated derogatory information, concerning (a) subversive activities occurring during his period of service, and (b) falsification in connection with security matters occurring during his period of service or pertaining to his entry into the service. The character of separation shall not take into account any limitations on performance of duty imposed for security reasons.

With reference to the significance and meaning of a discharge from the military service, the courts have held, in a case involving a soldier who

---

[19] Department of Defense Directive 5210.9, dated June 19, 1956.

145

deserted, later returned, was restored to duty, made up the time lost and, at the end of his term of service, received an honorable discharge:

the honorable discharge . . . was a formal final judgment passed by the Government upon the entire military record of the soldier and an authoritative declaration by it that he had left the service in a status of honor.[20]

It has also been held:

an honorable discharge connotes that the holder has been a member of the military organization of the country and that his conduct while in such organization has been such to justify the appropriate authorities to certify that it has been honorable.[21]

The Department of Defense in furnishing information concerning security separations stated that it is the Department's belief that, in the eyes of the public, the honorable discharge carries with it the Department's stamp of approval of the good character, trustworthiness, and loyalty of the former serviceman, as well as an attestation that his performance was satisfactory in all significant respects.[22]

In the case of *Harmon* v. *Brucker,* the district court stated that: [23]

the established policy of the military has been that the character of a discharge certificate is rooted in and fashioned from the conduct of a man during his term of service . . . support for the proposition that a discharge certificate was intended to be an unlimited military appraisal of the lifelong conduct of an individual rather than a reflection of the quality of military service rendered does not readily appear.

It is appropriate to note here that the United States Court of Appeals, in the same case,[24] expressed its view on this phase of the problem by stating:

an honorable discharge from the Army is . . . a mark of distinction. The courts cannot dictate to the Army that it must give this mark to an enlisted man when it finds on the basis of preinduction activities that his presence in the Armed Forces is not consistent with the national security.

The court of appeals also responded to the comments of the district court by stating:

It is suggested that the consideration of preinduction happenings is in conflict with the traditional policies of the Army. Most certainly we cannot order the Army to adhere to traditional practices.

In another case which involved considerations of preservice activity as the basis for determining the characterization of the soldier's discharge, Judge D. J. Edelstein, United States District Court, Southern District of New York, remarked:

It is contended that the procedure under AR–604–10, insofar as it purports to authorize proceedings based upon conduct antedating induction, is not authorized and is illegal. With this position, on the basis of assumptions made, I am in agreement. An honorable

---

[20] *U. S.* v. *Kelly,* 15 Wall. 34; 82 U. S. 34, 36 (1872).

[21] *In re Fong Chew Chung,* 149 F. 2d 905, 906 (1945). See also, *Ex parte Drainer,* 65 F. Supp. 410, 1946, affirmed 158 F. 2d 981; *Griffin* v. *U. S.,* 115 F. Supp. 509, 515, 1953; *U. S. ex rel Herschberg* v. *Cook, Commanding Officer,* 336 U. S. 210 (1949); 36 Am. Jour. p. 208; 6 C. J. C. Army and Navy, sec. 32, p. 415.

[22] Letter from Office of General Counsel, Department of Defense, dated Feb. 27, 1957, to Commission on Government Security.

[23] 137 Fed. Supp. 475, 477 (D. C. D. C., 1956).

[24] *Harmon* v. *Brucker,* C. A. D. C., No. 13230, Jan. 31, 1957.

discharge encompasses a property right, as well as civil rights and personal honor. . . . If an honorable discharge were denied to a soldier with an unexceptionable service record, on the basis merely of preinduction conduct, it would in my opinion be a deprivation of property without due process of law, and a regulation establishing a procedure for effecting such a denial could not be authorized by statute. . . . It would seem basic, therefore, that a soldier has a right to an honorable discharge if his military record merits it and that he cannot be held to answer in the consideration of his discharge, for matters extraneous to that record. . . . A procedure which postulates preinduction civilian conduct as the basis for a less than honorable discharge could not be countenanced and it must be concluded that such a procedure is legislatively unauthorized.[25]

A footnote to the supplemental opinion in this case reveals that the court took cognizance of the defendant's argument that the plaintiff's prior civilian conduct is properly evidentiary upon the plaintiff's subsequent security status in the Army. In answering this argument, the court commented:

There can be no doubt of the validity of that argument. The issue, however, to which it is addressed is not the determination of the security status of an individual soldier, nor even his retention in the Army, but the infliction of harm by means of a discharge without honor in the case of one who not only does not merit such a discharge on the basis of his actual service, but who was inducted with knowledge on the part of the Army, actual or constructive, of his civilian background.[26]

The Commission bases its recommendation on the simple proposition that a discharge from the Armed Forces, whether it be honorable or otherwise, reflects a determination of the individual's military service. This proposition precludes an interpretation that the discharge is a formal final judgment on any period of time other than the period spent in the military service to which the discharge refers. A policy which allows consideration of an individual's preservice activities as a basis for the character of his discharge rejects the principle that a discharge in essence represents an evaluation of the person's actual military service. Discharge under such a policy becomes instead an appraisal of a standard of conduct unrelated to the performance of the person's military duties. The Commission feels very strongly that every person in the Armed Forces, depending on the manner in which he performs his assigned duties, merits the type of discharge which most fairly represents an accurate appraisal of that performance, and that such a person has a right to receive a discharge based on his performance and on that factor alone.

The Commission has recommended that in loyalty separations the type of discharge given a serviceman should depend solely upon the conduct of such serviceman during his term of military service. The Commission believes that if the type of discharge given in loyalty separations continues to be other than that recommended,

---

[25] *Bernstein* v. *Herren*, 136 Fed. Supp. 498, 496 (S. D. N. Y., 1955), affd. 234 F. 2d 434 (2d cir.), cert. denied, 77 Sup. Ct. 60 (1956).

[26] Ibid., p. 499.

Congress should consider legislation providing a basis for judicial review of the type of discharge given in such separations.

Judicial review of the type of discharge or of the facts underlying the military separation leading to the certificate of discharge itself, has been consistently denied by the courts. The latest judicial expression on this matter is as follows:

> The courts have held many times that they have no power to review the administrative processes by which the President and Secretaries administer affairs of the Army, and this doctrine has extended to the nature of discharges from the service. . . .[27]

The Commission feels that the Department of Defense may choose to review its discharge policy on loyalty separations in light of the Commission's recommendation, which would preclude the necessity for recommending legislation in this matter. If its policy continues to be one other than that recommended by the Commission, it is believed that in order to protect the rights of the individual, Congress should consider providing legislation for judicial review in cases of other than honorable discharges in loyalty separations.

---

[27] *Harmon* v. *Brucker,* C. A. D. C. No. 13230, Jan. 31, 1957.

Document Classification Program

Introduction

Although there can be no serious objection to the premise that the executive branch has the right and duty to protect official papers and other material from unwarranted disclosure, serious objections have been raised by the public and the Congress to some of the practices and policies employed in carrying out that function. Recognizing these objections, the Administration has taken action to meet major criticisms of departmental and agency practices. The principal step toward clarification and simplification of Federal policies in the field was the issuance of Executive Order 10501, effective December 15, 1953. After studying this Executive order, the Commission on Government Security made detailed inquiries of 15 Federal departments and agencies concerned in varying degrees with problems of document classification and information control affecting the national security. All these departments and agencies cooperated in furnishing the information requested.

The Commission also considered the hearings and other detailed data compiled by the Special Subcommittee on Government Information of the House Committee on Government Operations during the 84th Congress in the course of the subcommittee's study of document classification practices and policies in the executive branch. In addition, the Interdepartmental Committee on Internal Security furnished information of value to the Commission in studying departmental and agency practices and problems involved in the document classification program. The comments and criticisms of scientists, engineers, and representatives of industry in respect to the operation and effect of the program have likewise been taken into account.

HISTORY

Introduction

The recognized right of the Federal Government to withhold certain types of information from unauthorized disclosure dates from the earliest days of the Republic. While the Founding Fathers would probably not have recognized their procedures as "document classification" the basic elements of their reasoning would have been the same as that prevailing today, namely the responsibility of Government to protect the interests of the people.

In retrospect, the problem of document classification in the early days was simple in comparison with the immense complexity of the problem today. The most casual study of the background of this problem reveals, however, that the differences arise from the natural growth and expansion of our country from the small, isolated society of thirteen colonies to the first class world power which the United States is today. The complexities of instantaneous worldwide communications plus the ever-lessening time element in intercontinental travel places us in an entirely different position from that of our Founding Fathers. In the interest of national and international security it is self-evident that we must build up protective barriers around our national secrets.

Early leaders and political philosophers were as keenly aware of the importance of an informed public as are the proponents of freedom of information today. For example, Thomas Jefferson wrote: "The basis of our Government being the opinion of the people, the very first object should be to keep that right; and were it left to me to decide whether we should have a government without newspapers, or newspapers without a government, I should not hesitate a moment to prefer the latter." [1] While one might prefer a compromise to this unequivocal stand it illustrates the importance attached to information availability even in that day. It should be apparent that it is no less important today.

Historical Background

From the beginning of our national existence a primary problem of document classification has been the difficulty of defining the areas of information which must necessarily be denied in the interests of national security and those areas of information which should be reasonably available to all. The trend in public and official viewpoints on these aspects is in itself an excellent index of the importance which we have historically placed upon document classification and information control.

From the beginning there has been universal acceptance of the fact that vital military information must be protected from unauthorized disclosure. There has likewise been general acceptance that diplomatic negotiations and correspondence should be subject to restrictions on its availability. The third category, neither military nor diplomatic matter, but that which is currently described as "the public's business," is the area over which the

---

[1] Thomas Jefferson, *The Writings of Thomas Jefferson*, Washington, D. C., 1905, vol. VI, pp. 55–57; cited in *Availability of information from Federal departments and agencies*, Twenty-fifth intermediate report, (House report), Committee on Government Operations, House of Representatives, 84th Cong., 2d sess., July 27, 1956, p. 100.

most controversy has taken place. The most trenchant proof of this is the fact that relatively little has ever been written against the right, and indeed necessity, to classify military or diplomatic information while volumes have been filled with argument for the right to full access to information about "the public's business". The basic difficulty, however, lies in defining the scope of the latter category.

While document classification as a form of combined censorship and information restriction has been a part of our national policy from the War of the Revolution, formal and pervasive procedures for document classification in the current sense are a comparatively recent development. Prior to World War II, in peacetime there were few formal restrictions on information availability; the major exceptions were the traditional restraints in the diplomatic and military fields. In others areas, information restrictions were based for the most part upon individual judgment, as situations arose.

The advent of World War I brought the first organized approach to document classification as a means of general restriction on public access to information. Censorship policies for control of published information commenced on March 24, 1917, with the promulgation of regulations by the State, War, and Navy Departments. Newspapers were asked to adhere voluntarily. One of the regulations requested that "no information, reports, or rumors, attributing a policy to the government in any international situation, not authorized by the President or a member of the cabinet, be published without first consulting the Department of State." [2]

On April 13, 1917, by Executive Order 2594, President Wilson created the Committee on Public Information, named George Creel as chairman, and World War I censorship formally got under way. Creel thought that censorship as practiced at that time was unworkable. He described the whole effort as of a piece with "the hysterical 'shush-shushing' that warned against unguarded speech, just as though every citizen possessed some important military secret." He said, at the end of the War, that "virtually everything we asked the press not to print was seen or known by thousands." Creel believed the answer to be "secrecy at the source" through action by the military departments without depending upon press judgment.

World War II

In World War II, a much more efficient and effective system of information control was employed. It was a system that profited by the mistakes of World War I. It separated propaganda and censorship and, in effect, supported by voluntary agreement the withholding of information which the Armed Forces thought dangerous to disclose. It was, in reality, a system for making effec-

[2] James Russell Wiggins, *Freedom or Secrecy*, Oxford University Press, New York, 1956, p. 95–96.

153

tive the theory of censorship at the sources of information that Creel had talked about at the end of World War I.

The first formal effort to withhold information in World War II came on December 31, 1940, when Secretary of Navy Frank Knox asked radio, news, and picture editors to avoid any mention of (1) Actual or intended movements of vessels or aircraft of the United States Navy, units of naval enlisted personnel or divisions of mobilized reserves, or troop movements of the United States Marine Corps; (2) New United States Navy ships or aircraft; (3) United States Navy construction projects ashore.[3]

During 1941 as America stepped up defense production and planning, information control tightened up. In September, the War and Navy Departments disclosed they were making plans for censorship of all outgoing communications. When the United States declared war, on December 8, J. Edgar Hoover was made temporary coordinator of all news and communications censorship. The President at this time appealed to press and radio to refrain from the publication of unconfirmed reports. Various Federal agencies took steps to curtail their information. The Weather Bureau, for example, began to restrict its reports.

When the first code of wartime practices for newspapers, magazines, and other periodicals was issued on January 15, 1942, wartime censorship was formally launched. The code was revised each 6 months thereafter. It described categories of news that were not to be published without appropriate authority, listing in 17 different clauses the information that required authorization before publication. The significant words in the operation of this wartime information code were "appropriate authority". The Office of Censorship did not undertake to suppress information that "appropriate authority" officially gave out. The Office of Censorship was terminated by Executive Order 9631, effective November 15, 1945.

By Executive Order 9182 of June 13, 1942, the Office of War Information (OWI) was established within the Office for Emergency Management (OEM). The OWI consolidated into one agency all foreign and domestic war information functions of the Government. This office combined the functions of several agencies dealing with various aspects of information availability: the Office of Facts and Figures, the Office of Government Reports, the Division of Information in OEM and the foreign information activities of the Office of the Coordinator of Information. The purpose of OWI was to "provide an intelligent understanding . . . of the status and progress of the war effort . . . policies, activities, and aims of the Government".[4] The Office of War Information was abolished by Executive Order 9608 of August 31, 1945. Some of its functions were liquidated, while others were transferred to the Bureau of the Budget and the Department of State.[5]

---

[3] *Ibid.*
[4] *U. S. Government Organization Manual, 1956–57,* General Services Administration, U. S. Government Printing Office, 1956, pp. 669–670.
[5] *Ibid.*

Following the end of hostilitites in World War II, the Security Advisory Board, which had functioned in a supervisory capacity in this field, as a part of the Office of War Information, survived the Office of War Information and continued to function as a part of the State-War-Navy Coordinating Committee—later the State-Army-Navy-Air Force Coordinating Committee. As part of Executive Order 9835, on March 21, 1947, the Security Advisory Board was directed to draft rules for the handling and transmission of documents and information which should not be publicly disclosed. The Security Advisory Board completed a preliminary draft of such minimum standards, but these rules had not been issued when the Security Advisory Board and its parent coordinating committee went out of existence.[6]

Cognizance of this unresolved problem was taken by the National Security Council in 1948, and the problem was subsequently transmitted to the Interdepartmental Committee on Internal Security (ICIS), which drafted new regulations establishing minimum standards for the handling and transmission of classified information in executive departments and agencies. These minimum standards were issued as Executive Order 10290 by President Truman on September 24, 1951.

When he took office in January 1953, President Eisenhower took notice of the widespread criticism directed at Executive Order 10290 by the press and public, and referred Executive Order 10290 to the Attorney General for recision or revision as deemed necessary. The Attorney General on June 15, 1953, wrote the President, detailing four objections from the standpoint of sound public policy with respect to Executive Order 10290 and its regulations. He recommended recision of that Executive order and the issuance of a new order which would protect every requirement of national safety and, at the same time, honor the basic tenets of freedom of information.[7]

The new Executive order was circulated in executive departments and agencies for comment and, after minor revisions, was signed by the President on November 6, 1953, as Executive Order 10501, effective December 15, 1953. This order is the present legal basis for classification. Its provisions will be discussed in detail later on, but briefly speaking, it differed from Executive Order 10290 in the following major respects: (1) It withdrew authority to classify information from 28 agencies of the Government; (2) in 17 other agencies it limited authority to classify to the agency head, without power to delegate; (3) it sharply limited the authority to classify only if required in the interest of the national defense of the United States; (4) it completely eliminated the *restricted* classification, one of the most controversial categories of classified information; (5) it explicitly defined

---

[6] Hearings before a subcommittee on reorganization of the Committee on Government Operations, United States Senate 84th Cong., 1st sess., on S. J. Res. 21, *A Joint Resolution To Establish a Commission on Government Security*, March 8, 9, 10, 11, 14, 15, 16, 17 and 18, 1955. Testimony of William F. Tompkins, asst. attorney general.

[7] *Ibid.*, p. 30.

for the first time the three remaining categories of classified information—*top secret, secret,* and *confidential,* in order to prevent indiscriminate use of the power to classify when specific interests of the national defense did not so require; (6) it provided for continuous review of classified material for the purpose of declassifying or downgrading the classification whenever national defense considerations permit; and (7) it made more definite and certain the procedures for handling classified information, so that employees would be more alert to the dangers of unauthorized disclosure.

Executive Order 10501, after defining the types of national defense information which may be classified in one of the three categories, sets forth minimum rules for the labeling of such information, for its dissemination, transmission, handling, storage, and disposition, and for review with a view to downgrading or declassification. It fixes upon the head of the agency the responsibility for protection of classified information, as well as for conformity to the regulations with respect to erroneous classifications, declassification and downgrading. Additionally, it limits access to such information to trustworthy personnel, and restricts such access and disclosure to those having a need to know the information.

Executive Order 10501 makes provision for the designation by the President of a member of his staff to receive, consider, and take action upon suggestions or complaints from nongovernmental sources relating to the operation of the order. It further provides that the National Security Council shall conduct a continuing review of the implementation of the order to insure that classified defense information is properly safeguarded in conformity with the provision of the order. This continuing review function has been assigned by the Council to the Interdepartmental Committee on Internal Security, discussed above.

Despite the declared purpose of Executive Order 10501, to recognize that ". . . It is essential that the citizens of the United States be informed concerning the activities of their government . . ." and the need that certain ". . . official information affecting the national defense be protected uniformly against unauthorized disclosure . . ." the Order has been subjected to continuous and sharp attack. These attacks have been led for the most part by leaders in the press and other information media as well as by numerous individuals in the legal field, and the world of science and scientific research.

In recognition of these attacks during the 84th Congress, the Special Subcommittee on Government Information of the House Committee on Government Operations held lengthy hearings under Congressman Moss to examine these complaints. These hearings and studies were the first major congressional effort to examine the document classification program.

Several agencies improved their information practices when the subcommittee was able to bring to the attention of the proper authorities complaints it had received from the press or the public. Following are some of the important developments, resulting from subcommittee hearings which have helped clear the avenues of access to Federal Government information:

1. The Department of Commerce, following a subcommittee hearing and letters from the subcommittees to the Department and the National Security Council, made public a previously classified section of the National Security Council document establishing the Office of Strategic Information and also made public the major portion of three previously classified reports on the progress of the OSI.

2. The Defense Department, following contacts with the subcommittee, announced at a subcommittee hearing the establishment of a panel to review declassification of historical documents and to set up firm guidelines to speed up declassification.

3. The Defense Department, following subcommittee hearings on the flow of scientific and technical information, announced a proposal to expedite the separation of basic information for distribution within the scientific community from scientific information available to military weapons.[8]

The subcommittee is continuing to conduct hearings during the 85th Congress on the information policies and practices of the Department of Defense.

LEGAL BASIS

Authority for the Program

As previously noted, the current legal authority for the document classification program is Executive Order 10501, which became effective December 15, 1953, and revoked Executive Order 10290.[9]

Executive Order 10501 is entitled "Safeguarding Official Information in the Interests of the Defense of the United States." In summary, it establishes the classification categories of "confidential," "secret," and "top secret." It is designed to regulate the day-by-day handling of national security information within the various executive agencies and departments by prescribing uniform procedures governing the classification, transmission, dissemination, custody, and disposal of such information. In addition, there is provision for review of the entire classification program to insure adequate protection of the national security as well as to insure that no information is withheld thereunder which the people of the United States have a right to know.

---

[8] *Availability of Information From Federal Departments and Agencies,* Twenty-fifth intermediate report (House Report 2947), Committee on Government Operations, House of Representatives, 84th Cong., 2d sess., July 27, 1956, pp. 80–81.
[9] 18 F. R. 7049.

Legal Justification for the Order

The preamble of the order contains the standard recitation that it was issued, "By virtue of the authority vested in me by the Constitution and statutes as President of the United States." Therefore, to be valid, Executive Order 10501 must be the product of a proper exercise of executive power derived either from executive authority conferred by the Constitution or from statutory authority, or both.

A. EXECUTIVE AUTHORITY CONFERRED BY THE CONSTITUTION.—Pertinent sections of the Constitution appear to contain no express authority for the issuance of an order such as Executive Order 10501. However, the requisite implied authority would seem to lie within article II which says in section 1: "The executive power shall be vested in a President of the United States of America"; and in section 2: "The President shall be Commander in Chief of the Army and Navy of the United States"; and in section 3: ". . . he shall take care that the laws be faithfully executed."

When these provisions are considered in light of the existing Presidential authority to appoint and remove executive officers directly responsible to him, there is demonstrated the broad Presidential supervisory and regulatory authority over the internal operations of the executive branch. By issuing the proper Executive or administrative order he exercises this power of direction and supervision over his subordinates in the discharge of their duties. He thus "takes care" that the laws are being faithfully executed by those acting in his behalf; and in the instant case the pertinent laws would involve espionage, sabotage, and related statutes, should such Presidential authority not be predicated upon statutory authority or direction.

B. STATUTORY AUTHORITY.—While there is no specific statutory authority for such an order or Executive Order 10501, various statutes do afford a basis upon which to justify the issuance of the order.

A statute frequently cited as affording some implied authority for the issuance of Executive Order 10501 is found in 5 U. S. C. A. 22, which authorizes the heads of departments and agencies, among other things "to prescribe regulations, not inconsistent with law, for . . . the conduct of its officers and clerks, the distribution and performance of its business, and the custody, use, and preservation of the records, papers, and property appertaining to it." The primary purpose is to afford a check or brake upon the general flow into the public domain of such agency information which might reflect upon internal management or proposed policy, and the publication of which could impede or prejudice efficient agency operation. The fact that such information may involve national security matters is not essential in giving proper effect to the statutory language.

The espionage laws have imposed upon the President a duty to make determinations respecting the dissemination of information having a relationship to the national defense. For example, 18 U. S. C. 795 (a) provides that "Whenever, in the interests of national defense, the President defines

158

certain vital military and naval installations or equipment as requiring protection against the general dissemination of information relative thereto, it shall be unlawful to make any photograph, sketch, picture, . . ., etc." Proceeding under this statute the President issued Executive Order 10104 which covers information classified by the agencies of the military establishments.[10]

In 18 U. S. C. 798 there is specific reference to the unauthorized disclosure of "classified information" pertaining to the cryptographic and communication systems and facilities. Furthermore, the term "classified information" is defined as information which for reasons of national security has been specifically designated by the proper government agency for limited or restrictive dissemination or distribution.

The most significant legislation, which set into motion the current document classification program, was enacted in 1947, when the Congress passed the National Security Act[11] in order to provide an adequate and comprehensive program designed to protect the future security of our country. To accomplish this avowed purpose the act provided for the creation of a National Security Council within the executive branch subject to Presidential direction. Its job is to consider and study security matters of common interest to the departments and agencies and to make appropriate recommendations to the President. Within the framework of this program, the Interdepartmental Committee on Internal Security (ICIS) came into being, and the activity of this committee was responsible for the issuance in 1951 of Executive Order 10290, which established the original document classification program. Thus it would appear that a document classification program is within the scope of the activities sought to be coordinated by the National Security Act of 1947, and that the issuance of an appropriate Executive order establishing such a program is consistent with the policy of the act.

Prior to issuance of Executive Order 10290, Congress had apparently recognized the existing Presidential authority to classify information within the executive branch when it passed the Internal Security Act of 1950.[12] Contained therein were provisions defining two new criminal offenses involving classified information.

Section 4 (b) of the act makes it a crime for any Federal officer or employee to give security information classified by the President, or by the head of any department, agency, or corporation with the approval of the President, to any foreign agent or member of a Communist organization, and section 4 (c) makes it a crime for any foreign agent or member of a Communist organization to receive such classified security information from a Federal employee.[13]

---

[10] 15 F. R. 597, Feb. 1, 1950.
[11] 61 Stat. 496, July 26, 1947.
[12] 64 Stat. 987–1031.
[13] 50 U. S. C. A. 783.

Conclusion

It is concluded, therefore, that in the absence of any law to the contrary, there is an adequate constitutional and statutory basis upon which to predicate the Presidential authority to issue Executive Order 10501.

PRESENT PROGRAM

Introduction

This survey, by definition, is concerned with the activities of the Federal Government as they involve policies and practices with respect to classified documents. It is not intended to cover information control policies and practices that do not involve material subject to the classified information provisions of Executive Order 10501. Although departmental and agency policies with respect to information control may impinge upon the area of document classification, they are governed by different criteria. The criteria of document classification involve application of narrowly defined standards of national security and defense. The criteria of information control, on the other hand, involve the broadest kind of standards. They range from the traditional claim against privileged information to the arguments for the "housekeeping" privileges required in the normal operation of the executive branch.

Scope of the Program

Although all Federal agencies have rules of some type to control documents and information in their possession, relatively few have the authority to restrict general availability of their material on grounds of its relevance to either national defense or security. Under Executive Order 10501 the authority to apply the top secret, secret, or confidential classification to Federal documents was severely limited. The following 28 agencies were denied authority to apply original classification to material originated by them:

AMERICAN BATTLE MONUMENTS COMMISSION
ARLINGTON MEMORIAL AMPHITHEATER COMMISSION
COMMISSION ON FINE ARTS
COMMITTEE ON PURCHASES OF BLIND-MADE PRODUCTS
COMMITTEE FOR RECIPROCITY INFORMATION
COMMODITY EXCHANGE COMMISSION
EXPORT-IMPORT BANK OF WASHINGTON
FEDERAL DEPOSIT INSURANCE CORPORATION

160

FEDERAL MEDIATION AND CONCILIATION SERVICE
FEDERAL RESERVE SYSTEM
FEDERAL TRADE COMMISSION
HOUSING AND HOME FINANCE AGENCY
INDIAN CLAIMS COMMISSION
INTERSTATE COMMERCE COMMISSION
MISSOURI BASIN SURVEY COMMISSION
NATIONAL CAPITAL HOUSING AUTHORITY
NATIONAL CAPITAL PARK AND PLANNING COMMISSION
NATIONAL FOREST RESERVATION COMMISSION
NATIONAL LABOR RELATIONS BOARD
NATIONAL MEDIATION BOARD
RAILROAD RETIREMENT BOARD
SECURITIES AND EXCHANGE COMMISSION
SELECTIVE SERVICE SYSTEM
SMITHSONIAN INSTITUTION
UNITED STATES TARIFF COMMISSION
VETERANS ADMINISTRATION
VETERANS EDUCATION APPEALS BOARD
WAR CLAIMS COMMISSION

The terms of Executive Order 10501 limited the authority for original classification to the agency head in the case of the following 17 agencies:

CIVIL AERONAUTICS BOARD
DEFENSE TRANSPORT ADMINISTRATION
DEPARTMENT OF AGRICULTURE
DEPARTMENT OF HEALTH, EDUCATION, AND WELFARE
DEPARTMENT OF THE INTERIOR
DEPARTMENT OF LABOR
FEDERAL COMMUNICATIONS COMMISSION
FEDERAL POWER COMMISSION
NATIONAL SCIENCE FOUNDATION
NATIONAL SECURITY TRAINING COMMISSION
PANAMA CANAL COMPANY
POST OFFICE DEPARTMENT
RECONSTRUCTION FINANCE CORPORATION
RENEGOTIATION BOARD
SMALL BUSINESS ADMINISTRATION
SUBVERSIVE ACTIVITIES CONTROL BOARD
TENNESSEE VALLEY AUTHORITY

The above group includes some of the major agencies or departments of the executive branch. For example, estimated on the basis of data published by the Civil Service Commission, the Department of Agriculture has about 85,000 employees in Washington and elsewhere; Health, Education, and Welfare, about 40,000; Interior has about 55,000; and the Post Office Department has about 510,000 employees in Washington and elsewhere. It is conceded that there is no necessary correlation between number of employees and the importance of certain agencies to Federal agency classified document production. However, the very fact that these major agencies had their classification authority curtailed was an important development in defining the scope of the present classification program. It should be noted that the response of these agencies to the Commission on Government Security interrogatory on document classification indicates that they are involved to only a negligible degree in production of material subject to classification under terms of Executive Order 10501.

Under the terms of Executive Order 10501, all agencies not denied authority or restricted as to classification authority were granted such authority. Among those whose authority was left undisturbed are: Atomic Energy Commission, Central Intelligence Agency, and the Departments of Commerce, Defense, Justice, State, and Treasury.

These represent the primary source of classified materal. No precise data are available as to the percentage of all classified material originated in these agencies, but it is estimated from data in the Commission files that they account for over 90 percent of all such material in the executive branch.

Mechanics of the Program

Executive Order 10501 forms the basis for the more detailed departmental regulations required in actual execution of the provisions of the order. Departments and agencies have adopted procedures for implementation of the document classification program as it affects their operations. In some agencies these regulations comprise only a few pages of a manual or memorandum. In other agencies regulations for all aspects of the classified document program comprise many pages of detailed data. The regulations of the Department of State pertinent to classified documents, for example, make up the major portion of the 98-page departmental manual on security regulations, published in January 1955.

Executive Order 10501 is a document of 20 sections. Each section, with the exception of the last two, deals with the classification program. An enumeration of the section headings of the order, along with quoting, paraphrasing, or summarizing their provisions provides an outline of the operation of the classification program.

Section 1 of the order, *Classification Categories*, sets forth the three designations top secret, secret, and confidential. The criterion of each category is the effect which the information in question would have upon national security. The order specifies that no other designation shall be employed to classify defense information. Other classifications such as "Agency use only," "Restricted to department use," etc., are thus excluded from the scope of the order.

Section 1 of the order provides:

Except as may be expressly provided by statute, the use of the classification "top secret" shall be authorized, by appropriate authority, only for defense information or material which requires the highest degree of protection. The top secret classification shall be applied only to that information or material the defense aspect of which is paramount, and the unauthorized disclosure of which could result in exceptionally grave damage to the Nation such as leading to a definite break in diplomatic relations affecting the defense of the United States, an armed attack against the United States or its allies, a war, or the compromise of military or defense plans, or intelligence operations, or scientific or technological developments vital to the national defense.

With respect to the secret category, the order states:

Except as may be expressly provided by statute, the use of the classification "secret" shall be authorized, by appropriate authority. only for defense information or material the unauthorized disclosure of which could result in serious damage to the Nation, such as by jeopardizing the international relations of the United States, endangering the effectiveness of a program or policy of vital importance to the national defense, or compromising important military or defense plans, scientific or technological developments important to national defense, or information revealing important intelligence operations.

With respect to confidential, the order states:

Except as may be expressly provided by statute, the use of the classification "Confidential" shall be authorized, by appropriate authority, only for defense information or material the unauthorized disclosure of which could be prejudicial to the defense interests of the Nation.

Section 2, *Limitation of Authority to Classify*, sets forth the definition of those agencies which have no responsibility to apply original classification to material and those which have partial authority for such action. The agencies in each category are listed in an addendum memorandum to the order. The section further specifies that heads of those departments and agencies having original classification authority shall "limit the delegation of authority as severely as is consistent," with the operations of their agencies. On the basis of responses to the Commission's written interrogatory on document classification, it appears that agencies try to limit actual original classification authority.

Responses to the interrogatory show agency efforts to control classification. The number of individuals possessing classification authority is indicated below:

1. ATOMIC ENERGY COMMISSION.—Seventy-five persons are authorized to classify information as top secret. Approximately 1,000 more employees have been granted original authority to classify documents as secret or confidential. This is 15 percent of the total Atomic Energy Commission employment.

2. CENTRAL INTELLIGENCE AGENCY.—Approximately 15 percent of the total number of employees are authorized to apply original classifications to documents or material.

3. DEPARTMENT OF COMMERCE.—There are approximately 593 employees in the Department who have authority to classify information originating in the Department. This figure amounts to about 1.3 percent of departmental employment.

4. DEPARTMENT OF DEFENSE.—In the Department of Defense as a whole, it is reported that "less than 20 percent" of the staff has the authority to apply original classifications. Within the three departmental components (Army, Navy, and Air Force) this figure varies considerably.

(*a*) In the Department of the Army, in Washington, approximately 1,640 persons are authorized to classify information at the secret or top secret level. This represents 5.2 percent of the total administrative, professional, or clerical personnel. This figure does not include those persons authorized to classify material as confidential.

(*b*) *Department of the Navy.*—In bureau and departmental areas, where the bulk of classified departmental material originates, approximately 12 percent of all personnel have authority to classify. This figure is subject to important qualification, however, in that it includes persons authorized to classify basic papers and research material that are never circulated out of the area in which it originates. There is significant variation within the Department as to the percentage of total individuals in any given component who can apply original classifications. In the Bureau of Aeronautics 490 individuals (17.7 percent of employment) have authority to classify. The response of the Navy Department affords an excellent example of concentration of actual classification as opposed to the authority to classify. In the Bureau of Aeronautics, while 17.7 percent of all employees have authority to classify, 2.35 percent, in fact, apply original classifications to 85 percent of the classified material originating in the Bureau.

(*c*) The Department of the Air Force reported that statistics were not available to show the number of individuals who have authority to classify defense information Air Force-wide.

5. DEPARTMENT OF STATE.—Any employee originating classified material has the responsibility of assigning the original classification; however, the final classification is determined by certifying officers. There are approximately 11,000 employees in the Department of State who possibly at one time or another could generate matter which in their opinion warranted a classification; however, there are approximately 2,200 [14] certifying officers situated worldwide who must assign the final classification.

The difficulty appears to be that, while relatively few agency officials (from 5 to 15 percent of all personnel) have authority to apply original classification, there is a great body of personnel in the "sensitive" agencies who have the authority to recommend original classifications. Although these recommendations may in theory be disregarded, it is believed that in fact the recommendations are usually followed by classification officials.

Section 3 of the order, *Classification,* deals with operational aspects of protection to be afforded classified documents. The section cautions against overclassification and unnecessary classification. In this section there is a provision that defense information originating with a foreign government or international organization shall be afforded the same or higher degree of protection given to it by the supplying agency.

Section 4, *Declassification, Downgrading or Upgrading,* is the longest section in the order. It provides the framework for departmental designation

---

[14] Department of State figures.

of persons or units to be responsible for continuing review of classified material so as to declassify or downgrade as soon as practicable.

The procedures and policies of some agencies with respect to downgrading are outlined below, as selected from their responses to the Commission's interrogatory:

1. ATOMIC ENERGY COMMISSION.—"AEC regulations require each person having custody of classified documents to keep them under review and to effect downgrading of these documents as soon as conditions permit. All top secret documents are required to be reviewed by classifying authorities or higher authority at intervals not to exceed 6 months."

2. CENTRAL INTELLIGENCE AGENCY.—"Agency classification control network has been established to control application of official classifications and to perform functions of reviewing classified material for the purpose of downgrading or declassification."

3. DEPARTMENT OF DEFENSE.—The Department recognizes the need for declassification activities, and in the past few years has taken various steps to establish a policy for declassification of documents. The latest action was taken in March 1957 when Secretary Wilson acted to implement some of the provisions of the so-called Coolidge report which in the month of November 1957 made a number of proposals concerning the information and document control policies of the Department. On March 28, 1957, the Secretary issued a directive which ordered the establishment of a Director of Declassification within the Office of the Assistant Secretary of Defense for Legislative and Public Affairs. The new office will have the task of working out programs and procedures for making classified documents available when they no longer require protection for reasons of national security. (The activities of this new office will not affect the operation of the Office of Security Review, which now has the responsibility of dealing with declassification of current information.)

The various services within the Department have their own policies and procedures for downgrading information. For example, in the Department of the Air Force the headquarters or activity which originates classified information is required to review continually such information with the view to downgrading or declassifying it. Additonally, before such information is retired to storage, it is again reviewed to remove the classification wherever possible.

4. UNITED STATES INFORMATION AGENCY.—"Agency has established procedures in accordance with Executive Order 10501. Any employee may request downgrading or declassification. Procedures have been established for applying automatic downgrading when applicable. Originating offices are instructed to maintain continuous review of all classified material for purposes of downgrading and declassification."

Two factors underlie the importance of the declassification and downgrading activities of departments and agencies. In the first place, such activities fulfill their directive under Executive Order 10501 to downgrade and declassify wherever possible, consistent with national security. In the second place, downgrading and declassification offer an opportunity to help solve the space problem and at the same time to reduce the cost of guarding material that actually could be afforded less expensive protection.

There are shown below typical responses from various agencies to the CGS written interrogatory on document classification illustrating their activities in the field of downgrading and declassification of classified material:

1. ATOMIC ENERGY COMMISSION.—Approximately 40,000 documents have been downgraded or declassified in the past 12 months. Approximately 14,000 cubic feet of space would be occupied by the documents thus downgraded or declassified.

2. CENTRAL INTELLIGENCE AGENCY.—In the period from December 1953 to July 1956, approximately 1,900 CIA documents have been downgraded and approximately 450 CIA documents have been declassified.

3. DEPARTMENT OF COMMERCE.—Although the Department has not kept statistics as to the number of documents which have been downgraded or declassified, approximately 58 standard file drawers (112 cubic feet) of classified documents have been declassified or destroyed in the year ending October 15, 1956. In addition, approximately 753 standard file drawers, approximately 1,500 cubic feet, of documents which were withheld under various statutory requirements were released (presumably declassified) in the same 12-month period.

4. DEPARTMENT OF DEFENSE.—In the Department of Defense there have been approximately 400 cubic feet of classified material downgraded in the past 12 months ending December 1956.

(a) Department of the Army has downgraded or declassified 1,030 linear feet of current files in the year ending December 1956 in the Washington establishment alone.

(b) Department of the Navy does not keep any records of declassification or downgrading.

(c) Department of the Air Force likewise has no information available on the extent of downgrading and declassification of its activities.

5. UNITED STATES INFORMATION AGENCY.—In the fiscal year ending June 30, 1956, 2,753 cubic feet of documents, both unclassified and classified, have been retired and 1,103 cubic feet destroyed.

Section 4 also provides special rules for establishing automatic declassification and downgrading. Industry has been especially critical of agency attitudes toward declassification. W. P. Gwinn, president of United Aircraft Corp., wrote Chairman Wright on October 11, 1956:

Finally, there is one more very important problem in this field which must be faced and solved. That is the delay and sometimes outright refusal of the military to release from security classification products having a commercial use. Let me say that we are not unmindful of the need to safeguard important technical knowledge in the aeronautical or other fields from falling into the hands of potential enemies. But, there comes a time when the need to safeguard disappears; sometimes because the "secret" has become general knowledge, sometimes because another and better method or device has been discovered, and sometimes for other reasons. When this happens, and the Government nevertheless continues diligently to classify and protect the old information, then it has lost its perspective and is wasting time and money. More concretely, the effect on the aircraft industry of overclassification or unnecessarily prolonged classification is very detrimental since it permits the capture of worldwide commercial markets by inferior products and by products of foreign nationals whose governments are not so bemused by the formalities of a security program.

Section 4 provides for disposition of transfer of classified current and dead-file material from one agency to another. Section 4 also provides procedures for agencies to employ in downgrading or upgrading the classification of material received from another agency. Agency responses to the Commission's interrogatory on document classification reveal few instances of agency action to either upgrade or downgrade documents received from other agencies.

Section 5 of the Executive order is entitled *Marking of Classified Material.* This section deals with operational and administrative procedures for applying the appropriate classification to classified documents. It details the procedure requiring that material be clearly stamped or otherwise marked and that containers for classified material be clearly designated. It appears to present no particular problem. Industrial contractors, moreover, have indicated no serious complaints as the section affects their operations, according to agency responses to the Commission's interrogatory.

The requirements for physical protection of classified material are set forth in section 6 of the order, entitled *Custody and Safekeeping.* This section provides that top-secret material must be given the most secure protection possible. It requires, moreover, only slightly less protection for secret and confidential data. This section also provides for action in the case of loss or compromise of classified data. Section 6 imposes serious and detailed administrative responsibilities on those agencies which originate any appreciable volume of classified material. To carry out these responsibilities, the agencies have established procedures for security officers, guard systems, and secure areas for document protection. These responsibilities have also been given, by delegation of authority, to industrial contractors involved in the defense program. Many contractors complained to the Commission on Government Security concerning the cost of their security program, despite the fact that a large part, if not all, of such operations may be charged to the cost of their Government work. Contractors, on the other hand, have apparently made few complaints to the various agencies.

In the Commission's written interrogatory on document classification to the executive departments and agencies, the question was asked: "Have industrial or other nongovernmental contractors indicated that the provision for custody and safekeeping of classified material as enforced by agency under provisions of Executive Order 10501, section 6, hampers their performance of agency contracts. . . ." The responses of several agencies especially concerned with the problem are given below:

1. ATOMIC ENERGY COMMISSION.—"There has been no indication from AEC contractors that provisions for the custody and safekeeping of classified information hampered the performance of contracts."

2. CENTRAL INTELLIGENCE AGENCY.—"The Central Intelligence Agency's high operational security requirements for custody and safekeeping of classified information causes some complaints but, to our knowledge, this has not hampered nongovernmental contractors in their performance of Agency contracts."

3. DEPARTMENT OF COMMERCE.—"The Department has received no indication that contractors are hampered by the provisions for the custody and safekeeping of classified material under section 6 of Executive Order 10501."

4. DEPARTMENT OF DEFENSE.—The Department of Defense indicated little direct complaint from contractors.

5. GENERAL SERVICES ADMINISTRATION.—"No industrial or nongovernmental contractors have indicated in any way that the provisions for custody and safekeeping of documents have hampered their performance of agency contracts."

Section 7, *Accountability and Dissemination,* details to some extent the administrative and operational functions required and authorized in section 6 of the order. It provides for maintenance of agency controls over classified material originating in the agency as well as control over data originating outside. In addition to emphasizing the "need to know principle" by stating that "Knowledge or possession of classified defense information shall be permitted only to persons whose official duties require such access in the interest of promoting national defense . . .," this section provides that such access shall be granted ". . . only if they have been determined to be trustworthy."

Agencies adhere to the principle closely as indicated in the responses of agencies to the Commission's interrogatory on that topic. Typical policies are outlined below:

1. ATOMIC ENERGY COMMISSION.—"The 'need to know' principle governs the control of classified information to which personnel of the AEC and its contractors have access. The statement of policy in this regard is contained in AEC manual, chapter 2101, enclosed, entitled 'Control of Classified Information.' Access to top-secret documents, to classified research and development reports and classified weapon data reports, among others, is controlled on the basis of need for the category of information involved. 'Need to know' requirement is a prerequisite to access to secret documents furnished to personnel in the civilian application program, but is not applicable to confidential documents furnished to such personnel."

2. CENTRAL INTELLIGENCE AGENCY.—"Classified information is disclosed only to those authorized individuals who require the information in the performance of their official duties."

168

3. Civil Service Commission.—"The Commission's regulations provide that knowledge or possession of classified defense information shall be permitted only to persons whose official duties require such access."

4. Department of Justice.—"Classified documents are made available only on a 'need to know' basis."

5. Department of State.—"The 'need to know' principle is applied."

Section 8 of Executive Order 10501 entitled *Transmission* provides the basic procedures for the protection of defense information while it is in transit, either within the agency or otherwise. Agencies and departments have, in turn, expanded these basic procedures to provide guidelines for their operations. There do not appear to have been any particular problems arising in the various agencies in carrying out provisions of this section of the order.

The procedures of typical agencies, as they stated in their responses to the Commission's interrogatory, are outlined below:

1. Central Intelligence Agency.—"Internal and external courier service for top secret and data classified 'secret' and below is performed by a regular organized courier unit. However, special couriers are designated as operational requirements demand."

2. Civil Service Commission.—"Where the situation warrants, the Commission uses special messengers and an appropriate receipt system for the transmission of defense information classified 'confidential,' and 'secret.' Where messengers are not used, this information is transmitted by registered mail. Defense information classified 'top secret' is transmitted as provided in section 8 (b) of the order."

3. Department of Defense—*Department of the Army.*—"The Department of the Army furnishes personnel to the Armed Forces Courier Service, a joint organization. In addition to this facility, command couriers are used on special occasions. These are officers who are designated, in orders, as couriers for specific missions."

4. Department of Labor.—"One special messenger is available; another is in the process of being cleared. Documents are usually delivered by hand, or, where appropriate, by registered mail."

Industrial contractors, however, have complained of the "unnecessary expense" incurred in carrying out regulations imposed upon them by Federal agencies in compliance with agency delegation of responsibility for protection of classified material in the possession of contractors.

Section 9, *Disposal and Destruction,* outlines the appropriate procedure for the disposal or destruction of classified material. (Some material, classified or not, is required to be kept for its historic or research value. It is then deposited in the National Archives.) The section further provides that certain "classified" material may be destroyed "only in accordance with the Act of July 7, 1943, 6.192, 57 Stat. 380, as amended, 44 U. S. C. 366–380."

Section 10, *Orientation and Inspection,* provides for the coordination and supervision of agency activitites generated as the result of the Executive order. It directs that adequate training programs be set up in the agencies so as to educate employees with the provisions of the order. The training programs vary from briefing of a few key individuals to more detailed orientation programs.

In response to questioning by the Commission on Government Security, the following agencies especially concerned with information security problems indicated the action taken toward employee training:

1. ATOMIC ENERGY COMMISSION.—The Atomic Energy Commission, through its Division of Classification Headquarters, conducts an active program for training certain employees, known as chairmen of classification committees, in applying proper security classifications to information. Classification appraisals of AEC field offices are also periodically conducted to determine whether local practices are in conformance with established policy. There are now eight classification committee chairmen who have received such training. These individuals in turn instruct those in their local areas who are concerned with the proper classification of information as to the correct procedures to be followed.

2. CENTRAL INTELLIGENCE AGENCY.—Prior to the time new employees commence their duties with this Agency, they receive an intensive security indoctrination which includes a briefing of their responsibilities under Executive Order 10501.

3. DEPARTMENT OF DEFENSE.—Upon entrance on duty or being permitted access to classified material, security instructions (administrative instruction No. 8) are issued and all persons are required to attend a security indoctrination. This indoctrination includes discussion of the security regulations and security lapses, a film on security, and an examination on security regulations. The lecture covers not only classification but also other aspects of security. All employees have attended at least one security indoctrination. The agency maintains a continuing program for emphasizing personal security consciousness in all phases of security.

4. DEPARTMENT OF STATE.—The Department of State has a program for training employees with respect to document classification and other related security requirements.

Section 11, *Interpretation of Regulations by the Attorney General,* provides the mechanism for agencies to request interpretation of the provisions of the Executive order. A few agencies indicated they have requested interpretation of various sections of the order. For example, the Civil Service Commission requested an interpretation on the relationship of Executive Order 10501 to Executive Order 10450, and the Department of Health, Education, and Welfare requested an interpretation of the requirement for assignment of classification to material.

Section 12, *Statutory Requirements,* insures that the provisions of the order do not contravene any statutory authority for dissemination, handling or transmission of classified information.

170

Section 13 is entitled *"Restricted Data" as Defined in the Atomic Energy Act.* This section provides that Executive Order 10501 shall not supersede any requirements of the Atomic Energy Act of August 1, 1946, as amended. There appear to have been no complex problems raised by agency interpretation of the provisions of this section. Specifically, the Atomic Energy Commission has not indicated any problems encountered in implementation of the section.

Section 14, *Combat Operations,* provides authority for the Secretary of Defense to make such modification of provisions of the order as may be dictated by military or combat-related conditions. The Department of Defense has issued directives to provide such modification.

Section 15, *Exceptional Cases,* provides for protection and transmission of defense material in certain instances out of the ordinary routine of agency operation.

Section 16 provides for *Review To Insure That Information Is Not Improperly Withheld Hereunder.* The order provides for designation of a member of the President's staff to carry out this function. Action has been taken to implement this provision. At present this function is performed by Gerald D. Morgan, special counsel to the President.

Section 17 provides for *Review To Insure Safeguarding of Classified Defense Information.* This section provides for continuing review of implementation of the order by the National Security Council (NSC) with respect to safeguarding information classified under the order. The responsibility for this function has been assigned by NSC to the Interdepartmental Committee on Internal Security (ICIS). That committee makes continuing surveys semiannually of agency implementation of Executive Order 10501.

Section 18, *Review Within Departments and Agencies,* provides for agency designation of individuals who are responsible for continuing review of the implementation of the order to insure that no information is withheld which the people have a right to know. At the same time it insures that information is properly safeguarded. Thus, this section provides for the dual function of releasing as much information as possible and withholding as much as necessary in the national defense. Agencies have generally assigned these dual functions to public information offices in liaison with security review officers.

Section 19, *Revocation of Executive Order 10290,* is self-explanatory.

Section 20, *Effective Date,* simply sets the effective date of the order as December 15, 1953.

171

RECOMMENDATIONS

NECESSITY

The Commission on Government Security is convinced that an adequate and realistic program for control over information or material of concern to national defense or security is vitally important to the objectives of our national security program.

It is obvious that we cannot afford to give unlimited access to information dealing with matters of defense or national security. We must be certain that adequate precautions are taken to insure that hostile eyes and hands do not gain access to information or material that our country wishes to safeguard. We must at the same time make certain that our people and our friends have access to all information or material which will help achieve our objective of peace and security. The basic problem of document classification, then, is how best to balance the one need against the other and still achieve the objective of peace and security. The necessity for this balancing is the reason behind document classification.

STANDARD AND CRITERIA

The Commission recommends that document classification policies and procedures in private industry having Federal Government contracts should conform with their counterparts in the executive branch.

While document classification in the industrial security program is based upon Executive Order 10501, as in the case of the program in the executive branch, the Commission believes that there should be basic uniformity of these programs in the interest of good administration as well as good national security policy. The Commission has received numerous complaints and suggestions for improvement from contractors who are affected by the classification programs enforced by executive agencies.

In the written interrogatory on document classification policies, practices and problems submitted by the Commission to the executive departments and agencies, there was included the following question: "Have industrial or other nongovernmental contractors indicated in any way that regulations for document classification as enforced by agency under provisions of Executive

172

Order 10501, section 1, hamper their performance of agency contracts? If so, describe, citing examples where possible." The replies indicate very little difficulty. Some agencies report little or no dealings with industrial contractors and so indicate in their replies to the interrogatory. The responses of other agencies indicate that they have prepared basic directives, regulations, handbooks, and manuals, which set forth the procedures under which defense information must be handled and guarded by industry contractors. These are based upon Executive Order 10501 for the most part, although other authorities are cited where appropriate. Examination of typical examples of the directive material indicates no significant variation in the security requirement for documents imposed upon industry from those practiced by the originating agency. In fact, the wording of various sections of such directives to industry are often taken directly from the pertinent sections of Executive Order 10501.

The question of possible variations between the basic order for document classification and the implementary directives applied to individual industrial operations has been studied by staff members of the Commission on Government Security having particular knowledge of the problems of industrial security. They concluded that variations are largely due to individual interpretations of the basic order. The Commission believes that effort by the executive branch to achieve conformity of purpose and direction from its industrial contractors will be repaid by more satisfaction with the necessary restrictions imposed.

The Commission recognizes the great contribution of American industry in the cause of national security and feels that the necessary restrictions should impose the smallest burden possible within the bounds of security.

The Commission recommends no change in the criteria established by Executive Order 10501 for evaluating the importance of information or material with respect to national security or defense, except as noted below with respect to the confidential classification.

Although there is a body of information or material which should be protected from hostile eyes and hands, all such information or material is obviously not equally important to defense or security. While disclosure of war plans, for example, might cause grave damage to the national security, disclosure of estimates of industrial capacity might cause none. Variable standards of security must be applied. To this end Executive Order 10501 provides a system for gradation of information or material according to its estimated importance to defense or security. The order establishes three categories: top secret, secret, and confidential.

The Commission recommends the abolition of the "confidential" classification of all future defense information and materials.

Representatives of industry, scientists, engineers, and other technicians have criticised the existing document classification program on three principal grounds:

(1) Overclassification of defense information and materials, disclosure of which would not substantially injure the national security.

(2) Since security at its best can only provide lead time in this highly technological age, this overclassification defeats its own purpose in that it retards the free exchange of information.

(3) The cost of handling, storing and transmitting classified information is excessive and imposes undue burdens in the light of the risk involved in the event of disclosure.

There would seem to be no serious complaint concerning the necessity of preserving the existing categories of top secret and secret under the criteria for such categories set forth in Executive Order 10501. The burden of the criticism is leveled at the confidential category.

The various departments and agencies having authority to classify, in response to the Commission's inquiries, almost uniformly have opposed the abolition of the confidential classification. The arguments advanced by these governmental departments and agencies in support of their position may be summarized as follows:

(1) Publication of matters now classified as "confidential" would have an adverse effect on the national security.

(2) If the classification were abolished, a substantial volume of the matter now classified as "confidential" would require upgrading to secret.

(3) The cost of reviewing and reexamining the great mass of matter now classified as "confidential", in order to determine the necessity for upgrading to secret, would be excessive.

The existing Executive order provides that defense information and material may be classified as "confidential" if its unauthorized disclosure could be prejudicial to the defense interests of the Nation.

While the Executive order, in connection with its definition of top secret, cites illustrations of consequences which would justify the classification of top secret, such as those leading to a definite break in diplomatic relations. or armed attack, or war, or the compromise of military or defense plans, intelligence operations, and scientific or technological developments vital to the national defense, and while similar illustrations are cited therein for the application of the classification of secret, it is significant that no illustrations are set forth in respect to the confidential category.

The phrase "could be prejudicial to the national security" describing confidential is so vague and broad as to furnish no reasonable basis for its application. In the course of its studies, the Commission has been furnished

174

with information classified as "confidential" which could have been so classified only by the widest stretch of the imagination.

Industry complains that frequently it must maintain elaborate procedures for the safeguarding of information that has been released to the public press by the cognizant security agency itself or by some other department or agency of the Government.

Restrictions upon the free exchange of information retard scientific and technological progress, and the leadtime so vital to the success of the defense effort may frequently be lost as the result of undue restrictions. The loss of such leadtime might in some instances threaten the very security which the restrictions are intended to protect although certain restrictions must be imposed on the exchange of information.

Estimates furnished to the Commission indicate that most classified information and material falls into the confidential category. Thus, the Department of Defense estimates that 59 percent of its classified material is confidential, as contrasted with 11 percent for secret, and 10 percent for top secret; the State Department indicates 76 percent for confidential, 20 percent for secret, and 4 percent for top secret; the Department of Commerce indicates 76.26 percent for confidential, 23.70 percent for secret, and 0.04 percent for top secret.

The Atomic Energy Commission estimates 49 percent for confidential, 49 percent for secret, and 2 percent for top secret. Only in the Central Intelligence Agency does the percentage of secret exceed the percentage of confidential, the figures in this Agency being 28 percent confidential, 61 percent secret, and 11 percent top secret.

It is difficult to reconcile the position in respect to the retention of the confidential classification taken by those governmental departments having industrial security programs with their practices in respect to clearance for access to confidential information and materials in their industrial security programs. Such clearance is granted not by the governmental department or agency but by the private industrial contractor, and such contractor is permitted to grant such clearance without the necessity of making an investigation of the individual seeking access and merely on the basis of his citizenship, plus certification that the private contractor does not have any derogatory information in his files relating to such individual.

It would seem that if the disclosure of confidential information and material could in any substantial degree adversely affect the national security, the function of granting clearance would not be delegated by the Government to the judgment of the individual private contractors; or that, even if such function were so delegated, adequate investigations would be required.

As noted above, one of the arguments advanced by the various governmental departments and agencies, in urging the retention of the confidential category is predicated upon the claim that in the event of the abolition of that category, a substantial number of documents heretofore classified as confidential would have to be upgraded to secret.

If this argument is sound, it would clearly seem that those departments and agencies of the Government which have been classifying defense information and materials as confidential, when in fact they should have been classified as secret, have been guilty of gross dereliction.

While in isolated instances there may be room for some latitude in determining whether specific information in the possession of unauthorized persons could prejudice national security as distinguished from causing serious damage to the national security, such as jeopardizing the international relations of the United States, or endangering the effectiveness of a program of vital importance to the national defense, the failure to observe the distinction on a large scale and in numerous instances would indeed be cause for grave concern.

There are no facts before the Commission which justify the claim, implicit in the argument thus advanced, that there has been such a consistent widespread underclassification, and the Commission is unwilling to assume that there has been any appreciable failure upon the part of classifying officers to observe the significant distinction between the criteria for secret on the one hand and confidential on the other. In the judgment of the Commission, only a minimum amount of upgrading would be necessary.

Any risk involved in the abolition of confidential, at least so far as the industrial security program is concerned, is minimized by the fact that the various industrial phases of a confidential contract are so dispersed as to make it virtually impossible for any employee to assemble the information to the detriment of the national security.

It is the view of the Commission that the criteria for the categories of top secret and secret, as contained in Executive Order 10501, are adequate to protect the national security, but that the disadvantages arising out of the confidential category, in the light of the risk, the nature of the information and materials falling within that category, and the cost and delay involved, outweigh any advantages to the national security to be derived from its retention.

Finally, it is argued by various Government departments and agencies that the cost of an immediate review and reexamination of information and materials now classified as confidential for the purpose of determining whether some should be upgraded to secret would be excessive.

The Commission has taken cognizance of this argument and, except as herein noted in the next recommendation, has proposed that abolition of the confidential category apply henceforth.

The Commission recommends that industry be permitted immediately to discontinue clearance of employees for existing contracts classified confidential.

While the recommendation as to the abolition of the confidential category is applicable only to future classifications, the Commission is of the view,

176

for the reasons set out in the preceding recommendation, that discontinuance of clearance for contracts that are presently classified as "confidential" should be made immediately operative in the industrial security programs. Contractors who in the past have concluded their own personnel investigations can be expected to do so in the future.

The Commission recommends that no additional security classifications be added.

As heretofore stated, the Commission is of the opinion that the top secret and secret classification categories as presently defined in Executive Order 10501 are sufficient to protect adequately the national security. On that basis, it has recommended the abolition of the confidential category. For the same reasons it is of the opinion that no new categories are necessary.

The Commission recommends that the power to apply defense classifications to documents or material under authority of Executive Order 10501 should not be expanded and that only those agencies now having this authority should continue to possess defense classification authority.

The Commission further recommends that agencies not having authority to classify or having only restricted authority maintain a continuing study of their need to classify, and if such need is found to exist, to make such fact known to the proper authority.

The document classification program concerns, directly or indirectly, the majority of all employees in the executive branch. Although Executive Order 10501 denied defense classification authority to 28 executive branch agencies and restricted such authority to agency heads in the case of 17 other agencies, it did not affect the authority of a number of major agencies. Among the agencies remaining unaffected were:

Agency	Number of employees [1]
Atomic Energy Commission	6,673
Civil Service Commission	4,450
Department of Commerce	47,065
Department of Defense	1,175,915
Department of Justice	30,520
Department of State	33,595
Department of the Treasury	78,424
Federal Civil Defense Administration	1,115
General Services Administration	27,100
U. S. Information Agency	11,496
Total	1,416,353

[1] As of Jan. 1, 1957.

The foregoing agencies possessing unqualified authority to classify information for reasons of national defense or security employ about 60 percent of all personnel in the executive branch of the Federal Government.

The executive departments and agencies which still have authority to classify are believed to include all those vested in any appreciable degree with original national security or defense responsibilities. A check of available file data and inquiries directed to the Department of Justice and elsewhere by the Commission staff, however, has not produced any document or material which would provide additional information for evaluating the basis for the decision to grant unlimited defense classification authority to these agencies. (There is likewise no such information from which to evaluate the basis for selecting the departments and agencies which were denied or restricted in their authority to classify.)

In the absence of information to the contrary, the Commission assumes that those agencies not affected by section 2 (a) and 2 (b) of Executive Order 10501 were, in fact, considered to be of particular importance to national security by the President at the time of issuing the order. The Commission has no evidence of shifts in the nature of work carried on by those agencies given the unqualified authority to apply original defense classifications to documents or other material. It must, therefore, be assumed that there have been no such changes since promulgation of Executive Order 10501.

In the intervening period of more than 3 years, the agencies whose classification authority was denied or curtailed have indicated little dissatisfaction with the restriction. The Commission on Government Security queried 15 executive departments and agencies on various problems of the document classification program, asking in the course of the query for any revisions needed in Executive Order 10501. Responses indicate little concern over classification limitations imposed by the Executive order. Agency reaction has been similar in the case of queries submitted to some 60 executive departments and agencies by the Interdepartmental Committee on Internal Security. In the course of hearings on their information policies and problems before the Special Subcommittee on Government Information (the Moss subcommittee) of the House Committee on Government Operations, moreover, witnesses for several leading executive agencies gave no indication that restrictions on their classification authority were impediments to their functions.

The agencies now denied authority to classify and the agencies whose power to originate classified material is restricted should maintain a continuing study of their need to classify in the interest of national security and, where such need is found to exist, should make the fact known to the proper authority.

The Commission recommends that the present restriction limiting original defense classification authority to agency heads in certain agencies should remain as at present subject to the proviso that,

in the event of the incapacity or necessary absence of the agency head, the individual acting in his stead may exercise the classification authority.

Section 2 (b) of Executive Order 10501 provides that in those departments and agencies having partial but not primary responsibility for matters pertaining to national defense, the authority for original classification of information or material shall be exercised only by the head of the department or agency without delegation. The departments and agencies subject to this restriction are set forth in the discussion of the present program.

It is the opinion of the Commission that this restriction of authority is desirable but that, in order to provide for administrative continuity, it should be made clear that in the event of the incapacity or absence of the head of the department or agency, the acting head thereof shall have the authority to classify.

The Commission recommends that every effort should be made in each agency to reduce the number of employees having the authority to classify or to recommend classification.

The Commission realizes that not all employees in agencies having unqualified classification authority have *de jure* authority to classify information under Executive Order 10501. Agency regulations based upon the order restrict original classification authority to certain employees ranging from minute fractions of all employees in some agencies to 15 to 20 percent in others, depending primarily upon the importance of classified documents in overall operations of the agency.

The Commission wishes to point out, however, that the relatively small number of individuals who have the authority to apply defense classifications to documents or material is overbalanced by the great number of individuals who in the course of their work have the authority to recommend defense classifications for documents or material within their area of activity. As a practical matter, these individuals have de facto authority to classify since it is patently impossible in most agencies for the responsible official to look behind the justification for each instance of document classification.

PROGRAM ADMINISTRATION

The Commission recommends that the executive agencies give particular attention to the requirements for fullest dissemination, consistent with national security, of scientific information and for fullest access, consistent with national security and the need to know,

179

to such information by scientists or others who may request such information or access.

The Commission recognizes the importance of scientific information to national security. The availability of such information, however, must be considered within the general framework of our requirements for guarding information in the national interest.

It has already been pointed out that unnecessary restrictions upon the dissemination of scientific and technological information may in the long run actually be detrimental to the national security. Positive contributions to national security through scientific and technological advancement must not be lost as the result of an overzealous effort to classify.

Adequate and intensive training programs of the kind heretofore suggested, close and frequent consultations with scientists, engineers, and industrial representatives; inspections and review by the Central Security Office; the abolition of the confidential category—all as recommended by the Commission—should contribute substantially to an improved balance between the need for protection of the national security and the need for free exchange of ideas and information.

The Commission recommends that all departments and agencies having original authority to classify documents under Executive Order 10501 should institute adequate document classification training programs for all personnel who originate or have responsibility for material which will require application of defense information classification.

It is generally agreed that many of the difficulties arising out of document classification programs in executive departments and agencies come from lack of basic familiarity with the program, its background, and especially its purpose.

Executive Order 10501 recognizes the need for employee training in document classification work. Section 10 of the order provides:

To promote the basic purposes of this order, heads of those departments and agencies originating or handling classified defense information shall designate experienced persons to coordinate and supervise the activities applicable to their departments or agencies under this order. Persons so designated shall maintain active training and orientation programs for employees concerned with classified defense information to impress each such employee with his individual responsibility for exercising vigilance and care in complying with the provisions of this order. Such persons shall be authorized on behalf of the departments and agencies to establish adequate and active inspection programs to the end that the provisions of this order are administered effectively.

In its interrogatory to selected executive departments and agencies concerning document classification, the Commission asked the following question: "Does agency have a program for training and indoctrination of employee with respect to document classification?" Virtually all agencies have some kind of training or indoctrination program. Their replies indicate that the scope of such programs varies with each agency, depending upon security requirements.

The nature of the training program should be determined only after consultation with scientists, engineers, technicians, and others familiar with all factors relevant to the protection of the national security and to the advancement of scientific and technological progress.

It must be borne in mind that there are no fixed formulas which can be automatically applied in this effort to protect the national security against compromise through underclassification without, at the same time, damaging national security by stifling scientific and technological progress.

Competence in the field of classification would require that the individuals with authority to classify or recommend classification should not only be persons of unusual judgment, but should be familiar with the processes which foster scientific and technological advance. While they should be fully aware of the dangers arising out of unauthorized disclosure of defense information and materials which would cause grave or serious damage to the national defense and to the national security, they should be equally aware of the impediments to national defense and security arising out of indiscriminate restrictions upon the free exchange of ideas and the free access to information.

The Commission recommends that the executive departments and agencies review, in consultation with industry, their provisions for training in all aspects of document classification as they relate to industrial contractors, changing them wherever found necessary.

In the course of this review and consultation, the agencies and industry should institute procedures for agency and industry personnel to be familiar with operations and problems common to each as well as peculiar to each. The Commission believes that closer liaison and appreciation of mutual problems is necessary. Industry feels that there is too little understanding of its special problems by executive agencies. Industry must, however, make more effort to call attention to these problems.

The Commission recommends establishment of the Central Security Office having review and advisory functions with respect to the Federal document classification program and to make recommendations for its improvement as needed.

The Commission believes that there are many advantages to be gained in creating an office to which the various Federal agencies could bring their problems of particular or common concern relating to the Federal security

181

program. Insofar as the document classification program is concerned, the Commission is convinced that the present system is not adequate to meet the needs of the program. For example, although Executive Order 10501 provides, in section 16, for a member of the President's staff to receive, consider, and take action on non-Government complaints relating to the order, it appears that little is actually accomplished through this method. This should be a full-time assignment, not an ad hoc function of a presidential staff member.

Executive Order 10501 also provides, in section 17, for continuing review by the National Security Council of the implementation of the order to insure that defense information is properly safeguarded. This function is now assigned by the Council to the Interdepartmental Committee on Internal Security as only one of several functions of importance to national security. The Commission believes that document classification problems warrant more attention. The Commission also feels that agencies should have the assistance of a specialized office in carrying out their duties under section 18 of the order.

The Commission wishes to emphasize that the foregoing comments regarding present implementation of assignments under the order are based primarily upon the conviction that the document classification program of the Federal Government deserves more specific consideration than is now possible.

A more extended discussion of the advisory and review functions of the Central Security Office in respect to the document classification program will be found in that portion of the report dealing with the proposed Central Security Office.

It is important to note, however, that the proposed Central Security Office will not have the power to review individual documents for the purpose of determining whether or not they are properly classified, but that such responsibility will continue to rest with the agency authorized officers. The review functions of the Central Security Office would be limited to a consideration of policies and procedures designed to guard against overclassification, to expedite declassification, and to suggest recommendations tending to make the security programs of all agencies and departments having authority to classify uniform, consistent, and effective.

Included in the policies and procedures which the Central Security Office should study for the purpose of making recommendations are the dangers of overclassification arising out of the fact that large numbers of individuals in the respective agencies have the power to recommend classification. The Central Security Office, in consultation with the heads of the departments and agencies having authority to classify, should conduct a continuing review of procedures due to this de facto authority to classify by employees normally authorized only to recommend classification.

Another subject which should be made a matter of close study is the administration of agency and department rules regarding the storage or destruction of classified material in the custody of Federal agencies and of private contractors having defense contracts. This problem is one of significant proportions and is the source of much dissatisfaction, particularly on the part of industrial contractors.

The Commission recommends no specific legislation for uniform penalties for violation of classification statutes and agency regulation at this time.

The question of uniform criminal penalties for violations of document classification statutes and agency regulations is not under consideration here. This recommendation refers only to uniform administrative penalties which may be imposed by departments and agencies, without original recourse to courts of law. Administrative penalties are not in the nature of statutory penalties and their provisions for similar infractions may vary considerably from one agency to another, or even within the same agency. For example, one agency may issue only an admonition to an employee for a first violation of regulations, suspend him for the second, and discharge him for the third, while another agency may follow another practice.

The Commission reviewed the manuals and regulations of several departments and agencies with reference to penalties for administrative violation of security regulations, including penalties for infractions of agency rules for classified information. There appears to be considerable latitude in their provisions as suggested above. The Commission, however, took cognizance of the fact that administrative penalty procedures in the various departments and agencies are integral parts of their housekeeping functions. They are not directed entirely toward the document classification program. For that reason and because of the impossibility, within the limited time and resources available, of assuming the task of collation and analysis necessary for adequate recommendations, the Commission decided not to recommend legislative action in this field at this time.

The Commission recommends that, except for the review and advisory functions of the Central Security Office which require legislation, the document classification program should be embodied in an Executive order.

The Commission is of the view that its recommendations regarding the document classification program should be implemented by an Executive order, and that legislation will be required only for the creation of the Central Security Office and to define its powers and duties in respect to such a program.

The Commission recommends the adoption of the provisions of Executive Order 10501 except as changed and modified by the foregoing recommendations.

The Commission has studied all of the provisions of Executive Order 10501 and finds no need for change, except as noted in the recommendations heretofore made.

Atomic Energy Program

Introduction

The Atomic Energy Commission was created by the Atomic Energy Act of 1946, and operates a security program which includes both civilians employed by the Federal Government and employees of industries with which the AEC has contracts. This security phase of the AEC is carried out by the Office of the Director of Security in Washington and the members of the 10 field operations offices.

About 95 percent of the security work is devoted to matters affecting the AEC's classified contractors and their employees. The AEC ranks second to the Department of Defense in the number of classified contractors involved, although the actual figures are only about 2,000 for the AEC as compared with 22,000 contractors for the Department of Defense. The AEC has handled about 500,000 cases involving clearance for employees of contractors, however, as compared with 3 million by the Department of Defense.

No other agency of government has any workload in industrial security which approaches the Department of Defense or the Atomic Energy Commission in size. The AEC's own personnel numbers about 6,500, 10 percent of whom are in Washington, and each of whom has a "Q" clearance based on a full field investigation by the Federal Bureau of Investigation. All AEC security regulations and procedures are contained in volume 2000 of the AEC manual, and there are no regulations which apply separately to the employees of contractors as distinguished from the employees of the Federal Government. This single set of regulations covering all aspects of security is a feature of AEC policy not found in the Department of Defense.

HISTORY

General

The announcement of the hypothesis of nuclear fission and its experimental confirmation took place in January 1939. In the spring of 1939, a group of American, British, and French scientists attempted to stop publication of further data by voluntary agreement, but the plan was vetoed by F. Joliot of France because of a previous publication in the "Physical Review." Consequently, publication continued freely for another year. At the April 1940 meeting of the division of physical sciences of the National Research Council, there was proposed the formation of a censorship committee to control publication in all American scientific journals. As a result there was formed the Reference Committee of the National Research Council to control publication policy in all fields of possible military interest.[1]

In 1939 President Roosevelt appointed the "Advisory Committee on Uranium," which was the only committee on uranium that had official status prior to the National Defense Research Committee (NDRC) which was formed in June 1940 and began recruiting scientists to work on urgent military problems. The Advisory Committee on Uranium became a subcommittee of NDRC, which in turn was a part of the Office of Scientific Research and Development (OSRD). From January 1942 until early summer of 1942, the uranium work of OSRD was directed by Dr. Vannevar Bush and Dr. J. B. Conant, who worked with the program chiefs and a planning board. In the summer of 1942 the Army Corps of Engineers was assigned an active part in the procurement and engineering phases, and organized the Manhattan Engineering District (MED) for that purpose. The period of joint OSRD and Army control continued through April 1943, but in May 1943 the research contracts were transferred to the Corps of Engineers and the period of complete Army control began.[2]

Reorganization of the atomic-bomb project occurred at the beginning of 1942, and a gradual transfer of the work from the Office of Scientific Research and Development auspices was made to the Manhattan District. The responsibilities of the metallurgical laboratory at Chicago originally included a preliminary study of the physics of the atomic bomb. Some preliminary studies were made in 1941, and early in 1942 G. Breit set into operation various laboratories for experimental study of problems that had to be solved before progress could be made on bomb design. J. R. Oppenheimer, of the University of California, gathered together a group of scientists in the summer of 1942 for further theoretical investigation, and undertook to coordinate their activities. This work was officially under the metallurgical laboratory, but the group devoted to theoretical studies operated largely at the University of California. By the end of the summer of 1942, when Gen. L. R. Groves took charge of the entire project, it was decided to expand the work considerably and, at the earliest possible time, to set up a separate laboratory.

In the choice of a site for the atomic-bomb laboratory, the all important considerations were secrecy and safety. It was, therefore, decided to establish the laboratory in an isolated location and to sever unnecessary connection with the outside world.

[1] A general accounting of the development of methods of using atomic energy, etc., H. D. Smith, p. 31.
[2] Edward S. C. Smith, "Applied atomic power," p. 70.

By November 1942 a site had been chosen at Los Alamos, N. Mex., on a mesa about 20 miles from Santa Fe.[3]

At the close of World War II the War Department, which had been charged with the development of atomic weapons, expressed the view that its job had been done and that, without legislation, the program was drifting and stagnating. In his message to Congress on October 3, 1945, President Truman stressed the necessity for legislation and specifically requested "an atomic energy commission whose members should be appointed by the President with the advice and consent of the Senate." The first Atomic Energy Act was approved August 1, 1946, and the commissioners were named on October 28.[4] The AEC, upon taking over from MED January 1, 1947, thereupon maintained in full force the security measures of MED and took under consideration their adequacy under the existing circumstances.[5] Congress declared that it is "the policy of the people of the United States" that the AEC shall carry out its broad statutory program "subject at all times to the paramount objective of assuring the common defense and security." [6]

Under the Act of 1946, AEC became responsible for developing a licensing system. Section 4 (e) provides that, unless appropriately licensed, no one shall produce, transfer, or acquire any facility for the production of fissionable material; section 5 (b) similarly restricts source material; while Section 7 states that a license is necessary to produce or export any device utilizing fissionable material.

In 1946 a technical information service for the Commission and contractor organizations was established, and a public information service was provided to supply information requested by press, radio, pictorial media, and citizens groups.[7] Late in 1947 these two services were combined for more effective operation.

Soon after taking office in 1946, the Commission enlisted the services of Rear Adm. Sidney W. Souers, first head of the United States Central Intelligence Group, and Frank J. Wilson, former chief of the U. S. Secret Service, to assist in a survey of the longterm security problem. As a result of the survey, AEC established in its staff headquarters an Office of Security and Intelligence to direct all of the security aspects of its program.[8]

A special panel was appointed in December 1949 to study the security system of AEC and its contractors. The panel made an intensive review over a period of four months, and returned an analytical report and recommendations. The Commission staff acted at once upon the analysis of deficiencies in the detailed organizational and procedural arrangements to protect physical, personnel, documentary, and other phases of security,

[3] "Applied atomic power," Edward S. C. Smith, p. 195.
[4] 1st semiannual report (AEC), p. 1, and "Atomic Energy," Teeple, p. 8.
[5] 1st semiannual report, p. 8.
[6] Act of 1946, sec. 1.
[7] 3d semiannual report, p. 3.
[8] 3d semiannual report, p. 29.

involving all divisions and operations offices, and to install corrective measures.[9]

During the first half of 1955, the procedures for resolving employee grievances, handling of separations, suspensions, demotions and other disciplinary actions, and other procedures were revised and improved.[10]

The Division of Inspection was established in September 1954. A small staff was organized to carry out the functions assigned to the Division in accordance with the provisions of section 25c of the Act of 1954. The director of the division has three assistants including an assistant director for investigations to investigate directly all questions of employees' conduct, fraud, etc., in AEC and contractor organizations.[11]

The Act of 1946 was amended in 1952, and was superseded by the Atomic Energy Act of 1954. In an AEC regulation dated August 30, 1954, all provisions of rules, regulations, and notices, published by the AEC in the Federal Register under the authority of the Act of 1946, and in effect immediately prior to the effective date of the Act of 1954, were continued in force to the extent that they were not inconsistent with the Act of 1954.[12]

The Act of 1954, among other things, sets up three committees as follows: (1) Joint Committee on Atomic Energy, composed of 18 members of Congress, to make a continuing study of AEC and resultant suggestions to Congress; (2) General Advisory Committee, composed of nine civilians, to advise AEC on scientific and technical problems regarding use and development of atomic power; and (3) Military Liaison Committee, composed of military men from the three services, which is a connecting link between AEC and DOD on military use of atomic energy.[13] This Act also authorizes AEC to promulgate its own security regulations.[14]

Personnel Security

When MED took over the development of atomic weapons in the summer of 1942, military security regulations were imposed for the purpose of protecting information. The principal methods of personnel security control included (*a*) investigations of individuals to determine eligibility for access to classified information, and (*b*) admission to installations only under exacting identification procedures. As aforementioned, MED security measures were initially adopted by AEC, but the Commission promptly met with the Attorney General and the FBI to establish procedures pertaining to personnel investigations and security violations.[15] During the first half of 1947, a program was initiated under which 6,500 applicants for employ-

---

[9] 8th semiannual report p. 178.
[10] 18th semiannual report, p. 96.
[11] 18th semiannual report, p. 99.
[12] 17th semiannual report, p. 104.
[13] Sections 21–28 and 201–207, AEC Act of 1954.
[14] Sec. 161.
[15] 2d semiannual report, p. 19.

ment by AEC, its contractors and licensees were investigated by the FBI; and all employees carried over from MED were being reinvestigated. Fifteen hundred former MED employees were reinvestigated during this six months' period.

During the latter half of 1947, AEC established a Personnel Security Review Board, composed of five prominent citizens to make recommendations to the Commission for further definition and codification of standards and criteria used in determining ineligibility for employment by AEC and its contractors, and to provide for administrative review. Vigorous efforts were made at this time to indoctrinate all personnel having access to restricted data with a full knowledge of their duties and responsibilities. Security kits containing training material and copies of "security education outline," a guide to the procedures involved in security, were distributed to managers of directed operations. Ten thousand copies of a general manager's instruction "responsibility for security" were also distributed.[16]

During 1948 the turnover of personnel among AEC and contractor operating employees was relatively small, but construction workers were being replaced continuously, and some of them had to be cleared. For example, more than 125,000 were employed in the construction of plant K–25 at Oak Ridge, although there were not more than 25,000 employed at one time. The administrative burden of considering security clearances continued to be great, and definite criteria had to grow out of experience gained in handling individual cases. Decisions made over a period of months gradually built up and refined a systematic catalog of the kinds of information which served to warn that a person under investigation might be a risk to the common defense and security.

In 1948, it became possible to delegate to the regional managers of operations the responsibility for screening cases—to grant clearances where no doubt existed, to refer others to Washington. Early in 1948 the Commission established the Personnel Security Review Board (PSRB) to advise it on personnel practices, criteria, and as to appropriate disposition of specific cases. Later in this same year, the Commission codified and simplified the results of its experience and, with the assistance of PSRB, developed a set of definitive criteria to serve as guides for determination. The new "criteria for determination of eligibility for security clearance" were published in the Federal Register on January 5, 1949. They are not exhaustive, but they contain the principal types of derogatory information that indicate security risk. Category (A) includes those classes of derogatory information that establish a presumption of security risk. Category (B) includes those classes of derogatory information where the extent of activities, the attitude, or convictions of the individual must be weighed in determining whether a presumption of risk exists.[17] With the criteria in effect, it was possible to extend to managers of operations the authority to make decisions

16 3d semiannual report, pp. 29, 31.
17 5th semiannual report, p. 122.

on clearance in a majority of cases. At the close of 1948, authority was being granted to managers of operations to initiate the aforementioned interim procedure for administrative review, although it was decided that headquarters would provide staff assistance and make surveys to assure that the security program is fairly and consistently administered.

Under the General Manager's directive (GM–80, effective April 15, 1948) complete processing of personnel clearance cases was delegated to the field office managers, except in those cases which were evaluated as containing substantially derogatory information about the person involved. Such cases remained the responsibility of the general manager.[18] The Commission, at this time, decided against further decentralization. In 1948 the Commission determined that a hearing procedure should be in effect to give the fairest possible hearing to employees whose eligibility for security clearance has been questioned. In April AEC issued an interim procedure pursuant to which employees would have the opportunity to appear before a local personnel security board which would make recommendations as to security clearance after weighing all of the evidence.

AEC security clearances are of two types: (1) "L" clearance for access to confidential information and for workmen employed in view of secret materials and equipment; and (2) "Q" clearance for secret and top secret access. The "L" is based on a national agency check and the "Q" on a full field investigation. (AEC manual, chap. 2302, 11–3–54.)

It was pointed out that loyalty is but one factor of consideration, and that the issues most often presented to local boards have been questions of character and associations, and not loyalty.

In 1948, the problem of confrontation of witnesses arose, and AEC announced its policy on this subject as follows:

In any hearing procedure based on information contained in investigative reports, one of the principal difficulties encountered is that of attempting to afford employees an opportunity to confront and cross-examine persons who have furnished information unfavorable to them. In the interest of the common defense and security of the United States, it is the Commission's duty to give appropriate consideration to all information which may be relevant to the security clearance of the person concerned. Under the Atomic Energy Act, the FBI report is the primary source of such information. There will be some cases in which important information comes from a source which the FBI has designated as confidential and which, therefore, the Commission may not properly disclose. In such a case, the employee will not have an opportunity to confront and cross-examine the person who supplied the information. It is hoped that it will be possible to keep these situations to a minimum, and that the sources of significant information bearing on the case can be available at a local board hearing.

The Commission recognizes that, where full confrontation is not possible, it is extremely important that the employee be protected against statements activated by bias or prejudice, or statements which result from simple lack of information, and that care be taken to check the accuracy of the information furnished. The Commission considers that one of the primary functions of the local board is to serve as an impartial body to do its best to evaluate all sources of information, and to elicit from the

---

[18] GM–80, effective Apr. 15, 1948.

employee and others all information necessary to clear up any misunderstanding which might otherwise result from lack of complete confrontation.[19]

As of July 15, 1948, there had been 15 hearings, with final action taken on six. Clearance was denied in only one of the six cases.[20]

During 1948 the Commission took steps to systematize its security education. It made clear to management and supervisory officials that the success of such a program depends upon their conscientious interest in promoting common understanding of security. All field offices received guides and sample talks to assist supervisors in indoctrinating employees in security principles. The Washington office of the Commission through security news letters, through posters, and through a series of pamphlets, the first two of which were issued in November, had the means for reaching employees informally and providing them with a medium for wide informal discussion of security problems.[21]

About 200,000 persons were investigated for security clearance during the 3-year period 1947–1950. In some 2,300 of the 200,000 cases, AEC instituted further review to determine whether clearance should be granted; approximately 700 were granted clearance after additional investigation, interview, or formal hearing, and the remaining 1,600 either resigned or terminated employment before a final determination by the AEC of their eligibility for clearance, or were denied clearance. The right to appeal adverse recommendations, originally available only to persons already in the program, such as those taken over from the MED, was opened on September 19, 1950, to applicants for AEC employment and to AEC contractors and licenses where access to restricted data is required.[22]

Employment by AEC and its contractors increased from 73,000 at the end of 1950 to 100,000 by the middle of 1951. To keep pace, AEC took steps to assure itself that no unnecessary FBI investigations were requested.

The Act of 1946 required personnel investigations by the FBI prior to clearance. The Act was amended in 1952 to permit certain investigations by the CSC. The Act of 1954 provides for investigations by the CSC with exceptions set forth in section 145 (c), (d) and (e). Under (e) the AEC may designate certain positions as highly sensitive and thus requiring an investigation by the FBI. All positions within AEC are classified as highly sensitive, consequently all AEC personnel undergo FBI investigations.

During the first 6 months of 1956, the Atomic Energy Commission revised its criteria and administrative review procedures for determining the eligibility for security clearance of persons in the atomic energy program or entering it. The Commission announced the revision on May 10, 1956, and published the regulation that same day in the Federal Register, to take effect immediately. The last previous revision, which took place in 1950,

---

[19] 4th semiannual report, p. 53.
[20] 4th semiannual report, p. 51.
[21] 5th semiannual report, p. 129.
[22] 9th semiannual report, p. 35.

extended to prospective employees the right of a hearing which had been limited to employees only.

Eight years of experience in the field of personnel security clearances, and the recommendations of representatives of the scientific community contributed to the 1956 revision. In January 1955, at a conference of the directors of eight Commission laboratories, it was recommended that a committee of scientific, legal, and security personnel be established to assist the Commission in revising the personnel security standards and procedures.

The revised review procedures and criteria apply to employees and applicants for employment with the Commission, its contractors, agents, licensees, holders of access permits, and other persons as designated by the general manager, concerning whom questions of eligibility for clearance have arisen. The new regulation also established standards under which reconsideration would be permitted for cases in which clearances previously had been granted or denied.

The policy in this field, as given in the regulations, declares:

It is the policy of the Atomic Energy Commission to carry out its responsibility for the security of the atomic energy program in a manner consistent with traditional American concepts of justice. To this end, the Commission has established criteria for determining eligibility for security clearance and will afford those individuals described in paragraph 4.2 (of the regulation) the opportunity for administrative review of questions concerning their eligibility for security clearance.[23]

The current criteria of derogatory information are set forth in the Federal Register, May 10, 1956, title 10, section 4.11.

Security of Documents and Information

The Commission in 1947 inherited from the Manhattan Engineer District a set of documentary and information controls and kept them in force as interim measures. In 1948, the Commission issued a "compilation of security instructions," which contained in looseleaf form the working instructions on security, including the original MED regulations still valid, as well as revisions and additions. The Commission meanwhile revised and simplified security instructions on document control. It also put into use two systems of cryptographic communications and devised security precautions for them.[24]

A Classification and Document Control Board was set up to establish criteria for classification of restricted data and to supervise procedures involved in the accounting for classified documents. Field units were formed to work closely with the Board.[25]

In 1948 AEC used a system of control over top secret documents involving (a) monthly report of top secret papers originated, destroyed, or

---

[23] 20th semiannual report, p. 117.
[24] 5th semiannual report, p. 127.
[25] 3d semiannual report, p. 30.

transferred, and (b) a semiannual inventory from each installation. A new system was inaugurated in January 1949 whereby a daily record is sent to headquarters listing top secret documents originated or destroyed, plus a receipt form for transfers.[26]

A revision of standards covering transportation of classified and other important documents and materials was formulated in 1951 and distributed throughout AEC operations. These standards include approved methods of shipment, use of receipts, and liaison with law enforcement agencies.[27]

As a result of discussions between AEC and DOD, an agreement was reached in 1952, whereby personnel of the Department of Defense and its contractors may be afforded access to restricted data by Commission personnel on the basis of military security clearances. Thereafter access to restricted data transmitted to the Department of Defense and its contractors was governed in accordance with clearance procedures of the agencies of the Department of Defense, based upon classification criteria jointly established by the Atomic Energy Commission and the Department of Defense. The agreement also provided that the Department of Defense and its agencies shall be responsible for safeguarding restricted data made available pursuant to procedures developed to implement this agreement. Requests for access to restricted data in the hands of Atomic Energy Commission personnel must be submitted in writing by a major administrative or higher military headquarters on a "need to know" basis, with the request indicating the clearance status of the individuals who are to be authorized to have such access.[28]

In 1953 AEC published a 4-volume, 3,000 page "reactor handbook," the most complete reference book existing in the field, for the primary purpose of providing atomic energy project scientists and engineers with a compilation of existing data.

As a continuation of the policy of cooperation with respect to release of technical information shared by the United Kingdom, Canada, and the United States as a result of their combined wartime efforts, the Sixth International Declassification Conference was held on April 8 to 10, 1953, at Chalk River, Canada. This Conference recommended changes in certain topics of the "declassification guide," in the light of developments since the previous conference in September 1951. The proposed revisions would permit the release of additional information concerning power reactors and associated technology. Agreement among the three nations on the categories of technical information to be released or declassified has resulted in uniform standards of secrecy for the fund of knowledge developed by the three nations in their atomic energy projects.[29]

During the first half of 1955 the AEC moved toward greater participation by industry in advancing the development of competitive nuclear power.

[26] 5th semiannual report, p. 128.
[27] 10th semiannual report, p. 62.
[28] 12th semiannual report, p. 44.
[29] 14th semiannual report, p. 61.

Toward this end, the Commission set up an expanded program for making classified information available to industry.[30] In order to discharge its regulatory responsibilities under the Act of 1954, the Commission established a Division of Licensing in March 1955 and took initial steps in setting up procedures under which private enterprise may assume the major responsibility in the developing of atomic energy for civilian uses. Proposed regulations covering licensing of production and utilization facilities, distribution of special nuclear materials, and safeguarding of restricted data were published in the Federal Register so that the public might have an opportunity to comment on them prior to the time when they would become effective. Regulations on access to restricted data relating to civilian uses of atomic energy were similarly published.[31]

During the last half of 1955, a constant flow of applications for access permits from a wide variety of industries, trades, and professions testified to the interest of private organizations and individuals in obtaining access to restricted data on civilian uses. An accelerated program was adopted to review Commission reports and other papers useful in civilian applications and to declassify or downgrade them whenever possible.

Encouragement of American industry was done previously on a limited scale by means of "study agreements" under which companies or groups of companies agreed to spend a certain amount of money on specific study projects and to submit reports to the Commission describing the results of these studies. Some 25 study groups, comprising a total of 81 companies, were granted access to restricted data under this program.

The study agreement program was replaced in April 1955 by a more simplified procedure under which restricted data relating to the civilian use of atomic energy, and classified as Confidential, could be made available to any applicant who evidenced a potential use or application of the information in his business, profession, or trade. The Government waived under section 152 of the Atomic Energy Act of 1954 all rights to inventions and discoveries arising out of access to such information. Where an invention or discovery was made or conceived in the course of, in connection with, or under the terms of an access permit, the applicant was required to waive potential claims against the Government arising from the imposition of secrecy orders on patent applications and all claims for just compensation under Section 173 of the Atomic Energy Act of 1954.

Under similar conditions, limited access was also granted to certain specific information classified as Secret, if the applicant could demonstrate that such information had an immediate or significant effect on his business, profession, or trade. In such cases, applicants must obtain full security ("Q") clearances and the Government will retain royalty-free, nonexclusive rights for governmental purposes in inventions and discoveries which result from such access.

---

[30] 18th semiannual report, p. 2.
[31] 18th semiannual report, p. 101.

Applicants for access must also agree to pay all established charges for security clearances, publication, reproduction, and other services furnished by AEC in connection with access permits.[32]

To service the industrial access permittees, as well as individuals and firms interested only in unclassified information, the AEC inaugurated in 1955 an accelerated industrial information program to provide written and graphic information, including unclassified and classified data on nearly every phase of science and technology developed within the national atomic energy program, excepting weapons technology and certain other limited defense-sensitive matters.

Under the AEC classified documentary service, the Commission authorized an expedited review for downgrading or declassification of approximately 20,000 classified reports in central files of the Technical Information Service at Oak Ridge. Industrially significant reports will be made available as unclassified, confidential, or secret to the permit holders.

Persons granted access permits receive immediately a listing of all available unclassified materials. When personnel and facilities clearances have been completed, the permit holders are apprised of all classified information available to them.[33]

Upon taking over from MED, AEC continued in effect the declassification of atomic energy data to the extent consistent with security, carried out on the basis of recommendations of a committee headed by Dr. Richard C. Tolman, which committee followed in general the established criteria codified by MED. In 1947 AEC was clearing technical articles for release at the rate of 100 a month.[34]

The Commission puts its basic classification policy into effect through the declassification guide for responsible reviewers prepared by the division of classification for Commission approval. This guide spells out by means of topics the types of information which may or may not be declassified, and assigns an appropriate classification to each topic. In the periodic revisions of the guide, a fine balance is struck between protecting information which is of national security interest and providing the maximum assistance to peaceful applications. Revisions of the guide take into account the information in the possession of the United Kingdom and Canada. Through annual tripartite declassification conferences, the three Nations keep their declassification rules consistent.

The present rules, since April 1955, have applied to the review of information currently arising in the atomic energy program. They also affect earlier information residing in classified papers and reports in files throughout atomic energy projects. The new rules have made thousands of these declassifiable, or at least eligible for downgrading to confidential.[35]

[32] 18th semiannual report, p. 102.
[33] 19th semiannual report, p. 96.
[34] 2d semiannual report, p. 15.
[35] 19th semiannual report, p. 98.

To step up this part of the program, the Commission completed in February 1956 a special accelerated review of much of the classified material accumulated throughout the life of the atomic energy program to determine the material which could be published or downgraded to a lesser category of classification.

The declassification guide, which provides current classification policy, was revised following each of the seven international consultations with the United Kingdom and Canada in earlier years. The eighth Declassification Conference was held in April 1956, and the Commission is currently considering the possibility of revisions involving declassification and also of downgrading a large body of material which will aid in the development of peaceful uses of atomic energy and in fundamental research in this field.

The last revision of the declassification guide was put into effect in July 1955. That version recognized that a great many reports about civilian power reactors no longer required the maximum protection of high classification. It has greatly facilitated industrial access to essential information.[36]

In the Commission's accelerated review of classified material, 30,773 research and development reports and informal memoranda were surveyed. The review was aimed at declassifying or downgrading the classification of a large accumulation of classified reports of potential use in the development of the atomic energy industry in the light of the current declassification guide. The review was done at the Oak Ridge, Tenn., operations office by a team of 35 scientists and engineers from major installations, under supervision by Commission staff.

It was a special stepped-up program within the larger program for continuous review of all currently produced technical reports carried on as normal procedure.

Of the 30,773 classified reports reviewed, 10,916 were declassified and are available to the general public; 8,574 were classified "confidential," and are available to private individuals and concerns with "L" or limited clearance, as well as those with "Q" or full clearances; and 11,283 remained in the "secret" classification. Approximately half of those in the last category are available to access permit holders with "Q" clearance who demonstrate a need for the information. The balance, or 4,700 reports, are not currently available to access permit holders because the reports are being reedited when possible so as to dissociate useful technology from its military application.

Since the special review team was disbanded, Commission staff has reviewed an additional 3,019 technical reports as part of its continuing program to declassify material for industrial use where this is possible without compromise to national security.[37]

In 1948 the Commission, with the advice of the Committee of Senior Responsible Reviewers, convened, as a Weapons Effects Classification Board, a panel of experts on weapons-effects data to recommend the proper

---

[36] 20th semiannual report, p. 63.
[37] 20th semiannual report, p. 63.

handling of a wide range of such data. The information considered by the Board is that which the National Military Establishment (NME) and the AEC believe should be distributed under special conditions to support the national defense in both military and civilian activities. These special conditions contemplate the dissemination of type B restricted data to NME personnel who do not have specific restricted data clearance, provided that the dissemination is in accordance with normal military safeguards. The Board urged that a considerable amount of weapons-effects data be determined to be unclassified and distributed for use in training of military personnel, and made publicly available. AEC and the NME have adopted an interpretive guide in accordance with the amended report of the Board.[38]

Physical Security

As previously stated, AEC kept in effect MED security regulations pending further study. After transfer of the atomic energy program from MED to AEC on the first day of 1947, security staffs of the managers of directed operations made 844 detailed inspections during the year. Protective devices to provide adequate mechanical safeguards were installed and an expanded guard force was created, bringing the total of guards employed to 3,100. An integrated survey system was established to provide a regular coverage of facility surveys. A headquarters inspection and survey unit was formed to advise the Commission in achieving an effective and consistent security policy, and to assist the managers in the accomplishment of that end.[39]

During 1948 the Commission took steps for the emergency defense of its vital facilities against attack. To this end, AEC collaborated with the NME in the development of plans for the emergency military protection of its key installations, plans which involve close coordination with the armed services.[40]

At the close of 1948 there were 1,270 installations requiring physical protection against intrusion, theft, espionage, and sabotage. This responsibility meant replacement of some wartime buildings and plants, additional construction, and a thorough check of all existing protective measures.

In its report to Congress in January 1951, the AEC stated that measures to protect property from sabotage and to maintain the security of its secret information were strengthened during 1950. Close liaison is maintained between AEC and DOD.[41]

During 1951, the Commission further improved its system of accounting for source and fissionable materials. This was accomplished in part by preparing a manual of procedural standards for source and fissionable ma-

---

[38] 5th semiannual report, p. 111.
[39] 3d semiannual report, p. 30.
[40] 5th semiannual report, p. 126.
[41] 9th semiannual report, p. 34.

199

terial accounting surveys. Physical protection and accounting control are the two principal safeguards against loss or misappropriation of source and fissionable materials. Physical protection against loss of these materials is incorporated in plant design and operating methods and includes such measures as building fences and providing guards. Accounting controls provide a record of materials to be compared with frequent and accurate measures of actual quantities on hand.[42]

Since the Act of 1954 provided that the Government retain ownership and control of special nuclear materials, at the same time encouraging the use of these materials in industrial applications of atomic energy, further accountability controls were developed by the Division of Source and Special Nuclear Materials Accountability.[43]

During the year 1945, the Manhattan Engineering District, which was then administering the atomic energy program, became greatly concerned over the possible diversion of final product at one of the production plants at Oak Ridge. Various physical security measures to prevent and detect diversion of material had been considered, and a decision was finally made to introduce the lie-detector for examination of all employees in one of the plant areas, since it was felt that the use of the lie-detector, plus the security clearance of all employees based upon an investigation, would provide a satisfactory guarantee of the security of the final product.[44]

As a result of a recent study of all available information including data on lie-detector use at Oak Ridge and its use in other activities, the Commission concluded that there was considerable doubt as to the utility of lie-detector techniques in the AEC security program. After weighing all of the factors involved in a lie-detector program, the conclusion was reached that the unfavorable factors outweighed whatever increase in AEC security might be achieved by its use.

Accordingly, on March 18, 1953, the AEC directed the discontinuance of the lie-detector program and limited its future use on a voluntary basis to specific cases of security interest when authorized by the general manager.

Labor Relations

AEC's predecessor, the Manhattan Engineer District, found it necessary to intervene in labor-management relations of cost contractors. On researcch and operations, union recognition was deferred by intervention of MED. The National Labor Relations Board was requested not to process any petitions for representation filed by unions. After the war, there were immediate demands that the restrictions against union organization be lifted. After a reexamination of security implications, the MED decided

---

[42] 11th semiannual report, p. 13.
[43] 18th semiannual report, p. 28.
[44] 18th semiannual report, p. 28.

(March 1946) to allow the NLRB to handle cases at Oak Ridge. Procedures were worked out to do this under special security controls. An examiner underwent a security investigation and was approved, then made a field study. Contractor and union representatives who had been similarly cleared appeared at secret hearings before the Board. The Board then published a description of the collective-bargaining unit found to be appropriate. Upon assuming operation of the program, the AEC sought to define its own role in relations between its contractors and labor unions. The Commission selected a committee of three labor relations experts (David Morse, George Taylor, and Lloyd Garrison) to analyze the proposed labor contracts negotiated after the NLRB representation elections. Their report, submitted on January 4, 1947, suggested the Commission should pass upon three major portions of labor contracts, i. e., labor expenditures, continuity of work, and security matters, but that, under a contract theory of operation, the Commission should not concern itself with the other provisions.[45]

In 1947 the plants at Oak Ridge were opened up for collective bargaining on an experimental basis, but, before extending to other areas, it was felt that the possibility of a formula had to be explored. Extensive discussions followed with contractor and union representatives and, in January 1948, AEC reported that it was moving in the direction of minimum intervention in relations between contractors and unions. Discussions continued in early 1948, but no formula was found. In June 1948 the President announced his intention to appoint a Commission on Labor Relations in the atomic energy field. The Commission studied the problem for six months and, in April 1949, submitted a report which was accepted by the President and AEC for a trial period of 2 or 3 years. The Commission recommended in effect that AEC should not intervene in labor-management relations as a whole, but that AEC had absolute and final authority in the area of security, and that security rules and their administration were not matters for collective bargaining. The report further recommended a labor relations panel of three members to be appointed by the President, and, in response thereto, the President appointed the same three men who had comprised the Commission. The panel is given full discretion in its handling of a dispute, but the procedures are designed to prevent unnecessary referrals to the panel's jurisdiction.[46] The overriding responsibility of the Commission for protecting the security of the program has led to situations which contradict normal collective bargaining practices. Nevertheless, the security of the program remains the paramount consideration.[47]

In 1948, when a serious question of loyalty to the United States arose in respect to certain officials of the United Electrical Workers, then affiliated with the CIO, the General Electric Company was directed to cease recognizing the union as representative of atomic energy workers in Schenectady. The union officials were not themselves employees of the contractor, but they

[45] 9th semiannual report, p. 75–76.
[46] 9th semiannual report, p. 76–80.
[47] Ibid., p. 82.

did exercise authority over employees and it was, therefore, considered that a threat to the security of the program might exist. AEC was upheld in this stand by a Federal court, after the union chose not to avail itself of an AEC offer of a hearing.[48]

When hearings are held before the NLRB, they are normally open to the public, as is the record of the hearing. When atomic energy cases first were allowed to come before the Board, secrecy was insisted upon. By September, 1948, however, the AEC had worked out methods for holding these hearings in a normal way, open to the public, without endangering security. A panel of NLRB trial examiners had been cleared for access to classified material so that, if it is alleged that information needed to support a position is classified, the trial examiner can talk privately with the party making this allegation, consider the materiality of the information and explore fully whether it can be presented in unclassified form. A representative of the Commission attends the hearings to assist on security questions. With the exception of these safeguards, the hearings now are carried out just as in any other industry and it has been possible for the NLRB to make its determinations without any classified material whatever coming into the open hearings.[49]

In 1949, the President appointed an atomic energy labor relations panel for jurisdiction in disputes which collective bargaining and normal processes of conciliation have failed to resolve.[50]

An AEC policy statement, "Security policies and practices in the area of labor relations," was issued May 8, 1951. The policies worked out within the framework of AEC's general objectives for labor-management relations in the atomic energy program provide for: (a) assurance that all participants in the atomic energy program are loyal to the United States, including those whose participation involves the exercise of negotiating and disciplinary authority over bargaining units; (b) assurances that determination of unit, jurisdiction, and similar questions will not breach security; (c) minimum interference with the traditional rights and privileges of American labor and management.

The statement codified a number of policies in effect throughout the program. It also established certain other policies and practices arising from recent experience at AEC installations. Policies are given on proceedings of the NLRB, loyalty of participants in the collective bargaining relationship, and clearance of union and other representatives.

On all matters of security at all Government-owned, privately operated atomic energy installations, the Atomic Energy Commission retains absolute and final authority, and neither the security rules nor their administration are matters for collective bargaining.[51]

---

[48] "AEC policy with regard to allegedly Communist dominated unions," undated, transmitted by AEC to CGS August 9, 1956.

[49] 9th semiannual report, p. 83.

[50] 10th semiannual report, p. 48.

[51] 10th semiannual report, p. 49–51.

LEGAL BASIS

The Atomic Energy Commission, like the Department of Defense, has major security responsibilities not only with respect to its own civilian personnel but also for employees of contractors having classified contracts with the Commission. Unlike the Department of Defense, however, the Atomic Energy Commission operates just one security program for both types of employees. For that reason, we here cover the legal basis of the Atomic Energy Commission's security program as it affects both its own personnel and those of its defense contractors.

Civilian Employees of the Commission

1. The security program of the Commission as it applies to its own personnel is based upon the provisions of the Atomic Energy Act of 1954 (42 U. S. C. 2011 et seq.). (*a*) Section 2165 thereof provides:

(*b*) Except as authorized by the Commission or the General Manager upon a determination by the Commission or General Manager that such action is clearly consistent with the national interest, no individual shall be employed by the Commission nor shall the Commission permit any individual to have access to restricted data until the Civil Service Commission shall have made an investigation and report to the Commission on the character, associations, and loyalty of such individual, and the Commission shall have determined that permitting such person to have access to restricted data will not endanger the common defense and security.

(*b*) Section 2190 thereof provides:

In the performance of its functions the Commission is authorized to—
(*d*) . . . The Commission shall make adequate provision for administrative review of any determination to dismiss any employee;

2. While these sections of the statute constitute an express statutory authorization to the Commission to establish a personnel security program for its own employees, reference should be made to the chapter on the federal civilian loyalty-security program for a discussion of the fact that the head of any department or agency has plenary control over the appointment and removal of his own employees, subject to statutory restrictions. Section 2165 (b) and section 2190 (d) of the Atomic Energy Act of 1954 constitute such a statutory restriction or limitation upon the Atomic Energy Commission, as well as an authorization to it.

3. Consideration must also be given to the relationship between the Atomic Energy Commission's personnel security program based upon section 2165 (b) and section 2190 (d), and the program authorized and provided for by Public Law 733 and Executive Order 10450, which apply to all Government agencies. In view of the fact that the Commission had been authorized by the Atomic Energy Act of 1946 to establish a personnel security program for

its own personnel, Public Law 733 of 1950 provided in section 2 thereof that—

Nothing herein contained shall impair the powers vested in the Atomic Energy Commission by the Atomic Energy Act of 1946 or the requirements of section 12 of that act that adequate provision be made for administrative review of any determination to dismiss any employee of said Commission.

Executive Order 10450 also recognized the existence of personnel security programs based upon statutory authorization other than Public Law 733, for section 10 of the Executive order provided that—

Nothing in this order shall be construed as eliminating or modifying in any way the requirement for any investigation or any determination as to security which may be required by law.

Shortly after the issuance of the Executive order, therefore, the Commission and the Department of Justice agreed that no change in the Commission's personnel security program would be required, particularly as the Commission was meeting at least the minimum standards specified by the President and the Department of Justice in the sample regulations of the Department of Justice.[52]

4. For the reasons set forth in the chapter on the Federal civilian loyalty-security program, there is no doubt but that section 2011 (b) and section 2190 (d) of the Atomic Energy Act of 1954 is a proper exercise of Congress' constitutional powers in this field.

Contractor Employees

1. The industrial security program of the Atomic Energy Commission is based upon the provisions of the Atomic Energy Act of 1954 (42 U. S. C. 2011 et seq.). Section 2165 thereof provides:

(a) No arrangement shall be made under section 2051 of this title, no contract shall be made or continued in effect under section 2061 of this title, and no license shall be issued under sections 2133 or 2134 of this title, unless the person with whom such arrangement is made, the contractor or prospective contractor, or the prospective licensee agrees in writing not to permit any individual to have access to restricted data until the Civil Service Commission shall have made an investigation and report to the Commission on the character, associations, and loyalty of such individual, and the Commission shall have determined that permitting such person to have access to restricted data will not endanger the common defense and security.

2. This section of the statute constitutes an express authorization to the Atomic Energy Commission for the establishment of an industrial security program.

3. There is, therefore, no question but that there is adequate statutory authority for the industrial security program of the Atomic Energy Commission.

---

[52] Atomic Energy Commission's answer to Commission on Government Security dated Aug. 9, 1956.

4. As is set forth in some detail in the discussion of the legal basis of the industrial security program of the Department of Defense, appearing below, Congress has the constitutional authority to enact legislation expressly providing for the exclusion or removal of private employees of Government contractors from jobs in which they have access to classified information or material, if the Government determines that such exclusion or removal is necessary in the national interest. It is clear that section 2165 (a) of the Atomic Energy Act of 1954 is a valid exercise by Congress of its constitutional authority to authorize an industrial security program.

PRESENT PROGRAM

The Atomic Energy Commission (AEC) was established by the Atomic Energy Act of 1946, which act was amended in 1952. The present atomic energy security program is governed by the Atomic Energy Act of 1954, which supersedes the act of 1946 as amended, and which provides that the commissioners may issue such rules and regulations as may be necessary to implement the Act.

Personnel Security

The procedures hereinafter outlined apply to employees (including consultants) of, and applicants for employment with, AEC, and its contractors, agents, access permittees and licensees and other persons designated by the General Manager of AEC.

A security clearance is based upon an investigation by the Civil Service Commission or the FBI, the extent of which is governed by the importance of the restricted data involved. The FBI handles all highly sensitive cases, and takes over all investigations in which derogatory information is uncovered by CSC or obtained by AEC. When clearance is granted access is permitted to that restricted data, materials, or areas which may be reasonably anticipated as being necessary in the performance of duties involved in the employment specified in the request for clearance.

Clearances are of two varieties: "L" clearance for confidential access, and for workmen who are employed in sight of secret structures and equipment; and "Q" clearance for secret and top secret access. "Q" clearance is required for all AEC employees and consultants, for employees of contractors and licensees in need of secret or top secret access, and for others in sensitive positions such as various hearing examiners, counsel, union representatives, and congressional investigators.

The decision as to security clearance is a comprehensive, commonsense judgment, made after consideration of all the relevant information, favorable or unfavorable, as to whether or not the granting of security clearance would endanger the common defense and security. Taken into account is the value of the individual's services and the operational consequences of denial of clearance. If it is determined that the common defense or security will not be endangered, security clearance will be granted; otherwise, security clearance will be denied.

Clearances for employees of a contractor are initiated by the submission of personnel security questionnaires and fingerprint cards by the contractor to the AEC Manager of Operations assigned responsibility for the administration of the contract. The AEC Operations Office determines whether an "L" or "Q" clearance is necessary, then, after screening for completeness, they are forwarded to the Civil Service Commission or the FBI for investigation. Upon receipt of completed investigations, the Operations Office screens the reports and, if no derogatory information has been developed, clearance is authorized. If derogatory information of a nonsubstantive nature (not falling within AEC's criteria for determining clearance eligibility) has been uncovered, the case moves to an analyst who reviews the file and recommends clearance on the record, or that the individual be informally interviewed. In either case, a second analyst or the chief of the local security division reviews the file and authorizes the clearance or the interview, and clearance after the interview.

The procedure in the case of AEC employees is similar, except that a contractor is not involved and a "Q" clearance in all cases is required.

Derogatory information of a substantive nature is divided into category A, for the more serious, and category B for the less serious information involving the individual or his spouse. Category A includes seditious acts, sabotage, espionage, association with objectionable foreign agents, membership in subversive organizations, significant falsification of personal history, willful security violations, mental illness, criminal tendencies, and drug addiction. Unless an individual can successfully rebut category A information, denial of clearance will follow.

Category B information is evaluated in light of time of occurrence, extent of activity, and present attitude of the individual. B items include advocating subversive political ideologies, associating with persons so advocating, affiliation with objectionable organizations or association with members of such organizations, presence of close relatives in Iron Curtain countries, rejection for military service, carelessness with classified information, immoral or disgraceful conduct, perversion, alcoholism, or refusing to testify regarding loyalty or misconduct.

These criteria are not exhaustive and AEC is not limited thereto. The criteria are subject to review and revision by AEC.

Upon receipt of a "hold" case, indicating adverse information, the AEC Division of Security may request additional investigation, may authorize the Manager of Operations [53] to grant clearance on the record, may recommend that the Manager of Operations conduct an informal interview in an effort to obtain satisfactory explanations of the adverse information, or may authorize an administrative review of the evidence.

Hearings

At present, anyone who is denied clearance because of adverse information may request a hearing. This privilege formerly was limited to current employees only and not to applicants. The individual is notified as to the substance of the derogatory information, together with his clearance status pending final determination, and if he does not respond within 20 days and request a hearing, his case will be decided upon the basis of the existing record.

If a hearing is requested, the Manager of Operations appoints a local hearing board and the individual is advised as to his right to challenge for cause, to be represented by counsel and to present witnesses. The board consists of 3 members and, if practical, 1 is an attorney and 1 is familiar with the individual's general field of work. The board members may include employees of AEC or the contractor, but an employee of the contractor may not hear a case involving another employee of the same contractor. As a matter of practice, the contractors do not furnish hearing board members. They feel that clearance is a matter between the Government and the individual, and that the contractor should not take part. The members are usually outstanding citizens of the community, and they must have "Q" clearances.

The Manager also appoints an attorney to serve as counsel to the board. He must have a "Q" clearance and may be an AEC employee or be specifically retained. It is his duty to advise the board concerning procedures and to advise the individual of his rights, but he may not participate in deliberations of the board or express opinions concerning the merits of the case. He must not assume the role of a prosecutor.

Legal procedure at the hearing does not follow trial court practices, and the utmost latitude is permitted with respect to relevancy, materiality, and competency. However, every effort is made to obtain the best evidence available. Hearsay evidence is accorded such weight as the circumstances warrant. The proceedings are not open to the public, and it is the duty of the chairman to guard against disclosure of restricted data to unauthorized persons.

---

[53] The country is divided into 10 districts, each headed by a Manager or Manager of Operations. The entire program is headed by the General Manager under the supervision of the Atomic Energy Commission.

Much consideration has been given to the question of confrontation of witnesses, but it has always been resolved in favor of protecting sources of information. If a hearing board decides that the presence of a witness is important, arrangements are made, if possible, for him to appear and be subject to examination and cross-examination. If he is unavailable, the reasons therefore are taken into consideration. If confrontation is not possible, the board may request that the witness appear privately for examination by the board.

Subpena power is exercised under the provisions of the AEC Act of 1954, section 161, which states that "the Commission is authorized to administer oaths and affirmations, and by subpena to require any person to appear and testify." Witness fees are the same as those paid by Federal courts. The board may request the Manager to arrange for additional investigation on any points which are material to the deliberations of the board and which the board believes need extension or clarification.

The recommendations of the board together with the dissent, if any, and the case record are forwarded to the Manager of Operations, who sends them with his recommendations to the General Manager. If the Manager of Operations recommends denial of clearance, the individual is notified and may request a review of his case by the AEC Personnel Security Review Board. The General Manager may refer a case to the Review Board, in which event the individual is also notified. In either case, the individual may submit a brief to the Review Board for consideration. After receipt of recommendations from the Review Board, the General Manager makes his final decision as to granting of clearance.

The General Manager may permit any individual to be employed by the AEC or have access to restricted data prior to completion of clearance procedure, but only under the most exceptional circumstances clearly consistent with the national interest. In cases where information is received which raises a question concerning continued eligibility, the Manager forwards to the General Manager his recommendation as to whether clearance should be suspended pending final determination. About 12 interim clearances have been granted since 1946.

Clearance for temporary employees of contractors is not handled differently from other cases at this time, although a study of such clearances is being considered. Ordinarily, an individual must be employed by the contractor before clearance is granted; but AEC has a preemployment clearance procedure applicable to certain technicians, scientists, and college seniors who are prospective employees.

Aliens may be cleared on the basis of calculated risk, but only if they have unique talents not possessed by an available United States citizen, and if the position involved is essential to the AEC program. As of December 1956, a total of five aliens had been so cleared.

In the event of marriage on the part of an employee or applicant, specified information must be forwarded to the appropriate investigative office for local agency check or for such investigation as may be warranted.

Requests for access by members of the Armed Forces and associated personnel are submitted by means of a prescribed AEC form, showing access needed, date of access, etc. The individual's military clearance must at least equal the classification of the material requested, in which case a separate AEC clearance is not necessary. Continuing access also may be arranged.

AEC regulations provide for clearance of NLRB trial examiners, Federal Mediation and Conciliation Service commissioners, various counsel, staff members of congressional committees, hearing board members, and certain union representatives. Union officials not requiring access, but who exercise authority over employees, may be checked upon request of the Manager of Operations. Congressmen may be granted access without investigation, but if derogatory information is brought to the attention of AEC, it is taken into consideration in connection with the proposed access. On one occasion a Congressman was denied access.

All AEC employees plus other selected individuals are reinvestigated every 5 years. Selections are made on the basis of personnel security questionnaires and other information within the knowledge of the Manager.

There also are regulations covering reaffirmation or extension of clearance, transfer of clearance, reinstatement of clearance, and termination of clearance. Each employee, upon termination, is interviewed and advised of his continuing responsibility. A security termination statement and a certificate of nonpossession, if required, is obtained. If the terminee is located at a remote installation, the security termination may be effected by correspondence.

In the employment of Government personnel, AEC is bound by civil service laws except that, to the extent the Commission deems such action necessary to the discharge of its responsibilities, personnel may be employed without regard to such laws. AEC has exercised the above exception and appoints officers and employees without regard to the civil service laws. The AEC manual requires that the character, associations, and loyalty of Government workers be of high order, with a standard of self-discipline and conduct both on and off the job.

Although AEC appoints and dismisses employees without regard to the civil service laws, AEC is bound by the Veterans' Preference Act of 1944. In the appointment of employees, the Veterans' Preference Act is administered by AEC. In the dismissal of employees, AEC is bound by civil service rules and regulations made pursuant to that act.

The foregoing discussion of personnel security is based on: "General Authority of Commission," 42 U. S. C. A. 2201; section 161, 68 Stat. 948; section 4, regulations of the AEC; and the AEC Manual, chapters 2301–2305, 2309–2318, and 4124.

Implementation of Regulations

The General Manager of AEC has issued security regulations in the General Manager's Manual, and the 10 AEC field operations offices issued implementing manuals to apply security in their areas of jurisdiction. Naturally they contain individual interpretations. It is important to note that one set of AEC security regulations covers contractors, AEC employees, all contractor employees, and consultants to AEC or contractors. Thus, any access to classified material is granted in accordance with one set of rules.

The staffing for the total AEC security program is very simple and consists of only two levels of operation. The security director is at Washington, and security directors are attached to each of the 10 field operations offices. In a few cases, area offices operate within geographical areas under the 10 operations offices. This simple organization permits rapid transmittal of problems to the Operations Offices Manager, or to the security director and the AEC General Manager at Washington. A very high percentage of personnel clearances is accomplished in the field. Complicated cases are the only ones transmitted for review by the security director at Washington. It is most significant that a request for investigation proceeds directly from the Operations Office to the office of the investigative agency at Washington (FBI or CSC). Each case is returned by the investigative agency to AEC at Washington, where within 24 hours it is checked off a status list and mailed to the point of origin (via the Operations Office if the point of origin was an area office). There it is evaluated and the final decision taken in most cases.

Control of Documents and Information

AEC uses the same levels of classification: confidential, secret, and top secret, which are employed in many other Government agencies. However, documents classified as "top secret" are relatively very few in number and are, of course, subject to special controls. AEC has prepared a classification guide which is available to all employees having authority to classify data. The guide is regarded by AEC as a document containing enough detail to enable proper classification decisions to be made.

During the first half of 1955 the AEC moved toward greater participation by industry in advancing the development of competitive nuclear power. A Division of Licensing was established and procedures were set up for this purpose. To obtain confidential information, the industry must show a potential use or application of the information and obtain necessary "L" clearances. For secret information, the applicant must prove an immediate or signficant effect on his business, trade, or profession, and obtain required "Q" clearances. Applicants must also agree to pay all charges for clearance, publication, reproduction, and other services furnished by AEC. Information concerning defense-sensitive matters will not be made available.

The Commission puts its basic classification policy into effect through the "Declassification Guide for Responsible Reviewers," prepared by the Division of Classification. The present rules, since April 1955, have applied to the review of information currently arising in the atomic energy program, as well as earlier information found in classified papers and reports in files throughout the atomic energy projects.

In the normal procedure, a report proposed for declassification is reviewed as to security and content by the coordinating organization director at the particular site. It then goes to a responsible reviewer, a scientist foremost in the particular field, who reviews it in light of the declassification guide and determines its appropriate classification. Finally, the report is reviewed by the Declassification Branch of the Division of Classification and, if the other reviews have indicated that such action is warranted, it is downgraded from secret to confidential, or is declassified and made available for distribution.

International declassification conferences are held by the United States, United Kingdom, and Canada for agreement on the categories of technical information to be released.

In order to accelerate declassification, a task force of some 40 persons was assembled at Oak Ridge, Tenn., in the fall of 1955 for declassification on a crash basis. With the assistance of contractor personnel, 31,000 documents were reviewed, of which 11,000 were declassified and 8,500 were downgraded to confidential. Originators of the material were notified of action taken and were asked to make the necessary corrections or to destroy copies. Out of that experience came the estimate that one qualified person can examine and dispose of one drawer of classified material in a day. Because of the success of the original task force, another was called to meet in January 1957 to carry out the same type of assignment.

In the top-secret category, AEC to date has been able to dispose of about 200,000 documents by destruction, declassification, or consolidation. It is estimated that 2,000 top-secret documents are being created each month (including all carbon copies), and that there are approximately 58,000 top-secret documents as a continuing total on hand.[54]

By agreement between the Department of Defense and AEC, the Department of Defense and its contractors are afforded access to AEC restricted data on the basis of military security clearances. The agreement also provides that the Department of Defense and its agencies shall be responsible for safeguarding restricted data made available by AEC.[55]

AEC recognizes the existence of information which does not affect the national defense but which is of a privileged nature and should receive only

---

[54] Capt. John A. Waters, Director, AEC Security Division, Jan. 2, 1957.
[55] AEC 12th semiannual report, p. 44.

such limited dissemination as is customary under standard industrial, professional, academic, and governmental practices.[56]

Physical Security

Operation of the AEC security system, with respect to a contractor, begins with the negotiation or letting of a contract for classified work. In the case of a negotiated contract, the premises to be used by the contractor are surveyed, before work commences, by a representative of the Manager of Operations. The purpose of this survey is to determine the adequacy of existing security measures in terms of AEC standards or to identify those measures which must be taken before facility approval for classified work can be granted. Following the initial security survey and approval, the plant is reinspected at regular intervals to ensure the maintenance of security safeguards.

Copies of all survey reports are transmitted to the Division of Security, Headquarters, where they are reviewed for adequacy. A master facility index is maintained by the Division of Security, headquarters, in which is recorded notice of facility approval, nature of work, ratings of periodic surveys, and other pertinent data.

On the initial contact with the facility, usually at the time of the initial survey, the contractor is briefed on the pertinent AEC regulations and provided with copies for his guidance. These include:

1. Physical Security Standards—(AEC Manual, ch. 3401).
2. Security of Matter in Transit—(AEC Manual, ch. 2402).
3. Control of Classified Information—(AEC Manual, ch. 2101).
4. Communications Security—(AEC Manual, ch. 2102).
5. Non-Defense Information—(AEC Manual, ch. 2104).
6. Procedures for Safeguarding Classified Documents and Other Classified Information—(Bulletin GM–SEC–5).
7. Security Education—(AEC Manual, ch. 2201).
8. Administration Handling of Violations and Related Matters— (AEC Manual, ch. 2601).

Additional instructions covering specific security problems or procedures are furnished the contractor when required.

AEC standards provide minimum requirements for safeguarding facilities, documents, and materials in accordance with their importance or classification. They prescribe, in detail, how classified documents must be marked, stored, transmitted and accounted for, reproduced, and destroyed. Physical safeguards such as fences, alarm devices, safes, vaults, lighting, and the use of guards and identification media for access control are covered as minimum requirements for various circumstances. The methods by which classified

---

[56] AEC manual, ch. 2104.

212

equipment and materials must be protected during transportation are also prescribed.

Each contract for classified work contains specific security provisions. Under the terms of the contract the contractor is obligated to comply with the provisions of the Atomic Energy Act and with the security regulations of the AEC.

Upon the completion of work under his contract, a determination is made that all classified matter has been removed from his premises or otherwise disposed of and there is no further security interest involved. The reestablishment of a security facility requires the same procedure as previously described.

Contractors' facilities are inspected by such Washington security representatives as may be required to ascertain the effectiveness of the Operations Office's inspection or appraisal programs.[57]

Security Education and Training

Each new employee who is to have access is given a security indoctrination lecture in which his specific security responsibilities are made known to him, and he is kept currently informed as to changes in regulations and procedures. Periodic lectures are given at intervals not to exceed 1 year, and more often if advantageous or if the nature of the work requires. Visual aid media is also recommended.

Security officials of AEC undergo on-the-job training whereby for the first 2 or 3 years they are periodically shifted to various positions concerning physical security, evaluation and clearance of personnel, relationships with contractors, training programs for contractors' employees, and classification subjects. Thus the official may eventually become qualified for the position of director of security for an area office or operations office.

During the operation of a classified contract, the contractor is required to establish and maintain a program of education designed to keep all employees continually reminded of their personal security responsibilities.[58]

Labor Relations

AEC retains absolute and final authority over all matters of security at Government-owned, contractor-operated installations. Security rules and their administration are not matters for collective bargaining, but AEC will consult with management and labor in formulating regulations that affect the collective bargaining process.[59]

---

[57] Operation of the AEC physical security program, Aug. 3, 1956.
[58] AEC Manual, ch. 2201.
[59] AEC Manual, ch. 2309.

Communist-dominated unions or unions whose officers have Communist affiliations may not represent atomic energy workers.[60]

AEC approves the principle of NLRB proceedings at atomic energy projects, but has requested that NLRB clear each case securitywise with local AEC representatives. The Commission prefers that NLRB cases be conducted in the normal, open fashion with special arrangements for security when necessary.[61]

RECOMMENDATIONS

NECESSITY

The necessity for an atomic energy security program has never been questioned. Because of the devastating power of the atom bomb and other possible destructive uses of nuclear fission, a security program will be necessary until there is complete international agreement on control and development of atomic energy.

STANDARD AND CRITERIA

The current AEC security program includes a standard and criteria applicable alike to Government and industrial employees. The Commission on Government Security believes that different standards and criteria should apply to (1) loyalty of government employees, (2) suitability of government employees, and (3) security of industrial employees.

The Atomic Energy Act should be amended to make the following standard and criteria applicable to employees of, and applicants for employment with, the Atomic Energy Commission:

1. The standard for denial of employment or the removal from employment shall be that, on all the information, there is reasonable doubt as to the loyalty of the individual to the Government of the United States.

2. Activities and associations of an applicant or employee which may be considered in connection with the determination of the existence of a reasonable doubt as to his loyalty may include one or more of the following:

---

[60] AEC Policy with regard to allegedly Communist-dominated unions, Aug. 9, 1965.
[61] AEC Manual, ch. 2309.

(*a*) Sabotage, espionage, or attempts or preparations therefor, or knowingly associating with spies or saboteurs;

(*b*) Treason or sedition or advocacy thereof;

(*c*) Advocacy of revolution or force or violence to alter the constitutional form of Government of the United States;

(*d*) Intentional, unauthorized disclosure to any person, under circumstances which may indicate disloyalty to the United States, of documents or information of a confidential or nonpublic character;

(*e*) Performing or attempting to perform his duties, or otherwise acting, so as to serve the interests of another government in preference to the interests of the United States;

(*f*) Membership in, affiliation or sympathetic association with any party, group, or association which the Congress of the United States, or any agency or officer of the United States duly authorized by the Congress for that purpose finds:

(1) Seeks to alter the form of Government of the United States by force or violence, or other unconstitutional means; or

(2) Is organized or utilized for the purpose of advancing the aims and objectives of the Communist movement; or

(3) Is organized or utilized for the purpose of establishing any form of dictatorship in the United States or any form of international dictatorship; or

(4) Is organized or utilized by any foreign government, or by any foreign party, group or association acting in the interest of such foreign government for the purpose of (a) espionage, (b) sabotage, or (c) obtaining information relating to the defense of the United States or the protection of the national security, or (d) hampering, hindering, or delaying the production of defense materials; or

(5) Is affiliated with, or acts in concert with, or is dominated or controlled by, any party, group, or association of the character described in (1) or (2) or (3) or (4) above.

(*g*) Membership in or affiliation with any organization which the Congress of the United States, or any agency or officer of the United States duly authorized by the Congress for that purpose, finds has adopted a policy of advocating or approving the commission of acts of force and violence to deny others their rights under the Constitution of the United States.

(*h*) Refusal to testify upon the ground of self-incrimination, in any authorized inquiry relating to subversive activities conducted by a congressional committee, Federal court, Federal grand jury, or any other duly authorized Federal agency, as to questions relating to subversive activities of the individual involved or others, unless the individual, after opportunity to do so, satisfactorily explains his refusal to testify.

(*i*) The foregoing enumeration shall not be deemed to exclude any other factors tending to establish reasonable doubt as to loyalty.

3. The following are recommended as suitability criteria for AEC employees and applicants:

(*a*) Any physical or mental unfitness for the position for which applied, including any physical or mental unfitness of a nature which in the opinion of competent medical authority may cause significant defect in the judgment or reliability of the employee with due regard to the transient or continuing effect of the illness and the medical findings in such case.

(*b*) Any criminal, infamous, dishonest, immoral, or notoriously disgraceful conduct, habitual use of intoxicants to excess, drug addiction, or sexual perversion.

(*c*) Any deliberate misrepresentations, falsifications, or omissions of material facts.

(*d*) Any behavior, activities, or associations which tend to show that the individual is not reliable or trustworthy.

(*e*) Any facts, other than those tending to establish reasonable doubt as to loyalty, which furnish reason to believe that the individual may be subjected to coercion, influence, or pressure which may cause him to act contrary to the best interests of national security.

(*f*) Recurrent and serious, although unintentional, disclosure to any person of documents or information of a confidential or nonpublic character.

(*g*) Refusal to testify upon the ground of self-incrimination in any authorized inquiry conducted by a congressional committee, Federal court, Federal grand jury, or any other duly authorized agency, unless the individual, after opportunity to do so, satisfactorily explains his refusal to testify.

(*h*) Dismissal from employment for delinquency or misconduct.

(*i*) Any legal or other disqualification which makes the applicant unfit for service.

4. In all cases where there is no charge as to the employee's loyalty, the suitability criteria and procedures must be used wherever possible to effect the subject employee's removal, if desired.

(*a*) In those situations in which the Chairman of the Atomic Energy Commission believes the national security can be adequately protected by transferring the employee to another position for which he is qualified and suitable, every effort shall be made to effect such transfer.

The Atomic Energy Act should be amended to make the following standard and criteria applicable to the industrial security program conducted by the Atomic Energy Commission:

1. Clearance shall be denied or revoked if it is determined, on the basis of all the available information, that access to classified information and materials will endanger the common defense and security.

2. Factors which may be considered in connection with the application of the foregoing standard shall include but not be limited to:

(*a*) Sabotage, espionage, or attempts or preparations therefor or knowing association with spies or saboteurs;

(*b*) Treason or sedition or advocacy therefor;

(*c*) Advocacy of revolution or force or violence to alter the constitutional form of Government of the United States;

(*d*) Intentional, unauthorized disclosure to any person of classified information or materials, or recurrent and serious, although unintentional, disclosure of such information and materials;

(*e*) Performing or attempting to perform his duties, or otherwise acting, so as to serve the interests of another government in preference to the interests of the United States;

(*f*) Membership in, affiliation or sympathetic association with any party, group, or association which the Congress of the United States, or any agency or officer of the United States duly authorized by the Congress for that purpose, finds:

(1) Seeks to alter the form of the Government of the United States by force or violence, or other unconstitutional means; or

(2) Is organized or utilized for the purpose of advancing the aims and objectives of the Communist movement; or

217

(3) Is organized or utilized for the purpose of establishing any form of dictatorship in the United States or any form of international dictatorship; or

(4) Is organized or utilized by any foreign government, or by any foreign party, group, or association acting in the interest of such foreign government for the purpose of (a) espionage, or (b) sabotage, or (c) obtaining information relating to the defense of the United States or the protection of the national security, or (d) hampering, hindering, or delaying the production of defense materials; or

(5) Is affiliated with, or acts in concert with, or is dominated or controlled by, any party, group, or association of the character described in (1) or (2) or (3) or (4) above.

(g) Membership in or affiliation with any organization which the Congress of the United States, or any agency or officer of the United States duly authorized by the Congress for that purpose, finds has adopted a policy of advocating or approving the commission of acts of force and violence to deny others their rights under the Constitution of the United States.

(h) Refusal to testify upon the grounds of self-incrimination in any authorized inquiry conducted by a congressional committee, Federal court, Federal grand jury, or any other duly authorized agency unless the individual, after opportunity to do so, satisfactorily explains his refusal to testify;

(i) Willful violations or disregard of security regulations, or recurrent and serious, although unintentional, violation of such regulations;

(j) Any illness, including any mental condition, of a nature which in the opinion of competent medical authority may cause sigificant defect in the performance, judgment, or reliability of the employee with due regard to the transient or continued effect of the illness and the medical findings in such case;

(k) Any behavior, activities, or associations which tend to show that the individual is not reliable or trustworthy;

(l) Any deliberate misrepresentations, falsifications, or omission of material facts in relation to security questionnaire, personal history statement, or similar document;

(m) Any criminal, infamous, dishonest, immoral, or notoriously disgraceful conduct, habitual use of intoxicants to excess, drug addiction, or sexual perversion;

(n) Any facts which furnish reason to believe that the individual may be subjected to coercion, influence, or pressure which may cause him to act contrary to the best interests of the national security.

Among security standards considered were (1) Reasonable grounds for belief of disloyalty, (2) reasonable doubt as to the loyalty, (3) will not endanger the common defense and security, (4) will not be inimical to the security of the United States, (5) clearly consistent with the interest of national security, (6) necessary or advisable in the interests of the national security, (7) efficiency of the service, and (8) is advisable in the interest of the United States. Each of these standards has appeared in recent years in either an act of Congress or in the regulations of a Government agency or department. It will be noted that, with the exception of No. (8), each embodies 1 of 3 principles: loyalty, security, and suitability; while No. (8) could include all 3. There is a tendency on the part of the public to group all three so far as denial of clearance is concerned, and to consider denial of clearance as a reflection upon the individual's loyalty. For this reason, both standards and criteria pertaining to loyalty should be clearly separated from standards and criteria pertaining to security and suitability. If a person is denied a Government position for reasons of suitability, no one should be given reason to believe that his loyalty has been questioned. This can best be brought about if loyalty is considered separately from all other factors. In the case of an industrial employee, the Government should be concerned with his loyalty and security only, and the determination as to his suitablity should be left entirely to his employer, the contractor.

For consideration of an AEC Government employee's loyalty, the Commission on Government Security has recommended the standard: "reasonable doubt as to the loyalty" as the standard most easily subject to a uniform interpretation and most clearly consistent with the needs of AEC. The phrase "reasonable doubt" is well known in legal and judicial circles and has been universally defined as a doubt which is not a fanciful or capricious doubt, but is the doubt which exists in the mind of a reasonable man after full consideration of the evidence presented.

The present AEC standard of "Will not endanger the common defense and security," while suitable for application to industrial employees who may be retained in the contractor's employ even though clearance is denied, is not suitable for application to present or prospective Government employees because it does not separate loyalty and security factors.

The recommended criteria under the loyalty standard are clearly consistent with concepts of loyalty, while the recommended suitability criteria will embrace any other derogatory information involving suitability or security.

219

Thus, if the employment of an individual is objectionable for reasons other than loyalty, he could be and should be denied clearance on grounds of suitability.

The current standard: "Will not endanger the common defense and security," appears in section 145b, Atomic Energy Act of 1954.[62]

The current criteria of derogatory information are found in Atomic Energy Commission regulations, section 4.11, promulgated under general authority of section 161 of the Atomic Energy Act of 1954. While an amendment to the act would not be necessary in order to effect a change in regulations, the Commission on Government Security believes that an amendment to the act would be more effective and, therefore, recommends new legislation, a draft of which appears on page 693.

INVESTIGATIONS

Under the current AEC program, personnel security investigations are conducted by the Civil Service Commission; however, applicants for positions which are declared "sensitive," including all AEC Government positions, are investigated by the FBI. If derogatory subversive information is developed by the Civil Service Commission, the investigation is completed by the FBI.

It is recommended that the Atomic Energy Act be amended to require all Atomic Energy Commission employee investigations to be conducted by the Civil Service Commission. The scope of investigation for Atomic Energy Commission employees should be the same as for employees of other Government agencies, and the scope of investigation for clearance in the Atomic Energy Commission industrial security program should be the same as that required for clearance in the industrial security program of the Department of Defense and other governmental agencies.

1. The foregoing would mean that as to personnel employed by the Atomic Energy Commission there would be a national agency check for nonsensitive positions and a full field (background) investigation by CSC for sensitive positions. As to the Atomic Energy Commission industrial security program, there would be a national agency check for clearance to

---

[62] It also appears in sec. 141 under the caption of "Policy" as follows: "It shall be the policy of the Commission to control the dissemination and declassification of restricted data in such a manner as to assure the common defense and security."

"atomic secret" and a full field (background) investigation by CSC for clearance to "atomic top secret."

It is the purpose of these and subsequent recommendations to bring the Atomic Energy Commission personnel program into line with the programs for employees of other Government agencies, and the AEC industrial program into line with the industrial security program of the Department of Defense and other governmental agencies. With types of clearances and scope of investigations placed on a parallel with other agencies, the door will be open for interchange of clearances. The recommendation for, and advantages of, transfer of clearance appear in the next chapter of this report and will not be repeated here, except to say that one of the most frequently heard objections to the Government system of clearances has been that of delay. Any system which eliminates repetition of investigations will, of course, speed up the process. Another frequent objection has been duplication of clearances with the resultant annoyances occasioned thereby. Along with delay and duplication go loss of personnel, loss of time, loss of efficiency, loss of morale, and loss of respect for government operations. The advantages of uniformity are obvious.

In the beginning the development of atomic energy was, of necessity, under the jurisdiction of a supersecret organization (Manhattan Engineering District) whose existence was known to a very limited few. Because of the necessity for conducting secret operations, AEC has been permitted to function under an act of Congress as an independent unit not subject to many of the rules, regulations, and procedures followed by other Government agencies. While the Civil Service Commission conducts routine security investigations for nearly all Government agencies and departments, AEC has decreed that each and every employee and consultant of AEC holds a "sensitive" position calling for a full field investigation by the FBI. In the opinion of the Commission on Government Security, the interests of the Government could best be served by permitting the Civil Service Commission to conduct all routine AEC security investigations, until and unless derogatory subversive information is developed, at which point the case could be completed by the FBI. The Civil Service Commission maintains the central index file, and is now well staffed with investigators who are adequately trained in conducting routine personnel investigations. CSC investigations are conducted at less cost and they release FBI agents for attention to other duties. While many of the functions of AEC are quite properly highly classified, it should no longer be considered as highly sensitive in all of its routine operations. On the other hand, AEC should now be placed on a par with other Government agencies in many aspects of its operations for purposes of uniformity and economy.

Although full field investigations for all AEC employees undoubtedly assure a higher degree of security, the Commission on Government Security

221

is of the opinion that such a complete coverage is unnecessarily expensive and time consuming. There should be a realistic division of AEC positions into sensitive and nonsensitive categories, with a clearance via a national agency check for the relatively nonsensitive positions.

AEC has certified all AEC positions as sensitive under authority of section 145e, Atomic Energy Act of 1954, which provides that AEC "shall certify those specific positions which are of a high degree of importance or sensitivity and upon such certification the investigation and reports required by such provisions shall be made by the Federal Bureau of Investigation instead of by the Civil Service Commission." Although the foregoing recommendation for investigations by CSC could possibly be implemented through a change in AEC policy whereunder AEC positions are not certified as sensitive, the Commission on Government Security is in favor of an amendment to the act, a draft of which appears on page 693. No change is recommended in section 145c which provides that in event information is developed which indicates questionable loyalty, the case shall be referred to the FBI; nor is any change recommended in section 145d which provides that in the national interest the President may from time to time cause investigations to be made by the FBI of any group or class.

Types of Clearance

It is recommended that the "L" (confidential) and "Q" (secret and top secret) clearances be abolished and that the AEC clearances be brought into line with the clearances for the rest of the Government by having two categories: "atomic secret" and "atomic top secret." The standards and investigation should be equivalent to those applicable to "secret" and "top secret" in the other agencies of the Government.

The Atomic Energy Commission could point to no significant advantage in retaining the "Q" label on clearances, and none is known to the Commission on Government Security. AEC pointed out that this nomenclature was established at a time when there was no well-organized security program in the Government, and the supposition was advanced that the "Q" and "L" labels were used to emphasize the AEC security problem. This particular "Q" label did serve to indicate that close scrutiny had been given the clearance procedure.

The "Q" and "L" types of clearance are provided for in the AEC Manual, chapters 2302–2304. They should be abolished by a change in regulations.

A. The evaluation of derogatory information relating to loyalty should be conducted by such officer as the Chairman of the Atomic Energy Commission shall designate for that purpose.

B. Such officer should perform the screening function and grant the individual involved an opportunity for an interview, at which he may offer his explanation of the derogatory information, prior to the issuance of a letter of charges. In the case of both applicants and employees, after the screening officer has reviewed the charges, there shall be placed in the individual's file the reasons for the decision to deny the application for employment or dismiss the employee, as the case may be.

C. The letter of charges shall be as specific and detailed as the interests of national security shall permit and shall include pertinent information such as names, dates, and places, in such detail as to permit reasonable answer thereto.

D. Prior to the issuance of a letter of charges, the security officer shall consult the legal officer as to—

(*a*) Whether the case is founded on loyalty or suitability criteria; and

(*b*) Whether the required specificity of the letter of charges and other procedural requirements have been satisfied.

E. The letter of charges shall contain a statement that a sworn answer thereto must be filed within a reasonable time. The Director of the Central Security Office shall by regulation prescribe such time.

F. The letter of charges shall also inform the individual involved of his right to a hearing.

G. The hearing shall be confined to the matters contained in the letter of charges. If, after the issuance of the letter of charges, the Government wishes to amend the letter of charges to add additional or different charges, the individual involved shall be allowed a reasonabe time in which to file his amended answer thereto.

H. The initial hearing on the letter of charges should be conducted by a hearing examiner rather than by a hearing board.

I. The hearing examiner should be under an independent central office in the executive branch.

J. The decisions of the hearing examiner should be advisory to the Chairman of the Atomic Energy Commission whose decision shall be final at this level of the clearance proceedings.

K. The hearing examiner should be appointed by the Director of the Central Security Office from an appropriate civil service register created for the purpose.

L. Hearing examiners should be full-time governmental employees with a sufficient number throughout the country to hear cases involving clearance under the port security and industrial security programs, as well as the atomic energy and civilian employee programs.

M. The hearing should not be open to the public.

N. Sufficiently in advance of the hearing to permit study by the hearing examiner, the Atomic Energy Commission should submit to the examiner the complete file on the individual and all pertinent supporting documents, plus a résumé of any administrative action and reasons therefor. At the hearing itself, a representative of the Atomic Energy Commission should be present to answer the questions of the hearing examiner and to assist the hearing examiner in any other appropriate way. He should not act as a prosecutor.

O. The Chairman of the Atomic Energy Commission should be the authority to designate the person or persons to represent the agency at the hearing, and such representative(s) should not participate in the formulation of the hearing examiner's decision. Such representative(s) need not be licensed attorneys.

P. The individual involved should be entitled to counsel of his own choice and the Government should not pay the fees of the individual's counsel.

Q. The hearing examiner should submit a written report to the Director of the Central Security Office for transmittal to the Chairman of the Atomic Energy Commission. Such report should contain the hearing examiner's findings of fact, decision, and reasons for his decision. A copy of the hearing examiner's report and a copy of the hearing should be sent to the individual involved upon receipt of notice of appeal.

R. An adverse decision of the Chairman of the Atomic Energy Commission may be appealed to the central review board of the Central Security Office at the request of the employee within time, and subject to procedures, to be prescribed.

The foregoing recommendations tie in with the Commission's recommendation for a Central Security Office set forth in the civilian employees program. The recommendations otherwise, except for making a distinction between loyalty and suitability qualifications, are substantially in line with current AEC procedures, and follow mainly the American concepts for dealing with controversial questions; such as the right to be informed of charges, the privilege of a hearing, and the right of counsel.

A hearing examiner is preferred over a hearing board because of the greater informality of procedure and ease in getting to the heart of the controversy.

A hearing examiner appointed by a Central Security Office would be capable of greater independence of action and judgment than that possessed by an examiner appointed by the Atomic Energy Commission.

The hearing should not be open to the public as open hearings would tend to discourage the appearance of witnesses and would subject the employee to additional unfavorable publicity which might do unwarranted violence to him and his reputation. The informal atmosphere of private hearings is more conducive to an impartial determination of the facts. Furthermore, open hearings would sometimes be inappropriate because classified information may be introduced.

The decisions of the hearing examiner or the Central Review Board should be advisory only to the Chairman of the AEC, in that the role of the examiner is principally that of a fact finder while the Chairman is in a better position to apply the facts to the standards of his own organization.

Conduct of proceedings is currently governed by AEC regulations, sections 4.15 through 4.18.[63]

CONFRONTATION

A. Confrontation of persons who have supplied derogatory information should be allowed to the maximum extent consistent with the protection of the national security.

B. Confrontation of regularly established confidential informants engaged in obtaining intelligence and internal security information for the Government should not be allowed where the head of the investigative agency determines that the disclosure of the identity of such informants will prejudice the national security. In such cases the report supplied by the investigative agency should contain as much of the information supplied by the informant as may be disclosed without revealing the identity of the informant and without otherwise endangering the national security.

1. If confrontation is not permitted under paragraph B, the hearing examiner should furnish the individual involved with the substance of the information obtained from such informant to the extent that such information is material to the consideration of the issues involved; and should read into the record the substance of such information and the evaluation as to reliability placed upon such confidential informant in the investigative report.

2. If the individual involved questions the accuracy or completeness of the information furnished pursuant to para-

---

[63] C. F. R., title 10, Atomic Energy, ch. 1.

graph 1 above, he may file with the hearing examiner a written statement setting forth in detail so much of the information challenged by him as to accuracy or completeness. If the hearing examiner is of the opinion that the additional investigation as to the specific matters challenged is required in the interests of ascertaining the facts, he should request the investigative agency to make such additional investigation. Information obtained as a result of the additional investigation should be treated in the same manner as provided for in the original investigation.

C. Derogatory information supplied by confidential informants other than those described in paragraph B should not be considered, over the objection of the individual involved, by any hearing examiner in arriving at his determination, or by any officer charged with the responsibility for making a final decision as to retention of an employee or as to clearance, unless such informants consent to the disclosure of their identity so as to enable the individual involved to obtain their testimony through the issuance of subpena or by depositions, orally or on written interrogatories.

1. Derogatory information supplied by identified persons should not be considered, over the objection of the individual involved, by any hearing examiner, in arriving at his determination, or by any officer charged with the responsibility for making a final decision as to the retention of an employee or as to clearance, unless the individual involved is given the opportunity to obtain the testimony of such identified persons through the issuance of a subpena, or by depositions, orally or on written interrogatories; if the individual involved is given the opportunity to obtain the testimony of such identified persons through the issuance of a subpena, or by depositions, orally or on written interrogatories, such derogatory information supplied by identified persons should be considered. Where an identified informant gives a statement on the condition that he will not be called upon to testify or otherwise be subject to subpena, the hearing examiner should have no authority to issue a subpena for, or require depositions from, such individual. If the identified person supplying the derogatory information is unavailable for service of subpena or the taking of his deposition, orally or on written interrogatories because of death, incompetency, or other reason, such derogatory information may be considered by the hearing examiner with due regard for the lack of opportunity for cross-examination. (It is not intended that the foregoing requirements of paragraphs C and C.1 apply to preliminary interviews preceding issuance of letters of charges.)

226

D. Nothing herein contained should be construed so as to require the investigating agency to exclude from its report any information derived from any source, but all information obtained should continue to be included in the report to be submitted to the appropriate agency.

E. Confrontation should be limited to evidence offered in support of any of the following charges:

1. Sabotage, espionage, or attempts or preparations therefor, or knowingly associating with spies or saboteurs;

2. Treason or sedition or advocacy thereof;

3. Advocacy of revolution or force or violence to alter the constitutional form of government of the United States;

4. Intentional, unauthorized disclosure to any person of classified information or materials;

5. Performing or attempting to perform his duties, or otherwise acting, so as to serve the interests of another government in preference to the interests of the United States;

6. Membership in, affiliation or sympathetic association with any party, group, or association which th Congress of the United States, or any agency or officer of the United States duly authorized by the Congress for that purpose, finds:

(a) Seeks to alter the form of government of the United States by force or violence, or other unconstitutional means; or

(b) Is organized or utilized for the purpose of advancing the aims and objectives of the Communist movement; or

(c) Is organized or utilized for the purpose of establishing any form of dictatorship in the United States or any form of international dictatorship; or

(d) Is organized or utilized by any foreign government, or by any foreign party, group or association acting in the interest of such foreign government for the purpose of (a) espionage, or (b) sabotage, or (c) obtaining information relating to the defense of the United States or the protection of the national security, or (d) hampering, hindering or delaying the production of defense materials; or

(e) Is affiliated with, or acts in concert with, or is dominated or controlled by, any party, group, or association of the character described in (a), (b), (c), or (d) above.

7. Membership in or affiliation with any organization which the Congress of the United States, or any agency or officer of the United States duly authorized by the Congress for that purpose, finds has adopted a policy of advocating or approving

the commission of acts of force and violence to deny others their rights under the Constitution of the United States.

8. Refusal to testify upon the ground of self-incrimination, in any authorized inquiry relating to subversive activities conducted by a congressional committee, Federal court, Federal grand jury, or any other duly authorized agency unless the individual, after opportunity to do so, satisfactorily explains his refusal to testify.

The current AEC regulations concerning confrontation, section 4.27 (m), applies to witnesses "whose testimony is important" and whose presence "is deemed by the Board to be necessary or desirable." The regulation should be changed to provide for confrontation under circumstances aforementioned.

SUBPENA POWER

A. Either the Government or the individual should be permitted to apply to the hearing examiner to issue subpenas, except as to confidential informants and identified informants who have given their information on the condition that they will not be called as witnesses. Such application should state the name and address of such witness, as well as the substance of the testimony to be presented by the witness. If the hearing examiner deems the evidence relevant and not merely cumulative, he may issue the subpena.

B. The witness should be compensated for travel expense and per diem, but where such costs are substantial, the hearing examiner may in his discretion require the parties to use deposition procedures.

C. The Government should bear the cost of Government witnesses, but the hearing examiner should not subpena a witness for the individual until the individual deposits with the Government sufficient funds to pay the travel and per diem costs of such witness. In the event that the individual is not cleared, the funds deposited by the individual should be used to pay for the individual's witness expenses. If, however, the individual is cleared, the funds deposited by the individual should be returned to him and the Government should bear the travel and per diem costs of the individual's witness.

The Commission believes that the right of subpena should be applicable where there is a right of confrontation, but this does not preclude the applicant for clearance, employee, or applicant for employment from furnishing affidavits or the testimony of witnesses he wishes to present and who are willing to appear voluntarily.

228

Where an individual is denied employment or clearance upon charges which reflect upon his loyalty, the consequences are much more serious than is the case where such denial is based upon grounds reflecting upon his suitability.

Where an adverse determination is predicated upon loyalty factors, the person involved should be given the fullest opportunity, consistent with the protection of national security, to defend himself.

The Commission, therefore, believes that where the criteria relating to loyalty are included in the charges in the areas above set out, the recommendations heretofore made in respect to confrontation and subpena be applicable.

Appearance of witnesses is governed by AEC regulations, section 4.27 (m), which provides that the Manager should arrange for witnesses to appear "if possible." Subpenas are authorized by the 1954 act, section 161c, which provides that AEC may issue subpenas for the purpose of making studies and investigations and obtaining information, and further provides for payment of witness fees and mileage. In the appendix of the AEC Security Manual, chapter 2302–04a, reference is made to the subpena power granted by the act. The regulation should be changed to provide specifically for the subpena power and to contain the additional provisions outlined above.

DOCUMENT SECURITY

A. The "secret" and "top secret" classification categories should be replaced by "atomic secret" and "atomic top secret" to bring the document classification program of the Atomic Energy Commission in line with that of the remainder of the Government. The classification "confidential" should be eliminated entirely, as recommended in chapter 3, *supra*.

B. The foregoinng recommendation should be confined to prospective application thereby obviating the necessity for immediate review of the documents already classified "secret" and "top secret," but a gradual review and reclassification of such documents should be carried on.

C. The new Central Security Office should conduct a continuing review of classification procedures and abuses thereof arising from the de facto authority to classify possessed by employees who nominally have authority only to "recommend" classifications.

D. Every effort should be made to reduce the number of employees having the authority to classify or to recommend classification.

E. The Atomic Energy Commission should institute an adequate document classification training program for all personnel who

originate or have responsibility for material which will require application of defense information classification.

F. The Atomic Energy Commission should be urged to give particular attention to the requirements of fullest dissemination, consistent with national security, of scientific information and for fullest access, consistent with national security and the need to know, to such information by scientists or to those who may request such information or access.

G. The Atomic Energy Commission should review, in consultation with industry, its provisions for training in all aspects of document classification as they relate to industrial contractors, changing them wherever found necessary. In the course of this review and consultation the Atomic Energy Commission and industry should institute procedures for the personnel of each to be familiar with the operations and problems common to each as well as peculiar to each.

H. The Central Security Office should maintain a continuing review of classification and declassification procedures and, for purposes of uniformity and effective program improvement, make advisory recommendations to the Chairman of the Atomic Energy Commission.

Overclassification, accumulation of classified documents, and delay in declassification have been the bases for frequent and continued complaints on the part of industry, research organizations, and the general public. AEC recognizes the problems growing out of accumulation and declassification, states that declassification is a monumental task, and further states that all practical steps are being taken to review classified documents for possible downgrading or declassification. Although much progress is being made, there should be a greater effort toward release of information which will contribute more to the nation's advancement than it will add to a potential enemy's military strength. Greater care should be exercised in the original classification to avoid the unnecessary expense of safeguarding, as well as the wasted manpower expended in review of overclassified documents. The best remedy lies in reduction of the number of employees authorized to classify or to recommend classification, plus an adequate training program for those charged with the responsibility of classifying. A Central Security Office would aid in establishing uniformity and effecting program improvement.

The current classification categories of top secret, secret, and confidential are provided for in section 6, AEC Bulletin GM–SEC–5. Elimination of the confidential classification, and substitution of atomic secret and atomic top secret for the currently used secret and top secret categories would require a revision in bulletin GM–SEC–5.

PHYSICAL SECURITY

The AEC system of physical security and facility clearance has been adequate, but it is recommended elsewhere in this report that a uniform clearance procedure be adopted after conference between the Director of the proposed Central Security Office, the Department of Defense, and other agencies having industrial security programs, and representatives of industry.

LABOR-MANAGEMENT RELATIONS

A. The present AEC program of labor-management relations should be continued.

The Commission on Government Security believes that the current AEC practice of permitting the National Labor Relations Board to conduct normal, open hearings concerning labor employed at AEC installations, subject only to AEC intervention regarding possible disclosure of restricted data, to be the most practical and equitable procedure. The Commission also agrees that AEC should retain final authority on matters of security at AEC plants, and that security rules and their administration should not be subject to collective bargaining. The history of labor-management relations at AEC installations has been satisfactory, it having been noted by this Commission that labor generally has been very cooperative.

CONSOLIDATION OF INDUSTRIAL SECURITY PROGRAMS

A. The Commission on Government Security recommends against consolidation of the AEC industrial security program with other industrial security programs in the Government.

The operation of the atomic energy industrial security program should be handled by AEC; subject only to such advice and guidance as may be furnished by the recommended Central Security Office, including coordination of industrial security manuals and the exchange of clearances between one industrial security program and another.

EDUCATIONAL AND TRAINING PROGRAMS

A. It is recommended that the Central Security Office of the Department of Defense conduct a training program for security officers throughout the Government and industry.

The Department of Defense school for security officers at Fort Holabird, Md., has met with almost universal approval, and a similar school has frequently been recommended for officials concerned with the industrial security phase of the atomic energy program. Although greater education of the general public in the Government's security aims is sometimes suggested, it is believed that such an educational program would be too impractical and expensive. Within AEC, the current programs for security education and training are considered adequate; however, the aforementioned recommended training program should be of benefit to future security officers.

The proposal for establishment of the training program is discussed in the section entitled "Industrial Security Program."

Industrial Security Program

Introduction

There are two types of industrial security programs: (1) those whose objective is the effective safeguarding of classified information and material in the hands of United States industry or foreign industry, and (2) those whose objective is the physical protection of defense-related facilities without classified contracts but which are deemed important to our national security.

Industrial security programs for the safeguarding of classified information and material operate through policies and procedures affecting physical security (the identification, receipt, handling, and storage of classified information and material) as well as personnel security (limitation of access to classified information or material to those individuals who have been cleared for access). Many Federal departments and agencies operate such programs, but the major security programs are those of the Department of Defense and the Atomic Energy Commission. (The AEC program is discussed separately on pages 187–232.) The program of the Department of Defense includes 22,000 contractor facilities with some 3 million employees.

The industrial security programs for the protection of defense-related facilities ("industrial defense programs") are primarily mobilization programs, i. e., setting up standards of physical protection (fire, trespass, vandalism, sabotage, and other acts) for those facilities without classified contracts which are presently on the standby list or otherwise of interest to our Government because of their importance to our Nation's productive capacity at a time of mobilization or war. The Office of Defense Mobilization, under Executive Order 10421, has policy formulation responsibility for the industrial security programs of approximately 13 authorized agencies, although only the Department of Defense currently has an operating industrial defense program.

The Commission has not gone into the subject of physical security as a separate item. This report covers numerous areas of physical security, but only as related to other specific items. To study and review the great countrywide complex of facilities requiring physical security would have been almost impossible, but the Commission recommends to Congress that a thorough review be given this subject.

HISTORY

Introduction

Although the term "industrial security" may be used in various senses, the regulations presently in force define it as "that portion of internal security which is concerned with the protection of classified information in the hands of United States industry." [1] On the other hand, industrial security has, in the past, been used in a broader sense, to include the protection of industrial facilities which are essential to support a wartime mobilization program from loss or damage by the elements, sabotage, or other dangers arising within the United States.[2] At any rate, a survey of the evolution of the present program and the problems that have been encountered along the way should lend a sense of perspective.

The World War II Period

Some industrial security measures were in force even prior to World War II. For example, the employment of aliens in aircraft plants was regulated by the Air Corps Act of 1926, and the Sabotage and Espionage Acts of 1917 provided general protection under criminal law. During the decade immediately preceding World War II, various Army and Navy security regulations were imposed upon defense contractors. In 1934, defense contractors were required to sign an agreement to adhere to secrecy precautions upon assumption of work of a secret or confidential nature, and the prime contractor was made responsible for secrecy precautions by his subcontractors.[3] In 1939, Army regulations required that classified information and material be so marked while in the hands of defense contractors. Inspectors at such defense facilities were directed to advise contractors as to their responsibilities for safeguarding classified material.[4] After studying the British experience, the FBI conducted plant protection surveys in vital defense facilities during 1938–40.

At the beginning of World War II, considerable confusion developed from the fact that both the Army and the Navy were engaged in administering the regulations dealing with industrial security. In order to avoid this confusion, the Navy agreed that the Army should assume responsibility for the handling of aliens, control of subversives, fingerprinting, and other procedures for the advancement of personnel security. Responsibility for

---

[1] Armed Forces industrial security regulation, sec. 1–217 (Sept. 1956).

[2] Memorandum of Secretary of Defense dated Oct. 12, 1949, Subject: Delineation of responsibility for industrial security.

[3] Army policy No. 329, Dec. 1934.

[4] Army regulation 380–5, June 1939.

supervising the industrial security program was delegated by the Secretary of War to the provost marshal general of the Army.[5]

The detailed implementation of the program included surveys and inspections of selected defense facilities as to such matters as armed guards, special alarm equipment, and other physical protection measures. A personnel security program was also instituted, although there was no requirement that individual clearances and letters of consent be issued. The personnel records of employees were checked. In addition, the internal security representative of the Army at the defense plant indicated that those suspected of disloyalty, those of questionable background, those in positions enabling them to acquire important classified information, and those in positions of particular trust should submit a personnel security questionnaire and thus become subject to possible investigation. Further, in order to identify those persons whose criminal records were definitely of such a nature as to endanger war production and impair the war effort, fingerprints were taken and checked.[6]

Early in 1942, the War Department instituted a program for the "Discharge of subversives from private plants and war department plants privately operated of importance to Army procurement." [7] A strenuous effort was made to accomplish this program with the voluntary cooperation of management and labor. The Army regulations, administered by the provost marshal general,[8] provided that when an adequate investigation revealed that there was good cause to suspect an employee of subversive activity (defined as sabotage, espionage, or any other willful activity designed to disrupt the national defense program), the military authorities could request the immediate removal of such individual from the defense project.[9] It was not required that the nature or source of the evidence be revealed, but administrative instructions stated that no employee should be suspended as a result of idle rumor, normal labor activity, gossip, or anonymous communication. Prior to requiring a removal, Army representatives were instructed to try to get the approval of management and labor representatives. "Where there is no good reason to the contrary and if the project representatives of the employees so desire, they should be given the option of handling the removal of any such individual from the project." [10] To minimize any possible injustice, the instructions called for exploration with management and labor of the possibility of arranging for other employment in non-defense work.

---

[5] Letter from the Secretary of War to the provost marshal general, War Department, Sept. 4, 1942.

[6] Memorandum No. 10, internal security section, Army Air Force material center, Mar. 8, 1943.

[7] War Department unnumbered circular, dated Feb. 5, 1942. This program was undertaken pursuant to the general authority of Executive Order 8972, dated Dec. 12, 1941, and was based on a joint memorandum, dated Jan. 10, 1942.

[8] Letter from the Under Secretary of War to the provost marshal general, Nov. 20, 1942.

[9] "Joint memorandum", dated July 31, 1943, contained in War Department pamphlet 32–4 "Suspension of subversives from privately operated facilities of importance to the security of the Nation's Army and Navy programs", dated Dec. 10, 1946.

[10] Ibid.

During the early part of the program, most of the removals were made from Washington, but later, when instructions had been disseminated, the function of effecting removal of subversives was largely performed by field representatives of the service commands.

Upon a written request within 30 days of the removal, the individual was entitled to such review as the provost marshal general provided. By authority of the Under Secretary of War,[11] the provost marshal set up a review committee, which ultimately became the Industrial Employment Review Board. If it appeared, after review, that removal had been without sufficient cause, the employee would be entitled to reinstatement.

Based on a study of a War Department historical monograph, one writer concludes:

> There would seem to be no doubt that the program was a success from a practical point of view. After a number of months of operation, it appears that the unions had only about five cases in which they were dissatisfied with the results of the program, and it further appears that in these cases satisfactory explanations were apparently made after appropriate investigation and review of the facts. It appears that something over 2,000 removals were effected in the course of the program. The monograph refers to the FBI as authority for a general statement to the effect that during the course of the War there was not a single case of damage proved to have been the direct result of sabotage.[12]

The Immediate Postwar Period to 1948

In 1946, the requirement was instituted that a contractor, before being given access to War Department classified data, must sign a secrecy agreement which provided that written consent must be obtained before any individual be permitted access to top secret or secret material.[13] In delegating authority to grant such consent, the Secretary of War stated:

> No consent will be granted unless, after full consideration of the evidence presented, it is determined that the employment of such individual, in the manner proposed, will not be inimical to the interests of the United States.[14]

This immediate post-war period was one of considerable confusion in the industrial security field. Following the cessation of hostilities, the Army was hampered by a severe curtailment of personnel and had to discontinue a number of security services which it had been administering. The Navy consequently had to assume much of the responsibility for enforcing the security of classified information entrusted to private Navy contractors. It was not until June 13, 1947 that Secretary of the Navy Forrestal wrote to the Secretary of War suggesting that the 1946 requirement of written

---

[11] Letter from the Under Secretary of War to the provost marshal general, dated Nov. 20, 1942.

[12] Memorandum from George MacClain, assistant general counsel to James L. Kunen, general counsel, National Security Resources Board, dated June 10, 1952.

[13] Army regulation 380–5, par. 67, dated March 6, 1946.

[14] Memorandum from the Secretary of War to the provost marshal general of the Army, the commanding general of the Army Air Force and the commanding general, Manhattan Engineer District, dated July 16, 1946.

clearance for employees of War Department contractors having access to top secret or secret material be made applicable to Navy contractors and be administered by the War Department for both the Army and the Navy.[15] Meanwhile, the Air Force was constituted as a separate military department and was beginning to administer its own industrial security program.

A Government committee stated that the responsibility at that time was divided among many Army, Navy, and Air Force agencies under the overall supervision of the provost marshal general of the Army. The result of this divided responsibility was reflected in plants of contractors holding contracts for one or more of the three services. Due to the lack of clearance criteria which could be used by all clearing agencies, individuals who had been cleared by one agency were found unacceptable to another. There were no comprehensive directives pertaining to the responsibilities and procedures for obtaining clearance. Clearances were based on outmoded directives which had been revised in part by written instructions, and in part by oral agreements among the various agencies involved. The partial decentralization of some portions of the wartime personnel clearance program and the complete decentralization of other portions resulted in confusion, misunderstanding, duplication of effort, and conflicting decisions in the field.

As an interim measure, pending general revision of the procurement-security program, the three military departments agreed in October 1947 to set up a central procurement-security board, to which the military field offices would send all cases where clearance did not appear to be justified.[16] Pursuant to this agreement, the *Army-Navy-Air Force Personnel Security Board (PSB)* was created March 17, 1948.[17] It was a three-man board, with one representative from each of the military departments, receiving its administrative services from the provost marshal general of the Army. Its functions were to grant or deny clearance for employment on aeronautical or classified contract work when such consent was required, and to suspend individuals, whose continued employment was considered inimical to the security interests of the United States, from employment on classified work. The Board was authorized to adopt its own rules of procedure; no specific criteria were promulgated.

During the year 1948, a great deal of attention was concentrated on the need to place the industrial security program, and the internal security program as a whole, on a more definite and certain basis. A Government study in 1948 recommended that:

> Provisions should be adopted for the security and protection in a practical, uncomplicated manner of classified information relating particularly to data of a military nature available to industrial organizations throughout the country.

---

[15] Letter from Secretary of the Navy Forrestal to the Secretary of War, dated June 13, 1947.

[16] Memorandum of interim agreement, Army, Navy, Air Force on clearance of alien and citizen employees of contractors (signed by the provost marshal general of the Army, the air provost marshal, and the chief, material division of the Navy) dated Oct. 9, 1947.

[17] Memorandum of agreement between the provost marshal general and the air provost marshal creating the Army-Navy-Air Force Personnel Security Board, dated March 17, 1948.

Contrary to procedures existing at the time, there should be uniform specifications emanating from the three departments of the National Military Establishment as regards the handling in industry of personnell clearances and of each category of contract wrought by the National Military Establishment.

In addition, only one agency should be charged with the responsibility of maintaining central records of firms cleared for work on classified contracts of the Departments of the Army, Navy, and Air Force. (In the course of this study, it was indicated that not infrequently three secrecy agreements and three personnel clearance procedures were in effect in one plant handling contracts for each of the Departments comprising the National Military Establishment.)

There should be formulated an intelligence program with specific responsibility being placed in one Department to ensure the security and physical protection of the Nation's vital industrial installations.

There should be established a similar program designed to ensure the security of the Nation's vital communication, transportation, and other public utilities.

Another Government committee in that year also recommended that the Secretary of Defense consider the establishment of a central industrial security office with appropriate power and personnel to exercise the functions which are designed to keep classified Armed Forces information from falling into the hands of potential enemies of the United States.

Secretary of Defense Forrestal requested the Munitions Board to examine this question in order to recommend specific plans and implementing directives to accomplish the desired coordination.

The Munitions Board was already working on the problem, having noted the existing lack of coordination and being conscious of its responsibility, under the National Security Act of 1947 [18] to coordinate internal security within the National Military Establishment with respect to industrial matters. A Munitions Board memorandum at this time emphasized the need for action to improve the security status of defense facilities through physical protection measures, relocation of plants located in concentrated areas, and dispersion of production of critical products among a number of producers. Along with these matters, which bulked large in the Munitions Board's concept of industrial security, the memorandum also noted the need for uniform security provisions in procurement contracts and uniform procedures for personnel clearances. The prevailing reaction of contractors to the existing situation was exemplified by a letter from the president of a large company:

No company would have any objection to filling out a personnel security form for each of its officers, directors, and other individuals having to do with procurement. Companies do object, however, and properly so, when asked to prepare a separate form not

---

[18] Sec. 213 (c).

only for each Service Department, but sometimes for various bureaus and technical services of the Military Departments.

At the present moment, the Navy, the Air Force, and the Signal Corps procurement district of Philadelphia are all seeking personnel security forms for various individuals within this company. No Department is willing to accept clearances given by another Department.[19]

In July 1948, the Munitions Board proposed the establishment of an industrial security committee, with representatives from each of the three Military Departments, noting that

It appears to be universally accepted that a high-level policy agency is essential to provide for uniform coordinated security procedures in the National Military Establishment. It further appears, but with less unanimity of opinion as to the form of organization and its position in the National Military Establishment, that an operating office containing Army, Navy, and Air Force elements, or an office jointly staffed by the three Departments is also essential.[20]

After approval by Secretary of Defense Forrestal, the Munitions Board Industrial Security Committee met in October 1948 under directives (1) to analyze the broad industrial security program—to assure all possible action for the protection of economic resources required for logistic support of a war program—and (2) to develop procedures for the protection of classified information in the hands of industry.[21]

By April 1949, an Industrial Security Division had been set up in the Munitions Board, with the following principal functions:

(1) To develop, coordinate and monitor plans, policies and procedures relative to industrial security matters within the National Military Establishment;

(2) To evaluate resources and facilities essential to industrial mobilization.

(3) To plan protection from physical hazard of all resources and technical information required for an industrial mobilization program.[22]

The Industrial Security Division included: (1) a security education officer; (2) a resource rating branch (evaluation of critical facilities and resources); (3) a resource protection improvement branch (physical security, camouflage, underground construction, dispersal, damage control, guards, fire forces, etc.); (4) a security program review branch (review of the operation and effectiveness of the industrial security program); and (5) a general security branch, with responsibility:

(a) To develop plans for the establishment and coordination of miscellaneous industrial security programs within the National Military Establishment;

---

[19] Letter from Thomas A. Hargrove, president of Eastman Kodak Co. to the Munitions Board, dated Apr. 20, 1948.

[20] Memorandum from the chairman of the Munitions Board to the Secretary of Defense, dated July 24, 1948.

[21] Munitions Board order No. 204, dated Sept. 29, 1948.

[22] Organization chart of Industrial Security Division Munitions Board, dated Apr. 6, 1949.

(*b*) To plan the establishment of a single agency to supervise the issuance of corporate or personnel clearances in order to maintain the security of classified military information in the hands of industry;

(*c*) To develop policies and procedures to prevent losses of scientific and technological knowledge to potential enemies through patent procedures, foreign reinsurance, alien control, technical aid contracts or other means;

(*d*) To formulate policies and procedures for the duplication of military industrial data vital to industrial mobilization by micro-filming or other process and to provide for their proper storage and dispersal;

(*e*) To develop uniform policies and procedures for the protection of classified information in the hands of industry and other Government agencies;

(*f*) To review legislation pertinent to industrial security matters; [23]

Thus it will be seen that, at the time when the industrial security program of the Department of Defense was getting into active operation in the Munitions Board in mid-1949, the concept of "industrial security" was rather broad; the program for the protection of classified material, and the personnel clearances which went along with it, were only one part of the industrial security program.

The Period From 1949 to 1953

During this period, the responsibility for developing and coordinating the industrial security program of the Department of Defense was centered in the Munitions Board, and numerous efforts were made to bring about greater uniformity and certainty in the program.

By means of memoranda to the Secretaries of the three Military Departments [24] and a directive establishing a Munitions Board charter,[25] the Secretary of Defense attempted to make clear that the Munitions Board had the responsibility for developing all policies, procedures and standards and for coordinating the activities of the Military Departments in the field of industrial security, which was defined to mean:

The effective protection of classified military information in the hands of United States industry, and of resources, premises, utilities and industrial facilities (not including military installations) which are essential to support a wartime mobilization program from loss or damage by the elements, sabotage, or other dangers arising within the United States, except armed insurrection and other serious disturbances which require the use of organized military force to restore the domestic tranquillity.

---

[23] *Ibid.*

[24] Memorandum: "Delineation of responsibility for industrial security," dated Oct. 12, 1949.

[25] Directive: "Munitions board charter," issued by the Secretary of Defense, Nov. 3, 1949.

The situation confronting the Industrial Security Division of the Munitions Board when it started to work on the problem has been described as follows:

Each military department had its own regulations for handling its own classified security information in industry. There was no cross-servicing between or among the Departments—each proceeded independently of the others. A company or an employee had to be cleared two or even three times in many instances. Some employees would be acceptable as a security risk to one Department but not to another for contracts of the same classification. The same held true for certain faciliites. There was no uniformity in the ground rules followed by management in protecting classified matter entrusted to his care.[26]

The effects of these practices were described as follows:

From management's point of view, this was confusing, wasteful, time-consuming, and caused the growth of a general disregard for security rules and practices in companies working on classified contracts, especially those doing work concurrently for technical services in two or more Departments. Compliance often became a matter of lip service. From the Military Department's point of view, long delays were encountered in getting clearances completed in the face of a constantly growing backlog of cases to be processed. Clearance of an individual cost between two hundred and three hundred dollars and duplications of this work were proving costly and time-consuming.[27]

Beginning in mid-1949, the Industrial Security Division in the Munitions Board began establishing Department of Defense policies as to various aspects of the program to protect classified information in the hands of industry, and the three Military Departments issued them in the form of Department regulations and orders. Some of the steps in this development follow:

Establishment of the central index file—June 15, 1949.

Issuance of a regulation governing visits to Department of Defense contractors—September 7, 1949.

Issuance of the security requirements checklist—September 26, 1949.

Issuance of a regulation governing security clearance of private contractors' facilities—February 27, 1950.

Issuance of a regulation governing security investigation and clearance of private contractors' employees—1950.

Issuance of a regulation governing assignment of departmental responsibilities for industrial security—June 22, 1950.

Issuance of Department of Defense industrial security manual for safeguarding of classified matters—January 18, 1951.

Issuance of Department of Defense security agreement—February 1, 1951.

Publication of a consolidated listing of Department of Defense contractors' facilities—May 29, 1951.

Establishment of uniform letters of consent—October 3, 1951.

---

[26] Briefing paper, "Department of Defense, industrial security program", Munitions Board, dated Mar. 31, 1953.

[27] Ibid.

Establishment of special clearance procedures for employees of Government activities (GAO, NPA, DPA, Renegotiations Board, etc.) (no set date).

Establishment of special clearance procedures for colleges and universities—April 3, 1952.

Establishment of operating procedures under U. S.-Canada industrial security agreement—May 22, 1952.

Although it was recognized that considerable progress had been made in correcting the previously existing situation, two difficulties were still encountered:

The Departments, in preparing their implementing regulations and orders, were often widely divergent in their interpretations of established policy. In addition, these were considered to be only "minimum" policy positions on matters covered. Thus, the Departments felt free to make their implementation of the regulations more stringent than the policy position if they wished. Consequently, the efforts to establish uniformity suffered under such an interpretation.[28]

It remained for the "Armed Forces industrial security regulation" to attack these defects. This regulation, to be discussed in the next section, was issued in 1953; it provided the field representatives of the three Military Departments with a single, uniform regulation to use in implementing the program for the protection of classified information in the hands of industry.

It should be noted that all during this period a large part of the work of the Industrial Security Division (known by 1952 as the Office of Industrial Security) in the Munitions Board was devoted to the evaluation of key facilities, in order to determine those facilities and necessary services most critical to a mobilization effort, and the promotion of a voluntary program on the part of management to secure those facilities by physical protection measures against a variety of hazards, including sabotage.

The Industrial Security Division was assisted, beginning in 1949, by an Industry Advisory Committee. However, it did not remain active, apparently because the membership, made up of top industrial executives, did not prove to be conversant with the detailed security problems involved in the specialized regulations being drafted in this period. It was not until 1955 that a reconstituted Industry Advisory Committee, composed largely of company officials principally concerned with security matters, became active again.

In 1949 the need arose for clear-cut criteria of derogatory information on which to base denial of security clearances. Accordingly in July of that year a set of six criteria was adopted for use by all military departments, the PSB, and the IERB. Also in 1949 the IERB was reconstituted and made responsible to the Secretaries of the three military departments instead of to the provost marshal general. It was composed of four members, including one lawyer, and was empowered to appoint regional appeal boards. However, such regional boards apparently were never created.

---

[28] Ibid.

In June 1950 the Personnel Security Board (PSB) was given additional functions and became responsible to the three Secretaries. This new Board administered the central index file, and decided all cases in which a military department recommended denial or revocation of clearance of industrial employees. In the event of an adverse decision by PSB, the individual involved could appeal for a hearing before the IERB.

The year 1952 witnessed a growing dissatisfaction within DOD concerning the granting of clearances by IERB, "to a number of persons alleged to be poor security risks." The board was eventually abolished in 1953. Even before this controversy there had been a movement toward a revision of the industrial security hearing and review system. Major deficiencies noted by the Army included the lack of a centralized administration and control, and the lack of a personal hearing before clearance was denied.

In April 1952 the three Secretaries authorized an ad hoc committee to draw up a charter for a reorganized industrial personnel security program to achieve, "as far as possible, the desired uniformity of principle, approach, and disposition of industrial security personnel cases, taking full account of the fact that the responsibilities for safeguarding military information rests with the heads of the respective departments." [29] However, because of objections voiced by the Chairman of the Munitions Board, there was a tentative compromise in June 1952, under which it was recognized that the Munitions Board would retain overall responsibility for establishing policies, procedures, and standards. Responsibility for operations on a case-by-case basis would rest with the military departments. An executive secretary, supported administratively by one of the military departments, would provide the overall direction and supervision of the administration and operational aspects of the program. All reference to the "Office of the Joint Secretaries" would be deleted. The IERB would continue to be located in the Munitions Board as the appellate agency for the overall program.[30]

The Period From 1953 to 1956

The year 1953 saw three major developments in the industrial security program of the Department of Defense: (1) the issuance of a uniform "Armed Forces Industrial Security Regulation" (AFISR); (2) the conversion of the Office of Industrial Security which had been under the Munitions Board to the Industrial Security Division under the Assistant Secretary of Defense for Manpower, Personnel and Reserve Forces; and (3) the establishment of regional Industrial Personnel Security Boards. These developments, and later modifications, will be discussed in that order.

---

[29] Memorandum of the three Secretaries, Apr. 29, 1952.

[30] Memorandum from the assistant to the joint Secretaries to the Chairman of the Munitions Board, June 5, 1952.

(1) *Issuance of AFISR.*—It will be remembered that, in spite of directives and regulations issued by the Department of Defense between 1949 and 1952 in the effort to promote uniformity in the program for the protection of classified material in the hands of industry, there was still considerable confusion, duplication and divergence of interpretation among the field offices of the three Military Departments. The files of the Department of Defense containing numerous letters from industry protesting this situation and requesting the issuance of a single, uniform regulation and the assignment of security cognizance at a contractor's facility to a single Military Department. For example, one letter protests "the constant duplication and repetition occurring in the accomplishment of facility and personnel clearances. This duplication impedes our defense effort, is wasteful in the expenditure of governmental and personnel, is costly to industry, and frequently results in adverse public relations." [31]   Other contractors complained that they were required to sign a new security agreement with every military activity for whom they did classified work and that they were required to process requests for personnel clearances through each such activity.[32]

It became apparent that if true uniformity was to be obtained in the development and application of security regulations in industry, a single regulation was necessary. The Armed-Forces industrial security regulation issued in 1953 served this purpose, superseding some 29 Department of Defense directives. Even where a contractor had classified contracts with more than one military activity, provision was made for handling security matters through a single "cognizant" department. Field representatives of all three Military Departments were to use this regulation in handling the security aspects of classified contracts. Cross-servicing was required and made simpler. Clearance was done in the name of the Secretary of Defense and was made acceptable to all Military Departments and their activities. The Armed Forces industrial security regulation was revised in 1955 and again in 1956, in the attempt to iron out continuing sources of difficulty.

(2) *Administrative reorganizations.*—Following the change of administration in 1953, and as part of a general reorganization of the Office of the Secretary of Defense, the Munitions Board was abolished as of July 1, 1953, and its functions were taken over by various Assistant Secretaries of Defense. The former Office of Industrial Security of the Munitions Board became the Industrial Security Division in a new office of domestic security programs under the Assistant Secretary of Defense for Manpower, Personnel, and Reserve Forces.

In October 1955, the office of domestic security programs was abolished and those functions of the Industrial Security Division which dealt with "industrial defense" (evaluation of key facilities and physical protection of defense plants) were placed under the Assistant Secretary of Defense for

---

[31] Letter from W. T. Van Atten, chairman, Armed Forces regional council, New York region, dated May 2, 1952.

[32] Letter from Stanford Research Institute, dated May 8, 1952; letter from Varian Associates, dated Oct. 31, 1952; letter from the University of Florida, Oct. 20, 1952.

Supply and Logistics in a new unit known as the Industrial Security Branch, Mobilization Planning and Statistics Division, Office of Planning and Review. Those portions of the Armed Forces Industrial Security Regulations (AFISR) which dealt with—not the protection of classified matter—but the protection of industrial facilities which are essential to support a wartime mobilization program from loss or damage by the elements, sabotage, or other hazards, were revised and issued as a separate "Armed Forces industrial defense regulation" in 1955.

Those functions dealing with the protection of classified matter in the hands of contractors remain under the Assistant Secretary of Defense for Manpower, Personnel, and Reserve Forces. The functions include the periodic revision of manuals and regulations and the monitoring and coordinating of the work of the three Military Departments as to facility and personnel clearances and as to the physical protection and handling of classified matter. This work is now done by the industrial security programs division, which is part of the Office of Personnel Security Policy created in 1955, under the Assistant Secretary of Defense (MP&R).

Under the auspices of the Department of Defense, a joint training course on industrial security (in the sense of the protection of classified matter in the hands of industry) for security officers of the three Military Departments was established in 1955 at Fort Holabird, Md., with the Army Intelligence School acting as executive agent; and in 1956 a similar course for security officers of defense contractors was established.

Since October 1955, an Industry Advisory Committee for Safeguarding Classified Information has met periodically with Department of Defense representatives to advise and assist in developing policies and procedures that will afford adequate protection to classified information and at the same time be practical from the standpoint of the requirements of industry.

(3) *Personnel security boards.*—Turning again to developments in the program for screening, hearing, and reviewing denials of clearance for access to classified information, the new Secretary of Defense, Charles E. Wilson, issued a memorandum in March 1953, to the Secretaries of the three Military Departments abolishing the Army-Navy-Air Force Personnel Security Board (PSB) and the Industrial Employment Review Board (IERB). He directed the three Secretaries to—

establish such number of geographical regions within the United States as seems appropriate to the workload in each region. There shall then be established within each region an Industrial Personnel Security Board. This board shall consist of two separate and distinct divisions, a Screening Division and an Appeal Division, with equal representation of the Departments of the Army, Navy and Air Force on each such division. The Appeals Division shall have jurisdiction to hear appeals from the decisions of the Screening Division, and its decisions shall be final, subject only to reconsideration on its own motion or at the request of the appellant for good cause shown or at the request of the Secretary of any military department.

The Secretaries shall within 30 days establish such regions and develop joint uniform standards, criteria, and detailed procedures to implement the above-described program.

247

In developing the standards, criteria, and procedures, full consideration shall be given to the rights of individuals, consistent with security requirements.[33]

Pursuant to these orders, the three Secretaries drew up a directive on the "Industrial personnel and facility clearance program," setting up three industrial personnel security boards in New York, Chicago, and San Francisco, with a screening division and an appeal division in each. Twenty-one criteria for the denial of clearance were set out.[34] This directive was issued by the three Secretaries without being referred to the Munitions Board for comment or concurrence.[35]

A period of considerable confusion and chaos existed after the abolition of the PSB and the IERB and the commencement of operations of the new regional boards. In October 1953, it was reported that the New York board had a backlog of over 300 cases,[36] and in February 1954, it was reported that "the screening division of the board in New York is apparently over a year behind in its cases and the backlog is considerable." [37]

In January 1954, Secretary of Defense Wilson authorized the Secretaries of the three military departments "to modify or overrule any decision of an Appeals Division of an Industrial Personnel Security Board when they deem such action to be in the national interest." [38]

In mid-1954, Secretary Wilson noted that:

A number of problems have arisen in connection with the Boards' operations which suggest another look at the program. In particular, the problems involved backlog of cases, lack of uniform application of procedures in the administration of the Boards, lack of uniformity in the statement of charges against individuals and failure to complete cases once they have been referred to the Board for action.[39]

The director of the office of domestic security programs commented:

There is dissatisfaction within the military departments on the present operation of the Boards, but, because of lack of any established leadership, the three departments have been unable to get together and solve the problems.[40]

The general counsel of the Department of Defense requested the Secretaries of the Army, Navy, and Air Force to review the industrial personnel security clearance and review program in July 1954. A working group was appointed from the staff of the general counsels of the three Military Departments and the Department of Defense and a representative of the Industrial Security Division. They produced a plan which included central admin-

---

[33] Memorandum from Secretary of Defense Wilson to the Secretaries of the Army, Navy, and Air Force and the chairman of the Munitions Board, dated Mar. 27, 1953.

[34] Directive, dated May 4, 1953, Subject: Industrial personnel and facility clearance program.

[35] Memorandum from Maj. Gen. F. R. Dent, military director, Munitions Board, to the acting chairman, Munitions Board, dated May 4, 1953.

[36] Memorandum from the director, industrial security division, to the director, office of domestic security programs, dated Oct. 1, 1953.

[37] Memorandum from the General Counsel of the Navy to the counsel, New York branch, dated Feb. 20, 1954.

[38] Memorandum from the Secretary of Defense to the Secretaries of the Army, Navy, and Air Force, dated Jan. 18, 1954.

[39] Memorandum from the Secretary of Defense to the Secretaries of Army, Navy, and Air Force, undated (approximately July 1954).

[40] Memorandum from the director, office of domestic programs, to the general counsel, Department of Defense, dated July 13, 1954.

istration in a new Industrial Personnel Security Review Division in the Office of Personnel Security Policy under the Assistant Secretary of Defense for Manpower, Personnel and Reserve Forces. Provisions were made for a central screening Board in Washington to pass upon cases in which one of the three Military Departments had recommended that clearance should be denied or revoked. Regional hearing boards were provided in New York, Chicago, and San Francisco, with review by a central review board in Washington. The criteria were refined and standard procedures were promulgated in the industrial personnel security review regulation of February 2, 1955.[41] A first annual report of the new review program was issued in September 1956.

LEGAL BASIS

Introduction

The industrial security program of the Department of Defense has as its objective the effective protection of classified information and material in the hands of United States industry through the use of specified policies and procedures for physical security (the identification, receipt, handling, and storage of classified information and material) and for personnel security (limitation of access to classified information or material to those individuals who have been cleared for access). These policies and procedures are set forth in two Department of Defense publications (the *Armed Forces Industrial Security Regulation* and the *Industrial Security Manual for Safeguarding Classified Information*) and the various implementing regulations of the three military departments. The industrial security regulation is directed to the military departments, while the industrial security manual is directed to those companies (contractors) who are bidding on or have entered into classified contracts with one of the military departments. The provisions of the industrial security manual are imposed contractually upon contractors through a "security agreement" (DOD Form 441), which is entered into by the contractor and binds him to observe and adhere to all of the provisions of the industrial security manual. In addition, each classified procurement contract entered into by a contractor contains a "military security requirements" clause, which obligates the contractor in a similar manner.

Statutory Basis of the Program

The operation of the industrial security program may thus be said to rest upon Government regulations and upon contractual obligations. These

---

[41] Department of Defense directive 5220.6, dated Feb. 2, 1955.

regulations and obligations do not, however, constitute the legal basis for the program as a whole.[42] Such a basis must be found in a statute which authorizes the executive branch of the Government (and the Department of Defense in particular) to establish this program.

It is clear that there is no statute (or Executive order) which expressly authorizes the Department of Defense to establish an industrial security program. A legal basis for the program may, however, be found in the implied authority contained in one or more of the following statutes (or Executive order) :

5 U. S. C. 22.—"The head of each department is authorized to prescribe regulations, not inconsistent with law, for the government of his department, the conduct of its officers and clerks, the distribution and performance of its business and the custody, use and preservation of the records, papers, and property appertaining to it." In addition to the general authorization contained in this act to prescribe regulations for the distribution and performance of the department's business, that part thereof which specifically authorizes the head of a department to prescribe regulations for the custody, use, and preservation of the records, papers, and property of the department has been uniformly held by the courts to authorize regulations prohibiting subordinate officers of the department from producing in court any official records of the department in obedience to a subpena duces tecum.[43]

It would seem that if the head of a department can preserve Government secrets from disclosure in court, where the public interest in justice may be thwarted, he can probably act to prevent disclosure of Government secrets to individuals in industry who may be unfriendly to the United States. The scope of the authority would also seem to extend to the protection of property the title to which is not yet in the United States, such as guns, ships, and airplane propellers being produced for the United States, because such property is, in the language of the statute, "appertaining to" the Department.

This statute refers to the "head of each department," which may refer to just the Department of Defense and not the Departments of the Army, Navy, or Air Force. Even if this restricted interpretation is accepted, the applicability of the statute to the military departments can be supported on the basis that the industrial security program is actually a Department of Defense program, operated by the three departments as agents of the Department of Defense.

This statute would therefore appear to authorize the industrial security program to the extent that such program is reasonably related to the distribution

---

[42] But see *Greene* v. *Wilson*, D. C. D. C., Civil Action No. 3561–54 (March 29, 1957), in which the court upheld the removal of Mr. Greene under an earlier industrial security program, apparently on the ground that there was a contract between the Government and Mr. Greene's employer: "It is fundamental when one presumes to accept a contractual offer then that offer must be accepted in terms, and one of the terms here, as has been said, related to security controls. The necessity for such is obvious. If the plaintiff's employer did not see fit to accept and conform, it had perfect freedom not to enter into the contract. On acceptance of the offer in terms, it was obliged in the circumstances to carry out its essentials, the presumed result of which was the loss by the plaintiff of his position."

[43] *Baske* v. *Comingore*, 177 U. S. 459 (1900) ; *In re Huttman*, 70 F. 699 (1895).

and performance of the department's business or is reasonably designed to protect Government secrets or defense production.

The National Security Act of 1947, as amended, 5 U. S. C. 171, is frequently cited in support of the industrial security program. Section 171a (b) provides that the Secretary of Defense shall have direction, authority, and control over the Department of Defense. Section 171a (c) (4) provides that "The Departments of the Army, Navy, and Air Force shall be separately administered by their respective secretaries under the direction, authority, and control of the Secretary of Defense." These sections grant the Secretary of Defense and the three military Secretaries the authority to administer their departments. It may well be argued that the power to protect the records and property of the department is an implied power of the head of the department who is responsible for administering the department.

18 U. S. C. 793 and 798 supply indirect authority for the industrial security program, for they clearly set forth the congressional policy that it is illegal for any person having defense or classified information to disclose the same to unauthorized persons or with the intent to injure the United States. The President, under article II, section 3, is directed to take care that the laws are faithfully executed by his subordinates. The industrial security program represents such an attempt, for it has as its objective the safeguarding from disclosure of defense or classified information.

41 U. S. C. 151, et seq.—The "Armed Services Procurement Act," authorizes each of the three military departments to negotiate procurement contracts of "any type" which in the opinion of the agency head will promote the best interests of the Government. This statute would appear to authorize the department head to prescribe any reasonable conditions in procurement contracts, including provisions for carrying into effect the mandate of 5 U. S. C. 22 above, namely, the preservation of the records, papers, and property appertaining to the department, although this interpretation of the act is weakened by the fact that the following subsection of the act may indicate that the type of contract referred to was a type of financial contract. The contracting authority provided for by this statute may therefore supplement the authority granted by 5 U. S. C. 22, and may be an additional legal basis for the industrial security program.

Executive Order 10501 (November 5, 1953) states that it ". . . is essential that certain official information affecting the national defense be protected uniformly against unauthorized disclosure," and provides in detail for and authorizes the classification, changes in classification, marking, safekeeping, and so forth, of such official information. In particular, section 5i of the order provides that when classified material affecting the national defense is furnished authorized persons in or out of Federal service, there shall be placed on such material a statement that the transmission or revelation of this material to an unauthorized person is prohibited by law. Section 7b further provides that "classified defense information shall not be disseminated outside the executive branch except under conditions and through channels authorized by the head of the disseminating department or agency, even though the person or agency to which dissemination of such information is proposed to be made may have been solely or partly responsible for its production." This order therefore supports and in fact authorizes the proper safeguarding of all classified defense information in the hands of industry, which is the objective of the industrial security program.

At various times the Department of Defense and the military departments have cited certain other statutes and Executive orders and constitutional provisions as supplying the legal basis for the industrial security program. These citations include:

1. Executive Order 10104 (February 1, 1950).
2. 50 U. S. C. App. 781–783.
3. 10 U. S. C. 310 (j).
4. 50 U. S. C. 781–826.
5. Executive Order 10421 (December 31, 1952).
6. 18 U. S. C. 2151–2156.
7. 5 U. S. C. 412.
8. 5 U. S. C. 181–4.
9. The United States Constitution, article II, section 2—the authority of the President as Commander in Chief to protect the Nation's secrets.

The statutes and Executive orders discussed or referred to above adequately authorize the Government to establish a program for the protection of classified information and material in the hands of private industry, although serious consideration might well be given to recommending the enactment of a statute expressly authorizing such a program and the particular policies and procedures to be used to implement the program.

Constitutional Basis of the Program

Aside from questions as to the statutory basis of the industrial security program, serious questions have been raised as to whether Congress has the constitutional authority to enact legislation authorizing an industrial security program, particularly where such a program provides for the exclusion or removal of designated employees of private defense facilities from those jobs in which they have access to classified information or material. Such questions do not, however, attack the constitutionality of the four statutes and the Executive order discussed above as supplying the legal basis of the industrial security program, for, as was emphasized above, these statutes and the Executive order do not deal directly with the subject of an industrial security program nor do they expressly authorize such a program.

Legislation expressly authorizing an industrial security program similar to that now in operation by the Department of Defense could be supported constitutionally as an exercise of Congress' power to: Declare war, raise and support armies, and provide and maintain a Navy—article I, section 8, clauses 11, 12, and 13; dispose of and make all needful Rules and Regulations respecting the Property belonging to the United States—article IV, section 3, clause 2; and the "inherent right of self-preservation."

The power of the Federal Government to wage war and provide for the Army and Navy—the "war powers"—is very broad in scope and authorizes Congress to enact all measures which are necessary and proper for carrying into execution such powers. As stated in *Hirabayashi* v. *United States*, 320 U. S. 81, 93 (1943):

> The war power of the National Government is the "power to wage war successfully." . . . It extends to every matter and activity so related to war as substantially to affect its conduct and progress. . . . It embraces every phase of the national defense, including the protection of war *materials* . . . from injury and from the dangers which attend . . . war. [Emphasis added.]

The war powers have been cited by the courts as the constitutional basis for a great variety of legislation covering many subjects including:

> Legislation authorizing the exclusion (removal) from designated areas of persons of Japanese descent, although there was no allegation that all such persons or any specific ones were disloyal to the United States. (*Korematsu* v. *United States*, 323 U. S. 214 (1944)); the Magnuson Act, which is the basis of the Coast Guard port security program. (*U. S.* v. *Gray*, 207 F. 2d 237 (1953) (C. A., 9th Cir.).) (*Parker* v. *Lester*, 227 F. 2d 708 (1955) (C. A., 9th Cir.)); legislation authorizing the construction of Wilson Dam. (*Ashwander* v. *Tennessee Valley Authority*, 297 U. S. 288 (1936)); legislation requiring the recovery of excess war profits. (*Lichter* v. *United States*, 334 U. S. 742 (1948)); legislation authorizing Federal housing for persons engaged in national defense activities (*United States* v. *City of Chester et al*; 144 F. 2d 415 (1944) (C. A., 3d Cir.)); rent control legislation. (*Woods* v. *Miller Co.*, 333 U. S. 138 (1948).)

In *Von Knorr* v. *Miles*, 60 F. Supp. 962 (1945) (D. C. Mass.), the court upheld on the basis of the war powers a statute and Executive order pursuant to which the commanding general of the First Service Command had directed a Government contractor to remove from employment on and access to work under War and Navy Department contracts the plaintiff Von Knorr, about whom derogatory information had been received by the Government. The court stated, in language very appropriate to the present industrial security program:

> Cities Service Oil Co. was operating what was in essence a private arsenal of our democracy. The supplies it was preparing were designed for the use of the Armed Forces of the United States. The processes which it was applying may have involved Government secrets, and, at the least, the data on volume and type of production, on transportation, and on like matters were confidential. Interference with such production processes, or disclosure of such confidential data, were dangers against which Congress was empowered to provide. And an obvious and logical provision was an order excluding from areas where there were such processes and data any person or persons in whom the Government lacked confidence.

Such an exclusion order is as plainly within the war power as the more drastic orders excluding persons from the public streets at nighttime, sustained in *Hirabayashi's* case, from an entire city, sustained in *Korematsu's* case, or from the Pacific Coast States, sustained in *Endo's* case, 323 U. S. p. 302, 'lines 16–20, 65 S. Ct. 208. All those orders interefered with employment, and on a much wider scale than here where plaintiff remains free to work for his former employer in jobs having no connection with war contracts and free to work for other employers in Massachusetts or elsewhere. It is true that the orders in those three Supreme Court cases were orders directed to an entire group on the basis of a military commander's doubts as to their loyalty, whereas here the order is directed to a particular person. But if that be a distinction, it would seem that the order here was more not less justifiable because it rested on views as to an individual's loyalty rather than a group's loyalty.

Moreover, quite apart from the precedents supplied by the cases of *Hirabayashi, Korematsu,* and *Endo,* it is clear on broad grounds of constitutional principle that an order excluding any person from a defense plant in war time is valid.

Two interests are in competition and must be considered: the Government's concern to prevent both sabotage and disclosure to the enemy of secret processes, statistics, and information; and the private individual's concern to go where he pleases and engage in such work as is offered him.

It is not mere rhetoric to say that the Government's interest in avoiding sabotage and espionage in wartime is one of its most vital concerns. National survival is quite literally at stake. Every schoolboy knows that the experience of this Nation during the last war and of continental countries during this war shows how easily a country's military efforts may be hampered by the admission to war plants of persons who on their face appeared unobjectionable. Saboteurs do not parade with foreign credentials of professional competence. And arsenals are not guarded if watchmen exclude only those in whose satchels they have already found bombs. To avoid grave risks, a prudent government may rationally favor a policy denying access to war plants not only by a person proved dangerous but also by any person in whom the Government lacks absolute confidence. (Pp. 969–70.)

This case would be on all fours with the present industrial security program except for the fact that it arose during wartime and the Court's decision refers to that fact in several places. The reasoning of this decision, however, is probably as applicable to an industrial security program in time of national emergency or international crisis as it is in time of war.

Although some of the cases cited above were limited factually and by the decision to wartime situations. there is reason to believe that only in the *Korematsu* case is the decision applicable exclusively to an actual war situation. In any case, the courts have generaly held that the war powers are not limited to wartime but may be utilized in preparing for war or in dealing with problems created by war. See *Ashwander* v. *Tennessee Valley Authority et al., supra,* in which the Court sustained the power of the Government to construct Wilson Dam as an exercise by Congress of its war powers, that is, for the purposes of national defense, although construction was not begun until 1917 and was completed in 1926. The Court stated:

While the district court found that there is no intention to use the nitrate plants or the hydroelectric units installed at Wilson Dam for the production of war materials in time of peace, "the maintenance of said properties in operating condition and the assurance of an abundant supply of electric energy in the event of war, constitute national defense assets." This finding has ample support. (Pp. 327–328.) (See also

U. S. v. *City of Chester et al., supra,* and *U. S.* v. *City of Philadelphia,* 56 F. Supp. 862 (1944) (E. D. Pa.).)

There would seem to be little doubt, therefore, but that a statute establishing an industrial security program would be held to be a necessary and proper execution of the war powers of Congress, particularly during the present critical international situation and the resultant national emergency.

A second source of congressional power in this field is article IV, section 3, clause 2, which empowers Congress to make all needful rules and regulations respecting the property belonging to the United States. The industrial security program has as its subject matter the protection of property belonging to the United States (classified information) or being produced for sale to the United States (defense production). A statute enacted by Congress to set up an industrial security program would certainly constitute a rule or regulation respecting property belonging to the United States.

In *Von Knorr* v. *Miles, supra,* the court said:

> In considering the constitutional authority of Congress in time of war to exclude a person from a plant having a Government contract for war supplies, it would perhaps be possible under some circumstances to invoke either the power of Congress to "make all needful Rules and Regulations respecting the * * * Property * * * of the United States," U. S. Constitution, article IV, section 3, clause 2. . . . However, the former alternative is unavailable in the case at bar since there has been no showing as to what contracts there were between Cities Service Oil Co. and the Government, as to when the Government had acquired or would acquire title to the supplies being furnished, as to the extent to which the Government had any property on the premises of the company, or as to the employment contracts of the company. I, therefore, leave unresolved the question whether the order of August 13, 1943, can be supported by the power of Congress under article IV, section 3, clause 2.

It should be noted that the present industrial security program affects only those private companies which do have a procurement contract with the United States and then only when Government classified information (property) is or will be furnished the contractor.

The opinion in the case of *Ashwander* v. *Tennessee Valley Authority, supra,* in which the Court relied upon article IV, section 3, clause 2, to support the constitutional authority of Congress to provide for the disposal of electric energy generated at Wilson Dam, referring to Story on the Constitution, the Court said:

> The grant was made in broad terms, and the power of regulation and disposition was not confined to territory, but extended to "other property belonging to the United States," so that the power may be applied, as Story says, "to the due regulation of all other personal and real property rightfully belonging to the United States." And so, he adds, "it has been constantly understood and acted upon." (P. 331.)

The power of Congress to enact legislation authorizing an industrial security program may also be found in an extra constitutional source, namely, *the "inherent right of self-preservation"* which exists among all sovereign powers, i. e., the protection of the national security from internal revolt or foreign domination. The industrial security program has as its objective the preservation and protection of classified defense information so as to prevent sympathizers or agents of foreign governments from obtaining such information and disclosing or transmitting the same to a foreign entity. Such a program is clearly designed to and is necessary in order to protect the national security from internal revolt or foreign domination.

The court stated in *Communist Party of the United States* v. *Subversive Activities Control Board*, 223 F. 2d 531 (1954) (C. A. D. C.) :

> Antipathy to domination or control by a foreign government, or even to interference on the part of a foreign government, is a basic policy in this Nation.

. . . .

> "Self-preservation is a high prerogative of any sovereignty. . . . It seems to us that, however high in priority the right of self-preservation is among the prerogatives of sovereign powers in general, it is peculiarly so in respect to the Federal Government presently established in this country. As we conceive the matter, the government established by our Constitution is an instrument for service, particularly for the protection of the people whose servant it is; it is a working tool, the value of which lies in its usefulness. Since it was created by the people for the security of the people, especially against foreign encroachment, it has supreme duties both to protect its own existence and in insure that unidentified efforts on behalf of foreign agencies devoted to its disestablishment do not occur. (P. 543.)

In this connection, see also *Dunne et al.* v. *United States*, 138 F. 2d 137 (1943) (C. A., 8th Cir.), where the court declared:

> Appellants state that "This statute must seek its validity and force in the vague and undefined 'right of self-preservation'". No such extremity exists. The statute is grounded upon specific constitutional grants of power. The preamble, setting forth the purposes of the Constitution, includes to "insure domestic Tranquility" and "to provide for the common defence," as well as to "secure the Blessings of Liberty." Article 1, section 8, clause 1, specifically grants to Congress the power to "provide for the common Defence." Clause 18 grants the power "To make All Laws which shall be necessary and proper for carrying into Execution the foregoing Powers." Article IV, section 4, is "The United States shall guarantee to every State in this Union a Republican Form of Government, and shall protect each of them against Invasion" and, upon application, "against domestic Violence." Thus, the Constitution expresses clearly the thoughts that the life of the Nation and of the States and the Liberties and welfare of their citizens are to be preserved and that they are to have the protection of armed forces raised and maintained by the United States with power in Congress to pass all necessary and proper laws to raise, maintain and govern such forces. (P. 140.)

. . . .

> Congressional enactments having the purposes of raising or *maintaining* armed forces have high standing because of their importance. (P. 141.) [Emphasis added.]

This language would seem appropriate with reference to the industrial security program, which is concerned with the production of defense materials for the use of and by the Armed Forces.

It may be concluded, therefore, that Congress does have the constitutional authority to enact legislation expressly authorizing an industrial security program for the protection of our national secrets and defense production. Aside from procedural questions under the due-process clause, there is little doubt but that an exclusion or removal program such as is currently in operation under the Department of Defense industrial security program would be considered as a reasonable means of achieving the congressional objective.

Procedural Due Process and the Industrial Security Program

A conclusion that Congress has the constitutional authority to authorize an industrial security program does not constitute a determination that all of the means (procedures) utilized in the present industrial security program of the Department of Defense, or of any other such program, are or would be immune from constitutional attack based upon the due process clause. Questions of due process have actually been raised with respect to this program, for in the field of security legislation and regulation such concepts as the right to work and the right of confrontation have run headlong into the concept of national security. This problem was well expressed by the Court in *Dunne* v. *United States, supra,* when it stated:

At the same time, they [congressional enactments having the purpose of raising or maintaining Armed Forces] must not limit the constitutionally protected individual liberties of the citizen to any greater extent than is reasonably necessary and proper to accomplish the important allowable ends of preserving the life of the Government and the States and their orderly conduct.

PRESENT PROGRAM

Scope of the Program

The industrial security program of the Department of Defense was devised to safeguard classified information and material in the hands of defense contractors. Security agreements made with the contractors limit access to classified matter to persons who have been cleared and who have a "need to know." Denial or revocation of clearance for access to classified material does not require that an employee be discharged.

Relatively few Government agencies and departments have industrial security programs. While the most comprehensive are those of the Atomic Energy Commission and of the Department of Defense, the number of classified contracts that may be let from time to time by other agencies is relatively small, and they therefore have not been individually treated. An examination however of the Department of Defense industrial security program includes such problems as may be incident to other governmental industrial security programs. A separate section of the Commission's report is devoted to the Atomic Energy Commission program.

As defined and limited, the industrial security program obviously does not constitute the entire Government program for the protection of defense industries against sabotage, espionage, and subversion. Other important factors are the criminal laws against sabotage and espionage, the provisions of the Subversive Activities Control Act barring members of Communist-action groups, when found to be such by the Subversive Activities Control

257

Board, from employment in defense plants, and the industrial defense program designed to prevent interruption of vital defense production.

Since the current industrial security program is focused upon safeguarding classified material, we may note here the three present levels of classification:

TOP SECRET.—Defense information and material, the unauthorized disclosure of which could result in *exceptionally grave damage* to the Nation.

SECRET.—Defense information and material, the unauthorized disclosure of which could result in *serious damage* to the Nation.

CONFIDENTIAL.—Defense information and material, the unauthorized disclosure of which could be *prejudicial* to the defense interests of the Nation.

Organization of the Program

Three fundamental documents set up the current program. The Armed Forces Industrial Security Regulation is the basic guide for Government security officers, and is not ordinarily distributed to defense contractors. The Industrial Security Manual establishes the requirements for safeguarding classified information in the hands of defense contractors. A copy goes to each contractor seeking plant clearance and he must sign an agreement to maintain the security safeguards it describes. The third important document is the Industrial Personnel Security Review Regulation which prescribes a uniform standard and criteria for determining which employees may have access to classified information. This third regulation also fixes procedures in case a military department recommends the denial or revocation of clearance.

Although each of the military departments has its own regulations and instructions to augment the basic policy documents, the industrial security program is carried out under the uniform direction of the Department of Defense.

Overall responsibility for developing policies, procedures, and standards lies with the Assistant Secretary of Defense for Manpower, Personnel, and Reserve. He is also responsible for assigning "security cognizance" (described below) of each defense plant to one of the three military departments.

The Director of the Office of Personnel Security Policy and his Industrial Security Programs Division are responsible for coordinating the industrial security operations of the Army, Navy, and Air Force.

The Assistant Chief of Staff, Intelligence, Department of the Army, supervises the central index file which concentrates current information from all three services regarding both personnel and plant security clearances.

The Defense Department has organized training courses for security officers of the military departments and of defense plants, conducted by the Army Intelligence School at Fort Holabird, Md. The Defense Department also furnishes industry with educational material on security, including motion pictures, posters, leaflets, cartoons, editorials, technical guidance, and a periodic industrial security letter.

The internal organization of the industrial security program in each of the three military departments is as follows:

ARMY.—Overall responsibility, the Assistant Secretary for Manpower and Reserve Forces. Staff supervision, Assistant Chief of Staff, Intelligence. Field administration (security cognizance, plant inspection, plant and personnel clearances, investigations), commanding general of each continental Army. Approval of bids and negotiations for classified contracts and plant clearance, procurement offices.[44]

NAVY.—Overall responsibility, Assistant Secretary for Personnel and Reserve Forces. Policy, Chief of Naval Operations. Coordination, Chief of Navy Material and Chief of Naval Operations, jointly. Field administration (clearances, cognizance, security inspections), Navy material, usually district inspectors. Contracts and classification, the procurement bureaus (Aeronautics, Ships, Yards and Docks, Office of Naval Research). Investigations, Office of Naval Intelligence.[45]

AIR FORCE.—Overall responsibility, Assistant Secretary for Manpower, Personnel, and Reserve. Staff supervision, the Inspector General and his deputy for security. Policy and liaison with Defense Department, Assistant for Security Plans and Policy (Deputy Inspector General for Security). Investigations, the Office of Special Investigations. Procedures, Office of the Provost Marshal. Field administration, the Air Materiel Command (8 Air Materiel areas, including 19 Air Procurement districts and 34 Air Force plant representatives) and the Air Research and Development Command (4 territorial suboffices).[46]

Plant Clearances

To avoid the necessity of a defense contractor dealing with more than one military department, the Department of Defense assigns each contract plant to the "security cognizance"—a term embracing jurisdiction and responsibility—of just one of the Armed Forces, even though the contractor may be doing classified work for several. However, each contracting department still performs some special functions to protect the security of its own classified information.

Before a defense contractor may have access to classified information, he must receive what the Defense Department calls facility clearance. The security office of the military department with jurisdiction over the plant in question first makes a survey to determine if the plant can provide the proper safeguards to keep classified material out of unauthorized hands. An investigation is then made to determine whether or not the firm—or the

---

[44] Army Regulation 380–131, Oct. 4, 1955.
[45] Secnav Instruction 5430.17, Mar. 16, 1954.
[46] Air Force presentation to the Commission on Government Security, June 29, 1956.

parent corporation, if the firm is part of a complex corporate structure—is foreign owned or controlled. The principal owners, officers, directors, and executive personnel having the need to handle classified material must be cleared individually. The contractor is then required to sign an agreement to abide by security regulations.

Should the firm appear to be foreign controlled or should any of the officials fail to obtain personal security clearance, the responsible military department recommends to the Defense Department that security plant clearance be denied, and the case is processed according to the Industrial Personnel Security Review Regulation. If plant clearance is revoked solely on the basis of lack of physical elements of security, the personnel clairances will not be withdrawn if the security lack is corrected within 6 months.[47]

Personnel Clearances [48]

Clearances under the industrial security program are not for employment; they are merely for access to classified material. The contractor himself may clear an employee for access to confidential material if the employee is a United States citizen and there is no information known to the contractor which indicates that the employee's access to confidential material is not clearly consistent with the interests of national security.

Access to higher levels of classification is granted by the security office of the cognizant military department only after Government investigation of the employee involved. For secret, a national agency check is made of the Federal Bureau of Investigation; Army, Navy, or Air Force; Civil Service Commission (in the case of ex-Federal employees); Bureau of Immigration and Naturalization (in the case of immigrants); House Committee on Un-American Activities, or other appropriate Government agency. For access to top-secret information, a full background investigation is made covering the subject's life since January 1, 1937, or since his 18th birthday, whichever is the later, seeking facts on his integrity, reputation, and loyalty to the United States.

The single uniform standard on which clearance is granted for access to classified material is that it is clearly consistent with the interests of national security.[49]

The Regulation lists 22 criteria for the application of the standard, adding that final determination must be on an overall, commonsense basis, founded on all available information.[50] The criteria:

    1. Sabotage, espionage, treason, sedition, or attempting, aiding, or abetting sabotage, etc.

---

[47] AFISR, sec. 2–111.
[48] Ibid., sec. 2–200.
[49] Industrial Personnel Security Review Regulations, sec. 12.
[50] Ibid., sec. 13.

2. Sympathetic association with a saboteur, spy, traitor, seditionist, anarchist, revolutionist, or a secret agent of a foreign government, or anyone advocating the overthrow of the United States Government by force or violence.

3. Advocacy of force or violence to overthrow the Government.

4. Membership in, or affiliation or sympathetic association with, any foreign or domestic organization, association, group, or combination of persons which is totalitarian, Fascist, Communist, or subversive, or which has adopted, or shows, a policy of advocating or approving the commission of acts of force or violence to deny other persons their rights under the Constitution of the United States, or which seeks to alter the form of government of the United States by unconstitutional means.

5. Intentional unauthorized disclosure of classified information.

6. Action in the interests of another government in preference to the interests of the United States.

7. Participation in the activities of an organization established as a front for an organization referred to under 4, when personally sympathetic to the subversive purposes of such organization.

8. Participation in the activities of an organization with the knowledge that it had been infiltrated by members of subversive groups under circumstances indicating that the individual was sympathetic to the infiltrating element or its purposes.

9. Participation in the activities of an organization referred to in 4, in a capacity where he should reasonably have had knowledge of the subversive aims or purposes of the organization.

10. Sympathetic interest in totalitarian, Fascist, Communist, or similar subversive movements.

11. Sympathetic association with a member or members of a group indicated in 4, ordinarily excluding chance or occasional meetings or normal business or official relations.

12. Currently maintaining a close continuing association or relationship with a person who has engaged in activities or associations of the type referred to in 1 through 10.

13. Close, continuing association of the type described in 12, even though later separated by distance, if renewal of the association seems probable.

14. Willful violation or disregard of security regulations.

15. Acts or associations indicating that the individual is not reliable or trustworthy.

16. Deliberate misrepresentations or material omissions from a personal security questionnaire, personal history statement, or similar document.

17. Criminal, dishonest, immoral or notoriously disgraceful conduct, habitual drunkenness, drug addiction, or sexual perversion.

18. Reckless or irresponsible acts indicating such poor judgment and instability that an individual might disclose classified information to unauthorized persons or otherwise assist them in activities inimical to the security of the United States.

19. Physical or mental illness which competent medical authority believes may cause deficiency in judgment or reliability.

20. Facts indicating that the individual may be subjected to coercion or pressures which may cause him to act contrary to the best interests of the national security.

21. Similar pressures which may be brought about by the presence of close relatives in a nation unfriendly to the interests of the United States, or in satellites of, or areas occupied by such nation.

22. Refusal by the individual, upon the ground of constitutional privilege against self-incrimination, to testify before a congressional or legislative committee, or Federal or State court or other tribunal, regarding charges of his alleged disloyalty or other misconduct.

Legitimate labor activities are not pertinent considerations.

Hearing and Appeal [51]

If the security office of the cognizant military department recommends denial of clearance, the case is forwarded through military channels to the Director of the Office of Industrial Personnel Security Review in the Department of Defense.

The case first comes before the Screening Board (in Washington, D. C.), and if this Board decides that clearance should be denied, it issues a statement of reasons indicating, in as specific detail as security considerations permit, the grounds for denial. A notice of suspension of clearance is issued simultaneously.

The employee is given the right to a hearing before one of three hearing boards (located in New York, Chicago, and San Francisco). He is given a transcript of the hearing which does not include confidential reports of the Federal Bureau of Investigation and other investigating agencies, nor does it contain information which might identify confidential informants or the source of confidential evidence. The hearing board is required to take into consideration the fact that the employee may have been handicapped in his defense by the withholding of classified information, or by his lack of opportunity to idenitfy or cross-examine persons who have been sources of information.

The hearing is not open to the public. The employee and his counsel have the right to be present throughout the hearing, but a witness may be present only while testifying. The board may request the attendance of witnesses, but the Government will not pay witness fees or travel expenses. Strict rules

---

[51] Industrial Personnel Security Review Regulation, secs. 15–26.

of evidence need not be followed. Hearsay evidence will be admitted, as will any material, oral or written, which in the minds of reasonable men is of probative value in determining the issues involved.

The hearing has two stated purposes: to permit the employee to present evidence on his own behalf, and to ascertain all the relevant facts to aid in reaching a fair and impartial decision.

The three-man hearing board reaches its decision by majority vote. The decision must be accompanied by findings as to each allegation set forth in the statement of reasons.

If the decision is not unanimous, the case is forwarded to the Review Board in Washington. Even if it is unanimous, if the Director of the Office of Industrial Personnel Security Review believes the case presents novel issues or unusual circumstances, he may send it to the Review Board. There is no general right of review.

If the case reaches the Review Board, it will be considered on the written record. Decision is by majority vote. Only the Secretary of Defense, or the Secretaries of the three military departments by joint agreement at the request of one of their number, may reverse a final decision of the Review Board to deny clearance.

If the decision is favorable to the employee, the military department which originally forwarded the case to the Department of Defense will reimburse him for loss of earnings resulting directly from suspension of his clearance.

The Program in Perspective

In an address to the ninth annual conference of the National Civil Liberties Clearing House in Washington, April 4, 1957, Mr. George MacClain, of the Department of Defense, quoted statistics to place the industrial security program "in proper perspective." Mr. MacClain, who is special assistant and legal adviser to the Director, Office of Industrial Personnel Security Review, had this to say:

Experience has shown that only a small proportion of the workers employed in United States industry will ever become the subject of an industrial security case. For instance, the work force in industry in the United States today is about 17 million. Yet during the 8-year period since 1949, the total number of all clearances granted has been only about 3 million. Between about July 1953 and the end of February this year, less than 3,000 cases have involved derogatory information that was sufficiently serious to require consideration by the screening board. Of these cases, 2,210 were processed under the former program from about July 1953 to April 1955; 517 came up under the present program between April 1955 and July 1956; the remaining 202 came up between July 1956 and February 1957.

Almost all of these cases have been finally settled as of today; 692 of them were closed out without a decision, principally because the individual left his job before screening board action was taken; 1,299 resulted in clearances, and 886 resulted in denial or revocation of clearance . . . a relatively negligible figure. . . .

Approximately 60 percent of the cases considered by the Central Screening Board since its establishment in 1955 have resulted in clearance for the individual concerned at that level. This figure contrasts with experience

263

under the preceding program 1953–55) where clearances were issued in only 37 percent of the cases by the regional screening boards. At the same time, when the cases unfavorable to the employee were subjected to the test of the hearing and review procedures, decisions reached by the Central Screening Board were sustained in approximately 60 percent of the cases, as compared with 44 percent sustained under the 1953–55 program.[52]

APPENDIX

CASES PROCESSED UNDER THE INDUSTRIAL PERSONNEL SECURITY REVIEW REGULATION

[Program established by DOD directive 5220.6, dated Feb. 2, 1955, effective Apr. 2, 1955]

(Figures cover period from Apr. 2, 1955, through Feb. 28, 1957)

A. Cases considered and disposed of by the screening board, hearing boards, and review board under current program_____ 719

1. Cleared by screening board_____ 333
2. Closed without final decision as a result of termination of employment or case withdrawn by submitting agency, etc._____ 154
3. Statements of reasons issued by screening board_____ 232

4. Final denial or revocation of clearance by director after failure of reply to statements of reasons_____ 64
5. Statements of reasons outstanding_____ 14
6. Referred to hearing board after reply to statements of reasons_____ 152
7. Referred directly to review board after reply to statements of reasons____ 2

8. Action of hearing board under 6 above:
    (a) Clearances granted_____ 42
    (b) Denial or revocation of clearance_____ 62
    (c) Pending_____ 33
    (d) Hearing board decisions referred to review board prior to announcement by director_____ 15
9. Action of review board under 8 (d) above:
    (a) Clearance granted_____ 4
    (b) Denial or revocation of clearance_____ 6
    (c) Pending_____ 5
10. Action of review board under 7 above:
    (a) Denial or revocation of clearance_____ 2
11. Total clearances after hearing and/or review_____ 46
12. Total denials or revocations of clearance after hearing and/or review____ 70

B. Cases decided under former programs reconsidered by the review board_____ 41

1. Sustained, previous denials_____ 14
2. Reversed, previous denials (cleared)_____ 27

C. Cases decided under current program reconsidered by the review board_____ 1
1. Sustained, previous denial_____ 1

---

[52] First annual report, Industrial Personnel Security Review Program, p. 5.

Statistics compiled by the Office of Industrial Personnel Security Review, Department of Defense.

For further statistics, see appendix B of first annual report on the industrial personnel security review program, 1956.

Physical Security and Visitors

The Industrial Security Manual gives detailed instructions for handling, safeguarding, and transmitting classified material. Not only must a contractor sign an agreement to follow the instructions but if his plant cannot meet basic storage requirements, he cannot submit bids on a classified contract. Top-secret information must be kept in a safe or a steel safe file having a three-position, dial-type combination lock. Secret or confidential material may be kept in a locked desk or file cabinet if a continuous watch is maintained by an officially assigned guard, or in a steel file cabinet secured by a steel bar and padlock of the three-position combination type. Confidential (modified handling authorized) information may be kept in a locked room or locked file cabinet or any other container with a locking device.

Secret and top secret must be accounted for by an inventory that must be maintained as a record for at least 10 years.[53] Top-secret material must be transmitted by cleared messenger approved in writing by the Government and never by mail. Top secret, secret, and cryptographic material must not be destroyed by the contractor (burning or pulping in the presence of witnesses) except by official approval.[54]

Control of visitors to a defense plant is required to prevent unauthorized access to classified information. When possible, visits should be approved in advance. The contractor is held responsible for confirming the visitor's identity and degree of security clearance, and must make a record of the visit and the nature of the classified material examined by the visitor, and keep the record for at least 10 years.[55]

The manual establishes 12 categories of visitors. Several categories, such as an interchange of employees between different plants operated by the same contractor; and the visit of subcontractors, venders, and suppliers require only that the visitor's clearance be checked with the cognizant military security office, but leave control in the hands of the contractor. Other categories require express approval by Government security and contracting officers. Military control is exercised in the case of foreign nationals, and representatives of the Atomic Energy Commission or other Federal agencies.[56]

The principal problem raised by these detailed regulations has been an alleged diversity of interpretation by various field representatives of the military departments.

---

[53] Industrial Security Manual, sec. II, 9a ff.
[54] Ibid., sec. II, 14.
[55] Industrial Security Manual, sec. V, 26, 27.
[56] Industrial Security Manual, sec. V, 28.

RECOMMENDATIONS

NECESSITY

An industrial security program is necessary as a result of the continuing effort to infiltrate industries vital to the security of the United States.

Two basic reasons suggest themselves for the necessity of an industrial security program in the United States, viz.: (1) the enigmatic character of Communist Russia's future actions as well as her openly avowed objective of world domination and her ruthless foreign policy; and (2) the sweeping and fundamental change in the nature of warfare within the past decade. Never before has the United States been faced by a foe possessed with more formidable means of destruction than today; never before has the importance of the maintenance not only of this country's safety, but the well-being of all nations, depended so much on the continuing development of advanced weapons and techniques, made available to our Armed Forces by science and the technological achievements of industry. Much depends, therefore, on our ability and efforts to safeguard advances in these fields. What good are advanced weapons made obsolete by reason of enemy counter-measures based on knowledge gained by infiltration and espionage in American industry? Industry, itself, has declared that an industrial security program is necessary and essential to our country's survival, and further that it is an added safeguard to our Government's secrets. No longer can a clear distinction be made between a nation at peace and a nation at war: the record of Communist infiltration into America's strategic industries is now established beyond challenge.

Continuation of Present Program

The Commission recommends that the present industrial security program should not be continued, but further recommends that the industrial security program be modified, as set forth herein in the subsequent recommendations.

STANDARD

The present standard should not be retained but should be modified as follows:

Clearance should be denied or revoked if it is determined, on the basis of all the available information, that access to classified information and materials will endanger the common defense and security.

America's scientific and industrial secrets need protection; one of the means to accomplish this is to restrict access to the same. By what standard shall an individual be denied access? It must be one that will prevent access to those whose character and conduct not only makes their trustworthiness doubtful but also unacceptable as trustees of such vitally important information. The present standard for denial of personnel clearance in the Department of Defense Industrial Personnel Security Regulations 5220.6 is: Clearance shall be denied or revoked if it is determined, on the basis of all the available information, that access to classified information by the person concerned is not clearly consistent with the interests of the national security.

The standard is extremely important because that is the test which the hearing examiner or the head of the responsible agency must apply in determining whether or not access should be denied. If loyalty alone were the standard, then the only ground for denial of access to classified matter would be that there is reasonable doubt as to the loyalty of the employee. But a loyal person might also be subject to pressures; he might be a loyal person with a criminal record; he might talk too much; or he might be a drug addict. Thus "loyalty" as a concept is not synonymous with that of "endangering the common defense", because the latter embraces more than just loyalty. Criticism has been leveled at the standard of "clearly consistent with national security" because as a concept it involves more elements than are involved in the question of whether or not national security would be endangered. The original Executive Order 9835 provided a standard of disloyalty which was later modified to read "reasonable doubt as to loyalty". Some cleared, because there was no evidence of disloyalty, were later denied clearance because the standard was changed to "reasonable doubt as to loyalty". Executive Order 10450 changed the standard to "clearly consistent with national security", and called for readjudication of persons who had been cleared under the previous standard of reasonable doubt as to loyalty. The standard here recommended is a slight modification of the standard used by the Atomic Energy Commission. It has been subjected to little criticism and generally accepted publicly and in government circles as much better than standards used in other security programs; it has worked better with less harm to individuals.

267

CRITERIA

The present criteria should not be retained, but should be modified as follows:

Factors which may be considered in connection with the application of the foregoing standard should include but not be limited to:

(*a*) Sabotage, espionage, or attempts or preparations therefor or knowingly associates with spies or saboteurs;

(*b*) Treason or sedition or advocacy thereof;

(*c*) Advocacy of revolution or force or violence to alter the constitutional form of Government of the United States;

(*d*) Intentional unauthorized disclosure to any person of classified information or materials, or recurrent and serious, although unintentional, disclosure of such information and materials;

(*e*) Performing or attempting to perform his duties, or otherwise acting, so as to serve the interests of another government in preference to the interests of the United States;

(*f*) Membership in, affiliation or sympathetic association with any party, group, or association which the Congress of the United States, or any agency or officer of the United States duly authorized by the Congress for that purpose, finds:

(1) Seeks to alter the form of Government of the United States by force or violence, or other unconstitutional means; or,

(2) Is organized or utilized for the purpose of advancing the aims and objectives of the Communist movement; or,

(3) Is organized or utilized for the purpose of establishing any form of dictatorship in the United States or any form of international dictatorship; or,

(4) Is organized or utilized by any foreign government, or by any foreign party, group, or association acting in the interests of such foreign government for the purpose of (*a*) espionage, or (*b*) sabotage, or (*c*) obtaining information relating to the defense of the United States or the protection of the national security, or (*d*) hampering, hindering, or delaying the production of defense materials; or,

(5) Is affiliated with, or acts in concert with, or is dominated or controlled by, and party, group, or association of the character described in (1) or (2) or (3) or (4) above.

(g) Membership in or affiliation with any organization which the Congress of the United States, or any agency or officer of the United States duly authorized by the Congress for that purpose, finds has adopted a policy of advocating or approving the commission of acts of force and violence to deny others their rights under the Constitution of the United States.

(h) Refusal to testify upon the ground of self-incrimination in any authorized inquiry conducted by a congressional committee, Federal court, Federal grand jury, or any other duly authorized agency, unless the individual, after opportunity to do so, satisfactorily explains his refusal to testify;

(i) Willful violations or disregard of security regulations, or recurrent and serious, although unintentional, violation of such regulations;

(j) Any illness, including any mental condition, of a nature which in the opinion of competent medical authority may cause significant defect in the performance, judgment, or reliability of the employee with due regard to the transient or continued effect of the illness and the medical findings in such case;

(k) Any behavior, activities, or associations which tend to show that the individual is not reliable or trustworthy;

(l) Any deliberate misrepresentations, falsifications, or omission of material facts from a personnel security questionnaire, personal history statement, or similar document;

(m) Any criminal, infamous, dishonest, immoral or notoriously disgraceful conduct, habitual use of intoxicants to excess, drug addiction, or sexual perversion;

(n) Any facts which furnish reason to believe that the individual may be subjected to coercion, influence, or pressure which may cause him to act contrary to the best interests of the national security.

The 22 criteria presently found in the Department of Defense Industrial Personnel Review Regulation 5220.6, have been reviewed as to clarity and the necessity of adding or eliminating some of them. As a result the Commission recommends a reduction in this number. For example, the present criteria numbers 12 and 13 read:

(12) Currently maintaining a close continuing association with a person who has engaged in activities or associations of the type referred to in . . . . A close continuing association may be deemed to exist if the individual lives at the same premises as, frequently visits, or frequently communicates with such person.

(13) Close continuing association of type described in subparagraph (12) above, even though later separated by distance, if the circumstances indicate that renewal of the association is probable.

Elimination of such multiple association criteria is recommended, because a close continuing association even though separated by distance carries with it an inherently contradictory concept. Individuals should not be deprived of rights by a factor of remote association, for in almost everyone's life may be found the situation of knowing someone who knows another person who might be of questionable character. On the other hand, associations which tend to show whether a person is reliable or trustworthy are retained in the recommended criteria. The refusal to testify at an authorized inquiry has been added, as well as provision for giving the individual an opportunity to explain his refusal to testify; it has been recommended also that the individual be accorded the right to question the scope of the inquiry of the committee under their authorization from Congress.

INDIVIDUALS COVERED

Prehiring Clearances

1. The Commission recommends that there should be a procedure available for prehiring clearances, and that preemployment clearance procedures should be made available to all employees requiring clearance.

2. It is recommended that the present requirement that an individual be employed before an investigation is conducted be eliminated, and that where the contractor certifies that he will employ an individual if such individual is cleared, an appropriate investigation for clearance be made.

3. Preemployment clearance procedures should be made available to all employees who are being considered for "secret" or "top secret" work.

There should be a procedure available for prehiring clearances, and preemployment clearance procedures should be made available to all employees requiring clearance. The present procedure whereby an industrial facility cannot request clearance of an individual until he actually enters on duty very often places the facility in an almost impossible situation. Although the individual is being hired to work on a spcific contract, he cannot have access to information in secret and top secret work until the Government has furnished its clearance and this sometimes takes several months.

The problem is what to do with the individual; although he is on the company rolls he cannot be given access to any of the information necessary

270

for him to do his job. It is granted that the possibility of interim clearance is a partial solution, but very often an agency has such a backlog of cases that even to get an interim clearance is time consuming, and can be done only in an emergency situation and in order to avoid crucial delays

As a solution to this situation, it is recommended that provisions be made for clearance procedures to be accomplished while the prospective employee is in an applicant status. If the individual withdraws from consideration during a preemployment investigation, it should be mandatory that the contractor immediately notify the clearing agency of the applicant's withdrawal from consideration.

Further, if the central index files contained all the Government accumulated information available on individuals, and was so organized to facilitate quick search, there appears no reason why the great bulk of industrial employees could not be speedily cleared making them available forthwith for work on classified contracts.

The Small Business Administration reported in a letter to the Commission on Government Security dated December 18, 1956, that in response to its questionnaire sent to members of its advisory boards throughout the country, the following information was received.

Question: Should a pool of cleared personnel be established?

Reply: Yes—132; No—26; No opinion—35; No answer—15.

The Commission on Government Security partial interrogatory-industrial security, dated September 13, 1956, asked:

IV.4. What are the advantages or disadvantages of waiting until a person is employed before beginning clearance procedure?

The answers were interpolated to reflect the views of the persons interviewed as to whether they favored prehiring clearance. Of 90 interviews, the results were as follows: Yes—45; Qualified yes—5; No—15; Qualified no—1; No comment—24.

While under the Atomic Energy Act, prehiring clearances are required, paragraph 19 of Defense Department industrial manual for safeguarding classified information (September 21, 1955) states that personnel clearance action for an individual may not be initiated prior to his actual employment. It is felt that this particular article in the Department of Defense instructions should be changed to enable the initiation of clearance on an individual person prior to actual employment.

Special Problems in Clearance of Aliens

The requirement that clearance procedures are not begun until immigrant aliens declare their intention to become United States citizens is unrealistic. It affords no additional security protection and should be eliminated. In lieu thereof, the alien should be

271

required to produce evidence that he is legally in the United States and entitled to work under the terms of his admission.

The clearance of aliens should be handled in the same manner as clearance of citizens. In the case of Canadian aliens without visas, the national agency check should include a check with the Royal Canadian Mounted Police. In the case of Mexican aliens without visas, the national agency check should include a check with the appropriate Mexican police officials.

Aliens under immigrant or nonimmigrant categories have been screened by the visa procedures prior to their admission to the United States and it thus seems unwise to recommend a second screening, particularly in view of the recommendation of the Commission that visa clearance procedures be strengthened by transferring such functions to the Immigration Service.

Relative to the problems in clearance of aliens, a pertinent section of DOD Armed Forces industrial security regulation, September 21, 1956, is quoted below:

2–203 *Requirements for Security Clearances for Contractor Personnel*

The requirements that shall be accomplished with favorable results prior to issuing letters of consent to facilities for the various categories of personnel security clearances are prescribed below. In addition, an immigrant alien to be eligible for a personnel security clearance shall have formally declared his intent to become a United States citizen before a naturalization court. In the event the individual refuses to execute Naturalization form N–315, clearance shall not be issued. The facilities shall be notified to this effect and the request for investigation shall be canceled. Security clearances that have been previously granted to immigrant aliens who do not intend to become United States citizens shall be administratively terminated by the security office of the cognizant military department, who will notify the individual, as well as management of the facility, of such action. These actions are not appealable. The central index file will be notified of such action through submitting a central index card—Personnel (DD form 264), noting under item 15, "Remarks," the facts of this matter. However, prior to the withdrawal of personnel security clearance under this provision, immigrant aliens shall be notified of the requirement and given a reasonable length of time to comply therewith. . . .

The declaration of intent serves no useful purpose and should be eliminated in favor of close security. A foreigner with intent to damage our nation would have no compunction about making a false declaration of intent, and the requirement may bar an honest foreigner who does not wish to make the declaration falsely. Therefore, the country loses his services.

A total of 70 contractors and security officers were contacted concerning alien clearance. Twenty-nine of this number or 40 percent, stated that the present regulations are adequate and create no problem. Twelve, or 17 percent, believe that the clearance procedure takes too long, and 7 of this number stated that because of the delay none are hired. An additional 16 stated that the regulations are generally satisfactory but should be altered to permit easier clearance of aliens. Eight believed that the declaration of intent to become an American citizen is meaningless. It was pointed out that if an alien came to this country for purposes of espionage, he would not hesitate to sign a false declaration of intent; but on the other hand, an honest alien may refuse to sign the declaration if he does not intend to become a citizen. Two believed that an alien cannot be thoroughly investigated. Two stated that a distinction should be made between aliens from friendly countries and aliens from the Communist-dominated countries. Another two informants believed there should be a central clearance agency for all aliens. Overall, a little more than half of the officials concerned with security believed that changes should be made.

Approximately 37,000 commuters who live in Canada and work in Detroit, owe their allegiance to the Queen. If they become United States citizens, they would lose their Canadian social pensions and benefits. Some of these individuals file the declaration of intent without actually intending to become citizens.

The American Society for Industrial Security, in a report to the Commission dated November 5, 1956, stated that the declaration of intent has little or no significance and that the requirement can result in losing the services of highly qualified aliens who do not wish to file a false declaration.

Expansion of Industrial Security Program

The Commission recommends that the industrial security program, which now authorizes the denial to designated individuals of access to classified information within a facility, not be expanded so as to authorize the exclusion of designated individuals from access to any part of a defense facility.

There is now a program which protects the classified information and materials phase of industrial security. Especially in view of the Commission's recommendation to abolish the confidential category, there will be many places in a plant where one could work without clearance for secret or top secret if the employer desires to continue the employment.

Any such bill as the Butler bill (S. 681, 84th Cong., 1st sess.) would have to be confined to the hard-core Communists and the investigative agencies of the Government have them well identified. In the event of war or insurrection, under title II of the Internal Security Act of 1950 they could be apprehended and detained.

Title I of the Internal Security Act of 1950 contains a provision, now under review by the United States Supreme Court, prohibiting employment of members of Communist-action groups in defense facilities.

To make such a program as that outlined in the Butler bill really effective would require screening of thousands of individuals not now subject to the security program, and the Commission regards such screening as objectionable and unnecessary.

The Commission believes that if an employee is discharged upon alleged security grounds, the present procedures under the National Labor Relations Act, as amended, provide adequate protection of the rights of the employee, as well as the employer. However, the Commission believes that the following should be made explicit by way of improving the present procedures:

Where an employee's clearance is denied or revoked for access to classified information and materials for the reason that such access would endanger the common defense and security, such denial or revocation of clearance by the Government shall not be the basis of any charge of unfair labor practice nor shall such decision be open to arbitration.

Where an employee is discharged upon the ground that he is an alleged security risk, and the employee or his representative contends that the discharge constitutes an unfair labor practice, or that such discharge was without just cause in violation of a collective bargaining agreement, and where there has been a hearing and adjudication in respect to said employee in connection with clearance, the transcript of the record including hearings, findings, and the decision, shall be made available to the employer and the employee and shall be admissible in evidence before the National Labor Relations Board or in any arbitration or other hearing.

Under Section 8 (a) (3) of the National Labor Relations Act, it is an unfair labor practice for an employer to discriminate against an employee because of his union activities, and the NLRB has the power to order reinstatement and back pay. The situation for consideration, therefore, is one in which the employer seizes upon the denial of clearance for access to classified matter as a pretext for discharging the employee. An unfair labor practice exists only where the employer's real reason for the discharge can be shown to be to discourage union activity.

Under section 10 (c) of the Act, the NLRB may not order reinstatement or back pay where an employee has been discharged "for cause". Apparently no cases have ever reached the NLRB in which an employer has discharged an employee after denial of clearance under the industrial security program. The problem of proof of anti-union motivation would be extremely difficult where the employer could point to the Government denial of clearance as cause.

The general counsel of the NLRB has refused to issue an unfair labor practice complaint, in the few cases in which the question has come up, on the grounds of insufficient evidence of employer intent to discriminate to discourage union activity. For example, see *NLRB General Counsel Administrative Ruling, Case No. 410* (October 24, 1952, 31 LRRM 1067), where it was held that an employer engaged in defense work, did not violate the NLRA by discharging an employee classified by the Army-Navy-Air Force Personnel Security Board as a security risk, and that although a possible discrimination might lie in the employer's refusal to assign the employee to unclassified work, the employer, in discharging the employee, followed a ruling of the State Board of Arbitration in a prior case that national security would be jeopardized by presence in the plant of individuals who had been classified as security risks. About 6 months after his discharge, the employee was reinstated to his old job after the employer was notified that the Industrial Employment Review Board had reversed the Security Board's determination. The employer had previously discharged six other employees who also had been classified as security risks by the Air Force. At that time, the State Board of Arbitration had ruled that the employer should not be required to reemploy the six employees.

Since a strike in 1949, which concerned the question whether an employer should dismiss so-called security risks or make room for them elsewhere, contracts between the employer and the union usually include a provision that the union will not contest any action the company reasonably may take to comply with its security obligation to the Government.

Collective Bargaining Agreements

The Commission believes that while the parties have the right to enter into collective bargaining agreements with respect to any matters they desire, any provision therein relating to industrial security must be consistent with and subject to the obligation of the contractor to protect the national security as required by contract, law, or regulation.

Labor-Management Relations

The Commission believes that the present laws can be strengthened by giving the National Labor Relations Board jurisdiction to inquire, by administrative hearings after appropriate notice, into the truth or falsity of the non-Communist oaths executed in compliance with section 9 (h) of the Labor Management Relations Act of 1947, and if the National Labor Relations Board finds that one or more of the union officers have falsely executed such oath, the union should thereupon be ineligible to utilize the facilities of the National Labor Relations Board in connection with labor-management disputes and grievances. When the union has cleared itself

of any taint it will be eligible to utilize the services of the National Labor Relations Board.

Measures must be taken to eliminate Communist domination of unions, and to exclude the Communist-dominated unions from bargaining positions in industrial plants having classified contracts.

The study and investigation of the Commission show that organized labor has generally been aware of the Communist problem and has cooperated with management in this regard. There is very little labor-management friction on this problem. It is believed, however, that the national security will be better protected by the above recommendation.

Prosecutions by the Department of Justice for filing of false non-Communist affidavits under section 9 (h) of the Labor-Management Relations Act of 1947 have resulted in eleven convictions and no acquittals. Only one of the defendants is actually serving a sentence in jail (Hupman); one defendant (Nelson) died after conviction; and one other defendant (Zenchuck) was given a suspended sentence after pleading guilty. Three of the convictions were reversed, two of which are to be retried. One case is pending before the Supreme Court and four cases are now pending before the courts of appeals; five cases are awaiting original trial.

The Gold Case [57]

On January 28, 1957, the United States Supreme Court reversed a conviction of Ben Gold for making a false statement under the non-Communist affidavit provisions of the Labor-Management-Relations Act and remanded the case to the District Court with directions to grant a new trial because of official intrusion into the privacy of the jury. Justices Reed, Burton, and Clark dissented on the ground that any presumption of prejudice to the defendant arising out of the incident had been rebutted in the hearing which the trial judge held on the matter. Mr. Justice Clark dissented on the additional grounds that proper judicial administration would be impeded by the failure of the Supreme Court to pass on a number of legal questions which are important in this and other cases:

    1. Applicability of the perjury rule of evidence to the false statement statute;

    2. Eligibility of Government employees to serve as jurors;

    3. Admissibility of evidence of prior activity in the Communist Party to disprove the sincerity of a resignation therefrom;

    4. The use of expert witnesses to prove continuing membership; and

    5. The correctness of the Court's charges as to membership in the Party.

---

[57] *Gold v. United States,* 25 *Law Week* 322, Jan. 28, 1957.

The incident which led to the order for a new trial was that an FBI agent, investigating another case in which falsity of a non-Communist affidavit was also charged, telephoned or visited three members of the petit jury or their families during the trial and inquired whether they had received any propaganda literature.[58]

The Justice Department has recently taken steps to invoke another type of sanction against the filing of false affidavits with the National Labor Relations Board. It obtained an indictment against fourteen officials and staff members of the Mine, Mill and Smelter Workers charging them with fraudulent conspiracy to obtain the services of the National Labor Relations Board through the filing of false affidavits. The case is pending before the United States district court in Denver.

It will be noted from the dissenting opinion in the Gold case above that a number of difficult legal questions remain to be resolved as to validity of convictions obtained for filing non-Communist affidavits. In spite of the legal obstacles in the way of criminal prosecutions in non-Communist affidavit cases, Department of Justice officials feel that the Taft-Hartley non-Communist affidavit provisions are worth retaining. As a result of such prosecutions, members of the unions involved are sometimes made aware of matters which lead them to remove the officers involved, or at least to place them in positions of less power. On the other hand, Senator Goldwater has recently introduced a bill in Congress to repeal the non-Communist affidavit provision of the Taft-Hartley Act.

Action of the National Labor Relations Board with Respect to Section 9 (h) of the Labor-Management Relations Act

Section 9 (h), requiring the officers of a union to file non-Communist affidavits as a condition to use the processes of the National Labor Relations Board, was added in the Taft-Hartley amendments of 1947, and its constitutionality was upheld by the United States Supreme Court in 1950. *American Communications Association* v. *Douds*, 339 U. S. 382, rehearing denied, 339 U. S. 990. The Court noted that Congress had considerable evidence before it, when it enacted this legislation, "that Communist leaders of labor unions had in the past and would continue in the future to subordinate legitimate trade union objectives to obstructive strikes when dictated by Party leaders, often in support of the policies of a foreign government. . . . The incident most fully developed was a strike at the Milwaukee plant of the Allis-Chalmers Manufacturing Company in 1941, when the plant was producing vital materials for the national defense program. . . . Congress heard testimony that the strike had been called solely in obedience to Party orders for the purpose of starting the 'snowballing of

---

[58] See *Gold* v. *United States*, 237 F. 2d 764 (C. A., D. C. Apr. 19, 1956).

strikes' in defense plants. . . ." The Court concluded that the first amendment does not require that a Communist "be permitted to be the keeper of the arsenal."

For a number of years, the National Labor Relations Board took the position, based on the language and legislative history of the Taft-Hartley Act, that it did not have the function of investigating and passing on the truthfulness of affidavits which had been filed. This was regarded as a matter for the Attorney General and the courts. (See *Craddock-Terry Shoe Corporation*, 21 LRRM 1194).

In 1952, however, the NLRB began to take some further steps to deny its processes to unions whose officers were involved in false affidavits prosecutions. The Department of Justice had instituted false affidavit proceedings against certain officers of the United Electrical, Radio, and Machine Workers of America and several other unions, and although the grand jury failed to indict, it sent word to the NLRB that the officers had declined to affirm the affidavits then on file with the Board. The NLRB then sent questionnaires to these officials asking them to reaffirm their oaths and to provide additional data on possible connections with the Communist Party. The Board indicated that it would void all certifications held by the unions and forbid their taking cases to the Board if the questionnaires were not answered satisfactorily.

A Federal district court enjoined the NLRB from proceeding with the questionnaires, ruling that the Board had no authority to inquire into the truth of the affidavits, and the decision was affirmed on appeal. *Electrical Workers* v. *Herzog*, 33 LRRM 2301, 33 LRRM 2197.

The NLRB then adopted a policy of denying the use of election machinery to unions with officials under indictment for false non-Communist affidavits, but the Federal courts held that the Board does not have authority to deny a union its compliance status by inquiring into the falsity of an affidavit filed by one of its officers. The rationale was that the Act does not deprive a union of its statutory benefits, because an officer had deceived the union as well as the Board by filing a false affidavit. *Farmer* v. *United Electrical Workers*, 33 LRRM 2196, 33 LRRM 2821.

The NLRB and a Federal district court later worked out a distinction that, where the union membership was shown to be aware of the fact that the union officer had filed a false affidavit, the union's compliance status could be withdrawn by the Board and the union could be deprived of its rights under the Taft-Hartley Act.

However, the Supreme Court has recently ruled that the Board does not have the power to take such action against the union. The Court said, "the only remedy for the filing of a false affidavit is the criminal penalty . . . we cannot find an additional sanction which in practical effect would run against the members of the union, not their guilty officers." *Meat Cutters* v. *The United States*, 39 LRRM 2149, 2150 (December 10, 1956) ; *Leedom* v. *Mine, Mill and Smelter Workers*, 39 LRRM 2146, 2147, 2149 (December 10, 1956).

The Commission recommends that investigation should be conducted according to a uniform procedure, and that the procedure should be as follows:

In the case of clearance for secret:

A national agency check conducted by the responsible industrial facility agency;

If derogatory subversive information is developed by the national agency check requiring further investigation, reference to the FBI for a full field investigation;

If nonsubversive derogatory information is developed by the national agency check requiring further investigation, such further investigation should be conducted by the investigative branch utilized by the responsible agency.

In the case of defense industrial contracts, the Office of Security in the Office of the Secretary of Defense should assign the investigation to the appropriate military investigative branch—i. e., OSI, ONI, G–2, or CIC.

In the case of other agency industrial contracts the investigative branch of such agency should make such further investigation; if it has none, such further investigation should be made by the Civil Service Commission.

In the case of clearance for top secret:

Each responsible agency through its investigative branch shall conduct a full field (background) investigation.

In the case of defense industrial contracts, such full field investigation should be assigned by the Office of Security in the Office of the Secretary of Defense to the appropriate military investigative branch—i. e., OSI, ONI, G–2, or CIC.

In the case of other agency industrial contracts, the investigative branch of such agency shall make the full field investigation; if it has none, such investigation shall be made by the Civil Service Commission.

If during the course of any full field investigation conducted by any of the above agencies there is developed derogatory subversive information, such investigatory branch should cease its investigation and transmit the case for full investigation by the FBI.

The Commission believes that the investigating agency should evaluate the need for classifying the informant as "confidential," as well as the reliability of the informant, but not evaluate the information provided by the informant.

Investigations by Government agencies should be conducted according to a uniform procedure,[59] but they should not all be performed by a single agency, nor should investigating agencies be required to evaluate the information; however, they should evaluate the sources.

Investigative reports in instances have been incomplete, or out of date, or based merely on a record check. The adoption of uniform investigative procedures and outlined in the foregoing recommendation will do much to eliminate these defects.

Screening Function—Charges

The Commission recommends that centralization of the screening authority for clearance is not necessary or proper, except that there should be a central screening program in the Office of Security in the Office of the Secretary of Defense.

As recommended by the Commission the screening board function should be retained in the Department of Defense industrial security program and:

> **It should be a segment of the Office of Security in the Office of the Secretary of Defense, and**

> **It should process its work directly with the recommended security office within the Department of Defense rather than through service command channels.**

> **Where there is derogatory information which has not been satisfactorily explained, the screening officer should send the employee a letter of charges and advise him of his right to a hearing. The applicant, within time prescribed by regulations, should file a sworn answer thereto together with any affidavits or other statements he may desire to submit. If he requests such a hearing, the screening board in the Office of Security in the Office of the Secretary of Defense should send the letter of charges and the reply thereto together with the file to the Director of the Central Security Office who should assign it to a hearing examiner. The decision of the hearing examiner should be advisory to the head of the responsible agency whose decision shall be final. An adverse decision by the head of the responsible agency may be appealed to the Central Review Board at the request of the employee within time and subject to procedures to be prescribed.**

The Department of Defense has issued a *First Annual Report*, dated September 13, 1956, titled *Industrial Personnel Security Review Program*. It contains charts and statistics on the accomplishments of the current hear-

---

[59] See full discussion and recommendations on Central Security Office, p. 89.

ing and review program and offers comparisons between the current and the superseded program. In the appendix of this document may be seen the full hearing and review regulations, 5220.6. On page 3, the report states:

The Screening Function

One area to which we have devoted careful attention relates to the Screening function—the initial determination, after a case is submitted by the Services, that either a clearance may issue, or that recourse must be had to a formal hearing. This area of the program is vital because it is at this point that a private citizen seeking clearance first becomes an active party to the proceedings. It is here that it may be necessary to tell him that his security status is in doubt. Then the results of investigation and the deliberations of Government may have their initial impact external to the Government. Here lies the threshhold to reaction at the job, family, and community levels.

Because this stage is of key importance, and because a denial results in the initiation of formal procedures with their inevitable consequences to the individual concerned, both financially and otherwise, this determination is now entrusted to the collective judgment of a central Screening Board. . . . Since this central Screening Board is located in Washington, it has been possible to develop a comprehensive liaison with the investigative agencies involved, and to create a working relationship which has meant that more detailed and specific information is more readily available. . . . Under our current procedures, approximately 60 percent of all the cases considered by that Board have resulted in a clearance for the individual concerned at that level. . . .

Significantly, suspension of an individual's clearance unnecessarily is avoided, and the serious reactions to such a suspension in terms of earning power, family tension, repect in the community and other adverse factors are minimized. (Under the provision of paragraph 26 of the regulation (industrial personnel security review regulation, February 2, 1955, No. 5220.6), a respondent who ultimately receives a determination in his favor is reimbursed for loss of earnings during the period his clearance was suspended.) Neither the fact that the Government has questioned an individual's security status, nor the specific information which has provoked these doubts, escape from the hands of the Department of Defense. The entire process is held confidential between the individual and his Government, and no one else, not even the employer, need be involved in any way when the case is closed by a clearance at the Screening Board Level. . . .

Statement of Reasons

Improved screening procedures have had their effect in another important area, that of informing the individual concerned, specifically and in detail, of the information which has led the Screening Board to withhold clearance.

In each case where the Screening Board determines that the record before it will not support a decision to grant access, formal proceedings are begun by providing the individual concerned with a statement of reasons. Prepared collectively by the Screening Board, this statement of reasons sets out the information supporting the decision that a clearance is not warranted, and states the issues in the case. It is the vehicle whereby the individual concerned is informed of the information which raises the security question. The more complete it is, the greater his ability to prepare himself fully, and to produce facts basic to a sound decision his case reaches the hearing level.

Through this machinery, the issues to be considered are sharpened and made more precise and definite. A foundation is thus laid which materially assists the Hearing Board members to render a fair and impartial judgment. Obviously, these results are as important to the Department of Defense as to the individual.

We have made striking progress in this area. . . .

281

SUSPENSION

Suspension of Clearance for Access to Classified Material

The Commission believes that where an employee has once been granted clearance, and derogatory information is received about him, present provisions for suspension are adequate for safeguarding:

The national security, and

That the individual's rights are not prejudiced pending a well-considered evaluation of the derogatory information.

The Commission believes that suspension for clearance should not in and of itself be the basis for discharge of an employee. While the employer has the legal right to discharge, it is believed that no person should be discharged merely on the ground that his clearance has been suspended. Under such circumstances an employee who has been removed from access under the suspension order may work on nonclassified information and materials.

The Commission believes that Government field offices should not exercise the power to make emergency suspensions, but that suspensions should be accomplished only at the Office of Security in the Office of the Secretary of Defense.

The Commission believes that at this juncture of proceedings, the reasons for suspension need not be complete and specific for within a reasonable time after the suspension and completion of any necessary investigation (and if not cleared by such investigation) an appropriate letter of charges will issue. Priority should be given to suspension cases.

Wherever possible in the light of the emergency requiring immediate suspension, an oral interview should be granted but should not be mandatory.

The first and most important distinction to be made between the Federal civilian employees security program and the DOD industrial security program is that in the latter program clearance relates only to access to classified defense information. Consequently, denial or revocation of a clearance to a contractor employee does not preclude his being employed on nonclassified work in the same plant or facility; however, if the only work that is being done at the industrial facility is of a classified nature, then suspension of clearance means loss of employment. (See industrial security manual for safeguarding classified information, DOD, September 21, 1956, section 1–3 (b).) Thus, the DOD industrial security program, and DOD regulations issued pursuant thereto, do not interfere with the contractors' prerogative of hiring, firing, promoting, or transferring for their own purposes. The

DOD industrial security regulations specifically provide that the person suspended from access to classified material need not be fired (industrial security manual, 1–3 (b)). But since a contractor can hire or fire, regardless of whether the Government suspends such individual's clearance, contractors may and do formulate policies involving suspension of employee's clearance, and some companies have the policy of firing such an employee.

If the derogatory information developed on an individual employee is serious enough, the emergency power of suspension of clearance (not employment) for access to classified information or material may be exercised, as provided for in the Armed Forces industrial regulation, DOD, September 1956. Thus, it may be seen that the Government field offices possess power to make emergency suspensions.

Perusal of the industrial personnel security review regulation, February 2, 1955, 5220.6, shows that the procedures established in this regulation are applicable to all cases in which a military department has recommended that clearance of a contractor employee be suspended (section 6.a. (2)), and also to all cases where once a clearance has been suspended even though employment has been terminated (section 6.b.). If the Screening Board concludes on the basis of the available information and in accordance with the standard and criteria that the case does not warrant a security finding favorable to the person concerned, it will prepare a statement of reasons which will be as specific and in as great detail as security considerations permit, in order to provide the person concerned with sufficient information to enable him to prepare his defense. Whenever the Board issues a statement of reasons, it will suspend any clearance previously granted to the person concerned. (Section 17 e.)

When there is a possibility that an individual's clearance for access to classified information may be suspended, the military department forwards the file to the director of the Office of Industrial Personnel Security, who will, upon receipt of the file and after ensuring that it has been properly prepared, transmit the same to the Screening Board for appropriate action.

The Screening Board will review each case referred to it by the director and will determine in accordance with the standard and criteria whether the reported information warrants (1) the granting or continuing of a clearance or (2) further processing. If an emergency suspension of clearance has been effected, the Board will review such action to determine its propriety. The Screening Board may request further investigation, or issue written interrogatories, or even arrange for an interview with the person concerned (sections 15, 16, and 17).

If the contractor has previously granted access to confidential material or if the Government has previously granted access to secret or top secret, and derogatory information comes to light, the military department concerned may suspend the clearance pending further investigation and action to revoke clearance under the industrial personnel security review regulation.

283

This action may be taken in exceptional cases, in which the information available indicates that retention of a security clearance would constitute an immediate threat to the security interests of the United States. Otherwise, all cases wherein derogatory information comes to light are forwarded for Screening Board consideration prior to suspension.

The Screening Board may determine at any time, while a case is pending before it, that an existing clearance should be suspended. Whenever the Screening Board concludes that a case does not warrant a security finding favorable to the person concerned and issues a statement of reasons, it will suspend any clearance previously granted.

The Office of Industrial Personnel Security Review in the DOD receives the case file from the military department concerned, and, after insuring that the case is properly prepared, forwards it to the Screening Board.

The Screening Board (located in Washington) after examining and evaluating the file, may request further investigation, issue a written interrogatory to the employee, or arrange an interview with him. If the decision is favorable, the Military Department concerned is instructed to issue a clearance (letter of consent), or permit the clearance to stand, and the case is closed.

If the decision is unfavorable, the employee is given a Statement of Reasons which will be as specific and in as great a detail as security considerations permit, in order to provide the employee with sufficient information to enable him to prepare his defense.

Further, suspension of clearance most assuredly is not presently, and ought not to be, in and of itself, the basis for discharge. However, some employers have voiced strong views to the contrary.

Government field offices already have the power to make emergency suspensions. If clearance is suspended by the DOD Screening Board (Office of Industrial Personnel Security Review), a specific statement of reasons is issued, and further, provision has been made for oral interview of the individual prior to suspension of clearance by the Screening Board.

Answer and Hearings

The Commission recommends the following hearing procedures for the industrial security program:

If the applicant for clearance requests such a hearing, the Screening Board in the Office of Security in the Office of the Secretary of Defense should send a letter of charges and the reply thereto together with the file to the director of the Central Security Office who should assign it to a hearing examiner.

The initial hearing on the letter of charges should be conducted by a hearing examiner rather than by hearing boards.

The hearing examiners should be under an independent central office in the executive branch. (See full discussion of Central Security Office and recommendations on page 89.)

The decisions of the hearing examiners should be advisory to the head of the responsibile agency whose decision shall be final.

The head of the responsible agency for all Armed Forces should be the Secretary of Defense. Although he should not be permitted to delegate his responsibility, he may designate any person within the Office of the Secretary of Defense to make such decisions on his behalf.

In all other departments or agencies having industrial security programs, the decisions of the hearing examiners should be advisory to the head of such department or agency.

The hearing examiners should be appointed by the head of the new Central Security Office from an appropriate civil service register created for the purpose.

Hearing examiners should be full time governmental employees with a sufficient number throughout the country to hear cases involving clearance under the industrial security program.

An adverse decision by the head of the responsible agency may be appealed to the Central Review Board at the request of the applicant for clearance within time and subject to procedures to be prescribed.

The Screening Board function should be retained in the industrial security program and, in consonance with the Commission's recommendation on the Central Security Office.

It should be a segment of the recommended Office of Security of the Office of the Secretary of Defense, and

It should process its work directly with the recommended Office of Security within the Department of Defense rather than through service command channels.

HEARINGS

Procedural Rights—Confrontation, Subpena, etc.

Supplementing the Commission's industrial security recommendation on hearing and review procedures, it further recommends that:

A. Confrontation, of the scope recommended in the civilian loyalty program, should be limited to evidence offered in support of any of the following charges:

1. Sabotage, espionage, or attempts or preparations therefor, or knowingly associating with spies or saboteurs;

2. Treason or sedition or advocacy thereof;

3. Advocacy of revolution or force or violence to alter the constitutional form of Government of the United States;

4. Intentional, unauthorized disclosure to any person of classified information or materials;

5. Performing or attempting to perform his duties, or otherwise acting, so as to serve the interests of another government in preference to the interests of the United States;

6. Membership in, affiliation or sympathetic association with any party, group, or association which the Congress of the United States, or any agency or officer of the United States duly authorized by the Congress for that purpose, finds:

(*a*) Seeks to alter the form of Government of the United States by forces or violence, or other unconstitutional means; or,

(*b*) Is organized or utilized for the purpose of advancing the aims and objectives of the Communist movement; or,

(*c*) Is organized or utilized for the purpose of establishing any form of dictatorship in the United States or any form of international dictatorship; or,

(*d*) Is organized or utilized by any foreign government, or by any foreign party, group, or association acting in the interest of such foreign government for the purpose of (1) espionage, or (2) sabotage, or (3) obtaining information relating to the defense of the United States or the protection of the National security, or (4) hampering, hindering, or delaying the production of defense materials; or

(*e*) Is affiliated with, or acts in concert with, or is dominated or controlled by, any party, group, or association of the character described in (*a*), or (*b*), or (*c*), or (*d*), above.

7. Membership in or affiliation with any organization which the Congress of the United States or any agency or officer of the United States duly authorized by the Congress for that purpose, finds has adopted a policy

of advocating or approving the commission of acts of force and violence to deny others their rights under the Constitution of the United States.

8. Refusal to testify upon the ground of self-incrimination, in any authorized inquiry relating to subversive activities conducted by a congressional committee, Federal court, Federal grand jury, or any other duly authorized Federal agency unless the individual, after opportunity to do so, satisfactorily explains his refusal to testify.

B. The Commission believes that the right of subpena should be applicable where there is a right of confrontation, but this does not preclude the applicant for clearance from furnishing affidavits or the testimony of witnesses he wishes to present and who are willing to appear voluntarily. If the individual involved presents an affidavit, and the Government has reason to doubt the affiant's veracity, the Government may subpena such affiant.

1. Either the Government or the individual should be permitted to apply to the hearing examiner to issue subpenas, except as to confidential informants and identified informants who have given their information on the condition that they will not be called as witnesses. Such application should state the name and address of such witness, as well as the substance of the testimony to be presented by the witness. If the hearing examiner deems the evidence relevant and not merely cumulative, he may issue the subpena. Under the same limitations, the hearing examiner may, on his own motion, subpena a witness.

2. In the exercise of his discretion to issue subpenas, the hearing examiner should consider such factors as the time and expense involved by reason of the travel requires.

3. The witness should be compensated for travel expense and per diem, but where such costs are substantial, the hearing examiner may in his discretion require the parties to use deposition procedures.

4. The Government should bear the cost of Government witnesses, but the hearing examiner should not subpena a witness for the individual until the individual deposits with the Government sufficient funds to pay the travel and per diem costs of such witness. In the event that the individual is not cleared, the funds deposited by the individual should be used to pay for the individual's witness expenses. If, however, the individual is cleared, the funds deposited by the individual should be returned

287

to him and the Government should bear the travel and per diem costs of the individual's witness.

C. The Commission further recommends that:

1. The evaluation of derogatory information relating to loyalty should be conducted by such officer as the head of the responsible agency should designate for that purpose.

2. The letter of charges should be as specific and detailed as the interests of national security permits and should include pertinent information such as names, dates, and places, in such detail as to permit reasonable answer thereto.

3. The letter of charges should contain a statement that a sworn answer thereto must be filed within a reasonable time. In order to establish uniformity among the departments and agencies as to the time within which the answer must be filed, the director of the Central Security Office should by regulation prescribe such time.

4. The letter of charges should also inform the individual involved of his right to a hearing.

5. The hearing should be confined to the matters contained in the letter of charges. If after the issuance of the letter of charges, the Government wishes to amend the letter of charges to add additional or different charges, the individual involved should be allowed a reasonable time in which to file his amended answer thereto.

6. The hearing should not be open to the public inasmuch as that would tend to discourage the appearance of witnesses and would subject the employee to additional unfavorable publicity which might do unwarranted violence to him and his reputation. The informal atmosphere of private hearings is more conducive to an impartial determination of the facts. Furthermore, open hearings would sometimes be inappropriate due to the necessity of considering classified information therein.

7. Sufficiently in advance of the hearing to permit study by the hearing examiner, the head of the responsible agency should submit to the examiner the complete file on the individual and all pertinent supporting documents, plus a résumé of any administrative action and reasons therefor. At the hearing itself, a representative of the responsible agency should be present to answer the questions of the hearing examiner and to assist the

hearing examiner in any other appropriate way. He should not act as a prosecutor.

8. The head of the responsible agency should be the authority to designate the person or persons to represent the agency at the hearing, and such representative(s) should not participate in the formulation of the hearing examiner's decision. Such representative(s) need not be licensed attorneys.

9. The individual involved should be entitled to counsel of his own choice and the Government should not pay the fees of the individual's counsel.

10. The hearing examiner should submit a written report to the director of the Central Security Office for transmittal to the head of the responsible agency. Such report should contain the hearing examiner's finding of fact, decision, and reasons for his decision. A copy of the hearing examiner's report and a copy of the hearing transcript should be sent to the individual involved upon receipt of notice of appeal.

PROGRAM AND ADMINISTRATION

Consolidation of the Industrial Security Program in a Single Agency

The Commission recommends that the industrial security programs of all agencies should not be consolidated in a single agency, but that an act of Congress should be passed, or an Executive order issued, specifying the policy and the major procedures governing all agencies of Government having need for an industrial security program.

The Commission does recommend consolidation of the industrial security programs of the various branches of the military services into a single, integrated program, devised, controlled, supervised, and operated by an Office of Security in the Office of the Secretary of Defense. This single program would cover all the security aspects of the military industrial security program.

Under such proposal, there would be a single set of regulations promulgated by the Defense Department binding on the Army, Navy, Air Force.

Security personnel, including inspectors, would work under and be subject to the Office of Security in the Office of the Secretary of Defense rather than to Army, Navy, or Air Force.

The requisite security personnel, including inspectors, would be transferred by the three services to the Office of Security in the Office of the Secretary of Defense for purposes of implementing this program.

In order to insure maximum uniformity, the industrial security provisions of any contract should be subject to approval of the Office of Security in the Office of the Secretary of Defense.

Existing legislation and executive orders have encouraged complexity by establishing two or more parallel systems of security and two agencies to administer the program. At present there are eight classifications of information, each indicating a different level of importance and a slightly different method of control. A variety of personnel clearances results in an excessive burden upon contractors, too often resulting in unnecessary delays, and duplication by Government agencies.

Interviews were held or letters received from 105 persons employed wholly or partly in the field of industrial security. Of the 105 persons responding, 5 stated that the security program is satisfactory in its present form, thus eliminating the need for either a single security agency or a single set of security regulations. Of the 88 who discussed the subject of a single security agency, 84 percent were in favor and 16 percent opposed. However, among the 88 aforementioned, some made conditional recommendations, and others did not have firm convictions on the subject. Most corporations were strongly in favor of a single agency to eliminate duplications, delay, waste of time and money, and confusion—chiefly to eliminate duplication of plant and personnel clearances.

Of the same 105, 73 discussed the advisability of a single set of security regulations, 95 percent were in favor and 5 percent opposed. Here again, some of the recommendations were conditional or indirect: many favored the proposal in order to allow interchange of all clearances, elimination of conflict between agencies, and elimination of divergent interpretations of regulations by representatives of various agencies. However, those opposed pointed out the difficulty of applying one set of regulations to the differing security needs of individual government departments.

It is believed that the industrial security programs of the three Armed Forces should be consolidated in the Office of the Secretary of Defense and that such Department of Defense industrial security program and those of the Department of Commerce, the National Science Foundation, the Atomic Energy Commission and other agencies of Government should be coordinated by the director of the Central Security Office.[60] It is further believed that the major policies and procedures should be expressed either in an act of Congress or an Executive order. Vesting responsibility in the Department of Defense will go far toward obtaining greater uniformity.

---

[60] See full discussion of Central Security Office on page 89.

Most of the advantages of consolidation without corresponding disadvantages can be achieved by the adoption of the foregoing recommendations.

Transfer of Clearance; Delay in Clearance

The Commission recommends that to avoid delay in contractor employee clearance there should be transfer of personnel security clearance between:

Government employment and industry

Military service and industry

One Department of Defense contractor and another

An Atomic Energy Commission contractor and a Department of Defense Contractor

Between one facility and another within the same company, all under the circumstances hereinafter set forth:

The creation of a central industrial security index in the Office of the Secretary of Defense should facilitate the exchange of clearances and eliminate duplicate investigations, fingerprinting, and the execution of unnecessary forms.

It is recommended that a current Department of Defense clearance for "secret" and "top secret" issued by the Office of Security in the Office of the Secretary of Defense, be recognized without further investigation by all facilities within the jurisdiction of the Department of Defense.

Where the standard for clearance as between agencies is the same and where the scope of the investigations is comparable and where the investigation in the opinion of the head of the transferee agency is current, the head of the transferee agency should accept the clearance in the absence of facts indicating to him the need for further evaluation.

It is further recommended that the Atomic Energy Act be amended to make it permissible for the Atomic Energy Commission, under the circumstances outlined in paragraph 3 above, to recognize an individual's current clearance granted by another agency without further investigation.

It is further recommended that the Atomic Energy Commission regulations be amended so that:

Both the "Q" clearance (secret and top secret clearances) and the "L" (confidential) clearance be abolished and that the Atomic Energy Commission clearances be brought into line with the clearances for the rest of the Government by having two categories, "atomic secret" and "atomic top secret"; that the standards and investigation for access thereto should be equivalent to those applicable to "secret" and "top secret" in other agencies of Government.

The heads of the various departments and agencies having industrial security programs shall confer with the Director of the Central Security Office for the purpose of establishing uniformity in the exchange of clearances as well as determining the duration for which a clearance shall be valid without a reinvestigation.

Rules and regulations concerning visitor control should be promulgated by the Office of Security in the Office of the Secretary of Defense in an effort to establish uniformity.

Clearance for Access to "Secret" and "Top Secret"

The Commission does not recommend that there be a single clearance for access to both "secret" and "top secret" information and material.

A national agency check is considered sufficient and proper for contractor employees who will have access to classified information and material up to and including "secret."

A full background investigation is considered necessary prior to clearance of contractor employees for access to "top secret" information and materials.

A national agency check could provide needed information for secret clearance with little loss of time, whereas a full background investigation is a necessity to meet the criteria for the top secret clearance.

Administrative Relationship Between the Office of Security in the Office of the Secretary of Defense and Field Offices

No more than one level of responsibility, operations, field offices and staff should be permitted to exist below the Office of Security in the Office of the Secretary of Defense.

Regional grouping of field offices may be arranged within the Office of Security in the Office of the Secretary of Defense for purposes of coordination but without administrative "ranking" or jurisdiction over any field office.

Orders, regulations, correspondence, instructions, cases for processing, and all other business of the Office of Security in the Office of the Secretary of Defense should flow directly to the field office from the Office of Security with information copies kept to a minimum.

Correspondence, cases for processing, mail, requests for guidance or clarification, and all other business of the field office should flow directly to the Office of Security in the Office of the Secretary of Defense from the field office with information copies kept to a minimum.

An analysis of the clearance procedures of the three military services shows that the clearances are granted at different organizational echelons. The Department of the Army's clearance procedure indicates that the determination as to whether a clearance will be issued, is made in the Army Area Headquarters, Industrial Security Division, G–2. Therefore, the Department of the Army, which has six army areas in the Zone of Interior, has six points where the personnel security questionnaires (PSQ's) are evaluated, and where the initial determination is made as to whether the contractor-employee will be issued a clearance.

The Department of the Navy and the Department of the Air Force have assigned the evaluation and clearance responsibility of their own industrial security program to the lowest possible operational level. The Navy has assigned this function to the field office known as Inspector of Naval Material (INSMAT) and the field offices of the naval procuring activities.

The Department of the Air Force on March 1, 1957 assigned the evaluation and clearance responsibility of its industrial security program to the lowest possible agency level.

In summary, therefore, the industrial security program of the Army is part of the intelligence function; however, the Navy and Air Force industrial security function is found in their procurement activities.

The following description of the route presently taken by a request for an industrial employee clearance in the Department of the Army is illustrative of the complex nature of the administrative path through which such request must flow.

DEPARTMENT OF THE ARMY

The Department of the Army has six Army Commands in the Zone of Interior. Within each Army area there are located Industrial Security Field Offices, the number depending on the procurement activity (e. g., Ordnance, Signal, etc.) within the Army area. For example, there are six industrial security field offices in the Second Army area covering the following States: Virginia, West Virginia, Kentucky, Maryland, Pennsylvania, Ohio, and Delaware. Whereas the Fourth Army area covering the central Southwest States of Arkansas, Oklahoma, New Mexico, Texas, and Louisiana, has only one, which is located at the Fourth Army Headquarters in San Antonio.

Generally, the Department of the Army's chain of command for request for clearances from and to the contractor employee is as follows:

1. The contractor submits the request for contractor-employee clearance to the procurement activity District Office, or the Industrial Security Field Office having security cognizance.

2. The Industrial Security Feld Office also occasionally receives request for clearances from Air Force and Navy Cognizant Offices in connection with Air Force or Navy contracts at the facility under Army cognizance.

3. The Industrial Security Field Office submits the PSQ [61] to the Industrial Security Division of G–2 of its Army Area Headquarters, which conducts background investigations if necessary.

4. They in turn forward the request for personnel clearance to the Assistant Chief of Staff Intelligence, Department of the Army, Washington, D. C., for a national agency check.

5. The district procurement activity office reports to the procurement activity of the Army Area Headquarters.

6. The Assistant Chief of Staff Intelligence, Department of the Army, processes the national agency check to the appropriate agencies.

7. The Assistant Chief of Staff Intelligence, Department of the Army, reports to the security branch of the Office of the Assistant Secretary of the Army for Manpower and Reserve Forces.

8. National agency checks are worked by FBI, ONI, OSI, INS, or other agencies and returned to ACSI.

9. Assistant Chief of Staff Intelligence receives completed NACs from appropriate agencies and returns the PSQ to the Army area headquarters.

10. The Industrial Security Division G–2 of the Army Area Headquarters analyzes the results of the NAGs and/or Background Investigations. If the results are satisfactory they issue the clearance. The Industrial Security Field Office is notified, as is the central index file and the facility.

11. The procurement activity of the Army Area Headquarters reports to the respective technical service, Department of the Army.

12. The technical service procurement activity reports to the Procurement Division of the Deputy Chief of Staff for Logistics, Chief of Staff, U. S. Army.

---

[61] Personnel security questionnaire (DD–48).

13. Deputy Chief of Staff for Logistics reports to the Assistant Secretary of the Army for Logistics.

14. Assistant Secretary of the Army for Logistics reports to the Assistant Secreary of Defense (supply and logistics) through the Secretary of the Army.

15. The Assistant Secretary of the Army for Manpower and Reserve Forces reports to the Assistant Secretary of Defense (Manpower, Personnel and Reserve) through the Secretary of the Army.

However, when sufficient derogatory information exists the case is referred to the Office of Industrial Personnel Security Review (OIPSR) in the Assistant Secretary of Defense (Manpower, Personnel and Reserve) for decision. These are the steps followed:

1. When the Industrial Security Division, Assistant Chief of Staff, Intelligence, Army Area Headquarters, analyzes the results of the national agencies checks and/or background investigations and sufficient derogatory information exists, it must make a determination as to whether the information warrants a recommendation of denial.

(a) Coordination and advice is sought from the Army Area Judge Advocate General and the Commanding General in conjunction with the Chief of Intelligence.

(b) Coordination and advice is sought from the procurement activity to determine the sensitivity of the contract. The procurement activity must seek further advice and coordination from its respective Technical Service in the Department of the Army, and it may require further coordination and advice from Deputy Chief of Staff for Logistics, Department of the Army.

2. Once determination is made that the derogatory information warrants the recommendation of denial, it is forwarded to the Assistant Chief of Staff, Intelligence, Department of the Army. An administrative review is conducted and a current status record of the cases submitted by the Army Area Headquarters is maintained.

3. When the Assistant Chief of Staff, Intelligence, determines that the information warrants the recommendation of denial, the case is referred to the Office of Industrial Personnel Security Review (OIPSR) in the Office of the Assistant Secretary of Defense (Manpower, Personnel and Reserve).

4. Office of Industrial Personnel Security Review (OIPSR) receives the complete case file including recommendation, the reasons therefore and all available information. After insuring that the case is properly prepared, it forwards it to the Screening Board (OIPSR).

5. The Screening Board (Office of Industrial Personnel Security Review) examines and evaluates the information and may at this point request further investigation, issue a written interrogatory, arrange and interview, or suspend any clearance in effect.

If the decision is favorable, the Army Area Headquarters is instructed to issue a letter of consent and the case is closed.

If the decision is denial, a statement of reasons is forwarded to the individual informing him of his right to answer in writing under oath and submit statements of affidavits; or he can appear before a hearing board in person or by counsel.

6. If the individual requests a hearing, the entire case file is forwarded to the Hearing Board (Office of Industrial Personnel Security Review). A decision is rendered, based on all available information. If the decision is not unanimous, the Director, Industrial Personnel Security Review, may forward the case to a Review Board (OIPSR). Hearing Board decisions when announced by the Director, Industrial Personnel Security Review, are final, subject only to reconsideration by Review Board at request of the Director, Industrial Personnel Security Review or the Secretary of the Army.

7. The Review Board (OIPSR) reviews each case and makes a determination on basis of the written record. It may adopt or reverse the findings of the Hearing Board.

8. The Review Board then returns the case to the Assistant Chief of Staff Intelligence Office which reviews on request, on behalf of the Secrtary of the Army, those Army cases in which final action has been taken by the Director, Industrial Personnel Security Review. Where warranted, the Assistant Chief of Staff of Intelligence may make a recommendation to the Secretary of the Army that the case be returned to the Industrial Personnel Security Review Office.

9. The Secretary of the Army may refer the case to the Director, Industrial Personnel Security Review, for reconsideration. Acting jointly with the secretaries of the other military departments, the decision of the Review Board (Industrial Personnel Security Review Office) may be reversed.

Security Cognizance of a Multi-facility Company

The Commission believes that all facilities of a multi-facility company should be assigned to the security cognizance of one governmental agency, and has taken this into consideration in the Commission's recommendation on the Office of Security in the Office of the Secretary of Defense, which will eliminate departmental security cognizance by the creation of such office.

Under the Department of Defense Armed Forces industrial security regulations (AFISR) effective December 1, 1956, security cognizance is assigned by DOD *by facility* to a single military department. There is nothing to prevent different facilities of a multi-facility company from being assigned to the security cognizance of different military departments. The selection for security cognizance depends upon nine considerations, such as dollar volume, volume of classified information, contract duration, contractor desires, etc., (AFISR, sec. 1–301).

The present Department of Defense practice of subdividing contractors' operational and organizational entities into separate units, under different security cognizance of various and often distant military security offices, further complicates and makes more difficult a contractor's security task. The confusion, complication, duplication, loss of coordination, loss of centralized security control and increased cost in time is apparent.

Implementing Documents

The Commission believes that the security manuals are too complex and technical, and that they are too vague, indefinite, and subject to varying interpretations.

The Commission has recommended the creation of an Office of Security in the Office of the Secretary of Defense, and that such office prepare a single manual for all three services. In preparation of such a manual, every effort should be made to avoid unnecessary complexity and vagueness in its content.

Departments and agencies outside the Department of Defense should review their respective industrial security manuals in a similar effort to achieve simplicity and clarity of expression.

It would be a part of the responsibility of the new Central Security Office, the creation of which has been recommended by the Commission, to maintain a continuing critical review of such manuals.

With the initiation of uniform industrial security regulations as evidenced by the Armed Forces industrial security regulations, and the industrial security manual for safeguarding classified information, there has been a vast improvement in the interpretation and application of industrial security procedures. However, these are still open to a considerable degree of interpretation, and the function of the security procedures is often hindered by such varying interpretations.

Standard and Uniform Interpretations of Regulations and Manuals

The Commission believes that there should be a more effective system of issuing and disseminating standard and uniform interpretations of the industrial security regulations and manuals.

The Commission's recommendation that there be one consolidated Office of Security in the Office of the Secretary of Defense will go far in achieving uniformity.

The Commission on Government Security partial interrogatory—industrial security, of September 13, 1956, asked: "III. 2. Granting that individuals should be allowed certain judgment in performance, is there too much interpretation of regulations permitted, and is uniformity of administration affected in this manner?" The Commission's partial interrogatory—industrial security, of November 1, 1956, asked: "12. Does excessive personal interpretation of security regulations by Government officials have an important effect on proper administration of the program?"

Out of 90 interviews conducted by Commission on Government Security representatives, the following tabulation shows results of answers to both questions: Yes—54; Qualified yes—3; No—14; Qualified no—1; No comment—18.

Federal Security Personnel

Investigation by the Commission on Government Security indicates that many security offices are understaffed and have difficulty in attracting competent personnel at the existing salary levels. Therefore, the Commission recommends that a survey or study be made by the new Office of Security in the Office of the Secretary of Defense to insure that the offices are staffed with sufficient competent personnel to handle the caseload. A study should also be made of the ways to achieve a higher and more uniform salary scale for security officers.

An area which needs considerable improvement involves the qualifications of Government personnel in what may be called the working level of industrial security. Apparently the Government has not yet appreciated the high professional caliber of personnel needed to work effectively in this sensitive area, as has been indicated by the alarmingly low wage scale being paid to many of these Government security specialists entirely incompatible with their responsibilities. Government security people engaged in evaluating loyalty and subversive information on contractor personnel should be highly qualified, competent and adequate if they are to do the job of protecting both the Government and individuals, on whom they initially pass judgment. A faulty and poorly-considered evaluation at this level may never come to the attention of either higher authority or the personnel of the screening, hearing, and review boards, and may strike deep at the roots of our entire effort to control subversion and disloyalty. A thorough-going reconsideration of job qualifications and salary rates paid to military security representatives should be made by the Civil Service Commission in order to attract to the field competent, well-trained and professional personnel.

Insufficient personnel has been a problem in operating cognizant offices, and as a result the actual physical inspections and rechecks required by the Department of Defense security regulations generally have not been properly performed. As an example, in one cognizant office assigned an expansive industrial area, Commission on Government Security representatives noted that only three employees were available for conducting facility inspections. These employees could perform approximately 750 facility inspections per year if one was made each day, but the number of inspections called for in that area was much greater than 750 per year.

Further, the quality of persons employed at grade GS–7 has generally limited performance records, and the availability of grade GS–9 for such work has occurred only recently. Because of the disparity of salary paid by industry and by Government, industry finds little difficulty in "pirating" Government field office employees. "Pirating" between the services also exists because of the varied pay standards of the three services for similar work.

Security Agreement and Contract Security Clause

The Commission believes that the security agreement and contract clause that binds the contractor to comply with subsequent revisions of security manuals is not unreasonable because the Government should retain the power to determine what are the appropriate security requirements. The requirement of bilateral consent would necessitate securing the approval of every contractor with which the Government has an industrial security contract. It is recommended, however, that the security manuals not be changed without prior consultation by the responsible agency with representatives of industry. Close cooperation between Government and industry is here essential.

It is further recommended that where changes in security requirements impose financial burdens upon the contractor not contemplated by the contract, the security costs shall be subject to renegotiation.

The Commission further believes that legal objections heretofore raised concerning the industrial security program in general, and in particular the reserved right of the Government in the security agreement and the supply contract to unilaterally change the manual, are without merit.

The Commission does not recommend that the security responsibilities of the contractor be embodied in a separate security agree-

299

ment thereby eliminating the security clause in procurement contracts. As recommended by the Commission in its recommendation on the Central Security Office, in order to insure maximum uniformity the industrial security provisions of any contract should be subject to approval of the Office of Security handling security in the Office of the Secretary of Defense. It is further recommended that all other agencies having industrial security programs should do likewise.   This need not be done by statute, but by regulations promulgated by the head of the responsible agency.

The objections to the legality of the industrial security program of the Department of Defense and the unilateral nature of the procurement contracts of DOD (as to subsequent changes in the DOD industrial security manual) are without substantial merit.

Arrangements for private contractors entering into a contract with Department of Defense for production of defense material call for a contractual agreement which is unilateral in nature, binding the contractor unequivocally to all subsequent revisions of the industrial security manual that may be issued by the Department of Defense. Few comments were noted on this topic in either the letters to the Commission from industry or interviews conducted by the Commission's representatives. However, the Commission was furnished detailed comments thereon by the United Aircraft Corporation, East Hartford, Connecticut, as an enclosure to a letter to the Commission from the President of that Corporation, Mr. W. P. Gwinn, under date of October 11, 1956.

Mr. Gwinn stated that United Aircraft Corporation's memorandum submitted to the Commission on Government Security was based on the Corporation's many years of experience as a Government contractor, and that while the memorandum thus furnished made no attempt to exhaust every facet of an old and troublesome problem, it did illuminate what the Corporation considered a critical aspect of the security program under examination. Mr. Gwinn alleged that the legal basis for regulations and directives issued by DOD (in the opinion of his Corporation) was doubtful [62] with the result, he claimed, that both Government and industry were uncertain of their fundamental rights and obligations.

The United Aircraft Corporation's memorandum contained a legal opinion attacking the unilateral character of the contractual relationships of industry with DOD contending that there is no firm legal basis for it, and that a sustained use of such procedures will result in establishment of individual units of private industry as mere agencies of the procurement departments of the Department of Defense. The final part of the United Aircraft Corporation monograph proposed a solution spotlighted on the criticized contractual aspects of the Department of Defense industrial security program.

---

[62] But, see discussion of legal basis of industrial program on p. 249.

The essence of the proposal is that a bilateral contract be used in contrast to the unilateral one now used; that the industrial security regulations be approached not from a military standpoint, which is unrealistic, but from a civilian management standpoint since the Department of Defense promulgated regulations must be adhered to not only by the contractors themselves but by the contractors' employees; that more emphasis should be placed on the obligations of the Government, such as requiring adherence to a reasonable classification program.

The only other significant comment received on this subject was that of the American Society for Industrial Security (ASIS) in their report to the Commission on Government Security under date of November 5, 1956. The ASIS finds that the security agreement (DD form 441) :

is legally objectionable since it binds the contractor to all future unilateral revisions of the Department of Defense Security Manual for Safeguarding Classified Information. The unilateral aspects of this arrangement are immediately offensive and create much concern within industry.

The obvious result of this procedure, ASIS further observed, is to find the Government projected into management functions, responsibilities and operating procedures, which could be best left in the hands of the contractor; that the use of security clauses in contracts unnecessarily involves procurement agencies in the administration of the security program; and further, that the use of both the security agreement *and* the security clause generates a needlessly complicated arrangement, a concomitant plague of diverse interpretations of regulations, a multiplication of procedures, and increased administrative costs.

Contract Officer vs. Security Officer

The Commission does not recommend that a contract be entered into by the security officer instead of the procurement officer, but in keeping with the Commission's recommendation on the Office of Security in the Office of the Secretary of Defense, in order to insure maximum uniformity, the industrial security provisions of any contract should be subject to approval of the Office of Security handling security within the Office of the Secretary in the Department of Defense.

When Commission on Government Security representatives discussed this subject with Government security personnel and with representatives of industry, most of the replies spoke of the problem in the sphere of operations in the field as contrasted to the activities of the entering into of procurement contracts with the military agencies.

The comments fell generally into two types. First, there is a source of friction in the field in the operations of contracting people and the security

301

people. Many pointed out that there should be greater cooperation; some pointed out that the contracting people investigating security requirements of contractors are ill qualified for security work. Second, contracting agency people stated that it is their primary responsibility to see that security provisions are carried out and, therefore, they must also be on the scene. Conflicting interpretations of regulations are bound to arise between the people of the contracting agencies enforcing security regulations and the Government security personnel from the cognizant agency offices. Opinions expressed in the interviews conducted by the Commission's representatives indicate that no one suggests that the contracting agencies and the security people be separated by water-tight compartments; each needs the advice of the other. The contracting people are relied on for their technical knowledge and implementation of the contract and the security people should be consulted as to the feasibility of maintenance of security requirements as called for by the contracts.

Overclassification

Overclassification of information retards scientific progress by confining knowledge to a limited number of persons.

The Commission recommends that the Office of Security in the Office of the Secretary of Defense prepare a comprehensive classification and declassification guide, and that all other agencies develop a similar guide for their respective operations. The new Central Security Office should coordinate such guides to insure maximum uniformity.

Personnel handling classification matters should be thoroughly trained and the number of persons authorized to classify material should be kept at a minimum.

By the Commission's recommendation on the Office of Security in the Office of the Secretary of Defense, it has been recommended that the industrial security provisions of any contract should be subject to approval of the Office of Security within the Office of the Secretary of Defense.

Adequate staff should be assigned to assure prompt declassification.

The application of the "need-to-know" policy should occur only on those occasions when there is sound reason to believe that the national security will be adversely affected.

There is a definite segment of opinion found in industry that visitor controls, clearance procedures, and "need to know" restrictions limit inventive and creative thought and impair industrial progress as well as industrial research and development. Some industrial firms supporting this opinion are

302

the Grumman Engineering Corporation, the Case Institute of Technology, the Clevite Research Center, the General Tire and Rubber Company, Brush Electronics Company, Hazeltine Corporation, Firestone Tire and Rubber Company, Rheem Manufacturing Company, the Burroughs Corporation, Lockheed Aircraft Corporation and the Garrett Corporation. Some firms taking the opposite view are the Philco Corporation, Curtiss-Wright Corporation, and the Chance-Vought Aircraft, Inc.

Lockheed Aircraft Corporation, Burbank, Calif., felt that the procedures do impede, but not seriously; but, the Garrett Corporation, Los Angeles, Calif., air research manufacturing company, felt that the procedures result in a general slowing up. The Goodyear Aircraft Corporation, Akron, Ohio, did not feel that clearance procedures represented restriction on the proper interchange of ideas; however, engineers at Goodyear Aircraft utilized common sense in matters pertaining to these procedures. Chance-Vought, manufacturers of aircraft, aircraft components and electronic equipment, stated that clearance procedures posed no problems at their plant. Republic Aviation Corporation stated that procedures should be modified so that persons on the same classification levels could discuss freely research and development ideas except on special projects which are highly classified; and although this would possibly be a calculated risk, it would not be to any great degree.

Much duplication of effort is due to the difficulty of obtaining background data, especially where an engineer is denied data because he is not currently working in that field and, therefore, lacks requisite need to know. Further, all of the services seem to apply the principle differently. If clearance procedures are strictly interpreted, they do represent a restriction of inventive and creative thought. Progress would be impaired if the regulations were strictly followed. Procedures shall be modified but not to the extent, however, where any unnecessary risk would be involved. A modified need-to-know could serve as a basis for a more generous interchange of ideas with a minimum of risk, and should allow discussions in related categories. In unrelated categories or unrelated subjects, a specific need-to-know should be established. There would be no additional risk involved if a person is kept within related categories, and there might even be some special advantages involved in procuring outside advice or outside thoughts on special projects. Engineers and scientists working too closely with a project are apt to become so closely associated with that particular item that outside thoughts or outside advice would help them to a great extent.

The strength of this country rests, to an important degree, on the continued advance in scientific knowledge, an advance which is accelerated by a free exchange of views, wide discussion, and critical examination of findings by our fellow scientists. For this reason it is urged that continued attention be given the problem of declassification of information, particularly of a scientific nature, whenever possible. It is believed that this will actually increase the country's military security if classification is confined only to those matters regarding which a policy of secrecy is clearly of the direct military importance as narrowly construed. This opinion applies to all types of restriction, such as visit authorizations and travel, as well as to the classification of documents and restriction of areas.

First and foremost, our security program must not in any way inhibit these technological achievements, or restrict the interchange of technical information between the specialists of known integrity, who are responsible in these fields. On the other hand, if this vital information is readily available to a potential enemy, we have sacrificed lead time and minimized the importance of the new developments to our defense efforts. Our security program has been established primarily to maintain as large a lead time for our scientists and technicians as must be realized, without interfering with their progress.

Under the present system, it is believed that a high percentage of the classified matter in industry is not vital or, in many cases, even significant information. No change in the systems will be effective until a new overall policy establishes exactly what information is vital to our national defense, based on the theory that classified matter must be held to the very minimum. Once this new method is evolved, it should be disseminated to the employee who creates classified information in the performance of his duties. We should insure that information which is not vital does not burden the security system.

Document Classification [63]

The Commission recommends the abolition of the "confidential" classification *as to all future* information and materials.

By confining the above recommendation to prospective application, there should be no need for immediate review of documents already classified "confidential," but a gradual review and declassification of such documents should be carried on.

The Commission further recommends that industry be permitted immediately to discontinue clearance of employees for access to contracts already classified "confidential."

The definitions of secret and top secret, in Executive Order 10501, are adequate to protect the national security. Only information and materials which clearly come within such definitions should be so classified.

The fact that the Government now permits private industry to clear employees for access to confidential information and materials, without requiring a security investigation of any sort and merely on the basis of a statement of citizenship, indicates that the degree of risk to the national security is not substantial.

---

[63] See full discussion of this topic on p. 151.

It may be expected that large business corporations will continue to screen their employees as a matter of sound personnel practice.

In the light of information available to the Commission from the Department of Defense, it is the opinion of the Commission that the risk is so small, considering the cost and delays incurred in the program, that the program is unjustified.

There have been many confidential documents made available to the Commission which, in the light of the definition of "confidential" within Executive Order 10501, could be so classified only by the greatest stretch of the imagination.

The industrial process is such that the various phases of a confidential contract are so dispersed that it would be virtually impossible for an employee to assemble this information to the detriment of the national security.

"Secret" and "Top Secret"

The Commission recommends that only the "secret" and "top secret" categories of defense information, as defined in section 1 of Executive Order 10501, remain as at present.

Executive Order 10501, section 1, provides that:

Official information which requires protection in the interests of national defense shall be limited to three categories of classification, which in descending order of importance shall carry one of the following deignations; top secret, secret, or confidential. No other designation shall be used to classify defense information, including military information, as requiring protection in the interests of national defense, except as expressly provided by statute. These categories are defined as follows:

(*a*) *Top secret.*—Except as may be expressly provided by statute, the use of the classification top secret shall be authorized, by appropriate authority, only for defense information or material which requires the highest degree of protection. The top secret classification shall be applied only to that information or material the defense aspect of which is paramount, and the unauthorized disclosure of which could result in exceptionally grave damage to the Nation such as leading to a definite break in diplomatic relations affecting the defense of the United States, an armed attack against the United States or its allies, a war, or the compromise of military or defense plans, or intelligence operations, or scientific or technological developments vital to the national defense.

(*b*) *Secret.*—Except as may be expressly provided by statute, the use of the classification secret shall be authorized, by appropriate authority, only for defense information or material the unauthorized disclosure of which could result in serious damage to the Nation, such as by jeopardizing the international relations of the United States, endangering the effectiveness of a program or policy of vital importance to the national defense, or compromising important military or defense plans, scientific or technological developments important to national defense, or information revealing important intelligence operations.

The Commission believes that there should be no Government regulation of defense information which is not classified. Therefore, it recommends abolition of the Office of Strategic Information in the Department of Commerce, unless other and logical reasons can be advanced for its continued existence.

The Office of Strategic Information (OSI) of the Department of Commerce furnishes, with interagency consultation, guidance to executive branch agencies on the publication of nonclassified information which may be prejudicial to the United States defense interest; coordinates government policies on the international exchange of nonclassified information with the Soviet Bloc; and furnishes guidance for the voluntary use of business and industry on problems relating to publication and exchange of such information.

Representatives of Soviet Bloc Missions are actively engaged in obtaining such unclassified information as industrial brochures and catalogs, production charts, blueprints and lay-outs, technical and research reports, aerial photographs of plants, etc. OSI advises United States industry that while there is no legal restriction on furnishing unclassified information to Communist countries, it is requested that an attempt be made to obtain useful information in return. OSI maintains a list of needed Communist documents. OSI is assisted in its program by the Library of Congress. The Library reports that it has been active in the field of international exchange since 1800, and that the program has been successful.

The Commission is of the opinion that except in time of war there should be no agency of Government censoring unclassified information and materials. It is unrealistic to believe that technical publications and catalogs of American industry, available to the public in the United States, would not be available to agents of foreign governments. To the extent that the Office of Strategic Information prevents the publication of unclassified material, it thereby impedes the free flow of scientific data to the American public and American industry. To the extent that the Office of Strategic Information seeks to prevent the distribution of information already published, it is unrealistic to believe that this restricts the flow of such information to hostile countries. The costs of the Office of Strategic Information are therefore unjustified. Adequate provision has already been made in other recommendations for the protection of any information the classification of which is necessary in the interests of the common defense and national security.

Uniformity, Reduction, and Review of Classified Material

The Commission recommends that the effort should be intensified to:
> **Insure uniformity of classification;**
> **Reduce the amount of classified material;**
> **Insure periodic review of classified material; and**
> **Insure proper control and disposition of classified material.**

Many of the problems connected with the safeguarding of classified matter in industry are probably due to the volume of such classified matter.

Greater caution should be exercised in the assignment of classification; classification should be evaluated on a more realistic basis. Attempts through classification to "hide the elephant in the middle of the prairie" serve only to weaken the entire security system by trying to safeguard more than it is possible to safeguard properly. A detailed classification system should be developed for all branches of the Department of Defense and other Government agencies having industrial security programs.

The Small Business Administration has reported that, in response to a questionnaire submitted by it to members of its Advisory Boards throughout the United States, 208 questionnaires being completed and returned, the answer to the following question: "20. Is overclassification of material prevalent in the industrial security system?"; Yes—74; No—44; No opinion—72; No answer—18. In response to the following question: "21. Is declassification generally found to be too slow?", the following replies were received: Yes—89; No—21; No opinion—76; No answer—22.

Alien Owned or Operated Facilities

The Commission believes that there is inadequate protection of classified matter in contracts made with or involving facilities in which aliens hold ownership or operating positions.

The Department of Defense does not know of any way to ascertain true ownership of a corporation if some device similar to the use of Swiss banks is utilized in obtaining ownership in American corporations. In spite of this, however, it is felt in DOD that there is no serious leakage of classified information to foreign sources because of this fact. This opinion is based on current precautions to investigate ownership and control of corporations. The present system, however, rests upon the requirement imposed upon cleared persons who later receive classified material, namely, that they shall not divulge any classified information or material to uncleared personnel or to unauthorized organizations. The device used is that of requiring a listing of corporate officers and stockholders who will not have reason to need access to classified information and to whom the same will not be divulged.

In its report of December 31, 1956, the subcommittee of the Senate Judiciary Committee to Investigate the Administration of the Internal Security Act and Other Internal Security Laws [64] recognized an inherent difficulty in such a situation in that it would be unrealistic to believe that classified material revealed to the officers who were cleared could be withheld by them from the owners of the corporation who had hired them.

In testifying before the subcommittee,[65] however, Jerome Fenton of the DOD said he did not think it was too unrealistic because the DOD assures itself there are no nominees of the foreign bloc on the Board of Directors and no officers or key employees selected by the foreign bloc.

Foreign Ownership and Control

The Commission believes that control of industrial enterprises having classified defense contracts, by hostile foreign governments or their nationals, constitutes a threat to the national security. The Commission recommends that the appropriate Federal authorities continue their efforts to devise ways and means whereby the identity of such governments or their nationals and the source of the funds used by them in obtaining such control may be ascertained, and whereby the national security may be protected where such control is found to exist.

Senator Olin D. Johnston has stated [66] that the evidence brought to attention of his subcommittee reflects the need for an investigation and possible legislation to protect the internal security of the United States against programs of certain foreign countries which permit undisclosed monies of citizens of all nations, including Communist ones, to invade the United States economy.

Mr. Arthur I. Bloomfield, senior economist, Federal Reserve Bank of New York, stated [67] the United States imposes no controls or restrictions over the inflow or outflow of foreign or American capital except certain controls over Chinese and North Korean dollar assets. In the absence of licensing, our knowledge of these movements of capital must be based upon reporting systems. Some foreign countries, such as Switzerland, have no restrictions with regard to capital flow in the United States. Dollar assets invested through Swiss banks are reported in our statistics as Swiss investments without regard to the actual ownership. The total amount of

---

[64] Sec. 5 of report.
[65] P. 1721, hearings, subcommittee to Investigate the Administration of the Internal Security Act.
[66] P. 1667, hearings, Johnston subcommittee, pt. 31.
[67] Pp. 1667–1682, hearings, Johnston subcommittee, pt. 31.

foreign assets and investments in the United States at the end of 1954 was approximately 26.8 billion dollars. It would be technically quite feasible for Russia or a satellite country to obtain dollars in this country through some other foreign bank and that money, from records presently maintained, would appear merely as held by a foreign country other than Russia or a satellite state. That money could presumably be used to buy shares in American industry.

Mr. Fred H. Klopstock, chief of the Balance of Payments Division, Federal Reserve Bank of New York, stated [68] the Swiss hold very substantial amounts of American corporate securities. At the end of 1954 these holdings amounted to 1.3 billion dollars. In addition, there would presumably be other Swiss long-term investments in branch plants here, or subsidiaries of Swiss companies. It is not known whether these holdings were held for citizens or residents of Switzerland or of other countries, but only that the money came from Switzerland and is being held in Swiss accounts or has been purchased for Swiss accounts. Present reporting requirements call for nothing but the domicile of the purchaser. If he is a resident of Switzerland, the investment is recorded as a Swiss investment regardless of the identity of the ultimate owner. Under present laws and regulations, there is no way to trace the ultimate owner.

M. Joseph Meehan, director, Office of Business Economics, Department of Commerce, testified [69] that our sources of information on acquisition and sale by foreigners of controlling interests in United States companies are incomplete. When purchases or sales are deliberately concealed, we would have no means to discover them.

Jerome D. Fenton, Department of Defense, stated [70] that full disclosure to each corporation of the identity of the owners of its stock would be helpful to the Department of Defense and that it should be the management's responsibility to determine what degree of foreign ownership constitutes a threat to them.

Offshore Procurement Program (OSP) and the North Atlantic Treaty Organization (NATO)

Offshore procurement program: **The present policy of not disclosing secret or top secret information or materials to a foreign government or industry except where there is a real need to know, and where the furnishing of such information and materials will result in a net advantage to the United States Government, should be continued. In such unusual cases, offshore procurement con-**

---

[68] Pp. 1690–1692, hearings, Johnston subcommittee, pt. 31.
[69] P. 1697, hearings, Johnston subcommittee, pt. 31.
[70] P. 1727, hearings, Johnston subcommittee, pt. 31.

tracts should be let only where the security requirements of our domestic industrial security program can be substantially met in such foreign country. The security requirements and standards for offshore contracts shall be covered by regulations promulgated by the Office of Security in the Office of the Secretary of Defense.

North Atlantic Treaty Organization: It is further recommended that NATO industrial facilities contracts involving classified materials and information to be performed in the United States be covered as to security requirements provided for defense industrial facilities applicants in the United States, and that as to such NATO industrial facility contracts to be performed in other countries, NATO should adopt reasonable standards of security for which the standards in effect in the United States might well serve as a yardstick. Where such standards cannot be substantially met in such foreign contracts, the contracts should be let only where there is a clear showing of a net advantage to NATO by the performance of the contract in such foreign country.

Offshore Procurement Program

The offshore procurement program was established by the Secretary of Defense in 1952, and is defined as the purchase, in friendly foreign countries, of military equipment, materials or services included in the material defense assistance program (MDAP). The basic objective of OSP is to expand and diversify the production bases of certain foreign countries (almost exclusively European) to such a level that in time of combat their production potential will be of strategic and logistic advantage to the United States. Consistent with this basic objective, OSP contracts occasionally are implemented to support other U. S. foreign policy objectives.

Under the terms of reference set up by DOD in 1952, the military departments were given contractual authority for the offshore procurement of defense materiel. Once a determination is made that the materiel should be procured, for strategic or other considerations, outside the United States, an overseas contracting officer of one of the military departments will proceed to negotiate a contract with a foreign government or firm for the materiel required. In the case of contracts let for the first time to an industrial facility in a particular country, it is also necessary to receive the approval of the "country team" (State, ICA, and Military Assistance Advisory Group officers) headed by our Ambassador, who must determine that the political, economic and military climate in the host country does not conflict with the national interest. If the contract involves the release of classified technical data, a physical security survey of the foreign facility is made by units of the "country team".

310

The United States position on the release of classified technical information to foreign governments or nationals is contained in the "Policy Governing the Disclosure of Classified Military Information to Foreign Governments" prepared by the State-Defense Military Information Committee (MICC). Under the "National Disclosure Policy" certain kinds of classified technical data can be given without prior MICC approval to NATO, and some designated countries, up to and including confidential. If the information to be released is of a higher classification or in a special category, the MICC can make an exception to the policy once it determines there is a real need to know, and that the furnishing of such information will result in a net advantage to the national interest.

Since it is difficult in most cases to meet the above conditions, there have been only a limited number of OSP contracts in the excepted category, and all but two of these have been let in the United Kingdom or Canada, where security standards are higher than in most foreign countries. All other classified OSP contracts let by one of the Military Departments were either in the non-excepted category (NATO countries, etc.) or declassified before work began on the project.

Once an OSP contract reaches the negotiation stage, the cognizant Military Department, through its overseas contracting officer, inserts a security clause in the contract which provides, in part, that the foreign government will afford to all classified information received substantially the same degree of security as that afforded by the United States, and will be treated by the recipient government as its own classified information of that security grading.

The number and dollar amounts of all OSP contracts have dwindled from 1.6 billion in 1953 to 60 million in 1956. Of the total of 2.8 billion appropriated for OSP activities since 1952, less than a fraction of 1 percent has been in classified contracts.

North Atlantic Treaty Organization Contracts

NATO is in the process of drafting regulations for implementation of an industrial security program necessitated by its activities calling for contracts with industry. Specifically, NATO seeks to provide an industrial security program designed to cover all aspects of the security problem inherent in the performance of NATO classified infra-structure contracts by United States firms at home or abroad. Thereafter, the Department of Defense Office of Personnel Security Policy should follow through with the generation and adoption of concrete proposals for protection of NATO generated security information in the hands of United States industry.

The Commission believes that there are unnecessary delays incurred in processing a clearance:

For "secret",

For "top secret", and

For immigrant aliens,

but notes that part of the delay may be occasioned by the Armed Forces waiting on one or more of the seven agencies whose files have to be checked in a national agency check. It is believed, however, that much of the delay can be avoided in the manner indicated below.

Investigation indicates that a substantial number of national agency checks have been pending 120 days or more and that a substantial number of background investigations have been pending six months or more. The FBI regards as delinquent all national agency checks pending in excess of three working days and all background investigations pending in excess of 45 calendar days. The Civil Service Commission reports an average of 60 calendar days to conduct a national agency check economically, and about 58 calendar days to conduct a background investigation. The elimination of the confidential classification, the creation of an Office of Security in the Office of the Secretary of Defense, direct operational and administrative communication between the Office of the Secretary of Defense and the various field offices, and the creation of a central industrial security index in the Office of the Secretary of Defense will all contribute to a solution of the delay problem.

As to delays for clearance of immigrant aliens, the Commission recommends elimination of the requirement that clearance procedures for immigrant aliens not begin until they declare their intention to become United States citizens and recommends that the clearance of aliens be handled in the same manner as the clearance of citizens.[71]

"Need to Know"

The Commission believes that the "need to know" test should be a prerequisite for access to classified material. However, the "need to know" should be applied on the basis herein below defined.

Access to classified information or materials should be granted to persons possessing the appropriate clearance:

Where such access is required in the performance of their duties, and

---

[71] See Commission's industrial security recommendation on special problems in clearance of aliens, p. 271.

Where the grant of access to such persons will not adversely effect the national security.

Appropriate management certification of "need to know" should be conclusive within the facility.

Definition of "Need to Know"

The Armed Forces industrial security regulations, DOD, September 1956, defines the term in section 1–211.1: "Need to know—The requirement that classified defense information shall be made available only to persons whose employment requires access (par. 1–201) and knowledge or possession in the interests of National Defense." (AFISR, p. 4.)

Section 1–201. "Access, accessibility. The ability and opportunity to obtain knowledge of classified information. An individual, in fact, may have access to classified information by being in place where such information is kept, if the security measures which are in force do not prevent him from gaining knowledge of the classified information." (AFISR, p. 3.)

Forty-six organizations and individuals expressed opinions concerning the need-to-know principle. Of this number, 34, or 74 percent spoke in favor of the principle as presently administered, including 5 who believed it should be narrowed or tightened to allow less access. These five were opposed by three who thought it was too restrictive and should be broadened. The 12 individuals (comprising 26 percent of the total contacted) who opposed the principle set forth 19 objections as follows: five stated that there were differences of opinion regarding interpretation of "need-to-know"; three said that "need-to-know" was not properly defined; three believed the principle should be applied by the contractor and not by the government; two thought the principle handicaps academic freedom; two stated that it furnished no risk protection or that those who wanted classified data could obtain it indirectly; one pointed out that there was no clear-cut responsibility for determining "need-to-know"; and, as aforementioned, three thought the principle should be broadened. Four recommendations, in addition to those indicated by the foregoing objections, were offered as follows: (1) Establishment of a system to handle approval of "need-to-know"; (2) Revision of the principle for freer access by engineers and scientists; (3) Adoption of a regulation whereby custody of information and authority to apply the "need-to-know" principle is not vested in the same person; and (4) Broadening the "need-to-know" principle to include any project on which the individual may be employed.

Trevor Gardner, former Assistant Secretary of the Air Force for Research and Development, stated on July 12, 1956,[72] that scientists, engineers, and physicists "need-to-know" all of the facts they can get their hands on, because

---

[72] P. 41, 25th Intermediate Report of the Committee on Government Operations, H. Rept. No. 2947, 84th Cong., 2d sess., 1956.

313

it is very difficult to ascertain which of them may develop a much needed idea. Applying the "need-to-know" criterion to a scientific situation results in the crippling of progress. It is often impossible to define what a scientist needs to know in order to accomplish his job.

Uniform Forms

The Commission believes that improvement can be achieved in formulation and use of uniform forms for use in facility clearances. Improvements can and should be achieved in the formulation and the use of facility clearance forms by unification in the Office of Security in the Office of the Secretary of Defense and by consultation between the Atomic Energy Commission, other departments and agencies having industrial security contracts, and the proposed new Central Security Office.

Personnel Security Questionnaires

The Commission recommends that the personnel security questionnaires be revised so that they would contain:
Simple language;
Only necessary information; and
Explanation of its purpose.
Also, there should be a uniformity of personnel security questionnaires for all agencies. Improvements can and should be achieved in the formulation and use of personnel security questionnaires by unification in the Office of Security in the Office of the Secretary of Defense, and by consultation between Atomic Energy Commission, other departments and agencies having industrial security contracts, and the proposed new Central Security Office.

The objections voiced by industry in this matter can be summarized as the following points:
There are too many variations as to type of forms required to be submitted, both as to personnel information and other; the need for standardization exists.
The same forms must be submitted too frequently; for example, submitting additional (repeated) clearance forms for the same type of work which is a mere continuation of a project on which the employee has already been cleared.
A simplification and reorganization of the forms is needed.

314

The imposition of special instructions and requirements over and above those called for by the instructions contained in the forms should be prohibited.

Visitor Control

The Commission recommends that there should be uniformity of processing visitor requests; that this can be best accomplished by uniform regulations formulated and agreed upon by the heads of the various agencies after consultation with the director of the Central Security Office and representatives of industry.

The Commission recommends that there be uniformity in the standards for the processing of requests for visits of contract personnel to military or Government installations. The standards for visitor control shall include the following:

Existence of the necessary clearance.

Establishment of the "need-to-know" to the satisfaction of the appropriate security officer as designated by regulations.

Appropriate identification of the visitor, including fingerprints and photographs.

Reasonable advance notice of the contemplated visit.

The establishment and administration of visitor controls under the industrial security program has been and continues to be a complicated and irritating problem. Opinion is rather equally divided on the questions whether visitor control procedures are generally satisfactory and whether they impede the interchange of creative ideas. The problem will always be difficult because of inherent ambiguity of the test—"need-to-know"—and because extraneous considerations tend to become involved, such as the conflict between the general desire to find out what other companies are doing and the natural reluctance of those companies to disclose more of their processes and techniques than is necessary.

The 90 industrial security interviews conducted by the Commission on Government Security between June and December 15, 1956, produced the following reactions to visitor control:

Question IV. 7. What has been your experience with procedures on control of visitors?

Answer: Satisfactory—28, Qualified satisfactory—3; Unsatisfactory —29; Qualified unsatisfactory—1; No comment—29.

Question IV. 8. Do clearance procedures, i. e., "need-to-know" and visitor controls, represent such restriction of inventive and creative thought as to impair progress of research or production by impeding proper interchange of ideas?

Answer: Yes—20; Qualified yes—16; No—35; Qualified no—1; No comment—18.

The Small Business Administration, in its questionnaire for the Commission on Government Security, asked the members of its advisory boards throughout the country, the following question: "Have proceedings controlling visitors been unnecessarily cumbersome?" The replies were as follows: Yes—38; No—112; No opinion—43; No answer—15.

Physical Security

Under the Commission's recommendations there will be single standards of physical security. The application of those standards by an Office of Security in the Office of the Secretary of Defense will achieve greater uniformity.

Of 30 corporate and Government officials concerned with security, contacted in reference to the above recommendation, 11 officials stated in general that the present physical security regulations are adequate; however, 10 of these added a recommendation or minor objection set forth below. Nineteen stated that the regulations are subject to varying interpretations, or that they are interpreted differently by various Government security officers. Another said that interpretation was too strict. Five complained of inflexibility of regulations, particularly in their application to local needs. Two believed that the physical security program was too costly and impractical. Two thought the regulations were not sufficiently instructive. One stated that there was a misuse of guards who should perform minor police duties only, and should not be trained to repel riots or armed attacks which they could not handle anyway. Included in recommendations was one for a single agency, and four for bringing the regulations up-to-date.

In addition to the above contacts, questionnaires were received from members of the Small Business Administration Advisory Board. Sixty-three members expressed no opinion regarding physical security. Of the 124 who expressed an opinion, 75 percent stated that the standards are understandable and adequate.

Transmission, Storage, and Disposition of Classified Material

The Commission believes that the present requirements for the handling of classified material are realistic and practical as to transmission. On document classification the Commission has recommended that no change be made in transmission procedures.

316

The Commission believes that the present requirements for the storage of classified material are not realistic and practical.

Classified material should be removed from each contractor's plant as expeditiously as possible.

Determination of material considered proper for retention by the contractor should be reached by the security officer negotiating with the contractor so as to provide the latter with an opportunity for stating his reasons for retention such as the prospect of continued Government work: That proprietary rights are involved; that manufacturing processes are involved; the development of engineering data; the necessity for the corporation keeping complete tax records, documents necessary in the prosecution or defense of legal actions, suits, claims or demands.

The Commission believes that the present requirements for the disposition of classified material are realistic and practical.

Current regulations as to disposition should be expeditiously enforced, subject to the condition set forth in the preceding paragraph.

The following is a résumé of the opinions or comments by 16 persons concerned with security in government or industry. Of this number, three government security officers stated that no problem exists. Among the remainder, six complained of storage problems, while one stated that storage was not a problem. Three of these six, plus one additional officer, stated that regulations call for retention of classified material far beyond its period of usefulness. Two with storage problems attributed them to the presence of excessive classified matter. Two recommended automatic declassification or disposal of classified documents at a predetermined date. One complained of cumbersome disposal regulations at the close of a project, particularly in the case of classified material produced by the contractor itself. One official stated that the use of locks, safes and fences is overemphasized, and one pointed out the lack of uniformity in regulations.

Universities

The Commission believes that classified research involves the same security procedures whether conducted by industry or universities and that the same security standards for personnel and physical security should apply.

The Commission believes that the Government should continue to clear university employees for access to classified material.

The Commission believes that there should not be a separate security manual prepared for university research and scientific grants.

Sixteen persons were contacted in reference to the handling of classified data by colleges and universities. Eight stated that present security regulations hinder scientific research, while one stated that the program has not been criticized at his university. Two expressed opinions on the question concerning clearance of university personnel, and both stated that all clearances should be granted by the Government only. One college objected to the repeated changes in the cognizant office, and to the low level of the security educational program, not suited to university professors. Purdue University stated that it is proper to classify defense "information" but basic scientific principles should not be classified. Two colleges stated that the Industrial Security Manual is unsuited to university needs.

In response to a questionnaire, 140 members of the Small Business Administration Advisory Board stated that a separate university security program is needed, and 56 held the opposite views.

Award of Grants and Contracts for Unclassified Research

The Government should not knowingly make grants for unclassified research where such research is to be conducted by or be subject to the direction and supervision of disloyal persons.

The Government should not undertake to screen for disloyalty, but it should be the primary responsibility of the university or other institution seeking the grant to certify that they have no information reflecting adversely upon the loyalty of the persons conducting the research.

In connection with grants or awards for unclassified research, no loyalty oath should be required by any department or agency of the Federal Government except where required by statute.

There is no law or Executive order which provides that Federal grants or contracts for unclassified research must be denied or cancelled upon receipt of derogatory information concerning the loyalty of an individual connected with the project. In the report of the Committee on Loyalty in Relation to Government Support of Unclassified Research, National Academy of Sciences (Bronk Report), it was recommended that the sole test should be "the scientific integrity and competence" of the individual; and that "criminal disloyalty" should be dealt with by the Department of Justice and not through administration of research grants. The Assistant to the President stated in August 1956 that the recommendations contained in the Bronk Report would be followed. The present practice of the Department of Health, Education, and Welfare is to bar those who (1) are Communists by admission or conviction, (2) advocate governmental changes through unconstitutional means, or (3) have been convicted of crimes involving the Nation's security, and, in the case of fellowships (but not in the case of grants for research) a loyalty oath and affidavit are required. The National Science Foundation follows the same procedure. The American Council of Education supports the Bronk Report in general, while the Special Committee to Investigate Tax-Exempt Foundations, House of Representatives, Eighty-third Congress, advocates a middle course. The Special Committee believes in taking risks in the field of natural sciences, but not in the fields of social and political sciences. The Special Committee reported evidence indicating that Communists have used scientific enterprises through a special form of infiltration to build up the reputations of scientists of hidden Communist persuasion and subsequently placing them in situations where they are able to engage in espionage.

Cost of the Industrial Security Program

The Commission believes that the departments and agencies conducting industrial security programs do not maintain adequate accounting records as to the costs of such programs. Considering the enormous costs of the industrial security programs, certainly the Department of Defense and other departments and agencies having such programs should establish a system of accounting for such costs. It is unrealistic that such a system of accounting has not been established in the past, and it is essential that it be established as soon as possible. Recognizing that it may be too expensive to require a highly-detailed cost analysis in this program, nevertheless we believe that there should be as much of a cost breakdown as is practicable.

In considering the cost aspect of the Department of Defense industrial security program, the Commission on Government Security was, after diligent effort, unsuccessful in obtaining comprehensive or reliable current or estimated future costs. Such cost figures were unobtainable because neither the Department of Defense nor the Armed Services maintain them. Figures made available to the Commission on Government Security gave only a partial cost picture at best, and reasons advanced for such deficiency were both illogical and unpersuasive.

319

Port Security Program

Introduction

Three hundred and fifty years ago the *Susan Constant*, the *Godspeed*, and the *Discovery* sailed into Chesapeake Bay and dropped anchor. The men who landed from those ships founded the first permanent English speaking settlement on this continent. They knew shipping was their lifeline.

Shipping continues to be a lifeline of the United States, a lifeline easily cut, vulnerable to "sneak" attack, as Senator Magnuson said on the floor of the Senate when the "Magnuson Act" was under debate. This Act, upon which the port security screening program is based, was approved August 9, 1950, shortly after the Korean crisis erupted.

As will be seen, studies of the Commission have verified the systematic infiltration by Communists and subversives into many of the maritime and waterfront unions. Its studies have also established the loyalty of the vast majority of maritime and waterfront workers, as is shown by these statistics: As of May 1, 1956, the Coast Guard had processed 435,894 applications for seamen's documents and 402,360 port security cards for waterfront workers. Denials of clearance were made in 1,835 cases of seamen and in 1,953 cases of waterfront workers.

The port security screening program is unique in that it is applicable to a group not necessarily having any contractual relationship with the Federal Government.

The Commission has found that the record of this program from its inception to the present is a significant chapter in the story of the struggle to safeguard the nation within the framework of our constitutional liberties. While the program is basically sound, the Commission has made specific recommendations for its improvement.

HISTORY

Coast Guard and Port Security

World War I.—The United States Coast Guard was created in an act passed January 28, 1915, by combining the then existing United States Life Saving Service and the Revenue Cutter Service. The new service, so Congress ordered, ". . . shall constitute a part of the military forces of the United States . . . shall operate under the Treasury Department in time of peace and operate as a part of the Navy . . . in time of war or when the President shall direct." [1]

By Proclamation issued December 3, 1917,[2] President Woodrow Wilson ordered the Secretary of Treasury to issue such rules and regulations as would put into operation Title II of the Espionage Act of 1917 which provided that "Whenever the President . . . declares a national emergency to exist by reason of actual or threatened war . . . the Secretary of Treasury may make, subject to the approval of the President, rules governing anchorage and movement of any vessel, foreign or domestic, in territorial waters of the United States, may inspect such vessel at any time, . . . and if necessary . . . may take . . . full possession and control of such vessel . . ." [3]

Proceeding under the Espionage Act, the Coast Guard during World War I maintained a port security force in excess of 41,000 officers and men. In addition over 10,000 volunteers served in the operation without pay.[4] However, the official end of the war terminated the Coast Guard war powers.

Pre-World War II.—Congress clearly defined Coast Guard jurisdiction in an Act passed June 22, 1936, vesting the service with full law enforcement powers. The Act authorized Coast Guard officials ". . . to make inquiries, examinations, inspections, searches, seizures, and arrests upon the high seas, and navigable waters of the United States . . .," but excluded from the jurisdiction certain inland waters. [5] The limitations upon "inland waters" were eliminated by amendment passed on July 11, 1941.[6] As presently constituted, Coast Guard authority extends "upon the high seas and waters subject to the jurisdiction of the United States . . ." [7]

Moreover, Congress enacted legislation providing for a Coast Guard Reserve and a Coast Guard Auxiliary. The Auxiliary consists of private owners of small craft who may make themselves and their boats available for use in certain operations of the service. An amendment in 1944 expanded the Auxiliary to include aircraft and radio.[8]

World War II.—The Japanese attack on Pearl Harbor plunged the United States into full-scale war. By Executive order the Navy was assigned full responsibility for protecting all United States vessels, harbors, ports, and waterfront facilities not directly operated by the Secretary of War from loss or injury by accident, sabotage, subversion or other causes of a similar

---

[1] 38 Stat. 800, Jan. 28, 1915; as amended, 14 U. S. C. A. 1. (1956 Ed.).

[2] 40 Stat. 1725, Dec. 3, 1917.

[3] 40 Stat. 217, June 15. 1917; 50 U. S. C. A. 191 (1956 Ed.).

[4] Hearings, S. Res. 41, Waterfront investigation, part I, subcommittee of the Senate Committee on Interstate and Foreign Commerce, 83d Cong., 1st sess., Testimony of Rear Adm. Raymond J. Mauerman, p. 402.

[5] 49 Stat. 1820, June 22, 1936, 14 U. S. C. 45 (1940 Ed.), 14 U. S. C. A. 2 (1956 Ed.).

[6] 55 Stat. 585, July 11, 1941, 14 U. S. C. 45 (1946) Ed.), 14 U. S. C. A. 2 (1956 Ed.). See also United States Coast Guard Captain of the Port Manual, p. 3, legal authority for activities of captain of the port.

[7] 63 Stat. 496, Aug. 4, 1949, 14 U. S. C. A. 2 (1956 Ed.).

[8] 55 Stat. 9, 11, Feb. 19, 1941, 58 Stat. 759, Sept. 30, 1944, 14 U. S. C. A. (1956 Ed.).

nature. The Secretary of the Navy promptly delegated this function to the Coast Guard.[9]

Supervision and enforcement of security operations in each port became the separate responsibility of the port captain who,[10] complying with the various statutes, executive orders, and regulations issued during the war, took steps to control the following activities:

(a) Protection of ports, harbors, vessels, piers, docks and other waterfront facilities against sabotage, accidents and negligence.

(b) Control of the anchorage and movement of vessels.

(c) Issuance of identification cards.

(d) Control of the loading and shipment of explosives and other dangerous cargoes.

(e) Promulgation of local rules within the authority of the Captain of the Port.

(f) Control of traffic in harbors and channels, (special conditions).

(g) Control of traffic from inlets and isolated harbors.

(h) Provision for boarding and examining parties.

(i) Enforcement of Federal laws on navigable waters within the jurisdiction of the Captain of the Port.

(j) Miscellaneous duties.[11]

Waterfront exclusion program.—The Commandant on April 15, 1942, ordered district officers and captains of the ports to ". . . . deny entrance and remove from all vessels, harbors, ports, piers, and waterfront facilities . . . all persons whose presence thereon is found . . . to be inimical to the national war effort by reason of, but not limited to, drunkenness, violations of safety orders, or subversive inclinations as demonstrated by utterances or acts." [12]

Thereafter, the foregoing measure was implemented by the waterfront exclusion program. The Commandant, on April 23, 1942, provided regulations for issuing Captain of the Port identification cards complete with serial numbers, photographs, fingerprints and signature of holder impressed by seal. Privileges extended the holder were based upon the color of his card. White cards were issued to United States citizens or citizens of allied or friendly neutral countries who earned their livelihood on vessels or on the waterfront facilities. Persons needing occasional access to vessels and facilities received buff cards. Temporary, single visit, or single trip cards were green. Pink cards signified the holder to be an enemy alien, seaman on a foreign vessel, or citizen of a country hostile to the United States.[13]

Limitations.—The effectiveness of the waterfront protective program was limited by several factors. Although the captains of the ports had authority

---

[9] E. O. 9074, February 25, 1942, 7 F. R. 1587. Thereupon, the Secretary of the Navy authorized such delegation by written order to the commander-in-chief of the fleet, dated April 29, 1942.

[10] Sec. 7, 55 Stat. 585, July 11, 1941; 14 U. S. C. 45 (1946 Ed.).

[11] Captain of the Port Manual, May 14, 1942, p. 9.

[12] Id., p. 113.

[13] Id., p. 21.

to guard installations when necessary,[14] personnel limitations required that such duty be restricted to emergencies. The Coast Guard patrolled the water side of facilities, and relied generally ,upon private owners and state and municipal authorities to safeguard the land side. Then, as now, the necessity for establishing special terminals for transfer of explosives, inflammables, or other dangerous materials, involved considerations of adjacent facilities, other shipping and commerce.[15]

With the termination of hostilities, the wartime port security program ended. Control of the Coast Guard reverted to the Secretary of Treasury commencing January 1, 1946.[16] However, its military function has continued since Congress had by law declared the Coast Guard shall be ". . . a military service and constitute a branch of the land and naval forces of the United States at all times." [17]

Communism in Maritime Unions

Through World War II.—Communist infiltration into the maritime unions became manifest by 1934. Party participation in the San Francisco dock strike of that year attested to the growing Communist influence in the West Coast unions.[18] As to East Coast infiltration, the following comments from an exhibit presented in hearings before a congressional committee presents the party's own measure of its successes and expectations:

First, a number of strikes have taken place aboard ship. These struggles are beginning to take on a mass and national character. For instance, the strike of 14 coal ports in Boston is an example. We have been able to initiate these struggles, extend them to other ports, broaden them out from individual ship strikes to larger mass struggles because we have carried on the policy of concentration. Our main energy was concentrated upon one company and 45 ship strikes were developed out of this concentration. As a result these struggles have become a lever which we are now using to set the masses into action and winning the mass of the workers.[19]

Significantly, another exhibit presented in the same hearings optimistically remeasured party progress in maritime infiltration by 1937:

Today, in the marine industry, the militancy of the workers is high, the consciousness of their strength is increasing. Powerful unions have been established which generally, have a wide degree of democracy. There is mass sentiment for and support of militant policies, progressive measures, and for the C. I. O. In this generally favorable situation, our party members have a chance to work with tens of thousands of workers. We are an influence in determining policies. Large numbers of seamen, longshoremen, and other workers from the industry have joined the party in various ports from coast to coast.[20]

---

[14] Id., p. 7–8; also E. O. 8972, December 12, 1941, 6 F. R. 6420.

[15] Id., f. n. 15, pp. 16–29.

[16] E. O. 9666, 11 F. R. 1, Dec. 29, 1945.

[17] 55 Stat. 585, July 11, 1941, amending the Act of 1915, 38 Stat. 800. 14 U. S. C. 1 (1946 Ed.); see also 63 Stat. 496, 14 U. S. C. A. 1 (1956 Ed.), August 4, 1949, changing words "land and Naval" to "armed," thereby designating the Coast Guard as "a branch of the armed forces of the United States at all times."

[18] "Investigation of Communist activities in the San Francisco area," Hearings before the Committee on Un-American Activities, House of Representatives, 83d Cong., 1st sess., December 2, 1953, p. 3175.

[19] Ibid., p. 3175.

[20] Id., 19, p. 3177.

That Communists dominated certain maritime unions by the end of World War II has been established through studies on how the leadership in those unions has consistently adhered to shifting patterns of the Communist Party line.[21] Thus, when Germany breached its nonaggression pact with Russia and invaded the Soviet Union in June, 1941, certain of the maritime unions called for United States support of Russia.[22] After the war, when Russo-United States relations became strained, the same unions continued to support Soviet policies, even though to do so put such unions in a position of openly opposing undertakings of the United States in both domestic and foreign matters.[23]

Wartime Communist Party Policy facilitated Communist infiltration into and recruitment of maritime labor. This was particularly so because the rank and file continued both to accept and to cooperate with the aggressive leadership the Communists afforded in labor matters. Nevertheless, numerous maritime employees have since come forward to explain how they deserted the Communist Party in disgust, when, with the end of the war, the Communists in the unions gave their anti-United States policies precedence over labor matters.[24]

Union control strife.—The post World War II shift by the Communist Party, following the pattern of Russian antagonism to the United States, set off a series of internal struggles for control of the maritime unions. In some instances, notably the National Maritime Union, CIO (NMU), non-Communist seamen physically ejected Communist Party members from their hiring halls.[25] Although they tried to do so, Communists failed to gain authority in and were otherwise consistently opposed by important A. F. L. unions, such as the International Organization of Masters, Mates and Pilots of America (MMP), the Seafarers International Union (SIU) and its affiliate, Sailor's Union of the Pacific (SUP).[26]

But charges of Communist domination in other unions compelled the CIO executive board to appoint trial committees to hear charges, make findings of fact and recommendations to the executive board. Subsequently, the CIO expelled nine affiliates, including three maritime unions, for the reason that such unions had for more than a decade invariably conformed

---

[21] "Public policy and Communist domination of certain unions," Report of the Subcommittee on Labor and Labor-Management Relations of the Senate Committee on Labor and Public Welfare, Senate Document No. 26, 83d Cong. 1st sess. (1953), p. 2.

[22] "Communist domination of certain union," Report of the Subcommittee on Labor and Labor-Management Relations of the Senate Committee on Labor and Public Welfare, Senate Doc. No. 89, 82d Cong., 1st sess. (1951), pp. 36, 51. 87.

[23] Id., pp. 37, 52, 88.

[24] "Investigation of Communist activities in the San Francisco area—part 5," Hearing before the Committee on Un-American Activities, House of Representatives, 83d Cong., 1st sess., Dec. 5, 1953, see testimony of James Kendall, pp. 3460–3491, for a detail of experiences in the wartime merchant marine, engaging first in Communist activities in a union of unlicensed seamen; later, as an officer, in a union of licensed officers.

[25] "Investigation of Communist activities in the New York City area—part 3," Hearing before the Committee on Un-American Activities, House of Representatives, 83d Cong., 1st sess., May 6, 1953, testimony of Robert Gladnick, p. 1383.

[26] Id., 24, testimony of James Kendall, pp. 3473–3490. See also, Senate staff report "Marine cooks and stewards union," infra, fn. 34, p. 8.

their policies to each shift in Communist Party policy.[27] Yet, over and above the CIO committee findings, other evidence taken at Congressional hearings further revealed the sinister danger to maritime security implicit in the Communist control of these unions.[28]

Communications.—The American Communications Association (ACA), expelled from the CIO in 1950, was criticized in 1942 by Admiral S. C. Hooper as ". . . the nucleus of the Communist Party cell in the United States communications . . . a well-known fact in the industry, and was shown by the fact that 7 out of 10 of its officers were known Communist Party members. . . ." In emphasizing the danger from such cells, the Admiral recounted the example of the Spanish Fleet in 1937:

> . . . 700 officers were murdered by the Communist Party cells in the fleet because of the fact that the radio operators delivered the announcement of the Communist revolution to their comrades rather than to the responsible ships officers, which permitted the revolutionists to commit the crimes, the officers not expecting it.[29]

Shipping.—Communist influence in the National Union of Marine Cooks and Stewards (MCS), has been detailed in a staff report to a Senate Subcommittee.[30] The report relates that in 1945, disregarding established union procedures, certain members of the MCS called a constitutional convention. By amendment, among other things they transferred administrative power over union funds and control over all port units to a general council made up of the president, secretary-treasurer and port agents of the union. Rank and file members unsuccessfully fought these moves principally because the main body of the membership was on the high seas serving the American war effort.[31] In 1950 the MCS was expelled from the CIO. Even as late as 1953 a declaratory judgment by a California State Superior Court against the union leadership, and the enforcement of its new constitution, had failed to dislodge the faction in authority.[32]

Nor had the National Labor Relations Board been able to wrest control over jobs from the group running the union hiring hall. Board case studies unfold the many individual stories of violence and vilification wreaked upon courageous anti-Communists who dared to file charges against the Union or undertake to defeat the entrenched forces in open elections. The futility of such efforts is summarized in the staff report:

---

[27] Id. 22, part I incorporates the complete reports of the CIO trial committees in each of the nine unions expelled.

[28] "Congressional investigations of Communism and subversive activities," Senate doc. No. 148, 84th Cong. 2d sess., compiled by the Senate Committee on Government Operations (July 23, 1956), contains a summary index of all such proceedings and reports by the United States Senate and House of Representatives from 1918 to 1956.

[29] Report of the Subcommittee to Investigate the Administration of the Internal Security Laws of the Senate Committee on the Judiciary (committee print, 83d Cong., 2d sess., Jan. 3, 1955, pp. 20–22). See also "Communist Party of the United States of America—What it is and how it works," a print by the same committee, 84th Cong., 1st sess., Dec. 21, 1955, pp. 97–99.

[30] "The marine cooks and stewards union." A case history of the tactics of Communist unionism, 1953, staff report to the subcommittee on labor and labor-management relations of the Committee on Labor and Public Welfare U. S. Senate, 82d Cong., 2d sess.

[31] Id., pp. 5–8.

[32] Id., p. 8, *Weber* v. *Marine Cooks and Sewards Association of the Pacific Coast*, 208, Pac. 2d 1009, Aug. 16, 1949.

Physical violence has been used against dissidents to discourage them in their opposition. In one case the wife of a member of the opposition groups was beaten in her home. The union hiring hall has at all times been a hazardous place for recognized opponents of the MCS administration to venture into. If they did so they risked being beaten or threatened by officers of the union or hangers-on around the union hall. Nor has the ship's galley or messroom provided a sure sanctuary from incitement to violence against the open anti-Communists. In short, the life of an active anti-Communist in the MCS has been lived against the ever-present threat of violence in his home, in the union hall, on the water front, and on board ship.[33]

The significance of such power over a maritime labor union is also expressed in the report:

The Marine Cooks and Stewards Union in its own right today represents between 3,000 and 4,000 seamen serving in the mess halls, galleys, and dining rooms aboard vessels plying between the Pacific Coast and Far East ports. The union, in addition to this source of strength and support, also has very close attachments and support from the International Longshoremen's and Warehousemen's Union headed by Harry Bridges. In a recent issue of the union newspaper, when the leadership felt that threats were being made about the way it operated its hiring hall, President Bryson called upon the owners and the Government to take heed of the fact that not only did they face the Marine Cooks and Stewards Union members but also the possible strike sanction of the Longshoremen of the West Coast and, in addition, the possible strike sanction of longshoremen in South Africa, Australia, and other countries where longshoremen's unions are closely associated with the World Federation of Trade-Unions.[34]

Waterfront workers.—The CIO expulsion from its ranks of the West Coast International Longshoremen's Union (ILWU) and the trials of its leader, Harry Bridges, are now matters of public knowledge. The Committee on Un-American Activities of the House of Representatives had this to say in 1951 about the ILWU:

This has 75,000 members. They have effective control of many ports in the U. S. A. and more than once have used it to paralyze shipping. Communist domination of this union in wartime could wreck the whole U. S. fighting power.[35]

Although references have been made to Bridges' Communist activities,[36] the CIO has stated that Bridges does not necessarily represent the union majority:

The reaction of Harry Bridges' own local to Bridges' attempt to foist the Communist Party line upon it in the current Korean crisis demonstrates that when the lines are clearly drawn, American workers are loyal to America, not to Russia.[37]

---

[33] Id., 30, p. 137. See also pp. 8–137.

[34] Id., p. 2.

[35] "100 things you should know about communism, series: In the U. S. A.,—and religion—and education—and labor—and Government and spotlight on spies." Committee on Un-American Activities H. Doc. 136, 82d Cong., 1st sess., May 14, 1951, p. 82.

[36] Id., 28, particularly see testimony of James Kendall, pp. 3475–3478, also part I, testimony of Don Resser, pp. 3057–3138; Id., 25, p. 2; "Communist infiltration of maritime and fisheries union," Hearings before the subcommittee of the Committee on Education and Labor, House of Representatives, 80th Cong., 2d sess., Oct. 18 thru 22, 1948. See testimony of Francis P. Foisie, president, waterfront employees organization of the Pacific Coast for discussion of strikes, slowdowns and their effect upon negotiation; see also "Labor management problems of the American merchant marine," Committee on Merchant Marine and Fisheries, House of Representatives. H. Rept. No. 1658, 84th Cong., 2d sess., Jan. 19, 1956, pp. 5, 15, 16, 21, for analysis of effect of strikes and slowdowns upon United States shipping.

[37] Id., 26, p. 95.

Moreover, the Commandant of the Coast Guard observed in testifying before a House of Representatives Committee that the majority of West Coast longshoremen requested port security cards despite the union's official policy opposing the screening program.[38] Finally, anti-Communist elements have made efforts to wrest power from the union leaders.[39]

Eastern waterfront.—The popular belief is that infiltration on the eastern seaboard has been blocked by the presence of other influences, such as alleged racketeering, dominating the International Longshoremen's Association, Independent (ILA, Ind.). Yet increasingly, evidence appears which shapes a growing pattern of Communit acvitity in that area.

In an all-out struggle with AFL Longshoremen's Union in 1954 for collective bargaining rights on the East Coast, and in political maneuvers in New Jersey to elect State assemblymen opposed to the New York Waterfront Commission for the New York Harbor, the ILA, Ind., accepted the collaboration of the United Electrical, Radio, and Machine Workers of America (UE), a union then notoriously in the control of Communists.[40]

Bridges himself appeared on the New York docks in 1955, ostensibly to study cargo-handling operations. He has maintained as a representative in the area an agent notoriously associated with eastern Communist Party activities for over two decades.[41] Bridges' agent was hired briefly by one I. L. A., Ind., local, under an assumed name until exposure by the press forced him to quit. It may be noteworthy that the same ILA, Ind., local in which Bridges' representative was known to have manifested an interest struck on December 27, 1956, in face of a United States District Court eighty-day injunction in effect against strikes by the ILA, Ind. The injunction had been issued November 25, 1956, in the public interest at the request of President Dwight D. Eisenhower, pursuant to the terms of the Labor Management Relations Act of 1947.[42]

Communist retrenchment.—But neither the CIO expulsion of the Communist unions nor the notoriety received from congressional exposure has deterred the Communist Party in its program of maritime union infiltration. Typically, the party has revised its tactics to hold its ground:

... The material from which to recruit was no longer available among workers ... Therefore, the Communist Party directed its intellectuals and white-collar worker members to leave their own chosen fields and to obtain employment in the basic industry. This the Communist Party did, starting late in 1948 and 1949.[43]

---

[38] "Study of operations of the United States Coast Guard," hearings before Committee on Merchant Marine and Fisheries, House of Representatives, 84th Cong., 1st sess., Mar. 22–25, 1955, p. 60.

[39] Id., 28, testimony of James Kendall, p. 3483.

[40] "Investigation of unauthorized use of passports—part I," hearings before Committee on Un-American Activities, House of Representatives, 84th Cong., 2d sess., testimony of William Aloysius Wallace, May 23, 1956, p. 4324.

[41] Id., 29, testimony of Robert Gladnick and Irving Charles Velson, pp. 1377–1422; Id., 44; hearings before the subcommittee to investigate the administration of the Internal Security Act and other internal security laws of the Senate Committee on the Judiciary, 84th Cong., 2d sess., June 21 and July 12, 1956, testimony of Velson and Jeff Kibre.

[42] *United States of America* v. *ILA Ind., et al.*, 147 F. supp. 425, Dec. 4, 1956.

[43] "Colonization of America's basic industries by the Communist Party of the U. S. A.," prepared and released by Committee on Un-American Activities, U. S. House of Representatives, Sept. 3, 1954, p. 13.

Finally, J. Edgar Hoover, in discussing the recent changes in tactics, described the following, as well as other measures adopted by the party:

. . . No longer are Communist Party membership cards issued; maintenance of membership records are forbidden; contacts of rank-and-file members are limited from 3 to 5—the basic club unit. Most of the local headquarters have been discontinued and party records have been destroyed. No evening meetings are permitted in headquarters without staff members present. Conventions and large meetings are held to the absolute minimum. The use of the telephone and telegraph are avoided.[44]

Port Security Under the Magnuson Act

The Honorable Emanuel Celler, explaining the bill which became the Magnuson Act, said:

. . . This bill permits the President . . . particularly to guard against, shall we say, Trojan horse ships bringing in atomic bombs or facilities for bacteriological warfare . . .[45]

The act.—The Magnuson Act became law August 9, 1950, during the period of growing public concern over Communist actions in Korea. The Act which amended Title II, the Espionage Act of 1917,[46] is more fully discussed in the next section of the report on port security, entitled "The Legal Basis."

Fundamentally, the bill corrected two weaknesses in the Espionage Act disclosed during World War II in the following manner:

First, by broadening the President's power for invoking port security measures, by including as an additional possible reason the threat of subversive activity, and by allowing the President to institute port security measures without declaring a national emergency. Second, by providing for regulations and measures to safeguard harbors, ports, and waterfront facilities, in addition to vessels.[47]

In support of the Act, Congressman Celler further advised:

. . . that only a few days ago five British ships enroute to Korea were sabotaged . . . The party line has openly urged comrades and fellow travelers everywhere to disrupt railroads, ships, and weapons and equipment bound for Korea. We must be vigilant.[48]

Sponsoring the bill before the United States Senate, Senator Warren Magnuson of Washington explained its purpose:

. . . This is not a national emergency measure; it is only a limited emergency measure to take care of the waterfront security of the Nation. It is to prevent the entry into our ports of foreign-flag ships without notice either to the Coast Guard or to the FBI, and enable them to make a search of the ships before they reach our territorial waters, in case they might have in their holds something which might be destructive.

. . . It would be impossible for destruction to come to any great port of the United States, of which there are many, as the result of a ship coming into the port with an

---

[44] Id., p. 15.
[45] Cong. Rec., vol. 96, part 8, p. 11220, July 27, 1950.
[46] 64 Stat. 427, Aug. 9, 1950, 50 U. S. C. 191, amending title II of the Espionage Act of June 15, 1917, 40 Stat. 220.
[47] United States Coast Guard Law Enforcement Text, ch. 9, p. 3.
[48] Id., 48.

atomic bomb or with biological or other destructive agency, without some liaison ashore. This would give authority to the President to instruct the FBI, in cooperation with the Coast Guard, the Navy, or any other appropriate governmental agency, to go to our waterfronts and pick out people who might be subversives or security risks to this country . . .[49]

Executive Order 10173.—In conformity with the Act, President Harry S. Truman, on October 18, 1950, finding that the security of the United States was endangered by subversive activity, issued Executive Order 10173. The order directed the Commandant of the Coast Guard to institute a maritime and waterfront employee screening program whereby he would exclude from vessels or certain restricted waterfront facilities any person whose presence thereon was found by the Commandant to be inimical to the welfare of the United States.

The President in the same order prescribed regulations to safeguard the physical security of United States ports. Coast Guard officials were required under the order to control vessel movements; visit and search any vessel or facility, and, when necessary, take possession; control handling of dangerous cargoes or explosives; report evidence of sabotage and subversive activity to the Federal Bureau of Investigation.[50] The additional duty of prescribing and enforcing measures to insure safety of ports was added by amendment.[51]

The screening program.—Public tension over Communist aggression in South Korea prompted security measures in the maritime industry even before passage of the Magnuson Act. A policy of keeping ships free from subversives was declared by representatives of both management and labor at a conference sponsored jointly by the Secretaries of Labor and Commerce on July 24, 1950. The President, through the Secretary of Treasury, directed the Coast Guard to put the conference policies into effect. The Coast Guard commenced screening all seamen signing ships' articles of agreement before United States deputy shipping commissioners.[52]

Passage of the Magnuson Act in the following month, and Executive Order 10173 in October 1950, vested the Coast Guard with full authority to proceed with a personnel screening program. Seamen denied shipping rights before October 24, 1950, received formal letters of denial from the Commandant, and were extended limited rights of appeal pending establishment of Coast Guard District hearing boards and the National Board of Appeals at Washington, D. C.

President Truman on December 16, 1950, proclaimed a state of national emergency growing out of the Korean crisis.[53] Thereafter, following public hearings, the Coast Guard on December 27, 1950, published official rules

---

[49] Id., p. 11321, July 28, 1950.

[50] Executive Order 10173, Oct. 20, 1950 (15 F. R. 7012), 33 C. F. R., chapter I, subchapter A., part 6.

[51] Executive Order 10277 Aug. 2, 1951 (16 F. R. 7541), adding sections 6.14–1 and 6.14–2 to Executive Order 10173.

[52] The incidents surrounding the labor-management conference have been related in a paper furnished the Commission on Government Security by Commander E. C. Hawley, U. S. Coast Guard, detailing the historic growth of the port security program.

[53] Presidential Proclamation 2914, Dec. 16, 1950, (15 F. R. 9029), 3 C. F. R. 1950 Supp.

and regulations, establishing clearance procedures, standards, and rights of applicants, both as to maritime and waterfront employees.[54]

Final authority to deny seamen access to maritime employment or waterfront employees the right to work on restricted facilities reposed then, as now, with the Commandant.[55] In either instance he shall not issue identification credentials to seamen or applicants for port security cards—

. . . unless he is satisfied that the character and habits of life . . . are such as to authorize the belief that the presence of such individual on board [a vessel or within a waterfront facility] would not be inimical to the security of the United States." [56]

Applicants denied clearance were notified in writing.[57] They might appeal to district hearing boards; thence, and finally, to the National Board of Appeals at Washington, D. C.[58]

Port security program administration.—Innovation of the port security program in 1950 posed extensive administrative problems for the Coast Guard. At the outset, programs were carried out in ten major ports by 4,772 officers and men.[59] Since the Korean War the program has been progressively reduced. By 1955 port security operational units personnel totaled 110 officers, 18 warrant officers, and 872 enlisted men. The operations included security checks on incoming vessels by 24-hour continuous harbor-entrance patrol at ten major and four minor ports. In addition, restricted zones of operations were established as required for handling military and explosive cargoes, and involved the need of shoreside and waterside patrols, preloading inspection of ships and facilities, issuance of permits, and actual supervision by trained personnel in loading of explosives.[60]

Considerable public controversy has been waged over the Coast Guard screening operations. The Communist Party and Communist-controlled unions at the outset aimed heated attacks at the program. However, constructive criticism both from maritime groups and the public press led to amendments of the regulations from time to time.[61]

At the estimated cost of $1,275,000 the Coast Guard by July 1, 1956, had considered 434,894 maritime and 402,360 waterfront employees' applications for clearance credentials. Final denials had been issued before May 1, 1956, to 1,953 waterfront employees and to 1,835 seamen.[62]

Hearing board.—The policy on hearing boards formulated in the labor-management conference of July 24, 1950, has been carried out in practice by

[54] 33 C. F. R. chapter I, subchapter K, section 121.01, *et seq.* (15 F. R. 9327), and subchapter L, section 125.01, *et seq.* (15 F. R. 7524).

[55] "Security of vessels and waterfront facilities," C. G.—239, published January 15, 1951, 33 C. F. R. 121.13 (c) for seamen; 33 C. F. R. 125.27 for waterfront employees.

[56] Quoted as amended by Executive Order 10277, 16 F. R. 7541 Aug. 2, 1951, amending section 6.10–7 of Executive Order 10173; and Executive Order 10325, 17 F. R. 4624, amending section 6.10–7 of Executive Order 10173. See C. G.–239, published May 12, 1952, replacing C. G.–239, published Jan. 15, 1951. Words in brackets apply only to section 6.10–7.

[57] C. G.–239, published May 12, 1952, 33 C. F. R. 121.15 (e) and 33 C. F. R. 125.27.

[58] Id. 57, 33 C. F. R. 121.19 et seq., and 33 C. F. . 125.

[59] Id., 4, p. 405.

[60] C. G. 239, published May 12, 1952.

[61] Id., 55.

[62] Letter from Acting Secretary of the Treasury, David W. Kendall, dated Nov. 19, 1956.

the Coast Guard. Applicants denied credentials have been afforded a right to a hearing before a three-member district board, one chosen from the ranks of labor, one from management, and a chairman with legal background from the Coast Guard.[63]

At the outset, the Coast Guard charged the chairmanship of local boards to members of its staff of thirteen civilian hearing examiners as an added and collateral duty to their main function, the hearing and deciding of marine casualty cases involving merchant marine personnel.[64]

Coast Guard personnel performed necessary clerical functions required by the boards. It is estimated that hearing examiners divided their time equally between security and marine casualty cases.

Prior to May 1, 1956, local hearing boards had sent recommendations to the Commandant in cases involving 2,329 maritime and 1,216 waterfront employees. Of these cases, 460 of the maritime and 71 of the waterfront employees were appealed to the Board of Appellate Review at Washington, D. C. All of these were heard.

As a consequence of several court decisions, the Coast Guard has issued revised regulations which are discussed in the section of this report entitled "The Present Program."

Present status of port security.—The port security program presently has diverged along two lines.

Initially, the Coast Guard, whether as an arm of the Navy in wartime or under the Secretary of the Treasury in peacetime, must protect American coasts and ports. The physical port security program calls for security preparedness in order to meet any condition that may arise; also, the Coast Guard must be alert to enforce additional measures as emergencies—or even war—may occur.

Secondly, the Coast Guard program for screening subversives from American ships and restricted waterfront areas must proceed under the new regulations. Meanwhile, complying with the decree of the ninth circuit court of appeals, the Coast Guard has commenced to issue clearance credentials to persons the Commandant had previously deemed to be security risks.

Thus, as the United States looks to the future of port security, the paramount question must be asked: Is the present security clearance program needed? As to this question, Acting Secretary of the Treasury David W. Kendall, writing in behalf of the Coast Guard, made the following observation:

Although it cannot be assumed that the Port Security Program has completely cleared the United States Merchant Marine of security risks, the Coast Guard believes that the existence of the program and the screening which has been done under it are an effective deterrent against infiltration of the United States shipping and waterfront activities by those bent upon sabotage or other subversive activities in this area.[65]

---

[63] C. G. 239, p. 58.
[64] See 46 U. S. C. for handling of marine casualty cases by the Coast Guard.
[65] Letter to the Commission on Government Security from Acting Secretary of the Treasury David W. Kendall, dated Nov. 19, 1956.

LEGAL BASIS

Introduction

This study of the current port security program which was begun after the start of the Korean war in 1950 will be limited to security clearance of seamen and harbor workers under the Magnuson Act, discussed later. It does not cover measures taken to protect the physical security of ports and shipping, supervision of handling explosives, guarding and supervision of restricted waterfront areas, the search of ships in American waters for weapons, examination of crewmen for technical skills, or such protective measures as the regulations of the United States Army Corps of Engineers relating to the navigation, anchorage, and unloading of vessels transporting explosives (33 C. F. R. 60–74). Neither does it include the Army and Navy programs for protection of piers and ports.

The port security program is administered by the Coast Guard and applies to all persons employed on United States registered merchant vessels of 100 tons gross or more, including barges and shipping on navigable inland waters. Vessels of less than 100 tons were exempted from credential requirements on the Great Lakes and "western rivers" by amendment to Coast Guard regulations on November 30, 1956. "Western Rivers" refers to the Mississippi and its tributaries, the Mobile, and the Red River, North (33 C. F. R. 125.53 and 95.03b).

Longshoremen must also be cleared before they may enter a port area designated by the Coast Guard as restricted. Although they may work in unrestricted port areas without clearance, a ship captain or crew member without clearance is completely barred from his vocation. The Commandant of the Coast Guard may restrict a port or lift restrictions at his discretion.[66]

Masters and crewmen of harbor craft such as water taxis, junk boats, garbage disposal boats, bum boats, supply boats, and ship-cleaning boats must have a port security card, Armed Forces identification, or one of the other credentials specified in 33 C. F. R. 125.09.

One distinctive feature of the port security program is that it applies to United States citizens whose private employers may not be under Government contract.

Statutory Basis for the Program

The basic statutory authority for the port security program is an amendment to the Act of June 15, 1917,[67] as amended, popularly referred to as the "Magnuson Act."[68] This statute in pertinent part provides as follows:

[66] For Coast Guard security regulations, see 33 C. F. R. 121 and 125.
[67] 40 Stat. 220, 50 U. S. C. A. 191 note.
[68] 64 Stat. 427, 50 U. S. C. A. 191.

335

Whenever the President finds that the security of the United States is endangered by reason of actual or threatened war, or invasion, or insurrection, or subversive activity, or of disturbances or threatened disturbances of the international relations of the United States, the President is authorized to institute such measures and issue such rules and regulations—

(a) to govern the anchorage and movement of any foreign-flag vessels in the territorial waters of the United States, to inspect such vessels at any time, to place guards thereon, and, if necessary in his opinion in order to secure such vessels from damage or injury, or to prevent damage or injury to any harbor or waters of the United States or to secure the observance of rights and obligations of the United States, may take for such purposes full possession and control of such vessels and remove therefrom the officers and crew thereof, and all other persons not especially authorized by him to go or remain on board thereof;

(b) to safeguard against destruction, loss, or injury from sabotage or other subversive acts, accidents, or other causes of similar nature, vessels, harbors, ports, and waterfront facilities in the United States, the Canal Zone, and all territory and water, continental or insular, subject to the jurisdiction of the United States.

The most important extension of authority granted by the Magnuson Act is the power granted the President to institute the security program whenever he finds that the national security is endangered. In short, the port security program does not require for its initiation a Presidential proclamation declaring a national emergency, which had previously been the prerequisite to invoking the statute.

The Magnuson Act was approved August 9, 1950, and was implemented October 18, 1950, by Executive Order 10173.[69] This Executive order was subsequently amended by Executive Orders 10277[70] and 10352.[71] The Executive orders vested the administration of the port security program in the Coast Guard and authorized the Commandant of the Coast Guard to issue regulations supplementing and implementing the Executive order. These regulations appear in 33 C. F. R., subchapter K, parts 121–125, inclusive. The first regulations were issued on December 27, 1950, and the most recent general revisions were released April 25, 1956, and April 27, 1956, to be effective May 1, 1956.[72]

Penalties for violation of the act are fixed by 50 U. S. C. A. 192, which provides:

SEC. 192. *Seizure and forfeiture of vessel; fine and imprisonment.*—If any owner, agent, master, officer, or person in charge, or any member of the crew of any such vessel fails to comply with any regulation or rule issued or order given under the provisions of this chapter, or obstructs or interferes with the exercise of any power conferred by this chapter, the vessel, together with her tackle, apparel, furniture, and equipment, shall be subject to seizure and forfeiture to the United States in the same manner as merchandise is forfeited for violation of the customs revenue laws; and the person guilty of such failure, obstruction, or interference shall be punished by im-

---

[69] 3 C. F. R. 1950 Supp. 141.
[70] Dated August 1, 1951, 3 C. F. R. 1951 Supp. 460.
[71] Dated May 19, 1952, 3 C. F. R. 1952 Supp. 77.
[72] Later amendments: *Nov. 30, 1956, 21 F. R. p. 9339; *Jan. 29, 1957, 22 F. R. p. 581; Sept. 22, 1956, 21 F. R. 7255; Dec. 4, 1956, 21 F. R. 9565; Jan. 21, 1957, 22 F. R. 502; *Mar. 7, 1957. 22 F. R. 1430 (asterisks designate more important changes).

prisonment for not more than ten years and may, in the discretion of the court, be fined not more than $10,000.

(a) If any other person knowingly fails to comply with any regulation or rule issued or order given under the provisions of this chapter, or knowingly obstructs or interferes with the exercise of any power conferred by this chapter, he shall be punished by imprisonment for not more than ten years and may, at the discretion of the court, be fined not more than $10,000.[73]

The program does not generally apply to alien crewmen, who must have passports with appropriate United States visas (22 C. F. R. 41.60) but are not screened otherwise, nor to aircraft flight crews nor to airports.

Constitutional Basis for the Program

While the port security program itself raises several important constitutional questions, as will hereinafter appear, the power of Congress to enact the Magnuson Act itself has not been seriously questioned.

In the only reported case in which there has been specific comment on the constitutionality of the Magnuson Act, *U. S.* v. *Gray*,[74] the court stated:

There seems to be no reason to doubt that the screening operation initiated by the Magnuson Act is a legitimate war measure.

This position was inferentially affirmed by the same court in *Parker* v. *Lester*,[75] when it stated:

We are in agreement with the determination of the district court that the Magnuson Act authorized the screening of seamen and the promulgation of regulations to accomplish that end. The district court correctly rejected the argument that the act did not authorize a screening program.

The "war power" of the Congress is found in article I, section 8, of the Constitution which, among other matters, empowers the Congress specifically to "provide for the common defense . . . to declare war . . . and to make all laws which shall be necessary and proper for carrying into execution the foregoing powers." This power has also been considered an attribute of sovereignty and has been given a very broad interpretation.[76]

The court noted in *U. S.* v. *Gray* (above) that the Magnuson Act was approved August 9, 1950, "shortly after the commencement of the military conflict in Korea." In *Parker* v. *Lester* (above), the court commented: "In 1950, during the Korean crisis, Congress enacted the so-called Magnuson Act."

Further, the Court in *Parker* v. *Lester* (above), said, "It may be taken for granted that in view of the emergencies referred to in the act and in the Executive order it was altogether appropriate to establish a system whereby persons who are security risks may be denied employment upon

---

[73] 40 Stat. 220, as amended by 54 Stat. 79 and by 64 Stat. 427.

[74] 207 F. 2d 237 (C. A. 9, 1953).

[75] 227 F. 2d 708 (C. A. 9, 1955).

[76] *Lichter* v. *U. S.*, 334 U. S. 742 (1948).

merchant ships. The existence of the emergency, the seriousness of the danger legislated against, and the necessity for such legislation, are for determination of other departments of the Government, not by us. We think it clear the screening of persons who are security risks is permissible as a matter of substantive due process. . . .

". . . No doubt merchant seamen are in a sensitive position in that the opportunities for serious sabotage are numerous."

However, the Magnuson Act is not limited in its application to a period of actual war, threatened war, invasion or insurrection. It may be invoked whenever the President finds that "the security of the United States is endangered by reason of . . . subversive activity." Consequently, constitutional authority other than the war power should be examined.

Article I, section 8, clause 3, of the Constitution provides that the Congress shall have power—

to regulate Commerce with foreign Nations and among the several States.

Chief Justice Marshall in 1824 in *Gibbons* v. *Ogden* [77] held that "commerce" includes "navigation." Subsequently, in *Pensacola Telegraph Co.* v. *Western Union Co.*,[78] Chief Justice Waite said, "The powers thus granted are not confined to the instrumentalities of commerce, or the postal service known or in use when the Constitution was adopted, but they keep pace with the progress of the country." It is under this clause that protective legislation for labor employed in commerce and navigation has been held constitutional.[79]

To illustrate that it was intended that the power of Congress in the matter of shipping should be broad and absolute, article I, section 8, clause 10, of the Constitution provides that Congress has the power—

to define and punish Piracies and Felonies committed on the High Seas and Offenses against the law of Nations.

And again clause 11 of the same section and article provides that the Congress shall have power to—

grant Letters of Marque and Reprisal, and make Rules concerning captures on Land and Water.

In short, the Constitution gave to the Congress power to deal with every danger known to its framers which might jeopardize shipping or commerce on the high seas. Subversion and sabotage are contemporary "piracies," from which the Nation must be protected.

The Congress has enacted measures [80] authorizing the examination and licensing of seamen, the regulation of conditions of employment and crimes at sea, and similar legislation.[81] Screening for security reasons may be deemed an extension of this type of legislation.

[77] 9 Wheat. 1 (1824), 22 U. S. 1.
[78] 96 U. S. 1 (1878).
[79] *Southern Railway Co.* v. *U. S.*, 222 U. S. 20 (1911); the Safety Appliance Act of 1893, 27 Stat. 531, was the legislation involved in this case.
[80] Many of the contemporary provisions are derived from the act of July 1790.
[81] For examples, see 46 U. S. C. A. 544–713; 33 U. S. C. A. 3, 451, 472, etc.

Further, article III, section 2, clause 1, of the Constitution which provides that "The judicial Power shall extend to . . . all Cases of admiralty and maritime Authority" has been held together with the congressional powers to justify the Longshoremen's and Harbor Workers Act [82] and thus is additional evidence of the broad authority of the Federal Government in controlling shipping and ports.

It is concluded, therefore, that the Congress had constitutional authority to enact the Magnuson Act, and that it may be lawfully administered in peacetime as well as during a war or national emergency, provided, of course, the President finds a danger to national security.

Federal Court Decisions

Regulations of the Coast Guard have come under review by the United States courts below the Supreme Court in several cases. The court of claims has also decided one case involving these regulations. The most important case is that of *Parker* v. *Lester*, cited above. In this case the appellants as plaintiffs below brought an action against officers of the Coast Guard in the San Francisco area and sought to enjoin the enforcement of security regulations. The plaintiffs were seamen and had been denied clearance on security grounds. The district court issued an injunction enjoining the Coast Guard officials from denying security clearance and from preventing the plaintiffs from being employed on merchant vessels unless certain information and bills of particulars showing the reasons for the denial of clearance were furnished. The plaintiffs appealed from the order of the district court,[83] asserting that it was inadequate. The court of appeals reviewed the Magnuson Act, the Presidential Executive order, and the regulations issued by the Commandant of the Coast Guard in detail.

The plaintiffs contended that the screening procedure under which they had been denied clearance constituted a denial of due process of law under the fifth amendment since the plaintiffs had not been given notice of specific charges and were refused the right to confront and cross-examine witnesses who allegedly furnished derogatory information.

The court pointed out that the plaintiffs were merely furnished a final statement to the effect that "no person shall be issued a document required for employment unless the commandant is satisfied that the character and habits of life of such person are such as to authorize the belief that the presence of the individual on board would not be inimical to the security of the United States." The court stated, "In short, the burden was placed upon the seaman, notwithstanding he knew neither the names nor identity of his accusers nor anything else about them."

[82] 33 U. S. C. A. 901–950; *Gudmundson* v. *Cardillo*, 126 F. 2d 521 (C. A. D. C., 1942).
[83] *Parker* v. *Lester*, 112 F. Supp. 433 (N. D. Cal. D. C., 1953).

The court also noted the weakness of the "so-called appeals" provided by the regulations, stating that the appeals boards are "without power to do anything other than make a recommendation to the commandant." The court noted the argument on behalf of the Coast Guard that the appellants had no standing because they had failed to exhaust their administrative remedies. The court further noted that the Coast Guard had amended its regulations subsequent to the decrees of the district court in an effort to conform to its holdings. In spite of this amendment, the court disposed of the argument as to the prior exhaustion of administrative remedies by stating that no rule "can deprive the court of authority to pass upon the issues here present," i. e., basic constitutional questions. The court then said:

The proceeding in the lower court was in no sense a proceeding to review administrative action. It cannot be, for the Magnuson Act, the Executive order, and the regulations contemplate no such review. Indeed, it is the position of the defendants, with which the trial court agreed, that the provisions of the Administrative Procedure Act including its provisions for judicial review, have no application here.

With this contention the court agreed. The court continued, "Plaintiffs were able to show and did show that the defendants through the application of the alleged void and unconstitutional regulations had deprived them of employment and were threatening further to deprive them of future work as merchant seamen."

The court noted that the plaintiffs had lost their opportunities for employment, some for months and some for years and would continue to suffer such loss if an injunction were not issued to restrain the enforcement of the regulations complained of. The court added:

It is apparent that the so-called appeal before the appeal boards is no remedy in fact or in law. The question of lack of due process of law in the procedures called for by the regulations in question is not only beyond the competence or power of the boards or of the Commandant to try and determine, but one which in the nature of the case, those officers would not undertake to consider.

The court affirmed the district court's determination that the Magnuson Act authorized the screening of seamen and the promulgation of regulations to accomplish that end. However, the court pointed out that the regulations do not provide for notice and an opportunity to be heard "as generally understood to be required by the provisions of the fifth amendment relating to due process." Further, the court noted deficiencies in the screening procedure: that the plaintiffs had not been given notice prior to the initial determination by the Commandant that they could no longer be employed; that the information furnished as to the reasons for the denial of clearance were inadequate and in no sense met the requirements of a bill of particulars and that the provisions for appeal as has been stated actually are not an appeal.

In conclusion, the court said:

The regulations as enforced and carried out by the Coast Guard operated to deny the plaintiffs due process of law and in consequence they are entitled to an injunction against the further enforcement of those regulations and of any act on the part of the defendants pursuant thereto which will operate or tend to deprive plaintiffs of their

340

employment as seamen upon merchant vessels. *In so deciding, we have no occasion to hold whether in subsequent attempts to carry out the objectives of the merchant seamen screening program regulations might be adopted which in some degree qualify the ordinary right to confrontation and cross-examination of informers.* It is sufficient to say that as framed and operated these regulations fall short of furnishing the minimum requirements of due process in respect to notice and opportunity to be heard. [Emphasis supplied.]

One judge dissented, stating he "would affirm the decision and order below" and would leave the constitutional "issue to the Supreme Court."

Following the decision in *Parker* v. *Lester* in 1955, the Government decided it would not seek a review by the Supreme Court. Instead the Coast Guard issued new regulations in an effort to comply with the criticism of the Court.

Subsequently, the Government contended that the plaintiffs in the case of *Parker* v. *Lester* should be refused clearance until they had been "screened and found acceptable under the new regulations." [84] The district court ruled adversely to this contention and entered a decree permanently restraining the Coast Guard from preventing their employment. From this decree the Government appealed. The Court of Appeals for the Ninth Circuit on August 27, 1956, again held that the plaintiffs were entitled to a permanent injunction against denying clearance of the plaintiffs. On October 1, 1956, the court denied a petition for rehearing. This order has now become final.

The Coast Guard screening program has been before the same court in other important cases, *U. S.* v. *Gray, U. S.* v. *Rodgers,* and *U. S.* v. *Wickliffe.* [85] These three cases were consolidated for purposes of the appeal. The defendants had been indicted for unlawfully entering upon and accepting employment on merchant vessels without first obtaining clearance as required by the screening program.

On behalf of the defendants, motions were made to dismiss the indictments. The trial court held that the regulations as administered by the Coast Guard violated the due-process clause in that the defendants were not adequately informed of charges upon which they were denied clearance nor were they accorded a fair hearing. The court found that the screening operation initiated by the Magnuson Act is a "legitimate war measure." The court also found that Executive orders and regulations of the commandant issued in implementation of this security legislation did not appear on their face to infringe the due process of the fifth amendment and depending upon the manner in which they were administered, the court observed that the regulations would appear to afford a fair means of reconciling the problems of security with those of individual freedom. The indictments were dismissed. It will be noted that in its subsequent opinion in *Parker* v. *Lester,* the court flatly stated the then effective regulations were null and void since they denied due process to the defendant and dis-

---

[84] *Lester* v. *Parker,* 235 F. 2d 787 (C. A. 9, 1956).
[85] 207 F. 2d 237 (1953) (C. A. 9).

341

tinguished the *Gray* case. The court, in *Parker* v. *Lester,* noted further that the case presented facts as to Coast Guard procedures unknown to the court when it decided the *Gray* case.

Eugene Dupree v. *U. S.*[86] was a suit for a money judgment. Dupree claimed he would have earned this money had the Coast Guard not refused to clear him. The court of claims held that for the purposes of its opinion, the court would assume that the failure to confront an applicant for a certificate of loyalty with his accusers is a denial of due process. Nevertheless, in this case the petition did not state a case as founded on the Constitution. In order to state such a case, facts must be alleged to show that except for the violation of his constitutional rights, the certificate would have been issued and the wages would have been earned. The plaintiff, Dupree, did not deny the truth of the charges or allege that they were insufficient grounds for refusing the certificate. The court, in its opinion, set out the bill of particulars furnished Dupree which contained 10 charges, several specific as to place and all specific as to date. The court said:

> Nor does plaintiff state a case of the violation of a statutory right. His master's license did not give him an unqualified right to sail as the master of a ship under any and all circumstances. In time of war or national emergency the Armed Forces and the country generally are dependent upon the preservation of the merchant marine, and the Congress has the undoubted power to adopt reasonable measures to safeguard it.

Since no case has yet gone to the Supreme Court, there is no decision from that Court upon the issues of confrontation, notice, appeal, and other aspects of due process under the fifth amendment in relation to the port security program. It would appear, however, that these basic rights must be recognized to the extent commensurate with protection of national security.

PRESENT PROGRAM

The U. S. Coast Guard

Generally the U. S. Coast Guard functions include the saving and protection of life and property, maritime law enforcement, providing navigational aids to maritime commerce and transoceanic air commerce, promotion of efficiency and safety in the American Merchant Marine and readiness for military operations.[87]

---

[86] C. C. No. 493–55, June 5, 1956, 24 L. W. 2569.

[87] Source material for the "screening program" was derived through interviews with Coast Guard officials heading divisions responsible for administration of port security and from the Coast Guard Law Enforcement Text (1954) ch. 9, pts. 1 through 6.

The Coast Guard operates now as a service in the Treasury Department. During time of war, providing the Coast Guard is transferred to Navy, district boundaries are realigned to conform with Naval districts.

Under authority of the Magnuson Act,[88] the President, on October 18, 1950, ordered the Coast Guard to set up the present port security program.[89] One aspect of the program deals with the screening of possible security risks from maritime and waterfront employees so that only those will remain whose presence on ships or restricted areas would not be inimical to the interests of the United States.[90]

The Commandant of the Coast Guard, through his staff, develops and implements the overall port security program. Within each Coast Guard district, the district commander and his staff together put into effect the operation approved by the Commandant. But immediate responsibility for security of vessels and restricted areas rests with the captain of the port. He administers the port security law enforcement functions provided for under Executive Order 10173, to assure the safety of United States harbors and vessels.

Actual screening, however, is a centralized function performed directly under the Commandant at Washington, D. C. Applications submitted at the proper Coast Guard offices in various American ports are forwarded to the Marine Vessel Personnel Division in the case of seamen, and, for port security cards, to the Intelligence Division, where they are processed for security clearance.

Credentials

Clearance programs.—As previously noted, the need for port security clearance grew out of the recognized danger from subversives, particularly Communists, who, at the outbreak of the Korean War, were working on ships and docks. Two screening programs, similar in most respects, were concurrently put into effect. The first procedure dealt with clearance of personnel manning the merchant marine; the second, with waterfront workers, and separate regulations were promulgated for each. (33 C. F. R. 121.01, *et. seq.*, covers maritime; 33 C. F. R. 125.01, *et. seq.*, covers waterfront workers.)

Merchant Marine.—No mariner may sail in the United States Merchant Marine on vessels in excess of 100 gross tons unless his credentials indicate he has been cleared for security by the Coast Guard. Coast Guard regulations identify this maritime clearance as "special validation endorsement for emergency service of Merchant Marine personnel," which means

---

[88] Pub. Law 679, 81st Cong., 2d sess., 64 Stat. 427, Aug. 9, 1950, 50 U. S. C. A. 191.

[89] Executive Order 10173, October 20, 1950, (15 F. R. 7005), as amended by Executive Order 10277, Aug. 2, 1951 (16 F. R. 7537) and Executive Order 10352, May 21, 1952 (17 F. R. 4607), 33 C. F. R. 1956 pocket supp. chapter 1, subchapter A pt. 1.

[90] 33 C. F. R. 121.03, 125.19.

343

that the applicant's Coast Guard merchant mariner's document has been stamped with the following words: "validated for emergency service," meaning he has been screened by the Coast Guard and properly cleared as to security.[91] The original document was issued by the Coast Guard under prior statutory authority, authorizing licensing or certification of persons to perform the duties called for by whatever marine license or certificate they may hold.

The Coast Guard shipping commissioner may check credentials at the time a ship's crew signs articles. Otherwise, the master of the vessel inspects his crew's credentials for security clearance. For that purpose a confidential list of individuals denied security clearance (commonly referred to as PDSC) is furnished to certain captains of the port and other Coast Guard officers by the Commandant. In cases where the ship's officials sign on employees, they may check with the proper Coast Guard office if a crewman's clearance is in doubt.

Waterfront employees.—Not having merchant mariner's documents in the first place, a waterfront worker, once screened, receives instead a "port security card." The card is laminated and bears the holder's photograph, signature, one fingerprint, personal description and other data. Lacking a card, a waterfront employee is not prohibited from working at his trade, but he may not enter any area designated by the Coast Guard district commander as "restricted." According to Coast Guard officials no permanently restricted areas have been thus set apart since the inception of the program.

Extent of clearance.—Whenever an area or facility is to be restricted, the captain of the port will give public notice in advance, and the inaccessible areas must be conspicuously marked. Fences and available guards may be used, sentries posted, and patrols and inspections ordered by the port captain to clear the area of unauthorized persons and prevent sabotage or accident.

In addition to waterfront workers port security cards are required of other employees, such as facility maintenance craftsmen, mechanics, teamsters, and railway employees operating equipment on the spur-lines at the restricted site.

Regardless of whether or not a port embraces a restricted area, operators and crews of most craft under 100 tons, including state and municipal harbor craft, must obtain port security or other credentials, such as police, fireman, or armed service identification, except on the Great Lakes and western rivers. However, operators of the following vessels, less than 100 tons, are excluded from security requirements: fishing boats and fishing fleets, dredges and craft equipped for salvage operations, river, pleasure and charter-hire craft and other small craft operating near port areas.

The Commandant may approve Coast Guard visitor identification for individuals who may occasionally enter the restricted area on public or private business, or for the operation, maintenance or administration of cargo or waterfront facilities. Application must be made to the officer detailed by

---

[91] C. F. R. 121.01; see also, Coast Guard Law Enforcement Text (1954), ch. 9, p. 30.

the captain of the port, accompanied by name, address, fingerprints and signature of the applicant and reasons for access to the area.

Certain crew members of foreign vessels, for instance a foreign vessel loading mutual defense assistance cargo, are furnished similar identification. Crewmen of American vessels not currently required to hold credentials must also obtain clearance if they operate in restricted areas, such as men without clearance aboard a vessel loading class A explosives.

Cooperating with other agencies.—The Army, Navy, and Air Force may close areas to certain personnel from time to time. The Coast Guard has no authority to screen personnel who enter these areas, responsibility being exclusively vested in the cognizant military agency.

The captain of the port, however, must maintain liaison with each of the military commanders. He must advise them of the existence and significance of the Coast Guard port security program so they may use it to keep unauthorized persons from harbor areas and vessels within the military reservation. Moreover, he must inform the commanders that casual or occasional vistors to waterfront facilities are not eligible for Coast Guard port security cards, and he must, upon request, cooperate fully with commanding officers by furnishing necessary patrols.

Army policy has been to bar military ports of embarkation to anyone without security documents. Liaison has been maintained with local Coast Guard authorities to recommend denial or revocation of an individual's card for cause.

Procedure

Authority.—Final authority to grant or deny security credentials reposes in the commanding officer of the United States Coast Guard. The Commandant may issue credentials if he believes an applicant's presence aboard an American ship, including certain harbor craft, or in a restricted port or harbor area, ". . . . would not be inimical to the security of the United States. . . ." His refusal may be based upon information appearing in the applicant's record indicating that his character and habits do not warrant his clearance. (33 C. F. R. 121.03; 33 C. F. R. 125.19.)

Neither district commanders nor port captains have evaluation authority, although the latter may attach to applications information which they believe should be considered.

As pointed out previously, denying validation of a mariner's document prohibits him from following his trade in the merchant marine. Although the refusal to issue a port security card is not so far-reaching, in effect it still limits the right to work at one's chosen trade.

Steps of procedure.—Applications for maritime or waterfront workers' credentials are screened by the same process.

1. APPLICATION—Applications for maritime credential endorsement are submitted at any one of the marine inspection offices; for port security cards,

at the closest port security unit set up by the captain of the port, and are then forwarded to the Intelligence Division, U. S. Coast Guard, Washington, D. C., for screening by the Marine Personnel Division for maritime, and by the Intelligence Division for waterfront employees.

2. INVESTIGATION—Screening consists of file checks for evidence of subversive or criminal conduct by the applicant which the FBI may have on file, and such further file checks with other intelligence agencies and state and local police as are deemed necessary.

3. EVALUATION—Cases which may result in a denial of application are referred to a special committee of three Coast Guard officials who examine the derogatory information. They may send the applicant a questionnaire to clear up uncertainties. Upon receipt of his sworn answers, the evidence in the file, and the information upon the application, the committee submits an evaluation of the case and a recommendation to the Commandant.

4. DECISION BY COMMANDANT—Any decision by the Commandant is completely within his own administrative discretion. He is not compelled to accept the committee's recommendation. If he denies the security credential, the applicant will be so notified, together with specific reasons. The applicant may answer or submit additional information within twenty days. However, if the response is still inadequate, the Commandant will refer the matter to the hearing board.

5. HEARING—Hearing boards are set up in each Coast Guard district. Applicants receive notice of hearing. Upon evaluation of testimony, additional evidence, and upon all prior information, the hearing board submits an opinion and recommendation together with the entire record to the Commandant.

6. DECISION BY COMMANDANT—Again the Commandant is not compelled to accept the hearing board's recommendation, but is free to make his own decision which will be transmitted to the applicant. If it is a denial, the applicant will be advised of his right to appeal within twenty days from receipt of the notice.

7. APPEAL—The National Appeal Board at Coast Guard headquarters, Washington, D. C., follows the same procedure established for the district hearing boards.

8. FINAL DECISION—Again the Appeal Board's opinion is not binding upon the Commandant. A denial at this juncture exhausts the applicant's administrative rights before the Coast Guard.

Applications

Subject matter.—Applications must be submitted in full, or contain written explanation in support of any omission and must be under oath. Apart from usual personal data and self-description, an applicant for a port security card must prove his citizenship, describe his military record, if any, and be properly sponsored. He must truthfully answer a questionaire as to any arrests and convictions, particularly of subversive crimes, or of crimes indicating a subversive propensity, such as arson or traffic in narcotics. Applicants for either validation of seaman credentials or for a port security card must satisfactorily explain any relation with members of or with organizations dominated by, or which might be dominated by agents of foreign governments.

Study of the sponsor system.—The responsibilities of the sponsor system and how it functions is under study now by the Coast Guard, as the provision has caused considerable difficulty in administering the program. During this period of study the requirement that there be a sponsor is not being enforced.

Who must file.—All holders of maritime credentials shipping on United States vessels of 100 gross tons or over, and all waterfront workers who may want jobs in restricted areas must file. In the latter case, inasmuch as no areas are presently restricted on a permanent basis, the purpose of the program is to build up a reserve of cleared craftsmen in each port. In addition, certain small-craft operators and crewmen must file.

Old timers and new.—Former merchant mariners who wish to return to sea must make application anew and be processed as in the original instance. Some applicants desire to sign on a merchant ship for a brief period. Nevertheless, they must apply for validation of their credentials, even for one trip.

Aliens.—Aliens admitted as permanent residents making trips to foreign countries as seamen must be cleared in the same manner as citizens. Before an alien can sign on an American vessel then in a foreign port he must be cleared by the American consul in the foreign country. Consular officials obtain such clearance by cabling the Secretary of State, who, in turn, seeks approval from the Coast Guard Commandant.

Records.—Records are kept at Coast Guard offices at which applications are received, credentials issued, and in the divisions concerned with screening. Captains of port offices responsible for maintaining such files must submit monthly reports to the Intelligence Division, Washington, D. C., summarizing according to class of work of applicants, the number of cards issued during the current month, and in total.

Action.—Once processed, the application form is returned to the port of origin. Photostatic copies of denial cases are maintained in the Intelligence Division. All denial case records of the proceedings are maintained in the Intelligence Division, Coast Guard Headquarters.

Screening

Administration.—Applications for maritime security validation endorsements and for port security cards are processed at Washington in a similar manner. However, the maritime program is administered through the Marine Vessel Personnel Division while the Intelligence Division screens waterfront workers.

Personnel.—No special qualifications for personnel actually engaged in screening waterfront and maritime employees are outlined in any Coast Guard regulation. The officials administering the programs must proceed on whatever general experience they have gained as Coast Guard officials. Otherwise, the only personnel involved in assisting the officers in charge of the port security program are seamen apprentices. They have no evaluation responsibility, but merely process papers for correct entries and completion of the application forms.

Certain civilian personnel participate in the port security program on the hearing and appellate review boards. They are subject to clearance under Executive Order 10450, controlling United States civil service employees, rather than Executive Order 10173, the basis for the port security program. They also receive no special indoctrination.

Indoctrination.—Officers and other personnel in the port security program felt they should receive indoctrination both in communism in the United States and in world communism, and in the tactics of subversion and infiltration. Study of the political and economic history of the United States, they believed, would also better prepare them for an assignment in the port security program.

Personnel interviewed in the port security program felt that officers and other personnel involved in the screening program should receive on-the-job training only, but no formal training. The Coast Guard has no school for training personnel to fill positions in the screening program. Actually, the personnel involved in making evaluations for the port security program is at a minimum. In practice, port security duties of Coast Guard personnel are collateral to their main duties.

No investigation.—There is no investigation as such upon which to base security clearance. Screening is limited to forwarding applications to the Federal Bureau of Investigation. The FBI makes a fingerprint and name check of each application, and returns all available information on each one to the Coast Guard.

The Coast Guard has no investigative unit for screening applicants for security clearance, as it holds it has no authority to request further investigation of any applicant. No money is appropriated for the Coast Guard to pay for an investigation by the FBI or any other investigative agency.

A working agreement has been set up between the FBI and the Coast Guard whereby the FBI flags cases of applicants. In the event any new information appears, it will be forwarded to the Coast Guard, and well may become the basis for denial or revocation of a clearance. Copies of both clearance denials and clearances granted are forwarded to the FBI and appropriate Federal agencies.

Purpose.—Whenever derogatory information is bared by an agency file check, the matter is evaluated by a committee of three comprised of the aforementioned division screening officers and a legal officer, who acts as chairman. This committee has been provided under the rules and regulations to expedite the screening process by eliminating, where possible, prolonged hearing board proceedings. Many applicants for port security cards or special validation endorsements may be cleared by the committee, thereby obviating recourse to a hearing. The committee prepares an analysis of each application and a recommendation both of which are forwarded to the Commandant. (33 C. F. R. 121.05 (e); 33 C. F. R. 125.29 (b).)

Qualifications.—Experience with seamen and dock workers and mature judgment in evaluating evidence are deemed to be sufficient qualification and training for members of the committee. Two of the present members have legal experience; the other, although he has no legal experience, has been a member of the Coast Guard since 1949, and has had first-hand experience with dock workers and merchant seamen.

Procedure.—Decisions of the committee are reached individually. If decisions cannot be reached separately, members of the committee are called into session by the chairman to resolve points of disagreement. Any member may write a dissenting opinion.

Evaluation.—Members of the committee evaluate information in each case to determine whether the applicant meets the requirement for clearance. In analyzing and evaluating the applications, the committee members are mindful of legal rules of evidence, even though these rules do not control the decision of the committee.

Captain James D. Craik, then chief of the Merchant Vessel Personnel Division, on March 24, 1955, testified before the Committee on Merchant Marine and Fisheries, House of Representatives. To a question on whether loyalty, Communism, or a matter of character and other things were involved in criteria evaluation, he responded that: " . . . As far as seamen are concerned, it is straight subversive acts and the recency of those subversive acts."

At the same hearing, Vice Admiral Alfred C. Richmond, Commandant of the Coast Guard, discussing the difference between criteria for longshoremen and seamen, stated: "It is only different to this extent, that we include waterfront workers convicted of certain crimes, such as arson, which, in our opinion . . . would make that individual a potential security risk. . . ." [92]

---

[92] Testimony of Capt. Craik, p. 58, and for Vice Adm. Richmond, p. 60, "Study of operations of the United States Coast Guard," Hearings before the Committee on Merchant Marine and Fisheries, House of Representatives, 84th Cong., 1st sess., Mar. 22, 23, 24, and 25, 1955.

Questionnaires.—If derogatory information is produced, additional clarification may be sought by formulating a questionnaire which is sent to the applicant. He is thereby given an opportunity to explain or refute the damaging information.

Notice.—If, upon review of completed questionnaire, the applicant is still believed to be ineligible for clearance, a notice by the Commandant is sent to the applicant, who may file an answer within 20 days. If he replies to the notice, his response is correlated with his file and evaluated.

Decision.—A final evaluation is made upon the applicant's record, and a recommendation as to whether to clear the applicant or refer the case to a hearing board is prepared. This recommendation is reviewed by each committeeman and, in the form approved, sent on to the Commandant for his decision. If clearance is denied, the matter is referred to a hearing board.

Hearing Boards

The board.—District security hearing boards are set up in all major ports and the Hawaiian Islands. The Commandant designates the board chairmen. Two other members are appointed, one from labor, the other from business, who are under contract with the Coast Guard. The latter two are taken from a panel selected by the Secretary of Labor. Ordinarily they are selected because of their association with maritime activities. Each civilian board member receives a full field investigation.

Qualifications.—No special training is required of members of the boards. However, they are briefed on the procedure. Ordinarily, they are interested in and associated with maritime activities, thereby having a knowledge of merchant seamen and longshoremen.

Notice.—The Coast Guard amended its rules, effective May 1, 1956, requiring that notice of the Commandant's denial ". . . shall be . . . specific, . . . and shall include pertinent information as to names, dates, and places in such detail as to permit reasonable answer . . ." to the extent that ". . . the interest of national security shall permit." [93]

Answer.—Applicants have 20 days to answer the Commandant's notice of denial, but the applicant's failure to answer the notice from the Commandant within the 20-day period provided for by the rules does not preclude him from further proceedings.

Appearance.—If the applicant does not appear after notice from the board, the board may proceed to hear the case in his absence. However, whenever an applicant fails to request an opportunity to appear, or, having so requested, fails to appear or be represented, and the Board hears the case in his absence, the individual concerned may make a new application. Extensions of time to appear are given for good cause.

[93] 33 C. F. R. 121.11 (a) ; 33 C. F. R. 125.35 (a).

Challenge.—Under the rules an applicant has the right to two peremptory challenges of hearing board members, one for each management and labor member. Otherwise he may challenge for cause, but must support such challenge by an affidavit, stating adequate grounds to disqualify the challenged member. (33 C. F. R. 121.17; 33 C. F. R. 125.41.)

Examples of reasonable grounds for challenge of a board member occurs where both board members and applicant were members of the same union. A merchant mariner may object to a board member from a maritime industry on whose ship the mariner had sailed and had trouble. Another cause for challenge may arise when the chairman of the Board of Appeals has already heard one previous appeal by same appellant.

Evaluation.—Boards decide each case on its merits. Federal Bureau of investigation reports are not binding on board recommendations or decisions. Seamen personnel files are available in the Coast Guard headquarters and may be checked to corroborate any statements made by the seaman as to what occurred on a certain date, at a certain place, or on board a certain ship.

Rehearing.—Any applicant may move to reopen his case; or, by filing a new application, he may obtain a reconsideration of the matter. In one instance an applicant moved to reopen the proceeding on five different occasions. Once the Board has transferred the record and its recommendations to the Commandant, jurisdiction to decide such motions rests with the Commandant, who has discretionary authority to refer the case back to the Board, or reconsider the matter himself.

A case may be opened on any grounds which the Commandant deems reasonable. No motion for rehearing has ever been filed upon grounds that the Board has acted arbitrarily or capriciously, or has rendered decisions without consideration of the substantial evidence on the whole record. However, it may be noted that the applicant does not see the opinion and recommendation of the Board.

Decision.—The Commandant receives a complete case, that is, the proceedings of the hearing, the charges, and reasons therefor; the FBI reports, reports of other intelligence agencies, and the rationale of the chairman of the board. On certain occasions he has remanded the case to the board for clarification of points.

National Appeals Board

The National Appeals Board sits in Washington, D. C., at Coast Guard headquarters. An applicant appealing from the denial of his security credentials after his case has been considered by a district hearing board may proceed under the rules precisely as he did before the hearing board. He has 20 days to file his appeal. Thereafter, the rules governing applicant's rights as to notice of hearing, challenge, and procedure at the hearing board level also hold good before the National Board of Appeals. (33 C. F. R. 121.23 (b) and (c) ; 33 C. F. R. 125.47 (b) and (c).)

The board chairman, a Coast Guard officer appointed by the Commandant, directs all board arrangements. The Secretary of Labor nominates two panels, one from labor and the other from management. From the panels the Commandant appoints one labor and one management member who, with the chairman, comprise a tripartite appeal board. Each civilian board member receives full field investigation before assuming his duties.

Qualifications.—As in the case of district hearing board members, no qualifying knowledge or experience peculiar to security screening matters is required. Nor is any training in such matters provided, other than a briefing on procedure prior to hearing a case.

Appearance.—If the appellant fails to appear or reply in 20 days, the board hears the case in his absence. In case of an adverse decision, the appellant may move for reconsideration or filing of a new application in the same manner as before the district hearing boards. The determination of such motions again rests with the Commandant, once the Board of Appeals has transferred the record and recommendation to him.

Procedure.—The Chairman of the Appeals Board advised that no differences in procedures were evident, in practice, between the district hearing boards and the appellate board.

Final evaluation by the Commandant.—The chairman of the National Appeals Board submits a transcript of the proceedings in each case with recommendations and the rationale of the Board to the Commandant. On this information the Commandant renders his decision. In some cases the Commandant has not agreed and has remanded the case to a board for a rehearing, additional testimony and new evidence.

Provided all prior proceedings have complied with regulations, and motions to reopen or reconsider were refused, a denial of the application by the Commandant is final. The appellant has no further remedy before the Coast Guard.

RECOMMENDATIONS

NECESSITY

A port security program is necessary to protect United States shipping, ports, harbor installations, and the Panama Canal from destruction and crippling damage by saboteurs and subversives.

The President of the United States, in issuing the Executive order which authorized the port security program, found that the security of the Nation is endangered by reason of subversive activity and that the country should be safeguarded against destruction from sabotage or subversive acts directed against vessels, ports, and waterfront facilities. A United States court of appeals has declared that there is "no doubt merchant seamen are in a sensitive position in that the opportunities for serious sabotage are numerous."

The Commission found that the conditions mentioned by the President and described by the court which led to the creation of the port security program continue to confront the Nation as there is substantial Communist control of certain maritime unions.

The overwhelming majority of merchant marine personnel and waterfront employees were found to be loyal, but the potential menace remains. We have noted that 1,835 persons were denied validated documents required for employment on merchant vessels and 1,953 persons were denied port security cards essential to employment at ports, which are extremely vulnerable to attack and destruction. For these and other reasons described in detail in the report, the Commission is satisfied that it is of utmost importance to the safety of the United States that the port security program be continued.

STANDARD

The Commission recommends that the standard for employment on a merchant vessel of the United States and for issuance of the documents required for employment on such vessel, as well as the grant of access to any vessel or any waterfront facility declared "restricted," shall be that such employment or access will not endanger the common defense or security.

An important reason for the establishment of the Commission on Government Security was the conflict within the Government over standards applicable in security matters. The Commission has found six different standards established in major security programs. If a degree of uniformity can be achieved, the Commission believes public respect and confidence in the security program will be greatly enhanced.

The Commission's studies revealed a lack of uniformity within the port security program itself. This becomes clear by noting the italicized phrases in the existing standards for (1) maritime employees and (2) waterfront workers quoted below:

(1) "No person shall be issued a document required for employment on a merchant vessel of the United States nor shall any person be employed on a merchant vessel of the United States *unless the Commandant is satisfied* that the character and habits of life of such person are *such as to authorize*

the belief that the presence of the individual on board would not be inimical to the security of the United States;" and

(2) A port security card will not be issued to a waterfront worker if there is *"information concerning the applicant for a Coast Guard port security card or a holder of such card which may preclude a determination* that his character and habits of life are *such as to warrant* the belief that his presence on waterfront vessels and port and harbor areas including vessels and harbor craft therein would not be inimical to the security of the United States." (Italic supplied.)

The rules for measuring "character and habits of life" are different although the basic standard "not inimical to the security of the United States" is the same.

The recommended standard has been tested by the Atomic Energy Commission in clearing employees of private industry for access to classified material. It has been found to be fair, workable, and adequate to safeguard the security of the United States.

The adoption of this standard will require an amendment to the presently effective Executive Order 10173 as amended by Executive Orders 10277 and 10352.

CRITERIA

It is recommended that factors which may be considered in connection with the application of the recommended standard shall include, but not be limited to:

1. Sabotage, espionage, or attempts or preparations therefor, or knowingly associating with spies or saboteurs;

2. Treason or sedition or advocacy thereof;

3. Advocacy of revolution or force or violence to alter the constitutional form of the Government of the United States;

4. Intentional, unauthorized disclosure to any person of classified information or materials, or recurrent and serious, although unintentional, disclosure of such information and materials;

5. Performing or attempting to perform assigned duties or otherwise acting so as to serve the interests of another government in preference to the interests of the United States;

6. Membership in, or affiliation or sympathetic association with any party or association which the Congress of the United States, or any agency or officer of the United States duly authorized by the Congress for that purpose, finds:

(*a*) Seeks to alter the form of government of the United States by force or violence, or other unconstitutional means; or,

354

(*b*) Is organized or utilized for the purpose of advancing the aims and objectives of the Communist movement; or,

(*c*) Is organized or utilized for the purpose of establishing any form of dictatorship in the United States, or any form of international dictatorship; or,

(*d*) Is organized or utilized by any foreign government, or by any foreign party, group, or association acting in the interest of such foreign government for the purpose of (1) espionage, (2) sabotage, or (3) obtaining information relating to the defense of the United States or the protection of the national security, or (4) hampering, hindering, or delaying the production of defense materials; or,

(*e*) Is affiliated with, or acts in concert with, or is dominated or controlled by, any party, group, or association of the character described in (*a*), or (*b*), or (*c*), or (*d*) above.

7. Membership in, or affiliation with, any organization which the Congress of the United States, or any agency or officer of the United States duly authorized by the Congress for that purpose, finds has adopted a policy of advocating or approving the commission of acts of force and violence to deny others their rights under the Constitution of the United States;

8. Refusal to testify upon the ground of self-incrimination in any authorized inquiry conducted by a congressional committee, Federal court, Federal grand jury, or any other duly authorized agency, unless the individual, after opportunity to do so, satisfactorily explains his refusal to testify;

9. Willful violations or disregard of security regulations, or recurrent and serious, although unintentional, violation of such regulations;

10. Any illness, including any mental condition of a nature which in the opinion of competent medical authority may cause significant defect in the performance, judgment, or reliability of the employee, with due regard to the transient or continued effect of the illness and the medical findings in such case;

11. Any behavior, activities, or associations which tend to show that the individual is not reliable or trustworthy;

12. Any deliberate misrepresentation or falsification of material facts in, or omission of material facts from, a personnel security questionnaire, personal history statement, or similar document;

13. Any criminal, infamous, dishonest, immoral, or notoriously disgraceful conduct, habitual use of intoxicants to excess, drug addiction, or sexual perversion;

14. Any facts which furnish reason to believe that the individual may be subjected to coercion, influence, or pressure which may cause him to act contrary to the best interest of the national security.

Present Coast Guard regulations prescribe different criteria for the employees of merchant vessels and for persons desiring access to waterfront facilities. The Commission also found wide diversity in the criteria utilized in the several security programs. Conflicting decisions and inequities are inevitable under such conditions, consequently the Commission is recommending uniform criteria for use in all security programs.

INDIVIDUALS COVERED

The Commission recommends (*a*) that the port security program continue to be applicable to:

1. All persons employed on merchant vessels of the United States of 100 gross tons or over, including those on the Great Lakes and on western rivers;

2. All persons desiring access to certain vessels presently specified in regulation 125.53; and

3. All persons regularly employed on vessels or on waterfront facilities declared to be "restricted," and all persons having regular public or private business connected with the operation, maintenance, or administration of vessels, their cargoes, or waterfront facilities declared to be restricted; and that

(*b*) Regulation 125.53 be amended to include in the program all persons desiring access to the vessels described therein on the Great Lakes and on western rivers.

The Commission is satisfied that the present port security regulations are sufficiently broad as to the individuals included with one exception. On November 30, 1956, the Coast Guard revised regulations 125.53 to exempt persons desiring access to vessels of less than 100 gross tons on the Great Lakes and western rivers. The Commission considers this action ill-advised, and it recommendation would require rescission of the November 30th amendment. This is an especially important matter since the St. Lawrence Seaway will soon be completed and foreign and domestic vessels will be operating on the Great Lakes in ever-increasing numbers. Ports on the Great Lakes give immediate and direct access to key industrial centers. It is vital that the Great Lakes and rivers be subject to the same precautions and security regulations as are coastal waters.

The Commission's satisfaction with the technical coverage of the regulations is not to be construed as satisfaction with the effectiveness of the port security program. As will appear in subsequent recommendations, the Commission found serious deficiencies in the present operations of this program. The change recommended by the Commission in the program's coverage can be accomplished by the issuance of a regulation by the Commandant of the Coast Guard.

INVESTIGATIONS

1. There should be a national agency investigation with respect to each maritime employee and port employee in restricted areas.

2. If derogatory subversive information is disclosed by the national agency investigation with respect to any person, the Commandant should request the Federal Bureau of Investigation to conduct a full-field investigation.

Studies made by the Commission have established that the Coast Guard has had no uniformity in standards or methods of securing information for clearing employees of vessels or waterfront facilities. It has learned also that the Coast Guard has no investigative section of its own and considers that it had no authority to make an investigation as such. Its practice has been, in some cases, to refer an application for security clearance to the Treasury Department and thence to the FBI for fingerprint and name check. Following a report from this check, the Coast Guard has on occasions contacted other Government intelligence agencies. There has been no uniform operational procedure in this matter.

The Commission was informed that at least some Coast Guard officials believe it advisable to have uniformity in practice. They agreed also that the scope of the preliminary investigation should include at least a national agency investigation. The Commission concurs with this view and has recommended a national agency investigation as the absolute minimum which should be made.

It appears that Coast Guard officials have heretofore acted without any definite policy as to when a full-field investigation should be requested. From a practical point of view, policies of the officials have been limited by the fact that funds available for an FBI full-field investigation were strictly limited or nonexistent. It will be recalled that the FBI performs these investigations on a reimbursable basis.

The Commission believes that, when derogatory subversive information is disclosed, the rule should be definite and certain that the Commandant must request a full-field investigation by the FBI.

To illustrate the importance of this proposed rule, there was one case which came to the Commission's attention wherein derogatory information was disclosed and clearance was refused. In this case, a full-field investigation was requested. It was found that the case was one of mistaken identity. A full-field investigation, therefore, is essential both to the security of the country and to the protection of the individual.

The Commission believes the investigation should be uniform for all persons and there should be no distinction between an officer and a part-time longshoreman on the docks. The Coast Guard has, in the past, considered that officers are generally members of the Naval Reserve and, therefore, a very limited security check has been made in such cases, a full investigation being regarded as an unnecessary duplication. The Commission does not concur in this view. The Commission believes that an officer is in a position where he may do great damage and that the same degree of care should be exercised in processing the applications of officers as of seamen, and that uniformity in administration is important in the basic matter of investigations.

The Commission is well aware, also, that one of the major criticisms directed to the Government security program has concerned the inequality and lack of uniformity in the type of investigation to which individuals are subjected, and it considers this one of the major areas in which both individuals and the Government will benefit from a uniform standard practice.

SCREENING FUNCTION

As to the screening function the Commission recommends that:

1. **The Coast Guard should continue to administer this function at the United States Coast Guard Headquarters;**

2. **The Coast Guard should discontinue its practice of assigning personnel part time to screening duties;**

3. **The Coast Guard should discontinue assigning personnel to screening duties without regard to training or experience in security work; and**

4. **The Coast Guard should promptly initiate and maintain a security training program for personnel assigned to screening duties.**

The screening function in the port security program is presently administered by the Coast Guard at its headquarters. The Commission approves this plan. The practice has been for the name of the applicant to be forwarded from the district in which he requests clearance to the Commandant. After the requested information is received, it is analyzed by a three-member committee, which then makes a recommendation for action by the Commandant. The decision of the Commandant is delivered to the applicant at the district office.

The Commission found that personnel is assigned to screening and other duties in the security program without regard to training or experience in security matters. *There are no special qualifications outlined in any regulation promulgated by the Coast Guard for personnel who carry out the port security program.* The Commission considers this to be a condition which should be promptly remedied.

The Coast Guard has no training program for officers and other personnel with security responsibilities. This situation should also be remedied promptly, and the recommendations as to the screening function may be accomplished by amending regulations issued by the Commandant of the Coast Guard.

DENIAL OF CLEARANCE

Final determination as to the issuance or denial of validated documents for employment on merchant vessels or port security cards for employment on waterfront facil.ties should continue to be the responsibility of the Commandant.

The President, by Executive order, has vested responsibility in the Commandant of the Coast Guard for the issuance or denial of clearance in the port security program. The Commission, believing that authority in a matter of such importance as security clearance should be definite, fixed, and centralized, recommends that this responsibility be continued.

NOTICE OF TENTATIVE DENIAL

When the Commandant is satisfied that the record of anyone applying for clearance contains derogatory information sufficient to support a tentative denial, he should give to the applicant for clearance a written statement of the reasons for such tentative denial. The statement shall be as specific and detailed as the interests of national security permit and shall include pertinent information, such as names, dates, and places, in such detail as to permit a responsive answer.

The revised Coast Guard regulations, which became effective May 1, 1956, provide that the Commandant, in issuing a denial of clearance, must give the applicant a statement of reasons for such denial. "Such notice shall be as specific and detailed as the interests of national security shall permit and shall include pertinent information such as names, dates, and places in such detail as to permit reasonable answer." This provision is essentially that recommended by the Commission. Regulations of the Coast Guard also provide that, in order to avoid additional procedures, the Commandant may notify the applicant to submit under oath further information. The notice recommended by the Commission would serve this purpose also.

359

As has been fully developed in this report, prior to the issuance of the above-quoted regulation, the notice given to the applicant by the Commandant was sharply criticized by the courts and held to be insufficient and void as not in compliance with constitutional requirements of due process.

Under the recommended procedures, the notice will be given concurrently with the issuance of a tentative denial, so that the applicant will not have to overcome a firm decision at the time of the initial hearing.

The Commission is firmly convinced that careful compliance with this recommendation will greatly improve effective administration and safeguard the rights of persons included in the program.

ANSWER

Regulations should require that the applicant be informed concurrently with the notice of tentative denial that a sworn answer must be filed within the time prescribed by regulations. The head of the Central Security Office should prescribe, by regulation, the time within which answers should be given to the Commandant.

Coast Guard regulations now in effect prescribe different time limitations within which employees of merchant vessels or waterfront facilities must reply to notice from the Commandant. For example, if it is a matter of revocation of a clearance previously made, a response to the inquiry from the Commandant must be made under oath within 30 days. It is also provided that the applicant or holder of a Port Security card or validated documents must reply within 20 days. This appears to be needlessly confusing.

The Commission considers that in order to introduce uniformity and system into the several security programs, the time limitations for response to notice of tentative denial should be fixed by the head of the Central Security Office.

HEARINGS

Procedures and Administration

The Commission recommends that the following hearing procedures be made applicable to the port security program:
1. The initial hearing on the notice of tentative denial should be conducted by a hearing examiner, rather than by hearing boards.
2. The hearing examiners should be under the Central Security Office in the executive branch.

3. The decisions of the hearing examiners should be advisory to the Commandant, whose decision should be final.

4. The hearing examiners should be appointed by the head of the Central Security Office from an appropriate civil service register created for the purpose.

5. Hearing examiners should be full time governmental employees, in sufficient number throughout the country to hear cases under the port security program.

6. An adverse decision by the Commandant may be appealed to the Central Review Board at the request of the employee within the time and subject to procedures to be prescribed.

7. The qualifications of a hearing examiner should be fixed by the Civil Service Commission after consultation with the head of the Central Security Office.

8. The experience of persons appointed as hearing examiners should include regular practice or technical work performed in a field appropriate to the Government's loyalty and security programs. The Civil Service Commission should prepare an appropriate job description and qualifications after consultation with the head of the Central Security Office.

9. There should be an appropriate initial training program and periodic in-training service, which, in addition to appropriate technical subjects, would provide for indoctrination in constitutional and related matters affecting port security.

10. The head of the Central Security Office should determine whether an applicant for clearance shall have the right to challenge hearing examiners either for cause or peremptorily, and fix the number of such challenges to be permitted.

11. The director of the Central Security Office should allocate the workload among the examiners and supervise the prompt disposition of such workload.

12. Hearings should not be open to the public.

13. Hearing examiners should be required in each case to submit a report which would include findings of fact.

14. A copy of the hearing examiner's report and a copy of the transcript of the hearing should be sent to the applicant for clearance upon receipt by the Central Review Board of notice of appeal.

15. The hearing examiner should submit a written report to the head of the Central Security Office for transmittal to the Commandant. Such report should contain the hearing examiner's findings of fact, recommended decision, and reasons for his decision.

16. The hearing examiner should be required to have prepared a verbatim transcript of the hearing. The applicant for clearance

would be entitled to be furnished a copy of the report of the examiner and the record, including the transcript, upon receipt by the Central Review Board of notice of appeal.

The Commission's studies disclosed delays and other defects in hearings held during the first few years the port security program was in operation. These delays may be attributed in part, at least, to the inadequate number of personnel assigned to security cases and the heavy backlog of applicants required to be screened at the program's inception. The Commission finds that present Coast Guard practice is to afford a hearing promptly. However, the Commission is not satisfied with Coast Guard practices in connection with hearings.

The most obvious defects flow from two sources: first, the lack of uniformity of rules, producing disparities in administration and expensive and unnecessary duplication of forms and investigations; second, the uncertainties and divergences resulting from the wide dispersion of responsibility among personnel lacking authority, adequate training, and central guidance.

It is considered that port security should be included in the proposed system for a Central Security Office. This system calls for qualified, adequately trained hearing examiners and an experienced appeal board, all in an independent office, removed from the climate that prevails in a particular agency or department or a particular area, and dedicated to their task.

The Commission believes that the establishment of a Central Security Office in the executive branch of the Government, with provision for competent, trained hearing examiners, and with the right to appeal to a Central Review Board, is necessary to achieve uniformity in the application of these programs, to eliminate unnecessary duplication of forms and investigations, and to provide definite, understandable standards and criteria to be applied by trained and qualified personnel.

Confrontation and Subpena Power

It is recommended that confrontation [94] be limited to evidence offered in support of any of the following charges:

1. Sabotage, espionage, or attempts or preparations therefor, or knowingly associating with spies or saboteurs;

2. Treason or sedition or advocacy thereof;

3. Advocacy of revolution or force or violence to alter the constitutional form of government of the United States;

4. Intentional, unauthorized disclosure to any person of classified information or materials;

---

[94] For full text of recommendations relating to confrontation, see Federal Civilian Loyalty Program, p. 66.

5. Performing or attempting to perform assigned duties or otherwise acting so as to serve the interests of another government in preference to the interests of the United States;

6. Membership in, or affiliation or sympathetic association with, any party or association which the Congress of the United States, or any agency or officer of the United States duly authorized by the Congress for that purpose, finds:

(a) Seeks to alter the form of Government of the United States by force or violence, or other unconstitutional means; or,

(b) Is organized or utilized for the purpose of advancing the aims and objectives of the Communist movement; or,

(c) Is organized or utilized for the purpose of establishing any form of dictatorship in the United States or any form of international dictatorship; or,

(d) Is organized or utilized by any foreign government, or by any foreign party, group, or association acting in the interest of such foreign government for the purpose of (1) espionage, or (2) sabotage, or (3) obtaining information relating to the defense of the United States or the protection of the national security, or (4) hampering, hindering, or delaying the production of defense materials; or,

(e) Is affiliated with, or acts in concert with, or is dominated or controlled by, any party, group, or association of the character described in (a) or (b) or (c) or (d) above.

7. Membership in, or affiliation with, any organization which the Congress of the United States, or any agency or officer of the United States duly authorized by the Congress for that purpose, finds has adopted a policy of advocating or approving the commission of acts of force and violence to deny others their rights under the Constitution of the United States.

8. Refusal to testify upon the ground of self-incrimination in any authorized inquiry relating to subversive activities conducted by a congressional committee, Federal court, Federal grand jury, or any other duly authorized Federal agency, unless the individual, after opportunity to do so, satisfactorily explains his refusal to testify.

It is recommended that the right of subpena should be applicable where there is a right of confrontation, but this should not preclude the applicant for clearance from furnishing affidavits or the testimony of witnesses he wishes to present and who are willing to voluntarily appear.

(a) In the exercise of his discretion to issue subpenas, the hearing examiner should consider such factors as the time and expense involved by reason of the travel required.

(b) Either the Coast Guard or the applicant for clearance should be permitted to apply to the hearing examiner to issue

363

subpenas, except as to confidential informants and identified informants who have given their information on the condition that they will not be called as witnesses. Such application should state the name and address of such witness, as well as the substance of the testimony to be presented. If the hearing examiner deems the evidence relevant and not merely cumulative, he may issue the subpena.

(*c*) The witness should be compensated for travel expense and per diem, but where the cost is substantial, the hearing examiner may in his discretion require the parties to use deposition procedures.

(*d*) The Coast Guard shall bear the cost of Coast Guard witnesses, but the hearing examiner shall not subpena a witness for the applicant for clearance until the applicant deposits with the Central Security Office sufficient funds to pay the travel and per diem costs of such witness. In the event that the applicant for clearance is denied validated documents or a port security card, the funds deposited by the applicant shall be used to pay for the applicant's witness expenses. If, however, the applicant is cleared, the funds deposited by the applicant shall be returned to him and the Coast Guard shall bear the travel and per diem costs of the applicant's witness.

Revised regulations of the Coast Guard presently provide that the hearing board "may, in its discretion, invite any person to appear at the hearing and testify. However, the board shall not be bound by the testimony of such witness by reason of having called him and shall have full right to cross-examine the witness. Every effort should be made to produce material witnesses to testify in support of the reasons set forth in the Notice of the Commandant, in order that such witnesses may be confronted and cross-examined by the applicant or holder." This regulation was issued after the Coast Guard procedures had been sharply criticized by the court of appeals for the ninth circuit.

The Coast Guard presently has no power to issue or request the issuance of subpenas.

PROGRAM ADMINISTRATION

It is recommended that:

1. The Commandant of the Coast Guard be vested with full authority to administer the port security program, including authority to issue regulations implementing the applicable Executive orders;

2. The final determination to issue or deny security clearance to employees on merchant vessels or waterfront facilities should be made by the Commandant;

3. Authority over recognized Army and Navy installations, such as the Brooklyn and Bremerton Navy yards, should continue to be vested in the cognizant military service; and

4. Coast Guard, Army, and Navy security clearance for persons employed on waterfront facilities should be recognized by each of the three services as interchangeable.

The Commission's study revealed evidence of conflicts between federal agencies in the manner of administering the security clearance for access to port areas. In some ports certain piers are designated for loading supplies for one or more branches of the Armed Forces, and the cognizant service, the Army, Navy, or Air Force, is held responsible for controlling access to these piers. The Coast Guard has had no authority for screening personnel who enter such areas. Rear Admiral Raymond J. Mauerman of the Coast Guard, testifying before the Senate subcommittee conducting waterfront investigations, in referring to jurisdiction over the Army and Navy docks, stated:

It is within their discretion (the Army or Navy) as to whether or not they insist upon their longshoremen having port security cards. This is a command function.

The Commission considers that it is important that administrative responsibility be clear, definite, and fixed. Hence, it recommends that the Coast Guard have full responsibility, except in recognized Army and Navy installations. In those installations, the cognizant military service should be responsible.

In an effort to remove annoying conflicts of authority, the Commission recommends that clearance certifications issued by the Coast Guard, the Army, or the Navy be interchangeable.

International
Organizations Program

Introduction

Henry Cabot Lodge, our Ambassador to the United Nations, has publicly stated that citizens of the United States who are employed by the United Nations and the other international organizations do not have authorized access to classified information. This is quite true, but it is also true that those who are disloyal to their country are nevertheless in an excellent position subtly to undermine our interests and influence our policies to the detriment of the national interest.

The findings of Federal grand juries, the public records of congressional committees, of the criminal courts are replete with indisputable evidence of ceaseless, determined efforts by Soviet agents to subvert our citizens in positions of strategic importance to engage in espionage, sabotage, and other disloyal activities. Gubitchev, Viktor Petrov, and other Soviet representatives have been declared *persona non grata* by our State Department, expelled from the United Nations and sent back to the Soviet Union because of definite evidence of their espionage, attempted espionage, coercion, blackmail, and other unprincipled and insufferable affronts to our hospitality.

It is abundantly evident that United States citizens employed in international organizations are prime targets for the deceptive and corruptive processes of Communist subversion. In the face of such clear danger, our Government is obliged to take every reasonable precaution to assure itself that its nationals in international organizations are men and women of loyalty and integrity.

HISTORY

The Problem

Does the Government security program of the United States, as it relates to United States participation in international organization, on the basis of applicable statutes, Presidential orders, and administrative regulations and directives, adequately protect "the national security, national defense secrets, and public and private defense installations, against loss or injury arising from espionage, disloyalty, subversive activity, sabotage, or unauthorized disclosures"? Of utmost importance to this study is the consideration that the international organizations' portion of the Federal security program affects United States citizens who are staff members of international organizations, i. e., these individuals are international civil servants, rather than employees of the American Government.[1]

Background of the "Independence" of the Secretariat

The idea of an international civil service divorced from national state control was established in practice under the League of Nations,[2] but the independent character of the Secretariat was not spelled out in the League Covenant, as it is under articles 100 and 101 of the United Nations Charter.

The Dumbarton Oaks proposals, the working draft from which evolved the United Nations Charter, did not provide for the independent status of the United Nations Secretariat. The independent character of the organization was not reflected in the Charter until the final drafting at the San Francisco Conference of 1945. In the interim, the United States and Canada worked on drafts of what eventually became articles 100 and 101 of the Charter.[3] Later, at the United Nations preparatory meeting in London in the fall of 1945, two concepts concerning the appointment of personnel to the United Nations were considered by the Preparatory Commission. One view was that the Charter should place exclusive appointive power in the hands of the Secretary General to insure the independence and international character of the organization; the other view was that, since member governments would be in a better position to judge the qualifications of candidates, appointments to the international staff should be subject to the approval of the candidate's national government. This latter proposition was offered by Yugoslavia with Soviet support. However, it was opposed by the United States and a majority of the Commission on the contention that it would jeopardize the independence of the Secretariat. Thus was recognized the exclusive and independent power of the Secretary General over his staff, i. e., independent from direct member state control.[4]

Although this provision was not included in the Charter, the Commission believed that "it was common sense that the staff should, as far as possible,

[1] United Nations. "Staff rules: Staff regulations of the United Nations and staff rules 101.1 to 112.8," Secretary-General's bulletin, ST/SGB/94/Rev. 4, 1955, p. 3. "Chapter I, regulation 1.1: Members of the Secretariat are international civil servants. Their responsibilities are not national but exclusively international. By accepting appointment, they pledge themselves to discharge their functions and to regulate their conduct with the interests of the United Nations only in view."

[2] U. S. Senate. 83d Cong., 2d sess., Review of the United Nations Charter: Compilation of staff studies prepared for the use of the subcommittee on the United Nations Charter of the Committee on Foreign Relations pursuant to S. Res. 126, Doc. 164, August 2 (legislative day, July 2), 1954, p. 346.

[3] U. S. House of Representatives. 83d Cong., 1st sess., hearings before the special subcommittee to investigate the Department of Justice, Committee on the Judiciary . . . on H. Res. 50, serial No. 2, pt. 1, February 19–May 12, passim, 1953, p. 300.

[4] Ibid., pp. 298–303.

be acceptable to the member governments, and also that the Secretary General would often require information regarding candidates from government or private bodies." [5] This was not to interfere, however, with the independent choice of the Secretary General.

Research indicates that the United States actually helped establish the independence of the Secretariat by directly supporting the incorporation of article 101, which along with article 100, provides the legal foundation for an independent Secretariat free from control or direction by any member state.[6]

Formative Years of the Secretariat

When the United Nations Secretariat was created in 1946, Secretary-General Trygve Lie was faced with the task of recruiting several thousand employees within a few months. Although references and previous employers were checked, and the normal personnel procedures of a business organization followed, the Secretariat had neither the time nor the facilities for a full investigation of each applicant for employment. Inasmuch as headquarters were located in the United States, it was only natural that a large majority of those hired were American nationals.[7]

Secretary General Lie followed the practice of asking member governments to propose candidates for United Nations employment, but he reserved the final decision to himself under article 100 of the Charter. Lie considered it both obvious and necessary that help be secured from member governments to insure high standards in the new Secretariat.[8] When a request for such information was made of the United States in 1946, Secretary of State James Byrnes said that the policy of the United States was to refrain from recommending United States citizens for employment or giving any official support or clearance to applicants and members of the staff.[9] The only official assistance rendered by the United States was the nomination of John B. Hutson to be Assistant Secretary General for administrative and financial services, and Abraham H. Feller to be legal counsel to the Secretary General. Secretary General Lie commended the motives of the United States in not wanting to impinge upon the independence of the United Nations, but felt that he was being deprived of much needed assistance. The Secretary General said, "After all, I had not asked the United States Government to tell me

---

[5] United Nations. Preparatory commission. Committee 6: Administrative and budgetary, summary record of meetings, supplement No. 6, PC/AB/66, Nos. 22 and 23, Dec. 22, 1945.

[6] U. S. House of Representatives. 83d Cong., 1st sess., hearings before the special subcommittee to investigate the Department of Justice, Committee on the Judiciary, on H. Res. 50, serial No. 2, pt. 1, February 19–May 12, passim, 1953, p. 300.

[7] United Nations General Assembly. Report of the Secretary-General on personnel policy, doc. A/2364, Jan. 30, 1953, pp. 4–7.

[8] Ibid., pp. 4–6.

[9] U. S. Senate. 82d Cong., 2d sess., hearings before the subcommittee to investigate the administration of the Internal Security Act . . . on activities of United States citizens employed by the United Nations, Oct. 13–Dec. 17, passim, 1952, app. E., p. 419.

whom I should appoint." [10]   All he had requested was assistance in finding qualified personnel and checking the records and character of American applicants.

It should be noted that the majority of staff members who were later called to testify before the Senate Internal Security Subcommittee in its investigations of the activities of United States citizens employed by the United Nations had been appointed originally in 1946–47, the period of rapid recruiting.[11]

In an effort to discover whether any American Communists were employed in the Secretariat, Secretary General Lie, during 1946 and 1947, directed informal requests for personnel data to the United States Government through the United States mission and also directly to the Department of State. Failing to receive any response, Secretary General Lie, on August 16, 1948, sent a list of 377 names of United States nationals employed on the Secretariat to the United States mission requesting that an effort be made to determine who and how many had been denied passports, such information not to be used as a basis for dismissal, but merely as a guide for further investigation.[12]

Eighteen persons on this 1948 list were later questioned by the Senate Subcommittee on Internal Security. In the months following the issuance of the 1948 list, Secretary General Trygve Lie repeatedly requested that the information be expedited. *Almost 2 years later,* adverse comments regarding a small number of individuals were received. "Subsequent written reports containing no adverse information were received, and on September 13, 1950, the Secretary General was informed that a check of all 377 names had been completed." [13]

Early State Department Policy

There are three general categories in which United States citizens are associated with the United Nations:

As United States representatives to the component organs of the United Nations; as members of the Secretariat; and as staff members of the United States delegation. The first group is selected by the President with the advice and consent of the Senate; the third group (members of the delegation staff) are selected under regular State Department procedure. The United States has jurisdiction over these two groups. However, it was the contention of

---

[10] Trygve Lie, "The personnel policy of the United Nations," reprinted from the United Nations Bulletin, vol. 14, No. 6, Mar. 15, 1953, New York: United Nations, Department of Public Information, p. 5.
[11] Ibid., pp. 5–6.
[12] Ibid., See also: U. S. Senate. 82d Cong., 2d sess., hearings before the subcommittee to investigate the administration of the Internal Security Act . . . on activities of United States citizens employed by the United Nations, Oct. 13–Dec. 17, passim, 1952, app. E, p. 419.
[13] U. S. Senate. 82d Cong., 2d sess., hearings before the subcommittee to investigate the administration of the Internal Security Act on activities of United States citizens employed by the United Nations, Oct. 13–Dec. 17, passim, 1952. App. E, p. 419.

Secretary of State James Byrnes that, "The United States Government has no authority whatever over appointments to the United Nations Secretariat. This is the responsibility of the Secretary General, Mr. Trygve Lie." [14]

At the time requests for assistance in securing personnel were being directed to the Department of State from the Secretary General, Alger Hiss was Director of the Department's Office of Special Political Affairs, a position to which he had been appointed by former Secretary Stettinius. The Deputy Director was John C. Ross. Both Hiss and Ross worked closely with Secretary Stettinius in the organization and conduct of the San Francisco Conference on International Organization in 1945. They continued to work closely with Mr. Stettinius when he was United States representative to the United Nations. The personnel staff of Mr. Stettinius and the Staff of the United States delegation were recruited primarily by this Office of Special Political Affairs, although appointments were not made until after a thorough investigation was conducted to determine competence, loyalty, fitness, and security. [15]

During the latter part of 1945, a number of applications for United Nations employment were received by the State Department from individuals within the Department, from other Government employees, and from individuals in private industry and professional fields who were interested in working for the United Nations. These were forwarded by the executive officer of the Office of Special Political Affairs headed by Hiss, to the Secretariat without comment or recommendation. [16]

On March 25, 1946, Hiss submitted a list of 78 names to the Secretary General. [17] On April 4, he learned that such practices might not be in accord with Secretary Byrnes' policy; nevertheless, on that same day, Hiss submitted a list of 284 names for the more responsible positions on the Secretariat. In a Department of State report dated May 28, 1953, William L. Franklin wrote that apparently Hiss sent out the list of 284 names "aware that it was uncertain whether the practice of making personnel suggestions to the Secretariat was in accordance with the Secretary's policies." This is shown by a memorandum Hiss wrote to Mr. Russell on April 4, 1946, and by memorandum of a conversation on the same day with another official of the Department. Hiss' memorandum to Mr. Russell stated:

. . . We are preparing for communication to you a general memorandum as to the attitude which the Department should take with respect to the whole question of Americans serving in the United Nations Secretariat. I talked to the Secretary about this subject in New York last week and I am familiar with the text of the Secretary's letter to Congressman Mundt of April 1. We have received word that in some cases the Secre-

---

[14] Ibid., app. D, pp. 414–415. In a letter from Dean Acheson to Senator Alexander Wiley, Oct. 12, 1952, Acheson stated: "It follows that United States nationals on the Secretariat do not represent the United States but are representatives of the United Nations insofar as their official capacity is concerned." Ibid., p. 305.

[15] Ibid., app. D, p. 415.

[16] U. S. House of Representatives. 83d Cong., 1st sess., hearings before the special subcommittee to investigate the Department of Justice, Committee on the Judiciary . . . on H. Res. 50 . . ., serial No. 2, pt. 1, Feb. 19–May 12, passim, 1953, p. 302.

[17] U. S. House of Representatives. 83d Cong., 1st sess., hearings before the special subcommittee to investigate the Department of Justice, Committee on the Judiciary, on H. Res. 50, serial No. 2, pt. 1, Feb. 19–May 12, 1953, pp. 313–314.

tariat will not wish to employ Americans unless they are satisfactory to the Department. Approval, we feel, would have to be on a formal written basis after careful consideration in each case. We will, as in the case of the suggestion of Mr. Hutson's name to Mr. Lie by the Secretary, also be asked to name people to fill particular Secretariat posts. Our proposals here, too, would have to be formalized and carefully screened. In addition, we can anticipate requests for suggested names of possible personnel for the Secretariat's independent consideration. In anticipation of requests of the latter kind, we have been preparing lists or rosters of qualified personnel. . . . Our present thought is that, if you and the Secretary approve, names from these lists might be supplied upon request without commitment or recommendation on the part of the Department, simply as names of persons which have been brought to our attention as possibly qualified for Secretariat posts. . . .

When Alger Hiss was replaced by Dean Rusk in 1947, Mr. Rusk attempted to modify Department policy to an extent. He recognized the responsibility of the Secretary General to hire his own employees, and stated that it was not his intention that the Department would interfere. However, Rusk felt, should the Secretary General request United States assistance, panels of qualified individuals should be submitted to the Secretary General by the Department from which the Secretary General could make independent selections. The plan was not put into effect. It would have cost $49,100, and funds were difficult to secure in the 1947–48 period. Rusk continued to ask the State Department to reconsider his proposals without success.[18]

The policy of the Department of State had changed little by 1949. In a letter to Byron Price, Acting Secretary General of the United Nations, Secretary of State Dean Acheson assured the Secretary General that the United States was fully aware of its responsibilities under article 100 of the Charter, namely, "to respect the exclusively international character of the responsibilities of the Secretary General and the staff and not to seek to influence them in the discharge of their responsibilities." Acheson stated that the United States had initially subscribed to the above provisions and continued to "support them wholeheartedly." [19]

United States-United Nations Secret Arrangement of 1949

On the initiative of the United Nations, in the summer of 1949, a principal assistant of the Secretary General conferred with John D. Hickerson, the then Assistant Secretary of State for United Nations Affairs. The Secretary General requested assistance from the United States in getting rid of undesirable Americans on his staff. A secret arrangement resulted from this conference under which the Secretary General, on his initiative, submitted lists of names of United States citizens employed or being considered for employment with the United Nations to the Department of State.

---

[18] Ibid., pp. 304–305.

[19] Dean Acheson, "U. N. Secretariat Procedures Upheld," *Department of State Bulletin*, vol. 21, Aug. 22, 1949, pp. 252–253.

The Department would conduct a "name check" investigation. All information secured through the Federal Bureau of Investigation and other agencies was then reviewed and evaluated by the State Department. If the information was derogatory, the Bureau of United Nations Affairs was notified so it could review the information and make proper comment to the United Nations. Evidence of a criminal or police record was forwarded in writing to the United Nations. If the agency check indicated that an individual was a member of the Communist Party or under Communist influence, the adverse comment was forwarded to the United Nations by word of mouth. Security practices made it impossible for the United States to send any information other than adverse comment to the Secretary General; e. g., "reject," "questionable," or "incomplete." It was the position of the State Department that failure to comment adversely was not intended to imply "clearance." [20]

In testimony before a House special subcommittee to investigate the Department of Justice, William L. Franklin, special assistant to the director, Office of Security, Department of State, March 23, 1953, explained the necessity for keeping the arrangement with the United Nations secret. The Department offered two basic reasons: "(1) it came close to violating the Department's policy of noninterference; (2) it might be interpreted as an instruction to the Secretary General as a violation of our obligations under articles 100 and 101 of the Charter." [21] Inasmuch as the arrangement was secret, all individuals participating in its implementation were instructed not to keep records. Only one person was selected to get the files together, and only one individual in the Bureau of United Nations Affairs was to receive the files for review and comment. Franklin further testified that "it was never intended that any clearances would be granted on these individuals, and . . . this was definitely and clearly understood by the representative of the United Nations." The United States was not assuming the responsibility for the loyalty of any persons employed by the Secretary General.[22]

Although initiated by the United Nations, the secret arrangement did not work out to the satisfaction of the Secretary General. Secretary General Lie stated that the degree of assistance afforded by the State Department did little more than to place him on notice that there was or might be something wrong about a staff member. The State Department told Secretary General Lie that an applicant should be "rejected" or was "questionable," but provided no supporting facts or evidence, nor gave any help in judging the pro-

---

[20] U. S. Senate. 82d Cong., 2d sess., hearings before the subcommittee to investigate the administration of the Internal Security Act . . . of the Committee on the Judiciary, on activities of United States citizens employed by the United Nations, October 13–December 17, passim, 1952, app. C, pp. 412–413. The agreement was the result of a request made by representatives of the United Nations to the Department of State. The agreement in part included a provision that the United States would furnish to the United Nations information concerning an American employee's, or prospective employee's, political affiliation or sentiment which might be of probable source of future injury to the United Nations. Ibid., app. D, p. 415.

[21] U. S. House of Representatives. 83d Cong., 1st sess., hearings before the special subcommittee to investigate the Department of Justice, Committee on the Judiciary, on H. Res. 50, serial No. 2, pt. 1, Feb. 19–May 12, passim, 1953, p. 307.

[22] Ibid., p. 307–308.

fessional qualifications of applicants. The Secretary General said that he "could not act on the basis of a mere adverse comment—usually expressed in a single word—without, in effect accepting instructions from the United States Government." [23]

The arrangement with the United States placed the Secretary General in an awkward position, inasmuch as he was of the general conviction that discharge could not be based on mere adverse comment reflecting on an employee's loyalty to the United States, especially in view of the fact that many of such employees had satisfactory or better efficiency ratings. Moreover, Secretary General Lie had to contend with a joint management-staff appeals board and an Administrative Tribunal which could demand a reversal of his decision or assess damages in lieu thereof. The major obstacle posed by the Tribunal was its insistence that the Secretary General render a statement of cause in discharging an employee. A further major consideration of the Secretary General was the necessity of protecting himself against charges that he was taking instructions from the United States Government—a violation of the Charter to which the United States was a signatory. [24]

In 1950, the Secretary General did dismiss several employees against whom he felt he had sufficient derogatory information upon which to base such action. However, the cases were appealed to the Administrative Tribunal charging breach of contract. The Tribunal found that even in cases of temporary employees, specific reasons for discharge had to be filed. The dilemma of the Secretary General was that he could not state reasons for dismissal without revealing information that was highly confidential. The following year, staff rules were amended to give the Secretary General the power to terminate temporary employees if he considered "such action . . . in the interest of the United Nations." Although this was of some assistance to the Secretary General, it nevertheless did not relieve him of the necessity for giving reasons for firing "permanent" employees. [25]

Of the more than 2,000 Americans in the Secretariat, the Secretary General had received "reject," "questionable," or "incomplete" warnings from the State Department on less than 3 percent.

Presentment of New York Federal Grand Jury

In March of 1952, Roy Cohn, an assistant United States attorney for the Southern District of New York, called Irving Kaplan, an employee of the United Nations, to testify before the grand jury. Kaplan had figured in congressional investigations of Communists in government. His testimony

---

[23] Trygve Lie, "The Personnel Policy of the United Nations," reprinted from *United Nations Bulletin*, vol. 14, No. 6, March 15, 1953, New York: United Nations, Department of Public Information, p. 6.

[24] U. S. Senate. 82d Cong., 2d sess., hearings before the subcommittee to investigate the administration of the Internal Security Act . . . of the Committee on the Judiciary, on activities of United States citizens employed by the United Nations, Oct. 13–Dec. 17, passim, 1952, app. C, pp. 412–413.

[25] United Nations General Assembly. Report of the Secretary General on Personnel Policy, doc. A/2364, annex I, Jan. 30, 1953, pp. 18–19.

.ed to the decision to call other United Nations witnesses. Between March and December 1952, numerous witnesses were called to testify at the inquiry into the disloyalty of certain United States citizens at the United Nations. "Witness after witness—American citizens on the Secretariat payroll—appeared before it (the grand jury) in response to its subpenas and pleaded the privilege against self-incrimination to defy all inquiries about Communist affiliations, espionage activities, and other conduct ranging from flagrant disloyalty to outright treason." [26] Of the nearly 100 witnesses heard by the grand jury, approximately half invoked the protection of the fifth amendment. A few admitted Communist Party membership, or Communist sympathy and service in the Communist cause.[27]

By the end of October 1952, a number of jurors felt the testimony indicated that a grave situation existed in the United Nations and that the facts should be brought to public attention; thus they expressed a desire to file a presentment. The presentment was extraordinary in that it identified witnesses by name and contained direct quotations from the testimony which had been taken in secret.

Myles J. Lane, United States attorney for the southern district of New York, suggested delay until the State Department could present its testimony. Moreover, he noted the possibility "that individual jurors might be subject to libel suits brought by persons named in the presentment, and that its irregularities in form might subject it to impounding by the court, thus defeating its purpose altogether.[28] The jury agreed to postpone the issuance of the presentment. It was later charged that the Justice Department had exerted undue pressure to call off the proceedings and quash the presentment.[29]

Adrian Fisher was named by Secretary of State Dean Acheson as State Department representative to appear before the grand jury. When asked to reveal the names of persons in the State Department responsible for the operation of the secret arrangement between the United States and United Nations, Mr. Fisher refused claiming these persons to be protected by executive immunity, and that disclosing their identity would be a breach of confidence by the Department.

According to a State Department report dated May 28, 1953, Secretary Acheson instructed Mr. Fisher to give the information requested by the grand jury if so instructed by the presiding judge rather than risk a contempt citation. Secretary Acheson reasoned "that if a departmental official refused to answer questions and accepted a contempt citation after a judge had directed him to answer, it would convince the public that the situation was very, very bad." It was unnecessary for Mr. Fisher to provide

[26] U. S. House of Representatives. 83d Cong., 1st sess., report to the Committee on the Judiciary by the subcommittee to investigate the Department of Justice pursuant to H. Res. 50 (committee print), 1954, p. 26.
[27] Ibid.
[28] Ibid., pp. 28–29.
[29] Ibid., p. 25.

such information, since the presiding judge failed to so direct him prior to the issuance of the grand jury presentment of December 2, 1952.

In November the Federal grand jury again decided to file a presentment. A new draft, prepared with the assistance of Roy Cohn, was unanimously approved by the jury. The final draft was unanimously agreed to and signed December 2, 1952. The grand jury stated that its inquiries indicated that there were "many . . . disloyal United States citizens . . . occupying high positions of trust in the United Nations"; thus it considered it its duty to advise "that startling evidence has disclosed infiltration into the United Nations of an overwhelmingly large group of disloyal United States citizens, many of whom are closely associated with the international Communist movement." Moreover, most of these individuals had long records of employment with the Federal Government prior to their employment by the United Nations or its specialized agencies.[30]

The evidence indicated that they had shifted from one Federal agency to another in a definite pattern. These persons assisted one another up through Government agencies into the United Nations.

The grand jury contended that the presence of these subversives in the United Nations and its related agencies was a menace to national security, since they were in policymaking positions charged with determination of how millions of dollars should be spent; occupied radio posts, and edited United Nations documents for world dissemination.

The presentment made the point that other member states of the United Nations had an effective control over their nationals employed by the United Nations through the issuance of passports, but that, as host nation, the United States had no such control. The grand jury implied that the United States should require passports of its nationals employed by the United Nations, the passport to be issued only after adequate loyalty check.

A brief review of the past relationship between the United States and United Nations took into account the operation of the secret arrangement of 1949. The grand jury charged that "in some of the most flagrant and obvious cases of disloyalty, the State Department gave the disloyal officials a clean bill of health to the United Nations." Moreover, the State Department refused "to furnish the grand jury with the names of the State Department personnel responsible for the faulty evaluations."

There were also instances of the United Nations failing to take action against an official concerning whom adverse reports had been supplied by the State Department.

The grand jury recommended the following action:

(a) No citizen of the United States shall hereafter be permitted to accept employment with the United Nations or any of its various divisions and departments or specialized agencies without prior clearance by a designated body of our own United States Government.

---

[30] Presentment of the Federal grand jury on disloyalty of certain United States citizens at the United Nations. App. I.

(b) That before a United States citizen may accept employment with the United Nations, he should be required to fill out an application form containing the questions designated to elicit the following information:

(1) Does the applicant have a criminal record? (and there should be the customary fingerprinting test as a supplement to this question).

(2) Is or was the applicant a member of any organization teaching and advocating the overthrow of the United States by force and violence?

(3) Was applicant ever known by any other name?

(4) Was applicant ever denied a passport by the United States Government?

(5) Has applicant ever been discharged or resigned from any United States Government employment, and, if so, under what circumstances?

(c) The recommendations made in (b) as to future applicants shall be applied at earliest opportunity to all present United States citizens employed in the United Nations and its specialized agencies.

(d) Another grand jury should continue our investigation at once.

Secretary General Lie commented critically on the activities of the Federal grand jury. Despite official requests for information on the grand jury proceedings, he received only hearsay reports. The Secretary General also noted that although he had been denied information on the ground that the proceedings were secret, there were periodic "leaks" to the press and radio. Secretary General Lie observed that the grand-jury presentment, while tending to cast discredit on the entire staff of the Secretariat, returned no indictment.

The Secretary General also sent a formal request for information to the United States Mission. In a letter addressed to Senator Austin, Chief United States Delegate, Mr. Lie wrote:

You are aware of my great concern over recent disclosures regarding United States citizens on my staff charged with having engaged in subversive activities and of the measures I have taken to meet this problem in a manner satisfactory to both the United Nations and its host country.

I should like to express my appreciation to you for the assistance given to me by the United States mission in regard to this problem and in particular for having made available to me the official records of the Senate Internal Security Subcommittee relating to personnel of the Secretariat. I have found these records most helpful.

In this morning's paper I have read the presentment of the Federal grand jury "on disloyalty of certain United States citizens at the United Nations" which was submitted to the United States district court yesterday. This presentment, as you are no doubt aware, contains a number of conclusions involving serious charges against members of the staff of the United Nations who are not specifically identified.

Mr. Lie, in view of the fact that these charges had been made public, requested that he be afforded the facts on which the conclusions of the grand jury were based. He assured Senator Austin that he would keep such information confidential.

This request of Mr. Lie was transmitted by Senator Austin to the Department of Justice. Senator Austin's reply to Secretary General Lie included in part the following:

As has been communicated informally to the Assistant Secretary General in charge of administrative and financial services, the representative of the United States has been advised that in the view of the Department of Justice that Department is forced to adhere

379

to its construction of rule 6 (e) of the Federal rules of criminal procedure as prohibiting the disclosure by that Department to the Secretary General of any testimony or proceedings before the Federal grand jury. . . ." (United Nations General Assembly, Report of the Secretary General on Personnel Policy, Doc. A/2364, Jan. 30, 1953, p. 9.)

One recommendation of the grand jury was effected when, on January 6, 1953, a second grand jury was empaneled to continue the investigation of disloyal Americans serving in international organizations. The presentment of the second grand jury, issued June 29, 1954, declared that although "certain allegations made in the presentment of December 2, 1952, reflected the condition prevailing up to that time, the situation has been improved, partly by reason of some resignations and dismissals, and principally because of the promulgation and operation of Executive Orders 10422 (January 9, 1953) and 10459 (May 27, 1953)."

The second presentment emphasized the fact that the United Nations and its specialized agencies are autonomous and "not subject to control by member Governments." Such being the case, the operation of the Executive orders is subject to the voluntary compliance of the organizations. The jury did not feel that there had been sufficient experience to evaluate the degree of cooperation that could be expected from these international organizations, but noted one case in which an individual employed by a specialized agency failed to respond to the jury's subpoena. He was judged to be in contempt by the district court, yet remained in the employ of the international organization. (He was later removed under International Organizations Employees Loyalty Board procedures.)

Investigations by Internal Security Subcommittee of the Senate Committee on the Judiciary

Meanwhile, the Senate Internal Security subcommittee, in conjunction with its investigation of the administration of the Internal Security Act and other internal security laws, began hearings on activities of United States citizens employed by the United Nations in October 1952. The previous May several American nationals employed by the United Nations had been called to testify before the subcommittee in connection with its investigations into the Institute of Pacific Relations. The hearings of the subcommittee concerning American nationals in international employ continued until March of 1954.

Among the witnesses appearing before the Senate subcommittee in the course of various hearings into the administration of the Internal Security Act was former Communist Elizabeth Bentley. Miss Bentley implicated Virginius Frank Coe as a participant in the Communist conspiracy. As early as 1948, Miss Bentley, in public testimony, had named Mr. Coe as having been a member of her espionage ring. Yet when subpenaed by the

Senate subcommittee in December 1952, Frank Coe still held the position of secretary of the International Monetary Fund. Since 1934 he had held a number of positions with the Government. At one time he was director of the Monetary Research Division of the Treasury Department.[31] In 1944 he was technical secretary of the Bretton Woods Monetary Conference which led to the creation of the International Monetary Fund and the International Bank. The Fund handles assets of between seven and eight billion dollars. In testifying before the Senate subcommittee, pleading privilege under the fifth amendment, Coe refused to answer numerous questions asking whether he was a Communist; whether he engaged in subversive activities; whether he engaged in espionage while technical secretary of the Bretton Woods conference, etc. Frank Coe was dismissed from his position as secretary of the International Monetary Fund several days after he appeared before the Senate subcommittee.[32]

The involvement of Alger Hiss in the Communist conspiracy had over the years been accumulated from many sources, among which were Miss Bentley, Whittaker Chambers, and Igor Gouzenko. Nathaniel Weyl confirmed Chambers' allegations that Hiss had been a member of the Harold Ware Communist cell, although Hiss denied this charge.[33]

J. Anthony Panuch, former Deputy Assistant Secretary of State in charge of security, testified that when he was associated with the Department, a move had been made to elevate the Office of Special Political Affairs to be the central key organization of the State Department. Alger Hiss, the Director of that Office, supported the proposal. The plan to make the Office of Special Political Affairs the superplanning and coordinating agency of the Department failed. Hiss, until his resignation in 1947, however, remained Director of the Office which initiated American policy on United Nations questions and serviced the American delegation to the United Nations. Mr. Panuch testified that at the time he was security officer, he was in possession of conclusive evidence that Hiss was involved in a Communist conspiracy. When the proposal was being considered to elevate the Office of Special Political Affairs, Panuch sent a memo to Donald S. Russell, Assistant Secretary of State, opposing the proposal. He had stated in that memo that Alger Hiss exercised "Svengali-like influence over the mental processes" of Edward R. Stettinius, Jr., United States delegate to the United Nations. The memo noted the extremely powerful position Hiss would be in if the proposal were accepted.[34]

Another witness before the Senate subcommittee was David Weintraub. He appeared on May 15, 1952, in connection with the subcommittee's inquiry

---

[31] U. S. Senate. 83d Cong., 1st sess., report of the subcommittee to investigate the administration of the Internal Security Act and other internal security laws to the Committee on the Judiciary . . . on interlocking subversion in Government departments (committee print), July 30, 1953, pp. 7–8. Other participants of the Communist conspiracy as named by Miss Bentley and Mr. Chambers who also were employees of the Treasury Department were Harry Dexter White, Harold Glasser, Victor Perlo, Irving Kaplan, Sol Adler, Abraham George Silverman, and William Ludwig Ullmann et al. Ibid., p. 29.

[32] Ibid., pp. 7–8.

[33] Ibid., p. 8.

[34] Ibid., pp. 9–10.

into the Institute of Pacific Relations. At that time, Weintraub was Director of Economic Stability and Development, Department of Economic Affairs, United Nations. The subcommittee charged Weintraub with being in "a unique position in setting up the structure of Communist penetration of governmental agencies by individuals who have been identified by witnesses as underground agents of the Communist Party. . . ." Weintraub had held a number of positions with the Federal Government. It appeared that through his efforts a number of underground Communists gained entry into Federal service and later into the international civil service. Weintraub denied Communist Party membership, although he admitted knowing a number of Government employees who had been accused in sworn testimony of being members of an underground Communist cell.[35]

A number of witnesses called before the subcommittee refused to acknowledge knowing David Weintraub on the contention that to do so might tend to incriminate them. His sister refused to state whether she was a member of the Communist Party. In 1943, Weintraub acted as adviser to the director general, Gov. Herbert H. Lehman, at the first council session of the United Nations Rehabilitation and Recovery Administration. Weintraub was secretary of the committee on supplies and later chief of supplies of United Nations Relief and Rehabilitation Administration.[36] (Weintraub resigned January 1953 from the U. N.)

Irving Kaplan, a several-time employee under David Weintraub and a protege of Weintraub's, was also a witness before the Senate subcommittee. Kaplan, following the usual pattern, had held numerous responsible positions with the Federal Government beginning in 1936, eventually reaching the Division of Economic Stability of the United Nations. Weintraub assisted him up the ladder all along the line. Both Kaplan and Weintraub had been involved in the Communist conspiracy by testimony of Whittaker Chambers.[37]

The ease with which individuals used the ladder up through Government service was described by Elizabeth Bentley. She testified that two of the best avenues for placing people were through Harry Dexter White and Lauchlin Currie, administrative assistant to the President. Part of her testimony went as follows: "Whoever we had as an agent would automatically serve for putting someone else in [Government]. . . . Once we got one person in, he got others, and the whole process continued like that. . . ."[38]

The subcommittee noted that past testimony of Bentley, Chambers, Budenz, Weyl, and others had indicated a purposeful design in Communist planning. Prior to the Second World War the major concern of the United States was in the economic field. The Communists were then infiltrating into the Agricultural Adjustment Administration, the Works Progress Administration, the National Recovery Administration, and other agencies. When the war was the major concern of the Government, these people shifted to the

---

[35] Ibid., pp. 10–11.
[36] Ibid., pp. 11–12.
[37] Ibid., pp. 12–13.
[38] Ibid., pp. 2, 14.

Board of Economic Welfare, the Foreign Economic Administration, the Office of Strategic Services, and similar agencies. At the conclusion of the war, these agents gravitated to the international organizations. These individuals "traveled to every continent as emissaries and representatives of the American people. They attended virtually every international conference where statesmen met to shape the future." [39]

One allegation of the Senate subcommittee was that although the Federal Bureau of Investigation had transmitted derogatory information on virtually all persons associated with the United Nations who appeared before the subcommittee to the Department of State years earlier, no action had been taken to remove these persons from their positions of trust and influence in the United Nations until after their appearances before the subcommittee. [40]

Among those named as part of the Communist conspiracy by Miss Bentley and Mr. Chambers were Harry Dexter White, Frank Coe, Harold Glasser, Victor Perlo, Irving Kaplan, Sol Adler, Abraham G. Silverman, and William Ludwig Ullmann. All had at one time been employees of the Treasury Department.

One of those named by Bentley and Chambers, Harry Dexter White, had been the "chief architect of the International Monetary Fund as well as its first United States executive director." Another reputed Communist, Harold Glasser, was the financial expert of the United States delegation which helped form United Nations Relief and Rehabilitation Administration; moreover, Glasser was Treasury "spokesman on this international body 'throughout its whole life.'" He had a predominant voice in "determining which countries should receive aid from United Nations Relief and Rehabilitation Administration, and which should not." A third alleged Communist, Frank Coe, "followed White as director of the Treasury Department's Division of Monetary Research." Coe later was to become secretary of the International Monetary Fund.

Twenty-seven witnesses called to testify by the Senate subcommittee investigating the activities of United States citizens employed by the United Nations "invoked the constitutional privilege against self-incrimination when asked about their connections with the Communist conspiracy. . . . For the most part, they held important positions in the Secretariat. . . . Almost all of them had previously held positions of similar importance in the United States Government." [41] The subcommittee was of the opinion that: "The pattern of the United Nations activity of American Communists bears strong resemblance to the pattern of the previous activity of such Communists in the United States Government, as described in the subcommittee's report on interlocking subversion in Government departments." [42]

---

[39] Ibid., pp. 20–21.
[40] Ibid., p. 25.
[41] U. S. Senate. 83d Cong., 2d sess., second report of the subcommittee to investigate the administration of the Internal Security Act . . . to the Committee on the Judiciary . . . on activities of United States citizens employed by the United Nations (committee print), Mar. 22, 1954, p. 3.
[42] Ibid., p. 49.

In an attempt to assess how such infiltration was possible, the subcommittee examined the background of the establishment of the Secretariat. It was noted that for 3 years, from 1946 to 1949, no safeguards were employed to keep persons disloyal to the United States from securing employment with the United Nations. "When the United States Department of State finally took cognizance of the situation respecting possible disloyalty of United States nationals employed by the United Nations, it was fully at the instance of the United Nations and not even partially as a result of initiative of any security officials within the State Department." [43] The subcommittee was referring to the secret arrangement of 1949 between the United States and the United Nations. In commenting on this arrangement, the subcommittee noted the declaration of the State Department which averred that under no circumstances did the State Department undertake to "clear" United States citizens employed by the United Nations, and that failure to make derogatory comment was understood by the United Nations not to imply clearance. In the opinion of the subcommittee, however, the secret arrangement "had the obvious effect of conveying to the United Nations the intelligence that when the State Department failed to make oral objections to an employee of the United Nations within a reasonable time after the name of such employee had been submitted by the United Nations, the Department had concluded . . . that there was not sufficient derogatory information to justify the Department in objecting to the continued employment of such person by the United Nations." When State Department witnesses were questioned as to how this differed from clearance, they were unable to explain.[44]

The subcommittee charged the State Department with failing to carry out its obligations under the 1949 arrangement with the United Nations. Not only might the Department's failure to forward derogatory comment be interpreted as "clearance," but also the "Department failed, over lengthy periods of time, to make any reports with respect to certain employees of the United Nations . . . in spite of the fact that security reports on such employees were heavy with derogatory information." [45]

The State Department did not bear the full brunt of the charges of the Senate subcommittee. On the basis of testimony during the hearings, the subcommittee charged that the United Nations did not investigate the background of its employees, even those in important positions, or if the United Nations was aware of their background it evidently was indifferent to the findings.[46]

The following conclusions were reached by the subcommittee:

(1) American Communists who had been officials of the United States Government penetrated the Secretariat of the United Nations after the United States Government had been apprised of security information regarding their conspiratorial activities.

---

[43] Ibid., p. 5.
[44] Ibid., pp. 5–6.
[45] Ibid.; see also fn. 27.
[46] Ibid., p. 26.

(2) American Communists have aided each other in securing employment in the United Nations.

(3) The pattern of the United Nations activity of American Communists bears strong resemblance to the pattern of the previous activity of such Communists in the United States Government. . . .

(4) American citizens, under Communist discipline, are particularly valuable to the world Communist conspiracy when employed in . . . the United Nations from which they can operate both here and abroad under the United Nations cover sometimes with diplomatic immunity, against the interests of the United States and in behalf of the Soviet Union.

(5) There is a Communist "fifth column" operating within the United Nations Secretariat. This "fifth column" includes American citizens * * * [and] also includes citizens of other non-Communist countries. The work of this "fifth column" necessarily is inimical . . . to the interests of the United States . . . and to the avowed interests and purposes of the United Nations itself.

(6) We believe that . . . American citizens [who refuse, on grounds of self-incrimination, to testify before properly constituted judicial or legislative agencies of the United States] are . . . unfit for Federal or United Nations employment.

(7) The existence of a "fifth column" in the Secretariat . . . brings into serious question the work of the United Nations agencies and also that of other international organizations.

(8) Communists within the United Nations are under discipline to conform with the world pattern of Communist activity, in which every available type of diplomatic agency is used as a "cover shop" for espionage and subversion.

(9) The hearings before the Senate Internal Security Subcommittee have been instrumental in revealing and securing the dismissal of a number of Americans with Communist records employed by the United Nations.

(10) Subsequent to . . . January 2, 1953, American representatives at the United Nations, together with the executive departments and in cooperation with the Secretary General, have instituted a number of safeguards against the activities and operations of American Communists within the United Nations. These safeguards should be improved and perfected.

(11) The same considerations of national interest which dictate that a Communist shall not be considered desirable for Federal employment are the basis for the conclusion that American nationals who are Communists must not be allowed to assume positions in the United Nations from which they can harm their country. We believe it can be demonstrated that citizens of any nation engaged in a conspiracy to overthrow that nation by force and violence are per se unfit for employment by the United Nations or any other international organization . . . we consider it the unquestioned right of the United States to demand that American nationals who join a conspiracy against their own country forego any opportunity to further that conspiracy through the United Nations or any other international organization. The United States should not assert or enforce this right through an attempt to coerce the United Nations with respect to its employment practices; but the United Nations can have no legitimate concern with restrictions and limitations which our Government, for its own protection, may choose to place upon its nationals.

(12) The presence, on the United Nations staff, of secret Communists from non-Communist nations operating under Soviet discipline, is detrimental to the purposes of the United Nations and specifically constitutes a violation of article 100 (1) of the Charter . . .

(13) Former Secretary General Lie showed awareness of the threat to American security when he dismissed American citizens from the United Nations Secretariat for refusing to answer the subcommittee's questions regarding their Communist activities.

(14) The Commission of Jurists, appointed by former Secretary General Trygve Lie to advise him, indicated its awareness of this threat to American security . . . (below).

(15) The action of the Administrative Tribunal in awarding indemnites, reinstatement, and legal costs to persons who are clearly a threat to the internal security of the United States, has done injury to the cause of the United Nations within the United States. (below)

(16) The decisions of the Administrative Tribunal reversing the Secretary General are unwarranted and demonstrate a totally erroneous conception of the world Communist conspiracy. (below) [47]

The 1952 investigations by the Senate Internal Security subcommittee came early to the attention of Secretary General Lie. The testimony of American nationals before the subcommittee led the Secretary General to conclude that those individuals had transgressed the staff regulations. Mr. Lie recognized the constitutional right of the witnesses to refuse to answer questions put to them by the subcommittee. However, he noted that there was no similar right to continued public employment by any person invoking the fifth amendment. Although the Secretary General recognized no national legal practice as binding upon the United Nations, he felt that the refusal of the witnesses to testify before the subcommittee had so discredited the Secretariat as a whole and imperiled the position of the United Nations in the United States that such persons should no longer be retained by the Secretariat.

Secretary General Lie was highly critical of the subcommittee's general practice of calling only those staff members to testify in open session who earlier had refused in closed session to answer questions about Communist Party membership, or who had admitted past membership. This practice gave the impression to the public that the Secretariat harbored numerous subversive Americans despite the fact that the witnesses were only about 1 percent of the Americans employed by the United Nations.[48] Nevertheless, the Secretary General did feel that staff members invoking the fifth amendment should be dismissed, inasmuch as they had not conducted themselves properly as international civil servants. Thus, he dismissed employees holding contracts and placed those with permanent contracts on compulsory leave.[49]

Investigation of the Department of Justice by the Special House Subcommittee of the Committee on the Judiciary

The presentment of the New York Federal grand jury had charged the State Department with clearing disloyal Americans for United Nations posts. Moreover, a number of charges had been made to the effect that the Department of Justice had attempted to put pressure on the grand jury to suppress

---

[47] Ibid., pp. 49–50.

[48] Trygve Lie, The Personnel Policy of the United Nations, reprinted from the *United Nations Bulletin*, vol. 14, No. 6, Mar. 15, 1953, New York: United Nations, Department of Public Information, pp. 8–9.

[49] United Nations General Assembly. Report of the Secretary-General on personnel policy, doc. A/2364, Jan. 30, 1953, pp. 11, 13–14.

its presentment. These charges led a House subcommittee on the Judiciary under Congressman Chelf to make an immediate investigation into the allegations that the Justice Department had delayed, interfered, and hampered the grand jury. The charges against the State Department were also considered by the special House subcommittee.

Testimony before the House subcommittee brought out the fact that Secretary of State Dean Acheson had known nothing about the secret United States-United Nations arrangement until October 8, 1952, when during the course of discussions between Secretary Acheson and Attorney General James McGranery over the forthcoming grand jury presentment, Adrian Fisher, legal adviser to the State Department, was called in and explained the workings of the highly secret arrangement.[50] The State Department prevailed upon the Justice Department to cooperate in delaying the presentment. One of Acheson's reasons for wanting the delay was that the General Assembly was about to begin sessions in New York, and he did not want the Assembly to be subjected to public attack. Attorney General McGranery was not opposed to the presentment, but did inform United States attorneys Lane and Cohn that he considered it premature. A suggestion was made that the State Department send a representative to advise the grand jury on the secret arrangement, and of the "possible international repercussions of its proposed charges." [51]

After the grand jury had been dissuaded from filing its presentment, there were unmistakable indications that attempts were made to delay proceedings. The appearance of a representative from the State Department was attended by a series of delays and postponements.[52]

Although Attorney General McGranery did not testify before the subcommittee concerning these events, "all the witnesses who had knowledge of his part in it concurred emphatically that he was in favor of the presentment from the outset, and that he imposed no delays or interference except only his request, on December 2, for time to examine the final version." [53]

In a statement before the House subcommittee, December 31, 1952, John D. Hickerson, Assistant Secretary of State for United Nations Affairs, briefly summarized the relevant points on the subject of disloyal Americans on the United Nations Secretariat. He stated that it was the opinion of the State Department that Americans subject to Communist discipline should not be employed by the United Nations, and that appropriate means should be used in trying to remove them. This view was shared by the Secretary General.

Hickerson made one comment of special note:

The Department has not had evidence justifying a conclusion that there was spying or espionage on the part of American citizens employed by the United Nations. If either

[50] U. S. House of Representatives. 82d Cong., 2d sess., hearings before the special subcommittee to investigate the Department of Justice, Committee on the Judiciary . . . on H. Res. 95 . . . serial No. 20, pt. 2, Aug. 26–Dec. 31, passim, 1952, p. 1730.

[51] U. S. House of Representatives. 83d Cong., 1st sess., report to the Committee on the Judiciary by the subcommittee to investigate the Department of Justice pursuant to H. Res. 50 (committee print), 1954, p. 29.

[52] Ibid., p. 30.

[53] Ibid., p. 32.

the Department of State or the Department of Justice had had evidence justifying such a conclusion, prompt action would have been taken under the criminal laws of the United States by the Department of Justice which has responsibility for enforcing these laws. These American employees have no immunity from our United States laws.[54]

Although Hickerson stressed the Department position that persons employed by the United Nations should be individuals of unquestioned integrity, he pointed out that "the security of classified information is not involved in this question. The employees of the Secretariat . . . do not have access to any United States security information." [55]

At the outset of the 83d Congress, the House subcommittee's mandate to continue the hearings was renewed. State Department witnesses testified that the United States, in the early stages of the development of the United Nations, had pressed hard for the principle that the permanent staff of the United Nations should be completely free from control by individual member nations. Such position was maintained despite strong opposition by Yugoslavia and the Soviet Union. This was the viewpoint that finally prevailed, and one accepted by Secretary of State James Byrnes and his successors, George Marshall and Dean Acheson.[56]

The subcommittee had been given detailed information regarding witnesses that had appeared before the New York Federal grand jury in 1952. This information indicated that in case after case, despite the transmittal by the Federal Bureau of Investigation to the State Department of highly derogatory information against these persons, the State Department either did not communicate adverse comment to the Secretary General or delayed action for periods of up to as much as 3 years.

During the entire life of the agreement the State Department submitted only 56 adverse comments: Eight with respect to applicants for employment by the Secretariat and 48 on persons who were actually employed by the United Nations. Fifteen of these persons had left or been placed on compulsory leave at the time of the grand jury's presentment in December 1952. The average time for processing cases under the arrangement, from the submission of the name by the Secretariat until the Department's comment in response, was approximately 1 year and 4 months.[57]

Secretary of State Dean Acheson, invited to appear before the House special subcommittee, refused to disclose the names of his staff members who had been responsible for working out the special arrangements with the United Nations saying that he and Hickerson would assume all responsibility for any defects in the program.[58]

Secretary Acheson's refusal was based on the contention that the evaluation process was not a single act; moreover, by direction of the President,

[54] U. S. House of Representatives. 82d Cong., 2d sess., hearings before the special subcommittee to investigate the Department of Justice, Committee on the Judiciary . . . on H. Res. 95 . . . serial No. 20, pt. 2, Aug. 26–Dec. 31, passim, 1952, p. 1755.

[55] Ibid., p. 1756.

[56] U. S. House of Representatives. 83d Cong., 1st sess., report to the Committee on the Judiciary by the subcommittee to investigate the Department of Justice pursuant to H. Res. 50 (committee print), 1954, pp. 34–35.

[57] Ibid., pp. 36–37.

[58] Ibid., p. 37.

names of those participating in the evaluating process could not be given out. It was Secretary Acheson's opinion that the evaluation process as related to United Nations employees was part of foreign relations and that the release of those names could jeopardize United States foreign policy:

It is apparent, at the outset, that a demand for the names of subordinate officials involved in any particular foreign relations task of the Department of State is, by itself, indicative that the task upon which they have been engaged is a matter of public controversy; if the subject matter itself were not a matter of controversy there would ordinarily be little motivation for any desire to identify subordinate officials connected with it.

A practice of making public these names would of necessity be a signal to all subordinate officials of the Department of State to avoid as best they could becoming involved in matters which were controversial, or, if unavoidable, for each to tailor his actions with respect to such a matter to what he conceived to be, at that time, the state of popular feeling or of any articulate portion of the public regarding it, even though he considered that action based upon that feeling or a portion of it to be contrary to the interests of the United States, as his own honest, considered, and trained judgment saw that interest. Not only that, he would be apt to document his precise contribution or attitude "make a record" on the controversy against the day when he would have to justify himself "on the record." [59]

Secretary Acheson defended his Department against the accusations of the New York Federal grand jury that both the State and Justice Departments were hampering the grand jury's search for disloyal Americans in the United Nations Secretariat.[60]

Dean Acheson's position was that the employment of United States citizens of doubtful loyalty might have been a threat to the national interest, but certainly not to United States national security:

These people in the United Nations did not raise a security question, because the people in the United Nations were not dealing with any matter where classified information of any sort, or matters having to do with our defense or security were involved.

That does not mean that it is a good thing to have these people in the United Nations, because I believe that the American employees of the United Nations should be the very highest type of loyal, true, American citizens; but let us be clear that they were not endangering the security of the United States. They were merely giving the United States a bad reputation and a black eye in the United Nations and they should not be there. . . .

Mr. KEATING. But do you not feel that the national security of the United States was involved in having disloyal American citizens in key positions in the United Nations?

Secretary ACHESON. I believe that the national interest of the United States was deeply involved, but I do not think that the security of the United States was involved.[61]

At the insistence of the subcommittee, the State Department finally made available the names of those officials of the Department responsible for the operations of the secret arrangement of 1949. William L. Franklin, special assistant to the Director, Office of Security, Department of State, testified

[59] U. S. House of Representatives. 82d Cong., 2d sess., hearings before the special subcommittee to investigate the Department of Justice, Committee on the Judiciary . . . on H. Res. 95 . . . serial No. 20, pt. 2, Aug. 26–Dec. 31, passim, 1952, p. 1710.

[60] Ibid., pp. 1742–1745.

[61] Ibid., pp. 1735–1736.

that because of the criticism of the evaluations these persons were all checked, and there was no doubt as to their loyalty, security, or integrity. Whatever shortcomings were present under the operations of the arrangement were explained as inherent in the restrictive nature of the arrangement itself, and the administrative complications and delays encountered in effectuating the program.[62]

Mr. Franklin, in a State Department report, explained in part the difficulties inherent in the secret arrangement. Between the fall of 1949 and March 1951, George M. Ingram, Bureau of United Nations Affairs, participated jointly with Joseph W. Amshey, Division of Security, in reviewing the investigative files supplied by cooperating agencies. Mr. Amshey evaluated the facts, and on this basis Mr. Ingram made the determination as to the proposed adverse comment to be conveyed to the United Nations.[63] Richard J. Kerry represented the Bureau of United Nations Affairs from March 1951 until December 1952. During this period he was assisted by Herbert F. Linneman until August 1952 and Thomas E. Hoffman of the Division of Security, from August till December 1952. Messrs. Linneman and Hoffman interpreted their respective roles as necessitating assistance to Mr. Kerry only when specifically requested. Mr. Kerry objected to assuming sole responsibility for making the adverse determinations and requested a return to the arrangement worked out by Ingram and Amshey. However, the workload on an extra-duty basis did not make such arrangement possible.[64]

Operation of this plan was handicapped by the necessity for secrecy, inasmuch as it was considered to be in possible violation of the Department of State's hands-off policy and also might have been construed as giving instructions to the Secretary General, a Charter violation. This being the case, FBI investigations were considered impossible. Moreover, only a few individuals were made aware of the arangement (Secretary of State Dean Acheson was not aware of the arrangement until the fall of 1952), and those participating in its operation did so on an extracurricular basis. An additional handicap to effective operation was that adverse security comments by the State Department to the United Nations were oral and usually consisted of a single-word evaluation, e. g., reject, without supporting evidence.[65]

At the conclusion of Mr. Franklin's testimony, Chairman Kenneth B. Keating made the following observation:

Your painstaking search is to be commended, but so far as I personally am concerned you have not helped a bit in establishing responsibility except that it was on the Department of State.

In other words, it looks to me as if the various divisions all sought and now seek to avoid responsibility for the long delay in submitting to the United Nations the adverse

---

[62] U. S. House of Representatives. 83d Cong., 1st sess., hearings before the special subcommittee to investigate the Department of Justice, Committee on the Judiciary, on H. Res. 50, serial No. 2, pt. 1, Feb. 19–May 12, passim, 1953, pp. 308–312.

[63] William L. Franklin, summary of investigation of 1949 secret arrangement between Department of State and the United Nations, Department of State report, May 28, 1953, p. 10.

[64] Ibid., p. 11.

[65] Ibid., pp. 50, 52–53.

comments which should have gone up long, long before they did as a result of the information furnished to the Department of State by the FBI.[66]

One person named by Franklin as having participated in the operations of the 1949 arrangement, was George M. Ingram, Director, Office of International Administration and Conferences. He voluntarily testified before the House subcommittee May 8, 1953. Testimony brought out that Ingram was not given any criteria or standard to apply in determining whether or not to make a derogatory comment on an employee or prospective employee of the United Nations.

The work under the secret arrangement was conducted by a few officials of the State Department as an extra duty. Robert A. Collier, chief counsel for the subcommittee, questioned why so serious a security function was undertaken on such a basis. Ingram stressed the necessity for secrecy and not keeping records by testifying that they did not want it known that such an arrangement existed, inasmuch as it might have resulted in the charge that the United States was attempting to influence the Secretary General in violation of Charter provisions. Collier suggested that had the organization been more tightly knit, fewer delays and slip-ups would have resulted.[67]

In answer to Chairman Kenneth Keating's question: "Do you consider that to have Communists or Communist sympathizers working in the United Nations was a threat to the security of this country?" Mr. Ingram replied: ". . . I think that a Communist or anyone under Communist influence is a danger to this country wherever he is. I do not think the security implications were of the same nature as you have with an individual on the staff of the State Department where they have access to classified and secret information and where they can represent themselves as being a United States representative." [68]

Representative Byron G. Rogers asked Mr. Ingram to comment on. charges that the State Department derogatory comments were not transmitted to the United Nations for as much as 16, 18, or even 24 months after requested. Mr. Ingram explained that the original name check might not have produced derogatory information, but that later information might have led to an adverse comment being made. Thus the time measure should not be from when the name was first submitted, but from when derogatory information was first uncovered.[69]

Ambassador Henry Cabot Lodge testified at the invitation of the subcommittee to explain the measures he and the State Department were taking to insure the loyalty of American citizens employed by the United Nations. Ambassador Lodge noted that under Executive Order 10422, searching, six-

[66] U. S. House of Representatives. 83d Cong., 1st sess., hearings before the special subcommittee to investigate the Department of Justice, Committee on the Judiciary, on H. Res. 50, serial No. 2, pt. 1, Feb. 19–May 12, passim, 1953, p. 797.

[67] Ibid., pp. 811–812.

[68] Ibid., p. 812.

[69] Ibid., pp. 813–814.

page forms inquiring into every phase of an individual's life history were distributed to some 2,000 United States nationals in United Nations employ. American employees in the United Nations were being fingerprinted and questionnaires being completed in the Headquarters area with the cooperation of Secretary General Lie. The large majority of the forms had already been returned to the State Department.[70]

Ambassador Lodge also testified that all personnel of the United States Mission to the United Nations were instructed not to reveal any top-secret material to Americans employed by the Secretariat, since they had not had security clearance; all American employees of the United States mission were being checked by the Federal Bureau of Investigation, and a security check was being made of the mission headquarters. Ambassador Lodge stated that he was doing everything humanly possible to insure security.

When asked to comment on earlier testimony by Dean Acheson to the effect that "the presence of Americans of doubtful loyalty in the United Nations staff was not a matter of affecting our national security in any way," Lodge said, ". . . I do not at all agree with Mr. Acheson on that. I think the presence of Americans of doubtful loyalty is definitely injurious to the best interests of the United States. I do not think they ought to be there.[71]

Ambassador Lodge expressed the opinion that the arrangements proposed under Executive Order 10422 were not in violation of article 101 of the Charter, since the United States was not suggesting who should be employed, but rather was screening American nationals, conveying derogatory comment to the Secretary General, and hoping that the Secretary General would cooperate.[72]

The conclusion of the House special subcommittee was that—

. . . the problem is well on its way toward solution. The subcommittee further feels that the Justice Department was drawn into this controversy by reason of its desire to cooperate with and back up the State Department, and that the situation created was the result primarily of an attitude of indifference to the problem by the State Department, coupled with the language of the United Nations Charter. If it is not believed under all the circumstances, that the action of the Justice Department amounted to such willful interference with the grand jury as to merit censure.[73]

The summary of the findings of the House special committee was that—

In connection with the grand-jury investigation of infiltration by subversive American nationals into the United Nations staff, it is clear that efforts were made to delay and impede the jury, but these efforts came principally from the Department of State and not from the Department of Justice. The State Department was gravely remiss, moreover, in not recognizing and dealing with the situation in the United Nations long before the grand jury brought it to light.[74]

[70] Ibid., p. 815.

[71] Ibid., pp. 815–816.

[72] U. S. House of Representatives. 83d Cong., Committee on Foreign Affairs, hearings, Feb. 2, 1954, p. 817.

[73] U. S. House of Representatives. 83d Cong., 1st sess., report to the Committee on the Judiciary by the subcommittee to investigate the Department of Justice pursuant to H. Res. 50 (committee print), 1954, p. 38.

[74] Ibid., p. 1.

Secretary General Lie was concerned with the problems arising from the presence of Americans of doubtful loyalty on the Secretariat. As a result of the proceedings before the New York Federal grand jury and the Internal Security Subcommittee of the Senate Committee on the Judiciary in 1952, Secretary General Lie, on October 22, 1952, decided to appoint a Commission of Jurists to advise him on proper action to take to meet the situation.[75] The three-member panel finally appointed included: Sir Edwin Herbert, of the United Kingdom, a prominent solicitor; William D. Mitchell, former attorney general under President Hoover; and Paul Veldekens, a Belgian professor of law at the Catholic University of Louvain. The jurists met November 14; their opinion was submitted November 29.

In the interim, Secretary General Lie took such action as he considered clearly within his authority. Temporary employees of the United Nations who had invoked the privilege against self-incrimination and against whom the Secretary General had additional adverse information were dismissed on the basis that continued employment was not in the interest of the United Nations. Permanent employees whose loyalty was in question were placed on compulsory leave.[76]

The following questions were submitted by the Secretary General for consideration by the Commission of Jurists:

(1) Is it compatible with the conduct required of a staff member for him to refuse to answer a question asked by an authorized organ of his government on the ground of the constitutional privilege against self-incrimination?

(2) What effect should be given by the Secretary General to the refusal of the United States Government to issue a passport to a staff member for purposes of official travel?

(3) In view of the Charter requirements and the staff regulations, what action should the Secretary General take when he receives information from an official source of the United States Government that a staff member of United States citizenship is alleged to be disloyal to his Government?

(4) In the course of inquiries by agencies of the United States Government, should the Secretary General make available archives of the organization or authorize staff members to respond to questions involving confidential information relating to official acts?

(5) If it appears that the Secretary General possesses no present authority to dismiss holders of permanent appointments on evidence of subsersive activities against their country or refusal to deny such activities, what new legal steps would be necessary and effective to confer such authority?

The opinion rendered by the jurists was based on a study of the Charter of the United Nations, headquarters agreement, staff regulations, statute of the Administrative Tribunal, and other basic documents.

Several points were uppermost in the jurists' mind when considering the above questions.

---

[75] United Nations General Assembly. Report of the Secretary General on personnel policy, doc. A/2364, Jan. 30, 1953, p. 11.

[76] Ibid., annex I, p. 19.

1. The special relationship existing between the United Nations and the United States as host nation.

2. The possible consequences of their opinion in other member nations.

3. The presence on the Secretariat of an individual whose home regime had changed and his resultant loss of citizenship or his becoming an unsatisfactory citizen.

The jurists had been commissioned to answer queries of the Secretary General as they related to United States nationals employed by the United Nations. They made the following observations:

The United Nations is not a superstate; it possesses no sovereignty and can claim no allegiance, but is an organization existing separate and distinct from its member states. Responsibility for the staff is vested in the Secretary General, acting independently and free from dictation or pressure by the individual member states. The jurists advised further that whereas Communist affiliation is no bar to the continued employment of non-American staff members, all of them are obligated to refrain from activities regarded as subversive by the United States, the host member of the United Nations.

The jurists declared that staff members retain their full legal rights including the privilege to invoke the fifth amendment, and that the exercise of this absolute right might result in unfavorable prospects of employment. Recognizing the fact that reliance on the fifth amendment in the United States might result in legislative or other consequences, the jurists recommended that the Secretary General dismiss all United Nations employees who invoke it; that he should not employ, and should dismiss from employment, any person concerning whom there are reasonable grounds for believing is, was, or is likely to be engaged in acts regarded as disloyal by the United States.

Derogatory information from member states, advised the jurists, should be accompanied by substantiating evidence, and necessitates a full inquiry by the Secretary General. Such evidence would be retained in the inviolable archives of the United Nations.

The jurists concluded:

The necessities of the international organization include the necessary independence of action required if the staff of the United Nations is to be a truly international civil service responsible to the United Nations in respect of its work. It must be recognized that this international civil service will inevitably include persons whose political, social, economic, and philosophical outlook differs from the beliefs and sentiments of many American citizens.

On the other hand, we believe that all members of the staff of the United Nations while living and working in the United States must wholeheartedly accept and abide by the laws of the host country whose protection they enjoy even if some of those laws run contrary to the beliefs and sentiments of some members of the staff. . . .

In relation to the five specific questions submitted to the Commission of Jurists, Secretary General Lie, in his report on personnel policy to the seventh session of the General Assembly, accepted their recommendations and conclusions, but he stated that he "did not bind himself to every argument or every single word contained in the opinion." [77] One such recommendation was that resort to the protection of the fifth amendment be grounds for dismissal as a fundamental breach of article 1.4 of the staff regulations. Mr. Lie felt that a refusal to answer questions put to an individual by a congres-

[77] Ibid., p. 11.

sional subcommittee destroyed the confidence which an international civil servant was required to maintain.

After accepting this recommendation of the Commission of Jurists, Secretary General Lie sought to give the employees involved a second chance. He notified them that they would be dismissed for a fundamental breach of staff regulation 1.4 unless, within 3 days, they notified the proper United States authorities of their intention to withdraw the plea of privilege and answer the pertinent questions put to them and so notify the Secretary General to this effect. None paid heed to the Secretary General's warning and the nine staff members holding permanent contracts who had resorted to the use of the fifth amendment were dismissed for not conducting themselves in a manner befitting their international status.[78]

Secretary General Lie gave the dismissed staff members indemnities and severance pay. This later proved to be a serious mistake on his part, inasmuch as such payment was one of the reasons the Administrative Tribunal overruled the decision of the Secretary General to dismiss. The Tribunal was of the opinion that had the Secretary General considered these dismissals to be on firm ground, he would not have attempted to ease the blow by giving indemnities and severance pay. Under staff regulations, when a staff member is summarily dismissed, he is not entitled to such severance pay.[79]

Executive Order 10422

In a statement released to the press, December 30, 1952, the Department of State announced the preparation of an Executive order (10422) to assure the loyalty of American citizens employed by the United Nations. The step was being taken to implement conclusions and recommendations of the United Nations Commission of Jurists.

On January 9, 1953, President Truman issued Executive Order 10422, which prescribed "procedures for making available to the Secretary General of the United Nations certain information concerning United States citizens employed or being considered for employment on the Secretariat of the United Nations."

The initial steps prescribed for the implementation of this order consisted in identifying data on American applicants or employees being forwarded by the administrative head of the international organization in question to the Secretary of State and also to the Civil Service Commission. The Commission would then make a full background check of all "locally" recruited American staff members and the Federal Bureau of Investigation would make a full field check of all "internationally" recruited American staff members and of American nationals against whom derogatory information

[78] Ibid., p. 11, annex I, p. 19.
[79] U. S. Senate. 83d Cong. 1st sess., hearing before the subcommittee to investigate the administration of the Internal Security Act . . . of the Committee on the Judiciary . . . on activities of United States citizens employed by the United Nations, pt. 3, Sept. 24, 1953, pp. 501–579.

might be uncovered. Reports of these investigations then went to the Regional Loyalty Board for evaluation with an opportunity for a Board hearing and appeals to the Loyalty Review Board. The standard to be applied in these cases represent a resolution of the question concerning reasonable doubt of the loyalty of the person involved to the Government of the United States based on all of the available evidence.

The criteria prescribed for the purpose of determining loyalty consisted of:

1. Sabotage, espionage, or attempts or preparations therefor, or knowingly associating with spies or saboteurs.

2. Treason or sedition or advocacy thereof.

3. Advocacy of revolution or force or violence to alter the constitutional form of government of the United States.

4. Intentional, unauthorized disclosure to any person, under circumstances which may indicate disloyalty to the United States, of United States documents or United States information of a confidential or nonpublic character obtained by the person making the disclosure as a result of his previous employment by the Government of the United States or otherwise.

5. Performing or attempting to perform his duties, or otherwise acting, while an employee of the United States Government during a previous period, so as to serve the interests of the United States.

6. Membership in, or affiliation or sympathetic association with, any foreign or domestic organization, association, movement, or group or combination of persons, designated by the Attorney General as totalitarian, Fascist, Communist, or subversive, or as having adopted a policy of advocating or approving the commission of acts of force or violence to deny other persons their rights under the Constitution of the United States, or as seeking to alter the form of government of the United States by unconstitutional means.

The Regional Loyalty Board or Loyalty Review Board, under the provisions of Executive Order 10422, transmitted its determinations together with the reasons therefor, stated in such detail as security considerations would permit to the Secretary of State for transmission to the administrative head of the international organization; and the Secretary of State would notify the administrative head of the organization concerned in all cases in which no derogatory information has been developed.

Executive Order 10422, was not the result of negotiations between the United States and the United Nations, but was welcomed by Secretary General Lie as "a progressive step toward making adequate information available." [80]

The Secretary General defended his policy of permitting the fingerprinting and interviewing of American staff members in the headquarters area against numerous criticisms made by member states as being in the best interests of the United Nations and not for the convenience of the United States. It was done to facilitate the implementation of Executive Order 10422 and thus expedite the clearing of the name of the Secretariat. No United States national was required by the United Nations to cooperate with the United States, although such cooperation was expected of them. [81]

---

[80] United Nations General Assembly. *Report of the Secretary-General on personnel policy*, doc. A/2364, Jan. 30, 1953, p. 12.

[81] Trygve Lie, The Personnel Policy of the United Nations, reprinted from the *United Nations Bulletin*, vol. 14, No. 6, Mar. 15, 1953, New York: United Nations, Department of Public Information, pp. 11–12.

The basis of the current loyalty program as it concerns United States citizens employed by international organizations is Executive Order 10422, as amended by Executive Order 10459, issued June 2, 1953, by President Eisenhower, effective May 27, 1953.   One minor amendment effected by Executive Order 10459 provided that short-term American employees of international organizations, i. e., those whose terms did not exceed 90 days, were to undergo only a national agency check.   A major change, necessitated by Executive Order 10450, of April 27, 1953, which had eliminated the Regional Loyalty Boards and the Loyalty Review Board, provided that reports of full field investigations be forwarded through the Civil Service Commission to an International Organizations Employees Loyalty Board.   Persons against whom there is derogatory information are availed an opportunity for a hearing before this Board.   The Board's determinations "with the reasons therefor stated in as much detail as the Board determines that security considerations permit" are transmitted as advisory opinions to the Secretary General through the Secretary of State.   The standard followed by the Board is the same as that provided in Executive Order 10422 for the guidance of the Regional Loyalty Boards and Loyalty Review Board.

Executive Order 10459 established in the Civil Service Commission an International Organizations Employees Loyalty Board "of not less than three impartial persons, the members of which shall be officers or employees of the Commission," to perform the functions of the defunct Regional Loyalty Boards and Loyalty Review Board.

The planned procedure under the confidential arrangement of 1949 differed in five major respects from that envisioned under Executive Order 10422.   First, and foremost, the old secret arrangement applied to United Nations Secretariat employees only.   It did not even extend to the specialized agencies of the United Nations.   Executive Order 10422, as amended, extended the security arrangements to United States nationals employed by all international organizations to which the United States was a member.   Moreover, the United States would now be able to give "clearance"—something not done under the old arrangement.   Authority now existed which would permit the establishment of formal investigative processes "comparable to those for Federal employees."   American employees had their rights better protected through the creation of hearings and appeals processes.   Lastly, the Secretary General was now to be afforded information upon which to justify his actions.[82]

---

[82] American citizens in the U. N. Secretariat: Department announcement of forthcoming Executive order, *Department of State Bulletin*, vol. 28, Jan. 12, 1953, pp. 61–62.

Assembly Consideration and Commentary on Report of Secretary General

Secretary General Trygve Lie's report on personnel policy, presented to the General Assembly on March 10, 1953, was followed by a full-scale debate in plenary session which resulted in an Assembly resolution expressing confidence in the Secretary General.

During the 4-day debate, most of the members evinced general support for the principles expressed in Mr. Lie's report—not without some reservations, however. Divergent views were expressed on the employment by the United Nations of anyone taking refuge in the fifth amendment. It was agreed that no grounds existed to support the charge that the United Nations was a "nest of spies." [83]

In a statement before the General Assembly, March 28, 1953, Ambassador Henry Cabot Lodge, Jr., attempted to defend the position of the United States and the report of the Secretary General with regard to American citizens in the employ of the United Nations.

Lodge stated that the United Nations could only be an effective force if it were supported by world public opinion. Senator Wiley, chairman of the Senate Foreign Relations Committee, had aptly expressed the prevailing opinion in the United States when he said that, "There is absolutely no place in the international Secretariat for a single American Communist or any American of doubtful loyalty . . . the United Nations should not become a haven for disloyal Americans or for espionage."

Ambassador Lodge noted in his address the request of the Secretary General that he be furnished information on current and prospective United States employees of the Secretariat to enable him better to assure that Charter standards were being met. Ambassador Lodge said the American Government agreed to do this. The information furnished the Secretary General would be regarded by the United States only as advice.

The American Ambassador assured the delegates to the Assembly that the United States was firmly convinced that the independence of the Secretariat had to be maintained. Moreover, the United States recognized the right of individuals to disagree with the policies of their governments, and that they should not be penalized for so doing. It was not the concern of the United States whether a man was a "Republican or Democrat or independent, so long as he meets the Charter standards of efficiency, competence, and integrity." Although Ambassador Lodge disagreed with several points in the Secretary General's report, on the whole he found it acceptable.[84]

Ambassador Lodge summarized the United States position as follows:

> The United States Government does not believe that persons engaged or who, based on their past and present record, seem likely to engage in subversive activities against any

---

[83] Assembly Votes Confidence in Direction of Personnel Policy, *United Nations Bulletin*, vol. 14, Apr. 15, 1953, pp. 269–72 ff.

[84] Henry Cabot Lodge, Jr., Maintaining Charter Standards for International Civil Servants, *Department of State Bulletin*, vol. 28, Apr. 27, 1953, pp. 620–23.

member state should be employed in an international organization. We will do all in our power to provide the Secretary General with the information necessary to enable him to make a determination on this matter. This does not constitute, nor is it intended to constitute, dictation to the Secretary General or other member governments. It is a service to the United Nations in the interest of maintaining a Secretariat which measures up to standards established in the Charter for international civil servants." [85]

As debate in the Assembly continued, Leslie Knox Munro, of New Zealand, supported the principle of a truly independent Secretariat. It was his contention that the broad membership of the Organization precluded it from acting "covertly." He continued: "Given the nature of the Organization's activities, there could be no good reason for any host state to use its sovereign powers in any way which interferred with the Organization's freedom."

The New Zealand representative warned that if national authorities attempted to exercise control over their nationals employed by the United Nations that the result would be the disintegration of the Secretariat into a "diplomatic corps of national groups, each playing for its own hand, and united by no moral bond stronger than the fact of being paid from a single budget and housed in a single building. . . ." [86]

Speaking for the Netherlands, Daniel Von Balluseck agreed that governments assuredly had the right to prohibit the affiliation of its own employees with any group, party or association, but that "an international organization could not and should not apply the different and changing national standards of each and all its members." He was of the contention that there should be established one international standard based on "the laws and interests of the Organization as a whole." Mr. Von Balluseck suggested the possibility of prohibiting members of the Secretariat from being members of any political party while in international service. [87]

Arne Lundberg, of Sweden, was also critical of the Secretary General's report. Lundberg was of the opinion that findings by member states, in extrajudicial proceedings, relative to the political activities of their nationals, members of the Secretariat, could not and should not be binding on the United Nations as a valid reason for discharge. [88]

Sir Gladwyn Jebb, of the United Kingdom, although giving support to the Secretary General in principle, felt that too much stress had been placed on the "special" position to be accorded a "host" state. It was his opinion that the jurists were overly concerned with the allegiance of staff members to their own governments and made "too little allowance for their allegiance to the international organization in which they worked." [89]

A number of other delegates spoke in defense of the Secretary General. Representatives of Poland and Byelorussia, however, were highly critical of Mr. Lie's personnel policies. They charged him with damaging the international character of the Secretariat and implied that Lie was a tool of

[85] Ibid.
[86] Assembly votes confidence . . ., *United Nations Bulletin*, Apr. 15, 1953, loc. cit.
[87] Ibid.
[88] Ibid.
[89] Ibid.

399

the United States and that he conducted "a purge" in the Secretariat on "the mere suspicion of so-called subversive activities." [90]

At the conclusion of the debate, a resolution was passed expressing confidence that the Secretary General would conduct his policies in accordance with the provisions of articles 100 and 101 of the Charter. Furthermore the Secretary General was requested to submit to the eighth session of the General Assembly a progress report on his personnel policy, and to make recommendations as "to further action that may be required of the General Assembly." [91]

Judgments of the Administrative Tribunal

In 1952, during the inquiries of the New York Federal grand jury and the Senate Internal Security Subcommittee, a number of United Nations temporary employees of United States citizenship were dismissed and certain permanent employees placed on compulsory leave by Secretary General Trygve Lie for their refusal to testify on the grounds of self-incrimination before these authorized agencies of the United States Government. The employment of those placed on compulsory leave was later terminated by the Secretary General following the recommendations of the Commission of Jurists.

The cases of 21 former United Nations staff members of United States nationality were appealed to the Administrative Tribunal of the United Nations on the contention that their discharge was illegal. Ten cases involved terminations of temporary appointments; 10 of permanent appointments; and 1 of summary dismissal of a permanent appointment for serious misconduct.

The seven-member Administrative Tribunal had been established by the General Assembly in 1949 with power to hear and pass judgment upon applications alleging nonobservance of contract and terms of appointment. Of the 7-member panel, no 2 could be nationals of the same state. The members of the Tribunal which dealt with the cases involving Americans of "doubtful loyalty" were: President, Madame Paul Bastid, of France; Lord Crook, of the United Kingdom; Sture Petren, of Sweden—vice presidents; and Omar Loutfi, of Egypt, alternate.[92]

Disputes involving the competence of the Tribunal were to be settled by the Tribunal itself. If the Secretary General determined the acceptance of a Tribunal order to be inadvisable or impossible under the original statute of the Tribunal, the Tribunal was to assess the amount of damages to be be paid by the United Nations.[93]

---

[90] Ibid.

[91] Ibid.

[92] Administrative Tribunal Delivers Opinions on Terminations, *United Nations Bulletin*, vol. 15, Sept. 15, 1953, p. 223.

[93] United Nations Administrative Tribunal statute and rules.

400

Of the 21 appeals by United States nationals, the action of the Secretary General was sustained in 9 of the cases involving temporary employees; in 1 case involving a temporary employee and in the 10 cases involving permanent employees, the Tribunal's rulings were against the Secretary General. Of the 11 cases which held for the employees, 4 of the findings provided for reinstatement, the balance to receive monetary awards. In the cases of the four ordered reinstated, Secretary General Lie refused reinstatement, referring the cases back to the Tribunal to determine damages on September 2. The Tribunal handed down compensation awards October 13.

The Tribunal found for the Secretary General in the cases of Kaplan, Middleton, Rubin, Kagen-Pozner, Sokolow, Saperstein, Van Tassel, and Marjorie and Herman Zap; the four ordered reinstated were Crawford, Svenchansky, Eldridge, and Glaser; monetary awards were given Gordon, Harris, Glassman, Older, Bancroft, Elveson, and Reed. The summary dismissal case of Eugene Wallach was ordered back to the Joint Appeals Board, since the Administrative Tribunal considered the original proceedings before the Board to be irregular and thus invalid.

The Secretary General has the option of refusing reinstatement under the statute of the Tribunal where he considers reinstatement inadvisable. The total amount of damages awarded by the Tribunal, including the four cases remanded by the Secretary General after refusal to reinstate, was $170,730, plus $300 for legal costs in each case.[94]

The decisions of the Administrative Tribunal were in part based on the following considerations. The Tribunal was of the opinion that the Secretary General was invested under staff regulations with discretionary powers in the termination of temporary appointments; however, such discretionary powers had to be exercised without improper motives. In refusing to recognize party membership as constituting grounds for dismissal, the Administrative Tribunal noted that staff regulation 1.4 recognized the right of staff members not to give up their political convictions. Therefore, it was the opinion of the Tribunal that membership in any particular party was not, of itself, justification for dismissal in the absence of other cause. The Tribunal held that permanent appointments could be terminated only in accordance with staff regulations; thus the Secretary General was obligated to indicate under which provision he was acting. The Tribunal was critical of the opinion of the Commission of Jurists which held that the Secretary General could go beyond the provisions of the staff regulations in terminating contracts of staff members—such was held to be in opposition to the nature of contracts and the regulations governing the same as established by the General Assembly. The term "unsatisfactory services" was considered not to apply to acts outside a staff member's official duties.

The Secretary General had dismissed a number of staff members for invoking the fifth amendment. The Administrative Tribunal pointed out that:

---

[94] AT/DEC/29, 31, 33–37, 39–42.

"Misconduct punishable under staff regulation 10 could be either misconduct committed in the exercise of a staff member's professional duties or acts committed outside his professional activities but prohibited by provisions creating general obligations for staff members. . . ." The Tribunal rejected the contention that resort to the fifth amendment constituted "serious misconduct." It noted the failure of any resort to pleading privilege to result in subsequent legal action. Moreover, the Tribunal stated: "This provision of the Constitution may be properly invoked in various situations which, because of the complexity of the case law, cannot be summarized in a simple formula." Continuing in the same vein, the Tribunal recalled that the Secretary General had paid termination indemnities to those summarily dismissed—a payment which was expressly forbidden by the staff regulations. In commenting on this action, the Tribunal stated: "The nature of serious misconduct appeared so disputable to the Secretary General that he granted termination indemnities, which are expressly forbidden by the staff regulations (annex III) in cases of summary dismissal." [95]

United States reaction to the judgments of the Administrative Tribunal was immediate and highly critical. Ambassador Lodge, testifying before the Senate Internal Security Subcommittee, on September 24, stated that he considered the turn of events to be "unjust and wrong and full of danger to the future of the United Nations." He observed that although the United States voted for the establishment of the Tribunal in 1949, originally the United States representatives had opposed the measure.

Ambassador Lodge was especially critical of the lack of United States representation on the Tribunal. "I think it is a very serious thing. When you stop to think of it, the spectacle of four foreign lawyers, sitting in Geneva, to interpret article [sic] 5 of the Constitution of the United States without any American representation being there, is in itself a fantastic contemplation. In addition, the fact that these individuals are making decisions which have a very great interest for American public opinion, without having a really correct understanding of the state of that public opinion, is in itself a most unsound device." [96]

The Ambassador stated that the United States delegation would try to get the staff regulations changed by the General Assembly so that the decisions of the Secretary General would be final. With respect to the rulings of the Administrative Tribunal, it was the opinion of the Legal Adviser in the Department of State that the General Assembly could overrule the Tribunal. However, this opinion was not shared by many other members of the United Nations.[97]

---

[95] AT/DEC/29 to 37.

[96] U. S. Senate. 83d Cong., 1st sess. hearings before the subcommittee to investigate the administration of the Internal Security Act . . . on activities of United States citizens employed by the United Nations, pt. 3, Sept. 24, 1953, pp. 496–497.

[97] Ibid., p. 498.

Report of the Secretary General on Personnel Policy, November 2, 1953

The debate of the General Assembly on Trygve Lie's report on the personnel policy of the Secretary General during the second part of the Seventh Session of the General Assembly resulted in the adoption of resolution 708 (VII). The resolution reviewed articles 100 and 101 of the Charter and then expressed confidence that the Secretary General would keep these points in mind when conducting the personnel policies of the Secretariat. A further report on personnel policy was requested by the Assembly.

Secretary General Dag Hammarskjold consequently submitted a report on personnel policy to the eighth session of the General Assembly on November 2, 1953. [98]

In the light of the judgment handed down by the Administrative Tribunal in the 21 cases involving United States nationals, Dag Hammarskjold made several recommendations to the General Assembly in an effort to strengthen his position as administrative head of the Secretariat. One point of special controversy involved the proper limits of permissible political activity on the part of staff members. Mr. Hammarskjold, in his report to the Assembly, stated that the political activity of a staff member of the United Nations, other than for criminal or subversive activity, should not "reflect unfavorably," ipso facto, on such employees—nor should such activity be regarded as "unsatisfactory service" or "misconduct." However, Secretary General Hammarskjold felt the relationship of the Secretariat with member states was such that it might be inadvisable for United Nations employees to engage in political activities. He stated that the decision as to the degree of permissible political activity should be that of the Secretary General, and that the decision should be free from arbitrariness and discrimination. If a staff member disagreed with the decision of the Secretary General, it was Hammarskjold's contention that "such a staff member [should] choose between continuing his political activities or remaining an employee of the United Nations." On this point, the Secretary General felt that the then current staff regulations provided him with only doubtful powers to make these decisions. He recommended that an explicit statement be added to the regulations prohibiting political activities other than voting "unless otherwise authorized in accordance with staff rules issued by the Secretary General." [99]

Hammarskjold considered that the phrases "unsatisfactory service" and "misconduct" were too limiting as bases of his removal powers. He recommended that an additional basis for removal should be "lack of integrity." This would give him more discretionary powers. The decision as to what constituted "lack of integrity" would be his based on the established facts and

---

[98] Dag Hammarskjold replaced Trygve Lie as Secretary General of the United Nations early in Apr. 1953.

[99] U. S. Senate. 83d Cong., 2d sess., review of the United Nations Charter: a collection of documents, subcommittee on the United Nations Charter, pursuant to S. Res. 126, doc. No. 87, p. 239.

his opinion as to their effects on the requirements of sound administration. The Administrative Tribunal would have the power to determine whether the Secretary General acted in an arbitrary manner. However, Hammarskjold stated that the Tribunal should accept his interpretations and evaluations as to what constituted "lack of integrity" and "political activity," inasmuch as such decisions involved considerations of administrative policy not open to a strictly legal review. It was hoped that the decisions of the Secretary General would gradually evolve into a body of principles which would be subject to review by the Administrative Tribunal.[100]

The Secretary General recommended, in addition to an amendment which would authorize the "termination of a permanent appointment if the Secretary General determines . . . that a staff member has shown lack of integrity," that there also be an amendment providing for termination "in the interest of good administration of the Organization" justifiable under the Charter standards.[101]

Acting on the report of the Secretary General, the General Assembly approved the following amendments to the staff regulations to give the Secretary General the additional powers requested:

Staff regulation 1.4 (*amended text*):
Members of the Secretariat shall conduct themselves at all times in a manner befitting their status as international civil servants. They shall not engage in any activity that is incompatible with the proper discharge of their duties with the United Nations. They shall avoid any action and in particular any kind of public pronouncement which may adversely reflect on their status, or on the integrity, independence and impartiality which are required by that status. While they are not expected to give up their national sentiments or their political and religious convictions, they shall at all times bear in mind the reserve and tact incumbent upon them by reason of their international status.

Staff regulation 1.7 (*amended text*):
Staff members may exercise the right to vote but shall not engage in any political activity which is inconsistent with or might reflect upon the independence and impartiality required by their status as international civil servants.

Staff regulation 9.1 (a) (*additional provisions*):
The Secretary General may also, giving his reasons therefor, terminate the appointment of a staff member who holds a permanent appointment—
(i) If the conduct of the staff member indicates that the staff member does not meet the highest standards of integrity required by article 101, paragraph 3, of the Charter;
(ii) If facts anterior to the appointment of the staff member and relevant to his suitability come to light which, if they had been known at the time of his appointment, should, under the standards established in the Charter, have precluded his appointment.

No termination under subparagraphs (i) and (ii) shall take place until the matter has been considered and reported on by a special advisory board appointed for that purpose by the Secretary General.

---

[100] Ibid., pp. 240–241.

[101] U. S. Senate. 83d Cong., 2d sess., review of the United Nations Charter: a collection of documents, subcommittee on the United Nations Charter, pursuant to S. Res. 126, doc. No. 87, Jan. 7, 1954, pp. 242–243. pp. 242–243.

Finally, the Secretary General may terminate the appointment of a staff member who holds a permanent appointment if such action would be in the interest of the good administration of the Organization and in accordance with the standards of the Charter, provided that the action is not contested by the staff member concerned.

Staff regulation 9.3 (b) (*additional paragraph*):

> The Secretary General may, where the circumstances warrant and he considers it justified, pay to a staff member terminated under the final paragraph of staff regulation 9.1 (a) a termination indemnity payment not more than 50 percent higher than that which would otherwise be payable under the staff regulations.[102]

With these additional powers, Secretary General Hammarskjold hoped that he would be able to dismiss an employee despite lack of sufficient evidence to convict in court—dismissal could now be hinged on the unsuitability of continued employment as evidenced by the facts.[103]

Aftermath of Judgments of Administrative Tribunal

The United States considered the judgments of the Administrative Tribunal to be prejudicial to its interests and sought to have the General Assembly annul the rulings of the Tribunal which had reinstated or awarded damages to dismissed loyalty risks on the contention that the Tribunal was subordinate to the General Assembly. The United States strongly protested the payment of damages to the 11 staff members of doubtful loyalty to the United States awarded by the Tribunal. Four arguments were offered to substantiate the United States position. The United States was of the opinion that the General Assembly had not only a legal right but also a responsibility to review and refuse to effect the decisions of the Tribunal, inasmuch as the Tribunal was a creature of the Assembly. Moreover, the Tribunal, it was averred, had exceeded its powers and misinterpreted its rules. A further charge was that the Tribunal had made serious errors of law in the application of staff regulations. Lastly, the United States considered that the Tribunal had made errors of judgment and fact in calculating the amounts of the awards.[104]

It was the considered opinion of the United States that the Administrative Tribunal was not a court, but rather a subsidiary body to the General Assembly which could be abolished at the discretion of the Assembly. Since such was the case, it followed that the Assembly could take less stringent measures and merely review the judgments of the Tribunal for possible revision.

In offering additional arguments in an effort to prevent the payment of monetary awards to United States citizens of doubtful loyalty, the United States noted that budgetary power lay with the Assembly. Since it would

---

[102] United Nations. Staff rules: Staff regulations of the United Nations and staff rules 101.1 to 112.8, *Secretary General's Bulletin*, ST/SGB/Rev. 4, 1955, pp. 4, 5, 47–48.

[103] U. S. Senate. 83d Cong., 2d sess., review of the United Nations Charter . . ., doc. No. 87, pp. 242–243

[104] *Yearbook of the United Nations*, 1953, p. 82.

not relinquish the same to the Tribunal, the Assembly could thus refuse to appropriate money to pay the awards.

Some member states agreed with the United States view that the Tribunal was subject to Assembly control. A strong argument supporting the American position was that the Secretary General was chief administrative officer of 1 of the 6 major organs of the United Nations, and was granted extensive powers by the Charter. Thus it was inconceivable that he would be subject to control by a subsidiary organ of the General Assembly.

The United States was not unopposed in its views, however. Many members felt that judgments of the Administrative Tribunal, if in accord with its statute, were final and without further appeal, and, moreover, the Assembly was legally bound to effectuate the awards as determined by the Tribunal. Their argument was that no principle existed under law to justify the refusal to pay compensation already awarded by the Tribunal, and that, for the sake of the prestige of the Organization, it had no alternative other than to comply with the judgments of the Tribunal; that to do otherwise would establish precedents dangerous to the moral authority of the United Nations, and influence future actions of member states when judgments of judicial bodies went against them.[105]

The General Assembly finally agreed to the passage of resolution 785A (VIII) which provided that the Assembly would ". . . submit the following legal questions to the International Court of Justice for an advisory opinion:

(1) Having regard to the statute of the United Nations Administrative Tribunal and to any other relevant instruments and to the relevant records, has the General Assembly the right on any grounds to refuse to give effect to an award of compensation made by that Tribunal in favor of a staff member of the United Nations whose contract of service has been terminated without his assent? (2) If the answer given by the Court to question (1) is in the affirmative, what are the principal grounds upon which the General Assembly could lawfully exercise such a right?

Advisory Opinion of International Court of Justice

The opinion of the Court was delivered on July 13, 1954, 9 to 3 in favor of the Tribunal. The three judges dissenting from the majority view were Judges Alvarez, Hackworth, and Carneiro.

Basically, the opinion of the Court was that the Assembly did not have the right on any grounds whatever to refuse to give effect to an award of compensation rendered by the Administrative Tribunal to a staff member whose contract of employment had been terminated without his assent. It was unnecessary for the Court to answer the second question submitted.

Several major considerations led the Court to form its opinion. For one thing, article 10 of the Tribunal's statute provided that: "Judgments shall be final and without appeal," and ". . . shall state the reasons on which they

---

[105] Ibid., p. 105.83–84.

are based." This the Court interpreted as establishing a truly judicial body; the judicial character of the Tribunal was confirmed by granting powers to rescind decisions of the Secretary General. In the opinion of the Court, no such power could have been conferred on a purely advisory or subordinate organ.[106]

The General Assembly, in the Court's opinion, was bound by the judgment of the Tribunal according to an established and accepted principle of law under which a judgment rendered by a judicial body is res judicata and has binding force between all parties to a dispute. With regard to the argument that the establishment of such a Tribunal was inconsistent with the exercise of the General Assembly's budgetary powers, the International Court noted that the budgetary power was not absolute. Thus if an expenditure arose out of an obligation, the Assembly had no alternative other than to honor its obligations.[107]

The United States insistence on the supremacy of the General Assembly to review the Tribunal's decisions was not upheld by the Court.

United States Reaction and Results Thereof

Reaction in the United States to the opinion of the International Court of Justice was almost immediate. The 83d Congress on August 20, 1954, passed House Resolution 262, wherein it was—

Resolved by the House of Representatives (the Senate concurring), That it is the sense of the Congress that the United States delegation to the United Nations should take all possible steps to prevent the General Assembly of the United Nations from authorizing or approving the payment, to the 11 American employees in the United Nations who were dismissed because of their refusal under the fifth amendment to answer proper questions before the Internal Security Subcommittee of the Senate, of the awards of damages (in a total amount of $179,420) made by the United Nations Administrative Tribunal and recently upheld by the International Court of Justice, and that no part of the funds heretofore appropriated, or hereafter appropriated by the Congress of the United States shall be used for the payment of such awards.

During the ninth session of the General Assembly, the United States delegation directed its energies against the injustice of the Tribunal awards. However, no attempt was made to defy openly the ruling of the International Court of Justice. As explained by Ambassador Lodge, to do so would have left the United States alone in the battle, inasmuch as the other members accepted the opinion of the Court. Moreover, any attempt on the part of the United States to defy the Court would have been powerful propaganda for the Soviet Union. The United States frequently challenges the Soviet Union to submit questions in dispute to the International Court. The inabil-

---

[106] Effect of awards of compensation made by the United Nations Administrative Tribunal, advisory opinion of July 13, 1954: International Court of Justice reports, 1954, pp. 50–53.
[107] Ibid., p. 53.

ity of the Soviet Union (or its unwillingness) to accept these United States proposals exposes the true nature of the Soviets to the world—therefore the United States could not afford to undermine the Court.[108]

After accepting the opinion of the Court that the Assembly was obligated to effect the decisions of the Administrative Tribunal, the American delegation fought to have a special fund established, contributed to by the employees, and not financed at all by the United States, from which to pay the awards. The United States also argued for the principle of judicial review over Tribunal awards. Both efforts were successful.

Considering the advisory opinion of the International Court of Justice which had held that, under the then current statute of the Administrative Tribunal, the General Assembly was obligated to effectuate the awards of the Tribunal, the Assembly passed resolution 888 (IX) on December 17, 1954, under which the principle of judicial review of the judgments of the Tribunal was accepted. Member states were requested to communicate to the Secretary General before July 1, 1955, "their views on the establishment of procedures to provide for review of the judgments of the Administrative Tribunal and to submit any suggestions which they may consider useful"; the Secretary General was invited to consult on the matter with the specialized agencies concerned; and finally there was established a special committee composed of Argentina, Australia, Belgium, Brazil, Canada, China, Cuba, El Salvador, France, India, Iraq, Israel, Norway, Pakistan, Syria, the Union of Soviet Socialist Republics, the United Kingdom of Great Britain and Northern Ireland, and the United States, to study the question of the establishment of procedures to provide for the review of the judgments of the Tribunal in all aspects and report to the Assembly at its 10th session.[109]

Primarily due to the efforts of the United States, the General Assembly passed a resolution which, in part, established a special indemnity fund as of January 1, 1955, to which the Secretary General was authorized to transfer $250,000 from staff assessments. A system of staff assessments had earlier been initiated in the Secretariat to which all staff members contributed in lieu of national income taxes. It was from this fund that money was to be taken to build the special indemnity fund from which all awards for compensation rendered by the Administrative Tribunal were to be paid. Such measure was to meet the objection of the United States to paying the awards out of regular United Nations funds—funds to which the United States contributes over one-third—since that would have resulted in using United States contributions indirectly to pay the awards rendered to Americans suspected of being disloyal to the United States.[110]

[108] U. S. House of Representaitves. 84th Cong., 1st sess., extension of remarks of Hon. Harold Ostertag. *Congressional Record* (daily edition, March 16, 1955, pp. A1787–1788.)
[109] *Yearbook of the United Nations*, 1954, p. 447.
[110] Ibid.

Report of the Secretary General on Personnel Policy to the Ninth Session of the General Assembly

October 28, 1954, the Secretary General presented a report on personnel policies to the ninth session of the General Assembly. Mr. Hammarskjold informed the Assembly that pursuant to its resolution 782 A (VIII), he had on March 15, 1954, created a five-member Special Advisory Board. Under the new arrangement, when allegations are made against any staff member, the Secretary General conducts a formal examination to determine the reliability of the source and whether the charges are of a sufficiently serious nature to warrant referral to the Special Advisory Board. If the source of the allegation was considered reliable and the charges sufficiently serious, the matter would be turned over to the Board. A function of the Board is to determine whether subparagraph (i) and/or (ii) of staff regulations 9.1 (a) apply in each case.

The Secretary General pointed out that "The Board was not a tribunal and would not decide upon, or even recommend, termination." It could however, suggest, under exceptional circumstances, that the Secretary General, at his discretion, "refrain from acting on the basis of the subparagraph which it might find to be applicable." After the Board determines which regulation is relevant, the responsibility for making the decision is in the hands of the Secretary General.

Dag Hammarskjold further informed the Assembly that inasmuch as the Special Advisory Board had taken over the functions of the Secretary General's advisory panel, that body had been discontinued.[111]

United States Reaction to the International Civil Service Advisory Board's Report on Standards of Conduct

In 1954, the International Civil Service Advisory Board released a report on standards of conduct in the international civil service. The Board was established by the Assembly in 1946 merely to *advise* "on the methods of recruitment for the Secretariat and on the means by which common standards of recruitment in the Secretariat and the specialized agencies may be insured." It has no power to enforce its recommendations.

In its 1954 report, the Board enumerated certain basic standards to be met by international civil servants. Among these were integrity, international outlook and independence, and impartiality. It was the considered opinion of the Board that staff members should avoid any action which would reflect on the name of the Secretariat, impair good relations between the organiza-

[111] United Nations General Assembly. Ninth session, personnel policy of the United Nations: Report of the Secretary-General, doc. A/2777, Oct. 28, 1954.

tion and member states, or destroy the confidence in the organization. It stated, ". . . any direct or indirect activity with a view to the overthrow of a government by force, including incitement or advocacy of such overthrow, is one of the gravest forms of misconduct." [112]

The report referred to possible conflict between national and international loyalties, concluding that under such circumstances ". . . the conduct of the international civil servant must clearly reflect his obligation to the international organization, and any appearance of disloyalty to that organization must be considered incompatible with his status. Acceptance of this principle may be made easier by the understanding that, from the long range point of view, legitimate national interests can only be served by the promotion of world peace and prosperity and the successful progress of the international organizations toward these objectives." It was the opinion of the Board that any staff member who could not accept this view was obligated to resign.[113]

The Board sought to emphasize two major points. First, that international organizations are made up of member states and that each secretariat is a service not a policymaking or controlling organ. Secondly, the function of the secretariat is to assist the representative organs in their work and in implementing their decisions.

On the question of the proper relations between staff members and governments, the Board pointed out that international civil servants are under no circumstances relieved of their obligations of citizenship "in matters unrelated to the work or interests of the international organization he serves." The executive head of the Secretariat will determine the matters related to the work and interest of the Organization, in the opinion of the Board.[114]

The report considered that staff members had the right to vote, but should refrain from political activities. Moreover, no staff member was to belong to a political party which was *illegal* in his own country. Also, the Board continued, "membership in any group, whether political or not, which imposes on the staff member an obligation to action incompatible with his oath of office and responsibilities as an international civil servant must be ruled out." [115]

Recent Developments at the United Nations

The special committee established under resolution 888 (IX), December 17, 1954, to study the question of procedures to provide for the review of judgments of the Administrative Tribunal made its report to the 10th session

---

[112] United Nations. International Civil Service Advisory Board, report on standards of conduct in the International Civil Service, COORD/Civil Service/5, 1954, p. 8.
[113] Ibid.
[114] Ibid., p. 11.
[115] Ibid., p. 11.

of the Assembly. The committee proposed that the Assembly create a screening committee which would have the power to request advisory opinions from the International Court of Justice. Individual member states were to be permitted to present their views regarding Tribunal judgments before this screening committee. If after a judgment of the Tribunal, the staff member involved, the Secretary General or any member state disapproved of the Tribunal's judgment, application could be made to the screening committee to request of the International Court an advisory opinion reviewing the judgment of the Tribunal.

The recommendations of the special committee were submitted to committee V of the Assembly for consideration. Some members objected to permitting member states the right to request review, since these members had no legitimate part of the dispute between the Secretary General, his staff and their relations with the Administrative Tribunal. Chester E. Merrow argued the United States case for the right to petition the screening committee on moral and legal grounds, i. e., each party should have equal rights before the screening committee.

On November 8, 1955, the General Assembly adopted a resolution amending the statute of the Administrative Tribunal. Any member state, the Secretary General, or an individual involved with a judgment of the Administrative Tribunal could, if in his opinion the Tribunal had exceeded its jurisdiction, or erred on the law or procedure, apply within 30 days to a screening committee made up of member-states representatives and request that the committee seek an advisory opinion of the International Court of Justice on the matter. Within 30 days after receipt of the petition, the committee was to decide whether there existed a substantial basis for the application. After submission of the case to the Court for an advisory opinion and after the rendering of such opinion, the Tribunal was to be directed to bring its judgment into conformity with the advisory opinion of the Court. The Secretary General was given the authority to advance one-third of the Tribunal's award to the staff member, so as not to handicap the employee while the above procedures were underway. However, if the Court ruled against the staff member, the money had to be returned. Either the staff member or the Secretary General could petition the Tribunal for a revision of the judgment if further evidence turned up within 1 year after judgment and 30 days after discovering the additional information. Subject to these provisions, the judgments of the Administrative Tribunal are final and without appeal. The Assembly resolution establishing the procedures further recommended that member states and the Secretary General refrain from making oral statements before the International Court of Justice.

LEGAL BASIS

I. Articles 100 and 101 of the United Nations Charter read as follows:

ARTICLE 100

1. In the performance of their duties the Secretary-General and the staff shall not seek or receive instructions from any government or from any other authority external to the Organization. They shall refrain from any action which might reflect on their position as international officials responsible only to the Organization.

2. Each member of the United Nations undertakes to respect the exclusively international character of the responsibilities of the Secretary-General and the staff and not to seek to influence them in the discharge of their responsibilities.

ARTICLE 101

1. The staff shall be appointed by the Secretary-General under regulations established by the General Assembly.

2. Appropriate staffs shall be permanently assigned to the Economic and Social Council, the Trusteeship Council, and, as required, to other organs of the United Nations. These staffs shall form a part of the Secretariat.

3. The paramount consideration in the employment of the staff and in the determination of the conditions of service shall be the necessity of securing the highest standards of efficiency, competence and integrity. Due regard shall be paid to the importance of recruiting the staff on as wide a geographical basis as possible.[116]

II. Executive Order 10422 issued by President Truman January 9, 1953,[117] as amended by Executive Order 10459 issued by President Eisenhower June 2, 1953,[118] prescribes procedures for making available to the Secretary-General of the United Nations certain information concerning United States citizens employed or being considered for employment on the Secretariat of the United Nations.

III. The provisions of Executive Order 10422, as amended by Executive Order 10459, are, by its terms, applicable to United States citizens who are employees of or are being considered for employment by other public international organizations of which the United States Government is a member "by arrangement between the executive head of the international organization concerned and the Secretary of State or other officer of the United States designated by the President."

IV. Executive Order 10422 recites:

(1) That the United States has ratified the Charter of the United Nations and is participating in the activities of the United Nations by virtue of the ratification of the said Charter and of the authority granted by the United Nations Participation Act of 1945; [119]

(2) That a Commission of Jurists has advised the Secretary-General of the United Nations that he should regard it as of the first im-

---

[116] 59 Stat. 1031, arts. 100 and 101 at p. 1052.

[117] 3 C. F. R., 1953, Supp., p. 57.

[118] 3 C. F. R., 1953, Supp., p. 81.

[119] 59 Stat. 619, as amended by 63 Stat. 734, 22 U. S. C. A. 287.

portance to refrain from employing, or to dismiss from employment, any United States citizen who he has reasonable ground for
believing has been, is, or is likely to be engaged in espionage or
subversive activities against the United States;

(3) That the Commission of Jurists has also advised that the United
States should make available to the Secretary-General information
on which he can make his determination as to whether reasonable
grounds exist for believing that a United States citizen employed,
or being considered for employment, has been, or is likely to be
engaged in espionage or subversive activities against the United
States;

(4) That the Commission has further advised that the independence
of the Secretary-General and his sole responsibility to the General
Assembly of the United Nations for the selection and retention of
staff should be recognized by all member nations;

(5) That the Secretary-General has declared his intention to use the
conclusions and recommendations of the opinion of the said Commission of Jurists as the basis of his personnel policy in discharging
the responsibility entrusted to him by the Charter and staff
regulations of the United Nations;

(6) That, in the participation by the United States in the activities of
the United Nations, it is in the interest of the United States that
its citizens who are employees of the Secretariat be persons of the
highest integrity, and not persons who have been or are likely to
be engaged in espionage or subversive activities against the United
States; and

(7) That it is in the interest of the United States to establish a procedure for the acquisition of information by investigation, and for
its transmission to the Secretary-General, in order to assist the
Secretary-General in the exercise of his responsibility for determining whether any United States citizen employed, or being employed, or being considered for employment, has been, is, or is
likely to be engaged in espionage or subversive activities against
the United States.

V. The Executive order states that it is issued "by virtue of the authority
vested in me by the Constitution, statutes and treaties of the United States,
including the Charter of the United Nations, and as President of the United
States."

VI. Paragraph 3 of Article 101 of the Charter quoted above states that
a paramount consideration in the employment of the staff shall be the necessity of securing "the highest standards of efficiency, competency and
integrity." [Italic supplied.]

The United Nations staff rules, as amended, give the Secretary-General
the power to base dismissals on "lack of integrity" or "in the interest of
good administration of the organization."

413

VII. Two legal questions arise in respect to the validity of Executive Order 10422, as amended by Executive Order 10459, namely:

(1) Does the program embodied in the Executive order violate Article 100 of the United Nations Charter as an impingement upon the independence of the Secretariat, or Article 101 of the Charter vesting responsibility for the appointment of the staff in the Secretary-General?

(2) Is the order within the constitutional power of the President?

VIII. As above noted, Section 3 of Article 101 of the Charter specifically states that the paramount consideration in the employment of the staff of the Secretariat shall be the necessity of securing the highest standards of efficiency, competency and integrity.

It would be difficult to reconcile the concepts of integrity and disloyalty. A person who was disloyal to his own country, who had engaged in or was likely to engage in espionage or other form of subversive activity would in all reasonable probability be lacking in the trustworthiness necessary to discharge his responsibility as an official or employee of the Secretariat of the United Nations.

The Commission of Jurists, to which the Secretary-General had turned for advice, recognized that a disloyal or subversive person should not be employed or retained in employment by the Secretariat.[120]

The Commission of Jurists, while specifically recognizing the obligation of each member nation to respect the independence of the Secretariat, specifically recommended that subversives should not be employed, and that it was the duty of member nations to make available to the Secretary-General information as to the subversive activity of employees or prospective employees.

It is generally believed that the United States, in making information available to the Secretariat as to United States citizens who are employed or are seeking employment by the United Nations, is not violating any provisions of the United Nations Charter respecting the independence of the Secretariat.

On the contrary, such a procedure is calculated to implement and to carry out the provisions of the treaty requiring the employment of persons of integrity.

It is to be noted that the Secretary-General retains exclusively the power of appointment and dismissal, and that the information furnished him through the loyalty program is merely for the purpose of giving him information relevant to his determination as to the fitness or unfitness of any employee or prospective employee.

Prior to the issuance of Executive Order 10422, the United States had furnished information to the Secretariat pursuant to an informal arrangement between the Department of State and officials of the United Nations.

---

[120] United Nations General Assembly, Seventh Session, Agenda Item 75, A/2264, January 30, 1953, Report of the Secretary General, Annex III.

Mr. Hickerson, an official of the State Department, testified at a hearing before the Subcommittee on Internal Security of the Committee on the Judiciary, United States Senate, on December 10, 1952, in the course of which the following comment was made:

Senator FERGUSON. When you say you had a tentative agreement, you certainly were not violating Section 101 or 100 by giving the Secretary information on the question of Communists.

Mr. HICKERSON. That is correct, sir.

Senator FERGUSON. So that ought to be clear on the record.

Mr. HICKERSON. That must be clear on the record. We did not violate Article 101. We gave confidential information.

Senator FERGUSON. He requested——

Mr. HICKERSON. On request, and the responsibility was wholly and exclusively that of the Secretary-General for any action taken thereon, in accordance with the Charter.

.   .   .   .

Senator O'CONOR. It is my understanding that the Department at no time sought, nor did it do anything which was violative of the Charter provisions as to seeking to instruct the Secretariat as to what it must do?

Mr. HICKERSON. That is correct, sir.

Senator FERGUSON. I realize the word "instruct" has a particular meaning here, because this is an international organization, and when the Secretary-General asked for information, to use it merely as he might see fit, you did furnish 37 to 40 adverse comments . . .[121]

Under the existing Executive order, a request for information emanates from the Secretary-General just as it did under the informal arrangement above referred to. The investigation is made only in respect to names submitted by the Secretary-General. Where no derogatory information is developed, the Secretary of State notifies the Secretary-General. Where derogatory information is developed, a hearing is held before the loyalty board, at which the person involved is given the opportunity to be heard. The findings of the board are transmitted to the Secretary of State to be forwarded to the Secretary-General. Thereafter, the ultimate decision is made by the Secretary-General.

IX. After a treaty has been ratified, it becomes the law of the land.

Article II, Section 1 of the Constitution, provides that "the executive power shall be vested in the President of the United States of America." The executive power to carry out the law includes the power to carry out a treaty which is part of the law of the land. The program embodied in Executive Order 10422, as amended, is believed to be a step in the implementation of Section 3 of Article 101 of the United Nations Charter, which prescribes that a paramount consideration in the employment of a staff will be the necessity of securing the highest standards of efficiency, competency and integrity. In providing a procedure whereby information as to subversive or disloyal activities of American citizens can be made available to the Secretary-General, the United States is furnishing material

[121] Hearings, Subcommittee on Internal Security, Judiciary Committee, U. S. Senate, 82d Cong., 2d sess., Oct. 13, 14, 15, 23, 24, Nov. 11, 12, Dec. 1, 2, 10, 11 and 17, 1952, p. 270, 272.

aid to the Secretary-General in the discharge of his responsibilities in procuring proper personnel for the Secretariat.

In addition to the executive power specifically lodged in the President by the terms of the Constitution, it has long been recognized that the President has broad powers in the conduct of foreign affairs.

Thus in *United States* v. *Curtiss-Wright Corporation*, 299 U. S. 304 (1936), the court describes this authority as "the very delicate, plenary and exclusive power of the President as the sole organ of the Federal Government in the field of international relations—a power which does not require as a basis for its exercise an Act of Congress but which, of course, like every other governmental power, must be exercised in subordination to the applicable provisions of the Constitution."

In *United States* v. *Belmont*, 301 U. S. 324 (1937), the President, in connection with the recognition of the Soviet Government and the resumption of normal diplomatic relations, entered into an agreement with the Soviet Government whereby the latter assigned to the United States all amounts due to that government from American nationals. This agreement was upheld as an international compact which the President had the right to make without the consent of the Senate. In the course of the opinion, the court said (p. 330): "Governmental power over external affairs is not distributed, but is vested exclusively in the national Government. *And in respect of what was done here, the Executive had authority to speak as the sole organ of that government.*" To the same effect is *United States* v. *Pink*, 315 U. S. 203 (1942).

In the exercise of the presidential power in the field of foreign relations, presidents have from time to time entered into agreements with other nations characterized as "executive agreements." While the source of the constitutional power to enter into such agreements is not entirely clear, and while its scope and extent have not been precisely defined or adjudicated, it has long been recognized.

The United States is participating in the activities of the United Nations, as set forth in Executive Order 10422, as amended by Executive Order 10459, by virtue of a ratification of the Charter, and by virtue of the authority granted by the United Nations Participation Act of 1945 *supra*. Other statutes governing the relationship of the United States and the United Nations are the International Organization Immunities Act of December 29, 1945, Public Law 291, 79th Congress, 22 U. S. C. A. 288,[122] and the Headquarters Agreement Act of August 1947, Public Law 357, 80th Congress, 22 U. S. C. A. 287.[123]

The Executive order recites that, in the participation by the United States of the activities of the United Nations, it is in our national interest that United States citizens who are employees of the Secretariat be persons of the highest integrity, and not persons who have been or are likely to be engaged in espionage or subversive activities against the United States.

---

[122] 59 Stat. 669.
[123] 61 Stat 756.

The power to enter into executive agreements in the field of foreign relations is generally believed to include the power to enter into any agreement which would benefit the United States in its participation in the activities of the United Nations.

Congress has recognized and implemented the Executive orders establishing the employees loyalty program for international organizations by appropriating funds necessary for its administration. For example, Public Law 428, 83d Congress, June 24, 1954, provides "for expenses necessary to carry out the provisions of Executive Order No. 10422 of January 9, 1953, as amended, prescribing procedures for making available to the Secretary-General of the United Nations, and the executive heads of international organizations, certain information concerning United States citizens employed or being considered for employment by such organizations, $400,000, together with not to exceed $500,000 of the unobligated balance of funds appropriated for this purpose in the 'Supplemental Appropriation Act, 1954': *Provided,* That this appropriation shall be available for advances or reimbursements to the applicable appropriations or funds of the Civil Service Commission and the Federal Bureau of Investigation for expenses incurred by such agencies under said Executive Order: . . ." [124]   A similar provision is in Public Law 112, 84th Congress, June 30, 1955. Public Law 623, 84th Congress, June 27, 1956, contains a similar provision and appropriates $487,500 for the fiscal year ending June 30, 1957.[125]

PRESENT PROGRAM

The revelations of the New York Federal grand jury and the Senate Internal Security Subcommittee concerning the activities of Communists in the United Nations indicated that the informal confidential arrangement of 1949, between the United States and United Nations for screening American citizens to be employed or employed by the United Nations, was unsuccessful in operation.

The declaration of the Federal grand jury presentment of December 2, 1952, that evidence had "disclosed infiltration into the United Nations of an overwhelmingly large group of disloyal United States citizens," and the recommendation of the United Nations Commission of Jurists that member states afford information on their nationals to the Secretary General of the United Nations, led to the issuance of Executive Order 10422, January 9, 1953, amended by Executive Order 10459, June 2, 1953.   Under these orders procedures were established for the screening of United States citizens applying for employment with or employed by international organizations, and

---

[124] 68 Stat. 274.
[125] 69 Stat. 199.

for the furnishing of information concerning such individuals to the administrative heads of these organizations to assist them in their independent personnel determinations.

Initial Procedures

Under the procedures instituted by the Executive order, all United States citizens applying for employment with or employed by an international organization complete an investigative questionnaire and a fingerprint chart. The information elicited by the questionnaire includes among other matters: personal data; dates and places of residence for the past 15 years; citizenship; military service; education; all employment; foreign countries visited since 1930; whether now or ever a member of the Communist Party or Fascist organization; whether a member of any foreign or domestic group advocating or approving acts to deny other of their rights, or seeking to alter the form of Government in the United States by unconstitutional means; past and present membership in all organizations; information concerning relatives; references; and, criminal record.[126]

The completed investigative form and fingerprint chart requested of the individual by the international organization are forwarded to the International Organizations Employees Loyalty Board of the Civil Service Commission for processing under the orders. Generally, the completed informational data is transmitted by the international organization directly to the Board, but in instances of international organizations headquartered outside the United States, the forms are transmitted through the foreign service posts of the Department of State to the Board.[127]

Investigative Stage

Once the identifying data have been received from the international organization, an investigation follows. All "locally recruited" applicants or incumbents undergo a "full background" investigation by the Civil Service Commission. All United States citizens applying for or employed on a short-term appointment, i. e., not to exceed ninety days, are given a "national agency check" by the Civil Service Commission. Any United States citizen being considered for or employed on the "internationally recruited" staff for a period in excess of 90 days is automatically subject to a "full field" investigation by the Federal Bureau of Investigation. Moreover, should derogatory information be uncovered by the Civil Service Commission in its conduct of a "full background" or "national agency check," the

---

[126] *Identification and personnel data for employment of United States cititzens*, form approved, Budget Bureau, No. 47–R119.1 and *supplemental*, No. 50–R254.

[127] Department of State response to Commission on Government Security interrogatory.

418

case is forwarded immediately to the Federal Bureau of Investigation for a "full field" investigation.[128]

The International Organizations Employees Loyalty Board

Upon completion of the investigation, a report is made available to the International Organizations Employees Loyalty Board for evaluation. It is on the basis of the evaluation of these reports and possible subsequent written or oral interrogatories and/or hearings that the board makes an advisory determination in each case. This determination is forwarded to the administrative head of the employing international organization for his information and guidance. It is to be remembered that these reports are merely of an advisory character, and do not circumscribe the freedom of action of the Secretary General or other employing administrative head.

The International Organizations Employees Loyalty Board is composed of seven members including a chairman, vice chairman, and an executive secretary. The Executive order requires that they be officers or employees of the Civil Service Commission; hence outstanding citizens are selected and appointed as excepted part-time employees of the Commission.

The power to appoint the members of the IOELB is vested in the Chairman of the Civil Service Commission. Originally, the members were appointed for a 1-year term. However, these positions are now in the excepted category without time limitation. The board members are rated at grade 15 and are compensated on a "when actually employed" basis. Present members of the board are: Chairman Henry S. Waldman, lawyer, past president of Union County Bar Association, New Jersey, former judge of Union County Juvenile and Domestic Relations Court; Vice Chairman H. Grady Gore, lawyer, engaged in real estate and financial activities in District of Columbia, member of Washington Board of Trade; Secretary George J. Kaufman, lawyer, legal counsel for a number of firms; members: Richard A. Bigger, corporation executive; Mrs. Katherine S. Carpenter, lawyer; Lawrence M. Gilman, elected to both Connecticut Legislature and State Senate, corporation president; Edmund L. Tink, Ph. D., educator. The executive secretary is appointed by the board.

The board frequently acts through panels of not less than three members as appointed by the chairman. These panels usually sit in Washington or New York, but may convene elsewhere for convenience.

All cases in which investigations have been conducted under the Executive order are referred to and reviewed by the Board. In consideration of what is termed a "clear" case, an examiner will review the file and prepare the recommendation. Reports are viewed in light of the standard and criteria as set forth in Executive Order 10422, as amended. The examiner's determination as to whether a report warrants a finding favor-

---

[128] Executive Order 10459.

able to an individual, or whether further processing of a case should be instituted with a view to possible unfavorable determination is based on the standard of whether, on the basis of all the evidence, there is a reasonable doubt as to the loyalty of the person involved to the Government of the United States. The applicable criteria include sabotage, espionage, treason, sedition or advocacy thereof, and advocacy or use of force to alter the constitutional form of Government of the United States.[129]

If, in the first instance, the examiner reaches a favorable conclusion involving the question of loyalty, his determination is that, on the evidence, there is not a reasonable doubt as to the individual's loyalty, and on this basis, he would recommend employment eligibility. This recommendation is then subject to review and approval by one board member.[130]

In cases involving a question of loyalty, the file is reviewed by an examiner and an analytical memorandum is prepared setting forth the pertinent facts, both favorable and unfavorable. It is possible that the facts may warrant a rating of eligibility for employment. However, if the situation is otherwise, the examiner prepares a letter of interrogatory, setting forth the facts, for which answers will be required. A second examiner reviews the case, and if he concurs in the initial action taken, the case proceeds to the executive secretary. If the two examiners are not in agreement, an attempt is made to reconcile the differences. When this is not possible, alternative recommendations are sent to the executive secretary for review. A decision to send the interrogatory requires the approval of the chairman of the board. A decision that no interrogatory is necessary to reach final determination requires the concurrence of three members of the board.[131]

When an interrogatory is sent out to the individual involved, he is apprised of the nature of the derogatory information and the facts and circumstances involved, in as much detail as security considerations permit, so as to afford an opportunity for answer in the form of defense or explanation and to submit affidavits. Answer is required under oath. The individual is given 10 days to reply to the interrogatory. In cases where derogatory information appears to be of a trivial nature, the matter may be resolved through the written interrogatory to the individual concerned or through an oral interview.[132]

When the completed interrogatory is received, it is reviewed by the original examiner, and, if the answer is considered to be satisfactory, the examiner recommends employment eligibility. This recommendation is reviewed by a second examiner. If he concurs, it then goes to three members of the board. If any of the three board members dissents, the case is submitted to the remaining members of the board. In cases where a hearing is deemed

---

[129] Executive Order 10422, as amended.
[130] Regulations of the International Organizations Employees Loyalty Board.
[131] Ibid.
[132] Regulations of the International Organizations Employees Loyalty Board, Aug. 19, 1953, 12 (b).

necessary, the chairman of the board must approve. Arrangements are then made to schedule a hearing, and the panel to sit at the hearing is designated.[133]

The individual concerning whom there is derogatory information is notified in writing of his opportunity to appear personally at a hearing; to be represented by counsel; to present evidence in his own behalf; and to cross-examine such witnesses as may be offered in support of the derogatory information. The hearing, conducted by a panel of not less than three members of the board, is conducted in such a manner as to protect from disclosure information affecting the national security. Testimony is given under oath or affirmation.[134]

Strict legal rules of evidence are not applied at the hearings, but reasonable bounds are required as to competency, relevancy, and materiality; moreover, due allowance is made for the effect of any nondisclosure to the individual of information or the absence of an opportunity to cross-examine informants who do not appear and testify. Both the Government and the individual concerned in the case may introduce such evidence as the panel may deem proper.[135]

Determinations of board panels are equivalent to determinations of the board. At the conclusion of the hearing, of which there is a full transcript, the examiner analyzes the case and submits his recommendation. The individual board members write their rationale. The board is required to make its determination promptly. Such determination is in writing, signed by the members of the panel, and states the action taken together with the reasons therefor. While the individual concerned is advised only of the conclusion, the determination of the board as well as a statement of reasons is rendered in each case to the Secretary of State for transmission to the administrative head of the international organization concerned.[136] Where the advisory determination is of an adverse character, the determination is accompanied by a statement of reasons in as much detail as the board deems security considerations permit. Along with the advisory determination may be included an "unevaluated" report on the individual's suitability, quite apart from any question of his loyalty, for the benefit of the head of the international organization concerned.[137] The communication of the determination through the Secretary of State to the administrative head of the international agency is expedited by the Office of International Administration, Bureau of International Organizations Affairs, Department of State. This office acts as liaison between the International Organizations Employees Loyalty Board and the international organizations on matters pertaining to

---

[133] Civil Service Commission response to Commission on Government Security interrogatory.

[134] Regulations of the International Organizations Employees Loyalty Board, August 19, 1953, 12 (b).

[135] Ibid., 15 (e).

[136] Regulations of the International Organizations Employees Loyalty Board, August 19, 1953, 16–18. A unanimous opinion is not required before a Board decision is issued. However, if a member of the board dissents, the administrative head of the international organization is not advised of such dissenting action. The majority decision is all that is transmitted.

[137] U. S. Department of State, exhibit No. 1, an enclosure submitted with the Department of State response to Commission on Government Security interrogatory.

the coverage of United States citizens employed on international organizations. In consultation with the International Organizations Employees Loyalty Board and the Office of Security and Consular Affairs in the Department of State, the Office of International Administration seeks to develop improved procedures to implement the Executive order and to facilitate the investigation of applicants for and incumbents in international employ and to clarify categories of individuals whose relationship with the international organization would exempt them from investigation under the order.[138]

International Procedures

Once the international organization has been apprised of the advisory determination of the International Organizations Employees Loyalty Board, through the Bureau of International Organizations Affairs of the Department of State, it is then up to the administrative head of that organization to make his independent decision whether to employ the individual, in the case of an applicant, or to dismiss or retain, in the case of an employee, on the basis of the advisory opinion of the board and such other information as he may have at his disposal. In the event that the International Organizations Employees Loyalty Board advises the Secretary General that an investigation has disclosed no derogatory information with respect to an applicant or employee, the Secretary General accepts this as implying "clearance." Should the determination of the board be that there does exist a reasonable doubt as to the individual's loyalty to the United States, several alternatives are open to the Secretary General. He can refuse to consider the United States determination as sufficient grounds for disciplinary action. In this case, the policy of the Department of State would be to make every effort to persuade the Secretary General that he is making an incorrect assessment of the board's determination. Nonetheless, the final determination is that of the Secretary General.[139]

On the other hand, the Secretary General might consider taking disciplinary action pursuant to the staff regulations. Little difficulty is encountered in the rules when terminating the employment of a temporary staff member, since under staff regulation 9.1 (c), such employees can be terminated at the discretion of the Secretary General. His powers are somewhat more circumscribed, however, in the case of a permanent employee. The appointment of a permanent staff member may be terminated under staff regulation 9.1 (a) if the post has been abolished; if his service is unsatisfactory; or, if he is incapacitated for reasons of health. Moreover, the termination of such permanent staff member is permitted if under subsection

---

[138] U. S. Department of State. Memorandum dated Aug. 1, 1956, enclosure No. 4, submitted with Department of State response to Commission on Government Security interrogatory.

[139] Department of State response to Commission on Government Security interrogatory.

(i) he should not meet the highest standards of integrity as required by article 101 of the Charter; or subsection (ii), "if facts anterior to the appointment of the staff member and relevant to his suitability come to light, which, if they had been known at the time of his appointment should, under the standards established in the Charter, have precluded his appointment."

No termination can be effected by the Secretary General under these last two categories until after submission to and consideration by a special advisory board appointed for that specific purpose.[140]

Finally, the Secretary General has the power to terminate any appointment should such termination be in the interest of the good administration of the Organization—if such action is not contested by the staff member involved.[141]

Upon receiving the advisory determination of the International Organizations Employees Loyalty Board, the Secretary General makes an initial examination of the case to determine whether the charges "emanated from a responsible source, did not involve mistaken identity and *prima facie*, were of a serious nature warranting consideration of the board." [142] No preliminary determination is made by the Secretary General at this time. If the conditions sought under the initial examination of the case are met, the matter is then referred to the Special Advisory Board. This board does not decide a case. Its function is purely of an advisory nature to the Secretary General. The board can suggest, for example, that the Secretary General refrain from taking action. The Secretary General makes his determination in the case after receiving the interpretation of the Board concerning the application of the relevant staff regulation to the facts. His decision might be that no action is necessary; on the other hand, termination or lesser disciplinary action might be the decided action.[143]

Should the Secretary General decide to terminate the appointment of an employee, the individual concerned has a right of appeal to a Joint Appeals Board, established by the Secretary General for the purpose of hearing appeals from administrative decisions alleging nonobservance of contract. The board is composed of three members, appointed as follows: a chair-

---

[140] United Nations. "Staff rules: Staff regulations of the United Nations and staff rules 101.1 to 112.8," *Secretary General's Bulletin*, ST/SGB/94/Rev. 4, 1955, p. 47. The special advisory board is composed of a chairman appointed by the Secretary General on the nomination of the International Court of Justice, and four other members appointed by the Secretary General in agreement with the staff council, a council elected by the staff to provide continuous contact between the staff and the Secretary General.

[141] United Nations. "Staff rules: Staff regulations of the United Nations and staff rules 101.1 to 112.8," *Secretary General's Bulletin*, ST/SGB/94/Rev. 4, 1955, p. 55. Staff regulation 10.2 permits summary dismissal of staff members for serious misconduct. A joint disciplinary committee, with staff representation, advises the Secretary General in disciplinary cases under regulaton 10.2. Cases involving the loyalty of United States citizens, however, are likely to be implemented under regulation 9.1, in view of the decisions of the administrative tribunal in the famous "21 cases" of 1953. An example of the disciplinary power exercised by the Secretary General was illustrated in the case of Viktor Petrov, former Soviet translator at the United Nations, who was separated from United Nations employ "without warning" for "attempting to obtain secret defense data on United States military aircraft." Kathleen Teltsch, "U. N. ousts a Soviet translator who sought U. S. plane secrets," *New York Times*, August 25, 1956.

[142] United Nations, General Assembly, Doc. A/2777.

[143] *Government Security and Loyalty Manual*, 4 : 6.

man selected from a panel appointed annually by the Secretary General after consultation with the staff committee; one member appointed annually by the Secretary General; one member elected annually by ballot of the staff.[144] Usually, the proceedings before the Joint Appeals Board are limited to the original written presentation of the case, together with brief oral or written statements and rebuttals. The board has the authority to call staff members of the Secretariat to give additional information. The production of additional documents may also be requested. Decisions of the board are by majority vote. The report and board recommendation are then forwarded to the Secretary General for his decision. Upon the rendering of the final decision by the Secretary General, the staff member concerned is notified of such decision along with a copy of the board's recommendation.[145]

Under all circumstances but one, the staff member concerned in a disciplinary case has still further recourse to appeals should the Joint Appeals Board rule against him. If the Joint Appeals Board unanimously determines the appeal to be frivolous, there is no further right to appeal. If, however, the board should decide against the staff member, or if it should rule in his favor and the Secretary General reject the recommendations of the board, or if the Secretary General fails to take action within 30 days of the opinion, or fails to carry out the board's recommendations within 30 days, the staff member can appeal the case to the Administrative Tribunal. Direct recourse to the Administrative Tribunal, thus bypassing the Joint Appeals Board, may be afforded under prior agreement with the Secretary General. It should be noted that the filing of an application for appeal to the Administrative Tribunal does not have the effect of suspending the execution of the contested decision.[146]

The Administrative Tribunal was established by the General Assembly by Resolution 351 A(IV) on November 24, 1949, "to hear and pass judgment upon applications alleging nonobservance of contracts of employment of staff members of the Secretariat of the United Nations or of the terms of appointment of such staff members."[147] The tribunal is composed of 7 members, no 2 of whom may be nationals of the same state. Three-member panels consider and judge each case. Membership is determined by appointment by the General Assembly for 3-year terms. Proceedings are usually conducted in public.[148]

Any staff member appealing his case to the Administrative Tribunal is permitted to do so in person, in either written or oral proceedings. He has the right to be represented by counsel or staff member of the United Nations

---

[144] United Nations staff rules, p. 57, Rule 111.2 ST/SGB/94/Rev. 4, New York, 1955.
[145] Ibid., pp. 57–59.
[146] United Nations. Administrative Tribunal, *Statute*, art. 7, pars. 2–6.
[147] Ibid., art. 2, par. 1.
[148] United Nations. Administrative Tribunal, *Statute*, art. 3, pars. 1, 2, and art. 8.

or one of the specialized agencies. Proceedings before the tribunal may be oral if so decided by the presiding member of the tribunal panel, or upon the request of either party to the case upon the approval of the presiding member. The parties to the case can call witnesses and experts to testify on their behalf. Witnesses take the following oath: "I solemnly declare upon my honour and conscience that I will speak the truth, the whole truth and nothing but the truth." Experts declare: "I solemnly declare upon by honour and conscience that my statement will be in accordance with my sincere belief." [149]

At any stage of the proceedings, the tribunal may request additional documentation or evidence as may be required. Oral testimony may be limited, if, in the opinion of the tribunal, the written documentation is adequate. [150]

Under article 9 of the United Nations Administrative Tribunal Statute, the tribunal is empowered to order the rescinding of a contested decision or the specific performance of the obligation invoked, if, in its judgment, the appeal is well founded. If within 30 days, the Secretary General should decide that in the interests of the Organization, the applicant should be compensated without further action, the tribunal determines the amount of compensation on the basis of the injury sustained. Except under unusual circumstances, such compensation does not exceed the equivalent of 2 years' net base salary of the appellant. The tribunal, subject to the request of the Secretary General and prior to determination of case merits, might also remand the case for processing under proper procedures, if it determines that such procedures as prescribed in the staff rules and regulations have not been observed. The appellant may be compensated, not to exceed the equivalent of 3 months' net base salary, by order of the tribunal to compensate for the loss incurred by procedural delays. Any compensation determined as obligated by the tribunal is paid by the United Nations or appropriate specialized agency. [151]

Article 10 of the tribunal statute provides that all decisions be by majority vote; that judgments are final and without appeal; and that such judgments state the reasons on which based. On November 8, 1955, the General Assembly amended the tribunal's statute wherein procedures were established for the screening of the tribunal judgments by a Screening Committee of the General Assembly with ultimate resort to the International Court of Justice for an advisory opinion, supra. Subject to this limitation, the judgments of the tribunal are final and without appeal.

---

[149] United Nations, Administrative Tribunal, *Rules*, arts. 12–14.

[150] Ibid., art. 15.

[151] United Nations, Administrative Tribunal, *Statute*, Arts. 9, 12. "The competence of the tribunal may be extended to any specialized agency . . . upon the terms established by a special agreement . . . made with each agency by the Secretary General . . . the agency concerned . . . [is] bound by the judgments of the Tribunal . . ." A number of specialized agencies utilize the Administrative Tribunal of the International Labour Organization.

Organizations Included

Pursuant to provisions of Executive Order 10422, as amended, the Department of State as of March 14, 1957, had made arrangements with the executive heads of the following 26 international organizations which employ American citizens:

UNITED NATIONS
Includes: UNITED NATIONS SECRETARIAT
OFFICE OF THE UNITED NATIONS HIGH COMMISSIONER FOR REFUGEES
UNITED NATIONS RELIEF AND WORKS AGENCY FOR PALESTINE REFUGEES IN THE NEAR EAST
UNITED NATIONS KOREAN RECONSTRUCTION AGENCY
UNITED NATIONS CHILDREN'S FUND

UNITED NATIONS EDUCATIONAL, SCIENTIFIC, AND CULTURAL ORGANIZATION
INTERNATIONAL CIVIL AVIATION ORGANIZATION
FOOD AND AGRICULTURE ORGANIZATION
WORLD HEALTH ORGANIZATION
INTERNATIONAL LABOR ORGANIZATION
INTERNATIONAL TELECOMMUNICATION UNION
INTERNATIONAL BANK FOR RECONSTRUCTION AND DEVELOPMENT
INTERNATIONAL FINANCE CORPORATION
INTERNATIONAL MONETARY FUND
PAN AMERICAN UNION
PAN AMERICAN SANITARY BUREAU
INTER-AMERICAN INSTITUTE OF AGRICULTURAL SCIENCES
INTER-AMERICAN DEFENSE BOARD
PAN AMERICAN INSTITUTE OF GEOGRAPHY AND HISTORY
INTER-AMERICAN RADIO ORGANIZATION
INTERGOVERNMENTAL COMMITTEE FOR EUROPEAN MIGRATION
GENERAL AGREEMENT ON TARIFFS AND TRADE
COTTON ADVISORY COMMITTEE
INTERPARLIAMENTARY UNION
INTERNATIONAL HYDROGRAPHIC BUREAU
CARIBBEAN COMMISSION
SOUTH PACIFIC COMMISSION
INTER-AMERICAN TROPICAL TUNA COMMISSION
INTERNATIONAL PACIFIC HALIBUT COMMISSION
INTERNATIONAL PACIFIC SALMON FISHERIES COMMISSION

RECOMMENDATIONS

NECESSITY

The Commission believes that an international organizations employees loyalty program is necessary to protect the national security.

An international organizations employees loyalty program is necessary because in recent years United States citizens of doubtful loyalty have held responsible positions on the United Nations Secretariat and as staff members of other international organizations. They have had the opportunity to participate in the policy decisions of these organizations to an extent which would permit them to influence policy adversely to our national security. Evidence secured by the Commission does not support a comment which has been made that the international organizations employees loyalty program is "actually harmful to the interests of the United States and its citizens," nor is there evidence to support the contention that the present loyalty program could set a precedent for other countries which might be detrimental to the national interest.

The extensive investigations of the New York Federal Grand Jury and the Senate Internal Security subcommittee uncovered a number of doubtfully loyal United States citizens employed by the United Nations and its specialized agencies. As a direct result of their findings, many employees were discharged from those organizations. Sixteen have been given adverse determinations by the International Organizations Loyalty Board and 162 were terminated prior to board action through resignations and other causes.

Paragraph three (3) of article 101 of the United Nations Charter provides that the highest standards of integrity are required for employment on the staff of the United Nations. It follows that any person who might engage in subversive activities does not meet this standard of integrity. The fact that these international civil servants do not have ready access to United States classified information does not preclude the possibility of compromise to the national security.

If the United Nations and other international organizations are to carry out effectively their worldwide responsibilities, they must have the respect and confidence of the member nations, particularly the United States, the host country to the majority of the international organizations. In order to engender maximum American respect for these organizations and their employees, and to minimize the possibility of any threat to our national security, it is necessary to have an international employees loyalty program designed to weed out those United States employees who might engage in subversive activities against their Nation.

427

One of the purposes of a loyalty program for United States citizens who are applicants for positions with, or employees of, international organizations is to make "suitability" information on such individuals available to the administrative head of an international organization without impairing his independence of action. However, the Commission stands opposed to all proposals which would require United States applicants or employees of international organizations to secure clearance from the Government before accepting employment, or as a requisite to continued employment, in such organizations.

The international status of an organization and its independence from control by a member state would not be impaired by the United States requesting the administrative head to cooperate in the execution of United States laws and regulations as they may affect international civil servants. The headquarters agreement specifically provides for such cooperation in certain respects.[152]

The Department of State has reported that the administrative heads of international organization wish to receive suitability information on all types of employees and that they give considerable weight to the findings of member governments when making their final determination to accept an applicant or terminate an employee. Although adverse suitability information will not automatically disqualify an applicant or an employee, it is a factor which the administrative head of an international organization takes into consideration in his decision to hire or not to hire, or, in the case of a permanent employee, to terminate his contract.

The United Nations Preparatory Commission, which met in London in 1945, felt that:

. . . it was common sense that the staff (of the United Nations) should, as far as possible, be acceptable to the Member governments, and also that the Secretary-General would often require information regarding candidates from government or private bodies.

This view was later upheld by Secretary-General Trygve Lie in his 1953 report to the General Assembly on the personnel policy of the United Nations. At that time the Secretary-General expressed not only the desirability of member states affording him information on prospective personnel, but also the practical necessity of such assistance:

The United Nations does not—and obviously cannot—have an investigation agency comparable to those at the disposal of national governments. Therefore, the United Nations must depend upon the governments of members for assistance in checking the character and record of staff members. The Secretary-General has had this assistance from many governments, but he has always reserved, and must always reserve, to himself the final decision on the basis of all the facts.

Reference has already been made to the legislation introduced in both the Eighty-third and Eighty-fourth Congresses which called for a Government security clearance as a prerequisite for employment and as a requisite

[152] Joint Resolution of the Congress, Aug. 4, 1947, 61 Stat. 756, 22 U. S. C. A. 287, note.

for continued employment in international organizations.   These measures have failed so far to receive the approval of Congress, and the Government departments most concerned have repeatedly expressed their opposition to such clearance requirements.   Spokesmen for the United States Mission to the United Nations, while reluctant to express an "official" opinion, felt that such a requirement might violate Articles 100 and 101 of the United Nations Charter.

STANDARDS AND CRITERIA

The Commission believes that the standard should be broadened to include security risks not arising out of doubt as to loyalty. The Commission therefore recommends the following standards and criteria:

1. The standard to be used by the board in making an advisory determination with respect to a United States citizen who is an employee of, or is being considered for employment by the United Nations should be whether or not, on all the information, there is reasonable doubt as to the loyalty of the person to the Government of the United States, or whether or not, on all the information, there is reasonable ground for believing that the person might engage in subversive activities against the United States.

2. Activities and associations of an applicant or employee which may be considered in connection with the determination of the existence of a reasonable doubt as to loyalty and of reasonable grounds for believing that the person might engage in subversive activities may include one or more of the following:

(*a*) Sabotage, espionage, attempts or preparations therefor, or knowingly associating with spies or saboteurs;

(*b*) Treason or sedition or advocacy thereof;

(*c*) Advocacy of revolution or force or violence to alter the constitutional form of Government of the United States;

(*d*) Intentional, unauthorized disclosure to any person, under circumstances which may indicate disloyalty to the United States, of documents or information of a confidential or nonpublic character;

(*e*) Performing or attempting to perform his duties, or otherwise acting while an employee of the United States Government during a previous period, so as to serve the interests of another government in preference to the interests of the United States;

(*f*) Membership in, or affiliation or sympathetic association with, any party or association which the Congress of the United States, or any agency or officer of the United States duly authorized by the Congress for that purpose finds:

(1) Seeks to alter the form of Government of the United States by force or violence, or other unconstitutional means; or,

(2) Is organized or utilized for the purpose of advancing the aims and objectives of the Communist movement; or,

(3) Is organized or utilized for the purpose of establishing any form of dictatorship in the United States or any form of international dictatorship; or,

(4) Is organized or utilized by any foreign government, or by any foreign party, group, or association acting in the interest of such foreign government for the purpose of (*a*) espionage, or (*b*) sabotage, or (*c*) obtaining information relating to the defense of the United States or the protection of the national security, or (*d*) hampering, hindering, or delaying the production of defense materials; or,

(5) Is affiliated with, or acts in concert with, or is dominated or controlled by, any party, group, or association of the character described in (1), (2), (3), or (4) above.

(*g*) Membership in or affiliation with any organization which the Congress of the United States, or any agency or officer of the United States duly authorized by the Congress for that purpose, finds has adopted a policy of advocating or approving the commission of acts of force and violence to deny others their rights under the Constitution of the United States.

(*h*) Refusal to testify upon the ground of self-incrimination, in any authorized inquiry relating to subversive activities conducted by a congressional committee, Federal court, Federal grand jury, or any duly authorized Federal agency, as to questions relating to subversive activities of the individual involved or others, unless the individual, after opportunity to do so, satisfactorily explains his refusal to testify.

430

(*i*) Any criminal, infamous, dishonest, immoral, or notoriously disgraceful conduct, habitual use of intoxicants to excess, drug addictions or sexual perversion.

(*j*) Any facts which furnish reason to believe that the individual may be subjected to coercion, influence, or pressure which might cause him to engage in subversive activities against the United States.

(*k*) The foregoing enumeration shall not be deemed to exclude any other factors tending to establish reasonable doubt as to loyalty or reasonable ground for believing that the person might engage in subversive activities against the United States.

The scope of subversive activities carried out by United States employees in international organizations since the Second World War has been exposed by several investigative bodies of the Government. Their findings indicate that not only should the present loyalty standard of Executive Order 10422 be retained but that it should be broadened to include security risks not arising out of doubt as to loyalty i. e., persons whose past conduct and/or present habits suggest a lack of reliability and trustworthiness to the extent that they might engage in subversive activities against the United States.

Although article 101 of the United Nations Charter precludes any standards beyond competence, efficiency and integrity, responsible officials of the world organization now agree that the conduct of an international civil servant must be such as to merit the confidence of *all* members of an international organization and his actions must never jeopardize the reputation or effectiveness of the entire organization. In 1953, the United Nations General Assembly, at the request of Secretary-General Hammarskjold, adopted additional regulations governing the conduct of United Nations employees which provided, in part:

Members of the Secretariat shall conduct themselves at all times in a manner befitting their status as international civil servants. They shall not engage in any activity that is incompatible with the proper discharge of their duties with the United Nations.

Further evidence in support of a more all-inclusive loyalty standard for United States employees of international organizations is contained in the 1954 report of the International Civil Service Advisory Board to the General Assembly on certain basic standards to be met by international civil servants:

. . . any direct or indirect activity with a view to the overthrow of a government by force, including incitement or advocacy of such overthrow, is one of the gravest forms of misconduct.

The criteria upon which adverse security determinations are made by the loyalty board under the present program are not sufficiently specific, in the light of past experience, to provide the board with the yardstick it needs to determine whether, on all the evidence, there is reasonable doubt as to a person's loyalty to the United States, or reasonable grounds for believing that the person might engage in subversive activities against the United States.

Executive Order 10422 does not delineate the nature and objectives of organizations and affiliations considered by the Government as subversive, but relies almost entirely upon the Attorney General's list of subversive organizations. While provision is made in the above recommendation for the Congress, or any agency or officer of the United States duly authorized by the Congress, to set forth lists of affiliations or organizations they consider to be subversive, an effort was made to define in clear and precise language the activities or purposes of an organization which would cause it to be placed in the subversive category.

Another shortcoming of Executive Order 10422 is the absence of any reference to invocation of the privilege against self-incrimination as a reasonable ground for casting doubt on a person's loyalty. Numerous United States employees of the United Nations and other international organizations in recent years have refused to testify before grand juries and congressional committees on the ground of possible self-incrimination. In 1952, a spate of such refusals to testify by United States employees of the United Nations forced the Secretary-General to reexamine United Nations personnel policies in order to determine if the refusal by an employee to answer a question asked by an authorized organ of his government, under his constitutional privilege against self-incrimination, was compatible with the conduct required of the United Nations staff member.

INDIVIDUALS COVERED

1. The Commission believes that United States citizens who are employees of international organizations come within the objectives and purview of the Government's personnel security program.

Even though American citizens are employed by international organizations, they are still viewed by other nations as representatives of the United States and its people. It is, therefore, essential to the United States that all such employees and particularly those in positions of high trust where they can guide, direct and control policy decisions which affect our national interest should be of unquestioned loyalty to the United States.

In view of the congressional position on this issue, and since the Commission has determined that United States employees of international organizations are in a position to injure the national security, it follows that such employees should be included in the Government's personnel security program.

2. The loyalty program should apply to locally and internationally recruited United States employees. In addition, short-term employees should be required to undergo a national agency check.

The Commission believes that the loyalty program should apply to both locally and internationally recruited United States employees, as well as short-term employees (not in excess of 90 days) of international organizations. Any attempt to differentiate between locally and internationally recruited employees, or to eliminate the provision of Executive Order 10459 which stipulates that a short-term employee must undergo a national agency check, would tend to weaken the program since it has already been established that United States citizens of doubtful loyalty have been recruited for the staffs of international organizations from all personnel categories. Although the Senate Subcommittee on Internal Security concluded that a majority of the reportedly disloyal United States citizens employed at the United Nations were on the internationally recruited staff, some members of the "fifth column" alleged by the Senate Subcommittee to have existed in the United Nations, had been recruited locally for their positions on the Secretariat.

Chairman Henry S. Waldman and members of the International Organizations Employees Loyalty Board, and others most concerned with the operation of the present loyalty program, contend that the program should continue to apply to all United States personnel on the staffs of international organizations, permanent and short-term employees, both locally and internationally recruited.

The Special Study Mission on International Organizations of the House Committee on Foreign Affairs, while noting the objections to the present program raised by various international organizations and agreeing to an acceleration of current procedures, concluded that in no instance should the standards and criteria established by those procedures be lowered or relaxed.

3. United States employees of international organizations owe their prime loyalty to the United States.

The Commission believes that United States employees of international organizations are not faced with a conflict between their loyalty to the United States and their loyalty to an international organization. This point was made manifestly clear by the Commission of Jurists when, in its report to the Secretary-General, it concluded that the United Nations is not a super state, nor can it claim the allegiance of its employees as demanded of citizens of a sovereign state. In its discussion of the legal relationship between the United Nations and the host country, the Commission of Jurists found:

. . . nothing in the Constitution of the United Nations or the provisions governing the employment of its staff which gives the least ground for supposing that there is or should be any conflict whatever between the loyalty owed by every citizen by virtue of

433

his alllegiance to his own State and the responsibility of such a citizen to the United Nations in respect to work done by him as an officer or employee of the United Nations.

In addition to the sound legal opinion on the conflict of loyalty issue handed down by the Commission of Jurists, the loyalty standard of Executive Order 10422, as amended, precludes any such conflict since it calls for "loyalty to the Government of the United States," a requirement which does not restrict or prevent an individual from faithfully discharging his duties and responsibilities as an employee of an international organization. It is also universally agreed that loyalty to one's own country is indispensable to meet the standard of integrity prescribed by Article 101 of the United Nations Charter.

INVESTIGATIONS

1. The Commission believes that the substance of the present loyalty program should be retained with certain modifications.

2. The following modifications of the present loyalty program are suggested, but should not be regarded as an exclusive list.

(*a*) Any person having prior security clearance as the result of previous Government employment should not be required to undergo another full field investigation as is presently required by Executive Order 10422, as amended. The investigative agency's report, or reports, should be furnished to the International Organizations Employees Loyalty Board, without a further investigation, if the reports are on a current basis, provided that the Loyalty Board should decide whether a report is sufficiently current and, if not, it shall order the investigation brought up to date. Except in the cases enumerated below, the head of one agency should not be compelled to accept another agency's security evaluation of an employee.

However, in the case of experts or consultants designated to represent the United States at conferences, or in similar short-term activities, the security clearance should be regarded as transferable, provided:

(1) They have been the subject of a full field investigation and

(2) They have been cleared under a standard at least as exacting as that used in the international organizations employees loyalty program.

(*b*) The Civil Service Commission should conduct all full field investigations.

434

(c) Applicants may be recommended by the Department of State for employment with international organizations on the basis of a clear national agency check, pending completion of the full field investigation. The employee should have no tenure rights until a report on the full field investigation was received and favorably evaluated. If such investigation has not been completed within three months, the Department of State will withdraw its recommendation.

(d) The name check and other processing through the International Organizations Employees Loyalty Board must be accelerated so as to avoid long periods of delay such as have occurred in the past.

The Commission recommends that Executive Order 10422 should be amended to accomplish the above suggested modification.

The substance of the program should be preserved because a total of 26 international organizations have accepted and cooperate in the implementation of the present program (none has refused to cooperate) ; the Department of State and the United Nations have confidence in the program; and experience to date indicates that the program has effectively deterred United States citizens of doubtful loyalty from seeking employment in international organizations. Since 1953, the number of United States applicants for employment in international organizations has averaged about 1,100 a year, and there has been only one rejection of an applicant.

However, certain modifications in the present program are needed to eliminate duplication and to expedite the processing of investigations and the adjudication of cases. Currently, an applicant for employment in one of the international organizations, even though he may have been the subject of a full field investigation and cleared for work in a sensitive agency of the Government, is subject to the clearance requirements of Executive Order 10422 which calls for another full field investigation or, at least, that the previous investigation be brought up to date. The restrictive nature of such requirements is obvious. Previously cleared United States scientists and other experts have been prevented from representing this country at international conferences because there was not enough time to allow for another full field investigation, and United States technical assistance personnel have been thwarted in their efforts to serve the Government overseas because of the rigid security requirements of Executive Order 10422. According to officials of international organizations interviewed by a Special Study Mission of the House Committee on Foreign Affairs:

The technical assistance programs being carried on in the international organizations have depended to a large extent on employment of experts from the United States. The drastic decline in the recruitment of such experts has resulted in a serious threat to the technical leadership which the United States has heretofore exercised in these fields. Organizations are hiring persons of other nationalities who not only are not as competent but who probably involve a much greater risk as far as the interests of the United States are concerned.[153]

Under Executive Order 10422 it is mandatory that the FBI make full field investigations of all internationally recruited personnel. If the Civil Service Commission were to make all full field investigations, except where derogatory subversive information is uncovered, it is estimated that this would result in a yearly saving to the Government of $100,000 to $150,000. The cost of a Civil Service Commission full field investigation is approximately $250.00. The cost of a detailed FBI investigation is $574.11 for applicant cases; $597.19 for full field loyalty investigations; and $113.55 for a preliminary inquiry.

HEARING PROCEDURES

The Commission believes that the procedures of the I. O. E. L. B. should be modified to expedite disposition of cases. Specifically it recommends dispensing with the review by a second examiner and the executive secretary, and that any Board member should be authorized to approve issuance of an interrogatory, thus eliminating the necessity for referral of such a matter to the chairman. Upon receipt of the interrogatory, the Commission believes that review by a second examiner and the executive secretary should be eliminated. The Commission believes the analysis of the file by an examiner after a hearing should be eliminated and the Board members should prepare a rationale and decision in each case. The preparation of the recommendations and rationale by examiners should be eliminated. The Commission recognizes that these recommendations describe specific items in a procedure which is subject to frequent change and, therefore, they are mentioned as illustrative of the type of modification which could, in the opinion of the Commission, expedite adjudication without sacrificing any basic right of an applicant to a fair adjudication.

The Commission believes that panels of the Board should be required to meet with sufficient frequency to insure prompt disposition of the cases. It considers that in the absence of unusual circumstances, a case should be decided in not to exceed 3 months after issuance of charges.

---

[153] *Report of the Special Study Mission on International Organizations and Movements . . . of the Committee on Foreign Affairs pursuant to H. Res. 113 . . . H. Rept. No. 1251, Feb. 25, 1954, p. 118.*

436

Executive Order 10422 requires that all United States citizens must be certified by the Board as to personal integrity before being hired by the United Nations or other international organizations. While this is a justifiable requirement, the overall program has suffered because the processing of cases by the Board consumes too much time. "Clear cases," i. e., cases with no derogatory information, require 60 to 75 days. Cases where derogatory information is uncovered normally require six to seven months, but some cases have taken considerably longer. Six such cases can be cited to show the time elapsed from date of receipt of reports to final determination:

CASE I.—Two years to final adverse decision. After a second hearing, five more months before the second, favorable decision.

CASE II.—One year for final decision; another year before second, favorable decision.

CASE III.—Seven and a half months elapsed. In this case employee failed to answer or appear.

CASE IV.—Three months before final, favorable decision. More than another year elapsed before second, favorable decision.

CASE V.—One year and nine months before adverse decision.

CASE VI.—Three years elapsed before final advisory recommendation.

The Board is powerless to grant on-the-spot or even quick clearances to United States citizens, a situation which prevents our people from obtaining temporary, seasonal or occasional employment in international organizations. In more than one instance alien college students living in Washington, D. C. were used as ushers for a local international function because United States college students could not be cleared in time to accept this type of "international" employment.

However, the Commission's recommendation that a national agency check be a requisite for the short-term employment of United States citizens in international organizations should eliminate clearance delays, and thus resolve the recruitment problem.

The Commission recommends that the International Organizations Employees Loyalty Board be reconstituted as follows:

1. Size: Nine members, one of whom should be designated chairman of the Board. Hearing panels should consist of three members.

2. Composition and qualifications: At least one-third of the members of the Board should be members of the bar and the member who is a member of the bar should serve as presiding member of a hearing panel. At least one member of each hearing panel (who may or may not be a lawyer member), should be appointed from the executive branch of the Government.

437

3. **Tenure**: The term of office should be for 3-year terms; the first appointments being staggered—one-third appointed for 1 year, one-third for 2 years and one-third for 3-year terms, and thereafter all appointments should be for 3 years. There should be no limitation on reappointment.

4. **Appointing authority**: The appointments of members of the Board shall be made by the President of the United States.

The Commission believes that the effectiveness of the international organizations employees loyalty program would be increased if the composition, tenure and qualifications of Board members were more consonant with the inherent responsibilities or Board membership.

The power to appoint the members of the Board is presently vested in the chairman of the Civil Service Commission. Members were appointed originally for 1 year, but are now in an excepted category and serve without time limitations. There are now seven members of the Board, one of whom is chairman, one vice-chairman, one secretary, and four members. A majority of the Board constitutes a quorum and not less than three members of the Board must be present at a hearing. There are no qualifications specified for membership on the Board. An examination of the records of present Board members shows a cross section of experience in law, banking, real estate, and education. It appears that none has had prior Federal Government experience. Board members currently serve on a basis of "when actually employed" and are compensated only for such time as they devote to Board work.

The present organization of the Board is not conducive to a prompt handling of cases and, since the scope of the loyalty program is so vast, exceptionally well-qualified people are needed to evaluate and adjudicate the many complex cases which come before the Board. While it is not necessary to establish a separate hearing authority apart from the present Loyalty Board, by increasing the number of Board members and, thereby, the number of available hearing panels, it would be possible to expedite the final disposition of cases.

EXECUTIVE ORDER AND LEGISLATION

While an international organizations employees loyalty program may be accomplished either by an act of Congress or an Executive order, the Commission believes that an Executive order is preferable because:

1. Primarily the matter is one which involves international relations;

2. Legislation is not needed in order to make the program effective inasmuch as the present program under the Executive order is acceptable and effective;

3. Although a statute could impose criminal penalties, and an Executive order cannot, there would be some doubt as to the constitutionality of legislation making it a crime to accept employment without obtaining clearance.

While there are other means available so long as the Secretariat recognizes and acts upon the principle that the employment of disloyal nationals is inconsistent with the standard of "high integrity," the machinery now in effect is best calculated to prevent the employment of disloyal Americans consistent with our obligation under the Charter.

The program currently in effect was established by Executive Order 10422, as amended by Executive Order 10459. While there is no doubt that these Executive orders are a lawful exercise of the President's executive power, it has been suggested that the loyalty program would be more effective if it were to be based upon an act of Congress rather than an Executive order.

One argument in favor of the Executive order stems from the premise that the conduct of our foreign relations is the responsibility of the President, and since the implementation of any loyalty program for United States citizens employed by international organizations involves the cooperation of foreign nationals, it becomes a matter of international relations and should be entrusted to the Chief Executive.

Legislation to prevent the employment of persons of doubtful loyalty by international organizations has already been introduced and is embodied in S. 3 of the Eighty-third Congress, as well as S. 782 and H. R. 772 of the Eighty-fourth Congress. S. 3 passed the Senate June 8, 1953. Neither house acted on S. 782 or H. R. 722 before adjournment of the Eighty-fourth Congress.

The bills proposed that before any United States citizen may accept employment in any international organization, he must first apply to the Attorney General for security clearance. The bills define, in some detail, what is to be included in the security clearance and prescribe the related duties of the Attorney General. The bills would require that any United States citizen employed by an international organization must register with the Attorney General and furnish him certain information. A violation of the provisions of the bill would be a crime with severe penalties upon conviction.

However, the question as to whether the enactment of legislation as proposed would be a valid exercise of congressional power is not a simple one. There is no clear precedent. The courts have recognized that there is an inherent right of self-preservation which exists among all sovereign powers,[154] but the Supreme Court has not yet passed on the constitutionality of certain acts of Congress directed against the Communist menace and its threat to our national security.[155]

While expressing the view that Congress has the power to legislate in this field, it cannot be said or implied that all the proposed legislation would be upheld against constitutional attack. Serious questions of due process of law arise, where criminal sanctions are imposed upon the exercise of the right to seek and retain employment. This is particularly true when clearance for employment is based not upon acts of subversion and espionage, but upon likelihood of future conduct based upon opinions, beliefs and associations of the individual seeking clearance.

There is also a need, based upon experience, for flexibility and prompt action in the loyalty program, which indicates that an Executive order would be preferable to an act of Congress.

There are other means available to the Government to prevent the employment by international organizations of disloyal United States citizens but, in view of the well-grounded Government and public arguments directed against the alternative measures proposed by Congress, and since a number of international organizations have come to accept and appreciate the value of the present loyalty program, it would be inadvisable to overhaul drastically the machinery currently in effect, particularly since present procedures guard the national security without compromising our obligations under the United Nations Charter or other international agreements.

CONFRONTATION

Caveat: The Commission has recommended that the international organizations employees loyalty program be implemented by Executive order, but it may be necessary to implement the subpena recommendation by legislation.

Confrontation, of the scope recommended in the civilian loyalty program, should be limited to evidence offered in support of any of the following charges:

1. Sabotage, espionage, attempts or preparations therefor, or knowingly associating with spies or saboteurs;

2. Treason or sedition or advocacy thereof;

3. Advocacy of revolution, or force or violence to alter the constitutional form of Government of the United States;

4. Intentional, unauthorized disclosure to any person, under circumstances which may indicate disloyalty to the United

---

[154] *U. S.* v. *Curtiss-Wright Export Corporation,* 299 U. S. 304 (1936).

[155] Internal Security Act of 1950, as amended 50 USC 781–826, and the Communist Control Act of 1954. Pub. Law 637, 83d Cong.

States, of documents or information of a confidential or non-public character;

5. Performing or attempting to perform his duties, or otherwise acting while an employee of the United States Government during a previous period, so as to serve the interests of another government in preference to the interests of the United States;

6. Membership in, affiliation or sympathetic association with, any party, or association which the Congress of the United States, or any agency or officer of the United States duly authorized by the Congress for that purpose finds:

(a) Seeks to alter the form of Government of the United States by force or violence, or other unconstitutional means; or

(b) Is organized or utilized for the purpose of advancing the aims and objectives of the Communist movement; or

(c) Is organized or utilized for the purpose of establishing any form of dictatorship in the United States or any form of international dictatorship; or

(d) Is organized or utilized by any foreign government, or by any foreign party, group or association acting in the interest of such foreign government for the purpose of (1) espionage, or (2) sabotage, or (3) obtaining information relating to the defense of the United States or the protection of the national security, or (4) hampering, hindering, or delaying the production of defense materials; or

(e) Is affiliated with, or acts in concert with, or is dominated or controlled by any party, group, or association of the character described in (a), (b), (c), or (d) above.

7. Membership in or affiliation with any organization which the Congress of the United States, or any agency or officer of the United States duly authorized by the Congress for that purpose, finds has adopted a policy of advocating or approving the commission of acts of force and violence to deny others their rights under the Constitution of the United States.

8. Refusal to testify upon the ground of self-incrimination, in any authorized inquiry relating to subversive activities conducted by a congressional committee, Federal court, Federal grand jury, or any other duly authorized Federal agency, as to questions relating to subversive activities of the individual involved or others, unless the individual, after opportunity to do so, satisfactorily explains his refusal to testify.

The Commission believes that the right of subpena should be applicable where there is a right of confrontation, but this does not preclude the applicant for clearance from furnishing affidavits or the testimony of witnesses he wishes to present and who are willing to appear voluntarily.

1. Either the Government or the individual involved should be permitted to apply to the hearing examiner to issue subpenas, except as to confidential informants and identified informants who have given their information on the condition that they will not be called as witnesses. Such application should state the name and address of such witness, as well as the substance of the testimony to be presented by the witness. If the hearing examiner deems the evidence relevant and not merely cumulative, he may issue the subpena.

2. In the exercise of his discretion to issue subpenas, the hearing examiner should consider such factors as the time and expense involved by reason of the travel required.

3. The witness should be compensated for travel expenses and per diem, but where the cost is substantial, the hearing examiner may in his discretion require the parties to use deposition procedures.

4. The Government should bear the cost of Government witnesses, but the hearing examiner should not subpena a witness for the individual involved until the individual deposits with the Government sufficient funds to pay the travel and per diem costs of such witness. In the event that the applicant is not cleared, the funds deposited by the applicant should be used to pay for the applicant's witness expenses. If, however, the applicant is cleared, the funds deposited by the applicant should be returned to him and the Government should bear the travel and per diem costs of the applicant's witness.

5. The Commission believes Congress should enact legislation giving the Civil Service Commission power to authorize the International Organization Employees Loyalty Board under its jurisdiction to issue subpenas to carry out the above recommendation.

Passport Security Program

Introduction

A passport has been defined generally as being in the nature of a political document allied to, and at times a part of, the conduct of foreign affairs.

Its usage in the United States goes back over the better part of 2 centuries. In the early stages it amounted in international law to a letter of safe conduct. Today it is an essential element to travel abroad by an American citizen.

The statutory authority to grant or withhold a passport was vested in the Secretary of State by the Congress 101 years ago, but this exercise of discretion in the issuance is actually grounded in the power over foreign relations placed in the Executive by the Constitution.

Passports have now become "big business." From a figure of 21,719 in 1912, the issuance or renewal of passports mushroomed to a total of 559,066 in 1956. In the 10 years from 1947 to 1956, inclusive, the Passport Office reported a grand total of 3,641,675. In the Passport Office files today there are more than 35 million documents incidental to the conduct of its business, covering the period from 1940 to date.

Whether Communists or those with sympathetic associations were entitled to passports has been a problem existing almost from the time of the Bolshevik revolution in 1917. Marked fluctuations in the policy of the Department of State in this respect have been reviewed.

The United States, like other nations, has had its full share of experience with Communist-inspired fraud and forgery and the full gamut of subtle devices employed in this field.

This Commission has closely studied the history of the passport security program. The record to date is not particularly impressive. Serious deficiencies have been noted.

Accordingly, the Commission has made 5 recommendations for legislation, 7 for changes in present regulations, and 10 for revision of operational procedures.

HISTORY

The United States Supreme Court in 1835 described the 19th-century concept of the passport as follows:

> There is no law of the United States, in any manner regulating the issuing of passports. . . . It is a document, which, from its nature and object, is addressed to foreign powers; purporting only to be a request, that the bearer of it may pass safely and freely; and is to be considered rather in the character of a political document, by which the bearer is recognised, in foreign countries, as an American citizen; and which, by usage and the law of nations, is received as evidence of the fact.[1]

In 1933, an Assistant Secretary of State defined American passports in these terms:

> The American passport is a document of identity and nationality issued to persons owing allegiance to the United States and intending to travel or sojourn in foreign countries. It indicates that it is the right of the bearer to receive the protection and good offices of American diplomatic and consular officers abroad and requests on the part of the Government of the United States that the officials of foreign governments permit the bearer to travel or sojourn in their territories and in case of need to give him all lawful aid and protection. It has no other purpose.[2]

Necessity and advisability for obtaining a passport.—The Constitution contains no express provision relative to the right to travel abroad or the necessity for a passport in order to leave the country. However, complaints contained in the Declaration of Independence against restrictions upon the right to travel indicate the high value placed upon that right by Colonial Americans.

Although Congress did not enact legislation governing the issuance of passports during the early days of our country, the Secretary of State has issued passports at least since 1796.[3]

As a matter of military necessity, Congress regulated the right to travel abroad during the War of 1812. That statute, which was passed in 1815, made it illegal for any person residing in the United States to enter territory occupied by the British without a passport.[4] Violation of the act was made punishable by fine or imprisonment. Similarly, during the Civil War, the Department of State prohibited anyone from going abroad or from passing the lines of the United States Army without a passport.[5]

When World War I began, American citizens were not required to carry passports when traveling abroad. However on November 14, 1914, the Department of State issued an order which said in part:

> All American citizens who go abroad should carry American passports, and should inquire of diplomatic or consular officers of the countries which they expect to visit concerning the necessity of having the passports visaed therefor.[6]

---

[1] *Urtetiqui* v. *D'Arcy et al.*, 9 Pet. 692, 698.

[2] 3 Hackworth, *Digest of International Law*, p. 435 (1942).

[3] *The American Passport*, published by the Department of State (1898), p. 77.

[4] 3 Stat. 195, 199–200.

[5] *The American Passport*, op. cit., pp. 49–50.

[6] 3 *Digest of International Law*, op. cit., p. 526.

By letter dated June 5, 1917, the Secretary of Commerce requested steamship lines not to accept as a passenger on any oceangoing vessel departing from the United States and bound for a foreign port, nor to permit the departure thereon as a passenger, any citizen of the United States unless such citizen has a valid passport issued by the Department of State.[7]

By act approved May 22, 1918, Congress gave the President the power to make it a criminal offense for any citizen to depart the United States unless he had a valid passport.[8] The act of May 22, 1918, was implemented on August 8, 1918, by President Wilson.[9] Thereafter it was unlawful for an American citizen to leave the United States without a valid passport. President Wilson also proclaimed that—

No citizen of the United States shall receive a passport entitling him to leave or enter the United States, unless it shall affirmatively appear that there are adequate reasons for such departure or entry and that such departure or entry is not prejudicial to the interests of the United States.

After the end of hostilities, American citizens could again leave the United States without passports.

Just prior to World War II, the Department of State replaced all outstanding passports with a new style document. By this means it was possible to remove all fraudulent or altered passports from circulation and also to remove passports from the hands of persons engaged in activities not in the best interest of the United States. A replacement passport was granted only after a thorough examination of the bona fides of the bearer.[10]

On November 14, 1941, the President of the United States proclaimed that "no citizen . . . or person who owes allegiance . . . shall depart from . . . the United States . . . unless he bears a valid passport issued by the Secretary of State. . . ."[11]

At the present time, it is provided by statute (66 Stat. 163, 190) that when the United States is at war or during the existence of a national emergency proclaimed by the President, if the President shall find that the interests of the United States require additional restrictions and prohibitions to those otherwise provided with respect to the departure of persons from and their entry into the United States, and shall so proclaim, it shall be unlawful, except as otherwise provided by the President, and subject to limitations and exceptions authorized by him, for any citizen of the United States, to depart from or enter the United States "unless he bears a valid passport." The President has made a proclamation which brings these provisions into effect.[12]

As shown above, during most of our history passports have not been required by this country of Americans who desired to travel abroad. How-

[7] 3 *Digest of International Law*, op. cit., p. 527.
[8] 40 Stat. 559.
[9] 40 Stat. 1829.
[10] 12 *Department of State Bulletin*, 1068 (1945).
[11] Proclamation 2523; 55 Stat. 1696.
[12] Proclamation No. 3004, 18 F. R. 489, which followed Proclamation No. 2914.

ever, the State Department has, at least since 1845, pointed out the desirability of obtaining such a travel document.[13]

In the general instructions in regard to passports, published in 1873 by the Department of State, it is said:

Citizens of the United States visiting foreign countries are liable to serious inconvenience if unprovided with authentic proof of their natonal character. The best safeguard is a passport from this Department, certifying the bearer to be a citizen of the United States.[14]

The State Department also advised Americans to secure passports if they were planning to visit countries which required such documents at their frontier.[15] By 1867 all Europe, except Russia and Turkey, had practically eliminated the passport. Since the end of the First World War, however, the majority of countries have required that foreigners entering their territories possess valid passports issued by the state of their nationality.[16]

Passports—By whom issued.—Before the establishment of the Federal Government, the States as well as municipal authorities had issued passports. This practice continued long after the adoption of the Constitution.[17] In 1856, Congress passed a statute declaring that the Secretary of State "shall be authorized to grant and issue passports, and cause passports to be granted, issued and verified in foreign countries by such diplomatic or consular officers, of the United States, . . . and no other person shall grant, issue, or verify any such passport. . . ." [18] Since 1856 a provision similar to the Act quoted above has been a part of the United States Code.[19] But even so, passports, or documents in the nature of passports, have occasionally been granted by governors of various States. Whenever the Department of State has been presented with evidence that a governor of a State has issued a passport, it has advised him of the statute prohibiting the issue of passports by other than the Secretary of State or persons duly authorized by him.[20]

Passport citizenship requirements.—There were instances in the 1820's of special passports being issued to foreigners.[21] In 1835, the Supreme Court referred to the practice of requiring "some evidence of citizenship" before issuing a passport.[22] In 1856 Congress specifically provided that passports could be issued only to citizens.[23] This was changed in 1863 and the Department of State could issue passports to "any class of persons liable to military duty by the laws of the United States." [24] After the Civil

[13] *The American Passport,* op. cit., pp. 46, 54.
[14] *The American Passport,* op. cit., p. 54.
[15] *The American Passport,* op. cit., p. 169.
[16] 12 *Department of State Bulletin,* 1066 (1945).
[17] *The American Passport,* op. cit., p. 37.
[18] 11 Stat. 60.
[19] Rev. Stat., sec. 4075; 22 U. S. C. 211a.
[20] 3 *Digest of International Law,* op. cit., pp. 470–471.
[21] *The American Passport,* op. cit., pp. 12–13.
[22] *Urtetiqui* v. *D'Arcy,* 9 Pet. 692, 698.
[23] 11 Stat. 60.
[24] 12 Stat. 754.

War, Congress again declared that passports could be issued only to citizens.[25] This law was codified into the Revised Statutes in 1874.[26] Since 1902 passports can be issued to all persons owing allegiance to the United States, whether citizens or not.[27]

Oath of allegiance.—At least as early as 1861 applicants for passports were required to take an oath of allegiance to the United States.[28] It is not improbable that the oath was originally intended to be a temporary measure which was to continue in force only during the Civil War; but the propriety of exacting a promise to support the Government from everyone who might ask from it the protection of a passport has been recognized by successive Secretaries of State since that time.[29] At the present time the applicant is required to take the following oath:

> Further, I do solemnly swear that I will support and defend the Constitution of the United States against all enemies, foreign and domestic; that I will bear true faith and allegiance to the same; and that I take this obligation freely, without any mental reservations, or purpose of evasion: So help me God.

It has been the practice of the Department of State to permit applicants for passports who so desire to make an affirmation in place of an oath of allegiance. However, the requirement for one or the other will not be waived.[30]

Growing demand for passports.—Passport activity in 1912 amounted to 21,719 passports issued and renewed. That American overseas travel increased after World War I is apparent from the State Department statistics which show that 160,488 passports were procured in 1920. The figure exceeded 200,000 in 1930, but receded considerably during the depression years that followed. As Hitler launched his European blitzkrieg in 1939, the number of passports issued and renewed dropped below 100,000 for the first time since 1919. With the prosperity following the war and the increased development of international air travel, the number of passports issued and renewed increased to nearly 300,000 by 1950. By 1956 this figure had risen to more than 559,000.

In 1950, in deference to congressional intent expressed in the Internal Security Act [31] and because leaders of the Communist Party had been convicted of violating the Smith Act, as well as because the Communists were actively supporting the aggressors in the Korean conflict, a stricter policy was inaugurated. Before initiating this new policy the Department of State also took into consideration its own experience that since the end of World War I American Communists and alien Communists illegally in possession

---

[25] 14 Stat. 54.

[26] Rev. Stat., sec. 4076.

[27] 32 Stat. 386; 22 U. S. C. 212.

[28] *The American Passport,* op. cit., p. 69.

[29] *The American Passport,* op. cit., p. 69; 3 *Digest of International Law,* op. cit., pp. 493–495; form DSP–11 (12–15–55) (Department of State passport application); 22 C. F. R. 51.23 (o) (1949 edition); Executive Order 4800 dated Jan. 31, 1928; Executive Order 7856 dated Apr. 2, 1938.

[30] 3 *Digest of International Law,* op. cit., p. 493.

[31] 50 U. S. C. 785.

of American passports had effectively carried on espionage, propaganda, and revolutionary activities on behalf of the Soviet Government and the international Communist movement.

Attack on the discretion of the Secretary of State to issue or refuse passports.—The carrying out of the stricter policy referred to above led to criticism of the Department of State's practices and procedures. As a result of this criticism, including that contained in a court decision adverse to the Department of State,[32] regulations were promulgated which made mandatory the discretionary policies which had previously been followed, and which provided for procedures in cases of persons refused passports.[33]

Five years have now elapsed since the court decided *Bauer* v. *Acheson.*[34] Until that time the discretion of the Secretary of State to issue or refuse passports had survived without serious contest as a necessary adjunct to the executive power to control foreign affairs.

Since the *Bauer* case, there have been several court decisions which indicate that the position once held, i. e., that the Secretary of State has absolute discretion in issuing passports, is necessarily undergoing a change.

Reorganization of the Passport Office.—The Passport Office was thoroughly reorganized in 1955. New and adequate quarters were acquired and revisions in procedure were effected. Today the Passport Office is geared to render fast, efficient service demanded by an ever more travel-conscious public.[35] However, security problems created by the need to prevent certain persons from traveling abroad are far from settled.

LEGAL BASIS

Introduction

There are three aspects to the legal problem presented by a study of passports: (*a*) foreign policy, (*b*) national security, and (*c*) the duty to reconcile those two obligations of the government with the citizen's need or urge to travel abroad.

The Constitution [36] invests the President with the "power, by and with the advice and consent of the Senate, to make treaties, provided two-thirds of the Senators present concur; and he shall nominate, and by and with the advice and consent of the Senate, shall appoint ambassadors, other public ministers and consuls . . ." By natural evolution, constitutional powers of the President in the area of foreign policy have been delegated in many

---

[32] *Bauer* v. *Acheson*, 106 F. Supp. 445 (1952).

[33] 22 C. F. R. 51.135–143.

[34] *Bauer* v. *Acheson*, ibid.

[35] Reorganization of the Passport Office, report of the Senate Committee on Government Operations, S. Rept. 1604, 84th Cong., 2d sess.

[36] Art. II, sec. 2, clause 2.

respects to the Secretary of State. One of those delegations has been in the area of passports.

A passport was defined in 1835 as a "document, which from its nature and object, is addressed to foreign powers; . . . and is to be considered rather in the character of a political document." [37] In 1874 Congress provided that no person other than the Secretary of State is authorized to "grant, issue or verify a passport." [38] This provision has continued in effect.

Statutes, Executive orders, and regulations

There are four statutes [39] of principal concern in the study of passports as related to security:

(1) 22 U. S. C. A. 211 (a):

Authority to grant, issue, and verify passports.—The Secretary of State may grant and issue passports, and cause passports to be granted, issued, and verified in foreign countries by diplomatic representatives of the United States, and by such consul generals, consuls, or vice consuls when in charge, as the Secretary of State may designate, and by the chief or other executive officer of the insular possessions of the United States, under such rules as the President shall designate and prescribe for and on behalf of the United States, and no other person shall grant, issue, or verify such passports.[40]

(2) 22 U. S. C. A. 212:

Who entitled to passport.—No passport shall be granted or issued to or verified for any other persons than those owing allegiance, whether citizens, or not, to the United States.[41]

(3) 8 U. S. C. A. 1185:

Travel control of citizens and aliens during war or national emergency—Restrictions and prohibitions on aliens.—(a) When the United States is at war or during the existence of any national emergency proclaimed by the President, . . . and the President shall find that the interests of the United States require that restrictions and prohibitions in addition to those provided otherwise than by this section be imposed upon the departure of persons from and their entry into the United States, and shall make public proclamation thereof, it shall, until otherwise ordered by the President or the Congress, be unlawful—

.   .   .   .   .   .

(b) After such proclamation as is provided for in subsection (a) of this section has been made and published and while such proclamation is in force, it shall, except as otherwise provided by the President, and subject to such limitations and exceptions as the President may authorize and prescribe, be unlawful for any citizen of the

---

[37] *Urtetique* v. *D'Arcy et al.*, 9 Pet. 692, 34 U. S. 692 (1835).
[38] Rev. Stats. 4075–4076 (1874).
[39] Exclusive of criminal provisions discussed *infra*.
[40] 44 Stat. 887.
[41] 32 Stat. 386.

United States to depart from or enter, or attempt to depart from or enter, the United States unless he bears a valid passport.[42]

. . . .

(4) 50 U. S. C. A. 785:

Denial of passport to members of Communist organizations.—(*a*) When a Communist organization as defined in paragraph (5) of section 782 of this title is registered, or there is in effect a final order of the Board requiring such organization to register, it shall be unlawful for any member of such organization, with knowledge or notice that such organization is so registered or that such order has become final—

> (1) to make application for a passport, or the renewal of a passport, to be issued or renewed by or under the authority of the United States; or
> (2) to use or attempt to use any such passport.

(*b*) When an organization is registered, or there is in effect a final order of the Board requiring an organization to register, as a Communist-action organization, it shall be unlawful for any officer or employee of the United States to issue a passport to, or renew the passport of, any individual knowing or having reason to believe that such individual is a member of such organization.[43]

It will be noted that there is no statutory requirement that a United States citizen or national must have a passport to depart from or enter into the United States in peacetime.

These statutes have been implemented by Executive orders and proclamations, specifically Executive Order 7856,[44] which contains detailed regulations governing applications for and the issuance of passports. A more important provision of that order, section 124, authorized the Secretary of State "in his discretion to refuse to issue a passport, to restrict a passport for use only in certain countries, to restrict it against use in certain countries, to withdraw or cancel a passport already issued, and to withdraw a passport for the purpose of restricting its validity for use in certain countries." By section 126 the Secretary of State was authorized "to make regulations on the subject of issuing, renewing, extending, amending, restricting, or withdrawing passports additional to these rules and not inconsistent therewith." Pursuant to this authority the Secretary of State has issued and subsequently revised regulations on this subject.[45]

The emergency provisions, 8 U. S. C. A. 1185, are invoked pursuant to Presidential Proclamation 2914,[46] which declared that world conquest by Communist imperialism is the goal of forces of aggression and proclaimed a national emergency. Later, Presidential Proclamation 3004,[47] found that "the exigencies of the international situation . . . still require that certain restrictions and prohibitions, in addition to those otherwise provided by law, be imposed upon the departure of persons from and their entry into the U. S."

---

[42] 66 Stat. 190, a slightly modified reenactment of act of June 21, 1941, 22 U. S. C. A. 223.
[43] 64 Stat. 993. "Board" refers to Subversive Activities Control Board, 50 U. S. C. A., 791.
[44] March 31, 1938, 3 F. R. 799, 22 C. F. R. 51.1–51.77.
[45] 22 C. F. R. 51–51.170, 52, 53.9.
[46] Dec. 16, 1950.
[47] Jan. 17, 1953, 3 C. F. R. 1953 Supp., p. 20.

The executive department urges that the long history of congressional enactments has established the intent of Congress that the Secretary of State, subject to the direction of the President, should have complete discretion in the field of passport issuance. Until recently, the courts have seemingly agreed that the discretion of the Secretary of State in this field is complete.

For example, in *Miller* v. *Sinjan*,[48] the court said:

> . . . a finding that plaintiff had ceased to be a citizen of the United States was not necessary to the action of the State Department in denying him a passport, for the reason that the granting of a passport by the United States is, and always has been, a discretionary matter; and a passport, when granted, is not conclusive, nor is it even evidence, that the person to whom it is granted is a citizen of the United States. . . . This has been the law both prior to the passage of any statute relating to the granting of passports as well as subsequent to such statutes, now embodied in sections 4075 et seq., Revised Statutes. . . .

The first shift in the position of the courts with reference to the unlimited discretion of the Secretary of State in the manner of the issuance of passports appears in *Perkins* v. *Elg*.[49] This was a case in which a passport had been denied the appellant, Miss Elg, for the reason that she was not a citizen. The plaintiff in the lower court, Miss Elg, had joined the Secretary of Labor, then administrator of immigration laws, and the Secretary of State as defendants. The lower court dismissed the bill of complaint as against the Secretary of State. The dismissal was upon the ground that the court would not undertake by mandamus to compel the issuance of a passport or control by means of a declaratory judgment the discretion of the Secretary of State.

Chief Justice Hughes, himself a former Secretary of State, said:

> . . . The Secretary of State, according to the allegation of the bill of complaint, had refused to issue a passport to Miss Elg "solely on the ground that she had lost her native born American citizenship." The court below . . . declared Miss Elg "to be a natural born citizen of the United States" and we think that the decree should include the Secretary of State as well as other defendants. The decree in that sense would in no way interfere with the exercise of the Secretary's discretion with respect to the issue of a passport, but would simply preclude the denial of a passport on the sole ground that Miss Elg had lost her citizenship.

Since 1950, the refusal and/or revocation of passports by the Secretary of State has been the subject of litigation in the lower Federal courts. While the Secretary has not been uniformly unsuccessful in this litigation, the decisions point in the direction of there being distinct limitations upon the Secretary's discretion where security and not foreign policy is the determining factor. No case has as yet been taken by the Government to the Supreme Court. The cases in point are reviewed, briefly, below.

Bauer v. *Acheson*[50] is the first of a series of what may be called 'passport security" cases. The plaintiff, a naturalized citizen since 1944, was in Paris,

---

[48] 289 F. 388 (C. A. 8, 1923).
[49] 307 U. S. 325 (1939).
[50] 106 F. Supp. 445 (D. C. D. C., 1951).

France, where she was employed as a journalist. She had gone to France in 1948 with a valid passport which was subsequently extended to January 1, 1952. On June 4, 1951, representatives of the Secretary of State seized plaintiff's passport and declared it had been revoked. The revocation was without notice or hearing and the reason given was that "her activities are contrary to the best interests of the United States." Plaintiff was informed that her passport would be returned to her, validated only for return to the United States, when she had completed travel arrangements for such return.

The plaintiff sued the Secretary of State, asking for a review under the Administrative Procedure Act [51] and for an injunction against the denial of her right to a passport. As the plaintiff raised constitutional questions, a three-judge constitutional court was convened to hear the case.

It was contended that the statutory authority of the Secretary of State to "grant and issue passports" and to "cause passports to be granted, issued and verified in foreign countries" did not include authority to revoke a passport. The court held that "the authority to issue passports necessarily implies authority also to regulate their use and to withdraw them."

The plaintiff further contended that the construction placed upon the passport control provisions by the Secretary of State that he could revoke and deny a passport without notice, hearing, and anything more than a generalized statement of the reason for such action,[52] is unconstitutional in that it violates the due process clause of the fifth amendment and ex post facto and bill-of-attainder provisions of the Constitution.[53]

The court held that neither the statute nor the regulation is a bill of attainder or an ex post facto law. The court held further that since the statute and regulation in question are susceptible of a constitutional interpretation, they are constitutional.

As to the question of the due process clause of the fifth amendment, the court held that while the "freedom to travel abroad, like other rights, is subject to reasonable regulation and control in the interest of the public welfare, . . . the Constitution requires due process and equal protection of the laws in the exercise of that control." The court, after a comprehensive discussion of the nature of passports, and of the requirements of due process, stated: "We conclude that revocation of the plaintiff's passport without notice and hearing before revocation, as well as refusal to renew such passport without an opportunity to be heard, was without authority of law. It follows that the Secretary of State should be directed to renew or revalidate the plaintiff's passport without the amendment making it valid only for return to the United States, unless a hearing is accorded her within a reasonable time." [54]

---

[51] 5 U. S. C. A. 1009.

[52] The regulations, 22 C. F. R. 53.8 (1949), provided "nothing in this part shall be construed to prevent the Secretary of State from exercising the discretion resting in him to refuse to issue a passport, to restrict its use, etc. . . ."

[53] Art. 1, sec. 9.

[54] Judge Fahy dissented from the opinion for the reason that the case should have been decided by one judge, rather than by a three-judge statutory court, and expressed no opinion on the merits.

454

The case of *Schachtman* v. *Dulles* [55] is an important passport security case. In this case, the appellant had sued in the Federal District Court of the District of Columbia to enjoin the Secretary of State from denying him a passport for the reason stated and for a declaratory judgment. The complaint was dismissed by the district court, the court holding that the denial was in the proper exercise of the Secretary's discretion and the court lacked jurisdiction. An appeal from this decision was taken to the Court of Appeals for the District of Columbia Circuit.

The court of appeals noted that Schachtman did not ask that the court require the Secretary to issue the passport, but only sought a ruling that the denial had been for legally insufficient grounds.

The court, in its opinion, did not "suggest that a passport is no longer a political document, or that its issuance is not allied to, and at times a part of, the conduct of foreign affairs." Continuing its discussion, the court pointed out that a passport is now essential to the lawful departure of an American citizen for Europe and the denial of a passport causes a deprivation of liberty. The court then said:

> The right to travel, to go from place to place as the means of transportation permit, is a natural right subject to the rights of others and to reasonable regulation under law. A restraint imposed by the Government of the United States upon this liberty, therefore, must conform with the provision of the Fifth Amendment that "no person shall be . . . deprived of . . . liberty . . . without due process of law."

The court observed that the case as presented did not involve procedural due process. There was no complaint the Secretary had failed to disclose the reason for his denial of the passport. A hearing of a sort was granted appellant and he was at least given an opportunity to state informally to an official of the Department the matters on which he relied in rebuttal of the reason given by the Department for refusing him a passport.

The court said:

> What is involved at the present stage is a question of substantive due process— whether the refusal for the reason given, as alleged in the complaint and undisputed thus far by the Secretary, was arbitrary.

The appellant's own statement in the complaint of the reason he was refused a passport was accepted as true, for the Secretary of State did not answer the complaint. The passport was allegedly denied for the reason that the appellant was chairman of the Independent Socialists' League which the Secretary of State understood had been classified by the Attorney General as both subversive and communistic. Subsequently, the Department of State informed the appellant that despite the evidence that the league had no connection with the Communist International and was hostile thereto, the Department felt that it would be contrary to the best interests of the United States to grant a passport to the head of an organization which had been classified by the Attorney General as subversive, especially as he desired to travel abroad on behalf of the organization.

---

[55] 225 F. 2d 938 (C. A. D. C., 1955).

The court said:

We think the complaint fairly read shows that the listing of the League by the Attorney General as subversive was the reason for the Secretary's refusal to issue the passport, that is to say, that except for such listing the fact that appellant was head of the organization and wished to go to Europe on its business would not have been considered by the Secretary as ground for rejection of his application.

The court further said:

It is not for us to determine, in this case at least, that a passport should or should not be granted, but only whether the reason given by the Secretary for its denial is sufficient. As to this we think the law must consider to be arbitrary, regardless of good faith, refusal of appellant's application only because the League was listed by the Attorney General as subversive when appellant in detail denies the correctness of this characterization, alleges lack of opportunity so to demonstrate, and when these allegations are not challenged by the Secretary. In these circumstances a sufficient basis for the action of the issuing authority apart from the mere listing must appear. For us to hold that the restraint thus imposed upon appellant is not arbitrary would amount to judicial approval of a deprivation of liberty without a reasonable relation to the conduct of foreign affairs.

Finally, the court said:

We must not confuse the problem of appellant's application for a passport with the conduct of foreign affairs in the political sense, which is entirely removed from judicial competence. For even though his application might be said to come within the scope of foreign affairs in a broad sense, it is also within the scope of the due process clause, which is concerned with the liberty of the individual free of arbitrary administrative restraint. There must be some reconciliation of these interests where only the right of a particular individual to travel is involved and not a question of foreign affairs on a political level.

Following the decision of the court in the above-styled case, the Passport Office issued a passport to Mr. Schachtman on August 2, 1955.

Shortly before the *Schachtman* case was decided, the same court, the United States Court of Appeals for the District of Columbia Circuit, issued an order, without opinion, in the case of *Dulles* v. *Nathan* [56] ordering the Department of State to accord a quasi-judicial hearing on the application of Mr. Nathan for a passport. The order was dated June 2, 1955, and directed that the hearing be held on June 7, 1955, and to be concluded within 3 days unless the court, upon application, should extend the time. The Passport Office issued a passport to Mr. Nathan on June 6, 1955; hence there was no necessity for a hearing.

The Passport Office refused a passport to Leonard Boudin. He filed suit, moved for summary judgment and a preliminary injunction. [57] In a memorandum decision, Judge Youngdahl held that section 51.170, when used in conjunction with section 51.135 of the passport regulations, does not comport with due process. The case was remanded to the Passport Office for a hearing within 20 days and the court directed "All evidence upon which the Office may rely for its decision under section 51.135 must appear on

---

[56] 225 F. 2d 29 (C. A. D. C., 1955).
[57] 136 F. Supp. 218 (D. C. D. C., 1955).

record so that the applicant may have the opportunity to meet it and the Court to review it." Both parties appealed from this decision, and on June 28, 1956, the decision was rendered.[58] The decision analyzes in detail section 51.135 [59] of the passport regulations.

Following the analysis, the court quoted in part from an affidavit filed by the Secretary of State in the district court: "The basis for my decision to deny the plaintiff further passport facilities rests on a pattern of associations and activities on the part of the plaintiff over an extended period of time leading to the conclusion that the plaintiff has been and continues to be a supporter of the Communist movement." The court then said: "For present purposes, we accept the Secretary's affidavit as a statement that he has found that Boudin is a supporter of the Communist movement even though such finding was not communicated in his letter notifying Boudin that issuance of a passport was precluded by 51.135 of the passport regulations."

The court then pointed out that the Secretary's finding did not conform to the requirements of the regulations, and the court stated: "We think that factual findings sufficient to bring the applicant within one of the classes described in section 51.135 are required before the Secretary may deny a passport under the authority of that regulation." The court added:

The matter must therefore be returned to the Secretary for reconsideration. He may conclude that a passport should be issued or that a further hearing is needed. But if he decides—with or without an additional hearing—that issuance of a passport would not be warranted under the regulations, he should advise Boudin in writing of the findings made, relating them to the sections relied on. We do not reach in the present posture of the case the contention made by Boudin that the Secretary cannot rely on confidential information in reaching his decision. But since that question may arise at a subsequent stage, we think the Secretary should—if he refuses a passport to Boudin after the further consideration we have ordered—state whether his findings are based on the evidence openly produced, or (in whole or in material part) on secret information not disclosed to the applicant. If the latter, the Secretary should explain with such particularity as in his judgment the circumstances permit, the nature of the reasons why such information may not be disclosed. . . . This will facilitate the task of the Courts in dealing with the question of the propriety of the Secretary's use of confidential information—a question which, we repeat, we do not now reach.

---

[58] 235 F. 2d 532 (C. A. D. C., 1956).

[59] § 51.135 *Limitations on issuance of passports to persons supporting Communist movement.*—In order to promote the national interest by assuring that persons who support the world Communist movement of which the Communist Party is an integral unit may not, through use of United States passports, further the purposes of that movement, no passport, except one limited for direct and immediate return to the United States, shall be issued to: (a) Persons who are members of the Communist Party or who have recently terminated such membership under such circumstances as to warrant the conclusion—not otherwise rebutted by the evidence—that they continue to act in furtherance of the interests and under the discipline of the Communist Party;

(b) Persons, regardless of the formal state of their affiliation with the Communist Party, who engage in activities which support the Communist movement under such circumstances as to warrant the conclusion—not otherwise rebutted by the evidence—that they have engaged in such activities as a result of direction, domination, or control exercised over them by the Communist movement;

(c) Persons, regardless of the formal state of their affiliation with the Communist Party, as to whom there is reason to believe, on the balance of all the evidence, that they are going abroad to engage in activities which will advance the Communist movement for the purpose, knowingly and willfully of advancing that movement.

A passport was issued to Mr. Boudin August 29, 1956.

On June 7, 1956, *Robeson* v. *Dulles* [60] was decided in favor of the Secretary of State. In this case appellant Robeson had applied for a passport. It was refused tentatively pending further information which he refused to furnish. Robeson then brought suit in the district court asking for a judgment that he be found entitled to a passport and that certain regulations of the Secretary of State and rules of the Board of Passport Appeals be declared invalid because they are in violation of the statutes of the United States, the United States Constitution, and the Declaration of Human Rights of the United Nations. The complaint asked for an injunction enjoining the Secretary of State from continuing to deny a passport and directing him to issue one. The complaint was dismissed by the district court, and Robeson appealed.

The opinion of the court of appeals pointed out the various administrative procedures with which the appellant refused to comply. Robeson had based his refusal on the grounds that the regulations were invalid and contended he should not be required to comply with them. The court said:

> Robeson failed to exhaust his administrative remedies. We think he was required to do so. He did not ask for a hearing but instead asserted the invalidity of the regulation providing for one. We cannot assume the invalidity of a hearing which has not been held or the illegality of questions which have not been asked. The judgment of the District Court should be affirmed.

The Supreme Court has refused jurisdiction. Presumably the law now stands as announced, that administrative procedures must be complied with before an applicant may resort to the courts.

A case which may go to the Supreme Court and permit an authoritative decision is that of *Dayton* v. *Dulles*. On February 6, 1956, by a memorandum decision, the district court found that "the denial of plaintiff's application for a passport was a reasonable exercise of discretion by the Secretary of State under valid regulations, and that it was not in violation of the due process requirements of the Constitution." Mr. Dayton appealed from this decision.

The court of appeals in its decision referred to its opinion in, and disposition of, the case of *Boudin* v. *Dulles*. The court stated that for the reasons given in that case the judgment of the district court was reversed and the case remanded for further proceedings not inconsistent with the opinion of the court. [61]

In compliance with the remanding order, the Secretary of State filed his "Decision and Finding in the case of Weldon Bruce Dayton" and sent a copy to Dayton. It was stated that the passport was denied under sec. 51.135 (c) of the passport regulations and because the issuance of a passport would be contrary to the national interest.

---

[60] 235 F. 2d 810 (C. A. D. C., 1950), certiorari denied Nov. 5, 1956.
[61] 237 F. 2d 43 (C. A. D. C., 1956).

The decision of the Secretary of State was divided into six numbered paragraphs. The first four numbered paragraphs were based on information contained in the open record and related various Communist associations and activities of the plaintiff. Other parts of the decision related several Communist associations and activities of the plaintiff based on confidential information contained in the files of the Department of State.

The Secretary found "that the applicant is going abroad to engage in activities which will advance the Communist movement for the purpose, knowingly and willfully of advancing that movement."

The Secretary further stated that the substance of the confidential information was revealed to the applicant during the consideration of his application and that to disclose publicly the sources and details of this information would—

be detrimental to our national interests by compromising investigative sources and methods and seriously interfering with the ability of this Department and the Executive Branch to obtain reliable information affecting our internal security.

The district court (December 21, 1956)[62] noted that "we now have a decision and findings by the Secretary of State made in conformity with the ruling of the Court of Appeals."

The court then considered the question of due process and stated that the full significance of the findings in certain parts of the Secretary's decision can be determined only by reference to other parts which are based on confidential information, the substance of which, however, was disclosed to the applicant. The sources and details were not disclosed, however, since the Secretary of State deemed that such disclosure would be detrimental to the national interest by compromising investigative sources and interfering with the ability of the executive branch to obtain reliable information affecting internal security. The Secretary of State further found that a full disclosure "would have an adverse effect upon our ability to obtain and utilize information from sources abroad and interfere with our established relationships in the security and intelligence area." The Secretary of State added that his decision and findings were based not only upon the confidential information referred to in the findings, but to other "confidential information contained in the files of the Department of State, the disclosure of which might prejudice the conduct of the United States foreign relations."

The court then stated:

In the light of the foregoing, it is my opinion that the denial of a passport to the plaintiff did not violate either procedural or substantive due process.

To hold otherwise would be to say that any citizen of the United States desiring a passport for the purpose of going abroad to engage in activities which will advance the Communist movement could force issuance of the passport unless the Secretary of State made disclosures detrimental to our national interest, affecting our internal security, and prejudicing the conduct of the United States foreign relations.

---

[62] 146 F. Supp. 876 (D. C. D. C., 1956).

459

The court reviewed authorities which had recognized the delicacy of foreign relations and their general immunity from judicial inquiry, and observed, "In addition to providing protection to the rights of individual citizens, the Constitution also recognizes interests of the Government and when conflicts arise, they can be resolved only by 'balancing the conflicting individual and national interests involved.' "

The court observed that the essence of the plaintiff's claim is that he is entitled to confrontation of all witnesses and that denial of such confrontation constitutes a denial of due process. In other words, the plaintiff contends a right of confrontation in administrative proceedings equivalent to that conferred on defendants in criminal actions. The court stated that this position was not supported by authorities.

Finally, the court said:

. . . the Court must accept the reasons advanced by the Secretary of State for not disclosing the source of the confidential information referred to, and, under the circumstances of this case, the manner and use of confidential information accords with both procedural and substantive due process.

An appeal to the Court of Appeals (D. C.) was noted February 15, 1957.[63]

Criminal sanctions

A discussion of the legal framework of the passport security program would be inadequate without comment upon statutory provisions defining crimes in this area.

Briefly summarized, the criminal sanctions relating to passports are as follows:

1. It is a crime willfully and knowingly to make any false statement in an application for a passport with intent to secure the issuance of a passport either for one's own use or for the use of another.[64]

The same section makes it a crime to use, willfully and knowingly, or furnish to another to use, a passport secured by any false statement.

2. A second statute [65] prohibits the forging, counterfeiting, mutilation, or alteration of a passport as well as the use of a forged, counterfeited, or mutilated passport.

3. It is also a crime willfully and knowingly to use or attempt to use another person's passport or to violate the terms and conditions of a passport or the rules regulating the issuance of passports or to deliver a passport to anyone for use of persons other than the one to whom it was issued.[66]

4. Violation of a safe conduct or passport duly issued under authority of the United States is a crime.[67]

---

[63] Civil Action No. 13717.
[64] 18 U. S. C. A. 1542.
[65] 18 U. S. C. A. 1543.
[66] 18 U. S. C. A. 1544.
[67] 18 U. S. C. A. 1545.

Besides the provisions contained in the Criminal Code, there are several other statutes concerning passports which are closely related to the security program and also impose a penalty for violation thereof. For example, as mentioned earlier, it is unlawful for any United States citizen to depart from or enter the United States without a passport in time of war or national emergency as specified in the statute and a penalty may be imposed on any such citizen who attempts to travel in violation of the statute.[68]

The most recent criminal provision relating to passports is contained in Title I, Section 6, of the Internal Security Act of 1950,[69] which provides that when a Communist organization as defined in the act is registered or there is in effect a final order of the SACB,[70] it shall be unlawful for any member, with knowledge or notice of such registration or order, to apply for a passport or the renewal of a passport to be issued under authority of the United States or to use or attempt to use such a passport. Further, the statute provides that it shall be unlawful for any officer or employee of the United States to issue a passport to or renew the passport of any such person.

One of the more important of the few criminal prosecutions for violation of the passport laws which has reached the Supreme Court is the case of *Browder* v. *United States*.[71] In this case, Earl Browder, who was at one time the leader of the Communist Party in the United States, traveled abroad on a passport obtained by false statements. He presented the passport in an effort to reenter the country and was indicted for a violation of title 18, section 1542, *supra*. While it was shown on the trial of the case that a passport was not required to reenter the United States on the date when Browder presented his passport, the Supreme Court affirmed his conviction and Judge Reed stated: "once the basic wrong under this passport statute is completed, that is, the securing of a passport by a false statement, any intentional use of that passport in travel is punishable."

Conclusion

In conclusion, it appears definite from the decisions of the courts of appeals that the statutes relating to passports are constitutional, and the power to issue passports includes the power to revoke them. The constitutionality of regulations relating to security was raised in the case of *Boudin* v. *Dulles*, and the court in remanding the case for further action by the Secretary of State reserved judgment on that issue.

Further, it is clear that an applicant for a passport must comply with the regulations and exhaust administrative remedies before resorting to the courts.

---

[68] 8 U. S. C. A. 1185.
[69] 50 U. S. C. A. 785.
[70] Subversive Activities Control Board authorized by title I, sec. 12, of the Internal Security Act of 1950, 50 U. S. C. A. 791.
[71] 312 U. S. 335 (1940).

On the other hand, the view of the Department of State that the courts have no jurisdiction to review the *manner* in which the Secretary exercises the discretionary authority conferred upon him by law, has not been accepted by the courts of appeals. The courts in the above-discussed cases have held that the exercise of the Secretary's discretion may not be arbitrary, that an applicant is entitled to a quasi-judicial hearing on the tentative denial of a passport, and that the applicant is entitled to be informed with some specificity as to the reasons for the denial and the evidence supporting those reasons. The court in the *Schachtman* case held that the denial of a passport is a deprivation of liberty and hence such denial must conform to the due-process provisions of the fifth amendment. Many questions remain to be resolved, especially the discretionary right of the Secretary of State to refuse to grant a passport for any reason believed by him to be in the public interest.

PRESENT PROGRAM

Jurisdiction over all American passport work both in the United States and abroad is vested in the Passport Office of the State Department.

Modern mechanized systems, filing and paper-handling techniques, and an improved internal accounting system enable the Passport Office to meet the growing demands for travel documents, now in excess of 500,000 annually and expected soon to exceed 600,000. Under the reorganized system, management control has been broken down into four divisions: administrative, legal, foreign adjudication, and domestic adjudication. Matters of security fall within the jurisdiction of the Legal Division.

Pertinent information is filed under the individual's name. The entire case file for any individual is immediately available via the master index in the Passport Office. Files are retained indefinitely. The Passport Office has no file-destruction program.

With more than 1,000,000 pieces of mail coming in annually and with thousands of telephone communications daily, serious information problems continuously confront Passport Office officials.

Information in the file may be made known to the applicant in keeping with security regulations. Information which would serve to disclose the identity of a confidential source, the concealment of which is necessary to national security, cannot be divulged. Nongovernmental inquiries on passport cases are denied information from the files.

Applications received between September 1, 1952, and August 1, 1956, amounted to 1,905,152. Of that number the following tentative refusals

462

of passports were made by the Passport Office under section 51.135 of the Code of Federal Regulations: [72]

Sept. 1, 1952, to June 30, 1953	79
July 1, 1953, to June 30, 1954	60
July 1, 1954, to June 30, 1955	116
July 1, 1955, to July 31, 1955	2
Aug. 1, 1955, to Aug. 1, 1956	18
Total	275
Final refusals (by the Passport Office):	
Jan. 4, 1954, to July 31, 1955	29
Aug. 1, 1955, to Aug. 1, 1956	None
Passports not issued because of failure or refusal of applicant to execute affidavits:	
Jan. 1, 1956, to Aug. 1, 1956	54

Following several court actions in recent years, the State Department has reversed itself and granted passports to individuals who were previously denied them.

Ehe new application for passport, which inquires as to present or past membership in the Communist Party, has not been in effect long enough to judge its effectiveness. However, the publicity given this new form in use only since September 1, 1956, increased the work of the Passport Office in cases involving derogatory security information. Intelligence sources have reported that Communists were instructed to make application on the old passport forms before the new ones were put into effect. Even with the old forms, however, applicants were sometimes required to furnish a separate affidavit regarding Communist Party affiliations.

Passport Regulations

When an application is received by the Passport Office all the names on the application are checked through the master index for possible derogatory information. If there is any, the pertinent files are checked for the full results of any investigation by an appropriate agency. The Passport Office will then have security information upon which to base the issuance or refusal of a passport.

Requests for inclusions of additional individuals on one passport involve the same type of check for every person named on the application.

Governors of outlying American possessions are empowered to issue passports to residents of those areas, provided the passport records in the respective territories are clear. In addition, copies of the applications are sent to the Passport Office in Washington for a check. If sufficient derogatory information is uncovered, the passport is cancelled.

---

[72] 22 C. F. R. 51.135.

Renewals.—Renewal applications go through the same security procedure as new applications. The information required in applying for renewal of a passport is the same type as that requested on the original application.

When a request for renewal of a passport is made abroad, the consul may renew the passport if the consulate files contain no stop notice or derogatory information furnished by the State Department.

Cancellation, revocation, and withdrawal.—Whenever action is taken which in effect bars an applicant from receiving or using a passport, he is accorded the same procedural rights as when a passport is initially refused.

In a foreign country, the American consul is instructed to pick up the passport and advise the individual of his rights. If the consul cannot locate the individual, the immigration authorities are requested to pick the passport up when the holder reenters the country.

When a person whose passport has been previously cancelled or revoked applies for a new passport, he is given the same procedural rights as any other applicant.

Lost passports.—Requests to replace lost passports are thoroughly examined by the Legal Division of the Passport Office. The master index and all pertinent files are carefully scrutinized for possible derogatory information before a new passport is issued.

If the request is made overseas, the American consul transmits it to the Passport Office in Washington where the master index and the files are checked. If no derogatory information is on file, the consul is authorized to issue a new passport.

Single trip passports.—A single-trip passport can be issued only abroad, solely to enable an American citizen to return to the United States. This type of passport is picked up by the immigration authorities at the point of entry. When a passport has been cancelled overseas, it may be necessary to issue a single-trip type passport for the individual's return to the United States.

Emergencies.—Although there are no emergency passports as such, a passport application may occasionally receive preferred attention to facilitate departure from the United States of an individual with urgent business or family reasons. In any event, the application goes through the usual processing but with unusual speed.

In cases of emergency processing which reveal derogatory information of not too serious a nature, or if the individual mentioned unfavorably in the files cannot be readily identified with the individual making application, a limited passport may be issued for the desired travel. However, the investigation is continued and if there is not sufficient information to warrant refusal of the passport, a full passport is issued. Otherwise immediate steps are taken to cancel the limited passport.

Federal personnel.—The employing agency must certify that each individual going abroad on official business has been cleared under the employee's security program. The master index of the Passport Office is also checked. The duration of the passport issued is contingent upon the duties to be performed.

Military personnel.—The military agency must certify that the individual is traveling in official status. The master index is checked. Adverse information is brought to attention of the appropriate Department, which usually cancels the request. There are few recent cases of this nature.

Members of the Armed Forces traveling in leave status follow the same passport procedures as private citizens. In addition, a copy of the individual's leave orders must be submitted with the application.

Exchange students are checked by the Security Office, Department of State, prior to submission of application in connection with the Fulbright Grant check. The master index is also checked.

American seamen need no passports if they are serving on American vessels. All American seamen must hold validated documents issued by the Coast Guard. If serving on vessels of foreign registry and the foreign government demands an American passport, the usual basic application is required. When a seaman must travel abroad to join his ship, he is issued a limited passport for that sole purpose.

American employees of international organizations.—In addition to the usualy check of the master index, a check is made with the Civil Service Commission to determine that the individual has been cleared by the International Organizations Employees Loyalty Board.

Cultural relations program.—While the individuals under this program are not Government employees, they are sent abroad at Government expense. Prior to making application, each individual has been checked by the Security Office of the State Department.

Security Control

The Bureau of Security and Consular Affairs,[73] as provided by the Immigration and Nationality Act of 1952,[74] controls administration of security matters within the Department of State.

The Passport Office is within the S. C. A. If at any stage of the procedure for processing of passports the Passport Office is of the opinion that a passport should not be issued for reasons of national security, the S. C. A. reviews the decision. Passport officials also consult with the legal adviser of the Department of State and with the Department of Justice. The Legal Division of the Passport Office cooperates with other Federal agencies in maintaining and searching files and records of passport applicants.

Since the adoption of new procedures in 1952, the Passport Office has had to add two attorneys to the Legal Division and several employees to the clerical staff.

---

[73] Hereinafter referred to as S. C. A.
[74] 8 U. S. C. 1104.

Reports to other agencies.—The Passport Office maintains close liaison with all Federal intelligence agencies to keep them advised on cases in which they are interested. Through the Interdepartmental Committee on Internal Security (ICIS), information concerning passport problems is furnished to the National Security Council, although no report is made to the Council on individual cases.

Procedure in Security Clearance Cases

Procedure is as follows: Applications are received by the cashier of the Passport Office and forwarded first to the index card section, then to the master index. (Master index goes back to 1906.) Any references to previous applications or actions are transmitted to the examiners.

If derogatory information appears in the master index, the application is passed on to the Legal Division without evaluation or recommendation. If the derogatory information is insufficient to warrant refusal, a passport is issued.

If the Legal Division recommends refusal, the application with recommendation for refusal is forwarded to S. C. A. If S. C. A. does not concur, the application is referred back and the passport issued. (S. C. A. in making its determination may confer with the legal adviser's office or the office of the Assistant Secretary of State for Administration).

If S. C. A. concurs in the recommendation that the passport be denied, the Legal Division of the Passport Office then writes a tentative refusal letter to the applicant. If the applicant does not answer, the application is considered abandoned.

If the applicant replies, a date for informal hearing is fixed by the Legal Division to suit his convenience. Information developed during the hearing is evaluated. If the hearing officers are satisfied that the information is not sufficient basis for refusal, a passport is issued.

If the hearing board decides to recommend refusal, the application, with the board's recommendation, is referred to S. C. A. If S. C. A. does not concur, the case is returned and a passport issued.

If S. C. A. does concur, the case is returned to the Legal Division and a final refusal letter advises the applicant he may appeal to the Board of Passport Appeals.

Security Cases

All passport applications are checked against the master index. The Passport Office has no facilities of its own to conduct an investigation, but information is constantly being furnished by other government agencies concerning applicants for passports. If a check of the master index does not turn

466

up the applicant's name, no additional check is usually made. The volume of applications received makes further investigation impracticable.

As a practical matter, the Passport Office includes in its index all pertinent names mentioned in connection with an investigation, besides the name being investigated. When an application is checked through the master index, and the name found in cross-reference, the original agency may be asked for clarifying information. Data in the State Department files may be very old and it may be necessary to obtain more up-to-date information from the FBI or elsewhere before making a passport decision. Further checks are sometimes indicated. Currently the Passport Office makes additional checks on applicants who are chemists and physicists.

Applicants who are the subject of derogatory information in security matters may be asked to give a complete explanation of their questioned activities. Confirmation of such explanations is handled by the FBI and the Security Office of the State Department.

Hearings

Approximately 100 informal hearings have been held since the 1952 passport regulations took effect. Hearings are scheduled on short notice at the convenience of the applicants. Long delays between date of tentative denial and hearings have occurred only when the applicant has not immediately requested a hearing. The average time between the date of a hearing and a final decision by the Passport Office is 6 weeks.

When letters of tentative denial of passports are sent to applicants, reasons for refusal, "as specifically as . . . security considerations permit," are given if they do not compromise confidential sources of information. According to Passport Office officials, the withholding of details furnished by confidential informants has not prevented applicants from requesting a hearing or appeal. Whenever an applicant has requested a "bill of particulars," it has been furnished in as much detail as consistent with security.

Even after a notice of final refusal is given, the door is always open for the applicant to reply. If as much as a year has elapsed between the notice of tentative denial and the applicant's reply, a new application may be requested from the applicant.

If, after requesting a hearing at the Passport Office, the applicant does not appear and no request has been made for a continuation to another date, the case is closed and the application is considered abandoned.

Informal hearings are conducted in the office of the chief of the Legal Division, Passport Office, Washington, D. C. Until early in 1956 no transcript was made, but a stenographic report is now kept. The applicant and his attorney are usually present at the hearing, as well as the Passport Office hearing officer and a Government attorney.

During the hearing, the applicant is permitted to call any witnesses he desires. The Government does not usually call witnesses. No spectators are present. A stenographic transcript of the hearing is furnished to the applicant as a matter of policy.

Upon completion of the hearing the transcript is reviewed by the hearing officer and the Government attorney who conducted the hearing. Their decision to issue the passport or recommend refusal is based on investigative reports weighed against the applicant's testimony at the hearing, or subsequent affidavits which the applicant may submit. The investigative reports appraise the reliability of informants. The Passport Office, as a rule, will not refuse a passport because of uncorroborated information from a single source.

If there is indication of bias, prejudice, or malicious misrepresentation, no adverse action is taken.

The applicant does not receive a copy of the hearing officer's report. Actually, the report is merely the recommendation of the hearing officer in the form of a memorandum to S. C. A. The decision reaches the applicant in the form of a valid passport or a final refusal letter.

As the applicant receives a transcript of the proceedings, he can file additional information in any form desired, usually in the form of an affidavit.

Board of Passport Appeals [75]

The Board of Passport Appeals was created on August 28, 1952. Prior to that time all decisions concerning passports were made by the Passport Office. However, while the Passport Office had the power of final determination in all applications, it was the practice in aggravated cases to obtain the comments from such interested offices as Office of Security and political desks. While the basic regulations concerning passport procedures were promulgated in August 1952, it was not until late 1953 that the Board of Passport Appeals was set up. It actually did not begin to function until early 1954 for the simple reason that there were no cases ready to be appealed until late 1953.

All members of the Board of Passport Appeals are appointed by the Secretary of State.

Before an applicant may file an appeal, he must have received a final determination from the Passport Office, exhausted all other administrative remedies, and completed all requirements of the Passport Office.

When a petition for appeal is filed, counsel for the Board determines that the petition for the appeal is in order. A mutually agreeable date is then arranged through the applicant or his attorney, usually within 30 days.

---

[75] Information on the Board of Passport Appeals was furnished to the Commission on Government Security by Mr. John W. Sipes, counsel, Board of Passport Appeals, Department of State, since Dec. 1953.

If the applicant requests additional information which is deemed not prejudicial to the interests of national security, it is furnished. When the applicant petitions for an appeal, and needs additional data, it is given to him if possible.

If he fails to appear before the Board of Passport Appeals after requesting a hearing, he is asked if he still wishes to appeal. If the circumstances so dictate, another mutually suitable date is arranged. Although it has never done so, the Board has authority to proceed without the applicant or his attorney present, and to make a recommendation based upon the written record. In some cases, the applicant is not present but is represented by an attorney.

Hearings are generally held at Washington. The applicant is placed under oath which is administered by the counsel for the Board. The interrogation during the proceedings is also conducted by the counsel.

The hearing before the Board of Passport Appeals is not an adversary proceeding, but is designed to determine all of the facts in order to make a fair and equitable decision.

When information concerning an applicant emanates from confidential sources that cannot be disclosed to the applicant, the credibility of the informant is evaluated by the investigating agency. Proceedings may be suspended at any time. Additional investigation may be requested to recheck or verify information.

Until recently the State Department would allow the applicant to review a transcript taken during a hearing at the Board of Passport Appeals Office. Such review was conducted under supervision, to prevent classified information in the testimony from being disclosed to unauthorized individuals. However, the policy has recently been changed, and the applicant is now furnished a copy of the transcript from which confidential information has been deleted.

The hearings are private and the privacy of the transcript must be maintained. However, when individuals have taken the Secretary's decision to court, the transcripts are available for examination in the court proceedings.

After a hearing has been completed, the applicant always retains the right to submit new information or evidence. He also has the right to request a new hearing on the basis of new information although the new hearing may not be granted, depending upon the nature of the new information.

When the recommendation of the Board is submitted to the Secretary of State, a confidential rationale is prepared. In the event that there is a dissenting opinion, two rationales are submitted.

The applicant does not receive a copy of the Board's confidential advisory opinion.

A rationale is transmitted with a memorandum from the Board to the Secretary through the Assistant Secretary of State for Administration. He has no authority to change the recommendation, but reviews it in order to be able to brief the Secretary if necessary. As a matter of practice, the Secretary has instructed the Assistant Secretary to refer each case to the legal adviser for review and opinion. The Secretary then decides whether to issue or refuse the passport.

RECOMMENDATIONS

NECESSITY

A passport security program is necessary to deter travel abroad by subversives bent on missions detrimental to the United States and to narrow as much as possible the sphere of Soviet international conspiratorial activity in the fields of espionage and propaganda.

Abundant evidence exists to support this finding. There is a long history of insidious use of travel documents, not only in the United States but in other nations of the free world, to further the Communist objective of world domination.

The passport is an important instrument in support of the recognized Communist technique of communication by personal contact. It has been employed over the years to insure the presence of American Communists and Americans under Communist discipline at Soviet centers for indoctrination and training, including the Lenin School in Moscow. It has been utilized by Communist sympathizers as a vehicle for their attendance at and participation in activities of international Communist propaganda organizations. It has been a device for the movement of Soviet agents and spies into and out of the United States and other free nations of the world.

The Internal Security Act of 1950, prohibiting the issuance of passports to members of Communist organizations registered or required to be registered by the Subversive Activities Control Board, enunciated the statutory necessity for travel restrictions in the following language:

Due to the nature and scope of the world Communist movement, with the existence of affiliated constituent elements working toward common objectives in various countries of the world, travel of Communist members, representatives, and agents from country to country facilitates communication and is a prerequisite for the carrying on of activities to further the purposes of the Communist movement.[76]

In retrospect, the Internal Security Act of 1950 can be viewed as a crystallizing force that terminated fluctuations of State Department passport policies and procedures prevalent for years.

---

[76] 50 U. S. C. sec. 781.

470

These fluctuations are reviewed in the following excerpts from one of the State Department's own documents:

The present attack on the passport policy is a part of a general Communist offensive against the security policies of the United States Government, policies painfully worked out after the Government's bitter experience with Communist espionage and propaganda activities in the United States and abroad. Paralleling the attack on our passport policies are current attacks on the port security program, the Government employees loyalty program, the industrial security program, and the visa program.

Several years ago a similar attack was made on the passport policies and procedures which were vigorously defended by Secretary Acheson in press releases of May 24, 1952, and June 18, 1952.

．　　　　．　　　　．　　　　．　　　　．

Shortly after the Bolshevik Resolution of 1917 this Government became aware of the scope and danger of the worldwide revolutionary movement and the attendant purpose to overthrow all existing governments, including our own. As a countermeasure passports were refused to American Communists who desired to go abroad for indoctrination, instruction, etc. This policy was continued until 1931 when Secretary Stimson reversed the previous rulings. Thereafter until World War II no persons were refused passports because they were Communists.

．　　　　．　　　　．　　　　．　　　　．

After the termination of hostilities and the return of travel to more normal conditions, the question came up as to whether the Department would issue regular passports to individuals if they were Communists. At first passports were refused, but the matter was reconsidered at the highest level of the Department in early 1948 and the decision was made that passports would be issued to Communists and supporters of communism who satisfied the Department that they did not intend, while abroad, to engage in the promotion of Communist activities. At the same time the decision was made that passports should be refused to persons whose purpose in traveling abroad was believed to be to subvert the interest of the United States. Later in the same year the policy was modified to permit the issue of passports to Communist journalists even though they were actively promoting the Communist cause. In September 1950 the Passport Division raised the question, in connection with pending passport applications by Communistic journalists, whether this policy should be modified. It was pointed out that ten members of the National Committee of the Communist Party had been convicted of violating the Smith Act; that the Communists were actively supporting the enemy position in the Korean war, and that the Internal Security Act of 1950 clearly showed the desire of Congress that no Communists should be issued passports of this Government.

The Department also took into consideration its own experience that ever since the end of World War I, American Communists and alien Communists illegally in possession of American passports had effectively carried on abroad espionage, propaganda and revolutionary activities on behalf of the Soviet Government and the international Communist movement and contrary to the foreign policy of the United States Government. The matter was referred to the Legal Adviser who agreed that it was the duty of the State Department to refuse passports to all Communists, including journalists.[77]

In the operation of its espionage apparatus in the United States, the Soviet Government has frequently interchanged its agents in Canada, Mexico, and this country, using fraudulent passports in the process.[78]

---

[77] Refusal of passports to Communists, State Department memorandum, May 29, 1956, pp. 1, 2.
[78] The Shameful Years, Thirty Years of Soviet Espionage in the United States, H. Rept. 1229, 84th Cong., 2d sess., p. 4.

471

Here in the United States, false naturalization and birth certificates have been employed in making applications for passports. False names have been used. Identities of other persons, many of them long since dead, have been assumed. Birth certificates of living persons have been bought, and there have been instances where municipal officials have been paid to record births and issue certificates for persons who never existed.[79]

Concealment of Destination

Since the Spanish Civil War there has been a great increase in the number of applicants concealing their true destination and purpose of travel.

During the Spanish war, between 2,000 and 3,000 Americans, who obtained passports for travel to some other country, went to Spain and joined the international brigade although their passports were stamped "not valid for travel to Spain." These Americans were required to turn over their passports to the headquarters of the international brigade in Albacete, Spain, "for safekeeping." Most of these passports eventually wound up in Moscow for alteration and possible use by Soviet agents. The United States, as a countermeasure, then replaced every outstanding passport in the world with a new-type document to prevent use of the old ones by Soviet agents.[80]

American supporters of international Communism have frequently certified that their trips abroad for business or pleasure contemplated visits only to certain designated countries. Upon arrival overseas, however, they have breached the restrictions stated in their passports and have passed through the Iron Curtain to become officials, delegates, and observers at conferences of Soviet-dominated propaganda organizations that have spawned infamous denunciations of the United States. Their passports, except for a few isolated instances, do not reflect entry or exit visas evidencing travel behind the Iron Curtain. These have been stamped on a slip of paper which was removed from their possession at the time of their return to the free world.[81] The detached visa device to conceal the fact of visits to the Soviet Union from agencies of the United States Government is known to have existed as far back as 1927.[82]

The Communist-inspired Asian and Pacific peace conference in Peking, China, in October 1952, which was attended by 15 American delegates, is a typical example of concealment.

Henry Willcox and his wife, Anita, of Long Island and Connecticut, despite their records of Communist sympathy, secured passports ostensibly

[79] Senate Internal Security Subcommittee hearings on "Scope of Soviet activity in the United States," pt. 27, app. I, p. 1497 and 1498.

[80] Pt. 23, hearings on scope of Soviet activity in the United States, Internal Security Subcommittee, Committee on the Judiciary, U. S. Senate, May 9–10, 1956, p. 1220–1222.

[81] H. Rept. 53, 85th Cong., 1st sess., annual report of Committee on Un-American Activities for the year 1956, p. 14.

[82] Report of the Subversive Activities Control Board (*Brownell* v. *Communist Party of the United States of America*), S. doc. 41, 83d Cong., 1st sess., p. 106.

to visit France and Turkey for business. Their passports carried the prevailing restriction against travel behind the Iron Curtain, but they showed up in Moscow and boarded a plane that took them to Peking, where Mrs. Willcox read a speech to the conference and Willcox served as vice chairman of the American delegation.

Endorsed Atrocity Propaganda

As delegates, they gave their endorsement to Communist propaganda accusing American troops of "horrible atrocities" in Korea. The following, an excerpt from an English-language broadcast from Peking by Louis Wheaton, another American who acted as an official at the conference, is a sample:

> . . . In one village in Korea more than 300 children were put into one warehouse and their mothers into another nearby. Gasoline was poured around the warehouse where the children were and set fire. The mothers, hearing the screams of their children, broke down the door and windows. As they were trying to save their children, these mothers were machinegunned by our troops. . . .

When Willcox returned to the United States he released to the press a statement by another American delegate, Hugh Hardyman, of California, that accused Americans of engaging in bacteriological warfare against women and children of North Korea and China. Hardyman, like Willcox and his wife, also had deceived the State Department by claiming he wanted to go to Australia. Instead, he went three-quarters of the way around the world, by way of New York and France, to get to Peking. He stopped off at Vienna, Austria, to attend another Soviet propaganda conference on the way home. The Willcoxes tarried temporarily in Warsaw, Poland, on their return trip although their passports were not valid for travel in that country.[83]

Willcox subsequently was a witness before the House Committee on Un-American Activities. When asked why he did not state in his passport application that he proposed to attend the Peking conference, Willcox replied, "I am sure that if I put that down, the passport would have been refused." [84]

Exhibiting utmost unconcern over their previous violations of passport restrictions, Willcox and his wife have taken the Secretary of State to court for refusing renewal. The United States District Court for the District of Columbia sustained the Secretary's action and the Willcoxes appealed. The Circuit Court of Appeals has remanded the case to the District Court for further proceedings in line with its decision in *Boudin* v. *Dulles*, 235 F. 2d 532.

Also summoned before the House Committee on Un-American Activities was Dr. John Adams Kingsbury. He, too, had been in Peking in 1952, in

[83] H. Rept. 53, 85th Cong., 1st sess., annual report of Committee on Un-American Activities for the year 1956, pp. 14, 15.
[84] Ibid., p. 14.

Moscow and Czechoslovakia, and had attended a conference of the World Peace Council in Vienna.

The committee asked him about the following quotation from his speech in Vienna:

Our democracy is dying. It is being beaten to death. Never before, except during the Goebbels era, has a campaign of lies met with as great a success as the present anti-Soviet hysteria in the United States. But most Americans, as in all other nations of this world, want peace. Because of the artificial creation of a mental disorder, the American people have been left neurotic.[85]

Dr. Kingsbury insisted he was quoting somebody but he could not remember who it was. Then, under prodding by committee counsel about what went on in Peking, Dr. Kingsbury declared:

There were exhibits of shells that were supposed to be dropped, containing insects which carried germs. There were microscopic exhibitions of the germs that were carried. There were various other things, a whole line of things. There were the statements by the men that were supposed to have dropped them. There were recordings by them. I spent about 2 or 3 hours there with the Chinese scientists going over this. I made no statement that it was convincing to me, but that it was very interesting evidence, and I said there was enough evidence there, the kind of evidence, that I thought should be presented to a grand jury in America to determine whether there is enough evidence there to convict.[86]

Condemned Own Governments

The committee also called several of the American delegates to the World Youth Festival held in Warsaw in 1955. All had concealed their purpose of travel, they were found to have been affiliated with the Communist Party and they refused to answer questions about their passport applications, their travel abroad, and their conduct at the conference.[87]

Of 1,905,152 applications received from September 1, 1952, to August 1, 1956, the Passport Office tentatively denied 275 for security reasons. There were final denials in 29 security cases by the Passport Office from January 4, 1954, to July 31, 1955, and none from August 1, 1955, to August 1, 1956. Final denials by the Secretary of State for 1955 for security reasons totaled 13. However, some indication of the deterrent effect of the program can be deduced from the figures showing that 54 passports were not issued between January 1, 1956, and August 1, 1956, "because of failure or refusal of applicant to execute affidavits" demanded by the Passport Office.[88]

[85] Hearings before Committee on Un-American Activities, House of Representatives, 84th Cong., 2d sess., May 24, 1956, p. 4412.

[86] Ibid., pp. 4424–4425.

[87] H. Rept. 53, 85th Cong., 1st sess., annual report of Committee on Un-American Activities for the year 1956, pp. 15, 16.

[88] Passport Office response to Commission on Government Security interrogatory, Oct. 3, 1956.

The efficacy of the passport security program can best be judged by the vigor of the Communist offensive to destroy it or render it innocuous and ineffective. The onslaught against it was spearheaded in 1952 by the Communist-controlled American Committee to Survey Trade Union Conditions in Europe, which undertook, as one witness described it, to do "everything in our power to raise such a hullabaloo that the Passport Office of the State Department would be so embarrassed that they would then stop denial of passports to certain individuals." [89]

The Passport Office is self-supporting and revenue producing. [90] The expense of the security program, therefore, is absorbed in the overall operating cost, thus distinguishing the Passport Office from other agencies of the Government whose security costs are assessed directly to the taxpayer.

For the reasons specified, we must conclude that a passport security program is a necessity and should be continued subject to changes and modifications delineated with more particularity hereinafter in this report.

LEGISLATION [90a]

In the legislative area, the Commission makes the following recommendations:

(A) Congress should enact legislation defining the standards and criteria of the passport security program. Such legislation should avoid limiting the program only to periods of national emergency as proclaimed by the President.

(B) The Internal Security Act of 1950 should be amended to specify the discretionary authority of the Secretary of State to issue passports in certain cases "strictly in the public interest."

(C) Title 8, U. S. C. A., section 1185 (b), should be amended to make it unlawful for any citizen of the United States to travel to any country in which his passport is declared to be invalid.

(D) A new subsection should be added to title 8, U. S. C. A., section 1185, making it a criminal offense willfully to refuse to surrender a passport which has been lawfully revoked.

(E) A new section should be added to the Immigration and Nationality Act of 1952 to require mandatory registration of the birth of a child to a United States citizen abroad.

The Commission suggests that the standards and criteria referred to in section A above governing the refusal to issue passports and the basis for

[89] H. Rept. 53, 85th Cong., 1st sess., annual report of Committee on Un-American Activities for the year 1956, p. 13.

[90] Reorganization of the Passport Office, published by the State Department, September 12, 1955, p. 5.

[90a] Commissioner Walter dissents as to part E only.

475

revocation of passports on security grounds should be drafted along the following lines:

Section 1.—Standards

Where there are reasonable grounds to believe that the purpose of the applicant in going abroad is to engage in activities which will further the aims and objectives of any party, group, or association, which the Congress of the United States, or any agency or officer of the United States duly authorized by the Congress for that purpose, finds:

1. Seeks to alter the form of Government of the United States by force or violence, or other unconstitutional means; or

2. Is organized or utilized for the purpose of advancing the aims and objectives of the Communist movement; or

3. Is organized or utilized for the purpose of establishing any form of dictatorship in the United States or any form of international dictatorship; or

4. Is organized or utilized by any foreign government, or by any foreign party, group or association acting in the interest of such foreign government for the purpose of (*a*) espionage, or (*b*) sabotage, or (*c*) obtaining information relating to the defense of the United States or the protection of the national security, or (*d*) hampering, hindering, or delaying the production of defense materials; or

5. Has adopted a policy of advocating or approving the commission of acts of force and violence to deny others their rights under the Constitution of the United States; or

6. Is affiliated with, or acts in concert with, or is dominated or controlled by, any party, group, or association of the character described in 1, or 2, or 3, or 4, above.

Section 2.—Criteria

For the purpose of section 1, "reasonable grounds" shall include but not be limited to—

(*a*) Membership in any party, group, or association described in section 1; or

(*b*) Prior membership in any party, group, or association, described in section 1, where termination of such membership was under circumstances warranting the conclusion that the applicant continues to act in furtherance of the interests of such party, group, or association; or

(*c*) Regardless of the formal state of his affiliation with any party, group, or association, described in section 1, has

476

engaged or engages in activities which further the aims and objectives of such party, group, or association, under circumstances warranting the conclusion that he engages in such activities as a result of direction, domination, or control exercised over him by such party, group, or association, or otherwise continues to act in furtherance of the interests of such party, group, or association; or

(*d*) Regardless of the formal state of his affiliation within a party, group, or association, described in section 1, has consistently over a prolonged period of time indicated through his actions that he adhered to the doctrine of such party, group, or association, as such doctrine is expressed in the actions and writings of such party, group, or association on a variety of issues, including shifts and changes in the doctrinal line of such party, group, or association.

Enactment of legislation in the passport field obviously is a clear and lawful exercise of the constitutional powers of the Congress. The Commission likewise feels that legislation will ease most, if not all, of the uncertainties arising out of administration and judicial determinations reflected by the litigation which occurred in 1955 and 1956.

The Commssion does not intend that the recommended legislation should interfere with the traditional discretionary authority of the Secretary of State in passport matters. Nor does it feel that the nature of the passport program is such that it should be brought within the scope of the Administrative Procedure Act of 1946 as amended.

The Commission also believes strongly that the national interest will be better served if procedures continue to be governed by regulations promulgated by the Secretary of State and grounded upon basic statutory authority along the lines suggested by this report.

In the case of *Dayton* v. *Dulles*, United States District Court for the District of Columbia, C. A. No. 4890–55, decided January 3, 1957, the court held that plaintiff's claim to right of confrontation in administrative proceedings equivalent to that conferred on defendants in criminal cases had no validity. The court held further that it—

must accept the reasons advanced by the Secretary of State for not disclosing the source of the confidential information referred to, and, under the circumstances of this case, the manner and use of confidential information accords with both procedural and substantive due process.

In that case the court also reviewed the authorities which had recognized the delicacy of foreign relations and their general immunity from judicial inquiry and observed:

In addition to providing protection to the rights of individual citizens, the Constitution also recognizes interests of the Government, and when conflicts arise, they can be resolved only by "balancing the conflicting individual and national interests involved."

This case has been appealed.

The Commission bases its recommendation that legislation not be limited to a period of national emergency as proclaimed by the President on the understandable premise that we cannot visualize in the foreseeable future any change in activities of the Communist Party and its threat to the American way of life.

Internal Security Act Change Urged

As mentioned earlier, the Internal Security Act of 1950 prohibits the issuance of passports to members of Communist organizations registered, or required to be registered, with the Subversive Activities Control Board. The act not only makes it unlawful for persons in this category to apply for issuance or renewal, but also makes it unlawful "for any officer or employee of the United States" to issue or renew a passport under these circumstances.[91]

The act makes no provision for the exercise by the Secretary of State of his discretionary authority in such matters.

It is understandable that the Secretary of State, in his role as director of the Nation's foreign policy, may consider it advisable to grant a passport under certain conditions. For example, the *Daily Worker's* correspondent was given a passport to attend the Geneva "summit conference" to forestall Communist propaganda that the established American press would present only the capitalist side of the meeting.[92]

There is also the possibility, by no means remote, that the Government's intelligence agencies, for the furtherance of their objectives, may want the Secretary of State to grant a passport to a known Communist.

As the Internal Security Act now stands, if the applicant is within the scope of the defined membership classes, it would be unlawful for the Secretary of State to issue or renew such a passport. We think this is unduly restrictive.

It is therefore the Commission's recommendation that section 785 (b) be amended to permit issuance or renewal of a passport when "personally directed by the Secretary of State for reasons deemed by him to be strictly in the public interest."

New Criminal Sanctions Recommended

In connection with its recommendation for new basic legislation in the passport field, the Commission has urged that the Congress shall not limit it to time of war or period of national emergency as proclaimed by the President.

---

[91] 50 U. S. C., sec. 785 (b).

[92] Testimony before subcommittee IV of the Commission on Government Security, July 17, 1956, pp. 81–83.

Adoption of this principle in any new legislation would, of course, require amendment of existing criminal statutes relating to passports to conform with the change. The Commission recommends that title 8, U. S. C. A., section 1185 (b), be amended to provide that "it shall also be unlawful for any citizen of the United States to travel to any country in which his passport is declared to be invalid," and that a new subsection be added to title 8 to make it a criminal offense willfully to refuse to surrender a passport which has been lawfully revoked.

These amendments, coupled with a program of strict enforcement, should go a long way toward preventing Communists and those with records of sympathetic association from traveling to Iron Curtain countries, there to participate in Communist-controlled international conferences from which emanate vicious propaganda aimed at the free nations of the world.

The Commission has carefully studied the prosecutive record. While it finds there were numerous prosecutions under the old section 220 of title 22 of the United States Code for making false statements in passport applications and that a number of the leading Communists in the country were jailed in the prewar period, there is no record of prosecutions in cases where a person made a false representation under oath respecting the country he intended to visit.

Earlier in this report, the Commission recited instances of attendance by Americans at conferences in Peking, China, and Warsaw, Poland, despite the fact their passports were stamped not valid for these places.

Still another facet of this complex situation which the proposed legislation is designed to correct is the following from a State Department report:

A great number of American Chinese visit Hong Kong and reside here for periods of at least 3 or 4 months. By leaving their American passports in the keeping of friends or agents in Hong Kong or Macau, they can travel easily to the mainland. The Chinese Travel Service, under Communist management, is quite active in Hong Kong.

Several cases of American Chinese entering Communist China come to the attention of the consulate each month. Some enter through Macau, others purchase Hong Kong identity cards and enter China from Hong Kong itself. Some use their United States passport names and are apparently known to the Communists as "overseas Chinese" from America. Others assume false identities . . .

The purpose for each of these visits is not known. Many apparently wish to visit their ancestral villages. Some may have business interests to protect or to further. Others may be couriers between certain elements in the United States and the "Socialist Fatherland." [93]

Mandatory Registration of Births Abroad

Recommendations for legislation by this Commission in the passport field include this final one proposing a new section be added to the Immigration and Nationality Act of 1952. It would require mandatory registration of

---

[93] Report on the problem of fraud at Hong Kong, dispatch No. 931, Department of State, p. 84.

any child born abroad to a United States citizen, with an express provision that failure to register raises the presumption that the child is not an American citizen.

The recommendation is prompted initially by the experience of the Department of State with the so-called Chinese fraud-type cases, but the principle of mandatory registration, it is felt, should have general application.

Provisions for registering the birth of Americans abroad are contained in the following sections of the State Department Foreign Service manual:

SEC. 286.12. Officers of Foreign Service are required, upon application of parents, to record the birth of a child when the child is an American citizen.

SEC. 286.15. In the event that the American parent of a child born abroad refuses to have it registered, an officer of the Foreign Service is without power to do more than urge the advisability thereof. When registration is refused, an officer should endeavor to obtain a certified copy of the registration of birth from the local authorities.

SEC. 286.3. A report of birth must be supported by evidence of citizenship of at least one parent.

These regulations have no present legal foundation; registration of births abroad now are not considered presumptive evidence of citizenship.

Threat Posed by Hong Kong Situation

The staff of this Commission has made an extensive study of the "problem of fraud at Hong Kong," as the Department of State describes it.

The following digest of a 98-page report from the American consulate at Hong Kong gives the background of the Chinese situation that has been causing the Department of State considerable concern over a period of years:

A criminal conspiracy to evade the laws of the United States has developed into so well organized a system at Hong Kong that—

1. Almost any Chinese with the proper resources may enter the United States even if ineligible under our immigration laws,

2. Adequate security precautions can hardly be taken to exclude Chinese Communist agents or criminal elements,

3. An alien Chinese can purchase American citizenship for (U. S.) $3,000. Terms: $500 down, balance after arrival in the United States, and

4. Thousands of dollars in American pensions have been collected annually by persons not entitled to them.

All of these problems are in turn based upon a single problem: Identity.

The major consular problem facing the American consulate general at Hong Kong has been the ease and frequency with which identities are bought and sold in the area. Most of these identities, moreover, represent persons who never actually existed.

How and why would such a situation come into existence?

An answer to this question requires a short look at the history of Chinese immigration to the United States.

This immigration began during the 1850's when Chinese coolies were first imported to work in the gold mines of California and on the construction of the

480

transcontinental railroads. When the proportions of this immigration became alarming, the inhabitants of the West began to fear that their part of the United States would become a predominantly Chinese area. Agitation led to the first of the exclusion acts in 1882. The Chinese greatly resented the exclusion acts and at first destroyed their effect by crossing the American borders illegally. If later questioned about how they entered the United States, these persons would claim that they had been born there.

If all the Chinese claiming birth in San Francisco prior to the earthquake and fire (which destroyed birth records) had in fact been born there, every Chinese female then in the United States (reliable census figures) would necessarily have given birth to more than 800 children. The Government, however, being unable to prove on an individual basis that the persons concerned had not been born in the United States eventually had to concede their citizenship.

When border control was tightened, a system for the creation of derivative citizenship claims was substituted. Every Chinese whose American citizenship had been conceded claimed sons after each subsequent visit to China. These nonexistent sons were paper citizens and their identity could later be sold to still other Chinese desiring to enter the United States. The immigration families created by these claims were characterized by large numbers of sons and few daughters, by a negligible rate of infant mortality, and by immediate application for entry to the United States as soon as the son was old enough to be a productive laborer.

This system has not yet been destroyed, although 83 years have elapsed since exclusion and 12 since the repeal of exclusion. When blood testing of the families of Chinese applicants for American passports was begun at Hong Kong in 1951, it could be estimated scientifically from the results that about 80 percent of the applicants then appearing were not related to their alleged parents as claimed.

When the exclusion acts were repealed in 1943, and when the wives and minor alien children of American-Chinese later became eligible for immigration to the United States regardless of quota limitations, many of these identities also went on sale. Between the 1940 census and the 1950 census, the Chinese population of the United States increased by over 50 percent, by far its largest increase since the decade just prior to the passage of the exclusion acts.

A brisk trade in fraudulent passport and visa identities continues in Hong Kong involving over one hundred shops acting as citizenship brokers. These brokerage firms act much as a real estate broker might in the United States taking listings of identities that have been created and matching them with persons who wish to gain entry to the United States. These shops and their clients in Hong Kong and the United States have no respect for American immigration, tax, selective service, tariff, narcotics, or other laws. For a period of almost three generations these persons have made a profitable business out of buying and sellings rights that exist under American law and by flouting all concomitant responsibilities.

The American consulate general at Hong Kong has done everything in its power to combat this system of fraud. During the last several years a total of 84 percent of all passport cases fully investigated at Hong Kong were proven fraudulent on one ground or another. In order to control the system whereby these identities are so commonly assumed, the consulate general has required that applicants for entry into the United States and for American pensions and allotments present some objective evidence that they are the persons they purport to be. It has been the experience of the consulate general that bona fide applicants seldom have serious trouble in establishing their identities.

The continuance of this system of illegal immigration under the present political situation poses a serious problem of national security, most particularly in respect to the security of the Chinese communities in the United States and loyal American citizens of Chinese race. Normal security controls (in respect to persons entering the United States) are of no value as long as false identities are as easily and as commonly assumed as at Hong Kong.[94]

The Commission has found that there are approximately 1,100 civil action cases pending in the Federal courts, most of them in San Francisco and New York, where Chinese plaintiffs denied passports under the provisions of section 503 of the Nationality Act of 1940 are seeking declaratory judgments to compel the Secretary of State to issue the passports. It has been estimated that approximately 300 of these cases will reach the court calendars during 1957, and that 1,000 new cases requiring extensive investigation will be added to the existing case load in Hong Kong. To combat the growing intensity of this problem, the Department of State has been compelled to assign more than 20 additional agents to augment the investigative force presently functioning in Hong Kong. It has also been necessary to increase the administrative and supervisory support for the Hong Kong investigative force in the headquarters of the Department's Office of Security in Washington.

Because of these factors, the Commission feels that it is premature to make any recommendations at this time, but appropriate congressional action should be forthcoming when the investigation action now being conducted by the Department of State is completed.

REGULATION

The regulations governing the operation of the Passport Office should be amended to provide that—

1. The Legal Adviser of the Department of State should determine the legal sufficiency of all passport denial cases before final action by the Secretary.

2. The stenographic transcript of all hearings in the Passport Office and before the Board of Passport Appeals should be made available to any applicant upon request, subject to security deletions.

3. In revocation cases, notice of intention to revoke and reasons therefor should be given and such notice and reasons may be furnished either before or after the passport has been picked up by a representative of the Department of State.

4. If revocation occurs abroad, the holder should be entitled to a hearing before any official abroad designated so to act by the Secretary of State.

5. Revocation cases should be accorded priority in disposition.

6. Revocation should occur where the holder, while abroad, engages in activities which would have justified denial in the first instance.

---

[94] Ibid; synopsis.

7. The degree of proof in revocation cases should be the same as required in issuance cases.

The Commission has carefully reviewed the regulations of the Department of State relating to the passport security program, and the contentions of the attacking parties in the litigation resulting from the enforcement of the regulations.

The regulations with security connotations pertinent to this discussion are set forth in 22 C. F. R. 51.135–51.143 and 51.151–51.170. They cover the limitations on issuance, state requirements for notice to applicants, and define hearing and appellate procedures.

Briefly, these regulations provide that passports will be denied (1) persons who are or have recently been members of the Communist Party; (2) persons, regardless of the state of their former affiliation with the Communist Party, whose activities support the Communist movement; and (3) persons, regardless of the state of their affiliation, as to whom there is reason to believe their purpose in going abroad is to advance the Communist movement. A further regulation provides that passports will be refused to persons whose activities abroad would (1) violate the laws of the United States, (2) be prejudicial to the orderly conduct of foreign relations, or (3) otherwise prejudice the interests of the United States.

The courts have thus far rejected the contention that the regulations are vague and ambiguous,[95] and an unlawful delegation of legislative power.[96]

In *Schachtman* v. *Dulles* (225 F. 2d 938, C. A. D. C. (1955)), the court observed:

> World conditions, and those in particular areas, as to which the Executive has special information and on the basis of which he is especially qualified to make decisions, bear upon the question. For reasons thus suggested, the issuance of passports throughout our history has been left to the judgment of the Secretary of State under Presidential regulation, and is subject only to constitutional safeguards. And even these must be defined with cautious regard for the responsibility of the Executive in the conduct of foreign affairs.

Misuse of Discretionary Authority Apparent

The Commission is in accord with the views thus expressed, as indicated by its recommendation for the amendment of the Internal Security Act of 1950 to spell out the Secretary's discretionary authority.

The Commission has scrutinized closely the 13 cases of final denials of passports by the Secretary in 1955. In 10 of the 13 cases the Secretary reversed himself and issued passports either as the result of court action or the threat of it. The other three cases are pending in the courts.

---

[95] *Dayton* v. *Dulles*, C. A. D. C. (1956), No. 13176, and D. C. D. C. (1956), civil action No. 4890–55.
[96] *Knauff* v. *Shaughnessy*, 338 U. S. 537; *Bauer* v. *Acheson*, 106 F. Supp. 445, U. S. D. C. D. C.; *Schachtman* v. *Dulles*, 225 F. 2d 938.

This desire to avoid testing out the merits of a case in a court of law has placed the Secretary in the unhappy dilemma of portraying decisions of the Passport Office and the Board of Passport Appeals as being evidentially deficient or his own decision as being arbitrary.

The decision of the Board of Passport Appeals comes to the Secretary in the form of an advisory recommendation. As a matter of practice but not of regulation, the Secretary has issued instructions calling upon the Department of State's Legal Adviser to review the legal aspects of a case before the Secretary is called upon to make his determination.[97]

The Commission believes that this responsibility should not be left to mere instruction, hence the recommendation that specific definition be given by amendment of present regulations. The administrative shortcomings which had an adverse effect on the passport security program initially appear to have been alleviated in more recent months. Basically, the defect has not been in the regulations themselves but in the way they have been administered.

The regulations and the procedures thereunder cast both the Passport Office and the Board of Passport Appeals in the role of triers of the facts. The proposed regulatory requirement for review of the entire record in any case by the Legal Adviser, and his certification of its legal sufficiency to meet a court challenge, should correct a serious problem.

Clarification Regarding Transcripts Needed

When the regulations were first adopted in 1952 to bar passport facilities to members of the Communist Party or supporters of the world Communist movement, no provision was made for a verbatim stenographic transcript of proceedings in the Passport Office. Although the regulations established a right to a hearing, the record consisted merely of notes or a memorandum of what transpired.

The rules under which the Board of Passport Appeals functioned, adopted in 1954, specified that "a complete verbatim stenographic transcript shall be made of hearings by qualified reporters, and the transcript shall constitute a permanent part of the record. Upon request, the applicant and each witness shall have the right to inspect the transcript *of his own testimony.*" [98] [Italics supplied.]

The procedures now in effect in the Passport Office provide for a transcript of testimony at that level, but this has been accomplished informally rather than by regulation, and did not become effective until 1956.

Until recent months, the Board of Passport Appeals permitted an applicant or a witness to review only his own testimony and this was done under supervision. The purpose of this control, it was stated, was to prevent any

---

[97] Passport Office response to Commission on Government Security interrogatory, Oct. 5, 1956.
[98] 22 C. F. R. 51.168.

classified information in the testimony from being disclosed to any unauthorized individuals.

The policy now is to make available to an applicant, upon request, a complete transcript of the testimony, subject to security deletions. The policy of the Passport Office has been brought into conformity with that of the Board of Passport Appeals.

However, the regulations have never been amended to make the transcript of testimony in the Passport Office mandatory, nor do they reflect the changes in policy that have occurred from 1954 to date. The Commission, therefore, recommends that this be done.

Revocation Procedures Need Revision

The Commission's study of the present procedures on revocation of passports indicates very clearly that considerable overhauling of the existing regulations is a necessity. At the present time the authority for the revocation procedure is derived from just one section of the regulations, 22 C. F. R. 51.143, which provides:

Applicability of sections 51.135 to 51.142.—When the standards set out in section 51.135 or section 51.136 are made relevant by the facts of a particular case to the exercise of the discretion of the Secretary under section 51.75, the standards in sections 51.135 and 51.136 shall be applied and the procedural safeguards of sections 51.137 to 51.142 shall be followed in any case where the person affected takes issue with the action of the Department in granting, refusing, restricting, *withdrawing, cancelling, revoking,* extending, renewing, or in any other fashion or degree affecting the ability of a person to use a passport through action taken in a particular case. [Emphasis supplied.]

From August 28, 1952, to September 1, 1956, approximately 245 passports were withdrawn pending determination of security questions. The Passport Office advises that many of those whose passports were withdrawn abandoned their efforts to have them reinstated. While unable to give the number of those eventually reinstated, the Passport Office indicated that the percentage was "small."

The Passport Office also asserted that "passport facilities are not withdrawn unless there is clear evidence that the case falls within section 51.135, stronger than would be necessary to sustain tentative refusal of any application." [99]

When proceedings are inaugurated to revoke a passport, the practice has been for a representative of the Department of State to secure, if possible, physical possession of the document. If the individual is already in the United States, the proceedings are conducted in a manner similar to that prevailing in ordinary cases of refusal. The same is true when the Department of State requests the immigration authorities at a port of entry to

[99] Passport Office response to Commission on Government Security interrogatory, Oct. 3, 1956.

pick up the passport of an individual who is on his way back to the United States. In these cases the holder of the passport is physically present in the United States and thereafter is able to avail himself of the prescribed hearing procedures.

The situation, however, differs when applied to an individual who is abroad when the move to revoke is made. The Department of State will notify the American consul in the country where the passport holder is believed to be located. The consul is directed to contact the individual and request surrender of the passport. The consul is also under instructions to advise the individual of his rights under the regulations. If the individual does surrender the passport, he is furnished with another valid only for return to the United States. If the passport holder declines, the consul has no way of enforcing demand for surrender. He can only give notice that the passport is no longer valid and cannot be legally used until it has been further validated.[100]

The ground rules for the application of the authority to revoke passports were clearly stated in *Bauer* v. *Acheson* in the District Court for the District of Columbia in 1951.[101] Because of the important constitutional questions raised by the complaint in this case, the plaintiff's motion to convene a three-judge court pursuant to 28 U. S. C. section 2282, was granted. The following excerpts from the court's opinion in that case are pertinent to the subject matter now under discussion:

It is clear that the authority to issue passports necessarily implies authority also to regulate their issuance and to withdraw them. The particular questions for inquiry in this case are whether a person who has received a passport may have it summarily revoked, during the period for which it was valid, without prior notice or opportunity for a hearing and on the bald statement that "her activities are contrary to the best interests of the United States," and whether the Secretary of State may refuse to renew such passport on the same statement.

This court is not willing to subscribe to the view that the Executive power includes any absolute discretion which may encroach on the individual's constitutional rights, or that the Congress has power to confer such absolute discretion. We hold that, like other curtailments of personal liberty for the public good, the regulation of passports must be administered, not arbitrarily or capriciously, but fairly, applying the law equally to all citizens without discrimination, and with due process adapted to the exigencies of the situation. We hold further that such administration is possible under the existing statute and regulations.

Since the act in question is susceptible of an interpretation which would permit due process, it follows that it is not in violation of the fifth amendment. The President's regulation authorizing withdrawal of passports is clearly within the intent of the Congress, and is susceptible of and must be construed as exacting notice and opportunity to be heard prior to any judgment effecting revocation or refusal to renew a passport. . . .

We conclude that revocation of the plaintiff's passport without notice and hearing before revocation, as well as refusal to renew such passport without an opportunity to be heard, was without authority of law. It follows that the Secretary of State should be directed to renew or revalidate the plaintiff's passport without the amendment making

---

[100] Passport Office response to Commission interrogatory, Dec. 20, 1956.
[101] 106 F. Supp. 445.

it valid only for return to the United States, unless a hearing is accorded her within a reasonable time.

Compliance with the rules set forth in the foregoing opinion appears to have been contemplated when 22 C. F. R. 51.143 was drafted in 1954. The same criticism that has been expressed by this Commission concerning other phases of the passport security program; i. e., the following of practices not in accord with the provisions of the regulations, holds true for the revocation cases that have been reviewed. The Passport Office response to a Commission interrogatory on December 20, 1956, in defining the procedures followed when a passport holder abroad is notified of the proposed revocation, states that the consular officer will discuss with the passport holder the information contained in the charges and afford him the opportunity to prepare a sworn affidavit in reply to those charges. It appears also that the individual is notified that he can have an informal hearing in the Passport Office in Washington and that, if he wishes to return to the United States for such a hearing, his passport will be validated for such return. The response to the interrogatory declares further that, if the passport holder does not wish to return, he can be represented at such informal hearing by his attorney and an opportunity will be given to his attorney to present any evidence in his behalf.

Compliance With Due Process Doubted

The Commission submits that this procedure hardly conforms to the principles of substantive due process, and entertains grave doubts that it can be regarded as meeting all of the requirements of procedural due process.

Review of all the passport cases that have reached the courts to date discloses that the courts uniformly decree the right to a quasi-judicial hearing before denial or revocation.

Under the present practice, the passport holder abroad is subjected to the inconvenience and heavy expense of traveling thousands of miles to get the hearing the law contemplates and guarantees, or he is left to the device of answer by affidavit and reliance upon such additional evidence as his attorney can submit in his behalf. Such circumstances can hardly be construed as constituting voluntary waiver of his right to a hearing. The Commission believes that the courts will not dismiss such a situation lightly.

This is the fundamental premise for the Commission's recommendation for a new regulation providing for a hearing abroad before any official of the United States designated by the Secretary of State.

Priority in disposition of revocation cases has been recommended by the Commission primarily because the holder of a passport is in a position different from that of an applicant. The issuance is an accomplished fact and the passport is in use if the person is abroad. Furthermore, in the case of a person abroad, notification of the proposal to withdraw the document is accompanied by warning that it cannot be legally used until it has been further validated. Theoretically, at least, it is in a state of suspension, and the holder thereof, if he refuses to surrender the passport upon demand, runs the risk of violating 8 U. S. C. A. 1543 and 1544 by any subsequent use.

The record previously cited of approximately 245 revocation cases over a 4-year period would indicate that the yearly average of around 60 cases lends itself readily to the establishment of a priority system.

The Commission finds itself strongly disagreeing with the present practice of withdrawing passports only when the evidence is "stronger than would be necessary to sustain tentative refusal of a new application."

There should be no variance in evidential standards. In the interest of consistency, there is no valid reason why the degree of proof should be different in revocation cases than that required for refusals in the first instance. Furthermore, if a passport holder engages in activities abroad which would have justified denial originally, the established criteria may still be applied.

OPERATION

In the operational phase of the passport security program the Commission makes the following recommendations:

1. The Passport Office, in cases of both tentative and final denials for security reasons, should comply strictly with the regulations requiring notice in writing and the reasons on which the decision is based "as specifically as within the judgment of the Department of State security limitations permit." [102]

2. Findings by the Board of Passport Appeals, which are only advisory in character and for the guidance of the Secretary of State, should not be furnished to an applicant.

3. The Secretary of State should make available to an applicant who is denied a passport for security reasons a copy of his decision and the findings upon which the decision is based, stated as specifically as security considerations will permit.

4. The present application should be amended to require the applicant to state whether, as the result of any security investigation or proceedings, he has been advised of an adverse finding.

5. A single fingerprint should be required on the application form and on the passport itself.

---

[102] 22 C. F. R. 51.137.

6. The Passport Office should make monthly reports to the Administrator of Security and Consular Affairs, listing the cases that have been pending for more than 60 days and the reasons for delay in disposition.

7. Qualifications should be specified for Passport Office employees who are charged with the responsibility for security decisions.

8. A training program for employees who may be called upon to make security decisions in the future should be inaugurated.

9. The present method of appointment and the basis for selection of members of the Board of Passport Appeals should be continued.

10. The Secretary of State should continue to exercise his own discretion as to the holding of hearings outside Washington.

The first three of the foregoing recommendations can be analyzed together because they comprise the heart of the operational phase of this program.

The Passport Office insists that (1) every effort is made to furnish the applicant with as much detailed information as security regulations will permit; (2) no present cases could be recalled wherein the withholding of certain details furnished by confidential informants precluded the applicant from responding sufficiently in his request for a hearing or appeal; and (3) if the applicant requests a bill of particulars, such will be furnished in as much detail as possible in keeping with security regulations.[103]

The staff of the Commission has reviewed the 13 cases in which final denials were made by the Secretary of State in 1955 on security grounds. In virtually every case the staff's findings as to specificity of charges are at complete variance with what the Passport Office says is the established pattern of operation.

Invariably the nature of the allegations was phrased in language that was too generalized. In many of the cases the files contained a wealth of information, a great deal of it from public sources, which would have permitted greater specificity. The charges frequently omitted dates and places which, in the opinion of the staff could very well have been supplied to the applicant without risk to security considerations or the disclosure of the identity of confidential informants.

The functions of the Board of Passport Appeals are clearly spelled out in the regulations.

---

[103] Passport Office response to Commission interrogatory, Sept. 27, 1956.

In 22 C. F. R. 51.140, it is stated:

It shall be the duty of the Board, on all the evidence, to advise the Secretary of the action it finds necessary and proper to the disposition of cases appealed to it, and to this end the Board may first call for clarification of the record, further investigation, or other action consistent with its duties.

And 22 C. F. R. 51.141 provides:

(a) In making or reviewing findings of fact, the Board and all others with responsibility for so doing under sections 51.135 to 51.143, shall be convinced by a preponderance of the evidence, as would a trial court in a civil case.

(b) Consistent and prolonged adherence to the Communist Party line on a variety of issues and through shifts and changes of that line will suffice, prima facie, to support a finding under section 51.135 (b).

To continue further, this is what the Passport Office asserts is the practice after proceedings before the Board:

With regard to the procedure followed when the recommendation of the Board of Passport Appeals is submitted to the Secretary of State, a confidential rationale is prepared reflecting the Board's decision. In the event that there is a dissenting opinion, two rationales are submitted, one reflecting the majority opinion and the other, the minority opinion. The rationale is signed by each member of the Board. A rationale is then overlaid by a memorandum from the Board to the Secretary through the Assistant Secretary of State for Administration. The Assistant Secretary has no authority to change the recommendation, but reviews it in order to be able to brief the Secretary if necessary. As a matter of practice, the Secretary has instructed that each case be referred to the Legal Adviser for any opinion on matters which may have legal aspects prior to sending it to him. The Secretary upon review of the Board's recommendation makes his determination as to issuance or refusal of the passport.[104]

Strict adherence to these procedural steps would seem amply to fortify the Secretary's final determination. As an appellate body, the Board has primary responsibility for assaying the sufficiency of the evidence. And the response to the Commission's interrogatory implies that the Legal Adviser also reviews the entire record prior to final decision by the Secretary.

The Commission's examination of the 13 refusal cases, however, refutes the foregoing contentions, and points up the fact that the Department's legal difficulties were self-made.

In nearly every case where court action was actually instituted or merely threatened, the legal adviser has been found on record with an opinion that the case was legally deficient, but such opinions are dated *after* the Secretary's decision and appeared only when litigation was imminent or actually begun.

The conclusion is obvious. Either the Board erred or the Legal Adviser was wrong. Because of the dilemma into which he was thrust, it was the duty of the Secretary to pinpoint the responsibility. There is nothing of record to show that he ever did.

---

[104] Passport Office response to Commission interrogatory, Oct. 5, 1956.

Remedy lies in following the clear lines of the recent court decisions. In *Dayton* v. *Dulles*,[105] where the appellate court remanded the case to the district court for further proceedings consistent with its opinion, the court said firmly that "the denial itself, rather than an affidavit filed in court after litigation has arisen, should specify the regulation upon which it rests" and should contain the findings upon which the denial is based.

The court also made reference to its previous ruling in *Boudin* v. *Dulles*,[106] that the Secretary should state whether his findings are based on the evidence openly produced, or (in whole or in material part) on secret information not disclosed to the applicant. If the latter, the court said, the Secretary should explain with such particularity as in his judgment the circumstances permit the nature of the reasons why such information may not be disclosed.

In the reconsideration of the *Dayton* case in the District Court, the Secretary complied literally with these instructions. The decision was in his favor.[107] The case is now back before the Circuit Court of Appeals, this time for review on the merits.

Proper Record Must Be Built

What needs to be understood in the future administration of the passport program is that a record capable of being sustained must be created right from the filing of an application up to and including final decision by the Secretary.

Greater specificity of charges is necessary at the outset. Having already recommended that a transcript of testimony be made available at the Passport Office level, the Commission believes that the record here be made as complete as possible.

The Board of Passport Appeals should concentrate on the full development of the findings upon which the Secretary must ultimately rely in those cases where the weight of the evidence indisputably supports the conclusion that a passport should not issue. Conversely, if the Board reaches the conclusion that the evidence is lacking in sufficiency, it should so advise the Secretary promptly.

Because the Board's decision may reflect confidential information and its function is only advisory, we consider it inadvisable to make it available to an applicant.

This works no hardship because, under our recommendation, the copy of the Secretary's decision and the findings upon which it is based henceforth will be given to the applicant. The findings and decision made by the Secretary in the *Dayton* case are in exactly the form the Commission contemplated in framing its recommendation.

---

[105] U. S. Court of Appeals, District of Columbia Circuit, No. 13176, Sept. 13, 1956.

[106] U S. Court of Appeals, District of Columbia Circuit, Nos. 13031, 13130, June 28, 1956.

[107] U. S. District Court, District of Columbia, civil action No. 4890-55, Dec. 21, 1956.

Change in Passport Form Suggested

In reviewing the cases of the 13 persons denied passports in 1955, the Commission observed that at least 5 had been employed at one time or another by the United States Government in a civilian capacity and that 1 of them had been terminated on security grounds. Three of the remaining eight had served in the Armed Forces of the United States.

The Commission also found that the personnel security questionnaire of the Atomic Energy Commission requires an applicant to answer if (1) he has ever, to his knowledge, been investigated by any branch of the Federal Government, and (2) he has ever been refused clearance by any branch of the Federal Government.

The Commission is of the opinion that an applicant for a passport may not be aware that he has ever been the subject of a security investigation, but certainly knows if, as the result of such investigation, he has ever been advised of an adverse finding. The Commission's recommendation for a change in the passport application has been framed accordingly.

While the Commission does not believe that every applicant for a passport should be required to submit a full set of fingerprints as part of the application, it does recommend that the form and the passport itself should make provision for a single fingerprint.

There is neither stigma nor inconvenience nor substantial cost to the Government involved in such a procedure. The old idea that fingerprints are associated only with criminality is fast disappearing, as evidenced by the millions of prints voluntarily submitted to the FBI to insure positive identification in recent years.

All Federal employees and members of the Armed Forces have been fingerprinted, and the single print is a requirement for port security cards. Fingerprints are now a requirement for drivers' licenses in many States.

Unnecessary Delays Encountered

The Commission has given close attention to the recurring complaints of unnecessary delay in disposition of cases involving security considerations.

It is not unmindful of the tremendous workload that has confronted the Passport Office. Ever since the end of World War II the boom in international travel has left its impact on the Passport Office. The number of passports issued or renewed annually has mounted steadily, and no leveling off is foreseeable.

The procedure thereafter is described as follows:

The time required to handle a passport when irregularities appear varies a great deal. In the preliminary stages of handling a passport application, particularly during the rush season, it may take from two weeks to a month for the application, with any pertinent derogatory information that may be uncovered, to reach the Legal Division of the Passport Office. Upon receipt in the Legal Division, the time consumed in further processing depends upon the amount and the gravity of the information concerning the applicant. Certain circumstances can arise which require additional checking concerning the applicant. For example, if the applicant's name is cross-referenced, that is, if his name with some derogatory notation has come up during the course of another investigation, it may be necessary to contact the FBI or other pertinent intelligence agencies in an effort to obtain full and clarifying informaton concerning the individual. A circumstance may also arise where information in the State Department files may be very old and it may be necessary to obtain more up-to-date information before making a decision. Under favorable conditions, if all information necessary to make a decision concerning an applicant is in the passport files, a case may be decided within 2 or 3 days. If in order to make a decision it is necessary to check with other intelligence agencies, it may take about 3 weeks. A case may arise where upon receipt of application it is determined that an affidavit is required from the applicant. This is usually handled within 4 or 5 days. (The new application forms contain a non-Communist affidavit which was not included on the old forms. In the case of the old forms it was sometimes necessary for a separate affidavit to be furnished by the applicant if the type of derogatory information indicated its necessity.) When a case is sent to the Bureau of Security and Consular Affairs, depending upon the volume of work, it may take from a few days to several weeks to handle. As a general rule, the time taken to process an application received in the Legal Division to the time a tentative refusal letter is forwarded is usually from 2 to 6 weeks. Upon the individual's reply requesting an informal hearing, such can be arranged at the applicant's convenience, and if necessary, within 48 hours. In cases where a hearing is held in the Passport Office and the hearing officers decide favorably, the applicant can be notified within 24 hours.

No instance can be recalled in which passports have been or are at present held up for an unduly long period of time.

Because of the variable factors which influence the time taken in processing a passport case, it is difficult to suggest any solution or make any recommendation, which would fit in all instances, to minimize or eliminate any delays which have occurred.[108]

The statement in the next to last paragraph of the foregoing is not supported by the facts. A review of security cases shows conclusively that delays ranging from several months to more than a year are the rule rather than the exception. Furthermore, the delays are not centered at any particular step in the proceedings.

The Commission has recommended, therefore, that the Administrator of Security and Consular Affairs institute a requirement for a monthly status report on all passport cases involving derogatory security information that have been pending more than 60 days. The Administrator should also make it mandatory that a statement of the reasons for the delay in such cases be included in the report.

In making its recommendations that qualifications be specified for Passport Office personnel making security decisions and that a training program

---

[108] Passport Office response to Commission interrogatory, Sept. 26, 1956.

be instituted for employees who will be making such decisions in the future, the Commission bases its action on the following:

There are no special qualifications laid down for work in the Passport Office. It is required, however, that each individual have the basic overall intelligence capable of appraising facts and of being able to exercise good judgment. It is desired that they have a legal background.

The persons selected for work in the Passport Office should be preferably young attorneys with a background training in the operation of the State Department. They should be afforded ample time, extending over a period of years, to familiarize themselves with passport procedures and the necessary background information concerning Communist activities. It is believed that if possible it is preferable to select these individuals from other offices within the State Department. The individuals who are presently responsible for passport security matters have had long and varied experience in this field and have acquired a thorough knowledge and understanding of the various operations.

It was the stated belief that the officials responsible for passport security matters have an adequate knowledge and understanding of their responsibilities in order to effectively and efficiently carry out their assignments.[109]

Members of the Board of Passport Appeals are designated by the Secretary of State and the regulations provide that the Board shall be composed of "not less than three officers of the Department." [110]

In selecting individuals to serve as members of the Board, positive efforts are made to appoint those "who have displayed balanced judgment and have demonstrated ability to make a determination on a set of facts and have displayed objectivity in their thinking. They must have a full realization of the realm of national security and foreign relations, fully recognize the rights of individuals and be free from any bias or prejudice." [111]

In the light of the smaller number of appeals, it appears that the Board is adequately staffed and the Commission accordingly recommends continuance of the present method of appointment and basis of selection.

The studies made by the Commission have not disclosed any particular necessity for the holding of hearings in passport cases outside of Washington, although there is some evidence that occasionally in the past, testimony has been taken in other cities. Aside from the recommendation that hearings be held abroad for revocation cases, the locale of future hearings should remain discretionary with the Secretary.

The Commission recognizes that its general recommendation with respect to confrontation found elsewhere in this report must be held to be not applicable to the passport security program.

It will be acknowledged that the Secretary of State, in making his decision to refuse or revoke a passport for security reasons, must weigh factors not to be found in other security programs.

Our recommendation for confrontation to the fullest extent possible consistent with the protection of national security takes into account the fact

---

[109] Passport Office response to Commission interrogatory, Sept. 27, 1956.
[110] 22 C. F. R. 51.139.
[111] Passport Office response to Commission interrogatory, Oct. 5, 1956.

that disclosure of the sources and details of confidential information related to the internal security would be detrimental to the national interest by compromising investigative sources and methods.

But these factors, when applied to decisions of the Secretary of State in passport matters, have even broader implications because disclosure of confidential information in the files of the Department of State could very well prejudice the conduct of United States foreign relations.

Security measures and foreign affairs, therefore, are so inextricably interwoven that greater application of the principle of confrontation conceivably could bring serious harm to the national interest.

As long as the substance of confidential information is disclosed to a passport applicant during the processing of the application and subsequent hearing, thus affording him opportunity to rebut, there will not be a serious departure from the degree of confrontation recommended by the Commission.

In the light of all the facts, the Commission sees no material need for a grant of subpena power in the passport field.

Civil Air Transport Security Program

Introduction

The operations of civil air transport extend into every part of the United States, thereby affording an extremely wide geographic opportunity for the commission of acts jeopardizing the internal security of the Nation. In 1955 there were 708 airports being served by 52 certified civil air carriers with a total operating capacity of 1,448 aircraft. At the conclusion of the fiscal year, ending June 30, 1956, the commercial airlines carried 39,171,181 passengers in domestic operations alone. This means that at some time during the fiscal year 1956 the equivalent of almost one-quarter of the population of the United States moved through our airports by air to various points within the continental limits of our country.

In addition to domestic operations, the American and foreign air carriers constantly moving in and out of our airports are of major importance when viewed from the standpoint of national security. The United States Immigration and Naturalization Service has compiled statistics showing that in the year ending June 30, 1956, more travelers crossed the Atlantic Ocean to and from the United States by air than by steamship.

Air transport is obviously more vulnerable to destruction, damage, or disruption of service by sabotage or overt hostile action than any other form of civilian transportation. Damage which would only cripple land or sea transport facilities is more likely to prove fatal to the operation of aircraft. A plane is not only susceptible to mechanical sabotage but is in even greater peril from explosives secretly loaded aboard than are other forms of transportation.

Aircraft personnel, amounting to a total of 122,124 workers,[1] also present unique problems in the field of national security. Although it is highly improbable that flight personnel would attempt to sabotage their own aircraft in flight, there is an ever-present danger to the internal security of the United States by reason of subversive individuals placed in strategic positions and who may serve as couriers for hostile powers or engage in espionage activities.

Congress has formally recognized the need for positive security measures in international and domestic air transport by enacting the Civil Aeronautics Act of 1950: "To establish security provisions which will encourage

---

[1] Pilots, copilots, stewards, stewardesses, dispatchers, meteorologists, mechanics, hangar and field workers, office employees, and others.

and permit the maximum use of civil aircraft consistent with national security," but little has been done to implement this basic legislation.

In analyzing the available data concerning the scope of the problem in air transport security and the present status of protective measures for the physical protection of airports and clearance of air transport personnel, the Commission on Government Security has concluded that with the exception of a few isolated and scattered precautionary measures, there is no coordinated peacetime security program for the civil air transportation industry.

LEGAL BASIS

As no program now exists for the security screening of personnel engaged in air transport, it is necessary to consider whether the appropriate executive agencies possess sufficient authority to establish such a program.

After the Korean war started in June 1950, the Congress became acutely aware of security problems and passed several measures which greatly broadened the authority of the executive department to act against subversives. The Internal Security Act, for example, was enacted September 23, 1950.[2] The Magnuson Act[3] passed in the same session of the Congress, although couched in general language, authorized the security screening of seamen and port workers.[4]   On September 9, 1950, an amendment to the Civil Aeronautics Act of 1938 was passed authorizing the Civil Aeronautics Board and the Secretary of Commerce *to undertake security measures relative to the regulation and control of air commerce and for other purposes.*[5]   [Italics supplied.]

The pertinent provisions of the amendment of September 9, 1950, as related to personnel security are the first two sections which state:

Section 1201.—The purpose of this title is to establish security provisions which will encourage and permit the maximum use of civil aircraft consistent with the national security.   Whenever the President determines such action to be required in the interest of national security, he may direct the Secretary of Commerce and the Civil Aeronautics Board to exercise the powers, duties, and responsibilities granted in this title to the extent, in the manner, and for such periods of time as the President considers necessary.

Section 1202.—The Board shall consider requirements of national security as well as safety of flight in air commerce, in exercising its powers and carrying out its responsibilities under title VI of this act.

The foregoing provisions are to be read with the first section of title VI of the act[6] which relates to airman certificates and provides in part:

(a) The Administrator of Civil Aeronautics is empowered to issue airman certificates specifying the capacity in which the holders thereof are authorized to serve as airmen in connection with aircraft.

---

[2] Public Law 831, 81st Cong., 64 Stat. 987–1031, 50 U. S. C. A. 781–826.
[3] 64 Stat. 427, 50 U. S. C. A. 191.
[4] *U. S.* v. *Gray,* 207 F. 2d 237, C. A. 9, 1953, and *Parker* v. *Lester,* 227 F. 2d 708, C. A. 9, 1955.
[5] 64 Stat. 825, 49 U. S. C. A. 701–704.
[6] 52 Stat. 1008, 49 U. S. C. A. 552–560.

(*b*) Any person may file with the Administrator of Civil Aeronautics an application for an airman certificate. If the Administrator of Civil Aeronautics finds, after investigation, that such person possesses proper qualifications for, and is physically able to perform the duties pertaining to the position for which the airman certificate is sought, he shall issue such certificate, containing such terms, conditions, and limitation as to duration thereof, periodic or special examinations, tests of physcal fitness, and other matters as the Administrator of Civil Aeronautics may determine to be necessary to assure safety in air commerce.

Subsection (*b*) further provides "That the Board may, in its discretion, prohibit or restrict the issuance of airman certificates to aliens. . . .

There are 9 sections in title VI; 7 contain references to the competency, skill, etc., of personnel. These sections are concerned with airman certificates, aircraft certificates; air carrier operating certificates, maintenance of equipment; air navigation facility rating; rating of schools, repair stations, and other agencies; form of applications; amendment, suspension, and revocation of certificates; and prohibitions. It is provided, for example, that any person who wishes to operate an air carrier must be investigated and approved by the Administrator. Any person engaged in operating, inspecting, maintaining, or overhauling equipment must observe all of the regulations issued by the Administrator and requirements of the law. The law sets out the qualifications and duties of inspectors. The law requires that persons engaged in repair stations or in school must meet requirements of competency established by the Administrator as may be necessary "in the interest of the public." Further, it is required that applications for any of the activities described in title VI shall be "in such form, contain such information, and be filed and served in such manner as the Administrator of Civil Aeronautics may prescribe and shall be under oath whenever the Administrator of Civil Aeronautics so requires."

The Civil Aeronautics Board is given authority to reexamine any airman, and, after investigation, and upon notice and hearing, to alter, amend, modify, or suspend, in whole or in part, any type of certificate, production certificate, airworthiness certificate, airman certificate, air carrier operating certificate, air navigation facility certificate, or air agency certificate, if the interest of the public so requires, or may revoke, in whole or in part, any such certificate for any cause which, at the time of revocation, would justify the refusal to issue a like certificate. There is also provision for the emergency suspension of certificates without notice. It is prohibited for any person to operate without certificates or in violation of the terms of the certificate or to do any of the things for which a certificate is required without such certificate. It is provided that special regulations may be prescribed as to airmen serving in connection with foreign aircraft, such regulations to be those required "in the interest of the public". As may be noted from a reference to the first section of title VI, the Board is specifically authorized to prohibit the issuance of airman certificates to aliens, in itself a security measure.

The law, therefore, sets out a complete and detailed system of examination and licensing of persons engaged in all aspects of air transport. The amendment added "national security" as a consideration of the Board in exercising the functions outlined above.

The authority of the Board to require pilot's licenses was questioned in *U. S.* v. *Drumm*, 55 F. Supp. 151, D. C. Nev. (1944). Drumm admitted habitually operating aircraft in flight without a pilot's license and contended the Civil Aeronautics Administration had no jurisdiction or authority over him. The court said in part:

> With respect to the contention of counsel for defendant and libelee that the action of the Civil Aeronautics Board in amending sections 60.30 and 60.31 of the Civil Air Regulations, in effect, prohibiting any person to pilot a civil aircraft unless such person "holds a valid pilot certificate" and the aircraft possesses an "airworthiness certificate," exceeded the authority of said Board, it is the conclusion of the Court that the same is without merit. It cannot be said from any evidence submitted or of which the Court may take judicial knowledge, that the findings of the Board were not well founded to the effect that there had been such increase in "aeronautical activity of the armed forces of the United States," the number of "certificated" and "uncertificated" pilots, that "any operation of any aircraft in the air space . . . either directly affects, or may endanger safety in, interstate, overseas, or foreign air commerce; . . . it is necessary that all pilots and aircraft . . . be certified . . . for the protection of safety in air commerce. . . ." Upon such findings, the amendments were within the powers conferred by the act of Congress creating the Board.

The legislative history of the act states that the executive departments and agencies concerned with air transport were doubtful of their authority to act in the interests of national security,[7] hence this bill was introduced. The report accompanyng the bill states:

> The purpose of the bill is to grant authority to the Secretary of Commerce and the Civil Aeronautics Board for the development and implementation of a plan for the security control of air traffic in time of war or when the national security is endangered.

The act of September 9, 1950, should be interpreted to add the words "and national security" to those provisions of title VI of the Civil Aeronautics Act of 1938 where the word "safety" appears. It therefore follows that the Administrator has under the act, as amended, authority to examine and test personnel engaged in air transport as he may determine to be necessary to the national security as well as to assure safety in air commerce.

The Civil Aeronautics Act, as amended, spells out in detail the authority to establish zones or areas in the airspace above the United States within which flights of aircraft will be restricted or prohibited. It is to these provisions the legislative history directs specific attention. Clearly, however, regulations relating to airspaces and safety zones cannot be enforced unless the personnel flying the planes are subject to the observance of such restrictions. A disloyal pilot could and would, if the occasion arose when it was to the detriment of the United States, violate regulations with impunity. It is clear that the amendatory act definitely authorizes the Board to establish a screening program.

---

[7] S. Rep. 2359, Interstate and Foreign Commerce Committee, August 14, 1950, to accompany S. 3995, 81st Cong., 2d sess.

In the debate in the House, Rep. Beckworth of Texas stated: [8]

"The Secretary of Commerce, under whom the CAA operates, feels that he does not have that authority with reference to security. He has it with reference to safety. In other words, he can cause a person to fly in a given area if safety demands it, but not if security demands it."

Senator Johnson, in the debate in the Senate,[9] stated:

"As we all know, in the present world turmoil we must prevent if possible a sneak attack by enemy aircraft such as occurred at Pearl Harbor when the United States was at peace with all the nations of the earth. The present law, the Civil Aeronautics Act of 1938, does not recognize national security considerations as one of the bases for the control, identification, and location of aircraft."

The authority of Congress to regulate air commerce and the similarity of air traffic with sea traffic is well stated in *Rosenhan* v. *United States*, 131 F. 2d 932, C. A. 10 (1942), in which the court said:

Congressional regulation of interstate air commerce in the interest of safety and efficiency is new and modern, but the law applicable thereto is of another generation. To sustain the broad and plenary power of the Congress to regulate interstate air commerce in the interest of safety and efficiency, we need but recur to the prophetic pronouncement of the Supreme Court of the United States, long before the skies were considered aeronautical highways, when it said: "Constitutional provisions do not change, but their operation extends to new matters, as the modes of business and the habits of life of the people vary with each succeeding generation. The law of the common carrier is the same today as when transportation on land was by coach and wagon, and on water by canal boat and sailing vessel; yet in its actual operation it touches and regulates transportation by modes then unknown,—the railroad train and the steamship. Just so is it with the grant to the National Government of power over interstate commerce. The Constitution has not changed. The power is the same. But it operates today upon modes of interstate commerce unknown to the fathers, and it will operate with equal force upon any new modes of such commerce which the future may develop." * * *

It cannot be doubted that if the Federal act is devoted to the promotion of safety and efficiency in interstate commerce, whether it be the stagecoach, sailboat, steamship, railroad train, motortruck, or airplane, if the act bears some reasonable and rational relationship to the subject over which it has assumed to act, the power is supreme and may not be denied, although it may include within its scope activities which are intrastate in character. "It is no objection to such an exertion of this power that the dangers intended to be avoided arise, in whole or in part, out of matters connected with intrastate commerce." * * *

The appellant contends that on a trial of the case he could have shown that the flight of his aircraft in the designated civil airway did not in any way endanger or interfere with safety in interstate commerce. We may concede that he could have shown that at the time the aircraft in question was in flight through, or upon, the designated airway no other aircraft was within dangerous range, but he cannot avoid the incidence of the Act by showing that these particular flights did not actually endanger interstate commerce. Congress has not seen fit to limit the question of safety in these circumstances to a manifestation of actual danger, rather it has sought to eliminate all potential elements of danger. The declaration that no aircraft shall operate in a designated civil airway, without having currently in effect an airworthiness certificate, evinces congressional judgment that such an operation is detrimental to the safety

---

[8] Congressional Record, vol. 96, pt. 10, p. 13977, 81st Cong., 2d sess.
[9] Id., pp. 13201 and 13202.

of those engaged in interstate commerce, or those who make use of its facilities. We cannot say that this exerted regulation does not have any reasonable relationship to the promotion of safety in air commerce, or that it does not rest upon any rational basis, when considered in the light of the broad legislative purpose. We conclude that such statutory precautions do not transcend the powers granted to the Congress over interstate commerce, or unduly encroach upon the powers reserved to the sovereign states.

It is noted that the construction of the act of September 9, 1950, adopted in this opinion is apparently the construction of Mr. Harris, a Member of Congress, who, on February 22, 1957, introduced in the Congress H. R. 5239, a bill "To authorize the imposition of civil penalties for violation of the security provisions of the Civil Aeronautics Act of 1938, and for other purposes," and specifically cites title VI in the bill; in other words, penalties will be imposed, in addition to those fixed by the act of September 9, 1950, for violations of security regulations issued pursuant to title VI, as amended.

While congressional regulation of interstate air commerce in the interest of safety, efficiency, and national security is new and modern, it is considered that the act of September 9, 1950, is adequate to support security screening of air transport personnel and other measures reasonably required for national security.

RECOMMENDATIONS

NECESSITY

The Commission on Government Security recommends a formal, industrywide security program in civil air transport. The program should be similar in scope and format to that now existing, or recommended by the Commission, for seaport security in our country.

Civil air transport operations reach into every part of the United States, affording the widest possible opportunity for action affecting the security of the country. The degree to which air transport penetrates the economic life of our country is illustrated by a few basic statistics. In 1955, there were 708 airports served by certificated civil air carriers.[10] (A "certificated carrier" is an airline holding route authority evidenced by a certificate of public convenience and necessity issued by the Civil Aeronautics Board (CAB) after formal procedures, including public hearings, and on the basis of public need and the fitness of the carrier.) The airports were served by 52 certificated carriers operating 1,448 aircraft.[11] In the year ending June

---

[10] Annual report of the Civil Aeronautics Board, 1956, p. 40.
[11] Ibid., p. 40.

30, 1956, airlines carried 39,171,181 passengers in domestic operations alone.[12]   This means that during the year the equivalent of nearly one-fourth of our total population traveled by air from our airports to points within the country.   The flow of so many people through such potentially vulnerable areas offers obvious danger to our national security.

Despite the wide geographical range of civil air transport, there is actually a high degree of concentration in activity.   For example, while in the year ending June 30, 1955, more than 9 million passengers moved through the airports of New York to or from 442 communities in the United States, Chicago, Boston, Washington, Miami, and Los Angeles accounted for about one-third of this traffic.[13]   Los Angeles, the largest west-coast hub for air traffic, handled nearly 3.5 million passengers in the year ending June 30, 1955, to and from 427 communities.[14]   The traffic concentration was similar to that for New York, with six cities providing a major share.[15]

There are several reasons for the unique vulnerability of air transport. In the first place, an aircraft is extremely susceptible to serious damage or destruction.   Mechanical failures may be fatal.   The potential danger of sabotage is clearly greater in aircraft operations than in other transport.

Aircraft personnel also present unique problems in security.   While it is improbable that flight personnel would attempt to sabotage their own aircraft in flight, there are opportunities for undetected damage to later flights. Ground and tower personnel, moreover, have ample occasion to commit acts of sabotage which might easily go undetected, or be charged to failures in judgment.   Mechanics and other maintenance workers and tower crews might engage in sabotage without being easily detected.

In view of the sensitivity of air transport facilities and aircraft to sabotage, it might be assumed that the Federal Government and the air transport industry had taken action to establish a security program for personnel and facilities.   In fact, however, little has been done, although basic legislative authority was enacted in 1950.

The carriers do check applicants for employment, but these procedures are not standardized throughout the industry, nor is there any formal coordination with or direction from the Federal Government.   There is no Federal program requiring personnel security clearances of air-transport employees.   The only personnel in the industry who receive such formal screening are those employed by the CAA, CAB, or other Federal agencies. These employees are subject to the screening applicable to all Federal applicants and employees.

---

[12] "Air Commerce Traffic Pattern, fiscal year 1956," CAA print; table 4, p. 6.

[13] *Federal Role in Aviation*, hearings before a subcommittee of the Committee on Government Operations. House of Representatives, 84th Cong., 2d sess., June 25–July 20, 1956. Testimony of Herbert H. Howell, Director, Office of Airports, CAA, p. 336.

[14] Ibid.

[15] Ibid.

STANDARDS AND CRITERIA

The Commission recommends that the standard for employment as a crew member on international flights shall be that such employment or access will not endanger the common defense or security.

Factors which may be considered in connection with the application of the foregoing standard shall include but not be limited to—

(1) Sabotage, espionage, or attempts or preparations therefor or knowingly association with spies or saboteurs;

(2) Treason or sedition or advocacy thereof;

(3) Advocacy of revolution or force or violence to alter the constitutional form of Government of the United States;

(4) Intentional, unauthorized disclosure to any person of classified information or materials, or recurrent and serious, although unintentional, disclosure of such information and materials;

(5) Performing or attempting to perform his duties, or otherwise acting, so as to serve the interests of another government in preference to the interests of the United States;

(6) Membership in, affiliation or sympathetic association with any party, or association which the Congress of the United States, or any agency or officer of the United States duly authorized by the Congress for that purpose; finds:

(*a*) Seeks to alter the form of Government of the United States by force or violence, or other unconstitutional means; or

(*b*) Is organized or utilized for the purpose of advancing the aims and objectives of the Communist movement; or

(*c*) Is organized or utilized for the purpose of establishing any form of dictatorship in the United States or any form of international dictatorship; or

(*d*) Is organized or utilized by any foreign government, or by any foreign party, group, or association acting in the interest of such foreign government for the purpose of (i) espionage, or (ii) sabotage, or (iii) obtaining information relating to the defense of the United States or the protection of the national security, or (iv) hampering, hindering, or delaying the production of defense materials; or

(*e*) Is affiliated with, or acts in concert with, or is dominated or controlled by, any party, group, or association of the character described in (*a*), (*b*), (*c*), or (*d*) above.

(7) Membership in or affiliation with any organization which the Congress of the United States, or any agency or officer of the United States duly authorized by the Congress for that purpose,

finds has adopted a policy of advocating or approving the commission of acts of force or violence to deny others their rights under the Constitution of the United States;

(8) Refusal to testify upon the grounds of self-incrimination in any authorized inquiry conducted by a congressional committee, Federal court, Federal grand jury, or any other duly authorized agency unless the individual, after opportunity to do so, satisfactorily explains his refusal to testify;

(9) Willful violations or disregard of security regulations, or recurrent and serious, although unintentional, violation of such regulations;

(10) Any illness, including any mental condition, of a nature which in the opinion of competent medical authority may cause significant defect in the performance, judgment, or reliability of the employee with due regard to the transient or continued effect of the illness and the medical findings in such case;

(11) Any behavior, activities, or associations which tend to show that the individual is not reliable or trustworthy;

(12) Any deliberate misrepresentations, falsifications, or omission of material facts from a personnel security questionnaire, personal history statement, or similar document;

(13) Any criminal, infamous, dishonest, immoral, or notoriously disgraceful conduct, habitual use of intoxicants to excess, drug addiction, or sexual perversion;

(14) Any facts which furnish reason to believe that the individual may be subjected to coercion, influence, or pressure which may cause him to act contrary to the best interests of national security.

The international operations of United States and foreign air carriers into and out of United States airports are of major importance to national security. While international traffic falls far short of the volume of domestic air traffic, it is nonetheless substantial. In 1955, 2,439,907 passengers were carried by aircraft to or from the United States.[16] Immigration and Naturalization statistics show that in the year ending June 30, 1956, more travelers crossed the Atlantic Ocean to and from the United States by air than by steamship.

It is of particular importance to note the relatively large number (in proportion to traffic performance) of personnel devoted to international air transport. These employees are in especially strategic positions to serve as secret couriers for hostile powers or to engage in actual espionage. The following table provides a summary of industry employment by general category of occupation:

---

[16] Unpublished data, Immigration and Naturalization Service, Feb. 28, 1957.

Position	Domestic traffic	International traffic	Total
Pilots and Copilots...........................	8,710	2,136	10,846
Other flight personnel........................	1,721	1,041	2,762
Stewards, stewardesses.......................	5,919	1,535	7,454
Dispatchers, meteorologists, etc...............	2,544	951	3,495
Mechanics...................................	23,747	5,420	29,167
Other hangar and field workers................	15,856	3,242	19,098
Office workers...............................	34,130	10,883	45,013
All other workers............................	2,841	1,448	4,289
Total..................................	95,468	26,656	122,124

SOURCE: *CAA Statistical Handbook of Civil Aviation,* Civil Aeronautics Administration, 1956 edition p. 71.

The Commission recommends that the standard for granting employment in or access to any airport facility declared "restricted" by the Civil Aeronautics Board (CAB) shall be such that access will not endanger the common defense or security.

The Commission believes that the same standards and criteria recommended above for crew members on international flights should also apply to employees having access to Civil Aeronautics Board (CAB) "restricted" facilities. Such employees could also constitute a substantial risk to the national security. In addition to their obvious opportunity for damage to operating and control facilities, they might also form important links in espionage. The Commission is convinced that these employees should, therefore, be subject to the same clearance requirement as flight personnel.

The Commission recommends that in any airport under the jurisdiction of the CAB, the CAB should have final authority as to admission to facilities it declares to be "restricted." This should not apply to recognized Army, Navy, or Air Force installations where the responsibility should remain in the cognizant military authority.

Civil air transport is intertwined with military air transport. In 1955 there were 304 military service installations located at 222 civil airports throughout the country.[17] In 1955, military aircraft accounted for 25 percent of all aircraft movement at commercial airports having CAA control towers.[18] The various operational problems which arise through such joint usage are the responsibility of the airport use panel of the Air Coordinating Committee.[19]

---

[17] *Federal Role in Aviation,* op. Cit. Testimony of Herbert H. Howell, p. 349.
[18] Ibid.
[19] Ibid.

508

The Commission feels that good administrative control procedures require that the agency having the responsibility for airport safety and the interests of national defense or security should also be given the authority for prescribing rules and regulations for carrying out such responsibility.

Subject to the limitations of the preceding recommendation, the overall responsibility for security in any airport should be vested in the Secretary of Commerce and in the Civil Aeronautics Board.

Federal regulation of civil aviation is now carried out by two agencies: the Civil Aeronautics Administration (CAA) and the Civil Aeronautics Board (CAB).

The CAB, an independent agency, prescribes the civil air regulations which deal with the competency of airmen, airworthiness of aircraft, and air traffic control. It issues certificates permitting persons to engage in air transportation as a business and is concerned with the economic regulation of air carriers. It investigates accidents in air transportation and compiles accident reports and statistics.[20]

The CAA is a bureau of the United States Department of Commerce, the Administrator of Civil Aeronautics exercising his functions under the direction and supervision of the Secretary of Commerce. The CAA constructs and operates the system of civil airways, maintaining air navigation aids along the airways and at landing areas. It maintains and operates the Washington National Airport, among other activities. It also makes provision for the control and protection of air traffic. CAA promotes safety through the certification of airmen, aircraft, and air agencies such as flight and ground schools, and checks the design, structure, and performance of new planes to insure the safety of the flying public.[21]

The Commission wishes to point out, furthermore, that the statutory responsibilities and functions of the CAA and CAB dealing with security and safety are so interrelated as to make it extremely difficult, if not impossible, to separate them into completely independent assignments.

The following excerpts from title XII (security provisions) of the basic statutory authority for civil air transport, the Civil Aeronautics Act of 1938, as amended September 9, 1950, demonstrate the close interrelationship of CAA and CAB in the field of security:

SEC. 1201.—The purpose of this title is to establish security provisions which will encourage and permit the maximum use of civil aircraft consistent with the national security. Whenever the President determines such action to be required in the interest of national security, he may direct the Secretary of Commerce and the Civil Aeronautics Board to exercise the powers, duties, and responsibilities granted in this title to the extent, in the manner, and for such periods of time as the President considers necessary.

---

[20] *CAA Statistical Handbook of Civil Aviation*, Civil Aeronautics Administration, 1956 edition, p. 1.
[21] Ibid.

Sec. 1202.—The Board shall consider requirements of national security as well as safety of flight in air commerce, in exercising its powers and carrying out its responsibilities under title VI of this act.

Sec. 1203.—The Secretary of Commerce is authorized to establish such zones or areas in the airspace above the United States, its Territories, and possessions (including areas of land or water administered by the United States under international agreement) as he may, after consultation with the Department of Defense and the Board, by rule, regulation, or order within such zones or areas, prohibit or restrict flights of aircraft which he cannot effectively identify, locate and control with available facilities: *Provided*, That the Secretary of Commerce shall consult with the Department of State before exercising the authority provided in this section with respect to areas of land or water administered by the United States under international agreement.

Clearance cards for access to military airport facilities declared "restricted" by CAB should be interchangeable whether issued by the Army, Navy, or Air Force.

This recommendation has no bearing upon requirements for access to military airport areas not under the authority of CAB. The Commission, however, is convinced that clearance requirements in those airports where CAB has the authority to designate restricted areas should be uniform in all branches of the military services. There may be good reason for variations in clearance requirements for access to civil air transport facilities and for access to military air transport facilites. The Commission, however, sees no reason for significant variations in such standards among the various branches of the Armed Forces.

INVESTIGATIONS

The Commission recommends that all crewmen on international flights should be subject to a national agency check. Where derogatory subversive information is developed during the course of such check, there should be a conversion to a full field investigation by the Federal Bureau of Investigation.

The Commission is convinced that national security requires at least the minimum standard of security investigation. It should impose little burden on the industry. In most instances it will entail scarcely more administrative activity than that incurred in the course of the routine check on references and past employment carried out by most employers as a matter of normal practice. The provision for FBI check in the case of derogatory subversive information should serve to deter job applicants who are aware of the routine nature of most personnel clearance procedures in private industry at present.

The Commission recommends that anyone seeking access to CAB "restricted" airport facilities should be subject to a national agency check. Where derogatory subversive information is developed during the course of such check, there should be a conversion to a full field investigation by the Federal Bureau of Investigation.

The Commission believes that the sensitive nature of large segments of air transport operations warrants application of at least these minimum requirements for security. They are no more rigorous than the present requirements for access to confidential information in the case of employees of industrial organizations working on Federal contracts.

SCREENING

The personnel screening function should be handled by the CAB. If, in considering derogatory information affecting national security disclosed by a national agency check, the CAB feels that additional investigation is necessary, the investigation should be made by the FBI. Derogatory information not affecting national security should be handled by the CAB.

The Commission believes that the separation of the screening function is required by good administrative procedure as well as by statutory requirements and the interests of national security. While the CAB is capable of handling the usual clearances required for employment, in the event a national agency check reveals derogatory information affecting national security the matter should be turned over to the FBI for full field investigation. The final determination of each case, however, should rest with the CAB.

CHARGES

In apprising an international flight crewman or an applicant for access to a "restricted" airport facility that there is derogatory information against him, the CAB should be as specific and detailed as the interests of national security permit. Pertinent information such as names, dates, and places in such detail as to permit reasonable answer hereto should be included.

The Commission believes that applicants should be granted all possible opportunity, consistent with national security, to rebut or explain any de-

511

rogatory information against them. This is not only a matter of fair play but it will also probably expedite the course of hearings. Applicants will be able to prepare a defense more expeditiously and thus avoid the necessity for requesting additional hearings to attempt rebuttal of charges which are not originally made specific but which may become so during the course of the hearing.

CONFRONTATION

The Commission recommends that in hearings arising out of the air transport security program, confrontation should be granted as provided in the port security program (p. 362).

HEARINGS

The Commission recommends that the following hearing procedures be employed in the air transport security program:

(a) The initial hearing on the letter of charges should be conducted by a hearing examiner rather than by hearing boards.

(b) The decisions of the hearing examiners should be advisory to the CAB whose decision shall be final.

(c) The head of the Central Security Office should determine whether an applicant for clearance shall have the right to challenge hearing examiners either for cause or peremptorily, as well as the number of such challenges to be permitted.

(d) The appointment of permanent hearing officers available throughout the country, in lieu of hearing boards, should expedite the hearing procedure.

(e) The Director of the Central Security Office should allocate the workload among the examiners, and supervise the prompt disposition of such workload, so as to minimize delay in hearings.

(f) Hearings should not be open to the public because to do so would tend to discourage witnesses, and would subject the applicant for clearance to unfavorable publicity, which might do unwarranted violence to him and his reputation. The informal atmosphere of private hearings is more conducive to an impartial determination of facts. Furthermore, open hearings would sometimes be inappropriate due to the necessity of considering classified information therein.

(*g*) Hearing examiners should be required to submit a report which would include findings of fact.

(*h*) A copy of the hearing examiner's report and a copy of the transcript of the hearing should be sent to the applicant for clearance upon receipt of notice of appeal.

(*i*) The hearing examiner should submit a written report to the head of the Central Security Office for transmittal to the CAB. Such report should contain the hearing examiner's findings of fact, decision, and reasons for his decision.

(*j*) The hearing examiner should be required to have prepared a verbatim transcript of the hearing. The applicant for clearance would be entitled to a copy of the report of the examiner and the record, including the transcript, upon receipt of notice of appeal.

The hearing procedures recommended are substantially the same as those recommended by the Commission for hearings in the port security program. The Commission has found that hearing procedures in the port security program now provide some of these safeguards to the national security as well as to the individual involved. The lack of a formal clearance program in the case of civil air transport, however, necessitates setting forth these basic guidelines for hearing practices.

For the Commissions recommendations concerning the Central Security Office, see the Federal Civilian Employees Loyalty Program.

The Commission recommends that the right of subpena should be applicable where there is a right of confrontation. This does not preclude the applicant for clearance, employee or applicant for employment from furnishing affidavits, or the testimony of witnesses he wishes to present and who are willing to appear voluntarily.

The Commission feels that to grant the right of confrontation without the power to subpena witnesses as necessary would largely vitiate the advantage gained by the right of confrontation.

Either the Government or the individual should be permitted to apply to the hearing examiner to issue subpenas; except as to confidential informants and identified informants who have given their information on the condition that they will not be called as witnesses. Such application should state the name and address of such witness, as well as the substance of the testimony to be presented by the witness. If the hearing examiner deems the evidence relevant and not merely cumulative, he may issue the subpena.

The witness should be compensated for travel expense and per diem, but where such costs are substantial, the hearing examiner may in his discretion require the parties to use deposition procedures.

513

The Commission recommends that the Government should bear the cost of Government witnesses in hearings under this program. The hearing examiner should not subpena a witness for the individual, however, until he deposits with the Government sufficient funds to pay the travel and per diem costs of such witness. In the event that the individual is not cleared, the funds deposited by him should be used to pay for his witness expenses. If, however, the individual is cleared, the funds deposited by him should be returned and the Government should bear the travel and per diem costs of his witness.

The Commission feels that this recommendation will reduce the possibility that individuals involved in hearings would subpena witnesses unnecessarily. It feels also that the provision for refund of costs when the individual is cleared is required in the interest of basic fairness to individuals unfairly accused. The provision for no refund in the event of no clearance is believed to be at least as fair treatment as the individual would receive in a civil court of law.

The Commission recommends that an adverse decision by the CAB may be appealed to a central review board of the Central Security Office at the request of the employee within time and subject to procedures to be prescribed.

Under security procedures now in effect with respect to employees in United States ports, an individual may appeal an adverse decision in a clearance hearing. This recommendation, therefore, serves only to establish the same procedure for individuals who may be denied clearance under the proposed air transport security program.

The Commission recommends that the final determination as to the issuance or denial of a security clearance for international flight crewmen or an applicant for access to "restricted" airport facilities shall rest with the CAB.

The Commission believes that CAB should have responsibility for final determination in air transport security cases. Although, as pointed out in a previous section, the CAB and CAA have closely related responsibilities in civil air transport, title XII, section 1202, of the Civil Aeronautics Act of 1938, as amended September 9, 1950, provides that "The Board shall consider requirements of national security as well as safety of flight in air commerce, in exercising its powers and carrying out its responsibilities under ttle VI (Civil Aeronautics safety regulations) of the act."

The Commission believes, furthermore, that the basic rules of good administrative procedure would not allow a joint jurisdictional responsibility in this matter. There is, of course, no reason why CAB should not consult with CAA as required in these matters.

PROGRAM ADMINISTRATION

The Commission recommends the following criteria, procedures, and practices with respect to individuals serving as hearing examiners of the new Central Securty Office:

(a) Hearing examiners should be under the jurisdiction of the Central Security Office.

(b) Hearing examiners should be full-time governmental employees, sufficient in number throughout the country to hear cases involving clearance under the aid transport security program.

(c) Hearing examiners should be appointed by the head of the Central Security Office from an appropriate civil service register created for the purpose.

(d) The qualifications of a hearing examiner should be fixed by the Civil Service Commission after consultation with the head of the Central Security Office.

(e) The Civil Service Commission should prepare an appropriate job description sheet and requisite qualifications after consultation with the head of the Central Security Office.

(f) The experience of persons appointed as hearing examiners should include legal practice or technical work performed in a field appropriate to the Government's loyalty and security programs.

(g) There should be an appropriate initial training program and periodic intraining service. In addition to appropriate technical subjects, this training should make provision for thorough indoctrination in constitutional aspects of security and related matters affecting Federal employment.

In the course of its study of the problems involved in establishing an adequate program for national security, the Commission has found that while various programs are established for this function there is often a lack of trained personnel to carry out the actual mechanics of these programs. This gap is a serious deficiency which should be remedied.

The program required by these recommendations is designed to remove the ad hoc aspect from the important function of hearing examiner in security proceedings, and to establish a career service for this activity. The Commission believes, furthermore, that the program recommended here for hearing examiners will emphasize the importance of security hearings to the individuals involved as well as to the Federal agencies holding them.

The recommendation that the Civil Service Commission determine the qualifications for hearing examiners parallels the current practice with regard to other technical or professional personnel in the Federal Civil Service. The Commission has, however, specifically recommended that the training programs, basic as well as in service, should provide for a thorough indoctrination in constitutional and other related aspects of the security problem. The Commission is convinced that a thorough grounding or "refresher" course in the reasons, justifications, and purposes of our national security program are urgently required for all individuals who are so intimately involved in the protection and maintenance of the security of the United States.

The Commission considers that the Civil Aeronautics Act of 1938, as amended, is adequate statutory authority to support a security screening program for air transport personnel as well as other measures reasonably required in that field for national security. The Commission recommends therefore that the necessary air transport security program should be implemented by Executive order.

Examination of the statutory authority granted by the act of September 9, 1950, indicates that it provides the necessary basis for instituting the air transport security program. The Commission believes, however, the various administrative functions which it has recommended in the program can be most expeditiously initiated and subsequently maintained by Executive order.

Immigration and
Nationality Program

Introduction

The United States is a Nation created by immigrants. The richness and diversity of its culture is without doubt due to the steady infusion of talents, traditions, and customs of the peoples of all lands. The immigrant was welcome and came to the United States without permanent restriction for the first century of the Nation's history.

Eventually it became necessary to place restrictions upon the admission of aliens. At the turn of the century, because of the disturbing rise of the anarchist movement, permanent legislation was enacted for the first time to exclude aliens who might attempt to overthrow the Government of the United States. Since 1917, because of the growing intensity of the Communist movement, other legislation has been enacted to exclude aliens who might attempt to overthrow the Government and also to enable the Government to follow the activities of aliens once admitted to the Unied States.

The Commission has studied the history of the measures taken by the Government and their effectiveness as administered. It has found that some of the legislation should be strengthened and that the administration of certain provisions of existing law should be improved.

In the following chapters, the materials examined by the Commission and its findings are described.

HISTORY

Nonimmigrants

The visa was first used to restrict immigration to the United States in 1882, but the Chinese Exclusion Act of that year applied to only one nationality (22 Stat. 58). The general practice of requiring aliens to obtain visas from American consuls abroad began as a wartime measure. A State Department order of April 17, 1917, required consular and diplomatic officers to refuse visas to enemy aliens and to warn all aliens applying for visas that they might be excluded. A joint order of the Departments of State and Labor dated July 26, 1917, required aliens traveling to the United States in wartime to present to an American consular officer abroad passports issued by the government of their allegiance. The consul could grant a visa or refuse it on the basis of public safety. The joint order was validated by the act of May 22, 1918 (40 Stat. 559).

To handle the extra work of issuing consular visas, a special Visa Section was set up in the Bureau of Citizenship of the State Department. On August 13, 1918, the Section became the Visa Office of the Division of Passport Control. Beginning December 1, 1919, the Visa Office operated as a separate unit, and on January 1, 1931, its title was changed by departmental order to the Visa Division. (S. Rept. 1515, 81st Cong., 2d sess., p. 319.)

The distinction between aliens coming to the United States for permanent residence (immigrants) and those who come temporarily with no intention of residing here (nonimmigrants) was first made in the Immigration Act of 1924 (43 Stat. 153). The nonimmigrant alien with whom this chapter is concerned is defined by section 3 of this act in six categories: (1) An official of a foreign government, his family, staff, and servants. (2) A tourist, or an alien visiting the United States temporarily for business or pleasure. (3) An alien in continuous transit. (4) An alien lawfully admitted who travels from one part of the United States through contiguous foreign territory. (5) A seaman on a foreign ship calling at an American port. (6) An alien entering the country to carry on trade under an "existing treaty of commerce and navigation."

In 1945 Congress amended the 1924 act, creating a seventh class of nonimmigrants to provide for the entry of alien personnel of the United Nations and other international organizations. (59 Stat. 669, 672.)

These seven basic classes of nonimmigrants were retained until the Immigration and Nationality Act of 1952, although in the interim some changes were made both by statute and regulation. The 1952 act established the classes as follows:

1. Foreign governmental officials are immigrants unless they qualify as follows:

   (i) an ambassador, public minister, or career diplomatic or consular officer who has been accredited by a foreign government recognized de jure by the United States and who is accepted by the President or by the Secretary of State, and the members of the alien's immediate family;

   (ii) upon a basis of reciprocity, other officials and employees who have been accredited by a foreign government recognized de jure by the United States, who are accepted by the Secretary of State, and the members of their immediate families; and

   (iii) upon a basis of reciprocity, attendants, servants, personal employees, and members of their immediate families, of the officials and employees who have a nonimmigrant status under (i) and (ii) above. (8 U. S. C. sec. 1101 (a) (15) (A).)

Thus before a foreign governmental official can be admitted as a nonimmigrant, he must not only be accredited by a foreign government which is recognized by the United States but he must also be accepted as such by the Government of the United States. However, once a visa has been properly issued to an accredited official of a foreign government as a nonimmigrant, it is conclusive evidence, when presented to the immigration authorities, of the official's proper classification.[1] Such a classification is important because certain provisions, which would otherwise prohibit the entrance of an alien, are either not applicable or may be waived. For example, the present law provides that upon a basis of reciprocity the provisions of 8 U. S. C. sec. 1182 (a) (28) (one of the sections prohibiting subversives from receiving visas or from being admitted into the United States) are not applicable to aliens seeking to enter as a nonimmigrant under paragraph (15) (A) (iii) of section 1101 (a) of title 8.[2] In other words, a servant or attendant to an ambassador or other public official of a foreign government who is a nonimmigrant pursuant to 8 U. S. C. sec. 1101 (a) (15) (A) (i) or (ii), may enter this country even though he—

    (a) is an anarchist,

    (b) advocates or teaches, or is a member of or affiliated with any organization that advocates or teaches opposition to all organized government.

    (c) is a member of or affiliated with the Communist Party of the United States.

In addition to the above, Congress also provided in the Immigration and Nationality Act of 1952:

> Upon a basis of reciprocity, accredited officials of foreign governments, their immediate families, attendants, servants, and personal employees may be admitted in immediate and continuous transit through the United States without regard to the provisions of this section except paragraphs (26), (27), and (29) of subsection (a) of this section.[3]

The requirements as to fingerprinting of all aliens applying for a visa "may be waived in the discretion of the Secretary of State in the case of any alien who" is an official of a foreign government.[4]

The 1952 act further provides that nonimmigrant visas may be granted foreign-government officials, alien students, or treaty traders, etc., even if they are normally ineligible as belonging to one of the 31 classes barred by 8 U. S. C. sec. 1182 (a), with two exceptions, if approved by the Attorney General and recommended by the Secretary of State or a consular officer. The exceptions are described in paragraph 27 which bars aliens who might engage in activities prejudicial to the public interest or endanger the national security; and paragraph 29, which bars suspected spies, saboteurs, and general subversives; aliens who might participate in activity intended to seize or overthrow the United States Government by force or violence; or potential affiliates with any group required to be listed under the registration required by the Internal Security Act (title 50, sec. 786).

---

[1] 22 C. F. R. 41.34.

[2] 8 U. S. C. sec. 1182 (d) (2).

[3] 8 U. S. C. sec. 1182 (d) (8). Pars. 27 and 29 deal with subversives and are explained subsequently. Par. 26 bars an alien from the United States unless he is properly documented.

[4] 8 U. S. C. sec. 1201 (b).

2. The provisions for temporary visitors' visas are substantially the same under the present law as under the 1924 act. The 1952 act describes this nonimmigrant as "an alien (other than one coming for the purpose of study or of performing skilled or unskilled labor or as a representative of foreign press, radio, film, or other foreign information media coming to engage in such vocation) having a residence in a foreign country which he has no intention of abandoning and who is visiting the United States temporarily for business or temporarily for pleasure." (8 U. S. C. sec. 1101 (a) (15) (B).

The requirement that the alien have permanent residence abroad restates the administrative regulations of the State Department in effect before 1952. (H. Rep., 82d Cong., 2d sess., p. 43.)

Another type of nonimmigrant is the "exchange visitor," defined by the United States Information and Educational Exchange Act of 1948 (62 Stat. 6), as amended by the Immigration and Nationality Act of 1952. The 1948 act authorized the Secretary of State to provide "for interchanges on a reciprocal basis between the United States and other countries of students, trainees, teachers, guest instructors, professors, and leaders in fields of specialized knowledge or skill." "Existing reputable agencies" may apply to the Secretary of State to sponsor a program under the exchange visitor program, and must assume certain obligations, such as notifying the Immigration and Naturalization Service if the alien ceases his prescribed activity. (22 C. F. R. 68.2 (a).)

3. The 1952 act redefined the aliens-in-transit class of nonimmigrants to specify that the alien must be in "immediate" as well as continuous transit through the country. The class now also includes aliens who qualify for transit privileges to and from the United Nations headquarters under paragraphs (3), (4), and (5) of section 11 of the headquarters agreement with the United Nations, which will be discussed later. Aliens with United Nations transit visas are admitted under the following conditions:

(a) That such alien shall proceed directly to New York City and shall remain continuously in that city during his sojourn in the United States, departing therefrom only if required in connection with his departure from the United States.

(b) That such alien shall be in possession of a valid visa or other form of valid authority assuring his entry into the country whence he came or to some other foreign country following his sojourn in the United Nations Headquarters District. (8 C. F. R. 214 c. 4.)

Aliens in transit who want to travel more extensively in the United States must apply for the broader visa on the same basis as any other alien.

4. The seaman class of nonimmigrants of the 1924 act was replaced in 1952 by a "crewman class" to include the operating personnel of foreign aircraft landing in the United States temporarily in pursuit of their calling and intending to depart on the same or another ship or aircraft. (8 U. S. C. sec. 1101 (a) (15) (D). The present statute excludes from nonimmigrant status alien seamen on fishing vessels based in American ports, who must have been legally admitted for permanent residence. (H. Rep. 1365, 82d Cong., 2d Sess., pp. 43–44.)

522

5. The provisions of the 1924 act applying to treaty traders was amended by Congress in 1932 to extend the nonimmigrant status to an alien trader's wife and unmarried children under 21. (47 Stat. 607–608.) The section was again amended in 1952 to provide that before a "treaty trader" may be admitted as a nonimmigrant, he must show that he intends "to carry on substantial trade, principally between the United States and the foreign state of which he is a national; or solely to develop and direct . . . an enterprise in which he has invested, or . . . is actively in the process of investing, a substantial amount of capital." (8 U. S. C. sec. 1101 (a) (15) (E).)

6. Prior to 1952, some students were admitted to the United States as nonimmigrants and some in the nonquota class. Since all students are ultimately to return to their own countries, Congress classed them all as nonimmigrants in the 1952 act and authorized visas for "a bona fide student qualified to pursue a full course of study and who seeks to enter the United States temporarily and solely for . . . study at an established institution of learning or other recognized place of study . . . approved by the Attorney General after consultation with the Office of Education of the United States, which institution or place of study shall have agreed to report to the Attorney General the termination of attendance of each nonimmigrant student. . . ." (8 U. S. C. sec. 1101 (a) (15) (F).)

7. The 1952 act also spells out more clearly exactly which aliens may be admitted as nonimmigrants because they are associated with international organizations. The visa of this class may be extended to five categories: (1) a principal resident representative of a foreign government recognized de jure by the United States and a member of an international organization enjoying privileges and exemptions under the International Organizations Immunities Act (59 Stat. 669), his staff and family; (2) other accredited representatives and their families; (3) accredited representatives whose governments are not recognized de jure by the United States or are not members of such international organizations; (4) officers and employees of such international organizations and their families; (5) attendants, servants, and personal employees of such representatives and their families. (8 U. S. C. sec. 1101 (a) (15) (G).)

The International Organizations Immunities Act referred to above exempts the staff of international organizations and the representatives of foreign governments to such organizations from United States laws governing entry and departure from the country, alien registration, fingerprinting, and the registration of foreign agents, just as members of diplomatic missions to the United States are exempt. (59 Stat. 669, 671–672; 22 U. S. C. sec. 288d (a).)

These exemptions, however, are conferred only upon a person who "shall have been duly notified to and accepted by the Secretary of State as a representative, officer, or employee"; or has been so designated by the Secretary prior to formal notification, "or is a member of the family or suite, or servant of one of the foregoing." (22 U. S. C. sec. 288e (a).)

An international organization, association with which confers such immunity, has been defined as a public "international organization in which the United States participates pursuant to any treaty or under the authority of any act of Congress authorizing such participation, or making an appropriation for such participation through appropriate Executive order as being entitled to enjoy the privileges, exemptions and immunities provided in said sections." (22 U. S. C. sec. 288.)

More than 20 organizations have been designated by Executive order as entitled to the privileges granted by the act.

THE HEADQUARTERS AGREEMENT.—On June 26, 1947, an agreement was signed by the Secretary General of the United Nations and the Secretary of State of the United States, granting certain privileges and immunities to aliens entering the United States on their way to or from the United Nations headquarters district in New York City. The Secretary of State acted under Executive order authorized by a joint resolution of Congress which stipulated, among other things, that nothing in the agreement shall diminish, abridge, or weaken "the right of the United States to safeguard its own security and completely to control the entrance of aliens into any territory of the United States other than the headquarters district and its immediate vicinity. . . ." (61 Stat. 756, 767–768.)

The agreement was made effective by an exchange of notes between the United Nations Secretary General and the United States delegate to the United Nations on November 21, 1947.

On December 18, 1947, the "immediate vicinity" of United Nations was defined by mutual agreement to include not only the headquarters district in Manhattan, but also the temporary United Nations headquarters then located at Lake Success, Long Island.

Section 11 of the headquarters agreement provides that—

The Federal, State, and local authorities of the United States shall not impose any impediments to transit to or from the headquarters district of (1) representatives of members or officials of the United Nations or of specialized agencies . . .; (2) experts performing missions for the United Nations or for such specialized agencies; (3) representatives of the press, or of radio, film or other information agencies . . . accredited by the United Nations . . . after consultation with the United States; (4) representatives of nongovernmental organizations recognized by the United Nations for the purpose of consultation under article 71 of the Charter; or (5) other persons invited to the headquarters district by the United Nations or by such specialized agency on official business. The appropriate American authorities shall afford any necessary protection to such persons while in transit to or from the headquarters district. . . .

Section 13 of the agreement further provides that: (a) United States laws and regulations governing the entry of aliens shall not infringe on the privileges granted in section 11, and that visas if required shall be granted promptly and without charge; (b) reasonable proof of eligibility shall be furnished by persons claiming rights under section 11; (c) they shall also comply with health and quarantine regulations; (d) except as otherwise provided, the United States retains full control over the entry of persons and things into American territory; (e) the Secretary General shall arrange with American authorities to register the arrival and departure of persons with visas valid only for transit to and from the headquarters district; and (f) the United Nations, subject to the foregoing, exclusively control the entry of persons and property into the headquarters district. (22 U. S. C. A. 287 note.)

During fiscal year 1947 some 3,800 members of international organizations entered the United States. In 1948 the figure rose to 4,050, and in fiscal year 1955 to more than 6,000. This influx of exempt aliens into the United States (since the United Nations headquarters district is within the boundaries of the United States) has presented some problems under our immigration laws. A special Senate subcommittee to investigate immigration and naturalization reported to the 81st Congress that: "Communist agents have used international organizations in this country as a vehicle for carrying on anti-American activity. The evidence in the files of the subcommittee shows conclusively that many representatives and staff members of international organizations are engaging in subversive activities beyond the proper scope of their duties of employment."

8. The Immigration and Nationality Act of 1952 established one new class of nonimmigrants, admitting under this visa an alien "who is of distinguished merit and ability" coming here temporarily to perform "services of an exceptional nature. . . ." Another subdivision of the new class would admit seasonal labor temporarily "if unemployed persons capable of performing such service or labor cannot be found in this country." A third type of alien made eligible for temporary admission as a nonimmigrant is the industrial trainee. (8 U. S. C. sec. 1101 (a) (15) (H).)

Visas for any labor imported under the new provision must be approved by the Attorney General in consultation with appropriate officials, after petition by the importing employer. (8 U. S. C. 1184 (c).)

9. Another new class of nonimmigrants was created by the 1952 act to admit "representatives of the foreign press, radio, film, or other foreign information media" temporarily "upon a basis of reciprocity." Wives and family are also included. (8 U. S. C. sec. 1101 (a) (15) (I).)

Any alien admitted as a nonimmigrant is subject to the following conditions:

(a) That while in the United States he will maintain the particular nonimmigrant status under which he was admitted or such other status as he may acquire . . . in accordance with the . . . law . . . .

(b) That he will depart from the United States within the period of his admission or any authorized extension thereof.

(c) That . . . he will not engage in any employment . . . inconsistent with . . . the status under which he is in the United States unless such employment . . . has first been authorized by the district director or the officer in charge having administrative jurisdiction over the alien's place of temporary residence in the United States.

(d) That he will not remain in the United States beyond a date 6 months, or in the case of a nonimmigrant admitted prior to the effective date of the Immigration and Nationality Act, 2 months, prior to the end of the period during which he will be eligible for readmission to the country whence he came or for admission to some other country, as evidenced by a valid passport or other travel document.

(e) That he will fulfill such other conditions as the admitting immigration officer . . . may impose . . . to insure that he will depart from the United States at the expiration of the time for which he was admitted, and that he will maintain the status under which he was admitted or which he may have lawfully acquired subsequent to his admission. (8 C. F. R. 214.2.)

Immigrants

Even before the United States became a sovereign nation, the American colonists were concerned with problems of immigration. One of the grievances against George III set forth in the Declaration of Independence was that the English King ". . . endeavored to prevent the population of these States; for that purpose obstructing the laws for naturalization of foreigners; refusing to pass others to encourage their migrations hither, and raising the conditions of new appropriations of lands."

Since 1776, however, the United States has received more than 40 million foreigners within its shores,[5] and its long immigration history has become rather complex.

Until about 1824, the several States controlled immigration according to their own desires. It was not until 1849 that the Supreme Court declared unconstitutional the State laws which taxed alien passengers arriving at New York and Massachusetts ports. (*Smith* v. *Turner* and *Norris* v. *The City of Boston*, 48 U. S. (7 How.) 283.)

The power of the United States as a sovereign nation to restrict, control, or prohibit the entry of aliens has been reaffirmed repeatedly by the Supreme Court, notably in 1904 in the case of *Turner* v. *Williams* (194 U. S. 279).

The power to deport was first exercised by Congress in passing the Alien Act of 1798 (1 Stat. 571) which authorized the President "to order all such aliens as he shall judge dangerous to the peace and safety of the United States, or shall have reasonable grounds to suspect are concerned in any treasonable or secret machinations against the government thereof, to depart out of the territory of the United States. . . ."

The Alien Act of 1798 expired with the century 2 years later and was not renewed. For the next 75 years there was no Federal legislation restricting the admission or requiring the deportation of aliens. From 1875 down to the present time, however, there has been a continuous history of laws which affect immigrants.

In 1875 Congress voted to exclude from the country certain types of criminals and women imported for the purposes of prostitution (18 Stat. 477). A few years later the ban was extended to convicts, lunatics, idiots, and potential public charges (22 Stat. 214). The year 1882 saw the passage of the first Chinese Exclusion Act (22 Stat. 58), and shortly afterward the

---

[5] Immigration and naturalization report for fiscal 1955.

expansion of the prohibition relative to contract labor (23 Stat. 332). Toward the end of the century Congress closed the doors to paupers, polygamists, "persons suffering from a loathsome or dangerous contagious disease," and those convicted "of a felony or other infamous crime or misdemeanor involving moral turpitude. . . ." (26 Stat. 1084.)

The assassination of President McKinley in 1901 inspired the first Federal legislation which linked immigration directly with security of the Government of the United States. The 57th Congress in 1903 voted to deny admission to the United States of "anarchists, or persons who believe in or advocate the overthrow by force or violence of the Government of the United States or of all government, or of all forms of law, or the assassination of public officials. . . ." The act also provided that "no person who disbelieves . . . in all organized government, or who is a member of . . . any organization . . . teaching such disbelief . . . or who advocates or teaches the duty, necessity, or propriety of the unlawful assaulting or killing of any officer or officers . . . of the Government of the United States or of any other organized government because of his or their official character, shall be permitted to enter the United States. . . ." (32 Stat. 1213, 1214, 1221, held constitutional in *Turner* v. *Williams*, cited previously.)

The flood of immigrants to America reached a record 1,285,349 during the year 1907. In this year Congress established a commission to "make full inquiry, examination, and investigation by subcommittee or otherwise into the subject of immigration." [6] The commission took 4 years to complete its report, which was published in 1911 in 42 volumes. The report was the basis of our first comprehensive immigration law, enacted on February 5, 1917. (39 Stat. 874, 875, 876.) Section 3 of this act contains substantially the same provisions regarding subversives as the acts of 1903 and 1907. In addition, the 1917 act provides that any person aiding a subversive to enter the United States is guilty of a felony, and that aliens who advocate the unlawful destruction of property are not admissible.

The first general requirement of visas to enter the United States was a wartime measure adopted in 1917. This was followed in 1918 by an act authorizing the President to proclaim further restrictions and prohibitions on entry and departure from the United States in the interests of "public safety." Such a proclamation was issued by President Wilson on August 8, 1918 (40 Stat. 1829).

Another act, passed on October 16, 1918, empowered certain Government officials to arrest and deport subversive aliens and declared their entry or attempted reentry to be a felony. (40 Stat. 1012.) This act was amended in 1920 to enlarge the class of subversive aliens to be excluded by adding those who advocated (1) the overthrow of the Government by force and violence, (2) the assassination of officials, (3) unlawful damage

---

[6] 34 Stat. 898, 909. This act contains provisions regarding subversives similar to the act of 1903.

or destruction of property, or (4) sabotage. (41 Stat. 1008.) The amendment also provided for deportation of members of subversive organizations.

In 1939 the Supreme Court ruled that the deportation provisions were valid only against aliens who were members of the subversive organizations when proceedings against them were begun. (*Kessler* v. *Strecker*, 307 U. S. 22.) However, when in 1952 the Supreme Court reviewed events following the 1939 decision, the Court pointed out [7] that—

The reaction of the Communist Party (to the above decision) was to drop aliens from membership, at least in form, in order to immunize them from the consequences of their party membership.

"The reaction of Congress was that the Court had misunderstood its legislation," and thereupon enacted the Alien Registration Act of 1940 (54 Stat. 670) which made mandatory the deportation of aliens who at any time had been members of prescribed organizations. This act also required fingerprinting of aliens seeking visas.

Meanwhile, the Immigration Law of 1917 had been modified in 1921 by legislation limiting the admission of aliens to 3 percent of the number of their particular nationality present in the country during the 1910 census. (42 Stat. 5.) And the Immigration Act of May 26, 1924 (43 Stat. 153), fixed quotas on ratios determined by nationality groups resident in the United States during the 1920 census. The 1917 and 1924 acts were our basic immigration laws until the present Walter-McCarran statute was enacted in 1952.

In 1940 Congress transferred the Immigration and Naturalization Service from the Department of Labor to the Department of Justice, and in 1949 allowed for the admission of not more than 100 aliens a year who might otherwise be barred but who would be certified by the Attorney General as in the interests of national security and "essential to the furtherance of the national intelligence mission." (63 Stat. 208, 212.)

In 1950, as "a result of evidence adduced before various committees of the Senate and House of Representatives" that a world Communist conspiracy exists, Congress enacted the Internal Security Act, then repassed it over President Truman's veto. (64 Stat. 987.) The act amended various immigration laws to strengthen security provisions applying to aliens. The most significant of these provided that present or former membership in the Communist or other totalitarian party was grounds for exclusion; the provisions for deportation were strengthened, and deportable subversives who willfully failed to depart within 6 months were made liable to imprisonment up to 10 years; the discretion of the Attorney General in admitting otherwise ineligible aliens was curtailed or eliminated; and all resident aliens subject to registration were required to report annually their changes of address.

The Immigration and Nationality Act (the McCarran-Walter Act) was enacted over President Truman's veto in 1952, and is now the basic statute

---

[7] *Harisiades* v. *Shaughnessy*, 342 U. S. 580, 593.

controlling immigration. (66 Stat. 163.) Auerbach, in his *Immigration Laws of the United States* (Bobbs Merrill, 1955), characterizes the 1952 act as follows:

> In general, the new law perpetuates the immigration policies of the earlier statutes with some significant modifications. Different from the earlier laws, the new act—
>
> > makes all races eligible to naturalization and eliminates race as a bar to immigration;
> >
> > eliminates discrimination between sexes with respect to immigration;
> >
> > introduces a system of selective immigration by giving a quota preference to skilled aliens whose service are urgently need in the United States;
> >
> > places a limit on the use of the governing country's quota by natives of colonies and dependent areas;
> >
> > provides an escape clause permitting the immigration of certain former voluntary members of proscribed organizations;
> >
> > broadens the grounds for exclusion and deportation of aliens;
> >
> > curtails procedures for the adjustment of status of nonimmigrant aliens into the United States to that of permanent resident aliens;
> >
> > and affords greater procedural safeguards to aliens subject to deportation.

The 1952 act continues the system of dual examination of aliens by consular officers who must grant them visas abroad and by immigration officers at the port of entry.

During the nearly 5 years the act has been in effect, various amendments have been suggested. The President has several times suggested changes, most recently in his immigration and naturalization message to Congress on January 31, 1957. In this message the President pointed out that many refugees, possibly thousands, when applying for visas, had assumed new identities to escape repatriation behind the Iron Curtain. The President suggested that some relief be granted this group who would otherwise be subject to mandatory deportation for such falsification. He also urged extensive changes in the present quota system and other matters not concerned with the security program.

The President's recommendations and the three bills pending in Congress in the early months of 1957 (H. R. 3364, introduced into the House by Representative Emanuel Celler of New York, and S. 1006 and S. 344, introduced into the Senate by Senator Arthur V. Watkins, of Utah) indicate that the immigration security program will receive much attention in the coming months.

LEGAL BASIS

Introduction

A sovereign nation may establish any rule it chooses for the admission or refusal of admission of aliens. As is so often true, the exercise of a basic power may have significant and varied effects upon the nation's affairs. So it is with the admission of aliens. This study is concerned only with the relation to national security of measures taken by the United States regulating the admission of aliens. There are two important categories of aliens, those who intend to make the United States their permanent home and those who do not. The first are designated as immigrants; the second as non-immigrants.

The Congress early asserted its authority to control immigration by passing the Alien Act of June 25, 1798,[8] which was the first Federal legislation dealing with the expulsion of aliens. This law expired 2 years after its enactment. There was no further legislation in this field until 1875, when the Act of March 3, 1875,[9] was enacted. This Act excluded from admission to the United States criminals and prostitutes and entrusted the supervision of immigrants to collectors of the ports. The Immigration Act of August 3, 1882,[10] added to the classes of inadmissible aliens: lunatics, idiots, and persons unable to take care of themselves without becoming a public charge.

The first legislative enactment providing for the exclusion of aliens because of proscribed opinions was the Act of March 3, 1903,[11] which made inadmissible: "anarchists, or persons who believe in, or advocate, the overthrow by force or violence the Government of the United States, or of all government, or of all forms of law . . ." The Immigration Act of 1917 [12] codified all previous immigration laws and added to the excludable classes of aliens. On October 16, 1918,[13] Congress enacted a law excluding alien anarchists and others believing in or advocating the overthrow of the Government, and also *persons who are members or affiliates of organizations which teach or advocate the overthrow of the Government*, etc., thus further expanding the security protection of the Act of March 3, 1903. On May 10, 1920,[14] an Act was passed calling for the deportation of alien enemies and aliens convicted of violation or conspiracy to violate various war statutes.

Immigration policy was governed by the Act of 1917 as amended by the Act of May 26, 1924,[15] until the Immigration and Nationality Act of 1952 was enacted. The 1924 Act was the first to make a distinction between immigrant and nonimmigrant aliens. This distinction has been continued in subsequent legislation. The 1952 Act, frequently referred to as the "Walter-McCarran Act",[16] is hereinafter referred to as the Act. It has been aptly described as the "first attempt to bring within one cohesive and comprehensive statute the various laws relating to immigration, naturalization, and nationality".[17] It contains most of the important statutory provisions

---

[8] 1 Stat. 570.
[9] 18 Stat. 477.
[10] 22 Stat. 214.
[11] 32 Stat. 1213.
[12] 39 Stat. 874.
[13] 40 Stat. 1012.
[14] 41 Stat. 593.
[15] 43 Stat. 153.
[16] 66 Stat. 163, 8 U. S. C. A. 1101–1503 (1952).
[17] Report No. 1365, Judiciary Committee of the House of Representatives, 82d Cong., 2d sess., to accompany H. R. 5678.

relating to immigrant and nonimmigrant aliens; among other matters, it specifies the several classes of nonimmigrants who may be admitted.[18]

A major effort to combat sedition and subversion through control of aliens within the United States was the Alien Registration Act of 1940.[19] Its provisions were incorporated in the Act and the Alien Registration Act was repealed.

Excluded from consideration in this study are the Displaced Persons Act, the Refugee Relief Acts,[20] the Mexican Migratory Labor Acts,[21] and other legislation of a temporary, emergent and/or limited nature. Also excluded will be provisions unrelated to security. The study will consider separately five primary topics, i. e., immigrants, deportation, naturalization, denaturalization, and nonimmigrants.

Statutory Provisions

A. IMMIGRANTS.—Before reviewing the provisions of the Act in the detail required, it is well to note section 8 of the Central Intelligence Act of 1949 which provides as follows:

Whenever the Director, the Attorney General, and the Commissioner of Immigration shall determine that the entry of a particular alien into the United States for permanent residence is in the interest of national security or essential to the furtherance of the national intelligence mission, such alien and his immediate family shall be given entry into the United States for permanent residence without regard to their inadmissibility under the Immigration Act or any other laws or regulations, or to the failure to comply with such laws and regulations pertaining to admissibility: *Provided*, That the number of aliens and members of their immediate families enter the United States under the authority of this Section shall in no case exceed one hundred persons in any one fiscal year.[22]

The Act in section 101 contains definitions. Of concern in this study are the following:

The term "immigrant", for purposes of the Act means "every alien except an alien who is within (certain specified) classes of nonimmigrant aliens." "Immigrant visa" is defined as a visa required by the Act and properly issued by a consular officer at his office outside the United States to an eligible immigrant.[23]

Certain terms are defined in this section to conform with the definitions contained in the Internal Security Act of 1950.[24] Among these are "organization," "communism," "totalitarian party" (this definition is: "an organization which advocates in the United States the establishment of a totalitarian

---

[18] 8 U. S. C. A. 1101 (a) (15) (1952).
[19] 54 Stat. 673.
[20] For example, the Act of August 7, 1953, 67 Stat. 400; 50 U. S. C. A. app. § 1971–1971Q.
[21] Act of October 31, 1949, 63 Stat. 1051, as amended by the Acts of July 12, 1951, 65 Stat. 119, August 8, 1953, 67 Stat. 500, March 16, 1954, 68 Stat. 28, and August 9, 1955, 69 Stat. 615.
[22] 50 U. S. C. A. 403 (H).
[23] 8 U. S. C. A. 1101.
[24] 64 Stat. 987, 50 U. S. C. A. 781–826.

dictatorship or totalitarianism"), "totalitarian dictatorship," "advocacy," "giving of support," etc. These definitions are applicable also to non-immigrants.

The Act in Section 212 specifies 31 classes of aliens who are ineligible generally to receive visas and who are excluded from admission.[25] The three most important classes from a security standpoint are described in paragraphs 27, 28 and 29. These paragraphs are condensed as follows:

1. Aliens who the consular officer or Attorney General knows or has reason to believe seek to enter the United States solely, principally, or incidentally to engage in activities which would be prejudicial to the public interest or endanger the welfare, safety, or security of the United States (Sec. 212 (a) (27)).

2. Aliens who are anarchists or who advocate or teach, or are members of organizations which teach opposition to all organized government, and aliens who are members of or affiliated with the Communist Party of the United States, any other totalitarian party of the United States, the Communist Political Association, the Communist or any other totalitarian party of any State of the United States, of any foreign state, or of any geographical subdivision of any foreign state, or any subsidiary, branch or affiliate of any branch or association or party, or the direct predecessors or successors of any association or party, regardless of name. Aliens not heretofore described who advocate the principles and doctrines of world communism or of a totalitarian dictatorship, or aliens who are members or affiliated with any organization required to be registered by the Subversive Activities Control Act, unless the alien did not know that the organization was a Communist organization. Aliens who advocate, teach, write, or publish anything in furtherance of the doctrines of Communist or totalitarian organizations and aliens who are affiliated with any organization which prints, publishes and circulates printed matter furthering such organizations.

It is provided that certain of the aliens described in this section may be given a visa if membership or affiliation with the Communist Party was involuntary or when the alien was under 16 years of age or automatic by operation of law or purposes of obtaining employment, food or other essentials of living, or defectors who at least 5 years prior to application have actively opposed the doctrines of the party. Such an alien must establish to the satisfaction of the Attorney General that he fulfills the requirements of these exemptions. The Attorney General must find further that "the admission of such alien into the United States would be in the public interest." The Attorney General must report to the Congress each alien who is admitted under the exception relating to defectors.[26]

---

[25] 8 U. S. C. A. 1182 (a) (27), (28), and (29). See also, 8 U. S. C. A. 1101 (a) (37) for a definition of totalitarian.
[26] Sec. 212 (a) (28).

3. Aliens with respect to whom the consular officer or the Attorney General knows or has reason to believe probably would after entry (a) engage in activities which would be prohibited by the laws of the United States relating to espionage, sabotage, public disorder, or in other subversive activities, or (b) engage in any activity, the purpose of which is the overthrow of the Government of the United States by force or other unconstitutional means, or (c) join or participate in the activities of any organization registered under the Subversive Activities Control Act.[27]

Section 221 specifies the terms and conditions for the issuance of visas to immigrants. Included among the conditions are the furnishing of personal information, photographs, registration, and fingerprinting.[28]

Section 261 provides that no visa shall be issued to any alien until he has been registered and fingerprinted.[29]

B. DEPORTATION.—The Act contains detailed procedures relating to the deportation of aliens. Security provisions relating to deportation are paraphrased below:

Section 241 provides for the deportation of aliens who are members or affiliates of the Communist Party, or any political subdivision thereof, or who have engaged in subversive activities described in section 212 (*a*) (27) and (29), above, and also those who have violated espionage and other security measures.[30]

Section 242 as amended September 3, 1954,[31] establishes procedures for the apprehension and deportation of aliens, including hearings before a special inquiry officer. The Attorney General is authorized to issue regulations providing for notice, representation and reasonable opportunity for the alien to examine the evidence against him and to cross-examine witnesses. The procedures established by this section in general follow the procedures established by the Internal Security Act of 1950.[32]

C. NATIONALITY AND NATURALIZATION.—For purposes of this study pertinent provisions of the Act relating to nationality and naturalization include the following:

Section 310 which fixes naturalization jurisdiction and initial naturalization procedures; and [33]

Section 313 which prohibits the naturalization of persons opposed to government, or law, or who are members of the Communist Party, or who favor totalitarian forms of government; the language descriptive of such organization and activities being similar to that of section 212 (a) (28) above. These provisions may be invoked in the case of an applicant for naturalization who at any time within ten years preceding the application

[27] Sec. 212 (a) (29).
[28] 8 U. S. C. A. 1201.
[29] 8 U. S. C. A. 1301.
[30] 8 U. S. C. A. 1251 ((a) (6) through (8), (a) (7) and (a) (17)).
[31] 68 Stat. 1232, 8 U. S. C. A. 1252.
[32] 64 Stat. 987.
[33] 8 U. S. C. A. 1421.

was or has been found to be within the classes enumerated in the section. Also contained in this section are the exceptions found in section 212 (a) (28), i.e., those whose membership was involuntary or when under 16 years, or who were defectors, etc.; [34] also it is required by section 316 (a) (3) that in order to be naturalized a person must be "attached to the principles of the Constitution of the United States." [35]

An exception is made in subsection (c) to certain requirements of the physical presence in the United States of an applicant for naturalization for an uninterrupted period of one year if the applicant is an employee of CIA.

Subsection (f) of this section provides that naturalization shall not be granted if proceedings are pending under Sections 13 and 14 of the Subversive Activities Control Act of 1950 against any organization of which the petitioner is a member or affiliate.

A petitioner for naturalization must sustain the burden of proof that he lawfully entered the United States for permanent residence according to section 318 which further provides that a petition for naturalization shall not be heard when an order of deportation or proceeding in deportation is pending against the petitioner.[36]

Under certain conditions set out in Section 331, an alien enemy may be naturalized.[37]

Procedures are established for the investigation of a petitioner for naturalization by section 335 [38] which also contains a provision that the Attorney General may waive this investigation.

The oath required to be taken prior to admission to citizenship includes a pledge to support the Constitution and laws of the United States. Section 337 (a).[39]

D. DENATURALIZATION.—*Section 340* as amended September 3, 1954, outlines the conditions upon which naturalization may be revoked; subsection (a) provides that

. . . refusal on the part of a naturalized citizen within a period of ten years following his naturization to testify as a witness in any proceeding before a congressional committee concerning his subversive activities, in a case where such person has been convicted of contempt for such refusal, shall be held to constitute a ground for revocation of such person's naturalization under this subsection as having been procured by concealment of a material fact or by willful misrepresentation.

Subsection (c) expressly provides for revocation of naturalization if a naturalized person within 5 years becomes a member of an organization, membership in which would have precluded naturalization.[40] Derivative citizenship of persons claiming citizenship through any such person is also

---

[34] 8 U. S. C. A. 1424.
[35] 8 U. S. C. A. 1427.
[36] 8 U. S. C. A. 1430.
[37] 8 U. S. C. A. 1442.
[38] 8 U. S. C. A. 1446.
[39] 8 U. S. C. A. 1448.
[40] 68 Stat. 1252, 8 U. S. C. A. 1451.

cancelled under certain conditions, but is not cancelled for denaturalization pursuant to subsection (a) cited above.

Section 349 outlines the conditions upon which a native born or naturalized citizen may be expatriated. Included in subparagraph (*a*) (9) as amended September 3, 1954, by the Expatriation Act of 1954, is the following:

. . . committing any act of treason against, or attempting by force to overthrow, or bearing arms against, the United States, violating or conspiring to violate any of the provisions of section 2383 of Title 18, or willfully performing any act in violation of section 2385 of Title 18, or violating section 2384 of Title 18 by engaging in a conspiracy to overthrow, put down, or destroy by force the Government of the United States or to levy war against them, if and when he is convicted thereof by a court-martial or by a court of competent jurisdiction.

Subsection (b) provides that

any person who commits or performs any act specified in subsection (a) ·shall be conclusively presumed to have done so voluntarily and without having been subjected to duress of any kind, if such person at the time of the act was a national of the state in which the act was performed and had been present in such state for a period or periods totalling ten years or more immediately prior to such act.[41]

E. NONIMMIGRANTS.—In addition to the basic Act, there are three other important statutes relating to nonimmigrant aliens; the International Organizations Immunities Act,[42] the U. S.-U. N. Headquarters Agreement, a Joint Resolution,[43] and the United States Information and Educational Exchange Act of 1948,[44] as amended, particularly as amended by the basic Act.[45] These acts are discussed later.

Generally both immigrants and nonimmigrants are required to have a visa before they may be admitted. Black's law dictionary defines a visa as "an endorsement made on a passport by the proper authorities denoting that it has been examined, and that the person who bears it is permitted to proceed on his journey." The term "nonimmigrant visa" [46] means a visa properly issued by a competent officer to an alien entitled to admission but who does not intend to reside in the United States.

The classes of nonimmigrant aliens as defined by section 101 of the basic Act [47] are as follows:

    (*a*) Foreign Government officials, ambassadors, ministers, etc., their families and employees.

    (*b*) Temporary visitors.

    (*c*) Aliens in transit.

    (*d*) Alien crewmen (both seamen and airmen).

    (*e*) Treaty traders.

    (*f*) Students.

---

[41] 68 Stat. 1146, 8 U. S. C. A. 1481.
[42] 22 U. S. C. A. 288 d (*a*).
[43] 22 U. S. C. A. 287 (note).
[44] 22 U. S. C. A. 1431—1479.
[45] 8 U. S. C. A. 1101 (*a*) (15) (F), 22 U. S. C. A. 1446.
[46] 8 U. S. C. A. 1101 (*a*) (15) (26) (1932).
[47] 8 U. S. C. A. 1101.

(g) International Organizations' representatives and personnel and persons accredited to them, and the families of such persons.

(h) Temporary workers of distinguished merit and ability.

(i) Members of foreign press, radio, film, or other information media, on a basis of reciprocity.

The privileges and immunities of international organizations are elaborated in the International Organizations Immunities Act,[48] and the U. S.-U. N. Headquarters Agreement.[49] The conditions of admission of students may be found in the Information and Educational Exchange Act of 1948 as amended.[49a] The admission of diplomatic representatives and their privileges and immunities are governed by 22 U. S. C. A. 252–254 and established usages of international law. However, the basic Act contains certain specific limitations upon the admission of aliens, including the diplomatic and international organization groups. These limitations, as related to security are identical for both immigrants and nonimmigrants, although there are some exceptions applicable only to nonimmigrants which will be discussed later. The most important sections, heretofore analyzed are paragraphs 27, 28 and 29 of section 212 (a) of the Act.

In general, officials of foreign governments, diplomatic ministers, and similar persons are not subject to the requirements for visas.[50] Persons in this class are expected to comply with reasonable requirements of identification either by having passports or other official documents to establish their identity and qualification for admission. They are exempt from fingerprinting. Members of the U. S. S. R. diplomatic staff and officials are admitted regardless of membership in the Communist Party, since paragraph 28 is not applicable to diplomatic and similar persons. However, under established procedures, any diplomatic official who interferes in United States affairs is subject to recall upon the request of the United States. Diplomatic personnel who come within the first security exclusion basis (par. 27), that is, aliens who the consular officer or Attorney General knows or has reason to believe seek to enter the United States solely, principally, or incidentally to engage in activities which would endanger the security of the United States are to be admitted only under such regulations as the President may provide.

The security regulations (par. 28) do not apply to a designated principal representative of foreign governments to an international organization, the accredited resident members of the staff of such representative and members of their immediate families except that such persons may be required to have appropriate identification documents. Further, their travel may be limited to going from their residence to the United Nations headquarters district and return. They may be required to proceed directly to New York City and to remain there continuously. Such an alien can only depart from the city of New York to leave the United States and, further, he must possess

---

[48] Note 35.
[49] Note 36.
[49a] Note 37.
[50] U. S. C. A. 1102.

a visa or other valid authority insuring his reentry into his country or other foreign country following his sojourn in the United Nations headquarters district.[51] Such persons must show before entry that their purpose in coming to the United States is not to engage in subversive activities (par. 27). In other words, representatives accredited to international organizations are not eligible to be admitted if the consular officer or the Attorney General believes that their purpose in entering the United States is to endanger the security of the United States.

However, persons other than an ambassador, public minister, or career diplomatic or consular officer, a designated principal resident representative of a foreign government to an international organization but who fall within the general classification of staff members, employees and members of families of such persons, are subject to the exclusion provisions (par. 27 and par. 29) discussed above. The provisions as to membership in Communist organizations do not apply to the staff members, etc. of embassies and international organizations who seek entry temporarily as nonimmigrants.[52]

A provision of the basic Act of particular contemporary interest is subsection (d) (5) of section 212.[53] This subsection authorizes the Attorney General in his discretion to parole into the United States temporarily *under such conditions as he may prescribe for emergent reasons or for reasons deemed strictly in the public interest,* any alien, but such alien shall not have the right to become a permanent resident. Further, the Attorney General is authorized to prescribe conditions including the execution of a bond for the admission of aliens under this so-called "parole" section. It is under this provision that many Hungarian refugees were admitted to the United States following the uprising in November, 1956.

The Attorney General is required to make a detailed report to Congress of his action waiving the security provisions (par. 28) and exercising certain other waiver authority extended to him.

It is provided that upon a basis of reciprocity, accredited officials of foreign governments, their families and personal employees may be admitted in immediate and continuous transit through the United States without regard to exclusion provisions other than paragraphs (26), (27), and (29) of subsection (a) of section 212.

The basic Act authorizes the President, whenever he finds that the entry of any aliens, or any class of aliens, would be detrimental to the interests of the United States, to suspend their entry under any restrictions he may deem appropriate.

The admission of nonimmigrant aliens in addition to the restrictions discussed above, may be for such time and under such conditions as the Attorney General may prescribe, including a requirement for bond.

It is further provided that an alien who is admitted as an officer or employee of a foreign government or of an international organization shall not

---

[51] 8 C. F. R. 214 (c) (4).
[52] 8 U. S. C. A. 1182 (d) (2).
[53] U. S. C. A. 1182 (d) (5).

be entitled to change his status and receive an immigrant visa except under strictly regulated conditions. Further, any alien who has received a visa to enter the United States in his own country, may, upon arrival in the United States, be excluded if found inadmissible under the basic Act. The Act provides that aliens, except diplomatic personnel or persons eligible as representatives of an international organization, must be registered and fingerprinted when they apply for a visa and must furnish copies of their photographs.[54]

A nonimmigrant visa is strictly limited as to time and nonimmigrants must register under the Act in the same manner as other aliens.

From a security standpoint, another important provision of the basic Act gives authority to the Attorney General to enter into contracts with transportation lines for transporting aliens in continuous transit through the United States to another country. In such cases the Attorney General may require the transportation lines to give bond and no transportation company shall land any aliens in the United States until it has entered into a contract as prescribed by the Attorney General. Generally, however, all aliens who wish to travel through the United States in immediate and continuous transit must meet the visa requirements of the Act.[55]

The importance of this provision has been noted by the Congress in a recent report on the administration of the basic Act which stated: "Every precaution must be taken to prevent any abuse of it which might endanger the security of the United States." [57]

Regulations of the Secretary of State [58] and of the Attorney General [59] *authorize waiving visas under specified conditions for nonimmigrant aliens who are being transported in continuous transit across the United States without stopover.*

There are provisions for special controls upon the entry and departure of alien crewmen.[60] Formerly, the term "seamen" was used; the change is a recognition of international air transport. The term "crewman" means "a person serving in any capacity on board a vessel or aircraft." [61]

The Act contains several provisions incorporating requirements previously found in regulations relating to alien crewmen. Whenever appropriate the same provisions apply to seamen and to the crews of aircraft. There are especially severe penalties for "jumping ship" without complying with requirements for fingerprinting and registration.

F. CRIMINAL SANCTIONS.—The Act contains detailed criminal sanctions for violations of its numerous provisions. The more important of those provisions relating to security are as follows:

---

[54] 8 U. S. C. A. 1201–1203.
[55] 8 U. S. C. A. 1228.
[57] Report on the administration of the Immigration and Nationality Act, House Committee on the Judiciary, February 28, 1955, pp. 3, 4, 8.
[58] 22 C. F. R. 41.6 (a) (2).
[59] 8 C. F. R. 212 (3) (b).
[60] 8 U. S. C. A. 1281.
[61] 8 U. S. C. A. 1101 (a) (10).

Section 215 makes it unlawful:

(1) For any alien during a war or national emergency to depart or attempt to depart from or enter or attempt to enter the United States except under such rules, regulations, etc., as the President should prescribe.

(2) For any person to:

(a) Transport or attempt to transport from or into the United States another person with the knowledge that the deportation or entry of that person is forbidden by this Section;

(b) Knowingly make a false statement in an application for permission to depart from or enter the United States;

(c) Knowingly furnish another a permit or evidence of permission to depart or enter not issued for that other person's use;

(d) Knowingly use a permit to enter or depart not intended for his use;

(e) Forge, counterfeit, etc., a permit to enter or depart;

(f) Use a forged, counterfeit, etc., permit to enter or depart.[62]

Section 214 (d) makes it a felony for any alien against whom a final order of deportation is in effect to fail to comply with restrictions imposed by the Attorney General.

Also, subparagraph (e) makes it a felony for an alien against whom an order of deportation is outstanding to willfully fail to refuse to leave the country, etc.[63]

Section 266 provides:

(1) Penalties for failure of parent of alien to apply for registration and fingerprinting as required;

(2) Penalties for false statements made in registration;

(3) That it is a crime for any person with an unlawful intent to counterfeit an Alien Registration Card.[64]

Section 271 requires masters and other personnel of ships, aircraft, transportation lines and others in related activities to prevent the unauthorized landing of aliens, and provides penalties for failure to comply with this provision. It also provides that the failure of an immigrant to present himself at the time and place designated by immigration officers shall be *prima facie* evidence of an unlawful landing.[65]

Section 273 makes it unlawful to bring into the United States aliens who do not have an unexpired visa and provides penalties for violation of the provision.[66]

Section 274 makes it unlawful to bring into the United States or to conceal or harbor any alien not lawfully admitted to the United States and provides a penalty for violation of this provision.[67]

---

[62] 8 U. S. C. A. 1185.
[63] 8 U. S. C. A. 1251.
[64] 8 U. S. C. A. 1306.
[65] 8 U. S. C. A. 1321.
[66] 8 U. S. C. A. 1323.
[67] 8 U. S. C. A. 1324.

Sections 275 and 276 provide penalties for the entry of an alien at an improper place, misrepresentation of facts and reentry of a deported alien.[68]

Relevant provisions from the Criminal Code, title 18, U. S. C. A. are as follows:

Section 1423 makes it a crime to misuse evidence of citizenship.

Section 1424 prohibits the impersonation of another person in any naturalization and citizenship proceedings or use of the evidence of citizenship of another person.

Section 1425 makes it a crime to procure citizenship or naturalization unlawfully.

Section 1426 provides penalties for forging papers related to an immigrant's arrival, naturalization and citizenship. The Act, section 402 (*a*), amends the Criminal Code, 18 U. S. C. A. 1546, which prescribes penalties for fraud and misuse of visas, permits and other entry documents. The more important change accomplished by the amendment is to include nonimmigrant visas among the documents which are not to be counterfeited or otherwise misused.

Section 1427 forbids the unlawful sale or disposition of naturalization or citizenship papers.

Section 1428 makes it a crime not to surrender a cancelled naturalization certificate after proper notice has been given.

Section 1429 (a new section) provides penalties for failure to answer a subpoena to testify at a final naturalization proceeding.

Of particular interest is section 277 which provides that any person who knowingly aids or assists any alien excludable under section 212 (*a*) (27), (28), and (29), the security provisions, to enter the United States or who connives or conspires with any person to allow, procure, or permit any such alien to enter, shall be guilty of a felony.[69]

Constitutional Basis

A. GENERAL PRINCIPLES.—Authority to formulate immigration policies rests exclusively with the Congress of the United States. As a sovereign nation, the United States has absolute power to regulate the admission of aliens into its domain.[70] With this power to regulate admission naturally follows the power of the United States as a sovereign to deport those aliens whom it determines are undesirable.

The Constitution [71] defines those persons who are citizens of the United States as:

---

[68] 8 U. S. C. A. 1325 and 1326.

[69] 8 U. S. C. A. 1327.

[70] *Hariseades* v. *United States,* 342 U. S. 580 (March 10, 1952). This case inter alia upheld the constitutionality of the Alien Registration Act of 1940; See also *U. S. ex rel. Avromovich* v. *Lehmann,* 235 F. 2d 260 (1956) ; *U. S. ex rel. John Turner* v. *Williams,* decided May 16, 1904, 194 U. S. 279.

[71] Constitution, amendment XIV, section 1.

All persons born or naturalized in the United States, and subject to the jurisdiction thereof, are citizens of the United States . . .

The Constitution vests in the Congress the authority "to establish a uniform rule of naturalization . . ." [72] The Constitution does not expressly provide for denaturalization proceedings; however, this authority would naturally follow from the authority to establish "a uniform rule of naturalization." It is also within the power of Congress to assert a considerable degree of control over aliens after their admission to the country. A major congressional enactment for the control of aliens was the Alien Registration Act of 1940,[73] presently incorporated in the basic Act.[74]

B. NATURE OF THE POWER OF CONGRESS.—As between the executive and legislative branches, it has been held that the delegation by the Congress to the Executive of the power to make rules and regulations concerning the entry of aliens was not invalid as representing an undue delegation of legislative power. In a case upholding the War Brides Act of 1945,[75] the Court said:

Normally Congress supplies the conditions of the privilege of entry into the United States. But because the power of exclusion of aliens is also inherent in the executive department of the sovereign, Congress may in broad terms authorize the executive to exercise the power, e. g., as was done here, for the best interests of the country during a time of national emergency. Executive Officers may be entrusted with the duty of specifying the procedures for carrying out the Congressional intent.[76]

C. FUNCTION OF THE COURTS.—Since 1798 Congress has vested the function of admitting aliens to citizenship exclusively in the courts. Commenting upon this the Supreme Court has said: "In exercising their authority under this mandate the federal courts are exercising the judicial power conferred upon them by Article III, section 2 of the Constitution." [77]

Federal Court Decisions

A. IMMIGRATION.—From the inception of legislative regulation of immigration, the Supreme Court has recognized the exclusive authority of Congress in this field. Summarizing the Supreme Court's view, Justice Frankfurter in a recent opinion, *Hariseades* v. *The United States,* stated in part:

The condition for entry of every alien, the particular class of aliens that shall be denied entry altogether, the basis of determining such classification, the right to determine hospitality to aliens, the grounds on which such determination shall be based, have been recognized as matters solely for the responsibility of the Congress and wholly outside of the power of this court to control. Courts who enforce the requirements imposed by Congress on officials in administering immigration laws and the requirement of Due

---

[72] Constitution, article I, section 8; *U. S.* v. *Macintosh*, 283 U. S. 605 (1931).

[73] 54 Stat. 670.

[74] 8 U. S. C. A. 1301–1306.

[75] 59 Stat. 659.

[76] *U. S. ex rel Knauff* v. *Shaughnessy*, 338 U. S. 543 (1950).

[77] *Tatum* v. *U. S.*, 270 U. S. 568 (1926).

Process may entail certain procedural observances. But the underlying problem of what classes of aliens should be allowed to stay are for Congress to determine . . .[78]

A landmark case in this field is the Chinese exclusion case *Chae Chan Ping* v. *The United States*.[79] In this case the appellant contested the constitutionality of the Chinese Exclusion Act of 1888, which was enacted as a result of public clamor protesting the influx of Chinese laborers into the United States, most of whom had entered pursuant to trade treaties.

In this opinion, the Supreme Court stated in part:

. . . that the Government of the United States through the Act of the Legislative Department can exclude aliens from its territory, is a proposition which we do not think is open to controversy. Jurisdiction of its own territory to that extent is an incident of every independent nation. It is part of its independency. If it could not exclude aliens, it would be to the extent subject to another power . . .

The case of *Shaughnessy* v. *United States ex rel Mezei* discusses the question of an alien's rights. The petitioner in this case was an alien resident of the United States who had traveled abroad and remained in Hungary for nineteen months. On his return to this country, the Attorney General ordered him permanently excluded without a hearing.[80] All attempts to deport petitioner failed and he was confined on Ellis Island. The U. S. District Court for the Southern District of New York sustained a writ of habeas corpus brought by petitioner. The Court of Appeals affirmed and certiorari was granted.

The Supreme Court in its opinion stated in part that the courts cannot retry the Attorney General's statutory determination that an alien's entry would be prejudicial to the public interest. The Court further held that *petitioner lost his status as a resident alien and thus his right to a hearing* by his protracted stay behind the Iron Curtain. Therefore, the Court determined he was an entrant alien or assimilated to that status for constitutional purposes.

In conclusion, the Court held that the alien's continued exclusion on Ellis Island does not deprive him of any statutory right and the petitioner's right "to enter the United States depends on the congressional will and courts cannot substitute their judgment for the legislative mandate." [81]

B. DEPORTATION.—Perhaps the leading case relating to deportation is *United States ex rel John Turner* v. *Williams*.[82] In this case, the Supreme Court stated:

Congress has the power . . . to establish regulations for sending out of the country such aliens as have entered in violation of the law and to commit the enforcement of such conditions and regulations to executive officers, that the deportation of an alien who is found to be here in violation of law is not a deprivation of liberty without Due Process of Law. . .

In another early case the Supreme Court established the principle that an alien, once within the jurisdiction of the United States, is entitled to due

---

[78] 342 U. S. 580 (Mar. 10, 1952).
[79] 130 U. S. 581 (1889).
[80] 22 U. S. C. A. 223.
[81] 345 U. S. 206 (1953).
[82] 194 U. S. 279 (1904). See also *Carlson et al* v. *Landon*, 342 U. S. 524, (1952). This case sustains certain provisions of the Internal Security Act of 1950 relating to deportation of Communists, etc.

process of law. This principle is considered in "The Japanese Immigrant Case," *Yamataya* v. *Fisher*,[83] which involved an attempted deportation of an alien without the formality of a hearing. The Supreme Court stated:

> But this court has never held, nor must we now be understood as holding, that administrative officers, when executing the provisions of a statute involving the liberty of persons, may disregard the fundamental principles that inhere in "due process of law" as understood at the time of the adoption of the Constitution. One of these principles is that no person shall be deprived of his liberty without opportunity, at some time, to be heard, before such officers, in respect of the matters upon which that liberty depends— not necessarily an opportunity upon a regular, set occasion, and according to the forms of judicial procedure, but one that will secure the prompt, vigorous action contemplated by Congress, and at the same time be appropriate to the nature of the case upon which such officers are required to act. Therefore, it is not competent for the Secretary of the Treasury or any executive officer, at any time within the year limited by the statute, arbitrarily to cause an alien, who has entered the country, and has become subject in all respects to its jurisdiction, and a part of its population, although alleged to be illegally here, to be taken into custody and deported without giving him all opportunity to be heard upon the questions involving his right to be and remain in the United States. No such arbitrary power can exist where the principles involved in due process of law are recognized.[84]

Several recent cases have raised constitutional questions with reference to certain deportation provisions of the Act. For example, *Sentner* v. *Colarelli*, in which petition for certiorari was filed January 29, 1957 in the Supreme Court. The style of the case presently is *Barton* v. *Sentner*, since Colarelli, an official of the Immigration and Naturalization Service, has been succeeded in office by Barton. In this case the district court, sitting as a three-judge constitutional court, construing subsection 242 (d),[85] held that certain paragraphs (6 and 7) in the order forbidding the alien to associate with members of the Communist Party were not "reasonable restrictions" designed to aid the Attorney General in ensuring that the alien will be available for deportation. The court said:

> The vagueness of paragraphs 6 and 7 has already been pointed out above; this vagueness would raise a substantial constitutional question, if the statute were construed to authorize these paragraphs.[86]

Further, the Court said:

> That part of section 242 (d) as construed in this opinion, which authorized the Attorney General to make an order of supervision, is valid and constitutional.

On May 20, 1957, the decision of the power court was affirmed by the Supreme Court.

---

[83] 189 U. S. 86 (1903).

[84] 189 U. S. 86 (1903). The same principle is applicable to aliens residing temporarily in the U. S. *Han-Lee Mao* v. *Brownell*, 207 F. 2d 142, D. C. D. C. 1953.

[85] Sec. 242 (d) in substance grants authority to the Attorney General to supervise within reasonable limits the activities of an alien against whom a final order of deportation has been pending for more than 6 months.

[86] 145 F. Supp. 569 (Oct. 1956). Paragraphs 6 and 7 in essence seek to prevent plaintiff from association with, or support of the doctrines and policies of the Communist Party, or any affiliate thereof, and from association with any person who plaintiff has reasonable ground to believe is affiliated with, or promoting, such activities.

On April 29, 1957, the Supreme Court rendered a decision in *United States* v. *Witkovich*,[87] a case involving the same section, 242 (d), but a different clause. Witkovich had been indicted on the charge that, as an alien against whom a final order of deportation had been outstanding for more than 6 months, he had willfully failed to respond to questions of the Attorney General. After various legal moves, the district court dismissed the indictment for failure to state an offense.

Examples of the type of questions Witkovich was asked are as follows: "Do you subscribe to the *Daily Worker?*" "Can you read in any other language other than Slovene and English?" "Since the order of deportation was entered in your case on June 25, 1953, have you attended any meetings of the Communist Party of the U. S. A.?"

The district court found that the questions listed in the indictment were not relevant to Witkovich's availability for deportation. The Supreme Court affirmed the decision of the district court, with two Justices, Clark and Burton, dissenting. In the majority decision, the Court, speaking through Justice Frankfurter, said:

Section 242 (d) is part of a legislative scheme designed to govern and to expedite the deportation of undesirable aliens, and clause (3) must be placed in the context of that scheme. As the district court held and as our own examination of the act confirms, it is a permissible and therefore an appropriate construction to limit the statute to authorizing all questions reasonably calculated to keep the Attorney General advised regarding the continued availability for departure of aliens whose deportation is overdue.

In the case of *Galvan* v. *Press*,[88] a case involving deportation, Justice Frankfurter, delivering the opinion of the Court stated in part:

Policies pertaining to the indirect entry of aliens and the right to remain here are peculiarly with the political conduct of government. In the enforcement of these policies, the executive branch of the Government must respect the procedural safeguards of Due Process, but that the formulation of these policies is entrusted exclusively to Congress has become about as firmly imbedded in the legislative and judicial issues of our body politic as any aspect of our government and whatever might have been said for applying the ex post facto clause, it has been the rule of this Court that it has no application to deportation.

Twenty years ago in *U. S.* v. *Parson* a Federal court held that aliens might be barred on the ground of beliefs. Parson, a Canadian, was ordered to be deported. He claimed that he was a "philosophical anarchist" and that the statute excluding anarchists violated the first amendment. The Court said:

An alien, when he seeks admission to the United States, does not have the power to command what we shall or shall not do. We have the right to exclude whomever we wish and for any reason whatsoever, because we do not approve an alien's political or social ideas, or he belongs to groups which are likely to become a public charge, or for other similar reasons.[89]

---

[87] No. 295, October term, 1956, U. S. Supreme Court, 140 F. Supp. 815.
[88] 347 U. S. 552 (1954).
[89] 22 F. Supp. 149, D. C. S. D. Cal. (1938).

The Court cited *Turner* v. *Williams,* in which as noted earlier, the Supreme Court had rejected a similar argument and had said:

Those who are excluded cannot assert the rights in general obtaining in a land to which they do not belong as citizens or otherwise.[90]

Perhaps the leading case relating to citizenship and expatriation is the case of *U. S.* v. *Wong Kim Ark.*[91] This case involved the question of the citizenship of a child born in the United States of parents of Chinese descent. When this case arose Chinese immigrants were ineligible for naturalization. The facts showed that Wong Kim's parents at the time of his birth were citizens of China but had a permanent domicile and residence in the United States. The special question in issue was whether on these facts Wong Kim became a citizen at birth. The Court in its opinion cited the first clause of the fourteenth amendment which defines as citizens of the United States "all persons born or naturalized in the United States, and subject to the jurisdiction thereof." The Court, declaring the petitioner to be a citizen of the United States, stated in part:

. . . Congress, having no power to abridge the rights conferred by the Constitution upon those who have become naturalized citizens by virtue of acts of Congress, *a fortiori* no act or omission of Congress, as to providing for the naturalization of parents or children of a particular race, can affect citizenship acquired, as a birthright, by virtue of the Constitution, without any aid of legislation. The Fourteenth Amendment, while it leaves the power where it was before, in Congress, to regulate naturalization, has conferred no authority upon Congress to restrict the effect of birth, declared by the Constitution to constitute a sufficient and complete right to citizenship. . . .

While it is conceded that Congress has authority to enact legislation providing that the performance of certain acts will expatriate a native born citizen, *Mackenzie* v. *Hare,*[92] nevertheless some of the Federal courts have gone quite far in holding unconstitutional certain expatriation provisions and in defining "duress."

A recent case in point is *Kuyikuro Okimura* v. *Acheson,* which originated in the United States District Court of Hawaii.[93] The plaintiff in this case was born of parents of Japanese descent in Hawaii in 1921. In 1934 he went to Japan. In 1943 he was inducted into the Japanese Army where he served until 1946. In 1947 he voted in a Japanese election. In 1949 he applied for passport to return to Hawaii, but his application was denied on the ground that he had lost his citizenship pursuant to section (c) and (e) of the Act.[94]

The Court in its opinion stated in part:

While the Constitution gives the Congress plenary power over citizenship by naturalization, it leaves the Congress no power whatever to interfere with American citizenship . . .

---

[90] 194 U. S. 279 (1904).
[91] 169 U. S. 649 (1898).
[92] 239 U. S. 299 (1915).
[93] 99 F. Supp. 887 (1951).
[94] 8 U. S. C. A. 1481 (a) (3) and (a) (5).

It is the holding of this Court that the only means of divesting one's self of United States citizenship is by voluntarily undergoing in a foreign state a process comparable to our own naturalization procedure.

Congress may not thus declare that by performing such and such an act, in or out of the United States, a citizen will become expatriated. Congress has been given control over only one means of creating United States citizenship, namely, by naturalization. It has the power to create and to condition that grant of citizenship, but it is wholly devoid of any power to destroy citizenship by birth . . .

This case was appealed to the Supreme Court. The Supreme Court remanded the case for specific findings as to the circumstances attending appellee's service in the Japanese Army and voting in the Japanese elections and reasonable inferences to be drawn therefrom.[95]

On the hearing after the remand, the district court [96] granted plaintiff's petition for papers certifying his United States citizenship and said: "This Court adheres to its belief that subsections (c) and (e) of section 801 of title 8, United States Code Annotated are unconstitutional." The mentioned sections are substantially similar to presently effective provisions of the Act.[97]

It would appear that the effect of the quoted decision has been largely nullified by a recent case, *Mitsugi Nishikawa* v. *Dulles*.[98] This case considered a factual situation very similar to that in the *Okimura* case, i. e., an American citizen conscripted into the Japanese Army.

In its decision the Court held that there is no presumption that one who is conscripted into armed forces of a foreign state enters so involuntarily that such service is not an act of expatriation, and all the circumstances must be looked at to resolve the question of voluntariness. The Court also said that the burden was on the petitioner to show that his conscription into the army was involuntary.

In its opinion the Court stated in part:

Appellant further contends that § 401 (c) of the 1940 Act which is here under consideration, is unconstitutional. This Court has already held other sections of the same Act, providing for expatriation, to be constitutional. There is nothing in these previous holdings of this Court to indicate that the same result should not be reached as to § 401 (c). Moreover, the many cases from other circuits, cited above, which have considered expatriation under § 401 (c) have assumed that it is constitutional. Appellant asserts that all persons born in the United States are citizens by virtue of the Constitution, and that Congress is powerless to enact laws which will deprive a native-born American of his citizenship absent a voluntary renunciation by such person. That Congress has such power was established in *Mackenzie* v. *Hare*. In our view, the claim of unconstitutionality lacks merit.[99]

C. NATIONALITY AND NATURALIZATION.—Naturalization has been defined by the Supreme Court in *Boyd* v. *Nebraska* as the "act of adopting a foreigner and clothing him with the privilege of a native citizen. . . ." [100] Chief Justice

[95] 342 U. S. 399 (1952).
[96] 111 F. Supp. 303 (1953) D. C. Hawaii.
[97] Section 349 (a) (3) and (5)—8 U. S. C. A. 1481 (a) (3) and (5).
[98] 235 F. 2d 135 C. A. (9th) (1956).
[99] Certiorari was granted by the Supreme Court Nov. 13, 1956 in *Mitsugi Nishikawa* v. *Dulles*.
[100] 143 U. S. 135 (1892).

Marshall, in stating the opinion of the Supreme Court in *Osborn* v. *The Bank of the United States*, said that:

> . . . a naturalized citizen . . . becomes a member of the society possessing all of the rights of native citizens and is in view of the Constitution on the footing of a native. The Constitution does not authorize Congress to enlarge or abridge those rights. Simple power of the national legislature is to prescribe uniform rules of naturalization and the exercise of this power exhausts it, so far as respects the individual.[101]

A naturalized citizen is subject at any time to having his good faith in taking the oath of allegiance to the United States inquired into, and the loss of citizenship, if not made in good faith, is confirmed in proper proceedings.[102]

A number of cases have arisen under the provisions excluding anarchists, Communists or other subversives from citizenship. Of these, a leading case is *Schneiderman* v. *U. S.*, in which the defendant had become a naturalized citizen in 1927. In 1939 the Government[103] insisted that he had procured his certificate illegally and had not "behaved as a person attached to the principles of the Constitution and the good order and happiness of the United States." The Supreme Court reversed the case for the reason that the evidence did not support the finding. It should be noted that the applicable statute did not provide adherence to Communist beliefs was incompatible with attachment to principles of the Constitution.[104]

D. NONIMMIGRANTS.—Principles applicable to nonimmigrant aliens are discussed at some length in *U. S. ex rel London* v. *Phelps*.[105] This was a case in which Mrs. London, a British subject of Russian birth, came to Canada on a British passport and sought a visa to enter the United States so she could visit her children in New York City. The visa was refused and she later appeared at the immigration office in Vermont. After a hearing she was declared to have entered the United States without a proper passport and was detained as an alien.

A writ of habeas corpus was sued out and the court, after hearing discharged the writ and remanded Mrs. London to custody.[106] Mrs. London appealed.

Executive Order 4125, dated January 12, 1925, provides, with certain exceptions, that aliens who are nonimmigrants "must present passports . . . duly visaed by consular officers of the United States." This order was promulgated under the Act of May 22, 1918,[107] as amended by the Act of March 2, 1921.[108] The former act authorized the President "when the United States is at war" to make reasonable rules, regulations and orders with respect to the entry and departure of aliens. The latter declares:

---

101 9 Wheat. 738 (1824).
102 *Johanessen* v. *U. S.*, 225 U. S. 227 (1912) and *Knauer* v. *U. S.*, 328 U. S. 654, 673 (1956).
103 Sec. 4, Act of 1906.
104 320 U. S. 118 (1943).
105 22 F. 2d 288, C. A. 2d (1927).
106 14 F. 2d 679, D. C., Vt.
107 22 U. S. C. A. 223–226.
108 22 U. S. C. A. 227.

. . . that the provisions of the Act of May 22, 1918, shall insofar as they relate to requiring passports and visas from aliens seeking to come into the United States, continue in force and effect until otherwise provided by law.

Mrs. London contended that the provisions of the 1918 Act and all other existing regulations were crystallized with the passage of the 1921 Act and that the President's power to modify or make new regulations was not extended. On this premise she hoped to have the Executive order of January 12, 1955, declared invalid and that she could enter from Canada without a passport and visa.

The appellate court rejected this premise and held "the adoption of an earlier statute by reference makes it as much a part of the later act as though it had been incorporated at full length, and brings in all that is fairly covered by the reference." The 1921 Act expressly continued the earlier Act insofar as it required passports and visas of nonimmigrant aliens.

The Court of Appeals continued:

Subsequent to March 2, 1921, Executive Orders have been promulgated both by President Harding and by President Coolidge under authority of the 1918 act as continued in the act of 1921. No decision has been cited which suggests any doubt of the validity of such orders, except *Johnson* v. *Keating*, 17 F. 2d 50 (C. C. A. 1). That case, however, holds merely that the President's powers were terminated as to immigrants. . . . The appellant in the instant case is avowedly not an "immigrant," but a temporary visitor, within the definition of that act, [1921] and, as such, is by section 3 expressly excluded from the provisions of the act of 1924. . . .

We conclude, therefore, that the Executive order of January 12, 1925, was a valid regulation, and required that the relator, before entering as a temporary visitor, present a passport duly visaed by an American consul. This accords with the holdings or dicta of all cases dealing with the problem which have been discovered. . . .

It is urged that, even if a visa "was lawfully imposed as a condition upon a nonimmigrant's entry, the giving of a visa" is a ministerial act, which the consul was bound to perform, and consequently the court should regard its omission as immaterial. With this we cannot agree. Certainly the giving of a visa "is not merely a ministerial act, because some inquiry on the spot, some determination of fact, is essential. It is admitted that the consul may withhold his visa" if he believes the passport not to be genuine, or not in the hands of the rightful holder. The instructions of the Secretary of State which supplement the Executive Order, also require the consul to "satisfy himself of the temporary nature of the visit" of the alien. *Whether the consul has acted reasonably or unreasonably is not for us to determine. Unjustifiable refusal to visa a passport may be ground for a diplomatic complaint by the nation whose subject has been discriminated against.* See 3 Moore's Digest 996. *It is beyond the jurisdiction of the Court.* [Italics supplied.]

In an early case, *Kaoura Yamataya* v. *Fisher*,[109] the court noted:

that among the aliens forbidden to enter the United States are those, of whatever country who are "paupers or persons likely to become a public charge." We are of opinion that aliens of that class have not been given by the treaty with Japan full liberty to enter or reside in the United States; for that instrument expressly excepts from its operations any ordinance or regulation relating to "police and public security." A statute excluding paupers or persons likely to become a public charge is manifestly one of police and public security. . . .

---

[109] 189 U. S. 86 (1903).

As to the alien's appeal for notice and an opportunity to be heard, the Court said:

Now, it has been settled that the power to exclude or expel aliens belonged to the political department of the government and that the order of an executive officer, invested with the power to determine finally the facts upon which an alien's right to enter this country or remain in it, depended, was "due process," and no other tribunal, unless expressly authorized by law to do so, was at liberty to reexamine the evidence on which he acted, or to controvert its sufficiency.

E. PROCEDURES.—The case of *United States* v. *Ettore Zucca* [110] involved an interpretation of Section 340 (*a*) of the Act. This subsection among other matters, prescribes procedures required to initiate revocation of naturalization. The pertinent language of the section reads as follows:

It shall be the duty of the United States District Attorneys for their respective districts upon affidavit showing good cause therefore, to institute proceedings in any Court. . . .

The Court held that this section was the only provision under which the U. S. attorney could institute denaturalization proceedings, and that the filing of an affidavit showing good cause therefore was a mandatory procedural prerequisite to maintaining a suit. Thus, the Court rejected the Government's argument that the U. S. attorney is a regular officer of the Government having inherent general authority to institute action upon his own initiative by information rather than by affidavit.

A recent case in which certiorari was granted April 1, 1957, *Nowak* v. *U. S.*,[111] apparently gives what may be considered a practical interpretation of the opinion in the *Zucca* case.

This case involved denaturalization proceedings against two aliens in which the sufficiency of the affidavit showing good cause filed pursuant to section 340 (a) of the Act was attacked in light of the Supreme Court's decision in *Zucca* v. *U. S.* The affidavit in the *Nowak* case consisted primarily of a recital under oath by the Attorney from the Immigration and Naturalization Service of the pertinent facts appearing in the official records of the Service, which set out the grounds for denaturalization.

In its short opinion the Court upheld the validity of the affidavit as satisfying statutory requirements as interpreted by the *Zucca* case. The pertinent language of the Court on this point was:

. . . in our judgment, the affidavit of an attorney of the Immigration and Naturalization Service of the United States Department of Justice reciting facts appearing in the official records, such as the affidavit filed in each of these cases, was an adequate compliance with the statutory requirements as interpreted in the *Zucca* case. The affidavit thus set forth sufficient evidentiary matters to show good cause for cancellation of the citizenship of each appellant. Fairly construed, the affidavit states facts appearing in the official records of the Immigration and Naturalization Service. It would be too stringent a requirement to hold that the good cause affidavit need embrace testimony of prospective witnesses. The affidavit in issue gave fair and sufficient notice of the facts charged as a basis for cancellation of citizenship of the appellants as to apprise them properly of the facts and reasons upon which their citizenship was sought to be revoked. . . . (p. 283)

[110] 351 U. S. 91 (1956).
[111] 238 F. 2d 282 (1956).

Conclusion

It is patently clear that it is completely within the power of Congress, exercising the inherent right of a sovereign nation, to enact legislation prescribing the terms and conditions upon which aliens may be admitted into this country.

It is also apparent, after a review of Supreme Court decisions relating to deportation, that Congress has exclusive authority to enact legislation providing for the deportation of aliens and that this power includes authority to delegate to executive officers the enforcement of conditions and regulations pertaining to deportation. In view of specific constitutional provisions authorizing the Congress to make rules of naturalization, Congress' power in this field is exclusive. Therefore, it would appear to be completely within the province of this constitutional grant that Congress has the power to enact legislation governing denaturalization of persons who are not citizens of the United States by birth.

Further, it is clear that in enacting the Walter-McCarran Act and related legislation governing the entry of nonimmigrant aliens, their conduct while in the United States, the length of their stay, and their ultimate departure, the Congress was exercising its constitutional powers.

There appears to be no serious question as to the constitutionality of the Walter-McCarran Act as a whole. This is not to say that serious questions may not be raised as to particular provisions of the Act from time to time.

PRESENT PROGRAM

Introduction

A visa is an endorsement on a passport or other travel document which entitles the bearer to travel to, and apply for, temporary or permanent admission into a country. It is not an entry permit.

All United States visas, whether nonimmigrant or immigrant, are issued by our consular officers overseas, but the authority for the admission of all aliens into this country is vested in the United States Immigration and Naturalization Service. However, few aliens with valid visas have been prevented from entering this country upon arrival at a United States port of entry. Those so excluded, for the most part, withheld information during their application for a visa.

The Visa Office of the Department of State supervises the overseas implementation of U. S. visa policies. It has administrative jurisdiction over nonimmigrant visas; gives guidance to consular officers abroad; recommends personnel for consular assignments; issues regulations to implement immigration laws; and maintains liaison with the Immigration and Naturalization Service. The General Counsel of the Visa Office renders opinions on legal questions and, to that end, cooperates with the legal staff of the Immigration and Naturalization Service to insure a uniform interpretation of current immigration laws.

United States visas may be issued by a commissioned consular officer at any of our embassies, legations, consulates general and consulates throughout the world. The senior consular officer at an embassy or legation is responsible, under the Chief of Mission, for all United States visa activities in the country to which he is assigned, but the right to issue visas is vested in all duly authorized consular officers at the principal post or at any consulate general or consulate within that country.

The Public Health Service of the Department of Health, Education, and Welfare is responsible for conducting all physical and mental examinations of aliens which are required by the immigration laws.

Application for Visas

The Immigration and Naturalization Act [112] hereinafter referred to as the Act, requires every applicant for a visa to make application therefor in such form and manner and in such place as shall be by regulation prescribed.[113] With a few exceptions (most notable being those in the case of nonimmigrants relating to crew list visas for alien crewmen) every alien shall make a separate application for a visa. An alien under 14 years of age or one physically incapable of executing an application may have an application for a visa executed in his behalf by a parent or guardian. If the alien has no parent or guardian, the application may be executed by any person having lawful custody of or a legitimate interest in such alien.

While the applications for immigrant and nonimmigrant visas are different, they require generally the same information,[114] i. e., full and true name, date and place of birth, age and sex, race and ethnic classification,[115] and personal description. In addition, the application for a nonimmigrant visa requires the alien's nationality, the purpose and length of his intended stay in the United States, his marital status and any additional information necessary to the identification of the applicant and the enforcement of the immigration and nationality laws. The applicant for an immigrant visa, among other things, is requested to present the following information: final destination, if any, beyond the port of entry; whether he is going to join a relative or friend, and whether he intends to remain in the United States.

All applicants for visas are required to present a valid and unexpired passport or other suitable travel document. However, certain exceptions

[112] 8 U. S. C. 1101 et seq.
[113] 8 U. S. C. 1202 (a) and (c).
[114] Ibid.
[115] This does not pertain to his religion. 22 C. F. R. 42.30 (a) and 22 C. F. R. 41.9 (a).

are specified. Included within the exceptions are (1) immigrants who are stateless, and (2) immigrants who are nationals of, and who are applying for an immigrant visa outside of a Communist-controlled country and who, because of their opposition to communism are unwilling to make application for passport to or unable to obtain passport from a government of such country. Applicants are also required to present other records such as military and prison records. All applicants must appear personally at the consular office in connection with their application and furnish three identical copies of their photograph which reflect a reasonable likeness.

Any alien who applies for a visa is required to be registered and finger-printed.[116] There are certain exceptions to this rule, the most noteworthy being children under 14 years of age,[117] aliens who are applicants for diplomatic visas or the equivalent thereof and aliens within the class of non-immigrants mentioned in section 1101 (a) (15) (A) and (G).[118]

An immigrant visa may be issued for a maximum period of validity of 4 months.

Types of Nonimmigrants

There are various groups of individuals admitted to the United States as nonimmigrants. In order to distinguish the groups, the consular officer in stamping a visa includes a certain symbol which is representative of the fact that the alien is a member of a certain class. The general classes of non-immigrants are as follows:

1. Ambassadors, public ministers, career diplomatic or consular offi-cers and members of their immediate family.

2. The attendant, servant or personal employee of the above class and members of their immediate family.

3. Temporary visitor for business or pleasure.

4. Alien in transit.

5. Alien in transit to United Nations Headquarters District under section 11 (3), (4) or (5) of the Headquarters Agreement.

6. Foreign government official, members of immediate family, attend-ant, servant or personal employee in transit.

7. Crewmen (seamen or airmen).

8. Treaty merchant, spouse and children.

9. Treaty investor, spouse and children.

10. Exchange visitor.

11. Student.

12. Principal resident representative of recognized foreign member government to international organization, his staff, and members of immediate family.

---

[116] 8 U. S. C. 1201 (b), 1301.
[117] 22 C. F. R. 42.38 (a) and 41.19 (a) (3).
[118] 8 U. S. C. 1201 (b).

13. Other representative of recognized foreign member government to international organization and members of immediate family.

14. Representative of nonrecognized or nonmember foreign government to international organization, and members of immediate family.

15. International organization officer or employee, and members of immediate family.

16. Temporary worker of distinguished merit and ability.

17. Other temporary worker, skilled or unskilled.

18. Industrial trainee.

19. Representative of foreign information media, spouse and children.

Diplomatic visas.—The term "diplomatic visa" means a nonimmigrant visa bearing that title and issued to a nonimmigrant in accordance with such regulations as the Secretary of State may prescribe.[119] Diplomatic visas may be of a regular or limited type. A regular diplomatic visa may be used during the period of its validity in making any number of applications for admission to the United States provided that the status of the bearer as a person entitled to a diplomatic visa is maintained. A limited diplomatic visa is valid for only one application for admission into the United States.[120]

Only certain classes of aliens may apply for regular and limited diplomatic visas. A listing of aliens eligible to apply for such visas may be found at 22 CFR section 40.4 (a) and (b).

A diplomatic visa may not be issued to anyone unless he would be entitled to receive a nonimmigrant visa. In addition he is required to present a valid diplomatic passport, or the equivalent thereof, issued by a competent authority of a foreign government recognized by the United States unless such requirement has been waived pursuant to the authority contained in section 212 (d) (4) of the Act.[121]

A diplomatic or consular officer to whom an alien applies for a diplomatic visa may require any reasonable evidence he deems necessary to establish the alien's eligibility to receive a diplomatic visa.[122]

Foreign governmental officials.—Whenever an alien in one of the classes described in section 101 (a) (15) (A) (foreign government officials) presents to the examining immigration officer a valid unexpired nonimmigrant visa duly issued to him by a consular officer, the immigration officer shall accept the consular officer's classification of the alien, and admit the alien if he is otherwise admissible to the United States, unless specifically directed to the contrary by the regional commissioner, after consultation with the Department of State. The period of the alien's admission shall not exceed such time as the Secretary of State continues to recognize the alien as a member of such class.[123]

---

[119] 8 U. S. C. 1101 (a) (11).
[120] 22 C. F. R. 40.3.
[121] 8 U. S. C. 1182 (d) (4).
[122] 22 C. F. R. 40.9.
[123] 8 C. F. R. 214 a. 1–a. 2.

Temporary visitors for business or pleasure.—An alien admitted to the United States as a temporary visitor for business or pleasure is admitted initially for a period not to exceed 6 months unless such alien intends to sojourn in the United States in more than one immigration district, in which event the period of initial admission shall not exceed 3 months.[124]

It is necessary for an applicant for this type of visa to establish that:

1. He has a residence in a foreign country which he has no intention of abandoning;

2. He is not classifiable as a student, a temporary worker or a representative of foreign information media;

3. He is proceeding to the United States temporarily for one of the purposes specified in section 101 (a) (15) (B) of the Act (for business or pleasure) ;

4. He intends in good faith and will be able, to depart from the United States at the expiration of his temporary stay;

5. He is in possession of a valid foreign visa or other form of permission to enter some foreign country upon the termination of his temporary stay; and that

6. He has made adequate financial provision to enable him to carry out the purpose of his travel to, sojourn in, and departure from the United States.[125]

If a consular officer receives an application from a commercial trader he has reason to believe may possible engage in business having to do with strategic material which will find its way into the hands of the Soviets, an exhaustive check of the intelligence research, commercial, and economic files in both the Department of State and Commerce is conducted, and recourse is also had to biographical files. Upon the evaluation of the information thus obtained, a consular officer makes his decision.

Alien crewmen.—An attempt was made to require all foreign crewmen to have individual visas by July 1, 1955.[126] This requirement was removed [127] and a new target date of December 31, 1956, was discussed but never implemented by an official order.[128] The enforcement of this provision of the law may yet take considerable time.

The present law permits alien crewmen to land temporarily in the United States by inclusion of the crewmen's names in the vessel's or aircraft's crew list if visaed by a consular officer.

Aliens employed on board a vessel or aircraft in a capacity not ordinarily associated with, or required for, normal operation and service on board the vessel or aircraft, or persons employed or listed as regular members of the crew in excess of the number normally required, shall be considered as

---

[124] 8 C. F. R. 214 b. 1.
[125] 22 C. F. R. 41.42 (b).
[126] See 19 F. R. 3504, June 16, 1954.
[127] See 20 F. R. 1097, Feb. 22, 1955.
[128] As of July 31, 1955, 42,921 visas in this classification had been issued.

passengers and shall be documented as any other passenger not employed aboard the vessel or aircraft.[129]

A consular officer who knows or has reason to believe that a crew list contains the name of an alien who is not a bona fide crewman, or who is otherwise ineligible to receive an individual visa as a crewman, shall either withhold the crew list visa until the name of such alien has been removed from the list by the master of the vessel or the commanding officer of the aircraft, or he shall issue the crew list visa excluding therefrom the name of any such alien listed as a member of the crew. In excluding an alien's name from a crew list visa, the consular officer shall place a notation below the visa stamp indicating the name of each crewman so excluded.[130]

Transit aliens.—An alien applying for a visa as a nonimmigrant transit alien shall establish specifically that:

1. He is proceeding to the United States solely for the purpose of passing in immediate and continuous transit through the United States to a foreign destination or to the United Nations Headquarters district;

2. He is in possession of a ticket for, or other assurance of, transportation to his destination;

3. He is in posssesion of sufficient funds to enable him to carry out the purpose of his transit journey, or has sufficient funds otherwise available for that purpose;

4. He is in possession of a valid foreign visa or other form of permission to enter some foreign country, provided that possession of such a visa or other form of permission shall not be required in the case of an alien proceeding through the United States for the purpose of applying for admission into Canada or some other country, if under the law or regulations of the country of destination, the alien would not be required to present a visa, or other form of permission as a condition of entry;

5. He intends in good faith, and will be able to depart from the United States at the expiration of the period for which he may be admitted.[131]

An alien to whom a visa is to be issued for the purpose of applying for admission solely in transit to the United Nations Headquarters District is informed by the consular officer that, if admitted, he may be subject to such restrictions in his travel within the United States as may be provided in the regulations prescribed by the Attorney General.[132] The Attorney General has promulgated a regulation that "such alien shall proceed directly to New York City and shall remain continuously in that city during his sojourn in the United States, departing therefrom only if required in connection with his departure from the United States.[133]

---

[129] 22 C. F. R. 41.60.
[130] 22 C. F. R. 41.67.
[131] 22 C. F. R. 41.51 (b).
[132] 22 C. F. R. 41.52.
[133] 8 C. F. R. 214 c. 4 (a)

Section 238 (d) of the Immigration and Nationality Act [134] provides that the Attorney General shall have power to enter into contracts including bonding agreements with transportation lines to guarantee the passage through the United States in immediate and continuous transit of aliens destined to foreign countries.

Pursuant to the Immigration and Nationality Act of 1952, the Attorney General and the Secretary of State have promulgated regulations waiving the requirement for visas for such aliens,[135] subject to certain specified conditions.

Treaty aliens.—Treaty aliens are of two types, treaty traders and treaty investors. An alien who applies for a visa as a nonimmigrant treaty trader under the provisions of section 101 (a) (15) (E) (i) of the Act is required to present evidence deemed necessary by the consular officer to establish that he is entitled to nonimmigrant status under that section. Such alien shall establish specifically that:

1. He is proceeding to the United States solely for the purpose of carrying on substantial trade principally between the United States and the foreign state of which he is a national, under and in pursuance of the provisions of a treaty of commerce and navigation between the United States and such foreign state;

2. He intends in good faith, and will be able, to depart from the United States upon the termination of his status; and that if he is employed or to be employed, his employer shall be a foreign person or organization and he shall be engaged in duties of a supervisory or executive character, or if he is, or is to be, employed in a minor capacity, he has special qualifications which make his services essential to the efficient operations of the employer. An alien employed solely in a manual capacity shall not be entitled to classification as a treaty trader.[136]

If the alien is applying for a nonimmigrant visa as a treaty investor under the provisions of section 101 (a) (15) (E) (ii) of the Act he must establish specifically that:

1. He seeks to enter the United States solely for the purpose of developing and directing the operations of an enterprise in the United States in which he has invested, or is actively in the process of investing, a substantial amount of capital; or in which his employer has invested, or is actively in the process of investing, a substantial amount of capital: *Provided*, That such employer is a foreign person or organization of the same nationality as the applicant and that the applicant is employed by such person or organization in a responsible capacity; or

2. He seeks to enter the United States as the spouse or child of an alien described above; and

---

[134] 8 U. S. C. sec. 1228 (d).
[135] 22 C. F. R. 41.6 (b); 8 C. F. R. 212.3.
[136] 22 C. F. R. 41.71 (b).

3. He is not applying for a nonimmigrant visa in an effort to evade the quota or other restrictions which are applicable to immigrants;

4. He intends in good faith, and will be able, to depart from the United States upon the termination of his status; and

5. The enterprise is one which actually exists or is in active process of formation, and is not a fictitious paper operation.[137]

Students.—An alien applying for a nonimmigrant visa as a student under the provisions of section 101 (a) (15) (F) of the Act is required to establish to the satisfaction of the consular officer that he seeks to enter the United States temporarily and solely for the purpose of pursuing a full course of study at an established institution of learning or other recognized place of study in the United States, particularly designated by him and approved by the Attorney General.[138]

An alien applying for a visa as a student must establish specifically that:

1. He has a residence in a foreign country which he has no intention of abandoning;

2. He is a *bona fide* student qualified to pursue, and seeking to enter the United States temporarily and solely for the purpose of pursuing, a full course of study as prescribed by the approved institution of learning or other recognized place of study which has accepted such student for study;

3. He is in possession of sufficient funds to cover his expenses or other arrangements have been made to provide for his expenses;

4. He has sufficient scholastic preparation and knowledge of the English language to enable him to undertake a full course of study in the institution of learning or other place of study by which he has been accepted, or if his knowledge of the English language is inadequate to enable him to pursue a full program of study in such language, the approved school or other recognized place of study is equipped to offer, and has accepted him expressly for, a full program of study in a language with which he is sufficiently familiar; and that

5. He intends in good faith, and will be able, to depart from the United States upon the termination of his status.[139]

When a prospective nonimmigrant student has been accepted for attendance, the appropriate officer of the approved institution of learning or place of study executes a Form I–20 which must be executed on the reverse side by the applicant before he is eligible for admission to the United States.[140]

International Organization Aliens.—An alien who applies for a visa under the provisions of 101 (a) (15) (G) of the Act must establish to the consular officer that he meets certain requirements which are set forth in detail in the Code of Federal Regulations.[141] In addition he must present evidence

[137] 22 C. F. R. 41.76 (b).
[138] 22 C. F. R. 41.80.
[139] 22 C. F. R. 41.81.
[140] 3 C. F. R. 214 f. 4–5.
[141] 22 C. F. R. 41.90.

of his status and of the means and destination of his travel to, or through, the United States. If the consular officer is in doubt he may require a confirmation of the status of such representative, officer, or employee from the appropriate foreign office or from the international organization concerned, and any other evidence considered necessary to establish the applicant's eligibility to receive a visa as a nonimmigrant under the provisions of section 101 (a) (15) (G), and other applicable provisions of the Act.[142]

An alien who seeks to enter the United States as a foreign-government representative to an international organization and who, at the same time, is proceeding to the United States on official business as a foreign-government official within the meaning of section 101 (a) (15) (A) of the Act if otherwise qualified is issued a visa as a nonimmigrant under the provisions of this section.[143]

Temporary Workers.—The question of importing any alien as a nonimmigrant under section 101 (a) (15), (H), (8 U. S. C. 1101 (a) (15) (H)),[144] in any specific case or cases is determined by the Attorney General, after consultation with appropriate agencies of the Government upon petition of the importing employer. This petition must be made and approved before any visa is granted.[145] The petition procedure is not applicable for aliens coming to the United States under the exchange visitor program provided for in the United States Information and Exchange Act of 1948, as amended (22 U. S. C. 1446.) [146]

If the alien is coming to the United States under clause (ii) of section 101 (a) (15) (H) there must be attached to the petition a clearance order bearing a statement from the United States Employment Service that:

(1) Qualified workers of the kind proposed to be imported are not available within the United States, and

(2) The employment service policies have been observed.[147]

If the alien is of distinguished merit and ability (clause (i) of section 101 (a) (15) (H) and seeks to enter the United States temporarily with the general intention of performing temporary service of an exceptional nature requiring such merit and ability, but has no contract or prearranged employment, he may be classified as a temporary visitor for business, under the provisions of section 101 (a) (15) (B) of the Act.[148]

---

[142] C. F. R. 41.91.

[143] 22 C. F. R. 41.92.

[144] That section provides: "The term 'immigrant' means every alien except an alien who is within one of the following classes of nonimmigrant aliens—

(H) an alien having a residence in a foreign country which has no intention of abandoning (i) who is of distinguished merit and ability and who is coming temporarily to the United States to perform temporary services of an exceptional nature requiring such merit and ability; or (ii) who is coming temporarily to the United States to perform other temporary services or labor, if unemployed persons capable of performing such service or labor cannot be found in this country; or (iii) who is coming temporarily to the United States as an industrial trainee . . ."

[145] 8 U. S. C. 1184 (c).

[146] 22 C. F. R. 41.100 (e).

[147] 8 C. F. R. 214h.41.

[148] 22 C. F. R. 41.100 (f).

Industrial trainees also enter pursuant to section 101 (a) (15) (H) of the Act. An "industrial trainee" is a nonimmigrant alien who seeks to enter the United States at the invitation of an individual, organization or firm, or other trainer for the purpose of receiving instruction in any field of endeavor, including agriculture, commerce, communication, finance, government, transportation, and the professions, as well as in a purely industrial establishment, regardless of whether any benefit, direct or indirect, accrues to the United States, employer or trainer, and regardless of the source of any remuneration received by the alien.

If the employer or trainer desires an extension of the temporary stay of an alien having a nonimmigrant classification described in Section 101 (a) (15) (H) of the Immigration and Nationality Act, he files an application in writing under oath. In the application, the employer or the trainer must include a statement describing the current and intended employment or training of the alien.[149]

REPRESENTATIVES OF FOREIGN PRESS, RADIO, FILM OR OTHER FOREIGN INFORMATION MEDIA.—In order to qualify as the representative of a foreign press, radio, film or other information medium within the meaning of Section 101 (a) (15) (I) of the Act (8 U. S. C. 1101 (a) (15) (I)), an alien must be accredited by a foreign medium having its home office in a foreign country, the government of which grants upon the basis of reciprocity similar privileges to representatives of such a medium having home offices in the United States.[150]

An alien applying for such a visa shall establish specifically that:

1. He seeks to enter the United States solely to represent in good faith a foreign press, radio, film or other foreign information medium, and that

2. He intends in good faith, and will be able to depart from the United States upon the termination of the status.[151]

Aliens admitted to the United States as representatives of the foreign press, etc., shall not be admitted initially for a period exceeding one year.[152] In addition the regulations provide that such a nonimmigrant is admitted upon the following conditions:

1. That he will not change the information medium or his employer by which he is accredited unless and until he obtains consent to do so from the district director having administrative jurisdiction over the district in which the alien resides in the United States, and

2. He will depart from the United States at such time as the Secretary of State determines that the reciprocity required by section 101 (a) (15) (I) of the Immigration and Nationality Act has ceased to exist.[153]

---

[149] 8 C. F. R. 214h.51.
[150] 22 C. F. R. 41.111 (b).
[151] 22 C. F. R. 41.111 (a).
[152] 8 C. F. R. 214i.1.
[153] 8 C. F. R. 214i.3.

An alien admitted to the United States as a nonimmigrant representative of the foreign press, etc., who applies for an extension of his temporary admission is required to attach to his application a statement in writing from his employer establishing that he is a representative of a foreign information medium in the United States and setting forth his current and intended activities and the reasons for the extension.[154]

Refusal of Visas

Immigrant Visa.—An informal refusal of an immigrant visa occurs when a consular officer, in a preliminary examination of an alien at a consular office, discovers cause for refusal of a visa and the alien, upon being so informed, decides not to execute a formal application. A formal refusal of an immigrant visa occurs when a consular officer declines to issue an immigrant visa after an alien has executed a formal application in the prescribed form and has paid the prescribed application fee.[155] If an immigrant visa is refused after formal application, the consular officer writes or stamps diagonally across the form, "Visa refused under authority of _____", and inserts the specific provision of law or regulation on which the refusal is based.[156]

Whenever an immigrant visa is refused, a memorandum of refusal is prepared on form 290. This is placed in the appropriate consular file. The action of refusing an immigrant visa is reviewed by the consular officer in charge of visa work at the post, and if he concurs in the refusal, he countersigns the memorandum of refusal. If the consular officer in charge of visa work at the post does not concur in the refusal, he shall refer the case to the Department for an advisory opinion.[157]

Nonimmigrant Visa.—Every alien is presumed to be an immigrant until he establishes to the satisfaction of the consular officer that he is properly classifiable within the nonimmigrant category.[158] However, certain grounds, such as illiteracy, polygamy, physical defects, and the possibility of becoming a public charge, are not grounds for refusing a nonimmigrant visa under certain specified conditions.[159] Certain classes of aliens can be denied visas only on certain specific grounds. For example, alien ambassadors, public ministers, career diplomatic or consular officers, and members of immediate families can be denied a nonimmigrant visa only when the applicant is persona non grata. Other foreign governmental officials or employees, and members of immediate families can be denied admission only for certain security reasons. The same is true of representatives, other than the

---

[154] 8 C. F. R. 214i.5.
[155] 22 C. F. R. 42.43 (c).
[156] 22 C. F .R. 42.43 (d).
[157] 22 C. F. R. 42.43 (b).
[158] 22 C. F. R. 41.17.
[159] 22 C. F. R. 41.17 (c).

principal resident representative of a recognized foreign member government to international organizations, and members of immediate families; representatives of non-recognized or non-member foreign governments to international organizations, and members of immediate families; and international organization officers or employees and members of immediate families. Similar exceptions are made for aliens in transit to the United Nations Headquarters District under the sections 11 (3), (4), or (5) of the Headquarters Agreement and for foreign government officials as well as for the principal resident representative of recognized foreign member governments to international organizations, their staffs, and members of their immediate families.[160]

In cases of refusal for reasons of national security the consul sends a written report in regard to the refusal in quadruplicate to the Visa Office security branch. This contains the biographical data and the grounds for refusal. One copy is retained by the Visa Office security branch, one copy goes to the Security Office in the State Department, one copy is sent to the Federal Bureau of Investigation, and the fourth copy goes to the United States Immigration and Naturalization Service. If considered advisable, a copy also goes to the Central Intelligence Agency. The consular officer also sends lookout cards to our central clearance offices in the country of application, the country of birth, the country of present nationality, the country of present residence and countries of past residence which constitute alerts against the possibility that the alien may try to secure a visa from some other consular post. If the information on the alien is considered to be exceptionally serious, the Visa Office security branch will notify all posts that if the alien applies, action in his case is to be suspended and the Visa Office security branch is to be notified at once.

Revocation of Visas

A consular officer is authorized to revoke a visa or other documentation under the following conditions:

    1. The consular officer knows, or after investigation is satisfied, that the visa or other documentation was procured by fraud, a willfully false or misleading representation, the willful concealment of a material fact, or other unlawful means; or

    2. The consular officer obtains information establishing that the alien was otherwise ineligible to receive the visa or other documentation at the time of issuance.[161]

In addition a consular officer is authorized to invalidate at any time a nonimmigrant visa or other nonimmigrant documentation in any case in which he finds that the alien has become ineligible to receive the visa or

---

[160] 22 C. F. R. 41.17 (d).
[161] 22 C. F. R. 41.18 (a); 22 C. F. R. 42.44 (a).

other documentation. However, the bearer of a nonimmigrant visa or other documentation which is being considered for revocation or invalidation shall, if practicable, be notified of the proposed revocation or invalidation and shall be given an opportunity to show cause why such action should not be taken.[162]

If the visa or other documentation is revoked or invalidated, the visa stamp or other documentation must be cancelled by writing the word "revoked" or "invalidated," whichever is applicable, plainly on the face thereof. Notice is to be given to the master, commanding officer or agent, etc., of the carrier or transportation line on which the alien is known or believed to intend to travel to the United States, unless the forms in the possession of the alien have been taken up and the visa cancelled. There is a similar provision with respect to notifying the Department of Justice.[163]

Security Aspects

Advisory Opinions.—Unless an advisory opinion by the Department is required or unless the consular officer submits the case of an applicant to the Department of State for possible 212 (d) (3) action,[164] a visa shall be issued or denied without reference to the Department of State. In cases where there is a refusal of a visa on security grounds, the officer making such a decision submits it to a board of three consular officers who also sign the refusal form. If there is not a concurrence in the decision the Visa Office is asked for an advisory opinion. If the visa is denied under the provisions of section 212 (a), (27), (28), or (29) of the Immigration and Nationality Act of 1952 (the security provisions), a detailed report on the circumstances leading to such action is submitted promptly to the Department, unless such action was based on the Department's advisory opinion, in which case a report on action taken will suffice.

Consular officers are required to submit to the Department for an advisory opinion, prior to visa issuance, applications for visas which fall in any of the following categories:

1. Any alien in whose case the consular officer is in doubt concerning the alien's eligibility to receive a visa so far as the provisions of section 212 (a), (27), (28), or (29) of the Act are concerned.

---

[162] 22 C. F. R. 41.18 (b) (c).

[163] 22 C. F. R. 41.18 (c) (d).

[164] That section provides: "Except as provided in this subsection, an alien (*a*) who is applying for a nonimmigrant visa and is known or believed by the consular officer to be ineligible for such visa under one or more of the paragraphs enumerated in subsection (a) (other than paragraphs (27) and (29), may, after approval by the Attorney General of a recommendation by the Secretary of State or by the consular officer that the alien be admitted temporarily as a nonimmigrant in the discretion of the Attorney General, or (*b*) who is inadmissible under one or more of the paragraphs enumerated in subsection (a) (other than paragraphs (27) and (29)), but who is in possession of appropriate documents or is granted a waiver thereof and is seeking admission, may be admitted into the United States temporarily as a nonimmigrant in the discretion of the Attorney General."

2. Any alien in whose case consular officers have been instructed not to issue a visa without prior referral of the case to the Department for an advisory opinion or in whose case the Department has previously rendered an adverse advisory opinion which is still outstanding.

3. Any alien to whom, within five years immediately preceding the application for a visa, a passport or other travel document has been extended or renewed, by the Government of the Union of Soviet Socialist Republics, or the Government or the authorities of any other Communist-controlled country, except an alien who is a national of such country, and as such is seeking to enter the United States as a foreign government official or as an international organization alien, and except an alien applying for a visa under section 201 of Public Law 402, 80th Congress, if his application has been submitted for clearance to the International Cooperation Administration or the Department's International Education Exchange Service.

4. Any alien who is requesting a visa for the purpose of conducting study or research for an extended period of time (several weeks or longer) at the University of California Radiation Laboratory, Berkeley, Calif., or at Brookhaven National Laboratory, Patchogue, N. Y., or any alien who is requesting a visa for the purpose of attending special training courses in radioactive tracer techniques at the Oak Ridge Institute of Nuclear Studies, Oak Ridge, Tenn.

5. Any alien who claims his past or present membership in any Communist Party is or was involuntary, or is or was solely when under 16 years of age, by operation of law, or for purpose of obtaining employment, food rations, or other essentials of living and where necessary for such purposes, within the purview of section 212 (a), (28), (I), (i).

6. Any alien who claims to be a defector as contemplated in Section 212 (a), (28), (I), (ii) of the Act and implemented by 22 CFR 42.42 (a), (28), (iii).[165]

In certain cases consular officers are required to ask the Department for an advisory opinion prior to the refusal of a visa. For example if the consular official believes that an alien is ineligible to receive a nonimmigrant visa under the provision of 212 (a) (28) of the Immigration and Nationality Act of 1952 and that alien's background, official business or personal affiliations are likely to make the denial of a visa a matter of public interest in the United States or abroad, a request for an advisory opinion must be made, even if the consular officer does not submit a recommendation as provided in section 212 (d) (3). In such a case, the issuance of a visa is not denied until the Department has advised the consular officer that the Secretary of State does not wish to recommend to the Attorney General the exercise of discretion under Section 212 (d) (3) of the Immigration and Nationality Act, or until the consular officer is informed that the Attorney General has refused to take such action.

---

[165] Department of State instruction, CA–1233, Aug. 19, 1954.

Whenever a consular officer contemplates the denial of a visa, in the case of an alien described above, pursuant to the provisions of Section 212 (a) (27) or (29), the denial of a visa should be deferred until the pertinent facts in the case have been submitted to the Department and the consular officer has been informed that the Department concurs with the conclusion that the facts in the individual case justify the application of section 212 (a) (27) or (29).

The procedure set forth in the above two paragraphs is followed, for example, in the cases of sports figures, persons associated with the arts in the broad sense, including singers, dancers, musicians, actors, artists, writers, beauty contestants, entertainers; leaders in government or politics; important businessmen; newspapermen; clergymen; any person affiliated with a pressure group which would be likely to make a public protest; ordinarily insignificant people who have been publicized on emotional grounds, such as personal tragedy, heroics, or anything which evokes public interest and sympathy.

Requests for advisory opinions are submitted to the Department of State by operations memorandum, unless the public relations aspect and the time factor warrant the submission of an advance request by telegram.

As the name indicates, the opinion is advisory. However, as a matter of practice, the consular officers do consider such opinions binding. If the consular officer seriously disagrees with the nature of the advisory opinion, he has the right to submit his own views as well as any clarifying information which tends to reverse the opinion. It may also be noted that the Visa Office periodically sends to all posts printed copies of advisory opinions for the guidance of consular officers who may rely upon the facts set forth in such opinions as precedents in cases of a similar nature they may be called upon to decide themselves.

If, after the receipt of a request for an advisory opinion, a security check in the United States is indicated on the basis of the consular officer's report, a request for such a check goes to the State Department, Office of Security, which maintains liaison with the Federal Bureau of Investigation, Central Intelligence Agency, Office of Naval Intelligence, Atomic Energy Commission, and G–2 (Department of the Army).

In addition to information from the above sources, the opinion also contains reports from the political, economic, biographical, and intelligence research areas of the State Department. Thus the consular officer has the benefit of all possible information from governmental agencies in the United States as a guide to his final evaluation.

Of the approximately 1,000 miscellaneous cases a month in the security branch of the Visa Office, between 450 and 550 are actual opinion requests that have to be processed. Included in the run of miscellaneous matters are cases where the consul will request advice on the complexion of organizations as a guide to his decision as to issuance or rejection of a visa. The Visa Office security branch will check such cases with the Intelligence Research, Political, and Security Divisions of the State Department and will also check the Attorney General's list.

PROTECTION OF INFORMANTS.—The source of security information is never divulged. In the course of an interview with an alien, a consular officer may skirt the basic information but he will never pinpoint it. The consular officer always exercises discretion in the conduct of such interviews.

PROTECTION OF THE APPLICANT AGAINST UNFOUNDED ACCUSATIONS.— In the case of signed or anonymous information, every available means will be followed in attempting to determine the validity of the derogatory information. At the present time, consular officers are permitted only to give the alien a citation to the relevant section of the law under which his application is being rejected.

PRIVATE BILLS.—In cases where private bills are introduced in Congress for the admission of aliens to whom visas cannot be issued administratively, the Visa Office security branch will make a security check and submit a report to the congressional committee handling such bills. If serious derogatory information is developed, the Visa Office liaison officer with Congress will submit a verbal report to the Congressman sponsoring a private bill for his guidance in dealing with his constituents.

Conditions of Nonimmigrant Status

An alien found admissible as a nonimmigrant under the Immigration and Nationality Act is admitted to the United States, but is permitted to remain in the United States only upon the following conditions:

1. That while in the United States he will maintain the particular nonimmigrant status under which he was admitted or such other status as he may acquire in accordance with the provisions of the Immigration and Nationality Act or which he may have acquired in accordance with the provisions of any prior law,

2. That he will depart from the United States within the period of admission or any authorized extension thereof,

3. That while in the United States he will not engage in any employment or activity inconsistent with and not essential to the status under which he is in the United States, unless such employment or activity has first been authorized by the district director or the officer in charge having administrative jurisdiction over the alien's place of temporary residence in the United States,

4. That he will fulfill such other conditions as the admitting officer, in his discretion, may impose or may have imposed to insure that he will depart from the United States at the expiration of the time for which he was admitted, and that he will maintain the status under which he was admitted or which he may have lawfully acquired subsequent to his admission.[166]

[166] 8 C. F. R. 214.2.

The application by an alien for an extension of the period of temporary admission shall be submitted as soon as the alien is aware that he will not be able to fulfill the purpose of his temporary stay within the period he has been authorized to remain in the United States. Such application must also be made not less than 15 or more than 30 days prior to the end of such period, unless the district director or officer in charge authorizes the filing of an application at an earlier date. Upon the receipt of an application the district director or the officer in charge shall cause such investigation to be made as is necessary to the proper disposition of the application. The application may be granted or denied upon such terms and conditions, including the furnishing of bond, as he may deem appropriate. There is no appeal from his decision.[167]

Waiver of Visas and Contiguous Land Borders

NONRESIDENT ALIEN BORDER-CROSSING IDENTIFICATION CARDS.—The Immigration and Nationality Act defines a border-crossing identification card as a "document of identity bearing that designation issued to an alien who is lawfully admitted for permanent residence, or to an alien who is a resident in a foreign contiguous territory, by a consular officer or an immigration officer for the purpose of crossing over the border between the United States and foreign contiguous territory in accordance with such conditions for its issuance and use as may be prescribed by regulation." [168]

The rightful holder of a nonresident alien Mexican border-crossing card may present such card in lieu of a nonimmigrant visa when applying for admission directly from Mexico and for admission to a port of entry situated along the Mexican border of the United States.[169]

A nonresident alien's border-crossing identification card may be issued to any alien who:

1. Submits satisfactory evidence that he is a Canadian citizen or a British subject residing in Canada, or a citizen of Mexico residing therein,

2. Presents a valid unexpired passport required of nonimmigrants unless the requirement is waived,

3. Desires temporary admission into the Continental United States for a period or periods of not more than 72 hours each, and

4. Is admissible to the United States.

The card may also be issued to an applicant who desires temporary admission to the United States for more than 72 hours if such applicant desires such card to facilitate admission and is a citizen of Canada or a British subject having his residence in Canada and is entitled to enter the United States

---

[167] 8 C. F. R. 214.41 (a).
[168] 8 U. S. C. 1101 (a) (6).
[169] 8 C. F. R. 212.11 (b).

under 8 C. F. R. 212.3 (*a*) and (*b*) without presenting a visa, border-crossing identification cards, or passport.[170]

WAIVER OF PASSPORT, VISA, AND BORDER-CROSSING IDENTIFICATION CARD.—The requirement that aliens will not be admitted to the United States unless they are in possession of a passport valid for a period of six months, etc., and which requires aliens to have at the time of application a valid non-immigrant visa or border-crossing identification card [171] has been waived on a reciprocal basis by the Secretary of State and the Attorney General acting jointly [172] in the cases of certain aliens. Included are citizens of Canada who have their residence in Canada and who are making application to visit the United States from Canada or from and after a visit solely to some place in foreign contiguous territory or adjacent islands.

Nationality

A. *Naturalization:* The Act provides subversives may not be naturalized as citizens of the United States.[173]

No alien may be naturalized unless he can prove:

1. An understanding of the English language, including an ability to read, write, and speak words in ordinary usage in the English language (does not apply to a person who is physically unable to comply therewith or to any person who was fifty years of age at the time of the effective date of the Act and who has been living in the United States for periods totaling at least 20 years.) [174]

2. A knowledge and understanding of the fundamentals of the history, and of the principles and form of government, of the United States.[175]

3. That he was lawfully admitted for permanent residence.[176]

4. That immediately preceding the date of his petition for naturalization he has resided continuously in the United States for at least five years during which he has been physically present in the United States for periods totaling at least half of that time and has lived within the State in which the petition was filed for at least six months.[177]

5. That he has resided continuously within the United States from the date of the petition up to the time of admission to citizenship.[178]

6. That during the period referred to above he has been, and still is, a person of good moral character who is attached to the principles of the Constitution of the United States.[179]

---

[170] 8 C. F. R. 212.11 (c).
[171] 8 U. S. C. 1182 (a) (26).
[172] This was done in pursuance of the authority contained in 8 U. S. C. 1182 (d) (4) (B).
[173] 8 U. S. C. 1424.
[174] 8 U. S. C. 1423 (1).
[175] 8 U. S. C. 1423 (2).
[176] 8 U. S. C. 1427 (a) (1).
[177] 8 U. S. C. 1427 (a) (1).
[178] 8 U. S. C. 1427 (a) (2).
[179] 8 U. S. C. 1427 (a) (3).

These requirements are somewhat modified in the case of former cititzens of the United States, spouses and children of cititzens, aliens with service in the Armed Forces, alien seamen, and persons performing religious duties abroad.

A person who has petitioned for naturalization shall, in order to be and before being admitted to cititzenship, take in open court an oath:

1. to support the Constitution of the United States;

2. to renounce and abjure absolutely and entirely, all allegiance and fidelity to any foreign prince, potentate, state or sovereignty of whom or which the petitioner was a subject or citizen;

3. to support and defend the Constitution and laws of the United States against all enemies, foreign and domestic;

4. to bear true faith and allegiance to the same; and

5. (a) to bear arms on behalf of the United States where required by law, or (b) to perform noncombatant service in the Armed Forces of the United States when required by law, or (c) to perform work of national importance under civilian direction where required by law.[180]

B. *Denaturalization:* A court order admitting a naturalized citizen to citizenship may be revoked and the certificate of naturalization cancelled on the ground that the order and certificate were procured by concealment of a material fact or by willful misrepresentation. Refusal on the part of a naturalized citizen within a period of 10 years following his naturalization to testify as a witness in any proceeding before a congressional committee concerning his subversive activities, in a case where such person has been convicted of contempt for such refusal, is held to constitute a ground for revocation of such person's naturalizatiton as having been procured by concealment of a material fact or by willful misrepresentation.[181]

At present the application for a petition for naturalization contains several questions relating to subversive activities. The questionnaire asks if the individual is or has been within the previous 10 years a member of the Communist Party, and also if the individual is or has been within the previous 10 years a member of an organization which advocates the overthrow of the United States Government by force and violence. Most subversive denaturalization cases are based on a false statement to these or other specific questions in the petition for naturalization.

Deportation

As could be expected, Congress specifically provided that Communists or members of any other totalitarian party are included within the classes of deportable aliens. Also among the other classes of aliens who are deportable are aliens who are members of, or affiliated with, any organization

[180] 8 U. S. C. 1448; 8 U. S. C. A. 1–1280 (aliens and nationality), p. 85.
[181] U. S. C. 1451 (a).

during the time it was registered or required to register under Section 786 of title 50 (Internal Security Act).

While the deportability of an alien is being determined, he may be arrested and taken into custody on warrant of the Attorney General. Pending final determination of deportability, the alien may be continued in custody or released on conditional parole. Any competent court has authority to review and revise the Attorney General's determination concerning the alien's detention, and release him on bond or parole, if it is conclusively shown in habeas corpus proceedings that the Attorney General is not proceeding with reasonable dispatch.[182]

After a final order of deportation has been issued, the Attorney General has six months, or, if judicial review is had, then six months from the date of the final order of the Court, within which to effect the alien's departure from the United States.

The Attorney General is authorized to withhold deportation of any alien within the United States to any country in which, in his opinion, the alien would be subject to physical persecution.[183] A claim of physical persecution may be considered at any time after an order of deportation becomes final. In all cases except exclusion cases the alien is granted a temporary stay of execution pending a final determination of the application. It is the policy of the Immigration and Naturalization Service not to consider claims of physical persecution made by excluded aliens.

The Act also gives the Attorney General the power to suspend deportation and adjust the status of the alien to that of one lawfully admitted in certain cases.[184] One of the classes includes aliens who are deportable on subversive grounds for an act committed or status acquired subsequent to entry into the United States. Such an alien must continuously have been present in the United States for a period of not less than ten years immediately following the commission of an act, or the assumption of a status, constituting a ground for deportation. In such a case the alien must prove that during all of such period he has been of good moral character. He is not eligible if he has been served with a final order of deportation. The person must be one whose deportation would "in the opinion of the Attorney General, result in exceptional and an extremely unusual hardship to the alien or his spouse, parent, or child, who is a citizen or an alien lawfully admitted for permanent residence." [185]

If the alien meets the above requirements, the Attorney General may, in his discretion, suspend deportation. In such a case a complete and detailed statement of the facts and pertinent provisions of the law must be reported to the Congress with the reasons for such suspension. If the Congress passes a concurrent resolution stating in substance that it favors the suspension of deportation, the Attorney General may cancel the deportation proceedings.

[182] 8 U. S. C. A. 1–1280 (aliens and nationality), p. 62; 8 U. S. C. 1252 (a).
[183] 8 U. S. C. 1253 (h).
[184] 8 U. S. C. 1254 (a).
[185] 8 U. S. C. 1254 (a) (5).

If, within the time specified, the Congress does not pass a concurrent resolution or if either the Senate or the House of Representatives passes a resolution stating in substance that it does not favor the suspension of deportation of such alien, the Attorney General shall thereupon deport such alien as provided by law.[186]

RECOMMENDATIONS

NECESSITY

Security controls over aliens seeking admission to the United States on temporary visits for business or pleasure, or for permanent residence, are necessary.

The question of the necessity for a security program covering aliens can be considered only against the broad backdrop of American history.

Migration to America was the greatest mass movement in all history. Not only did it change the face of a continent but its impact has been felt, in varying degrees, in virtually every corner of the globe.

Historians agree that a full-scale evaluation of American immigration is achievable only after much more intensive and specialized study becomes an accomplished fact. Vast areas of the subject remain unexplored; measurements of the effects can be, at best, but shaky generalizations.

As was pointed out in the legal basis for the security program for immigrant and nonimmigrant aliens, the Congress first provided for the exclusion of aliens because of proscribed opinions in the Act of March 3, 1903, and broadened the security base in the Act of October 16, 1918. Subsequent enactments in 1920, 1924, and 1940 are now embodied in the Walter-McCarren Act (Immigration and Nationality Act of 1952) which is the controlling statute covering immigration, naturalization and deportation matters and regulating the admission of immigrants, those who intend to make the United States their permanent home, and nonimmigrants, those who do not.

Statistics of the Immigration and Naturalization Service of the Department of Justice offer convincing proof that the screening of aliens applying for admission to the United States is a necessary governmental function. For the fiscal year ending June 30, 1956, more than 1,000,000 aliens were admitted, 321,625 of them for permanent residence. Admission of quota and nonquota immigrants alone for the period of July 1, 1950 to June 30, 1956, totaled more than 1,400,000.

---

[186] 8 U. S. C. 1254 (e).

Class	1951	1952	1953	1954	1955	1956
Aliens admitted................	670,823	781,602	656,148	774,790	858,736	1,007,884
Immigrants........................	[1]205,717	265,520	170,434	208,177	237,790	321,625
Quota immigrants.................	156,547	194,247	84,175	94,098	82,232	89,310
Nonquota immigrants..............	49,170	71,273	86,259	114,079	155,558	232,315
Wives of United States citizens.....	8,685	16,058	15,916	17,145	18,504	21,244
Husbands of United States citizens.	822	793	3,359	7,725	6,716	5,788
Children of United States citizens...	1,955	2,464	3,268	5,819	5,662	4,710
Natives of Western Hemisphere countries....................	34,704	47,744	58,985	78,897	92,620	122,083
Their spouses...............	337	455	1,127	1,119	1,059	1,398
Their children..............	233	209	987	510	595	551
Persons who had been United States citizens....................	[2]39	32	104	427	87	44
Ministers of religious denominations.	376	338	244	263	194	210
Their spouses...............	129	96	69	57	50	55
Their children..............	228	146	74	65	68	85
Employees of United States Government abroad, their spouses and children......................	[3]	....	2	4	9	2
Refugees.....................	[4]	....	....	821	29,002	75,473
Other nonquota immigrants.......	1,622	2,938	2,124	1,227	997	672

[1] An immigrant is defined in statistics of the Service as an alien admitted for permanent residence, or as an addition to the population.
[2] Under the Immigration Act of 1924, this class covered only women who had been United States citizens.
[3] New classes under the provisions of the Immigration and Nationality Act.
[4] Refugees admitted under the Refugee Act of 1953.

Despite the precautions taken to exclude individuals who constitute a threat to our national security, an occasional subversive does succeed in gaining admission. From July 1, 1950, to June 30, 1955, it was necessary to deport 177 subversive aliens.

The volume of nonimmigrant traffic yearly also points up the necessity for security investigations before the issuance of visas by consular officers abroad. Admissions of nonimmigrant aliens rose steadily for each of the four fiscal years preceding June 30, 1956. The figure was 485,714 for fiscal 1953; 566,613 for fiscal 1954; 620,946 for fiscal 1955, and 686,259 for fiscal 1956.

The breakdown showing the types and numbers of nonimmigrants admitted for fiscal 1956 follows:

Foreign government officials... 27,109
Temporary visitors for business.. 72,265
Temporary visitors for pleasure... 399,704
Transit aliens.. 65,214
Treaty traders and investors.. 1,619
Students... 28,013
International representatives... 5,190
Temporary workers and trainees[1]...................................... 17,077
Representatives of foreign information media............................ 697
Exchange aliens.. 17,204
Returning resident aliens.. 52,136
Other classes.. 31

[1] Does not include 15,152 agricultural laborers admitted under section 101 (a) (15) (H), Immigration and Nationality Act.

The foregoing figures do not reflect the inward movement of aliens over the Canadian and Mexican borders which also has been rising steadily for the past decade. The statistical records of the Immigration and Naturalization Service list each and every arrival of the same person separately. Border crossings by aliens rose from a total of 44,620,010 for fiscal year 1951, to a total of 61,611,311 for fiscal 1955.

LEGISLATION AND REGULATION

The Immigration and Nationality Act of 1952 should be amended to (1) transfer the functions of visa control, except for diplomatic and official visas, from the Department of State to the Department of Justice and (2) authorize the Attorney General to maintain offices and personnel abroad to carry out the visa functions without the concurrence of the Secretary of State being a requisite for such action.

The question of making the Department of Justice, through its Immigration and Naturalization Service, solely responsible for the travel documentation of all aliens, except diplomats and foreign government officials, is not new.

Over the years it has been a subject for consideration by the executive branch of the Government and by congressional bodies. It was studied by the professional staff of the Senate Subcommittee to Investigate Immigration and Naturalization in the 80th Congress in 1948. The Commission on Organization of the Executive Branch of the Government (Hoover Commission) recommended the transfer of the visa function to the Department of Justice in 1949.

Transportation companies, in particular, have been vigorous complainants against a system which imposed heavy financial burdens upon them because screening and documentation of aliens by consular officers abroad was ruled, for one reason or another, to be deficient when the aliens reached a port of entry and became subject to the scrutiny of immigration officers.

The following statement of Welburn Mayock, counsel for American President Lines, Ltd., typifies the dilemma of the transportation companies:

In the last 5 years, American President Lines, Ltd., has paid an estimated $550,000 in detention expenses for aliens and citizens treated as aliens who came on its vessels. The immigrants were detained for additional screening by the immigration officers. Each of such immigrants carried a visa or travel documents signed by a consular official. Each immigrant had been examined medically by the consular service before he was allowed to secure passage. Some of these immigrants were detained for months— even as much as a year—at the expense of the company. This tremendous expense was assessed although we had done no wrong, had been guilty of no negligence, but had simply performed our legal duty as a public carrier in receiving and transporting persons duly screened and documented for passage by consular officers of the United States.[187]

[187] Joint hearings before the subcommittees of the Committee on the Judiciary, 82d Cong., 1st sess., on S. 716, H. R. 2379 and H. R. 2816, p. 184.

The Walter-McCarran Act (Immigration and Nationality Act of 1952) established the Bureau of Security and Consular Affairs in the Department of State and placed the Visa Office within this bureau.

The duties of the Visa Office are described generally as follows:

Gives guidance to visa issuing officers abroad; staffs consulates with visa personnel; issues regulations to implement the law; controls quota system; establishes quota for any new country; and maintains liaison with the Immigration and Naturalization Service.

The General Counsel of the Visa Office gives decisions in questions of law interpreting the Walter-McCarran Act; serves under the general direction of the legal adviser of the Department of State; and cooperates with the appropriate legal officer of the Immigration and Naturalization Service to insure the uniform interpretation of the Act.

The duties of embassies and legations are principally to process applications for diplomatic and official visas. The consul general attached to an embassy is the supervisor of all consular officers located within the country where the embassy is located and has the status of a diplomatic officer.

Generally speaking, the embassies and legations handle the issuance of diplomatic and official visas and consular officers handle the issuance of all nonofficial visas. Under certain circumstances the ambassador can delegate authority to a consular officer somewhere in the country to issue a diplomatic or official visa. As an example—if a French diplomat who is in Marseilles wants to secure a diplomatic visa, it is not necessary for him to apply to the American Embassy in Paris; the ambassador in Paris will authorize the U. S. consul at Marseilles to issue such a visa. In some cases, embassies or legations may also issue the nonofficial type of visa but as a general rule this function is confined almost entirely to consular officers.[188]

.   .   .   .

Dual System of Examination of Aliens

The act continues the dual system of examination of aliens seeking to enter the United States through the issuance of consular officers abroad of visas to qualified applicants and through the examination by immigration officers at ports of entry of aliens who have obtained visas. This procedure follows the usual international practice. The jurisdiction of the two services does not overlap, but close liaison is maintained to insure a uniform interpretation of the law.

.   .   .   .

Consular officers are responsible under the law for the issuance or refusal of visas. The Department of State is responsible for the general supervision of the administration of the act, insofar as the Department of State and the Foreign Service are concerned. The Department of State may instruct consular officers regarding interpretations of the law and may furnish them with advisory opinions concerning other phases of the work. The Department of State may also obtain reports from consular officers in individual visa cases under an informal visa review procedure with a view to determining whether the action taken or contemplated is in accord with the law and regulations.

In the course of a year, consular officers examine several hundreds of thousands of visa applicants, issue visas to aliens who qualify under the law, and refuse visas to those who fail to qualify thereunder.[189]

---

[188] Visa Office response to Commission interrogatory, Sept. 21, 1956.
[189] Visa work of the Department of State and the Foreign Service, published by the Department of State, 1953, pp. 1 and 2.

The Immigration Service has advocated for some time a system of pre-inspection of aliens abroad to determine their admissibility before they leave for the United States.

Section 103 of the Walter-McCarran Act confers upon the Commissioner of Immigration, under a delegation of power from the Attorney General, the authority to establish offices and detail employees of the Service to duty in foreign countries, "with the concurrence of the Secretary of State."

This Commission has been advised by the Commissioner that repeated efforts have been made to secure the necessary concurrence of the Secretary but his consent has been withheld.

Additional Points by Commissioner

The Commissioner also makes these points:

1. Under the present system, it is impossible for the Service to carry out its responsibilities satisfactorily. The Service knows nothing about the alien when he arrives at a port of entry and factors evidencing inadmissibility can be developed only by interrogation, an extremely difficult proposition even for skillful and experienced inspectors.

2. Having two agencies of the Government involved in the determination of admissibility is inefficient, ineffective and wasteful.

3. Aliens who already have gone through the procedure of obtaining visas from consular officers are unable to understand why they should not be admitted merely on proof of identity.

4. The place to investigate an alien is at the point where he lives and the determination of his admissibility or inadmissibility at this juncture can save a great deal of trouble. Once the alien reaches the United States, he has recourse to administrative procedure and court reviews and, as the record so clearly shows, is in a position to make it difficult for the Government to deport him.

5. Personnel stationed abroad can develop contacts and sources of information important to a determination of whether an alien is a threat to the security of the United States. Employees abroad also can help stop stowaway and smuggling activities of aliens.

Position of Department of State

The Commission has been assured by officials concerned with visa matters in the Department of State that the Department's position today remains substantially the same as that expressed when the Hoover Commission recommended transfer of the visa function to the Department of Justice.

It has also been stressed that the Walter-McCarran Act left undisturbed the authority of consular officers to issue or refuse visas, first established in the Immigration Act of 1924.

The position of the Department encompasses the following eight points:

1. It is the practice for officers of the Visa Office and the Immigration and Naturalization Service to consult regarding proposed regulations affecting consular administration of the immigration laws. It would make little difference if the regulations were to be prescribed by the Attorney General with the concurrence of the Secretary of State but it would be necessary for the Department of State to approve policy and regulations relating to the issuance of visas since matters involved therein may affect the conduct of foreign relations and are therefore of concern to the Department of State.

2. The bulk of the security information pertaining to aliens abroad is procured by missions and consulates from appropriate sources in the countries where they are located. Additional information is available in some cases from political reports regarding aliens involved in activities of a political nature, from the Department of State files, and from various sources in the United States including the Central Intelligence Agency, the Intelligence Offices of the Army and Navy, the Narcotics Division of the Treasury Department, and the Federal Bureau of Investigation of the Department of Justice. The Department of Justice, which operates in the domestic field, does not have *superior facilities* to furnish security information relating to aliens abroad applying for visas. On the contrary, the facilities are not as extensive since the Department of Justice does not have the information available to the consuls abroad.

3. The Department of State has readily available specialized knowledge and experience of the political officers who have intimate acquaintance with conditions in every area of the world and is therefore able to evaluate security reports in the light of political conditions and trends abroad at least equally as well as the Department of Justice in cases involving political considerations. It is not believed, therefore, that the Department of Justice has *superior facilities* to evaluate security information relating to aliens abroad applying for visas.

4. Prior to 1924, consular officers had no statutory authority to refuse visas to immigrants who desired to come to the United States. The admissibility of aliens was determined at a port of entry by the immigration authorities after the aliens had severed their ties abroad and had come to the United States. This was a single check of aliens seeking to enter the United States. Under it, aliens often suffered great hardship after having made a long journey to the United States only to find that they were inadmissible under the law and after exclusion had to return abroad and attempt to re-establish themselves. Under this system, too, background information from the alien's home country was unavailable to the immigration officer and aliens were admitted who might have been held to be inadmissible had full information regarding them been available. After long study and careful considera-

tion of the problem, Congress provided in the Immigration Act of 1924 for a *double check* of aliens by separate independent agencies of the Government; first, by consular officers of the Foreign Service of the Department of State before they issued visas, and second, by immigration officers of the Department of Justice after the aliens arrived at a port of entry. The Act of 1924 placed directly on consular officers responsibility for the issuance or refusal of immigration visas. If a double check was considered essential (in 1924) to protect the United States against criminals and other undesirables, it is even more necessary in the present critical condition of the world to use the double check provided through the prophetic foresight of Congress, to screen upon security, as well as upon other grounds, aliens seeking to enter the United States.

5. Under existing procedures for issuing regulations, it is necessary for the two Departments to consult with a view to obtaining concurrence before regulations are promulgated. There would be little advantage to be gained if the functions of the Visa Office were to be transferred to the Department of Justice for the reason that the Secretary of State would have to concur in policy and regulations in any case to see that any proposed changes do not adversely affect the conduct of foreign relations.

6. The issuance of visas to aliens directly involves relations between the United States and the foreign countries of which the aliens are nationals. The lawful refusal of a visa to a prominent person often involves discussion through diplomatic channels and may even inspire retaliatory action. Political conditions in a country often affect the determination of the eligibility of an alien for a visa and Foreign Service officers are trained for and have the primary responsibility for evaluating such conditions. In this connection, questions constantly arise as to whether the entry of an alien would be contrary to the national interest or national safety and are referred to the Visa Office by the consuls for consideration and instruction. In many cases, questions of policy and trade relations must receive full consideration as well as security. If the review of visa cases were to be placed in the hands of the Department responsible for security alone, there might be an over-emphasis on this phase of the case.

7. Cases constantly arise in which the political divisions of the Department have an interest and officers in these divisions very frequently consult officers of the Visa Office regarding them. Frequently, too, prompt action is necessary. It has been a great facility to such officers to have immediate personal and telephone access to officers within the Department having knowledge of the immigration laws and regulations to discuss the facts or to clear an urgent telegram. This facility would be greatly reduced if the functions of the Visa Office were transferred to another agency.

576

8. The Department of State and the Foreign Service are the internationally accepted channels for communication with foreign governments and except in routine cases it would not be wise to permit communications in potentially controversial cases to be handled by another agency except through the Visa Office of the Department of State.

Viewpoint of the Hoover Commission

The task force report on foreign affairs (appendix H) prepared for the Commission on Organization of the Executive Branch of the Government in January 1949, page 104, and subsequently adopted as a recommendation of that Commission, contained the following views:

The Visa Division (now Office), on the other hand, presents a problem of another nature. It is responsible for establishing standard requirements and practices for the administration of immigration and other laws governing the entry and departure of aliens and their travel to and from the United States. These duties, however, must be performed in collaboration with the Department of Justice, which has similar functions. At present the State Department is responsible for issuing visas which permit aliens to come to the United States, while the Department of Justice, through the Immigration and Naturalization Service, is responsible for admitting aliens into the United States. This situation merits analysis at this point.

In addition to providing general administrative direction to the American consular officers in the discharge of their statutory obligations with regard to operation of the visa system, the Visa Division maintains control over the allotment of immigration quotas. Again, in collaboration with the Immigration and Naturalization Service, it develops policies governing alien travel to and from the United States. The Immigration and Naturaization Service, however, has statutory control over the admission of aliens into the United States.[190] Moreover, most of the information in which visas are granted or denied is furnished by the Department of Justice.

Thus, the situation in connection with the issuance of visas is confusing because of the division of authority between the Departments of State and Justice. Specifically, both have joint policy, regulatory and procedural responsibilities in the issue of visas, and whereas the State Department grants the initial visa to an alien the Justice Department has the final authority to approve or disapprove the visa on the basis of its independent judgment. Furthermore, there has been considerable criticism of the manner in which the visa system operates, and this criticism appears to have some merit. The State Department, for instance, has not brought its visa regulations and procedures up-to-date nor have consular officers or visa division personnel been adequately trained.

The logical solution to the visa problem lies in the transfer of the Visa Division functions to the Department of Justice. Diplomatic visas, however, should remain under the jurisdiction of the Secretary of State.

The Commission on Government Security has deliberated at length over the implications of the Hoover Commission recommendation. On the basis

---

[190] Prior to 1924 aliens wishing to enter the United States bought passage and presented themselves to immigration and naturalization officials at the port of debarkation for admission to the United States. The Immigration Act of 1924 was designed to relieve aliens of the unnecessary expense of coming to this country if they were unqualified for entry. Therefore, the Act placed the responsibility of issuing visas on consular officials so that an alien could proceed to the United States with reasonable assurance he would be admitted upon arrival.

of our own analysis of all facets of this complex question, we arrive at the same conclusion.

To insure maximum security in this area, responsibility properly must be concentrated in the agency the Congress has always intended shall make final determination of admissibility or inadmissibility. To achieve that goal, there must be a realignment to insure complete control by the Immigration Service from the time the alien first makes application for a visa right down to the moment he first sets foot on the American shoreline.

To accomplish this purpose, it necessarily follows that employees of the Immigration Service must be stationed abroad.

The Commission recommends that the deportation sections of the Immigration and Nationality Act of 1952 be amended to provide that:

1. Issuance of both immigrant and nonimmigrant visas to, or the use of bonded transit without visa by, the nationals of any country which refuses to accept a deportee who is a national, citizen, or subject of such country, should be suspended, and such suspension should remain effective as long as such country persists in refusal to accept said deportee. This provision should not apply to diplomatic personnel.

2. Any alien against whom a final order of deportation has been outstanding for more than 6 months should be returned to custody under the warrant which initiated the proceedings against him and should be retained until his deportation can be effected when the Attorney General, in his discretion, considers such action necessary to protect the national security or public safety.

3. The conditions under which aliens awaiting deportation shall be subject to supervision by the Attorney General should be defined with greater specificity than presently stated in section 242 (d), and should include provisions that the Attorney General, in performing the function of supervision, should not be limited only to assuring that the alien shall be available for deportation.

4. The Attorney General should have the power, specified by statute and not by regulation, to order a deportable alien under supervision to refrain from subversive activities or associations, with any violation of such order to be a criminal offense punishable by fine or imprisonment, or both.

A number of alien Communists who have been under a final order of deportation, some of them for years, and who have long been devoted advocates of the overthrow of the Government of the United States by force and violence, continue to be residents of American cities simply because no other nation will take them. Some courts have ruled that the Attorney General can supervise them only under "reasonable restrictions" limited solely to insuring that they will be available for deportation, when and if it can ever be arranged.[191]

The Immigration and Nationality Service, in its annual report for the fiscal year ending June 30, 1955, stated:

Difficulties in securing travel documents for aliens deportable to the U. S. S. R., Poland, Czechoslovakia, Rumania, Hungary, Albania, and the mainland of China were responsible in large part for a record 10,967 pending unexecuted orders of deportation at the end of the year. Deportation may never be accomplished in a large number of these cases becauses of inability to obtain travel documents. In 229 of these cases the orders of deportation were based on subversive grounds.

One year later the Service had 10,874 unexecuted orders and 191 were based on subversive grounds.

As of June 30, 1956, the Service reported that the number of subversive cases pending investigation totaled 9,520.

In the 6-year period from July 1, 1950, to June 30, 1956, the Service succeeded in ridding America of only 193 subversives by the deportation process, an average of 32 a year.

The following excerpt from the report of the Committee on the Judiciary, House of Representatives report No. 1192, 81st Congress, 1st Session (pages 8 and 9) is illustrative of conditions:

First is the case of Frank E. Spector, born in Odessa, Russia, and now living in Los Angeles, California. He served a jail sentence in California in 1930 and was ordered deported by the Attorney General that same year, being a person who advocates and teaches the overthrow by force or violence of the Government of the United States. Spector showed up in Los Angeles about 1921. Since then he has had a record of continuous activities and leadership in the Communist party. Last year (1949) he defied the authority of the California State Senate and was threatened with contempt. He was told that contempt might be ground for deportation from the United States. In reply Spector [192] retorted, "You are too late, Mr. Tenney, my order of deportation has been issued 21 years ago and I am still here." The Attorney General's comment on Spector is as follows: "As a result of numerous refusals on the part of Russia to issue a travel document to the alien, he is free to travel in the United States and continue his communistic activities. He has been openly and usually defiant of this Government's efforts to carry out the law in his case. We have no means whereby he can be taken into custody. In view of his ability as a leader and organizer, he is a distinct threat to the national security of the United States."

The second case is that of Badrig Selian, 50, a native of Turkey. He is an active member of the Communist Party and one of their most important publicists in the United States. In 1930 his deportation was ordered but refused by Turkey and by Syria, which now controls his birthplace. Of his own free will he left the United States last year (1949) after the Government had failed throughout 18 years to get him out of the country.

---

[191] *Sentner* v. *Colarelli*, 145 Supp. 569, affirmed by Supreme Court, May 20, 1957; *U. S.* v. *Witkovich*, 140 F. Supp. 815, affirmed by Supreme Court, Apr. 29, 1957.

[192] The Immigration and Naturalization Service informed the Commission on Government Security that Spector was still in the United States as of May 1, 1957.

Concerning the Selian case the Attorney General says that—

This Communist declined to leave the United States, and since no country of origin would take him we were obliged to permit him to remain here at large. When it suited his own purposes, however, he was able through his own efforts to obtain a passport. Selian, we believe, would have departed years earlier had the alternative been indefinite detention as authorized in the Hobbs bill.

Next case: Joseph Bernard, alias Charles Murphy, 55, is probably a native of Switzerland. He came to this country as a visitor and stayed. In 1934 he was sentenced in Salt Lake City, Utah, for 5 years for indecent assault. In 1943 he was again sentenced for taking indecent liberties with female children. This sex criminal is allowed to continue at large in the United States as a potential menace to the health and morals of children with whom he may come into contact. He is under order to be deported but remains at large because under existing law we cannot send him to the country he came from, Canada, which refuses him, and without his consent we cannot send him to any other country.

Another case: Mones Chomsker, 63, of New York City, a native of the portion of Poland that is now within Soviet borders. He has at least a dozen aliases. He has been convicted at least 30 times on charges of larceny, theft, professional thief, and assault. His sentences have ranged from 30 days to 3 years. He was ordered deported, but Soviet Russia refused a passport. This alien is a confirmed criminal mandatorily deportable under our laws but the Department of Justice under existing laws is unable to effect his departure. He remains at large, a continuous and continuing menace to the peace and safety of our country.

"Another deportable alien, John Mastin, 50, was born in England and migrated to Canada, wherefrom he came to the United States. He has a long record of convictions for larceny, robbery, and burglary. Since Great Britain is unable to locate a record of his birth in England, a passport is refused. We are unable to deport this alien under existing law even though he is a habitual criminal. We cannot keep him in detention but must allow him to remain at large.

And still another, Joseph Vandervelt, 48, of Detroit, Michigan, is a native of Belgium. His record speaks for itself. He married and is the father of four children. He applied for and was put on relief in Detroit during 1934 by falsely representing himself to be a nativeborn citizen. He claims to be physically unable to work although medical examination disclosed that he is fit for work. He admits that he falsely claimed birth in the United States in order to secure relief money. In 1944 he was given 6 months to 10 years sentence for indecent liberties with a 3-year old girl. He is now in jail. The Attorney General says: "This alien, although able to work, has refused or avoided employment. He secured relief funds fraudulently and has been imprisoned for a sex crime. His family has derived little or no support from his efforts during the past 14 years. Upon his release from prison it will be necessary to allow him to remain at large, a burden to the community and a threat to the morals of children."

The Selian case, cited in the foregoing, points up another interesting fact, that important Communists, when confronted by the possibility of detention or imprisonment, have no difficulty in obtaining travel documents when it suits their convenience. Selian resisted deportation for 18 years and then left of his own accord.

Nor is his case an isolated one. Irving Potash, after serving one term in prison for violation of the Smith Act, got out of the country when faced with prospect of having to serve another. He is back in prison again, this time for having returned to the United States illegally.

Two other notorious Communists, John Santo and J. Peters, alias Alexander Stevens, fled to Hungary where they promptly assumed high Communist positions. Peters, head of a Soviet espionage apparatus in the United States, became supervisor of all publications going to Hungarian Communist Party members and sympathizers throughout the world. Both he and Santo, who had a long record of Communist activity in American labor circles, were assisted in leaving the United States by the American Committee for the Protection of the Foreign Born,[193] shown by testimony before the House Committee on Un-American Activities to be a subversive organization.

In last year's revolutionary outbreak in Hungary, Santo got across the border into Austria ahead of the rebels. He has since been trying to seek sanctuary in the United States on a claim that he has reformed.

These facts and the cases cited lead naturally to the conclusion that there should be more vigorous enforcement of section 242 (e) of the Immigration and Nationality Act, which provides severe penalties for willful failure or refusal to depart or to apply for travel document necessary for such departure, once a final order of deportation has been issued. If this is coupled with an alternative of detention when the final order of deportation is more than six months old, and a firmer United States attitude toward countries refusing to take back their nationals is adopted, at least some of the present abuses can be corrected. There is even the possibility that the Communist countries, when confronted with the restrictions on issuance of visas this Commission proposes, might change their attitude toward acceptance of deportees in the interest of promoting travel of their nationals. The proposed suspension would not be applicable to diplomatic personnel of countries involved.

Courts Used to Delay, Defeat Expulsion

Aliens deportable on subversive or criminal grounds have taken full advantage of the relative newness of the Immigration and Nationality Act of 1952 and the fact that it takes some time to build up a body of judicial interpretations and precedents.

Attacks on the validity of the deportation order, either by habeas corpus proceedings or suits for review and injunctive relief, challenging of the constitutionality, of the basic act, petitions for judicial review of denial of administrative relief, charges of unfairness at hearings and lack of compliance with the Administrative Procedure Act are some of the long series of legal maneuvers pursued. There are cases where simultaneous suits have constitutionality of the basic act, petitions for judicial review of denial of Columbia, and successive suits based upon virtually the identical allegations

---

[193] Hearings before subcommittee No. 1, Committee on the Judiciary, House of Representatives, May 25, 1949, p. 24.

have been filed in some jurisdictions.   In some instances, overcrowded dockets create long lapses of time between the filing and ultimate hearing by a trial judge.

Thus, we frequently encounter the incongruity of seeing aliens whose entire course of conduct in the United States has been devoted to seeking to destroy our Constitution cloaking themselves in its protective principles.

In recommending that the Congress define by legislation, and not leave to regulation, the restrictions to be invoked in the cases of aliens to be supervised by the Attorney General pending deportation, the Commission is moved in part by the following from *Sentner* v. *Colarelli*, previously cited and since affirmed by the Supreme Court (May 20, 1957):

Beyond the terms of the Immigration and Nationality Act of 1952, evidence of the legislative purpose may be found in other statutes bearing on the same subject. It is well known that Congress has enacted many statutes in the field of subversive activities. It seems hardly likely that Congress by the general language of Section 242 (d), has authorized the Attorney General to add to these regulations any new restrictions he may desire, applying to individual deportable aliens. When Congress sought to confer upon the Attorney General the power to detain aliens without bail, on the ground that their freedom might be harmful to the national security, Congress set forth this power specifically. Section 242 (a). . . . If Congress were to confer any further power to regulate subversive or potentially subversive activities of deportable aliens, one would hardly expect the power to be conferred by general language of this sort. On the contrary, the record of Congressional regulations in this area indicates that Congress considers itself competent to regulate such activities, and considers that it has already dealt with such activities in a satisfactory manner.

Persecution Claim Pressed

Even as this report is being written, the Immigration and Naturalization Service is undertaking an exhaustive investigation of so-called section 243 (h) cases under which aliens under a final order of deportation make application for a stay based on the claim that to be returned to certain countries will subject them to physical persecution.

There is some evidence already that abuses have occurred.   The applications for section 243 (h) relief have enabled some aliens to delay deportation for a year or more.

The following, from a Commission survey report, illustrates abuses in this area:

(1) A Chinese seaman illegally in the United States was taken into custody in 1950. He was given a hearing and a warrant of deportation was issued in July 1951. By applying for adjustment of status under both the Displaced Persons Act of 1948 and the Refugee Relief Act of 1953, the alien was able to withhold deportation until 1955. In November 1955 the alien filed an application to stay deportation under Section 243 (h). In December 1956 the INS deferred action on that application until July 1, 1957. In January 1957 the alien left the United States of his own volition and went to Red China.

Unless it can be shown that the conditions in Communist China changed radically between November 1955 and January 1957, it appears that this alien's invocation of section 243 (h) was not made in good faith.

(2) A husband and wife, both Chinese aliens in the United States, and subject to a deportation order, applied for discretionary relief under section 243 (h). The husband, who was to be deported to Communist China, was granted his application and a stay was issued. The wife, who was to be deported to Formosa, was denied her application. Subsequently, the husband was interviewed by the Service when it was learned that he intended to leave the United States. He expressed in the interview that his intention was to depart with his family for Communist China.

This appears also to be a case where section 243 (h) was not used in good faith. The essential point of both these cases is the fact that a person will not go voluntarily to a country where he earnestly believes he will be subject to physical persecution.[194]

The Commission suggests that the results of the Service's inquiry into section 243 (h) cases should be made available to the Judiciary committees of the House and Senate as soon as it is completed.

The Commission finds that the admission to the United States of any large group of aliens en masse creates a security problem.

The Commission recommends that the parole provision of the Immigration and Nationality Act of 1952 be amended to clarify with greater specificity the intent of Congress relative to its use.

The Commission further recommends that the status of refugees who have been, or in the future will be, admitted under such emergency conditions should not be changed until sufficient time has elapsed to ensure the adequate screening of all such refugees.

The Commission also recommends that the Federal Government sponsor an appropriate Americanization program for all refugees ultimately granted permanent status.

When the revolutionary strife broke out in Hungary in October 1956, the United States, along with other nations of the free world, was faced with the problem of what had to be done with the thousands of refugees who poured across the border into Austria.

A White House directive from President Dwight D. Eisenhower, dated November 7, 1956, authorized the admission of 5,000 Hungarian refugees under the Refugee Relief Act of 1953. A second directive about December 1, 1956, authorized 21,500 admissions, some under the Refugee Relief Act, and the majority under the parole provision of the Immigration and Nationality Act of 1952. On or about January 3, 1957, there was a third directive authorizing continued processing under the parole provision. This was done because the Refugee Relief Act expressly provided that no immigrant visa could be issued thereunder after December 31, 1956.

Through April 25, 1957, the admissions totaled 31,806, with 6,284 being brought to the United States under the Refugee Relief Act and 25,522 under the parole provision. As of the same date, 125 had been returned

---

[194] Memorandum of interview by Commission's representative at Immigration and Naturalization Service, Feb. 4, 1957.

583

to Austria and 5 of these were security cases, according to the Immigration and Naturalization Service.

On January 1, 1957, the Vice President of the United States, Richard M. Nixon, submitted a report to the President based upon a personal inspection tour of the processing centers in Austria.

These are the pertinent excerpts from his report:

The quality of the people who fled Hungary is of the highest order. For the most part they were in the forefront of the fight for freedom and fled only when the choice was death or deportation at the hands of the foreign invaders or temporary flight to a foreign land to await the inevitable freedom for Hungary. The large majority are young people—students, technicians, craftsmen, and professional people. There are many family units, including a large number of children.

> .   .   .   .

The problem of checking the security backgrounds of the refugees is not as difficult as usual, due to the fact that in addition to the usual documentary evidence available in such cases, direct evidence is being volunteered by other refugees who are well-informed as to the identity of spies and agents in their communities.

I am convinced that if the screening process which is presently in effect is continued the Hungarian refugees who are admitted to the United States will present no significant risk of internal subversion in this country.

> .   .   .   .

Our policy should be based on the following principles:

> .   .   .   .

Until Congress passes appropriate legislation, admission of Hungarians to the United States should be continued under the parole procedures now in effect.

> .   .   .   .

An amendment to the Immigration and Nationality Act should be presented to the Congress for immediate consideration which would:

    (a) Regularize the status of Hungarian refugees brought into the United States under the parole procedure.

> .   .   .   .

It has been suggested that no change in the law is needed and that the whole problem of refugees from Communist countries can be handled adequately under the parole provisions of the present Act.

While the Attorney General has interpreted the parole provisions so as to cover the 15,000 Hungarian refugees who have been admitted up to this time, and while I believe that the applications of additional Hungarian refugees should be processed under that provision between now and the time the Congress has an opportunity to consider amendments to the Act, the circumstances and the limits under which this provision should be applied in the future should be spelled out by the Congress.

As the Attorney General has stated, neither he nor any other administrative official should have unlimited authority to admit aliens to the United States on a parole basis. It is obvious that such power, if arbitrarily used, could completely circumvent the basic purposes and objectives of the Immigration Law. (Emphasis supplied.)

Excerpts From President's Messages

In his state of the Union address to the Congress on January 9, 1957, the President said:

584

The recent historic events in Hungary demand that all free nations share to the extent of their capabilities the responsibility of granting asylum to victims of Communist persecution. I request the Congress promptly to enact legislation to regularize the status in the United States of Hungarian refugees brought here as parolees. I shall shortly recommend to the Congress by special message the changes in our immigration laws that I believe necessary in the light of our world responsibilities.

The President's special message went to Congress on January 30, 1957, and these are the pertinent excerpts from it:

Most of the refugees who have come to the United States have been admitted only temporarily on an emergency basis. Some may ultimately decide that they should settle abroad. But many will wish to remain in the United States permanently. Their admission to the United States as parolees, however, does not permit permanent residence or the acquisition of citizenship. I believe they should be given that opportunity under a law which deals both with any other like emergency which may hereafter face the free world.

First, I recommend that the Congress enact legislation giving the President power to authorize the Attorney General to parole into the United States temporarily under such conditions as he may prescribe, escapees selected by the Secretary of State, who have fled or in the future flee from Communist persecution and tyranny. The number to whom such parole may be granted should not exceed in any one year the average number of aliens who over the past 8 years have been permitted to enter the United States by special acts of Congress outside the basic immigration system.

Second, I urge the Congress promptly to enact legislation giving the necessary discretionary power to the Attorney General to permit aliens paroled into the United States who intend to stay here to remain as permanent residents. Consistent with existing procedures, provision should be made for submission of the cases to Congress so that no alien will become a permanent resident if it appears to the Congress that permanent residence in his case is inappropriate. Legislation of this type would effectively solve the problem of the Hungarian escapees who have already arrived and, furthermore, would provide a means for coping with the cases of certain Korean orphans, adopted children, and other aliens who have been granted emergency admission to this country and now remain here in an indefinite status. This should be permanent legislation so that administrative authorities are in a position to act promptly and with assurance in facing emergencies which may arise in the future.

Before proceeding to the discussion of the problems posed by the foregoing recital of the facts, the Commission acknowledges that the President and the present Administration has handled an extremely difficult and delicate situation with commendable regard for America's historic humanitarian principles.

We regard it as indisputable that the vigorous and forthright action by the President and the difficult decisions he was called upon to make were motivated by the determination to put America in the forefront of nations offering sanctuary to those fleeing from Communist oppression.

We hold strongly to the belief that Congress never intended that the parole provision should be used for the implementation of the Nation's foreign policy. Furthermore, review of the legislative intent in so far as the parole provision is concerned demonstrates conclusively that Congress had in mind individual emergencies and not "mass" emergencies.

Formal Opinion of General Counsel

The general counsel of this Commission analyzed the situation and submitted a formal opinion which is reprinted herewith:

Section 212 (d) (5) of the Immigration and Nationality Act of 1952 reads as follows:

> "The Attorney General may in his discretion parole into the United States temporarily under such conditions as he may prescribe for emergent reasons or for reasons deemed strictly in the public interest any alien applying for admission to the United States, but such parole of such alien shall not be regarded as an admission of the alien and when the purposes of such parole shall, in the opinion of the Attorney General, have been served the alien shall forthwith return or be returned to the custody from which he was paroled and thereafter his case shall continue to be dealt with in the same manner as that of any other applicant for admission to the United States."

The foregoing provision on its face purports to give the Attorney General discretion to parole under such conditions as he may prescribe for emergent reasons, or for reasons deemed strictly in the public interest, *any* alien applying for admission to the United States.

No restriction is placed upon the number of aliens that may be admitted by the Attorney General under this section.

The only case which has been found in which this section has been cited is *Chin Ming Mow et al.* v. *Dulles et al,* 117 F. Supp. 108. This case involved the application by the plaintiffs for an order restraining the Attorney General from executing an exclusion order. The Court mentioned the parole provision by stating:

> "The Attorney General has discretion to parole excluded aliens for emergent reasons or reasons deemed in the public interest under Section 212 (d) (5) of the Immigration Act of 1952, 8 U. S. C. A. 1182 (d) (5). Otherwise, there is no provision for release of an excluded alien, nor was there under the statutes existing prior to December 24, 1942. . . .
>
> "The application for a stay and bail in the instant suit places no reliance upon the foregoing provisions, as well as it might not."

The language used in this section would seem to be free from ambiguity, and it might be persuasively argued that the absence of ambiguity prevents resort to legislative history in order to ascertain the intent that the Congress had in respect to the subject matter of this section.

Recourse to legislative history, however, may be permissible in the light of a decision of the Supreme Court of the United States in *U. S.* v. *Public Utilities Commission of California,*[196] wherein the Court said:

> "Where the language and purpose of the questioned statute is clear, courts, of course, follow the legislative direction in interpretation. Where the words are ambiguous, the judiciary may properly use the legislative history to reach a conclusion. *And that method of determining congressional purpose is likewise applicable when the literal words would bring about an end completely at variance with the purpose of the statute.*" (Emphasis supplied.)

The legislative history of the Immigration and Nationality Act of 1952 includes report No. 1365, 82d Congress, 2d session, House of Representatives, report to accom-

---

[196] 345 U. S. 295, L. C. 815 (1952).

pany H. R. 5678, "to revise the laws relating to immigration, naturalization, and nationality, and for other purposes," which contains the following pertinent comment:

Discretionary authority

Having concluded that failure by an alien to meet the strict qualitative tests will disqualify him for admission to the United States, the committee is of the opinion that any discretionary authority to waive the grounds for exclusion *should be carefully restricted to those cases where extenuating circumstances clearly require such action and that the discretionary authority should be surrounded with strict limitations. . . .* (Emphasis supplied.)

.   .   .   .   .

"Discretionary authority is vested in the Attorney General in paragraph (5) of section 212 (d) to parole into the United States temporarily otherwise inadmissible aliens for emergent reasons or for reasons deemed strictly in the public interest. *Such parole shall not be regarded as an admission of the alien, and when the purposes of such parole shall have been served, the alien shall forthwith return or be returned to the custody from which he was paroled and shall continue to be dealt with in the same manner as any other alien applying for admission.* The provision in the instant bill represents an acceptance of the recommendation of the Attorney General with reference to this form of discretionary relief. The committee believes that the broader discretionary authority is necessary to permit the Attorney General to parole inadmissible aliens into the United States *in emergency cases, such as the case of an alien who requires immediate medical attention before there has been an opportunity for an immigration officer to inspect him, and in cases where it is strictly in the public interest to have an inadmissible alien present in the United States, such as, for instance, a witness or for purposes of prosecution."* (Emphasis supplied.)

The two specific illustrations set out in the report above quoted would seem to indicate that the parole provision was intended to cover isolated, individual cases as distinguished from large groups of individuals to be admitted thereunder en masse.

More persuasive than the history above quoted is the fact that in April 1953 at a time when the parole provision was already in the law, the President and the Congress deemed it necessary to enact special legislation to cover the admission of large numbers of escapees from the Iron Curtain through the adoption of the Refugee Relief Act of 1953.

The very purpose of the Refugee Relief Act was to make it possible to admit political refugees such as are presently being admitted under the parole provision.

The Congress, in the exercise of its legislative judgment, concluded that a limited number of refugees in limited areas should be granted admission for a limited period of time.

It would seem, therefore, that the parole provision of the 1952 Act is, in substance, being used to effectuate an extension of the Refugee Relief Act of 1953 for a period beyond that prescribed by the Congress.

In the circumstances above set forth, while a literal construction of the parole provision might justify the admission of more than 25,000 escapees thereunder, such construction would, in my judgment, in the language of the Supreme Court in *U. S.* v. *Public Utilities Commission,* supra, "bring about an end completely at variance with the purpose of the statute."

For the reasons above stated, I am of the opinion that the admission of the 25,000 or more Hungarian refugees is not validly authorized under the parole provision of the Immigration and Nationality Act of 1952.

The Commission is satisfied, on the basis of its own investigation, that the screening that took place, first in Europe and then upon arrival of the aliens at Camp Kilmer, N. J., did not meet acceptable standards. The magnitude of the project precluded it.

In making the statement, the Commission is mindful of the tremendous task that was thrust upon the responsible services without warning. Personnel rushed to Austria from other points in Europe and from the United States were compelled to deal with an extremely difficult situation. In the early stages they worked almost around the clock, but the sheer weight of numbers limited the application of security measures almost entirely to the securing of accurate background information as to each alien.

There is even serious doubt that there was full compliance with the requirements of the Refugee Relief Act as to those processed under it.

Section 1971–i (a) provides that no alien shall be issued a visa or be admitted unless there shall first have been a thorough investigation and written report made and prepared by such investigative agency as the President shall designate regarding his character, reputation, mental health, and eligibility under the Act. The President designated the Department of State to make these investigations and reports.

The Act also stipulates that no person shall be issued a visa or admitted unless complete information shall be available regarding the history of such person covering the period of at least two years immediately preceding his application. This provision, however, may be waived if there is concurrence by the Secretaries of State and Defense and such waiver is determined by them to be in the national interest. This waiver was executed on November 20, 1956.

John Rieger, who is in charge of the refugee relief program in the Department of State, was interviewed by a Commission representative on January 25, 1957. He admitted that no separate report had been prepared in each case. He stated there is a separate document pertaining to each case which consists of the application for visa and the visa itself. The interviews with the applicants were not recorded, reported, or written up in the ordinary cases. Whatever writing was done in questionable cases was not retained.

Mr. Rieger said he feels that the statutory requirement was satisfied by the particular manner in which they went about processing the applicants. He stated there should be some indication of the investigation in each file. He also stated some documentation had since been prepared in Vienna, but that no written reports were prepared at the time of actual processing. He also said that there is no document in these files similar to the regular report prepared in cases under the Refugee Relief Act other than those involved in the Hungarian emergency.

The Commission subsequently directed specific questions on this point to the Administrator of the Bureau of Security and Consular Affairs in the Department of State. Here are the questions and his replies:

Q. Was a thorough investigation made with regard to each of the six subject matters enumerated in Section 1971–i (a) of the Act in the case of each person fleeing Hungary on or after October 23, 1956, prior to the issuance of a visa?

A. The answer to this question depends upon the meaning of the term, "thorough investigation." To the best of the knowledge, information, and belief of the Administrator a thorough investigation was made but it must be conceded that the investigation was not as extensive for the Hungarians fleeing after October 23, 1956, as for those who fled earlier because of the waiver of the two-year history requirement and the impossibility of doing neighborhood and employment checks in Hungary. Except as waived, the investigations were made by the agency responsible; e. g., State Department as to character, reputation and personal history; Public Health Service as to physical and mental health. In each case, the consular officer and immigration officer, who jointly determined eligibility, had to be satisfied.

Q. Was a written report of the investigation prepared in each case handled during the emergency?

A. With respect to the Hungarians fleeing after October 23, 1956, the completed application form, the Public Health Service officer's report of examination, the completed questionnaire devised by the immigration officer, the security record checks with United States Government agencies and Austrian local police and security agencies, and the signature of the visa and immigration officers indicating that they had reviewed these items and interviewed the applicant were together treated by the consular and immigration officers as the written report in each case.

Q. Were the required investigations and reports made and prepared in each case handled under the Act other than the cases handled in the emergency after October 23, 1956?

A. Yes. In the cases other than Hungarian emergency cases the foregoing information and the additional information gathered in during the 2-year history were summarized in a singe document as the written report.

The Commission feels that these facts speak for themselves and serve to emphasize the importance of the Commission's recommendation that the Congress should not take any steps to "regularize" the status of the Hungarian parolees until sufficient time has elapsed to ensure they have been adequately screened.

When the Hungarian emergency was in its early phases, our Government negotiated a hasty agreement with the Austrian Government that any refugees rejected by the United States could be returned to Austria by July 1, 1957. The Commission has since been advised that subsequent negotiations have resulted in an agreement by the Austrian Government to permit refugees to be returned indefinitely.

The parole provision, as previously stated, provides that such parole shall not be regarded as an admission of the alien "and when the purposes of such parole shall, in the opinion of the Attorney General, have been served the alien shall forthwith return or be returned to the custody from which he was paroled."

Since the solution can come only from the Congress, this Commission urges prompt attention by both the administration and the legislative branch to the substance and the form that must be embodied in remedial legislation.

The Commission recommends that subsection (*a*) of section 340 of the Immigration and Nationality Act of 1952 be amended by striking out "upon affidavit showing good cause therefor" and inserting in lieu thereof "upon their own initiative or upon the filing with them of an affidavit showing good cause therefor." The Commission also recommends that a new sentence be added to subsection (*a*) to provide that "the complaint in any proceeding instituted under this section shall be sworn to by the United States attorney filing it."

The recommendation for this change in the present law is based upon the decision of the Supreme Court of the United States on April 30, 1956, in *United States* v. *Ettore Zucca*, reported in 351 U. S. 91.

The case originated in the southern district of New York where the defendant was naturalized on January 4, 1944. The Government moved to cancel on the ground that the defendant's naturalization had been illegally procured and that he concealed material facts and wilfully misrepresented others. The basis for the allegation was that Zucca had been a member of the Communist Party from 1925 to 1947.

The district court dismissed the case because of the Government's failure to file the affidavit required by the Act. The United States Court of Appeals for the Second Circuit affirmed the decision.

The Supreme Court granted certiorari because the third, fifth, and District of Columbia circuits had taken the same position in other cases as the second circuit in the Zucca case, while the seventh and ninth circuits favored the contrary position. Certiorari was also granted "because of the importance of the question in the administration of the Immigration and Naturalization Laws."

The statute in question (section 340 (a)) provides:

It shall be the duty of the United States attorneys for the respective districts, upon affidavit showing good cause therefor, to institute proceedings in any court specified in subsection (a) of section 310 of this title in the judicial district in which the naturalized citizen may reside at the time of bringing suit, for the purpose of revoking and setting aside the order admitting such person to citizenship and canceling the certificate of naturalization on the ground that such order and certificate of naturalization were procured by concealment of a material fact or by willful misrepresentation, and such revocation and setting aside of the order admitting such person to citizenship and such canceling of certificate of naturalization shall be effective as of the original date of the order and certificate, respectively: Provided, that refusal on the part of a naturalized citizen within a period of ten years following his naturalization to testify as a witness in any proceeding before a Congressional committee concerning his subversive activities, in a case where such person has been convicted for contempt for such refusal, shall

590

be held to constitute a ground for revocation of such person's naturalization under this subsection as having been procured by concealment of a material fact or by willful misrepresentation. If the naturalized citizen does not reside in any judicial district in the United States at the time of bringing such suit, the proceedings may be instituted in the United States district court in the judicial district in which such person last had his residence.

Contrary to the Government's contention, the Supreme Court held that this section was the only provision under which the United States Attorney could institute denaturalization proceedings, and that the filing of an affidavit showing good cause therefor was a mandatory procedural prerequisite to maintaining a suit. Thus, the court rejected the Government's argument that the United States Attorney, as a legal officer of the Government having inherent general authority to institute upon his own initiative any civil action on behalf of the United States, could, therefore, file a denaturalization complaint ab initio without any supporting affidavit. The court likewise rejected the Government's contention that the filing of a verified complaint by a United States Attorney satisfied the affidavit requirements of section 340 (a).

Chief Justice Warren delivered the majority opinion. Justices Reed and Minton joined Justice Clark in the dissent. Justice Clark said in his opinion that "my major objection to the decision today is the extreme burden placed on the Government in cases such as this," and he warned that the decision "may well submerge the denaturalization procedure established by Congress in a morass of unintended procedural difficulties."

That the Supreme Court decision in the Zucca case did not end the confusion is apparent in *Nowak* v. *United States*, 238 F. 2d 282, decided by the sixth circuit on November 26, 1956.

This case involved denaturalization proceedings against two aliens in which the sufficiency of the affidavit showing good cause filed pursuant to section 340 (a) of the Immigration and Nationality Act of 1952 was attacked in light of the Supreme Court decision in the Zucca case. The affidavit in the Nowak case consisted primarily of a recital under oath by the attorney from the Immigration and Naturalization Service of the pertinent facts appearing in the official records of the Service, which set out the grounds for denaturalization.

In its short opinion the Court upheld the validity of the affidavit as satisfying statutory requirements as interpreted by the Zucca case. The pertinent language of the Court on this point is worth noting:

In our judgment, the affidavit of an attorney of the Immigration and Naturalization Service of the United States Department of Justice reciting facts appearing in the official records, such as the affidavit filed in each of these cases, was an adequate compliance with the statutory requirements as interpreted in the Zucca case. The affidavit thus set forth sufficient evidentiary matters to show good cause for cancellation of the citizenship of each appellant. Fairly construed, the affidavit states facts appearing in the official records of the Immigration and Naturalization Service. It would be too stringent a requirement to hold that the good cause affidavit need embrace testimony of prospective witnesses. The affidavits in issue gave fair and sufficient notice of the facts charged as a basis for cancellation of citizenship of the appellants as to apprise them properly of the facts and reasons upon which their citizenship was sought to be revoked . . .

The annual report of the Immigration and Naturalization Service for the fiscal year ending June 30, 1955, discloses that investigators completed 5,346 denaturalization investigations and the citizenship of 197 naturalized citizens was revoked. Eight of the revocations involved fraudulent concealment of membership in subversive organizations.

The Commission believes that its recommendation for the amendment of Section 340 (a) will facilitate the administration of laws relating to denaturalization.

The Commission recommends that the Immigration and Nationality Act of 1952 be amended to require the Attorney General to report to Congress the number and circumstances of waivers granted by him and the Secretary of State jointly under section 212 (d) (4) on the basis of unforeseen emergency, reciprocity, and immediate and continuous transit.

The Commission further recommends that the Department of Justice should amend its regulations to make the Immigration and Naturalization Service solely responsible for the custody of all aliens traveling under bonded transit contracts negotiated by the authority of section 238 (d) and not permit the service to delegate such responsibility to any nongovernmental agency.

The Commission also recommends that all transportation companies that are parties to agreements executed under section 238 (d) should be required to maintain records covering aliens traveling in bonded transit for at least 3 years.

The Immigration and Nationality Act, in section 238 (d), authorized the Attorney General, on behalf of the United States, to enter into contracts, including bonding agreements, with transportation lines to guarantee the passage through the United States in immediate and continuous transit of aliens destined to foreign countries.

The Attorney General, by subsequent regulation, delegated his power to the Commissioner of Immigration.

These agreements are more generally known as "bonded transit" or "travel without visa" contracts. In tracing the history of, and experience with, these contracts the Commission has found that this particular section of the Act has been the source of much difficulty. Moreover, there has been a corresponding disregard for strict enforcement, not only of provisions of the Act itself, but the contracts the Act authorizes.

The standard contract in such cases (form I–426) specifies that the transportation line shall not accept for passage through the United States any alien who is inadmissible to the United States under the immigration laws, or who does not have confirmed connecting and onward reservations continuously from the point of foreign embarkation to at least the next country beyond the United States. If found inadmissible, the alien is to be returned to the port of embarkation at the expense of the line.

In its study of the bonded transit situation, the Commission has found that the waiver provisions of the Immigration Act have been invoked by both the Attorney General and the Secretary of State in a manner inimical to the security of the United States.

Under section 212 (a) (28), citizens of Russia and the satellite nations, with certain exceptions, are ineligible to receive visas and are excluded from the United States. Section 212 (a) (26) excludes aliens who are not in possession of valid nonimmigrant visas at the time of application for admission, or passports valid for six months from the date of expiration of the initial period of admission or contemplated period of stay.

But section 212 (d) (4) permits the waiver of the Section 212 (a) (26) requirement for travel documents by the Attorney General and the Secretary of State jointly on the basis of unforeseen emergency, reciprocity, or immediate and continuous transit under section 238 (d) contracts. And section 212 (d) (3) gives the Attorney General discretionary authority to admit temporarily any alien who is inadmissible under section 212 (a) (28) or who has been granted a waiver of the requirements of section 212 (a) (26).

The section 212 (d) (4) waiver has been made a blanket waiver, has been embodied in regulations and is applicable to all bonded transit cases.

The Commissioner of Immigration, under his delegation of authority from the Attorney General, permitted at least six contingents of Russians to enter the United States in bonded transit during the last half of 1956, by the exercise of his authority to waive excludability under section 212 (d) (3).

Furthermore, the Secretary of State permitted landings of Russians at points in the United States not designated as ports of entry for Soviet bloc nationals in violation of a National Security Council directive and joined with the Attorney General in a waiver of documentary requirements for Russian athletes returning from the Olympic games in Australia on the ground that it was an "unforeseen emergency." These athletes also landed in an area barred to Soviet bloc nationals by the National Security Council directive.

The explanation offered to this Commission was that this was all done to avoid creating incidents "which might be used unfavorably toward the United States."

The Commission has found, too, that the regulations which originally decreed that aliens traveling in bonded transit must be in custody of an officer of the United States at all times when not aboard an aircraft in flight through the United States were so loosely interpreted in stages so that the custody eventually was vested in the airlines.

One airline, in April 1956, included a bulletin in its passenger traffic manual of instructions to personnel which stated: "Guarding of TRWOV's during their United States transit is no longer required. No mention need be made of this fact unless it is known that the passenger is aware that this formerly was required when transiting the United States as a TRWOV."

The Commission has evidence that aliens traveling under this arrangement have been "lost in transit" and there are indications that it has been going on for several years. The issue received attention at meetings of staff representatives of the House and Senate Judiciary Committees and representatives of the Department of State and the Immigration and Naturalization Service on March 12 and April 23, 1953. The following appears in the record of the meeting of this group on March 12, 1953:

> The transit bond procedure authorized in sections 212 (d) (4) (C) and 238 (d) of the Act, and implemented in 8 CFR 212.3 (h) and 22 CFR 41.6 (h) was discussed. Certain complaints by the airlines were considered which on one hand stressed the heavy financial burden placed on them by the necessity of paying INS for guard service furnished under the bonding agreement, and on the other hand the relatively small number of aliens which during last year were "lost in transit." It was recognized, however, that the present transit procedure does present a security risk in that it affords an opportunity to otherwise inadmissible aliens to pass through the United States with considerable ease and to make contacts with subversive elements in this country. It was also pointed out that INS has turned back in recent weeks a considerable number of aliens who, upon arrival in this country, were found to be inadmissible and therefore not qualified for the transit bond procedure. It was also stressed that since the initiation of the transit bond procedure the volume of transit business by airlines has considerably increased so that the expense required for guard service appears relatively insignificant.
>
> The question will be further discussed at a subsequent meeting after INS has supplied data on the number of aliens turned back at the time of arrival at a United States port of entry and on the number of aliens who were "lost in transit."

At a meeting on April 23, 1953, the following observation was noted:

> The transit bond procedure authorized in sections 212 (d) (4) (C) and 238 (d) of the Act was again discussed. In line with a decision reached on March 12, INS reported that the number of aliens "lost" under this procedure is relatively small, but that the security risk involved in this procedure cannot be measured by the number of aliens "lost" but rather by the opportunity for contact with subversive elements in this country which is afforded aliens in transit under bond unless they are under guard of an officer of the United States whenever they are not in flight.
>
> In view of this observation it was unanimously decided not to consider any general modification of existing procedure, but in appropriate cases in the discretion of the immigration officer in charge it is believed use of the telephone by the transient alien may be permitted.[196]

Aliens "Lost in Transit"

The Commission also obtained evidence that Pan-American Airways "lost" three Chinese in December 1955, and four in October 1956. The three Chinese who disappeared in December, 1955, were enroute from Hong Kong to the Dominican Republic. At San Francisco they transferred from Pan-

---

[196] Report of a Senate Subcommittee of the Committee on the Judiciary, H. Rept. No. 1570, 84th Cong., 1st sess.

American Airlines to United Airlines and were flown to New York. There they disappeared. A later check with authorities of the Dominican Republic showed that they never arrived there and the results of this investigation indicated that their sponsorship was a sham and that they never intended to arrive in the Dominican Republic.

The four who disappeared in October 1956, in San Francisco, also came to the United States by way of Pan-American from Hong Kong, but they were apprehended subsequently and returned to Hong Kong. A representative of the airline advised the Commission that Pan-American was fined $2,000 and also had to pay the expenses incurred in rounding up these aliens and returning them to Hong Kong.

The Commission has made repeated efforts to ascertain from the Immigration and Naturalization Service the number of aliens "lost in transit" since January 1, 1953. The Service insists that there is no way for them to determine from its records the exact number of such cases. However, one official of the Service did volunteer the statement that the increase, if any, in the number of "abscondees" would be in the period of carrier custody.[197]

With the exception of the incident involving the Russian athletes in December, 1956, the other cases of travel by Russian contingents in bonded transit through the United States occurred in connection with the holding of an international conference of scientists in Mexico City in August. Two of these incidents involved Scandinavian Airlines, Inc. A group of nine Soviets arrived in Los Angeles without prior warning on August 20, 1956. This group had been issued regular C–3 transit visas which specified that they were to be admitted only at the port of entry in New York. This was apparently not noticed by airline employees at Copenhagen, Denmark. Los Angeles is a barred area for Soviet bloc nationals. The nine Soviet scientists departed for Mexico City after a 3-hour wait for clearance from the State Department.

A second group of nine Soviets was allowed to arrive in Los Angeles after a long exchange of messages between Copenhagen and Los Angeles had clarified that they would be traveling under bonded transit and after the Immigration and Naturalization Service has secured official permission from Washington. When the second group reached Copenhagen they, too, held C–3 transit visas calling for entry at the port of New York only. To avoid misunderstanding they were taken to the United States Embassy in Copenhagen where their visas were cancelled so that they could qualify for travel under the bonded transit procedure. After their arrival in Los Angeles, the State Department had to be contacted again and a waiver was obtained after a three-hour delay.

The main body of Russian scientists, however, transited the United States under arrangements negotiated with the Paris office of Pan-American. The Commission has been advised by a reliable source in the Government that the original travel plans by the Russian scientists called for them to be transported by KLM (Royal Dutch Airlines) to Montreal and then over the

[197] Commission on Government Security memorandum, Nov. 15, 1956.

United States into Mexico City. The Soviet secret police looked with dis-
favor on these arrangements because the reservations provided for small contingents spread over too many days. Consequently, Pan-American's office
in Paris on August 20th received a request for better accommodations from
a Czechoslovakian airline in Prague.

It is to be noted that Pan-American at the time was negotiating through the
Department of State for the privilege of extending its international routes to
Moscow. Pan American's Paris office arranged for the transportation of a
total of 40 Soviet scientists from Paris to New York under the bonded transit
procedure.

Pan-American's records indicate that the proposed travel of the Russians
by this method was communicated to the Immigration Service at 10 a. m. on
August 21st. Neither Pan-American in Paris nor New York had any information at that time as to the type of passports that had been issued to the
scientists. Pan-American was advised by the Immigration inspector at Idlewild Airport that he did not anticipate any trouble and that the worse that
would happen would be that the Russians would be placed in Immigration's
custody.

The Russians arrived in New York in three groups, 12 on August 22, 19 on
August 23 and 9 on August 24. The first contingent left Paris for New York
at 3 p. m., New York time, on August 21. It was not until almost an hour
later that Pan-American in Paris sent a teletype message to New York advising that all of the Russians were carrying civil passports valid for one month.

This information was communicated to the Immigration Inspector at Idlewild Airport who instructed Pan-American to transmit the information to
Washington. The Washington office of the Service approved the bonded
transit arrangement for the entire group of 40 at 5 p. m., on August 21, on
condition that each of the three contingents would be kept under guard while
on the ground in the United States between connecting flights.

The first and third contingents were routed to Mexico City from New York
by way of Chicago and Dallas with brief stopovers in both cities. The second
contingent was routed to Mexico City by way of Houston, Tex.

Contacts With Russian Embassy

The Commission obtained from Pan-American a memorandum which is
a chronological recitation of the handling of the three contingents after their
arrival in New York. This shows that, with the permission of the Immigration Service, the Russians were permitted to make telephone calls to and
receive calls from the Russian Embassy; that they were also allowed to take
pictures; that a representative of the Soviet Consulate visited with the first
group; that a representative of the Russian Embassy was permitted to visit
with the second group and to accompany them on a 4-hour bus tour of
New York City, and that the expenses for the handling of the Russians while

they were between flights in New York totaled $538.85 exclusive of transportation charges. All three groups were under the supervision of a private detective service.

The Commission has also been advised that the Russians sought to return to Europe from Mexico City under bonded transit with a planned stopover in New York City. The records of the Department of State show that when information as to the arrival of Russians in New York was first brought to the attention of the Department, it was made known to Immigration that the Department would be pleased if the Russians were refused admission and sent back to the port of embarkation. After receiving information that the Russians desired to stop over in New York on the trip home, the Department of State asserted that this could be done only if the Russians presented themselves at the American Embassy in Mexico City and applied for regular C–3 visas which would have required that they be fingerprinted. This the Russians refused to do and their return to Europe was accomplished through arrangements with airlines that did not transit the United States.

Eleven more Russian nationals arrived at Idlewild Airport in New York on August 30, 1956, via Scandinavian Airlines en route to an international industrial exhibit in Montreal. Eight of these had diplomatic passports and the remaining three had ordinary passports. None had visas. The holders of the diplomatic passports were permitted to continue to Montreal after an attache of the Russian Embassy in Washington had contacted the Department of State with a request for such permission on the plea that the plane had been "misdirected." The Immigration Service accordingly waived their inadmissibility pursuant to section 212 (d) (3). The three holders of the ordinary passports were ordered excluded and were put on a plane bound for Gander, Newfoundland, where they subsequently secured accommodations to Montreal.

Foresaw "Emergency" Months Ahead

With the reference to the arrival of Soviet bloc nationals returning to Russia from the Olympic games in Australia in December, the Commission received advance notice from Pan-American that the group of 18 would arrive in Los Angeles on December 12th. The Commission requested from the Department of State a report as to the circumstances under which this entry was being allowed. A reply was received on Decmber 28 which confirmed the information in the hands of the Commission that this contingent had been granted a waiver on the basis of "unforeseen emergency." The letter clearly shows that the Attorney General and the Secretary of State had "foreseen" that this "unforeseen emergency" was going to occur in December when the waiver was agreed to jointly by the Attorney General and the Secretary of State as far back as August 9th. The excuse offered was that "it did not appear to be in the best interests of the United States to refuse to cooperate

597

with the holding of the Olympics or to do anything which might be interpreted as interference with competitors to the American teams."

As in the case of the Russians in Mexico City, the December contingent
did not apply for visas and therefore they were not fingerprinted. In the
group were newspapermen, coaches, and trainers. While they were in Los
Angeles a tour of Hollywood was arranged by Pan-American before their
departure for Copenhagen.

The Commission has also secured from the Immigration Service a copy
of a memorandum which indicates that the Department of State authorized
the issuance of C–3 visas to six members of a Soviet agricultural mission for
transit through the United States. The Department of State imposed the
condition that during their stopover periods they be confined to the Honolulu
and Los Angeles airports which are not specifically approved as ports of entry
for Russian nationals. This occurred in November. The Immigration Service agreed to carry out these instructions provided that each of the aliens
concerned was given written notice at the time of the issuance of the visas
that the Department of State was requiring this confinement.

As a direct result of the chain of events in August, Pan-American on September 6th dispatched to all system traffic and sales managers a bulletin
prescribing new restrictions relative to the carrying to the United States
of aliens holding passports issued by a Communist government. The memorandum explained the conditions under which holders of diplomatic and
official passports would qualify but warned that the holder of a civil passport
does not qualify for transit without visa.

This occurred just about the time that this Commission was manifesting
considerable interest in the situation. In the course of the Commission's
investigation, we were continuously reminded by the Immigration Service,
representatives of airlines, and trade associations that there are no instances
of record where a subversive has ever gained admission to the United States
in bonded transit. This by no means discounts the possibility that it has
happened or that it can happen, even though there is no present official knowledge of such an occurrence. The Commission also desires to point out that
the airlines and the Immigration Service have both admitted that no
security check is made of airline or non-governmental agency personnel
assigned to maintain surveillance of aliens traveling in bonded transit.

The Commission has been furnished with information indicating that
airline revenue from bonded transit is currently running at a rate of approximately $5,000,000 annually. Immigration has supplied the Commission
with figures showing 13,251 such transits in 1951; 18,072 in 1952, and
16,989 in 1953. The Service has been unable to supply any figure for 1954
because these statistics were not kept separately in that year. For the
period of January 1, 1955, through October 1956 this type of traffic approached the figure of 30,000.

The attention of the Commission has also been directed to the fact that
the airlines are in the difficult position of not being in position to determine

598

the eligibility for admission to the United States of any alien seeking to travel in bonded transit. One official to whom the suggestion was made that a telephone call to the Embassy might produce such a decision retorted that this had been tried and that the airline was advised that such information was confidential.

The Commission has also explored with the Immigration Service the method of control on the verification of departures. The Service's Form I–419 is executed in triplicate with the original being on file at the port of entry; the other two copies are surrendered at the point of departure from the United States and these are forwarded to the port of entry to be matched with the original.

It might be pointed out that there is nothing to prevent the airline from turning in the duplicates of the I–419 which would indicate that there had been a departure even though the alien in transit got "lost" somewhere along the line. Unless there is verification by an immigration official that the alien was in fact on board the plane when it departed from the United States, there is no assurance that the alien would not disappear somewhere in transit.

Other Agencies Also Apprehensive

The Commission also has examined reports of other intelligence agencies which express apprehension about the way the bonded transit arrangement has been carried out. These reports stress that an alien boards a plane abroad without the Government being in possession of any fingerprints, photographs, biographical or other identity record which would assuredly present a problem in the case of any alien who is "lost" in transit.

Coincident with the Commission's active interest in the bonded transit situation, the Department of State dispatched a letter to the Commissioner of Immigration expressing deep concern about the effect of the bonded transit procedure on security of the United States.

A copy of this letter has been furnished to the Commission and is reprinted herewith.

It has come to the attention of this Department that a group of Soviet nationals, who recently arrived in the United States without visas, were permitted by your Service to proceed through the United States to Mexico under the so-called bonded transit procedure. This Department is deeply concerned about the effect this application of the bonded transit procedure may have on the security of the United States.

As you know, on the various occasions when the bonded transit procedure was the subject of discussions between your Service, this Department and the staff members of the Senate and House Subcommittee on Immigration, the unanimous view was expressed that every precaution must be taken to prevent any abuse of it which might endanger the security of the United States.

In the light of the more recent developments this Department has reached the conclusion that it can agree to a continuation of the documentary waiver now contained in 22 CFR 41.6 (b) (2) and 8 CFR 212.3 (h) only if it receives assurance from your

599

Service that nationals of Iron Curtain countries who are seeking admission as aliens in bonded transit shall remain in the custody of an officer of the United States at all times they are not aboard an aircraft which is in flight through the United States. This Department is of the opinion that the relinquishment of custody in such cases to custodians other than officers of the United States would constitute a severe risk to the security of the United States.

Considering the threat to the national security which may result from an abuse of the bonded transit procedure, I should like also to suggest that the entire question of bonded transit be reexamined by a committee of representatives of your Service and this Department in consultation with the appropriate committees of the National Security Council. This committee should examine, among other problems, in which type of cases the Commissioner has approved custody other than that by officers of the United States whenever such custody appeared not practicable. I am concerned about this problem in view of the language contained in paragraph 5 of form I–426, which suggests that in certain instances transit aliens are left to the supervision of the carrier without being in the actual custody of immigration officers or other custody approved by the Commissioner. Such arrangement, it would appear, would not live up to the terms of the joint waiver on which the present bonded transit procedure is based.

Also, I should like to suggest that the committee examine the relationship of the bonded transit procedure to the recommendation of the National Security Council that nationals of Iron Curtain countries be admitted only through certain designated ports.

As you know, this Department has agreed to the waiving of the visa requirement in the case of aliens in bonded transit with the understanding that such aliens be otherwise eligible for admission to the United States. I realize that this condition is contained in paragraph (e) of form I–426. In this connection the committee should examine the basis on which immigration officers have determined that aliens in bonded transit are not excludable, particularly under the provisions of sections 212 (a) (27), (28), and (29) of the Immigration and Nationality Act with respect to nationals of Iron Curtain countries.

In order to emphasize the condition of the documentary waiver, now contained in form I–426, I propose that the joint waiver be amended so as to express specifically that it should apply only if its beneficiaries are found admissible to the United States under the immigration laws.

While this Department, like your Service, has been making every effort to facilitate the flow of bona fide nonimmigrant travel to and through the United States, it appears that we should now reexamine whether steps taken to further this purpose have been or may be abused by those inimical to the United States.[198]

The Commission, in its efforts to secure all available information with reference to the travel of the various Russian contingents, has discovered that records of reservations and other papers material to our inquiry were not being retained by the respective airlines involved. One airline disposes of reservation records after 30 days and another does not maintain them beyond three months. For that reason the Commission has recommended that in the case of aliens traveling in bonded transit the regulations be amended to make it mandatory that any records pertaining to such accommodations and the flights involved be maintained for at least three years.

With reference to the responsibility for guarding of TRWOV aliens, the Commission sees no reason why the Immigration Service should be per-

[198] Letter from Robert F. Cartwright, Acting Administrator Bureau of Security and Consular Affairs, to General Swing, Commissioner of Immigration and Naturalization. This letter was received by General Swing, Oct. 3, 1956.

mitted to divest itself of the responsibility. The regulations accordingly should be amended to restore this arrangement to the original provision of 22 CFR, section 41.6, i. e., that "at all times such alien is not aboard an aircraft which is in flight through the United States he shall be in the custody of an officer of the United States." The original arrangement requiring the airlines to reimburse the United States for the guard service required by this regulation should also be restored.

The Commission has noted with considerable interest that the Department of State early this year agreed to a proposal made by the Immigration Service to exclude from waiver provisions entered into under section 212 (d) (4) (c) of the Immigration and Nationality Act, citizens and residents of the Union of Soviet Socialist Republic, Estonia, Latvia, Lithuania, Poland, Czechoslovakia, Hungary, Rumania, Albania, Peoples Republic of China, Peoples Democratic Republic of Korea (North Korea Regime), German Democratic Republic, and North Viet Nam (Viet Minh). However, the April 6th *Federal Register* published proposed changes in regulations regarding bonded transit which included, among other things, a plan to make the decision to impose custody discretionary with the district director of the Immigration Service at the port of entry.

The Commission inquired as to the reason for this change and asked to be advised if the Secretary of State and the Attorney General were concurring in the necessary waiver. Immigration was also asked to explain why Yugoslavia and Bulgaria were not included in the list of regions excluded from the use of bonded transit.

Under date of April 23, 1957, General Swing submitted the following reply:

The proposals to limit the ports of entry at which aliens may enter the United States without visas in direct transit and to exclude nationals of the Union of Soviet Socialist Republics and satellite countries from participation was the result of a careful study with the view toward strengthening the security aspects of the procedure. Background information usually available on other individual applicants for admission as nonimmigrants is usually unavailable in the direct transit cases, but the Service felt warranted in its assumption that nationals and residents of Iron Curtain countries would generally be inadmissible to the United States.

With reference to your question as to custody of direct transits, the proposal that the alien "remain in such custody as the district director having administrative jurisdiction over the port of entry may direct," would make no change in the present procedure, since the district director and officers serving under his supervision now determine the manner of custody of direct transit aliens.

The proposed publication of this waiver was taken up with the Department of State which concurred, in principle, although the details of the proposals have not been cleared. Final publication of the waiver will, of course, require a joint concurrence of the Departments of State and Justice.

At the request of the Department of State, Yugoslavia was not included in our original list of countries. Bulgaria was inadvertently omitted in the exchange of correspondence between this Service and the Department of State. The omission was subsequently discussed informally with a representative of that Department who expressed the view that Bulgaria should be included. This addition will be made.

601

Contrary to the statement that there has been concurrence by the Department of State, the Commission has been told that the Department does not agree with the recommended change as to discretion being given to the district director at the port of entry. The position of the Department of State is that such an arrangement "reflects a weakness of the safeguards presently enforced."

This Commission has reviewed the quality of the "safeguards presently in force." We believe that it has been clearly shown that the only adequate safeguards are those recommended by the Commission.

The Commission recommends that section 290 of the Immigration and Nationality Act of 1952 be amended to limit the central index of the Immigration Service to those aliens who enter the United States with travel documents.

Section 290 of the Act (8 U. S. C. 1360 (a)) provides:

There shall be established in the office of the Commissioner, for the use of security and enforcement agencies of the Government of the United States, a central index, which shall contain the names of all aliens heretofore admitted to the United States, or excluded therefrom, insofar as such information is available from the existing records of the Service, and the names of all aliens hereafter admitted to the United States, or excluded therefrom, the names of their sponsors of record, if any, and such other relevant information as the Attorney General shall require as an aid to the proper enforcement of this chapter.

The Immigration and Naturalization Service maintains a record of all aliens excluded from the United States, a record of all immigrants admitted to the United States, and a record of all "documented" nonimmigrants admitted to the United States. The Service also maintains a record of all aliens who enter the United States illegally and are subsequently discovered. It does not maintain a record of nonimmigrants admitted to the United States where documentary requirements are waived by regulations. The major instance where documentary requirements are waived is in the case of Canadian citizens and British subjects residing in Canada who enter the United States across the Canadian border.

Immigration feels that section 290 can be technically construed to require that the Service maintain a central index on nonimmigrants admitted where documentary requirements are waived by regulation. However, no attempt has been made to comply with section 290 in this regard because of the tremendous difficulties involved. It has been estimated that any attempt to comply with this provision would cost about $2,000,000 per year. In the year ended June 30, 1956, there were 26,097,673 crossings of the Canadian border by aliens in the aforementioned classes. In view of the absence of adequate appropriations and the lack of the necessary manpower, the Commission recognizes the impracticability of maintaining the central index under a literal interpretation of Section 290.

602

The Commission recommends that the function of issuing visas to alien crewmen be transferred from the Department of State to the Department of Justice, consistent with our previous recommendation for the transfer of all visa functions in this manner, and that the immigration service fix a definite date, as intended by Congress, by which all foreign crewmen will be required to have individual visas.

One of the more difficult problems in connection with the administration of immigration laws has always concerned the handling of alien seamen. For the past several years, more than one million alien seamen entered United States ports. The Immigration Service has had the continuing problem of dealing with alien crewmen who desert their ships or otherwise overstay the period for which they had been allowed sojourn in the United States. The number of deserting alien seamen by years follows:

1950	2,410
1951	3,591
1952	3,021
1953	2,317
1954	1,963
1955	2,376
1956	2,968

Section 221 (f) of the Immigration and Nationality Act of 1952 (8 U. S. C. section 1201 (f)) provides:

Each nonimmigrant shall present or surrender to the immigration officer at the port of entry such documents as may be by regulation required. In the case of an alien crewman not in possession of any individual documents other than a passport *and until such time as it becomes practicable to issue individual documents,* such alien crewman may be admitted, subject to the provisions of this part, if his name appears in the crew list of the vessel or aircraft on which he arrives and the crew list is visaed by a consular officer, but the consular officer shall have the right to exclude any alien crewman from the crew list visa. (Emphasis supplied.)

An attempt was made to require all foreign crewmen to have individual visas by July 1, 1955.[199] This requirement was removed [200] and a new target date of December 31, 1956, was discussed but never implemented by an official order. As of July 31, 1955, 42,921 visas in this classification had been issued.

Early in this session of Congress an administration-sponsored bill was introduced which would amend section 221 (f) to eliminate the requirement for individual documents on the ground that this requirement of the Act has proved to be difficult to administer, unduly burdensome, and unnecessary. This Commission believes that the views expressed by the special subcommittee of the Committee on the Judiciary, House of Representatives, as re-

[199] 19 F. R. 4504, June 16, 1954.
[200] 20 F. R. 1097, Feb. 22, 1955.

flected in House Report No. 1570, 84th Congress, 1st Session, are more persuasive. This report said:

The fact that enforcement of the requirement of individual visas for crewmen has proved impracticable affords reason to question the wisdom of the continuation of the specific requirement in the law. On the other hand, the consideration of the security and well-being of this country, which led to the inclusion of such requirement in the statute, remain more vital than ever at the present time. An alternative to issuance of individual visas could be a system of clearance of crewmen in United States ports. This system would involve the issuance of revocable permits which would be valid for repeated entries over a stated period of time. The requirement of the visaed crew list need not be changed under such a system.

The Commission believes that a substantial security problem is involved and that an acceptable system for the issuance of visas or some similar type of documentation can best be handled by the Immigration Service in the performance of its duties at the various ports of entry.

The Commission finds that the present procedures for the investigation of applicants for immigrant and nonimmigrant visas are adequate to protect the security of the United States, but, consistent with the previous recommendation for transfer of the visa functions, the Commission recommends that the Immigration Service be given the responsibility for investigation of applicants for visas.

The Commission finds that personnel having authority to review, revoke, or invalidate immigrant and nonimmigrant visas appear to be adequately trained in security matters as a result of recent training programs. Consistent with the previous recommendation for the transfer of the visa function to the Department of Justice, the Commission recommends continued emphasis on security matters in the training of visa personnel and an adequate training program for personnel engaged in the discharge of such functions.

OPERATION

The Commission recommends that the present provisions of the Immigration and Nationality Act of 1952, relative to the fingerprinting of immigrant and nonimmigrant aliens, be continued in force in view of its other recommendation that all Americans be fingerprinted when applying for passports.

In the case of immigrants coming to the United States, they are admitted as potential cititzens. It is advisable, therefore, that fingerprints be secured to facilitate the check on possible subversive or criminal activities. The Commission is aware of the agitation that has prevailed for some time to relax the fingerprinting requirements as applied to nonimmigrant aliens on the plea that this would facilitate travel. It has been alleged that the fingerprinting of aliens is discriminatory. No such claim may be made in the future since the Commission's recommendations would require in this regard of the aliens no more than is required of citizens of the United States. The Commission does not share this view on the premise that it would represent a serious weakening of security measures.

The present Act permits waiver in the discretion of the Secretary of State of fingerprint requirements for certain diplomatic personnel and officials of foreign governments. As an example of the exercise of this discretion, the Department of State on February 1, 1957, amended its regulations to eliminate the fingerprinting requirement in connection with C–3 visas issued to a foreign government official, members of his immediate family, attendant servant, or personal employees in transit through the United States.

The Commission finds that the present laws, regulations and procedures governing the admission of diplomatic personnel and officials of foreign governments appear to be adequate under the circumstances of international practices to protect the security of the United States if they are rigidly enforced. The Commission recommends discontinuance of the practice of admitting artists and others under the guise of their being official government employees. This practice appears to be in violation of the law.

Ample evidence exists that diplomatic missions of Russia and some of her satellites are not channels for peaceful international relations, but are merely new avenues of intrigue. An address by Attorney General Herbert Brownell before the Inter-American Bar Association Conference in Dallas, Tex., on April 17, 1956, effectively summarized Russian diplomatic activities. The address contained the following:

The spy and the spy ring are the forerunners of revolutionary and subversive movements working through local branches of the International Communist Party, through front organizations, and, as experience has demonstrated, through Iron Curtain embassies and commercial establishments. The spy system of the Communist Party of the Soviet Union extends into all of our countries. Here and there some frightened defector, seeking asylum from some alert government officer, uncovers a bit of its tangled web. You may remember the spy ring exposed in Canada in 1945 when Igor Gouzenko, a code clerk in the Soviet Embassy in Ottawa, Canada, set off a series of exposures which revealed how the Soviet Union was able to steal atom secrets during World War II. Later, in 1954, Lattimer Petrov, the Third Secretary in the Soviet Embassy in Canberra, revealed how, for more than ten years, the Soviet Union had operated an espionage network in Australia, a network which operated out of the Soviet Embassy, and which reported directly to Moscow. More recently, alert representatives of the Iranian Government captured a Major Skuzentzov, the Deputy Soviet Military Attaché of the Soviet Embassy in Teheran, in the very act of receiving secret Iranian air force documents for copying and transmission to Russia. You will observe that each of these spy rings was being operated out of the Soviet Embassy. This accounts for the intense interest of the Governments of the Soviet Bloc in locating new diplomatic establishments in as many of the capitals of the world as possible.

In support of the recommendaton for discontinuance of the practice of admitting Soviet Bloc nationals in the guise of official government employees, the Commission cites the following memorandum received November 13, 1956, from the Commissioner of Immigration:

The following are some nationals of Russia or satellite countries who have entered the United States with official visas issued by the Department of State and available information does not indicate that they are in the category of persons normally considered as government officials.

1. *Soviet pianist, wife, and interpreter.*
   Purpose: Giving concerts in the United States.
   Group included: Pianist, wife, and interpreter.
   Sponsored by: Columbia Artists, Inc., New York.
2. *Soviet cellist.*
   Purpose: Concert tour.
   Group included: Russian cellist, accompanist, and interpreter.
   Sponsored by: Columbia Management Artists, Inc.
3. *Five Soviet Baptists.*
   Purpose: To attend convention of Baptist World Alliance.
   Group included: Soviet churchmen.
   Sponsored by: Baptist World Alliance.
4. *Eight Soviet churchmen.*
   Purpose: Tour of the United States.
   Group included: Church officials.
   Sponsored by: National Council of Churches.
5. *Polish pianist.*
   Purpose: For a recital tour.
   Group included: Pianist and husband.
   Sponsored by: National Concert and Artist Corporation, New York.

The number of foreign government officials who have been admitted for the years ending June 30, 1952 to June 30, 1956, are as follows:

1952	1953	1954	1955	1956
22,267	24,502	23,095	26,288	[1] 27,109

[1] Table 3, Aliens admitted by classes under the immigration laws: Years ended June 30, 1952 to 1956, United States Department of Justice, Immigration and Naturalization Service.

For the year ending June 30, 1955, 273 Russian government officials were admitted into the United States. During the same period of time 385 government officials from Yugoslavia, 88 from Czechoslovakia, 68 from Hungary, 5 from Latvia, 11 from Estonia, 4 from Lithuania, 202 from Poland, 56 from Rumania, and 5 from Bulgaria also were admitted.[201]

For the year ending June 30, 1956, 311 Russian government officials were admitted to the United States. During the same period 309 government officials entered from Yugoslavia, 112 from Czechoslovakia, 72 from Hungary, 7 from Latvia, 7 from Estonia, 13 from Lithuania, 216 from Poland, 101 from Rumania, and 2 from Bulgaria.[202]

[201] Table 16, nonimmigrant aliens admitted, by classes, under the immigration laws and country or region of birth: Year ended June 30, 1955, United States Department of Justice, Immigration and Naturalization Service.
[202] Nonimmigrant aliens admitted by classes under the immigration laws and country or region of birth: Year ended June 30, 1956, United States Department of Justice, Immigration and Naturalization Service.

The Commission finds that the present laws, regulations, and procedures governing the admission of personnel of certain foreign governments accredited to or employed by international organizations to the United States appear to be adequate under the circumstances of international practices to protect the security of the United States if they are rigidly enforced.

There have been instances where personnel of certain foreign governments accredited to or employed by international organizations have acted from time to time as espionage agents on behalf of their government. During the past year instances of espionage were uncovered involving Russians employed by the United Nations. When the cases were brought to the attention of the Secretary-General, these employees were summarily dismissed. One of those expelled was seeking classified information from an employee of an aviation corporation manufacturing two of the latest American fighter planes.

"The term 'international organization' means any public international organization which has been designated by the President by Executive order as being entitled to enjoy the privileges, exemptions, and immunities provided for in the International Organizations Immunities Act (59 Stat. 669)." [203]

Approximately twenty organizations have been designated by the President as International Organizations entitled to enjoy the privileges, exemptions and immunities conferred by the International Organizations Immunities Act.

For the year ending June 30, 1955, 6,003 international representatives entered the United States. Included in this figure were 250 from Russia, 3 from Bulgaria, 2 from Estonia, 74 from Czechoslovakia, 7 from Hungary, 2 from Latvia, 1 from Lithuania, 82 from Poland, and 10 from Rumania.

For the year ending June 30, 1956, 5,190 international representatives entered the United States. Included in this figure were 225 from Russia, 15 from Bulgaria, 52 from Chechoslovakia, 11 from Hungary, 1 from Latvia, 4 from Lithuania, 63 from Poland, 10 from Rumania, and 37 from Yugoslavia.

The Commission finds that the present procedure which permits admission to the United States of former Communists under certain conditions adequately safeguards the security of the United States.

The present regulations of the Department of State stipulate that in the case of any alien who claims that his past or present membership in the Communist Party was involuntary or who claims to be a defector, no visa

---

[203] 22 CFR 41.90 (h).

607

shall be issued until the consular officer has submitted to the Department of State a request for an advisory opinion. Section 212 (a) (28) (I) of the Immigration and Nationality Act (66 Stat. 163) is the pertinent statute covering cases of this kind. These are the provisions:

(I) Any alien who is within any of the classes described in subparagraphs (B), (C), (D), (E), (F), (G), and (H) of this paragraph because of membership in or affiliation with a party or organization or a section, subsidiary, branch, affiliate, or subdivision thereof, may, if not otherwise ineligible, be issued a visa if such alien establishes to the satisfaction of the consular officer when applying for a visa and the consular officer finds that (i) such membership or affiliation is or was involuntary, or is or was solely when under sixteen years of age, by operation of law, or for purposes of obtaining employment, food rations, or other essentials of living and where necessary for such purposes, or (ii) (a) since the termination of such membership or affiliation, such alien is and has been, for at least five years prior to the date of the application for a visa, actively opposed to the doctrine, program, principles, and ideology of such party or organization or the section, subsidiary, branch, or affiliate or subdivision thereof, and (b) the admission of such alien into the United States would be in the public interest. Any such alien to whom a visa has been issued under the provisions of this subparagraph may, if not otherwise inadmissible, be admitted into the United States if he shall establish to the satisfaction of the Attorney General when applying for admission to the United States and the Attorney General finds that (i) such membership or affiliation is or was involuntary, or is or was solely when under sixteen years of age, by operation of law, or for purposes of obtaining employment, food rations, or other essentials of living and when necessary for such purposes, or (ii) (a) since the termination of such membership or affiliation, such alien is and has been, for at least five years prior to the date of the application for admission actively opposed to the doctrine, program, principles, and ideology of such party or organization or the section, subsidiary, branch, or affiliate or subdivision thereof, and (b) the admission of such alien into the United States would be in the public interest. The Attorney General shall promptly make a detailed report to the Congress in the case of each alien who is or shall be admitted into the United States under (ii) of this subparagraph; . . .

The Department of Justice has no jurisdiction on the issuance of advisory opinions. This is strictly an administrative matter within the Department of State. However, there are some factors which require liaison between the Visa Office and the Department of Justice. For instance, if an alien has been deported at one time and makes application for a visa, the permission for his reapplication for admission to the United States must come from the Immigration and Naturalization Service. Without this permission, the consular office has no authority to issue a visa. The other case is where an alien applies for a visa to visit the United States. If, in the opinion of the Consul, such alien is ineligible for a visa because of the provisions of section 212 (a) (28), the consul may not issue the visa until the Attorney General has given the authority for temporary admission as provided in section 212 (d) (3) of the Act. The same also applies with respect to aliens claiming to be defectors, or who claim past or present membership in any Communist Party is or was involuntary.

Advisory opinions are rendered in both immigrant and nonimmigrant visa cases. When a consular officer submits a request for an advisory opinion, the request will contain the consular officer's views and recommendations. While the opinions are considered to be advisory and, in fact, do not contain specific instructions as to the course of action to be pursued, the consular officer, as a matter of practice, will consider the advisory opinion binding. If he seriously disagrees with the nature of the advisory opinion, he has the right to submit the views he may hold and any clarifying information which might tend to reverse the opinion but there is no instance of record where a consular officer has decided a case in a manner contrary to the reasoning of the opinion. It may also be noted here that the Visa Office periodically sends to all posts printed copies of advisory opinions for the guidance of consular officers who may rely upon the facts set forth in such opinions as precedents in cases of a similar nature they may be called upon to decide themselves.

The consular officer, in his request for such an (advisory) opinion, will forward to the Visa Office all of the derogatory information, investigative reports, a report as to his interrogation of the alien, together with comments as to the eligibility or ineligibility of the applicant and his recommendations. If a security check in the United States is indicated on the basis of the consular officer's report, a request for such a check goes to the State Department, Office of Security, which maintains liaison with FBI, CIA, ONI, AEC, and G–2. The advisory opinion will also embody reports from the political, economic, biographical, and intelligence research areas of the State Department. Thus, the consular officer, when he receives the advisory opinion, has the benefit of all possible information from governmental agencies in the United States as a guide to help him in making his final evaluation.

The system of safeguards employed in cases where visas are refused very likely can be considered to be controlling with reference to revocations. An explanation of the action taken by the consular officer on refusals is therefore in order. The consul sends a written report on refusal in quadruplicate to the Visa Office security branch. This contains the biographical data and the grounds for refusal; one copy is retained by the Visa Office security branch, one copy goes to the Office of Security in the State Department, one copy is also sent to the FBI, and the fourth copy goes to the Immigration and Naturalization Service. If considered advisable, a copy also goes to CIA. The consular officer also sends lookout cards to the central clearance office in the country of application, the country of birth, the country of present nationality, the country of present residence and countries of past residence which constitute alerts against the possibility that the alien may try to secure a visa from some other consular post. If the information on the alien is considered to be exceptionally serious, Visa Office security will notify all posts that if the alien shows, action on his case is to be suspended and Visa Office security is to be notified at once.

In one category (applicants who may presently receive visas but who previously were denied visas for reasons of security) would be included former Nazis, former Fascists, collaborationists, black marketeers, etc. Visas would be issued in such cases if the consular officer was satisfied on the basis of new investigations that the particular alien does not now represent a threat to the security of the United States. It should be emphasized that this does not apply with reference to membership in the Communist Party or any organization or association that is or has been Communist controlled. The test in the Communist cases is whether or not there was membership "at any time." Thus, aliens claiming that their membership was involuntary, or the so-called defector type, would be handled in accordance with the procedure previously outlined.

It may be well at this point to review briefly the general activity in the security branch of the Visa Office. Of the approximately 1,000 miscellaneous cases a month, between 450 and 550 are actual opinion requests. Included in the run of miscellaneous matters are cases where the consul will request advice on the complexion of organizations as a guide to his decision as to issuance or rejection of a visa. The Visa Office security branch will check such cases with the intelligence research, political, and security divisions of the State Department and will also check against the Attorney General's list.[204]

Occasions have arisen where an alien has been inscribed in a Communist organization by some third party without his knowledge. As a case in point, this is known to have been done by a foreign manufacturer dealing with a Communist union. The manufacturer would furnish the names of certain employees to the union and would pay their dues but the persons might not know that this occurred.

The Commission finds that the temporary admission of alien students and exchange aliens under present procedures does not create a security problem for the United States.

The Commission has received from the Immigration Service the following figures showing the admissions of alien students and exchange aliens for the fiscal years ending June 30, 1952 through June 30, 1956:

	1952	1953	1954	1955	1956
Students	8,613	13,533	25,425	27,192	28,013
Exchange Aliens		12,584	15,260	16,077	17,204

For the year ending June 30, 1955, 27,192 aliens were admitted as students. These students come from the following countries:

Austria	78	Germany	306
Belgium	56	Greece	287
Bulgaria	5	Hungary	75
Czechoslovakia	57	Ireland	14
Denmark	30	Italy	191
Estonia	15	Latvia	8
Finland	35	Lithuiana	14
France	223	Netherlands	188

[204] Visa Office response to Commission on Government Security interrogatory, Sept. 21, 1956.

Norway	107	India	532
Poland	100	Israel	127
Portugal	33	Japan	462
Rumania	56	Palestine	69
Spain	251	Philippines	541
Sweden	28	Other Asia	2,205
Switzerland	70	Canada	5,606
United Kingdom:		Mexico	3,518
England	280	West Indies	3,942
North Ireland	16	Central America	1,950
Scotland	31	Other North America	95
Wales	7	South America	4,069
U. S. S. R	32	Africa	333
Yugoslavia	42	Australia and New Zealand	90
Other Europe	165	Other countries	295
China	558		

Mr. Russell L. Riley, director of the International Educational Exchange Service, Department of State, was interviewed on February 13, 1957. The interview was arranged for the purpose of determining whether the international educational exchange program had experienced any security difficulties.

Mr. Riley said that there has not been a single case where any person brought to this country under the program has ever been returned to his native country for security reasons. In addition, Mr. Riley reported that he had reviewed approximately 6,000 cases and had requested consular posts abroad to furnish him with any information indicative of an anti-American attitude or expression by any of the persons who had been in the United States under the program. The net result, according to Mr. Riley, was eleven cases, and most of the 11 were reported to have made statements about the United States that were critical in nature but the subject matter of such criticism was, for the most part, innocuous. As an example, one person had been critical of the tremendous output of comic books and magazines.

Mr. Riley also made the following statement:

Foreign nationals coming to this country under the Department of State's international educational exchange program have presented no serious security problems because of the screening process which takes place before they are selected. Before any person is given a grant the investigative agencies whose services are available to the United States Government are requested to check to determine whether or not derogatory information is available on the proposed grantee. On the basis of a review of the results of these inquiries a determination is made as to whether the awarding of a grant would not be prejudicial to the interests of the United States. It should also be recalled that immigration regulations preclude the issuance of visas to individuals who do not meet necessary security requirements.

While it is not our practice to assume that all applicants who meet visa requirements are automatically eligible for grants, it is our practice that any foreign national who does not meet visa requirements is automatically ineligible to receive a grant.

611

ADDITIONAL FINDINGS

The Commission finds that the temporary admission into the United States of certain representatives of the foreign press, radio, film, or other information media creates a security problem.

It is known that this particular field has been used as a cover for Soviet espionage activity. Nevertheless, this is a calculated risk the United States must take inasmuch as the United States wishes the representative of its press, radio, film, or other information media to have similar privileges in other countries.

The Commission finds that waiver provisions of the Immigration and Nationality Act relating to immigrants have not been invoked in a manner inimical to the security of the United States.

The Commission's study has revealed no evidence of abuse of the few authorizations for waivers applying to immigrants.

The Commission believes that the present provisions of the Immigration and Nationality Act relative to the registration of both immigrants and nonimmigrants should be continued.

The Commission believes that the relevant sections of the Immigration and Nationality Act dealing with security measures (8 U. S. C., section 1182, (a), (27), (28), and (29)) adequately protect the security of the United States.

The Commission believes that the penalty provided in section 276 of the Immigration and Nationality Act for reentry or attempted reentry into the United States of an arrested, excluded, or deported alien, is adequate and should not be changed.

The Commission finds that the present laws and regulations relative to naturalization are adequate for the protection of the security of the United States.

Criminal Statutes

Introduction

The Commission, pursuant to its mandate under Public Law 304,[1] reviewed the provisions of all applicable statutes bearing upon national security. It is the purpose of this chapter to sum up briefly those criminal statutes and other provisions which the Commission believes after due consideration to be of primary importance in the security field. For the most part they have been codified and placed in Title 18 of the United States Code.

There are certain criminal statutes which per se are concerned with specifically punishing acts posing serious threats to our national security. Included in this class are the treason, espionage, sabotage, and sedition statutes, in addition to the singularly important penal sections of the Atomic Energy Act of 1954, as amended. There are other criminal statutes of secondary importance in the security field, which when the occasion arises are readily adaptable to the prosecution of individuals committing criminal acts having important security considerations. In this category there are included the general conspiracy statute, and the false statement, perjury, and theft of Government property statutes. In addition to a short résumé of the above criminal provisions, there is also included the Commission's legislative recommendation punishing as an offense the unlawful disclosure of vital defense information.

There is another class of penal provisions which do not stand alone as primary criminal statutes but are adjunct penalties designed to insure compliance with purposes of a parent or principal statute. In this group are the penal provisions accompanying the laws governing the issuance of passports; the Foreign Agents Registration Act of 1938, as amended; section 9 (h) of the Labor Management Relations Act of 1947 calling for the filing of non-Communist affidavits by union officials; and registration provisions of the Subversive Activities Control Act of 1950, as amended. Where these laws have not been dealt with in other sections of this report, they will be touched upon in this chapter.

In addition to the criminal statutes, some treatment will be given to two other subjects of vital importance in the security field. The first of these is the procedural device provided by the Immunity Act of 1954, which authorizes a grant of absolute immunity from future criminal prosecution to witnesses reluctant to testify on fifth amendment grounds before con-

---

[1] 84th Cong., 69 Stat. 595 (1955) ; Public Law 786, 70 Stat. 634 (1956).

,gressional investigating committees or in judicial or grand jury proceedings. The second topic is the controversial subject of wiretapping. Attention will be given to its present legal status, and to the Commission's recommendations to authorize Federal law-enforcement officials under proper safeguards to wiretap in security cases.

PRIMARY CRIMINAL STATUTES

A. Treason

The common ancestor or forerunner of all Federal criminal statutes in the security field is the constitutionally defined offense of treason.[2] To be guilty of the high crime of treason, a citizen must do either one or both of two things. He must either levy war against the United States or adhere to their enemies giving them aid or comfort. Consequently, no other acts than those defined in the Constitution can be declared by statute or otherwise to be treasonable. Complementing this restrictive definition of treason is a self-contained rule of evidence which simply states that "no person shall be convicted of treason unless on the testimony of two witnesses to the same overt act, or on confession in open court."[3] However, Congress does have the constitutional authority to fix the punishment, and in 18 U. S. C. 2381 is found the statutory definition of treason carrying a possible death penalty.[4] In the succeeding section, 18 U. S. C. 2382, Cogress has defined and punished the crime of "misprision of treason" as the concealing and failing to disclose to proper authorities by any person owing allegiance to the United States any act of treason against the United States of which such person shall have had knowledge.

Due to the limited and restrictive definition of treason, no such crime as a constructive treason can be included thereunder. This was so determined in the earliest judicial expression on this subject by the Supreme Court. In the case of *Ex parte Bollman*, the Court, speaking through Mr. Chief Justice Marshall, confined the meaning of levying war against the United States to actual engagement and not to preparation or conspiracy to levy war.[5] While recognizing the intentional restriction imposed by the Constitution, Chief Justice Marshall in this same case pointed the way for Congress to deal legislatively with those acts akin to treason when he stated:

Crimes so atrocious as those which have for their object the subversion by violence of those laws and those institutions which have been ordained in order to secure the peace

---

[2] Art. III, sec. 3, U. S. Constitution.
[3] Ibid.
[4] Ch. 645, 62 Stat. 807 (1948).
[5] 4 Cranch 75 (1807).

and happiness of society, are not to escape punishment because they have not ripened into treason. The wisdom of the legislature is competent to provide for the case; . . ."

In this regard Congress has taken appropriate action by enacting other criminal statutes attacking the various forms of subversive activity, treasonable in nature and equally as destructive of national security.

B. Espionage and Related Statutes

Prominent among the statutory offenses enacted by Congress and relating to matters of national security are the espionage laws found in title 18, sections 791 through 798.[7] The activities covered therein by these sections go far beyond those limited to any dictionary definition or popular concept of the term "espionage."

The obtaining of national defense information for the benefit or use of foreign nations or its subsequent transmittal is the primary target of the espionage laws. However, equally as criminal is the conspiracy and attempt to do any of the above as well as the receiving or obtaining of national defense information with reason to believe that such information was to be used in violation of the espionage laws. In addition, the willful refusal to turn over national defense information upon proper demand by lawful authority and the loss or compromise of national defense information through gross negligence is also included in the statutory proscription. The penalties prescribed for violation of the espionage laws are severe. A conviction of transmitting national defense information to a foreign nation in violation of section 784 carries a possible death penalty or an alternative maximum life sentence. No distinction is made between war and peacetime espionage under this section. Other penalties call for prison terms up to 10 years or a fine up to $10,000 or both.

Perhaps the most notorious case of recent origin prosecuted under the espionage laws was the infamous Rosenberg affair. In this connection, it should be noted that, while the Rosenbergs engaged in the trafficking of atomic energy secrets during the embryonic period of the development of the atomic bomb in World War II, their activities continued until 1950. As a result, some of their later activities were substantial enough to support an indictment charging violations of the Atomic Energy Act of 1946, as amended.[8] Former section 16 of the act defined and punished as a crime any espionage dealing strictly with atomic energy information classified under the term "restricted data." To avoid any conflict with applicable

[6] Ibid., p. 126.

[7] 62 Stat. 736, 737, 738 (1948), 65 Stat. 719 (1951), 67 Stat. 133 (1953), 70 Stat. 216 (1956).

[8] Formerly 42 U. S. C. A. 1810, Ch. 724, 60 Stat. 755 (1946), Ch. 633, 65 Stat. 692; amended by act August 30, 1954, Ch. 1073, 68 Stat. 958, 959, with similar provisions now found in 42 U. S. C. A. secs. 2274, 2275, and 2276. Penalties prescribed carry possible death penalty or life imprisonment upon the recommendation of a jury, with the alternative sentence of a prison term up to 20 years and a maximum fine of $20,000. Other penalty provisions involve a maximum sentence of 10 years and a $10,000 fine.

sections of the espionage statutes, the act further provided that the penal provisions contained therein would not operate to exclude any other applicable provision of law, therefore insuring that a prosecution brought under the espionage statutes involving the peddling of atomic energy secrets could not be adversely affected.[9] The Supreme Court interpreted the language of this section in like manner in its opinion rejecting the various contentions of the Rosenbergs in the appeal from their conviction for wartime espionage.[10]

Other provisions of the espionage statutes prohibit the unauthorized photographing and sketching of national defense installations and facilities;[11] the use of any aircraft or other contrivance in making any unauthorized photograph or sketch of defense installations;[12] and the unauthorized publication and sale of photographs of defense installations.[13] Each of these provisions carries a maximum penalty of 1 year in jail and a $1,000 fine. Recent amendments to the Atomic Energy Act of 1954 prohibit the photographing or sketching of atomic energy installations without first obtaining the permission of the Atomic Energy Commission.[14] An addition to the espionage statutes enacted in 1950 is designed to protect the vital cryptographic and communication intelligence facilities, procedures, and methods of the United States. This statute carries a maximum penalty of 10 years in prison and a $10,000 fine for the unauthorized communication or use in any manner prejudicial to the United States of any information concerning the above which has been properly classified for reasons of national security.[15]

Since espionage cases may frequently involve national security information of the highest classification, the Government is confronted with the serious problem of how far such information can be compromised in the course of a prosecution. Were it not for certain other criminal provisions in title 18 which can be adapted to prosecutions in security matters, a defendant who may have met with the greatest success in securing our most precious secrets, may also have secured an advantage in warding off a successful prosecution. To prevent just such a dilemma, two other general criminal statutes can be used in certain instances to provide additional counts in an espionage indictment. Section 2071 of title 18 defines and punishes the concealment, removal, or mutilation of Government documents, papers, and records;[16] and section 641 of title 18 punishes any individual who embezzles, steals, purloins, or knowingly converts any money, property, records, or anything of value belonging to the United States or any department or agency thereof.[17]

---

[9] Formerly 42 U. S. C. A. 1810 (b) (6), now 42 U. S. C. A. 2279, *supra.*

[10] *Rosenberg* v. *United States,* 346 U. S. 273 (1953), reconsideration denied 346 U. S. 324.

[11] 18 U. S. C. A., sec. 795.

[12] 18 U. S. C. A., sec. 796.

[13] 18 U. S. C. A., sec. 797.

[14] Act of Aug. 6, 1956, ch. 1015, sec. 6, 70 Stat. 1070, 42 U. S. C. A. 2278 (b).

[15] 18 U. S. C. A., sec. 798.

[16] Ch. 645, 62 Stat. 795, carries a maximum penalty upon conviction of 3 years in prison and a $2,000 fine.

[17] Ch. 645, 62 Stat. 724, carries a maximum penalty upon conviction of 10 years in prison and a $10,000 fine. If the value of the property is less than $100, then the maximum penalty is 1-year sentence and a $1,000 fine.

By adding additional counts where possible charging violations of these two statutes, the Government would not be compelled to establish the national defense character of the evidence introduced beyond proper identification and proof of ownership. As a result it may be possible to avoid publication of the contents of highly classified documents.

A recent case of this kind is the Judith Coplon prosecution, in which the indictments included, apart from the espionage counts, other counts charging both conspiratorial and substantive violations of 18 U. S. C., section 2071.[18]

There are several other penal provisions dealing with the unauthorized disclosure of many types of information which should be considered along with the espionage statutes. 18 U. S. C. 1905 is aimed at punishing the unauthorized disclosure by an officer or employee of the Government of what is generally termed "confidential information." [19] Such information comprises that which would normally come to a Government employee in the course of his daily duties and would involve such things as confidential statistical data, trade secrets, processes, and similar matters. No official classification is attached to such information, but this does not exclude the fact that it could involve information relating to national defense. Also applicable to Government employees is 18 U. S. C. 952, which punishes the unauthorized disclosure or transmission of any coded matter by anyone having custody or access to an official or diplomatic code.[20]

Section 783 (b) of title 50 punishes the unauthorized disclosure of "classified information" by an officer or employee of the Government to any person whom such officer or employee has reason to believe is a member of a Communist organization or represents a foreign government.[21] This statute deals directly with information affecting national defense which has been officially classified by the proper governmental agency for reasons of national security. In prosecutions for violations of this section, it would appear that the burden of proof would be limited to the identification of the information as being classified so as to prevent any collateral attack leading to possible compromise and disclosure.

The Commission found to its dismay that one frustrating aspect of this overall security problem is the frequent unauthorized disclosure without subversive intent of classified information affecting national security. Several instances were noted where information emanating from the Department of Defense, and subsequently determined to have been classified, has found its way through various media into the public domain, when in deference to the interests of national security more restraint should have been exercised before dissemination. Airplane journals, scientific periodicals,

---

[18] *Coplon* v. *U. S.*, 191 F. 2d 749 (1951), cert. denied 342 U. S. 926.

[19] Ch. 645, 62 Stat. 791, carries a maximum penalty upon conviction of 1 year in prison and a $1,000 fine.

[20] Ch. 645, 62 Stat. 743, carries a maximum penalty upon conviction of 10 years in prison and a $10,000 fine.

[21] Ch. 1024, title 1, sec. 4, 64 Stat. 991, carries a maximum penalty upon conviction of 10 years in prison and a $10,000 fine.

and even the daily newspaper have featured articles containing information and other data which should have been deleted in whole or in part for security reasons.

In many instances the chief culprits responsible for any unauthorized publication of classified material are persons quite removed from Government service and therefore not amenable to applicable criminal statutes or other civil penalties. Congressional inaction in this particular area can be traced to the genuine fear of imposing undue censorship upon the bulk of information flowing from the various governmental agencies, and which the American people, for the most part, have the right to know. Any statute designed to correct this difficulty must necessarily minimize constitutional objections by maintaining the proper balance between the guarantee of the first amendment,[22] on one hand, and required measures to establish a needed safeguard against any real danger to our national security.

The Commission recommends that Congress enact legislation making it a crime for any person willfully to disclose without proper authorization, for any purpose whatever, information classified "secret" or "top secret", knowing, or having reasonable grounds to believe, such information to have been so classified.

The Commission believes that such a legislative enactment would act as a genuine deterrent to those who, without giving serious thought to the overall security picture but without pernicious or subversive intent, deliberately compromise vital defense information for the sake of publicity or for any commercial or other purpose.[23]

C. Sabotage

The statutes dealing with acts of sabotage are found in sections 2151 through 2157 of title 18.[24] The purpose of these sections is to punish the willful destruction of national defense utilities, materials or premises. In addition, the willful production of defective war material is punishable as sabotage. These sections further differentiate between those acts constituting wartime sabotage and similar acts committed in times of peace. The distinction lies only in the degree of proof required to establish criminal intent. Proof that a particular act of sabotage was done with reason to believe that such act may injure or interfere with or obstruct the United States is sufficient to convict for wartime sabotage.

In a prosecution for peacetime sabotage, it falls upon the Government to prove the specific intent in each case. Penalties prescribed for acts of sabotage include maximum prison sentences of 10 to 30 years, and a fine of up to $10,000.

---

[22] "Congress shall make no law . . . abridging the freedom of speech, or of the press; . . ."
[23] See Commission's legislative draft, p. 739.
[24] Ch. 645, 62 Stat. 798–800; Ch. 175, 67 Stat. 133, 134; Ch. 1261, 68 Stat. 1216–1218.

D. *Seditious Conspiracy and the Smith Act*

The crime of seditious conspiracy is found in 18 U. S. C. 2384.[25] The language contained therein is based upon an old statute enacted in 1861.[26] As the name indicates, "seditious conspiracy" is a conspiracy having as its objectives any of the following overt acts: To overthrow, put down or destroy by force and violence the Government of the United States, levy war against the United States, or interfere, prevent, or hinder the execution of any law of the United States or to wrongfully seize or take away Government property. Proof of an overt act is not required.

While the avowed purposes of the Communist conspiracy would be expected to culminate in the overt acts proscribed above, this statute has not been used to date against the leaders of the Communist Party in the United States. In their subtle approach, the Communist hierarchy made sure that their position in advancing the Communist conspiracy would lend itself to the more passive role of teaching and advocating the party line. Consequently, the Government has resorted to the pertinent provisions of the Smith Act.

The provisions of the Smith Act were first enacted in 1940 and are found in 18 U. S. C. 2385.[27] This act provides a maximum penalty of up to 20 years in prison and a $20,000 fine for anyone convicted of teaching or advocating the violent overthrow of the United States Government, or the government of any State, Territory, district, or possession thereof. In addition, the willful publication or distribution of any material with the intent to accomplish the above purposes or the organizing or holding of a membership in any group or organization which advocates such overthrow with knowledge of the aims and purposes of such organization is also prohibited. Equally criminal and subject to the same penalty is a conspiracy to do any of the foregoing acts. From its inception this act was intended to combat and resist the organization of Fascist and Communist groups owing allegiance to foreign governments whose operations and activities were clearly contrary and dangerous to the Government of the United States. The first Communist Party cases to be prosecuted for violations of this act were instituted in 1948 and resulted in conviction of the 11 members of the governing body of the Communist Party, USA, for conspiracy [28] to teach and advocate the violent overthrow of the United States Government.

Since 1948 some 103 party leaders and minor officials have been successfully prosecuted on conspiracy charges involving violations of the Smith Act. The Government, in each case, has demonstrated and proven that the

---

[25] Ch. 678, sec. 1, 70 Stat. 623, carries a maximum penalty upon conviction of 20 years in prison and a $20,000 fine.

[26] R. S., sec. 5336.

[27] Ch. 678, sec. 2, 70 Stat. 623.

[28] Until the act of July 24, 1956 (note 27), a conspiracy to violate the provisions of former 18 U. S. C. A. 2385 was prosecuted under the provisions of the general conspiracy statute in 18 U. S. C. A. 371 (ch. 645), 62 Stat. 701).

Communist Party as it functions in the United States is indeed a vicious and active conspiracy, dedicated to the proposition that the Government of the United States must be overthrown by unconstitutional means, and that these individuals actively and with full knowledge participated in acts designed to further the objectives of this conspiracy.

Of vital importance to the Government's security program are two cases, now pending for decision before the Supreme Court in which the respective defendants stand convicted under the membership clause of the Smith Act.[29] The indictments returned therein charged in substance that these two defendants well knew that at all times during the period in which they were members of the Communist Party, this organization was a group which teaches and advocates the overthrow of the Government of the United States by force and violence, and that they subscribed to the aims and objectives of the Communist Party with the intention of bringing about their complete fulfillment as quickly as possible.

Recently the Supreme Court held that a state could not punish seditious acts against the United States on the ground that Congress has preempted the field through the passage of the Smith Act.[30]

E. The False Statement and Perjury Statutes

The false statement and perjury statutes have played an important role in combating Communist and other subversive activity. 18 U. S. C. A. 1001 provides for the punishment of up to 5 years in prison and a $10,000 fine for anyone who has been convicted of willfully and knowingly making any false or fraudulent statement or representation in any manner within the jurisdiction of any department or agency of the United States.[31] The purpose of this section as indicated by congressional intent is to protect against the perversion and corruption of the functions of Government agencies and departments through deceptive practices.

18 U. S. C. A. 1621 defines the offense of perjury, making it a crime for any person willfully to give false testimony on a material fact after having been duly sworn under an oath or affirmation, properly administered, and required by any law of the United States. A conviction for perjury under this statute is punishable by imprisonment up to 5 years and a $2,000 fine.

Besides being the applicable statute for prosecutions involving the filing of false non-Communist affidavits under the provisions of section 9 (h) of the Taft-Hartley Act, convictions for violations of 18 U. S. C. A. 1001 have been obtained against persons who have falsely concealed their Communist affiliations in job applications for Federal employment, in applications for security clearances by the Department of Defense, and in similar

---

[29] Scales v. United States, 227 F. 2d 581 (1956), certiorari granted 350 U. S. 992; United States v. Lightfoot (1956), 228 F. 2d 861, certiorari granted 350 U. S. 992.

[30] Commonwealth of Pennsylvania v. Nelson, 350 U. S. 497 (1956).

[31] Ch. 645, 62 Stat. 749.

622

applications filed with the Atomic Energy Commission.[32] Perjury convictions were obtained in several cases against individuals who denied affiliations with subversive elements and activities before Federal grand juries [33] or other judicial proceedings.[34]

F. Registration Statutes

As was indicated earlier there are other statutes which contain adjunct criminal provisions intended to enforce compliance with the statutory duties. The duty imposed as well as the accompanying procedures to be followed are civil in nature. These procedures may vary from the purely ex parte administrative to the more formalized quasi-judicial adversary hearing. These adjunct-penalty provisions are for the most part severe, and are intended to punish either willful noncompliance or fraudulent compliance with the statutory purposes. Two registration statutes of grave import are the Foreign Agents Registration Act of 1938, as amended,[35] and the Subversive Activities Control Act of 1950, as amended.[36] In addition to these acts, some attention should be given to section 9 (h) of the Labor Management Relations Act of 1947, which, while not properly a registration statute, requires officers of unions desiring to use the facilities of the National Labor Relations Board in settling labor disputes to file non-Communist affidavits.[37]

(a) *Foreign Agents Registration Act of 1938, as amended.*—The purpose of this act is to afford a means of identification through mandatory registration of those agents and their foreign principals, who engage in subversive acts or in the spreading or dissemination of foreign propaganda within the United States. Registration requires them to make public the nature of their employment, thus subjecting their statements and activities to visible inspection and to the pressure brought to bear by the force of public opinion. Congress believed that as long as the activities of these foreign agents are kept out in the open and in the public eye as far as possible, there is less chance of deception being practiced upon the American people, if what they are being fed from abroad can be properly identified as nothing more than political propaganda.

Section 20 (a) of the Internal Security Act of 1950 [38] amended the Registration Act by broadening the definition of the term "agent of a foreign principal" to include persons who are well versed, or who have received assignments and instructions in the espionage, counterespionage and sab-

---

[32] Statement of the Attorney General of the United States for the Commission on Government Security, Sept. 5, 1956.

[33] *United States* v. *Hiss,* 185 F. 2d 822 (1950), cert. denied 340 U. S. 948; *United States* v. *Perl,* 210 F. 2d 457 (1954).

[34] *United States* v. *Remington,* 208 F. 2d 567 (1953), cert. denied 347 U. S. 913.

[35] 22 U. S. C. A. secs. 611–621.

[36] 50 U. S. C. A. secs. 781–798.

[37] 29 U. S. C. A. 159 (h).

[38] Ch. 1024, tite 1, sec. 20 (a), 64 Stat. 1005.

otage tactics of a foreign government or political party. The twofold objective of this amendment was to provide a valuable firsthand source of information and material regarding various foreign espionage and sabotage systems, while at the same time providing our Government with the possible opportunity of gaining some preliminary knowledge about the plans and designs of foreign espionage and sabotage agents before they have a chance to carry them into execution.

From a practical standpoint, the Department of Justice found one serious evidentiary obstacle which can forestall successful prosecutions for a violation of section 29 (a); that is, the necessity of proving the existence of the principal-agent status. The Department recommended to Congress that appropriate amending language be enacted. Congress acceded to the request of the Department, and H. R. 3882, as passed by the Congress, became Public Law 893 on August 1, 1956.[39] This act completely repealed the troublesome section 20 (a) of the Internal Security Act of 1950 and substituted in lieu thereof a separate registration statute unconnected with the Foreign Agents Registration Act, which provides that any individual who has received instructions or assignment in foreign espionage or sabotage, or who has knowledge of foreign espionage or sabotage systems, must register with the Attorney General. Willful failure to comply with the registration requirements, or the filing of any false statement thereunder, is punishable up to 5 years in prison and a $10,000 fine.[40]

(b) *Subversive Activities Control Act of 1950, as amended.*—The second important registration act is the Subversive Activities Control Act of 1950, as amended, which was enacted as part of the Internal Security Act of 1950. The registration provisions of this act are aimed primarily at groups and organizations which are either Communist-action or Communist-front organizations. As defined in section 3 of the act, a Communist-action organization is one which is substantially directed or dominated by the foreign government or organization controlling the world Communist movement and operating to advance the objectives and purposes of this movement. A Communist-front organization is defined as one substantially controlled or dominated by a Communist-action organization and operated for the purpose of giving aid and support to the dominating authority.

The obligation to initiate registration under the act lies with the organization and upon failure of such organization to register within the time prescribed with the Attorney General, he can then petition the Subversive Activities Control Board, created under the act, to hold hearings to determine whether registration is required. The hearing provided before the Board shall be a full and fair hearing subject to the applicable provisions of the Administrative Procedure Act. The findings of the Board must be supported by a preponderance of the evidence and any order entered therein shall

---

[39] 70 Stat. 899. 900.
[40] 50 U. S. C. A. secs. 851–857.

not be final until the party aggrieved has exhausted his opportunity of judicial review.

Whenever any organization registers, or an order for registration has become final, the act imposes other duties and sanctions upon both the organization and its officers and members. Such things as annual reports disclosing full membership and financial data must be filed by a registered organization. They are also denied a tax-exempt status. In the event an organization has failed to comply with a final order to register, then the obligation to register individually falls upon all members of a Communist-action organization and upon the officers of a Communist-front organization. Other restrictions falling upon individual members include denial of passport privileges and denial of Federal employment or employment in defense facilities. The penalties imposed upon individuals for a willful failure to register or to file required statements and annual reports, or to file a false or fraudulent statement include a fine up to $10,000 or imprisonment up to 5 years, or both such fine and imprisonment.

To date no organization has voluntarily registered. Pending in the courts for judicial determination is the first and most important decision to come down from the Board, in which it found that the Communist Party, USA, was in fact a Communist-action organization, subject to the registration requirements of the act. Undoubtedly, the Supreme Court will have to determine the validity of the entire registration program when it ultimately comes to grips with serious constitutional issues raised by the Communist Party case.[41]

(c) *Section 9 (h), Labor Management Relations Act of 1947, as amended.*—Unique in the field of statutory law designed to combat the threat of Communist infiltration into the labor movement is section 9 (h) of the Labor Management Relations Act of 1947, as amended, better known as the Taft-Hartley Act. This section requires the filing of non-Communist affidavits with the National Labor Relations Board by the officers of any union desiring to use the facilities of the Board in connection with the investigation and settling of labor-management disputes. The affidavits must state that the affiant is not presently a member or affiliated with the Communist Party and that he does not believe in or is not a member or affiliated with any organization advocating or teaching the overthrow of the Government by force or violence or by any illegal or unconstitutional means. The penal provisions of 18 U. S. C. A. 1001 are made specifically applicable in case affidavits containing false statements have been filed. Because the wording of section 9 (h) requires only a denial of present membership in any of the proscribed organizations, a prosecution for filing a false affidavit will generally call for proof that the affiant has held membership both prior and subsequent to the execution of his affidavit, and under such circumstances

---

[41] On its initial review of the case, the Supreme Court reversed the judgment of the United Court of Appeals, affirming the findings of the Board and remanded the case to the Board for the introduction of additional evidence. The court found it unnecessary to reach the constitutional issues. *Communist Party of the United States of America* v. *Subversive Activities Control Board,* 351 U. S. 115 (1956).

as to infer that his membership has in fact been a continuous one. On occasion union officers holding Communist Party memberships have sought to avoid the effect of section 9 (h) by going through the motions of publicly tendering their formal resignations from the party before executing the required affidavit. However, such performances would not deter a prosecution for a violation of 18 U. S. C. A. 1001 if the evidence shows thereafter a continuing membership.

THE IMMUNITY ACT OF 1954

A résumé of applicable criminal statutes in the security field would not be complete without mentioning one of the important procedural weapons which Congress has seen fit to give Federal law-enforcement officials. The Immunity Act of 1954 [42] establishes a procedure in the investigation of cases involving national security where, in spite of a valid claim of the fifth-amendment privilege against self-incrimination, a reluctant witness can be compelled by court order to testify under a grant of absolute immunity against future prosecutions involving any incriminating matter which may be disclosed. Failure to so testify under a valid court order is punishable as a contempt of court, while giving false testimony on material facts is punishable as perjury. The view that a Federal statute granting absolute immunity from future criminal prosecution cannot displace the constitutional guarantee against self-incrimination was rejected as early as 1896, when the Supreme Court upheld the act of February 11, 1893, amending the immunity provisions of the original Interstate Commerce Act of 1887.[43] The act became the model for other subsequently enacted immunity provisions, particularly in the field of Federal regulatory legislation. The Immunity Act of 1954 followed the same pattern, and on March 26, 1956, the act survived its initial constitutional attack when the Supreme Court judicially approved the provisions of section (c) of the act as granting an immunity against future criminal prosecution broad enough to supplant the protection afforded by the fifth-amendment privilege against self-incrimination.[44] Section (c) of the act applies to proceedings before grand juries and cases in Federal courts. Sections (a) and (b) have reference to the investigative proceedings before either House of Congress or any authorized committee thereof, and it was only until recently that first applications for appropriate court orders pursuant to these sections were issued in favor of the Senate Internal Security Subcommittee against four reluctant witnesses.[45]

---

[42] 18 U. S. C. A. sec. 3486, 68 Stat. 745.

[43] *Brown* v. *Walker*, 161 U. S. 591 (1896).

[44] *Ullman* v. *United States*, 350 U. S. 422 (1956).

[45] *In re Glasser, McElrath, Oka,* and *Symonds,* misc. docket No. 6, 7, 8, 9, 57—U. S. District Court for the District of Columbia. Appropriate order signed by District Judge Pine on April 10, 1957. Notice of appeal filed April 11, 1957.

WIRETAPPING

The most controversial weapon employed by Federal law-enforcement officials in the investigation of internal security matters is the use of wiretaps. A great deal of vital information on the subversive operations of both individuals and groups has been uncovered through the wiretapping technique. However, under present law such information cannot be used in Federal prosecutions for violations of our security statutes. Because of this prohibition as construed by the courts, the Department of Justice has consistently and strongly urged over the years the necessity for legislation which would make evidence obtained by wiretaps admissible in criminal prosecutions. Realizing the importance of this matter from a security standpoint, the Commission has reviewed the history of Federal legislation and the pertinent Supreme Court decisions with a view to making definite recommendations on this subject.

Back in the early thirties a joint committee of Congress was busily engaged in preparing legislation to transfer jurisdiction over all radio, telegraph and telephone facilities to the newly created Federal Communications Commission. An amendment to the Radio Act of 1927 was prepared, and in 1934 the bill as proposed passed Congress with few changes.[46] Included, and the subject of little debate at the time of passage, was a section 605 which contained the following prohibition:

. . . No person not being authorized by the sender shall intercept and divulge or publish the meaning of such intercepted communication to any person. . . .[47]

This section 605 of the Federal Communications Act is the current statutory law on the subject of wiretapping and the focal point of present-day controversy.

Prior to the enactment of section 605 of the Federal Communications Act, two other temporary wiretapping measures have appeared on the statute books. The first of these was a wartime provision passed in 1918 at a time when the Federal Government was operating the telephone system.[48] In broad language it forbade all forms of wiretapping for the duration of World War I, and expired by its own terms in July of 1919 when the Government returned management of the telephone system to its owners. The other temporary measure was enacted in 1933 as a rider to an appropriation bill.[49] It provided that no part of the appropriation could be used in connection with any wiretapping activity to procure evidence of violations of the National Prohibition Act.

Throughout this period, congressional activity has witnessed the introduction of some forty-odd bills in both Houses of Congress. The purposes have

[46] 48 Stat. 1103.
[47] 47 U. S. C. A. sec. 605.
[48] 40 Stat. 1017.
[49] 47 Stat. 1381.

been varied, ranging from an absolute ban on all wiretapping, to granting limited controlled wiretap authority to Federal law-enforcement officials in the investigation and detection of subversive activity, security violations, and specified Federal offenses. One bill managed to survive in both Houses but failed in final passage because minor variations between the House and Senate versions could not be ironed out before Congress adjourned.[50] Three others have managed to pass at least one House.[51]

Federal case law on wiretapping as declared by the Supreme Court began in 1927 with the decision in *Olmstead* v. *United States*.[52] The Court ruled in this case that all wiretapping activity and other communications interceptions did not per se violate either the fourth amendment proscribing unreasonable searches and seizures, or the fifth-amendment protection against self-incrimination. No wiretapping statute was involved in the *Olmstead* case, but subsequent Supreme Court decisions have been concerned with section 605 of the Federal Communications Act.

As interpreted by the Court, section 605 prohibits Federal law-enforcement officials from testifying to the contents of intercepted communications in any Federal criminal proceeding.[53] The prohibition extends to intercepted communications which are intrastate.[54] Any evidence which is the product or the derivative result of a wiretap is also inadmissible in Federal criminal cases.[55] On the other hand, the use of detectophones and other eavesdropping equipment is not an interception within the meaning of section 605,[56] nor does a third person not a party to an intercepted communication have any legal standing under this section to challenge its admissibility into evidence when sought to be used against him.[57] Finally, section 605 does not operate to effect a binding rule of evidence upon State courts so as to exclude such evidence in state proceedings.[58]

Upon the completion of its study, the Commission arrived at one basic conclusion, which apparently has universal support from both sides of the wiretapping controversy; namely, that there is an immediate need for legislative action in this area. From the standpoint of our national security, the need is even more demanding, and in this connection the Commission has taken particular note of the aforementioned *Judith Coplon* case as being a prime example of a legalized miscarriage of justice occasioned by dutiful judicial interpretation of section 605 of the Federal Communications Act.

[50] S. 3756, 75th Cong., 3d sess. (1938).
[51] H. J. Res. 553, 76th Cong., 3d sess. (1940); H. J. Res. 310, 77th Cong., 2d sess. (1942); H. R. 8649. 83d Cong. (1954), 2d sess.
[52] 277 U. S. 438.
[53] *Nardone* v. *United States*, 302 U. S. 379 (1937).
[54] *Weiss* v. *United States*, 308 U. S. 321 (1939).
[55] *Nardone* v. *United States*, 308 U. S. 338 (1939).
[56] *Goldman* v. *United States*, 316 U. S. 129 (1942); *On Lee* v. *United States*, 343 U. S. 747 (1952).
[57] *Goldstein* v. *United States*, 316 U. S. 114 (1942).
[58] *Schwartz* v. *Texas*, 344 U. S. 199 (1952).

Judith Coplon, a former Justice Department employee, had been indicted separately in two cases, one arising in the southern district of New York and the other in the District of Columbia, each charging her with conspiracy to defraud the United States and attempting to deliver defense information to a foreign agent.

In the New York case [59] her conviction was reversed on the grounds that the FBI arrest without a warrant was invalid, and that the trial judge erred in denying to the defense the opportunity at pretrial to inspect the wiretap records upon which the judge had concluded that the FBI wiretapping had in no way furnished the leads to that evidence introduced at trial. The reasons for denying inspection were predicated on the Government's refusal to compromise national security information. An additional ground for reversal was the refusal by the trial judge to permit the defense reasonable inquiry into the question of whether the information which initiated the investigation was procured by wiretapping. That Judge Learned Hand may have felt that the present law governing the admissibility of wiretap evidence in Federal courts had frustrated the immediate ends of justice can be gathered from the following words in his opinion:

For all the foregoing reasons, the conviction must be reversed; but we will not dismiss the indictment for the guilt is plain. . . .[60]

The final chapter in the Coplon matter took place in the District of Columbia when, after affirming her conviction in the district court, the United States Court of Appeals reversed a subsequent order of the lower court denying defendant's motion for a new trial on the grounds of newly discovered evidence relating to wiretapping.[61] The case was remanded for further proceedings and remains in that status today.

The Commission recommends that a separate wiretapping law be enacted which would eliminate the evidentiary disability ascribed to information procured by wiretapping in criminal prosecutions only for violations of our security laws. This new statute would permit Federal law-enforcement officials, and selected military intelligence agencies, to employ the wiretapping technique in the investigation of security violations but only upon the specific authorization of the Attorney General.[62]

Such a statute, by lifting the evidentiary disability and placing the responsibility solely in the hands of the Attorney General, would lend itself to uniformity in administration and consistency in judicial interpretation.

In Public Law 304 the Congress declared as a matter of policy that there should be a sound Government program "for vigorous enforcement of effective and realistic security laws and regulations."

---

[59] *United States* v. *Coplon*, 185 F. 2d 629 (1950); certiorari denied 342 U. S. 920.

[60] Ibid.

[61] See footnote 17 on p. 618.

[62] See Commission's legislative draft, p. 737. Commissioner Stennis dissents and Commissioners Noel and Murphy abstain.

The inadmissibility of evidence obtained by wiretap in criminal prosecutions for violation of espionage and related security laws constitutes, in the judgment of the Commission, a serious obstacle to the vigorous enforcement of such laws.

The requirement that authorization for the wiretap be obtained personally from the Attorney General should allay any apprehensions that the authority will be used indiscriminately for the mere purpose of invading the privacy of American citizens.

Special Studies

Central Security Office

Perhaps the most important recommendation made by this Commission is the one urging the creation of a Central Security Office in the executive branch of the Federal Government directly responsible to the President.

The Commission's recommendation concerning the nature, jurisdiction, and operations of the proposed Central Security Office will be found on page 89 of this report relating to the civilian employees loyalty program. In brief, it would provide coordinative control in the civilian employees program, the industrial security program, the port security program, the proposed civil air transport security program, and the document classification program. It also would provide hearing examiners to hear cases of organizations contesting their designation to the Attorney General's list. The purpose of this paper is to indicate in detail some of the considerations which led to this recommendation.

The urgent need for such a Central Security Office became apparent to the Commission after an intensive study of current programs, review of congressional hearings and contemporary writings, examination of official case files and correspondence, interviews and written exchanges with representatives of Government and industry, and the advice of other knowledgeable individuals and organizations. Some 15 months of study has shown that the uncoordinated and often inefficient and ineffective loyalty-security programs now in force seriously need central direction of a type permitting the sound conduct of official business yet insuring that neither the Government's security is jeopardized nor the rights of the individual infringed.

The most obvious defects disclosed by the Commission's study were—

1. Lack of uniformity in the preparation and application of rules and regulations.

2. Lack of coordination between agencies and between divisions of the same agency.

3. Duplication of forms and records.

4. Duplication of investigations and clearances.

5. Wide dispersion of responsibility among personnel.

6. Lack of training and guidance of personnel.

7. Lack of uniformity in screening procedures.

8. Lack of uniformity in hearing procedures.

9. Absence of provision for appellate review.

10. Failure to keep proper records.

To help correct these and other deficiencies noted, the Commission on Government Security has made a number of basic recommendations in the various programs examined as set forth throughout this report. The Commission believes that in addition it is imperative that provision be made for central coordination in those programs.

Although the function of the proposed Central Security Office would be purely advisory, with final authority still retained by each respective department or agency, the proposed Central Security Office would insure uniformity of rules and procedures in all programs by continuous coordination and consultation. It would provide a body of trained, competent hearing examiners who would serve all departments and agencies and review appeals in loyalty and security cases. It would advise the President in matters of laws, Executive orders, and directives related to the operation of the various programs.

The recommended Central Security Office would have no authority to examine files, documents, or material within any agency but would be limited in its inspection duties to an examination and appraisal of rules, regulations, and procedures of the various agencies of Government in the implementation of loyalty-security programs.

Under Executive Order 10450, which established the present civilian security-loyalty-suitability program, no one authority has overall responsibility for supervision or coordination. Each department or agency makes its own rules, holds its own hearings, and makes final disposition of questionable security cases, with no provision under the order for an appeal outside the agency. True, the Civil Service Commission under section 14 of the order is charged with making a continuing study of the security program and of reporting deficiencies and unfair treatment of employees to the National Security Council semiannually.[1] However, as the Chairman of the Civil Service Commission told a Senate subcommittee, the operations of the Commission "are of a service type"; even section 14 of Executive Order 10450, ". . . requiring us to make a study of the application and implementation of the program . . . does not give the Commission any authority to make changes in content or the subject matter of the program."[2]

Furthermore, the Chairman testified at the same hearing that he did not feel that the Civil Service Commission had any "major responsibility in terms of coordination" of the security program.

The National Security Council to whom the Civil Service Commission once reported, was established in 1947 to ". . . advise the President with respect to the integration of domestic, foreign, and military policies relating to the national security. . . ."[3] The executive secretary of the Council, however, in a letter to the Commission on Government Security dated January

---

[1] Now the Civil Service Commission is obliged to report directly to the President although the Executive order has not been formally amended.

[2] Hearings before a subcommittee on reorganization of the Committee on Government Operations, U. S. Senate, 84th Cong., 1st sess., S. J. Res. 21, March 8–18, 1955, p. 501.

[3] Title 50, U. S. C., chap. 15, sec. 402 (a), 1952 ed.

3, 1957, declared that the Council, "being solely an advisory body to the President, does not have any enforcement authority over the several departments and agencies concerned with the implementation of Executive Order 10450."

Section 12 of the order makes the Department of Justice responsible for furnishing agency heads with the names of organizations designated to the so-called Attorney General's list, while section 13 charges the Attorney General with advising agency heads on establishing and maintaining appropriate employee security programs. Acting under this authority, the Department of Justice did issue sample regulations in the beginning of the program for the assistance of each agency in preparing its own security regulations and held a few conferences for security personnel. Assistant Attorney General W. F. Tompkins, testifying before a Senate subcommittee of the Committee on Post Office and Civil Service, 84th Congress, 1st session, made clear, however, that the function of the Department of Justice is purely advisory and that "individual agency heads have the complete responsibility and authority."

An attempt was made to coordinate the present civilian security program with the creation, in January 1955, of the Personnel Security Advisory Committee. Mr. Thomas J. Donegan, a special assistant to the Attorney General, and former chairman of the Interdepartmental Committee on Internal Security of the National Security Council, was made chairman.

Besides Mr. Donegan, the Personnel Security Advisory Committee was originally composed of representatives of the Atomic Energy Commission; Civil Service Commission; Departments of State, Treasury, and Defense—although the Defense Department's two most important programs, military personnel and industrial security, do not come within the jurisdiction of the committee. In April of this year the committee functions were taken over by the Internal Security Division of the Department of Justice.

The jurisdiction of the committee was never clearly spelled out. It was created at a time when there was great criticism of the diverse handling of similar cases by different agencies and its principal task was to resolve such conflicts. In any event, receiving the assistance of the committee was a voluntary matter with the interested agencies, and the committee had no authority either to review the civilian security program or promulgate suggested changes in it. It had no budget and its staff was assigned to the chairman on a temporary basis from other agencies. Chairman Donegan himself was on the payroll of the Internal Security Division of the Justice Department and his correspondence appeared on the letterhead of the Executive Office of the President.

Although functioning for more than a year, the existence of the Personnel Security Advisory Committee was not formally recognized by the Cabinet until March 23, 1956, when it was authorized to coordinate executive branch security matters with the work of the Commission on Government Security.

635

One of the weaknesses of the present security program which would be corrected by the creation of a Central Security Office is the desultory nature of hearing board operations. The Civil Service Commission maintains a roster of Government employees available to serve on hearing boards in civilian employee security cases. While precise statistics are not available, the Civil Service Commission has advised that some 290 employee and applicant cases are processed monthly by the Commission and other departments and agencies involving loyalty-type information. Under the proposed Central Security Office, all of such cases which could not be otherwise resolved would be heard by specially trained and qualified hearing examiners under the supervision of the Central Security Office. Today each department or agency—with the exception of the Atomic Energy Commission—furnishes names from its own personnel to hear cases originating in another agency. The Atomic Energy Commission maintains its own hearing board roster selected by its ten field operations managers.

The Civil Service Commission roster listed over 1,800 names on April 1, 1957. Of these, approximately 230 were available to sit on hearing boards in Washington, 17 in the Canal Zone, and approximately 1,600 in the field, including both civilian and military personnel.

Nearly all departments and agencies reported difficulties and delays in actually empaneling a hearing board. The proposed Central Security Office, by providing a body of full-time, trained hearing examiners available to all agencies would help correct these difficulties.

The lack of central coordination, with resulting loss of efficiency found in the civilian employee program is reflected in varying degrees in other programs as well.

In the industrial security program each of the three military services conduct their own programs. Separate related programs are operated by the Atomic Energy Commission, the Department of Commerce, the National Science Foundation, and other agencies. The Commission on Government Security has recommended that the three programs of the military services be consolidated in the Office of the Secretary of Defense.[4] This, however, is not sufficient in view of the separate activities of the other agencies in this field. It therefore has recommended that limited overall coordination of the industrial security program be effected through the Central Security Office. It feels that through conferences with representatives of industry and government and through examination and evaluation of procedures and practices it can help correct deficiencies, eliminate unnecessary duplication of jurisdiction or responsibility, and establish greater uniformity. Further, the Central Security Office hearing examiners would also be available to hear cases of individuals whose qualifications for clearance for access to classified information and materials are questioned.[5]

---

[4] See p. 235, Industrial Security Program.

[5] Information concerning the present hearing board system of this program and the Port Security Program is set forth, *infra*.

The port security program is an integrated one within the United States Coast Guard. The proposed Central Security Office would provide hearing examiners to hear cases of seamen and waterfront workers whose qualifications for clearance are questioned. It would also aline Coast Guard clearance rules and regulations with those for similar Federal programs.

The document classification program by virtue of section 17 of Executive Order 10501 is subject to a continuing review by the National Security Council. The Council in turn has delegated this responsibility to its Interdepartmental Committee on Internal Security. The Executive order thus recognized the need for coordination within this program. The Commission submits, however, that the responsibility for active review and coordination is improperly placed within the jurisdiction of a policy recommending and nonoperating agency. It feels that such responsibility is a natural concomitant of the other duties which under the recommendations would be vested in the Central Security Office.

The Commission believes that the proposed Central Security Office should, through the resulting increase in uniformity and efficiency, have a decided effect in reducing present security costs particularly in the matter of hearings.

Comparison of the cost of hearings under the present security programs and probable costs under the proposed Central Security Office is difficult to make for several reasons: The complexity of the cases varies, and consequently the time involved; there are no statistics showing the salary level of hearing board members in all cases; and some boards are composed of part-time examiners still responsible for regular duties at their own agencies. However, a few figures are available indicating the trend of current costs:

The Atomic Energy Commission, for instance, assigning to the Executive Order 10450 program a percentage of the overall salary costs equal to the percentage of the overall case load represented by Executive Order 10450 cases, produced the following statistics:

June 1953 (3.3 percent of total cases)	$3,037
Fiscal year 1954 (2 percent of total cases)	22,093
Fiscal year 1955 (3.7 percent of total cases)	40,070
Nine months fiscal 1956 (6.3 percent total cases)	51,074

As of April 1, 1956, AEC had 6,340 employees. The annual turnover ranged from 18 to 24 percent.[6] From January 1, 1954, to October 26, 1956, 27 AEC employees served on personnel security boards. Boards having an AEC member heard 78 cases, all but 2 involving contractor personnel. In the two cases involving AEC employees, one member of the board hearing the cases was an AEC employee. All AEC employee or applicant cases were heard by boards composed in their entirety of persons outside the agency.[7] The average time between notification of charges and date of hearing was 63 days, and between date of hearing and final decision, 188 days.

---

[6] Letter from AEC to Commission on Government Security, Aug. 9, 1956.
[7] Letter from AEC to Commission on Government Security, Oct. 26, 1956.

The AEC's industrial security program processed 33,243 persons for "Q" clearances during the past fiscal year, and 9,783 for "L" clearances. Nine hearings were held during the same period. Assigning to the industrial security program the difference between total salary costs of the overall caseload and the costs allotted to the civilian employees program, we reach the following cost estimates:

June 1953 (96.7 percent of total cases)............................	$88,996
Fiscal year 1954 (98 percent of total)............................	1,082,557
Fiscal year 1955 (96.3 percent of total)............................	1,042,903
Nine months fiscal 1956 (93.7 percent of total)....................	759,624

At present the Department of Defense operates industrial personnel security hearing boards in San Francisco, Chicago, and New York. Each of the boards has a number of full-time, as well as part-time, employees. When the boards meet, the chairman, who is a permanent employee, is assisted by two other board members.

Statistics issued by the Director, Office of Personnel Security Policy, Office of the Assistant Secretary of Defense (Manpower, Personnel, and Reserve), indicate that for the period April 2, 1955, through February 28, 1957, a total of 719 cases were considered by the screening board, the hearing boards (referred to above), and the review board. Of this number, 333 were cleared by the screening board and a total of 152 were eventually referred to the hearing boards after a statement of reasons had been issued by the screening board and replied to by the individuals concerned. During this period, therefore, these three boards considered 152 cases, or approximately 6.6 per month.

The Coast Guard, which handles the port security program, has set up tripartite hearing boards in 11 major United States port areas, including Hawaii and Alaska. Each board consists of a Coast Guard examiner, who acts as chairman; and one representative each from labor and management. Coast Guard statistics for fiscal 1954 (believed to be a representative year) show a total of 671 hearings, of which 365 concerned port security cards and 306 document validation. Of these cases, 33 were appealed, requiring an average of 80 man-hours per case. There are 13 full-time examiners assigned to Coast Guard hearings, and one officer assigned to serve part time as chairman of the National Appeals Board.

The approximate personnel cost of Coast Guard hearings during the fiscal year 1954:

National Appeals Board:		
Commander (half time on security)....................	$5,000	
Secretary..	4,250	
Panel members......................................	10,869	
		$20,119
Local hearing boards (estimated)................................		60,000
Total estimated costs......................................		80,119

Coast Guard estimates for succeeding years were: 1955, $124,400; 1956, $97,920; 1957, $87,000; total for 3 years, $309,320.

Should the Central Security Office be created as proposed, the new program would include a security program for civil air transport [8] which would be comparable to the port security program. It is estimated that the air transport program would involve screening some 22,000 flight personnel, of whom 5,000 are in international traffic.

Under the Commission's recommendations hearing examiners would be available full time for each of the programs to be used as needed. Their training and experience should lessen the time presently needed for hearings. Their central supervision should insure uniformity in the conduct of hearings with greater justice provided for both the Government and the individual concerned.

In an effort to get a cross section of opinions concerning the problem, the Commission considered the opinions of large numbers of knowledgeable individuals and organizations in and out of Government.

Arguments in favor of placing responsibility for coordinating the loyalty-security programs within a single office outweigh those against.

Opinion inside the Government seems about evenly divided. Of the 40 agencies canvassed by the Commission on Government Security, slightly more than half (52.5 percent) opposed the idea of a central office. Some 37.5 percent stated that there is such a need, and 10 percent declined to take a position.

Many of those responding in the negative were referring to a central agency which would have final decisions over all programs, and final word on case appeals to the exclusion of the department heads and agencies. Actually the Commission's recommendation would not divest agency heads of their present authority. The Central Security Office recommendation in case appeals or in administrative operations would be advisory only. The coordinative functions of the Office would complement the responsibilities and authorities of the agency head and not be in derogation of them.

Some of the opinions reviewed by the Commission are summarized here:

The director of the commission on law and social action, the American Jewish Congress, after reviewing some of the defects in the present program, stated before a congressional subcommittee in August 1955: [9]

. . . today there is no central regulation of this program. An employee cleared by one agency can still be discharged by another. There is no central review board, and therefore you have considerable variance in the types of program that are administered from department to department. It would be the function of such a civilian commission to supervise this program, to insure uniformity, to prevent arbitrary action, to prevent the discharge of employees in the name of security in order to make way for deserving members of one party or another.

---

[8] See p. 499, Civil Air Transport.
[9] Hearing before a subcommittee of the Committee on Post Office and Civil Service, U. S. Senate, 84th Cong., 1st sess., pursuant to S. Res. 20, Aug. 30, 1955, p. 518.

The American Jewish Congress, in a report specially prepared for the Commission dated March 1957, formally recommended:

An independent civilian commission, composed of distinguished lawyers, retired judges, and other persons of acknowledged impartiality, integrity, and intelligence, chosen from outside the government, without regard to party, and high level representatives of those government agencies most concerned with security, should be set up for general administrative control of the operation of the security program.

The American Jewish Congress suggested that its proposed "security commission" with the cooperation of the agencies involved would catalog positions as sensitive and nonsensitive; serve as a final board of appeals; supervise and regularly review the steps taken by agencies under the security program; and assist in preparing a course of training of security personnel. Procedural regulations of the security commission would apply uniformly in all agencies unless exception were granted because of the unique nature of the problems in a particular agency. The security commission would review all formal charges before they were lodged against employees.

The Reverend John F. Cronin, S. S., Assistant Director of the Department of Social Action, National Catholic Welfare Conference, made several personal recommendations to the Commission in a letter dated July 20, 1956, regarding centralization of some phases of the security mechanism. He recommended that definite standards, applying to all security boards or officers, be centrally drawn up and promulgated; that, as soon as practical, a central training program for security officers be instituted and that all security officers and board members take such a program; that there be a central review board with the right to supervise findings of lower boards; and that the administration subject the program to continuing review so that failures may be detected and corrected at the earliest opportunity. Father Cronin commented that determination of loyalty and security matters is a highly specialized and demanding occupation and should not be assigned to persons without special training; that only fully competent hearing officers will dare to clear a person they consider loyal in the face of some contrary evidence, and on the other hand, to withhold clearance, when necessary, in spite of great pressures in the other direction; and that competence in hearing officers involves thorough knowledge of the Communist conspiracy and its methods of operation.

The special committee of the association of the bar of the city of New York recognized the need for a unified approach to the problem and in its report issued in mid-1956 [10] recommended:

1. The Office of Director of Personnel and Information Security should be established in the Executive Office of the President.

2. The Director should be appointed by the President subject to confirmation by the Senate and serve at the pleasure of the President.

---

[10] Report of the special committee on the Federal loyalty-security program of the association of the bar of the city of New York, Dodd, Mead & Co., 1956, pp. 7–8. The committee also recommended that the office should act as a central screening board (p. 11).

3. The Director should have the primary responsibility of conducting a continuous review of and supervision over:

(*a*) The personnel security programs in order to assure efficiency, uniformity, and fairness of administration, consonant with the interests of national security.

(*b*) The classification of information so that information should be classified only as the interests of national security actually require.

4. In the performance of his responsibility, the Director should make recommendations to the President, which, when embodied in regulations prepared by the Director and approved by the President, would be binding upon the departments and agencies concerned.

The director, American Civil Liberties Union, Washington, D. C., in testifying before a subcommittee of Congress,[11] strongly urged the committee to recommend the setting up of a centralized review agency to which employees might appeal an adverse decision. The director also stated:

Our experience has more than conclusively shown the need for a process by which security cases might be reviewed by an agency operating independently from the employer agency.

Under the old loyalty program an employee or an applicant has the right to have an adverse decision by a local board reviewed by the Loyalty Review Board.

The way to overcome the politically motivated security officer or agency head is a return to the independent hearing and review board system.

The President's Temporary Commission on Employee Loyalty, in its report dated March 22, 1947,[12] stated:

Existing law imposes the responsibility for the conduct of the internal affairs of each department or agency in the head thereof and principles of sound administrative management and executive accountability require that the present arrangement be left undisturbed.

However, so that the loyalty procedures operative in each of the departments and agencies may be properly coordinated, the Commission believes that a centralized advisory body should be established within the Civil Service Commission. Such advisory body shall advise departments and agencies on loyalty problems, disseminate to the departments and agencies information pertinent to loyalty matters, coordinate employee loyalty policies and procedures, conduct such studies and surveys and make such rules and regulations as it deems appropriate to the proper effectuation of the loyalty program, and from time to time, make such recommendations to the President as it deems necessary to the maintenance of employee loyalty.

The Interdepartmental Committee on Internal Security (ICIS) of the National Security Council in a report submitted to the President on April 29, 1952, in participation with the Civil Service Commission, while recognizing that final authority in a given case must rest with the agency head, concluded: [13]

---

[11] Hearings before a subcommittee of the Committee on Post Office and Civil Service, U. S. Senate, 84th Cong., 1st sess., pursuant to S. Res. 20, May 26 through Sept. 28, 1955; at p. 937.

[12] The Commission's study led to the issuance of Executive Order 9835 in March under which appeals were permitted to the Loyalty Review Board located in the Civil Service Commission.

[13] Hearings before a subcommittee of the Committee on Post Office and Civil Service, U. S. Senate, 84th Cong., 1st and 2d sess., pursuant to S. Res. 20 and S. Res. 154, Dec. 1, 2, 1955, and Jan. 6, 1956, pp. 1352–1353.

4. There should be provision for a central review of procedures established by department and agency heads for the administration of an employee security program, to determine compliance with prescribed minimum standards. The best method of assuring that procedures for the administration of an employee security program in a department or agency comply with prescribed minimum standards is to require that they be reviewed by a central body either before or after being issued. It is not intended to imply that such central review will be for any purpose other than determining compliance with minimum standards to be prescribed by the President for an employee security program. Nor is it intended that the body assigned this review function have authority to prescribe additional rules or regulations which may be binding upon departments and agencies.

It appears both reasonable and practicable that the Civil Service Commission should be designated as the body to review and advise departments and agencies concerning their procedures under the employee security program.

5. There should be provision for a limited central review of decisions of department and agency heads to terminate employees on security grounds. In his letter to the executive secretary, National Security Council, the President expressly asked that consideration be given to whether provision should be made for central review of decisions made in the various departments and agencies under employee security programs. The ICIS has given serious consideration to this question and to the implications involved therein. It has reached the conclusion that provision for appeal to some central body from removal decisions in security cases is desirable and in the public interest from the standpoint of assuring that the employee has been given his procedural rights and has had a fair opportunity to be heard, and that the decision of the agency head is supported by substantial evidence; i. e., that it is supported by such relevant evidence, more than a mere scintilla, such as a reasonable mind might accept as adequate to support the conclusion even though the reviewing agency is of the opinion that it would have reached a different conclusion had it passed on the matter originally.

Industrial organizations overwhelmingly favor administrative security centralization. Of 105 persons responding to inquiries of the Commission, 88 discussed the need for centralization to eliminate duplication, delay, waste of money, and confusion. Of the 88, 84 percent favored a central office, mostly to eliminate duplication of plant and personnel clearances. The Commission has recommended, as indicated previously, that the Office of the Secretary of Defense coordinate the industrial security work of the three military services, but that the Central Security Office assist in developing uniformity throughout the overall program under which responsibility is shared by other nonmilitary executive agencies.

In view of the above considerations the Commission has recommended the establishment of a Central Security Office headed by a Director reporting directly to the President. Its principal responsibilities in summary would be to promote uniformity and efficiency through coordinative supervision of the loyalty-security programs within its jurisdiction. This would be accomplished through a small but competent staff of hearing examiners to hear personnel cases; through a Central Review Board to hear appeals and through a small administrative staff to insure unanimity of approach not only within particular programs but where possible among the various programs. The task of insuring loyalty among Federal employees and determining that other individuals within the Federal purview meet established security standards is a major responsibility of Government. Cer-

642

tainly the foremost consideration should be that basic policies determined by Congress or by Executive order or regulation are constant and consistent in essence and uniform in application. Experience has proven that for years the opposite has been true, resulting in inequities to both the nation and the individual.

In making its recommendation for central coordination, the Commission has kept in mind at all times the delicate balance which must be observed between agency authority and total governing policy; between national security and individual rights. It believes that its recommendations not only retain those balances in proper perspective, but provide a vehicle of government administration in which they may more properly and effectively succeed.

Attorney General's List

In 1939, Congress took the first legislative step in recent years toward insuring the reliability of Government employees by enacting section 9A of the Hatch Act.[1] This was a broadly worded statute prohibiting employment by the Government of members of "any political party or organization which advocates the overthrow of our constitutional form of government," and providing that "any person violating the provisions of this section shall be immediately removed from the position or office held by him." [2]

In June 1940 Congress enacted Public Law 671 which authorized the War and Navy Departments and the Coast Guard to remove summarily any employee in "the interests of national security." [3]

To implement the Hatch Act mandate, the Civil Service Commission on June 20, 1940, issued departmental circular No. 222, stating that the Commission "will not certify to any department or agency, the name of any person when it has been established that he is a member of the Communist Party, the German-American Bund, or any other Communist, Nazi, or Fascist organization."

On June 24, 1940, Congress provided, in a rider to the Emergency Relief Appropriations Act of 1941, that "no alien, no Communist, and no member of any Nazi Bund organization shall be given employment or continued in employment on any work project prosecuted under the appropriation contained in this joint resolution." [4]   And in the Selective Training and Service Act of September 16, 1940, Congress declared its policy to be that whenever an employment vacancy resulted from induction into the armed services "such vacancy shall not be filled by any person who is a member of the Communist Party or the German-American Bund."

In June 1941, Congress appropriated $100,000 for the Federal Bureau of Investigation "to investigate the employees of every department, agency,

---

[1] 5 U. S. C. 118 (j).

[2] On Aug. 9, 1955, Congress repealed this section, replacing it with Public Law 330 (84th Cong., 1st sess., ch. 690, 69 Stat. 624), which bars the acceptance of Federal employment by any person who "(1) Advocates the overthrow of our constitutional form of government . . ."; "(2) Is a member of an organization that advocates the overthrow of our constitutional form of government in the United States, knowing that such organization so advocates." Every employee (except temporary emergency employees for less than 60 days) is required to execute an affidavit that he does not fall within these and other categories of the act; violation is made a felony, punishable by fine of $1,000 or imprisonment for not more than 1 year and a day, or both.

[3] Acts of June 28, 1940, and July 2, 1940, 54 Stat. 679, 50 U. S. C. App. (1946 ed.), 1156.

[4] Sec. 14 (f) of the act of June 24, 1940, 54 Stat. 611, 620.

and independent establishment of the Federal Government who are members of subversive organizations or advocate the overthrow of the Federal Government," and directed the Bureau to report its findings to the agencies and to Congress.[5] In 1941 also, Congress began the practice of attaching riders to the regular appropriations acts—a practice which continued during World War II and for a number of years thereafter—barring compensation to "any person who advocates, or who is a member of an organization that advocates, the overthrow of the Government of the United States by force or violence: *Provided,* That for the purposes hereof an affidavit shall be considered prima facie evidence that the person making the affidavit does not advocate, and is not a member of an organization that advocates, the overthrow of the Government of the United States by force or violence: *Provided further,* That any person who advocates or who is a member of an organization that advocates the overthrow of the Government of the United States by force or violence and accepts employment, the salary or wages for which are paid from any appropriation contained in this act, shall be guilty of a felony, and, upon conviction, shall be fined not more than $1,000, or imprisoned for not more than 1 year, or both."

The appropriation for the Federal Bureau of Investigation investigations pointed up the questions raised by this series of acts: What organizations were "subversive" and who was to determine that fact? It will be noted that Congress included no organizations by name in the acts, except in the Selective Training and the Emergency Relief Appropriations Acts; nor did it set up machinery for a definition of "subversive" which would be binding on all departments; nor did it name or empower any specific agency to make a determination.

In order that the Federal Bureau of Investigation might carry out its mandate to investigate despite the omissions in its Appropriations Act, the then Attorney General, Francis Biddle, June 1941, advised the Federal Bureau of Investigation that the Communist Party and the German-American Bund, named in the acts mentioned above, and seven other organizations came within the congressional intent.[6] This intent appears to have been made out from the language in the act dealing with advocacy of overthrow of the Federal Government, together with the legislative history of the act.

On March 16, 1942, the Civil Service Commission, pursuant to Executive Orders 9063 (7 F. R. 1075) and 9067 (7 F. R. 1407), adopted War Service Regulation II, section 3 (7 F. R. 7723), providing that an applicant might be denied appointment if there is "a reasonable doubt as to his loyalty to the Government of the United States," and stating that this matter might be considered in determining whether removal of an incumbent employee will "promote the efficiency of the service." These regulations were rescinded in 1946, with the cessation of armed hostilities.

---

[5] Pub. Law 135, 77th Cong.

[6] Memorandum, The Federal Loyalty-Security Programs, submitted to Commission on Government Security by Attorney General Brownell under covering letter dated Dec. 11, 1956.

The various departments and agencies of the Government were still left in doubt as to what constituted "subversive organizations" and as to the use, interpretation, and weight to be given to the Federal Bureau of Investigation reports on employees which were being furnished to them. Several of them asked the Attorney General for advice and guidance, in view of a number of cases which had arisen. In April 1942, the Attorney General, therefore, established an interdepartmental committee, composed of Under Secretary of the Interior John J. Dempsey, chairman; Assistant Secretary of the Treasury Herbert E. Gaston; Under Secretary of Commerce Wayne C. Taylor; and Francis C. Brown, Solicitor of the Federal Deposit Insurance Corporation. Edwin D. Dickinson, special assistant to the Attorney General, was assigned to the committee as executive secretary.[7]

This committee made a study of the problem of organizations, based on a mass of data available in the Department of Justice. In collaboration with the War Policies Unit of the War Division of the Department of Justice, brief statements concerning 14 of the so-called front organizations—Communist, Fascist, or Nazi—were distributed among the departments and agencies concerned for confidential use in administration under Public Law 135. Other "fronts" were made the subject of continuing study. Data compiled by the House of Representatives Special Committee To Investigate Un-American Activities was carefully appraised, in addition to Justice files, and the results of these studies were made available to the departments and agencies concerned. "All information released to the departments and agencies was accompanied by a caveat indicating limitations on its use and warning against inferences which might have resulted in misunderstanding." [8] During its existence, the committee designated some 32 organizations. They were not termed "subversive," but membership therein was considered relevant to an inquiry concerning fitness for public employment.[9] It also prepared and released a memorandum to the departments and agencies describing Federal Bureau of Investigation procedure in investigating complaints made under Public Law 135, explaining the nature and purpose of the interview accorded the employee by the Bureau at the conclusion of each investigation, pointing out limitations inherent in the reports and the necessity for further departmental procedures wherever there was substantial doubt as to appropriate disposition.[10]

---

[7] Report to Hon. Francis Biddle, Attorney General of the United States, from the Interdepartmental Committee on Investigations, pursuant to Public Law 135, June 30, 1942. (Reproduced pp. 83–87, hearings before the Humphrey subcommittee on Government Operations, U. S. Senate, 84th Cong., 1st sess., on S. J. Res. 21, Mar. 8–18, 1955.)

[8] Report to Hon. Francis Biddle, Attorney General of the United States, from the Interdepartmental Committee on Investigations, pursuant to Public Law 135, June 30, 1942. (Reproduced pp. 87–88, hearings before the Humphrey subcommittee of the Committee on Government Operations, U. S. Senate, 84th Cong., 1st sess., on S. J. Res. 21, Mar. 8–18, 1955.)

[9] Memorandum, The Federal Loyalty-Security Programs, submitted to Commission on Government Security by Attorney General Brownell under covering letter dated Dec. 11, 1956.

[10] Report to Hon. Francis Biddle, Attorney General of the United States, from the Interdepartmental Committee on Investigations, pursuant to the Public Law 135, June 30, 1942. (Reproduced p. 88, hearings before the Humphrey subcommittee of the Committee on Government Operations, U. S. Senate, 84th Cong., 1st sess., on S. J. Res. 21, Mar. 8–18, 1955.)

The "Attorney General's list," as it came to be called, made its first public appearance on September 24, 1942. On that date Congressman Martin Dies of Texas, in reply to statements made as to the usefulness of investigations carried on by the House Committee on Un-American Activities, read on the floor of the House of Representatives excerpts from what he termed "a photostatic copy of the confidential memoranda which was distributed to the heads of the respective departments, in which he [the Attorney General] branded 12 organizations as Communist controlled." [11] (The "respective departments" are not identified.) The excerpts read actually contained the names of nine organizations.[12] Each of the excerpts, headed "strictly confidential," began with the following caveat:

NOTE.—The following statement does not purport to be a complete report on the organization named. It is intended only to acquaint you, without undue burden of detail, with the nature of the evidence which has appeared to warrant an investigation of charges of participation.

It is assumed that each employee's case will be decided on all the facts presented in the report of the Federal Bureau of Investigation and elicited, where a hearing is ordered, by the board or committee before which the employee is given an opportunity to appear.

Please note that the statement is marked "Strictly Confidential" and is available only for use in administration of the mandate of Public Law 135.

It then went on to describe at some length the organization, membership requirements, history, leadership, and program of the named organization, and discussed the extent of Communist control over it.[13]

On February 5, 1943, President Roosevelt issued Executive Order 9300, citing as his authority therefor title I of the First War Powers Act, 1941, and his powers as President. This order established, within the Department of Justice, a new Interdepartmental Committee on Employee Investigations, composed of five members appointed by the President from among the officers or employees of the "departments, independent establishments, and agencies of the Federal Government."

Executive Order 9300 remained in effect until March 21, 1947, when President Truman revoked it and issued Executive Order 9835,[14] which instituted the so-called loyalty program. Citing as authority the Constitution and statutes of the United States, including the Civil Service Act of 1883 (22 Stat. 403), as amended, and section 9A of the act approved August 2, 1939 (18 U. S. C. 61 (i)), and his powers as President and Chief Executive of the United States, the order set up a Loyalty Review Board and, in part III, section 3, directed:

---

[11] Congressional Record, vol. 88, pt. 6, 77th Cong., 2d sess., 1942, p. 7442.

[12] The American League Against War and Fascism—The American League for Peace and Democracy; American Peace Mobilization (later [1942] called American People's Mobilization); American Youth Congress; League of American Writers; National Committee for the Defense of Political Prisoners and National Committee for People's Rights; The National Federation for Constitutional Liberties; National Negro Congress; Washington Cooperative Book Shop; and Washington Committee for Democratic Action.

[13] Congressional Record, vol. 83, pt. 6, 77th Cong., 2d sess., 1942, pp. 7442–7448.

[14] 12 F. R. 1935.

The Loyalty Review Board shall currently be furnished by the Department of Justice the name of each foreign or domestic organization, association, movement, group or combination of persons which the Attorney General, after appropriate investigation and determination, designates as totalitarian, Fascist, Communist, or subversive, or as having adopted a policy of advocating or approving the commission of acts of force or violence to deny others their rights under the Constitution of the United States, or as seeking to alter the form of government of the United States by unconstitutional means.

> (a) The Loyalty Review Board shall disseminate such information to all departments and agencies.

The list was forwarded by the Board in December 1947, and made public by printing in the *Federal Register* on March 20, 1948 (13 F. R. 1471); at that time it comprised 82 organizations, 35 of which were named for the first time.

The list as disseminated after October 21, 1948, did, in a sense, characterize the organizations, for they were listed under the six headings set up by the order (totalitarian, Fascist, etc.).[15] Those named ranged from the Klu Klux Klan and Silver Shirt Legion of America, to the Communist Party, USA; and the Jefferson School of Social Science. Because of some duplications and additions, the exact number included on this list is difficult to compute, but one copy [16] included over 150 names, the bulk of them Communist. The practice of using descriptive headings was abandoned when Executive Order 9835 was revoked by Executive Order 10450 in April 1953.

The first, and thus far the only, real Supreme Court review of the list came in 1951 in *Joint Anti-Fascist Refugee Committee* v. *McGrath.*[17] In this case the Refugee Committee, the National Council of American-Soviet Friendship and its affiliates, and the International Workers Order sued in Federal district court for injunctive relief. They recited irreparable damage from being listed without hearing, both in terms of public support and of harassment by administrative agencies of State and Federal Governments with which they dealt. The district court granted the Attorney General's motion to dismiss on the ground that no claims were stated on which relief could be granted. The Court of Appeals affirmed.

Justice Burton announced the judgment of the Supreme Court, but no opinion of the Court, in itself, commanded a majority. Five Justices held that the plaintiffs had standing to sue, although there was disagreement as to whether this arose from injury to the organizations or from a standpoint of vindicating the rights of their members. Four Justices agreed that listing without notice and hearing was improper, either on constitutional grounds or as a violation of Executive Order 9835. Justice Burton held that the Government's motion to dismiss admitted, for purposes of the decision, that the Attorney General had acted arbitrarily, and took no position

---

[15] 13 F. R. 6135.

[16] Appendix F, Commission on Government Security Hearings, Humphrey subcommittee of the Committee on Government Operations, U. S. Senate. 84th Cong., 1st sess., on S. J. Res. 21, Mar. 8–18, 1955, p. 949 ff.

[17] 341 U. S. 123 (1951).

on the broader issues. Three dissenting Justices (Reed, Vinson, and Minton) would have upheld the judgments of the courts below. Justice Clark did not participate in the case.

On remand to the district court, cross-motions of both the plaintiffs and the Attorney General for summary judgment were denied, as was the plaintiff's petition for a temporary injunction.[18] In this action, the Attorney General filed long affidavits giving reasons for listing each of the organizations; these are summarized in the opinion. He also argued that security considerations would not permit disclosure of many confidential reports and sources of information on which his determinations were based. The district court did not resolve this issue in its opinion. Plaintiff's petition for certiorari directly to the Supreme Court to review the denial of the temporary injunction was denied; [19] appeal to the court of appeals resulted in affirmation of the denial.[20] In the same opinion, the appellate court reversed a subsequent dismissal of the suits because of mootness; the Attorney General had in the meanwhile set up the hearing procedure outlined below, and had argued that the court case was moot pending the plaintiffs availing themselves of this administrative procedure. The appellate court ordered the district court to reinstate the case and give the plaintiffs time to ask for a hearing under the new procedure. They did not file for such a hearing within the 10 days allowed, however, and the district court held that their failure to act constituted acquiescence in the designation. This decision was affirmed by the Circuit Court of Appeals on February 28, 1957. The International Workers Order forwarded a letter of protest to the Attorney General on June 12, 1953, indicating that the organization neither acquiesced in the designation nor wished to participate in a hearing.[21]

It appears that as a result of opinions expressed by members of the Supreme Court in the *McGrath* case, Attorney General Brownell published, on May 6, 1953, Attorney General's Order No. 11–53,[22] which provided:

SEC. 41.1. (a) Within 10 days after effective date of Executive Order 10450 of April 27, 1953 (3 C. G. R., 1953 Supp.), each organization which has been designated by the Attorney General pursuant to paragraph 3 of part III of Executive Order 9835 of March 21, 1947 (3 C. F. R., 1947 Supp.), may file with the Attorney General . . . a written notice that it contests such designation. Failure to file a notice of contest within such period shall be deemed an acquiescence in such designation.

(b) Whenever the Attorney General after appropriate investigation proposes to designate an organization pursuant to Executive Order 9835 or Executive Order 10450, or both, notice of such proposed designation shall be sent by registered mail to such organization at its last known address. If the registered notice is delivered, the organization, within 10 days following its receipt or 10 days following the effective date of Executive Order 10450, whichever shall be later, may file with the Attorney General . . . a written notice that it desires to contest such designation. If the notice of proposed

---

[18] 104 F. Supp. 567 (D. C. D. C., 1962).

[19] 345 U. S. 911 (1953).

[20] 215 F. 2d 870 (D. C. D. C., 1954).

[21] Letter to Commission on Government Security from Warren Olney III, Acting Deputy Attorney General, June 28, 1956.

[22] 18 F. R. 2619, 28 C. F. R. sec. 41.1, et seq.

designation is not delivered and is returned by the Post Office Department, the Attorney General shall cause such notice to be published in the *Federal Register*, supplemented by such additional notice as the Attorney General may deem appropriate. Within 30 days following such publication in the *Federal Register*, such organization may file with the Attorney General . . . a written notice that it desires to contest such designation. Failure to file a notice of contest within such period shall be deemed an acquiescence in such proposed action, and the Attorney General may thereupon after appropriate determination designate such organization and publish such designation in the *Federal Register*.

A number of procedural rules for the hearing itself are also included in the Attorney General's order.

It should be noted that this hearing is held within the Department of Justice, for the purpose of determining whether an organization should be included on the Attorney General's list, which is prepared for the information of Federal officials and employees and for the convenience of persons about to enter Federal service. It is entirely separate from, and should not be confused with, hearings before the Subversive Activities Control Board, an agency independent of the Department of Justice, which makes determinations under the Internal Security Act of 1950 leading to the compulsory registration of organizations and their members and other sanctions. The SACB hearing of the Communist Party, for example, lasted for over a year and produced a transcript of 14,403 pages, with nearly 600 documents offered in evidence.

As of June 28, 1956, 15 organizations which had been on the list prior to Executive Order 10450 had requested an opportunity to contest, 12 of them failed to comply with procedural rules set forth in the Attorney General's order and consequently received no hearing. Three complied with the rules and received a hearing, but the decision had not been announced as of this writing. The remainder of the organizations listed prior to Executive Order 10450 did not request an opportunity to contest, and a large number of these were probably no longer in existence. Also as of June 28, 1956, the Attorney General had proposed 90 organizations for designation under Executive Order 10450 which had not previously been listed under Executive Order 9835. Each of these was individually notified of its proposed designation and afforded the opportunity to contest; 87 of these failed to comply with the rules and were formally designated, while three were in the process of contesting. Of the three, only one, the National Lawyers Guild, upon receiving notice of proposed designation, filed suit in Federal court and also filed a notice of contest. On June 11, 1956, the Supreme Court denied the Guild petition for rehearing, and it therefore is proceeding with the administrative contest.[23]

Executive Order 10450,[24] which became effective thirty days after its issuance on April 27, 1953, revoked Executive Order 9835, but retained so

---

[23] Letter to Commission on Government Security from Warren Olney III, Acting Deputy Attorney General, June 28, 1956.
[24] 18 F. R. 2489.

much of it as pertained to the Attorney General's list. "Section 12. . . . and the Department of Justice shall continue to furnish the information described in paragraph 3 of part III of the said Executive Order 9835, but directly to the head of each department and agency." This order also provided (sec. 8 (a) (5)) that: one of the elements of an employee's or applicant's history concerning which information was to be elicited by investigation, "membership in, or affiliation or sympathetic association with, any foreign or domestic organization, association, movement, group, or combination of persons which is totalitarian, Fascist, Communist, or subversive, or which has adopted, or shows, a policy of advocating or approving the commission of acts of force or violence to deny other persons their rights under the Constitution of the United States, or which seeks to alter the form of government of the United States by unconstitutional means," should indicate the necessity for investigations. Executive Order 10450, with the excerpts quoted, is presently in effect.

A copy of Civil Service Commission Form 385, Revised November 1955, in the files of the Commission on Government Security, has the following title: "Organizations Designated Under Executive Order 10450." Just under this, in smaller type, is the statement: "Compiled from memoranda of the Attorney General dated April 29, July 15, September 28, 1953, January 22, 1954, April 4, September 21, and October 20, 1955." In smaller type, the caveat: "This list is prepared solely for the information of Federal civilian officers and employees and for the convenience of persons completing applications for Federal employment. Membership in or affiliation with a designated organization is one factor to be considered by the departments and agencies of the Federal Government in connection with the employment or retention in employment of individuals in Federal service." An earlier (April 1955) edition added this to the preceding: "This may vary depending upon the nature of the organization and of the individual's participation." Indeed, they did vary with the several agencies, thereby adding confusion to a program fast becoming topheavy with complexity and lack of uniformity.

Civil Service Form 385 of November 1955 is the latest published list, and contains 287 names.

USES OF THE ATTORNEY GENERAL'S LIST

From the foregoing, it becomes apparent that the list has undergone considerable change in application, format, and size since 1941. These changes resulted partly from statutory and administrative requirements, and partly from public pressures.

In its inception, the list was designed for the confidential use of agency heads and their personnel officers in resolving questions arising in their implementation of certain statutes and regulations. It was not a list, in the usual sense of the word, but a series of short summaries of the information available to the Department of Justice concerning each organization; these were designed to acquaint those responsible with the possible degree of danger arising from an employee's affiliation with the organization. This danger also was a factor of the employee's activity in the organization—an organizer of it might be in a different category from a casual member.

In 1948, however, a change occurred. The list began to be printed in the *Federal Register,* and thus became officially a public, instead of a confidential, document. The practice also appears to have begun about this time of showing it to employees or applicants for their information and guidance in signing the required oaths that they were not members of subversive organizations—which were not otherwise identified in the oaths themselves. It will be recalled that criminal statutes applied to those who accepted Federal employment while holding membership in such organizations.

Present practice of at least some Government departments and agencies appears to be to print the list as an integral part of certain questionnaires and of the required oath of nonmembership.

The widespread public knowledge of the list's contents may have served a useful purpose in putting citizens on notice of possible loss of employment from too active membership in one of the named organizations. However, its publication also gave it a certain character, in the public mind, of a judicial determination, which apparently it was not intended to have. The activities of the Subversive Activities Control Board, which is designed to make judicial determinations (with attendant safeguards) and require public registration of organizations and their members, may eventually replace this function of the Attorney General's list. The tremendous time and effort required for hearings before this Board, together with possible necessity of disclosing confidential information or informants, should be borne in mind, however, in view of the fact that some 20,000 new employees are hired each month.

In some individual Federal employee cases, it appears that those making loyalty or security determinations have interpreted the regulations under which they operated to require automatic dismissal of any person who claimed, or was found to have had, any affiliation with a named organization, or associated with a person so affiliated. This, of course, distorts the list's purpose from that of merely supplying one factor to be investigated and to be borne in mind in making decisions, to that of an automatic disqualifier. The following quotation is pertinent here:

The nature and purpose of the Attorney General's list of subversive organizations is greatly and quite generally misconceived.

This list is issued pursuant to Executive Order 10450, which constituted in effect a request by the Executive for advice from the Attorney General. Thus, the list of subversive organizations, and any changes in or additions thereto, is advice from the chief law officer of the Nation to the Executive; much like a communication from an attorney to his client.

Placing the name of an organization on this list does not constitute an adjudication with respect to the nature of that organization, but is only a discretionary act by the Attorney General, by virtue of which he communicates to the President his advice

653

that the organization in question is such that unexplained, or unsatisfactorily explained, membership therein by an individual is a factor to be considered in a security evaluation of that individual. The Attorney General is saying to the Executive:

> In my judgment, as your lawyer, you ought to consider the question of the unexplained or unsatisfactorily explained membership of a man in this organization when you are reviewing his security file or determining his security status.

Membership or affiliation in one or more of the organizations on the Attorney General's list is only one factor to be considered in the evaluation of a security case.

Unfortunately, some of the trappings of adjudication appear to surround or precede the exercise by the Attorney General of his discretion in placing an organization on his subversive list. The Attorney General, of course, has a right to use whatever procedure he sees fit to help him in exercising his discretion in this regard. Since he has elected to utilize procedure paralleling in part that which would be used in an adjudication proceeding, it is not unnatural that there should be some misunderstanding of the true situation.

The committee considers it important that there should be widespread public understanding of the fact that hearing procedures instituted by the Attorney General as a preliminary to the placing of an organization on the subversive list were and are voluntary and discretionary with the Attorney General, and need be pursued or continued only so long as the Attorney General finds them needful or desirable in helping him make determinations preliminary to the exercise of his discretion with respect to what advice he shall give the President respecting subversive organizations.

While it is technically true, in a legal sense, that no sanctions flow from the fact that an organization is listed as subversive by the Attorney General, it is clear that, in a practical sense, there is a detriment, if not to an organization itself, certainly to members of the organization who are known as such, by virtue of such listing. For instance, a contractor-employer on a job where security rules are in effect normally will not employ a person whose application for employment includes derogatory information, and information respecting an organization on the Attorney General's subversive list is commonly treated as derogatory, even though unevaluated.

The practical effect of this is that, in most cases, a person who has been a member of an organization cited by the Attorney General as subversive, and who discloses that fact in his application for employment, cannot get a job on a project where clearance is required.

This situation is, of course, not a fault flowing directly from the existence of a list of organizations concerning the subversive character of which, in the judgment of the Attorney General, that official has advised the Executive; but flows, rather, from a system which, for the sake of expediency, has permitted the nature of the Attorney General's list to be misconceived, and the list itself to be misused.[25]

The Legislative Reference Service of the Congress made a survey of State and local government legislation in the subversive field. Its findings, insofar as they have been completed, are reproduced in "Security and Constitutional Rights" (hearings before the Hennings Subcommittee on Constitutional Rights of the Committee on the Judiciary, U. S. Senate, 84th Cong. 2d sess., pursuant to S. Res. 94, November 14–29, 1955) at p. 249 ff. It lists three categories: (1) State and local governments which have adopted acts or regulations which contain an express reference to the United States Attorney General's list; (2) State legislative committees conducting investigations which had made use of the United States Attorney General's list; and (3)

---

[25] Subversive Activities Control Act of 1950, report of the subcommittee to investigate the administration of the Internal Security Act and other internal security laws to the Committee on the Judiciary, U. S. Senate, 84th Cong., 1st sess., Washington, 1955, pp. 4–5.

State and local governments which have adopted acts or regulations which do not expressly include any reference to the United States Attorney General's list, but where it seems likely that the list would be used as a guide by those carrying out the program. Pertinent sections of the acts or regulations are quoted, covering some 18 pages. (Research on the third item listed above has not yet been completed.)

Apparently the States and localities have not attempted to cover the field entirely; the bulk of their activity pertains to public employees, including public-school teachers. Some of them have, however, seen fit to deal with matters such as loyalty of taxicab drivers, the barring of Communists from cities, loyalty of candidates of public office, loyalty of members of the bar, exclusion of subversive "political" parties from the ballot, loyalty of voters, loyalty of persons visiting State institutions of higher learning, loyalty of authors of schoolbooks, loyalty of insurance agents and brokers, loyalty of users of public school property, loyalty of jurors, and so forth. Some of these acts and regulations, particularly those requiring automatic dismissal of any person claiming or found to have membership in a named organization, have been the subject of court tests.

The following is an example of the use to which the Attorney General's list is presently put by an agency of the Federal Government. Any person legally holding a current valid merchant marine license or certificate, or an applicant for such a document, may make application for a special validation endorsement for emergency service. Persons eligible may apply for a port security card. In either instance, the Coast Guard rules provide:

Applications . . . shall be made under oath upon a form prescribed by the Commandant.[26]

Applicants in both instances are required to fill out questionnaires, attached to and made a part of each application. Both questionnaires contain 14 questions drawn up to elicit from the applicants information of present or past conduct bearing upon whether or not the issuance of credentials to them would be inimical to the interest of the United States. Item 14 in both questionnaires is stated as follows:

Are you now, or have you ever been, a member of, or affiliated or associated with in any way, any of the organizations set forth below?

Thereafter follows a list of almost 300 organizations. If the applicant answers "yes" to any one or more of the organizations, he must give full details in writing.

---

[26] 33 C. F. R. 121.05 (b) for merchant mariners, and 33 C. F. R. 125.21 (a) for waterfront employees.

Confrontation

One of the most controversial issues arising out of the operation of the various loyalty-security programs of the Government involves the question as to whether an individual under charges on grounds relating to loyalty or security should be accorded the opportunity to confront and to cross-examine under oath confidential informants who have furnished the derogatory information upon which the charges are based. Concerning confidential informants, J. Edgar Hoover, director of the Federal Bureau of Investigation, in appearing before the Loyalty Review Board operating under Executive Order 9835 in 1947, made the following statement:

Now as to the matter of confidential informants. That, of course, is a problem that you have to pass on. I just want to outline to you gentlemen the three types of informants that we have contact with. The first type is what we call the top secret or highly confidential informant. Under no circumstances will we disclose his identity. That informant is one who may be in high rank in the Communist Party. It has been necessary for us to have informants in some of the higher subversive movements in the country. Those informants may have furnished us information concerning certain individuals who are now employed in the Government service, and consequently, when we initiate the investigation we may find that John Doe, an employee of the Department of Agriculture, has been reported by such confidential informant as having been a member of the Party, having Communist membership card so-and-so. That information would be included in the report to the employing agency. To identify that informant would destroy the informant for our subsequent work. It would very likely imperil the informant's life.

The second type of informant is what we call the contact; that is, a person that we would not employ. It would be a professional man, a banker, a lawyer, a doctor, or some person of high standing in the community with whom we have had contacts for many years and who would not accept Government employment, but who is an outstanding, reliable source. . . . So we would record that confidential informant T–1 or T–2 has advised as follows. We would evaluate the informant by saying he is a leading member of the New York bar, and we can vouch for his thorough reliability. When that type of man gives us information in confidence, we of course are going to treat it in confidence.

The third type of informant is the next-door neighbor or fellow employee. Many times in many other types of investigations fellow employees will come in and give us information concerning some other employee in their office. It may be a superior officer. On some occasions he insists that his identity be treated in confidence. We endeavor to try to find out whether he is activated by malice, and, if he is, we try to explore that and establish the background for his hostility. He may be somewhat hysterical or overwrought as to some matter of administrative procedure that he may think he has been the victim of. Those are necessarily the functions of an investigator in interviewing a person like that. But if that person says he wants to be kept confidential we must not use his name. We will ask these employees as to whether they are willing to make a signed statement. If they will not make a signed statement, we will reflect that in our report, and that is for the evaluation by the loyalty board and the employing agency. We ask the employee if he would be willing to testify. If he says he will not, we observe that reaction and put that in the report.

Now the only other alternative that we have in that situation is a matter of policy for this committee to determine. . . . And if you decide that we should follow it, we will. We will instruct our agents that before they go in to interview that they advise the person that anything he says he must be prepared to testify to. I frankly don't believe we will get any information that way. . . .

The function of the Bureau is a fact gathering and fact finding agency. We intend merely to get the information to run down allegations of disloyalty and to incorporate them in our records, giving the sources of information where it will not affect the security of our country. But, where the person giving us information insists upon being treated as confidential, we will not give the source of the information. . . .

There has been some criticism and comment, I am told, about these designations of T–1, T–2, etc. I think it is a very simple problem. If it is the desire of this Board that the identity of confidential informants be given, I am perfectly willing to advise everyone in advance that they must be ready to testify. If they won't give it to us under those circumstances, we won't take the information. We can't afford, in the Bureau, to violate confidences.

Although Mr. Hoover in the foregoing statement referred to three types of confidential informants, broadly speaking they fall into two categories: (1) regularly established informants employed by an investigative branch of the Government for the purpose of obtaining intelligence information, and (2) lay persons such as the prominent citizen, the neighbor or fellow employee who are willing to supply information as to a particular individual only upon condition that their identity be withheld.

The name of the regularly established confidential informant engaged in intelligence work does not appear in the report of the investigative agency. He is characterized by a symbol such as T–1, and his identity is frequently withheld from the head of the agency charged with responsibility for final decision as to the retention or clearance of an employee.

The name of the casual confidential informant falling within the second category above referred to may or may not appear in the investigative report, depending upon the circumstances under which he has consented to the disclosure of his identity; and where his name is not disclosed in the report, he is likewise characterized by a symbol such as T–2.

While the investigative agency does not undertake to evaluate the information which is developed during the course of an investigation, it does evaluate the reliability of the confidential informant. The evaluation of informants by the Federal Bureau of Investigation is carefully done. The interviewing agent, in dictating his report, indicates on the last page the identity of the informant and includes sufficient data to justify the evaluating terms used. This report is reviewed in an FBI field office by a supervisor who passes on the agent's judgment. Subsequently, the agent in charge of that office personally approves the report, including the evaluation of informants. The report is then sent to FBI Headquarters in Washington where a supervisor, a section chief, an assistant director, and an assistant to the Director personally read and approve the report. When the report leaves the office of the assistant to the Director, the last page of the report containing the identity and data describing the informant is detached before the report is mailed to the agency requesting it. The evaluation relates only to the extent of reliability of the informant and not to the reliability of the information furnished.

The term *confrontation* is defined as follows: "In *criminal law,* the act of setting a witness face to face with the prisoner, in order that the latter may make any objection he has to the witness, or that the witness may identify the accused. The constitutional right of confrontation does not mean merely that witnesses are to be made visible to the accused, but imports the constitutional privilege to cross-examine them." [1] (Emphasis supplied.) Other authorities on the subject have stated that the chief purpose, the indispensable feature, of confrontation is cross-examination,[2] and that if the opportunity for cross-examination has been secured, the function of confrontation is acomplished.[3] Wigmore points out that a secondary advantage is gained by the personal appearance of the witness, "The judge and jury are enabled to obtain the elusive and incommunicable evidence of a witness' deportment while testifying, and a certain subjective moral effect is produced upon the witness,[4] but that the advantage arises not from the confrontation of the opponent and the witness but from the witness' presence before the tribunal."[5]

Obviously, the issue of confrontation arises only in those situations where the Government employee, or the privately employed individual subject to a loyalty or security program, is granted the right to a hearing in connection with charges relating to his fitness for employment or eligibility for clearance. Such a hearing is not, of course, a criminal prosecution or trial.

It was established at an early date that heads of departments and agencies in the executive branch of the Government were at liberty to hire and fire at will in the absence of statutory limitation. Discharges could be made without cause, without notice, and without hearing unless the Congress had made contrary provision.

For more than a hundred years the Congress, with few minor exceptions, had imposed no limitations on the powers of the executive branch in this respect.

The Civil Service Act of 1883 contained only one limitation, namely that employees in the competitive civil service could not be discharged for making or refusing to make a political contribution or for rendering or refusing to render a political service.

In 1912 the Lloyd-LaFollette Act was adopted. This act provided that removal or suspension without pay of permanent employees in the competi-

---

[1] *Black's Law Dictionary,* 4th edition, 1951.
[2] *Wigmore on Evidence,* vol. 5, 3d edition, par. 1362.
[3] *Greenleaf on Evidence,* 16th edition, vol. 1, sec. 163f.
[4] *Wigmore on Evidence, supra.*
[5] *Ibid.*

tive civil service could be only for such cause "as will promote the efficiency of the service." But although the act required (1) notice in writing and the reasons therefor, (2) a reasonable time in which the employee might reply in writing, (3) a consideration of such reply by the department or agency, and (4) a written decision containing the reasons for the adverse action, it expressly provided that:

No examination of witnesses nor any trial or hearing shall be required except in the discretion of the officer or employer directing the removal or suspension without pay.[6]

Under the Veterans Preference Act of 1944, veteran preference eligibles who have completed their probationary or trial period are entitled to (1) notice, (2) a reasonable time for answering and for furnishing affidavits in support of such answer, and (3) a right of appeal to the Civil Service Commission.[7]

From the foregoing it is clear that as a matter of traditional policy, hearings, with the accompanying right to present evidence, constituted the exception rather than the rule. Notwithstanding this policy, the executive and the legislative branches of the Government have recognized the need for hearing where employment or clearance is to be denied on loyalty or security grounds.

Executive Order 9835, promulgated by President Truman March 21, 1947, provided that:

An officer or employee who is charged with being disloyal shall have a right to an administrative hearing before a loyalty board in the employing department or agency. He may appear before such board personally, accompanied by counsel or representative of his own choosing, and present evidence on his own behalf, through witnesses or by affidavit.

Public Law 733, 81st Congress, which authorizes suspension and termination when deemed necessary or advisable in the interest of national security, provides that prior to termination employees who have completed their probationary or trial period and who are citizens of the United States shall be entitled to a hearing "by a duly constituted agency authority for this purpose."

Executive Order 10450, promulgated by President Eisenhower in April 1953, provides by implication for a hearing, and the regulations adopted by the various department and agency heads to implement the Executive order do so in express terms.

This departure from what may be regarded as the normal procedures, it can be fairly inferred, stems from the recognition of the grave effects which an adverse determination based upon loyalty or security grounds have upon the reputation and the earning power of the individual involved.

Under the old loyalty program embodied in Executive Order 9835, and under all the current security programs, the individual is not permitted to confront or to cross-examine the "confidential informant," whether he is

---

[6] 5 U. S. C. § 652 (a).
[7] 5 U. S. C., § 863.

regularly engaged in intelligence work, or is a casual confidential informant who has given his information under a pledge of confidence. As to all other persons who have supplied derogatory information, it is the policy of the executive branch to encourage their appearance.

The Attorney General, the Honorable Herbert Brownell, Jr., in a letter to President Eisenhower dated March 4, 1955, approved by the President shortly after its receipt, expressed this policy as follows:

Even though the statute does not provide subpoena power for witnesses, every effort should be made to produce witnesses at Security Board hearings to testify in behalf of the Government so that such witnesses may be confronted and cross-examined by the employee, so long as the production of such witnesses would not jeopardize the national security.

A subcommittee of the House of Representatives Committee on Civil Service in a report of investigations with respect to employee loyalty policies and practices stated as follows:

The Commission (CSC) feel, and the Committee (subcommittee) agrees that it would not be administratively feasible to endeavor to apply standard judicial procedure to a consideration of loyalty cases. Unless it is possible to obtain information under a pledge that the source of inform~~~~~~~~~~~~~~~ divulged, the Government will not be given ad~~~~~~

~~~~~~

~~~erican Bar Association on Com-
~ cognizance of the problem in

-commonly called "informers" has
~ almost every sphere—except em-
~ ample protection afforded against
~ is occasionally presented by in-
urity—undisclosable source. The
~st the individual rights is thus

use of such undisclosed informa-
~ontation. It is the view of this
disclosed information should be
~e, nevertheless, in the ultimate

~ to the extent consistent with
~ has created a doubt as to his
responsible officials, to gamble
~ in him which does not exist.'

ral, the statement of the
before the Richardson
~d the report of the sub-
in above quoted make it
~ntial informants are not
making his defense but

loya.
nat~

by what are genuinely regarded to be overriding considerations of national security.

On the other hand, equally loyal and patriotic individuals, groups and organizations who have made a study of the problem, motivated by a recognition of the damage which results from an adverse determination, and by the view that every precaution must be taken to insure that no injustice shall result, advocate elimination or at least substantial modification of the existing practice.

Representative of the view that the practice of denying confrontation should be completely abolished is the following statement submitted by the American Jewish Congress at the invitation of the Commission: [10]

Use of Undisclosed Evidence—First among the protections evolved by our law is the right to face one's accusers. *We, therefore, urge that all actions taken in security hearings be based on evidence placed in the record and that the use of evidence not disclosed to the accused be ended.*

A rule requiring confrontation would present no serious problem in the case of casual witnesses such as neighbors, fellow employees, classmates and other informants not regularly used by investigative agencies. The argument that such persons will not give information if required to testify openly serves only to reveal the unreliability of such backroom gossip. Experience in actual security cases shows that, when it can be exposed and challenged, the so-called information supplied by casual informers rarely results in an adverse decision. A prime example of this is the case of Abraham Chasanow. On the other hand, the anonymity given to such informers is an open invitation to scandalmongers, crackpots and personal enemies. If a person is not willing to testify openly and subject his story to the test of cross-examination, his statement should not be used by the Government in a way damaging to another person.

A more serious question is raised in the case of the paid professional informer. Plainly, there is no need for the Government to shield the identity of such witnesses as Budenz, Bentley and Philbrick who have long since abandoned their undercover work. However, the argument can be made that, if a person is still acting as a concealed operative, putting him on the stand would destroy his continuing value. In answer, it must be said that recent recantations by and discrediting of paid Government witnesses and informers such as Matusow, Crouch, and Johnson, have cast so much doubt on their reliability as to make their continued use open to serious question. Moreover, in almost all cases where an undercover agent supplies evidence against an employee, his information can be used as leads to develop independent evidence that can be used at a hearing, thereby obviating the necessity of exposing the agent.

What then would be the effect of barring the use of secret testimony? In the exceedingly rare case in which an undercover agent has the only evidence against an employee that can be obtained, the Government would have to choose between using the agent at a hearing, thus ending his undercover services, and leaving the employee in his position while protecting the Government by routine intelligence procedures. This is the same choice as the Government now faces in criminal proceedings, where the use of secret informers is, of course, absolutely barred. There is no evidence that our security is in danger because of this wholesome rule in criminal proceedings.

It is an unfortunately specious argument to confuse an administrative hearing in an essentially employer-employee relationship with a criminal prosecution. In such an administrative hearing the employee is not being

[10] Statement of the American Jewish Congress submitted to the Commission on Government Security on the Federal employees security program, Mar. 1957, pp. 24–26.

prosecuted as a criminal, and the procedures of a criminal trial are therefore not applicable.

Others would modify the program by according the right to confront and cross-examine the casual confidential informant while denying the opportunity to do so in respect to the regularly established confidential informant.

Typical of this view are the following statements:

Mr. Ernest Angell, chairman of the board of directors, American Civil Liberties Union, testified in behalf of that organization and criticized the present program because:

There is no requirement at the present time that the accusers of an employee shall be disclosed to the employee affected or even that the accuser be identified, and the employee has no right to confront or cross-examine the accusers.[11]

. . . .

The FBI counterespionage agent and the like can well have his identity kept a secret from the employee—but there is no reason why the security board itself should not cross-examine him closely in the absence of the employee.

The casual private informant, however, should be required to submit to cross-examination.[12]

Former Senator Harry P. Cain in an address delivered before the Seventh Annual Conference on Civil Liberties said:

The Government employs undercover agents, paid informers, and casual informers for whom it wishes to guarantee anonymity. This is a touchy question but I think it not indiscreet to refer to my understanding of the casual informer. Most of us have been casual informers from time to time. Investigators ask us what we know or desire to say about our friends, coworkers, associates, and acquaintances. Should we not be willing to say under oath and at a hearing what we have freely said, be that derogatory or praiseworthy, within the four walls of our home or office? If we are unwilling, should we not be required to support our judgment or retract it.[13]

Joseph Amann, president, Engineers and Scientists of America, Washington, D. C., in a letter dated April 19, 1954 to Honorable John A. Hannah, Annual Conference on Civil Liberties said:

The individual involved (accused) should have the right to hear the testimony of adverse witnesses and be afforded an opportnnity to cross-examine them. How else does one establish credibility of witnesses? An exception might apply to Government undercover agents but should most certainly not apply to those from whom such undercover agents obtain derogatory information and whose value to a security program is as incidental as that of any other loyal American citizen. Spite cases help only those who do not wish a defense program to succeed.

The procedural rights which we suggest are those provided or contemplated by the sixth amendment.

As an alternative to confrontation it has been suggested that hearing officers or boards should examine the confidential informant privately for the purpose of satisfying themselves as to the reliability of such confidential

---

[11] Hearings before a subcommittee on reorganization of the Committee on Government Operations, U. S. Senate, 84th Cong., 1st sess., on S. J. Res. 21, p. 484, Mar. 8–18, 1955.

[12] Hearings before a subcommittee on reorganization of the Committee on Government Operations, U. S. Senate, 84th Cong., 1st sess., on S. J. Res. 21, Mar. 8–18, 1955, p. 485.

[13] Hearings before a subcommittee on reorganization of the Committee on Government Operations, U. S. Senate, 84th Cong., 1st sess., on S. J. Res. 21, p. 677, Mar. 8–18, 1955.

informants and the truthfulness of the information they furnish. This policy is reflected in the revised regulations of the Atomic Energy Commission issued in May 1956.[14]

Under the new regulation, when a hearing board determines the presence of a witness is important to the resolution of material issues, the board is required to request the appropriate Commission officials to arrange, if possible, for the witness to appear, and be subject to examination and cross-examination. If the witness is unavailable, the reasons therefor are to be considered by the hearing board in making its determinations. Also, when the disclosure of the confidential nature of the sources of information are not possible, the hearing board may request the Commission to arrange for the witness to testify privately and be subject to questioning by the board.[15]

A similar approach is embodied in the recommendation of the special committee of the Association of the Bar of the City of New York on the Federal loyalty-security program, wherein it is recommended that:

> The identity of an informant who regularly provides or is employed to provide secret information should not be disclosed by requiring his appearance before a screening board or a hearing board or otherwise identifying him, whenever the head of the department or agency which obtained such information shall certify that the identification or presence of such an informant would be detrimental to the interests of national security. To the extent practicable and consistent with the interests of national security, certificates should be accompanied by data which would aid the board in evaluating the evidence given by the informant, including a statement of whether he obtained the information at first hand or through hearsay.
>
> As to all other witnesses, including casual informants, and with due consideration of the national security and fairness to the employee
>
> (a) the screening board should determine whether it desires a witness to appear before it for interview, and
>
> (b) the hearing board should determine whether the witness should be produced for cross-examination, or whether because of special circumstances he should be interrogated by the board without the employee being present, or whether his evidence should be given to the board in other ways, such as by an affidavit or a signed statement. So far as consistent with the requirements of national security, a hearing board should make available to the employee the substance of all evidence it takes into consideration which was given by any witness whom the employee has not been permitted to cross-examine.[16]

JUDICIAL OPINIONS

The issue as to the constitutional right of a Government employee to confront and to cross-examine persons supplying derogatory information has been before the Supreme Court of the United States on two separate occasions, *Bailey* v. *Richardson* [17] and *Peters* v. *Hobby*.[18]

---

[14] Title 10, chap. 1, pt. 4, sec. 4.27 (m), AEC security clearance regulations.

[15] P. 118, title 10, chap. 1, pt. 4, sec. 4.27 (m), AEC security clearance regulations.

[16] Page 14, report of the special committee on the Federal loyalty-security program of the Association of the Bar of the City of New York.

[17] 341 U. S. 918 (1951).

[18] 349 U. S. 331 (1955).

The plaintiff in the *Bailey* case was a Government employee who was removed under the loyalty program embodied in Executive Order 9835. She contended that the failure to accord her the right to confront and to cross-examine the individuals who provided the derogatory information upon the basis of which she was discharged violated the sixth amendment to the Constitution, which provides that in all criminal prosecutions the accused shall be entitled "to be confronted with the witnesses against him," and the fifth amendment to the Constitution which provides that no person shall be deprived of life, liberty, or property without due process of law. The court of appeals for the District of Columbia had ruled adversely to the employee on both of these points.[19]

A majority of the court held that the sixth amendment applied only to criminal prosecutions and was not applicable to the determination by the executive to dismiss subordinate employees at will subject only to congressional limitation.

The majority further held that the due process requirements of the fifth amendment were not applicable to the discharge of a Government employee upon the theory that Government employment was neither a property nor a contract right, and in this connection the court said: [20]

We are unable to perceive how it could be held to be "liberty". It is not "life." . . . Never in our history has a Government administrative employee been entitled to a hearing of the quasi-judicial type upon his dismissal from Government service. Due process of law is not applicable unless one is being deprived of something to which he has a *right*. (Emphasis supplied.)

The case was affirmed in the Supreme Court by an equally divided vote, and without written opinion.

Peters v. *Hobby* involved an action wherein the services of the plaintiff had been terminated notwithstanding the fact that he had been cleared after a loyalty board hearing. It was contended that the failure to accord Dr. Peters the right to confront and to cross-examine the persons supplying the derogatory information constituted a violation of the due process requirements of the fifth amendment.

The court concluded that the Loyalty Review Board did not have the authority to review the case where a favorable finding had previously been made, and it disposed of the case upon this ground without reaching the constitutional issue.

The doctrine laid down by the court of appeals in *Bailey* v. *Richardson*, affirmed by the Supreme Court, has not been overruled or repudiated, but two later Supreme Court decisions bear directly on the problem, *Wieman* v. *Updegraff*[21] and *Slochower* v. *Board of Higher Education of the City of New York*.[22]

---

[19] 183 F. 2d 46 (C. A. D. C., 1950).
[20] 182 F. 2d 46, 57.
[21] 344 U. S. 183 (1952).
[22] 350 U. S. 551 (1956).

In the *Wieman* case the majority of the court held that the constitutional protection of the fourteenth amendment extended to a public servant whose exclusion pursuant to a statute is patently arbitrary or discriminatory.

In the *Slochower case*, the court said:

> To state that a person does not have a constitutional right to Government employment is only to say that he must comply with reasonable, lawful, and nondiscriminatory terms laid down by the proper authorities.

In both *Wieman* and *Slochower* the action of State authorities dismissing the respective individuals involved was vacated by the Supreme Court on the basis that such action constituted a violation of due process under the fourteenth amendment, where the procedures followed are arbitrary and discriminatory.

The current security programs of the Government extend to the granting of clearance for access to classified information and material in the industrial security program and to the clearance of seamen under the port security program. In respect to the latter, the due process of law requirements of the fifth amendment were invoked in an action brought by seamen on behalf of themselves and others falling within the same class in connection with the then existing Coast Guard regulations in the case of *Parker* v. *Lester*.[23]

In that case the Court of Appeals for the Ninth Circuit held that the due process clause of the fifth amendment was applicable to the screening program under which seamen were screened for clearance. The court further held that the then existing Coast Guard regulations were invalid as a violation of the due process of law clause, in that they did not provide for notice of charges with such particularity as would adequately inform the individual of the basis for denial of clearance to the degree that would adequately afford him an opportunity to marshal evidence in refutation of the charges.

The court indicated that a fair résumé of the evidence against the seamen might be acceptable in lieu of confrontation and cross-examination.

The Government did not apply for writ of certiorari in the Supreme Court to review this decision, and the Coast Guard subsequently amended its regulations in an attempt to comply with the requirements of the opinion of the court in *Parker* v. *Lester*.

The use of confidential information as the basis for the denial of a passport under the passport security program has been attacked as a violation of due process of law. This issue reached the Court of Appeals for the District of Columbia in *Boudin* v. *Dulles*[24] and *Dayton* v. *Dulles*.[25] In these cases the court of appeals did not pass upon the issue but remanded the cases for further consideration with directions that, in the event the Secretary of State denied a passport on the basis of confidential information, he should so state, together with an explanation as to the nature of the reasons why such information could not be disclosed.

---

[23] 220 F. 2d 708 (1955).
[24] 235 F. 2d 532 (1956).
[25] 237 F. 2d 443 (1956).

On reconsideration the passport was issued to Boudin but denied to Dayton. In connection with the denial of a passport to Dayton, the Secretary of State stated that he had reached his conclusion in part on the basis of confidential information contained in the files of the Department of State, the disclosure of which might prejudice the conduct of United States foreign relations. Dayton brought a proceeding in the District Court of the United States for the District of Columbia to review this action. The district court held that denial of the passport on the basis of confidential information under the circumstances did not violate either procedural or substantitve due process.[26] An appeal from the decision of the district court is now pending in the Court of Appeals for the District of Columbia.

In *Jay* v. *Boyd* [27] the use of confidential information in connection with the decision of the Attorney General to refuse to suspend an order of deportation was attacked. A majority of the court held that suspension of an order of deportation was an act of grace and could not be demanded as a matter of right, and that the use of confidential information pursuant to the statute authorizing such use was not invalid. Chief Justice Warren and Mr. Justice Douglas dissented upon the ground that the use of confidential information was not authorized by the statute. Mr. Justice Frankfurter dissented upon the ground that where the Attorney General invoked the statute, the decision as to the use of confidential information and the effect to be given thereto had to be made by him personally and could not be delegated. Mr. Justice Black dissented upon the ground that the use of anonymous information to advocate deportation was not consistent with the principles of a free country.

Even if it be conceded that the interests of the government employee in his job, or that the interests of the individual employed by private industry who requires clearance for access to classified information and material, or the interests of the seaman who requires clearance in order to pursue his livelihood, are of such a nature as to be subject to the due process requirements, it does not follow that they are thereby entitled to the rights of confrontation and cross-examination.

"Due process of law" is not a fixed and static concept but is fluid in its nature.[28] The necessary requisites of due process of law under a given set of circumstances may be far more stringent than they are under other circumstances. In determining what constitutes due process of law in the loyalty-security program, the courts must take into consideration not merely the possibility of injustice to an individual but the appropriate safeguards that are necessary to adequately protect the national security.

Under Public Law 304 the Commission is charged with the dual responsibility for the development of a sound program for the adequate protection of the national security and for the administration of such a program in a

---

[26] 146 Fed. Supp., p. 76. For a more detailed discussion, see legal basis for the Passport Security Program.
[27] 351 U. S. 345 (1956).
[28] *Betts* v. *Brady*, 316 U. S. 455, p. 462 (1942).

manner which will protect the national security and preserve basic American rights.

We are of the view that the term "rights", as used in Public Law 304, is not to be construed as being limited merely to those interests recognized by the law and enforceable in court. The term, in our judgment, includes all the protective measures which fair-minded men would accord in the light of all the relevant circumstances and of the competing claims of the respective interests to be balanced.

The Commission finds that the disclosure of the identity of the regularly established confidential informant, who is employed by an investigative branch of the Government for the purpose of obtaining intelligence information which would enable the Government to cope with subversive attempts at its overthrow, would compromise the national security so long as such individual is engaged in such work.

While some advocates of full confrontation [29] recognize the need of preserving secrecy as to the identity of the regularly established confidential informant, they propose that the Government should be restricted to the choice it must make in connection with a *criminal* prosecution, namely, disclosure of the identity of the informant or abandonment of the use of the information supplied by him. Under this view the Government would be compelled to pay as the price of nondisclosure the retention in employment of, or the grant of clearance to, an individual where there was information indicating that such employment or clearance constituted a threat to the very security which nondisclosure was intended to protect. The Commission does not believe that the exaction of such a price is reasonable.

A proceeding by the Government to determine the fitness of an individual for employment or for clearance for access to classified information is not a criminal prosecution but merely an administrative process designed to ascertain the facts. Accordingly, in its recommendations as to confrontation heretofore set out in the report in connection with the individual programs to which the recommendations are applicable, the Commission does not provide for confrontation and cross-examination of the regularly established informant.

Reference is made in the statement of the American Jewish Congress, earlier referred to in this report, to doubts as to the reliability of such regularly established confidential informants arising out of their alleged recantations. To date it has not been established that evidence given by them was false or perjurious.

It should be clearly borne in mind that the regularly established confidential informant is not employed for the primary purpose of investigating any particular Government employee or any particular private employee subject to a security program. Such informant is employed for the purpose of ascertaining the facts as to the activities and plans of subversive groups and

---

[29] For example, statement of American Jewish Congress quoted above at p. 662.

organizations. During the course of such work he makes reports to the investigative agency with which he is in close contact. As an incident or byproduct to his principal function, he reports concerning all individuals as to whom he has gleaned information with respect to their activities and associations. It may be that such an individual is an employee of the Government or a worker in private industry subject to a security program; and during the course of the investigation as to his eligibility for employment or fitness for clearance, a check discloses that information concerning him is contained in the files as a result of reports made by the regularly established confidential informant.

From this it would appear clear that there would be no motive for a regularly established confidential informant to dig out or invent derogatory information as to any particular Government employee or privately employed individual. Moreover, an investigating agency has ways and means of checking the facts reported by the regularly established confidential informant for the purpose of determining his reliability.

While the Commission's recommendations do not permit confrontation or cross-examination of the regularly established confidential informant except where the head of the investigative agency is of the opinion that his identity may be disclosed, there are safeguards in connection with the use of the information furnished by such informant which can be afforded and which the Commission has recommended.

Among these safeguards are the following:

(1) The hearing examiner must furnish to the individual against whom charges have been preferred the substance of the information obtained from the regularly established confidential informant to the extent that such information is material to the consideration of the issues involved.

(2) The hearing examiner must read into the record the substance of such information and the evaluation as to the reliability placed upon such informant in the investigative report.

(3) The individual may file with the hearing examiner a written statement setting forth in detail as much of the information as is challenged by him as to accuracy or completeness.

(4) If the hearing examiner is of the opinion that additional investigation as to the specific matter challenged is required in the interest of ascertaining the facts, he may request the investigative agency to make such additional investigation.

In other recommendations the Commission has urged that the letter of charges be specific, including names, dates, and places, where the national security will not be prejudiced.

The Commission has recommended that charges be heard in the first instance by adequately trained and qualified hearing examiners under the jurisdiction of the proposed Central Security Office and has provided for an appeal to a Central Review Board.

669

As has been heretofore pointed out, it is the policy of the Government to encourage the production of witnesses so long as national security is not thereby jeopardized.

In the first annual report of the industrial personnel security review program issued by Mr. Jerome D. Fenton, director, Office of Personnel Security Policy, Department of Defense, he states: [30]

> In practice, the hearing boards not only invite the categories of witnesses listed in this instruction, but urge them to appear, and seek to impress upon each of them the importance of his role as a witness. Obviously, this sharpens the general instruction to the boards that, in evaluating the probative effect of information attributed to an informant, they shall take into account his refusal to appear as a witness and face cross-examination.
>
> A continuing effort is made to induce confidential witnesses to doff their cloak of anonymity, and to determine from the investigative agencies whether conditions have not so changed as to permit their special informants to appear and testify.

The amended Coast Guard regulations [31] in the port security program provide:

> Every effort shall be made to produce material witnesses to testify in support of the reasons set forth in the notice of the Commandant in order that such witnesses may be confronted and cross-examined by the applicant or the holder.

In the course of its deliberations the Commission has noted and given careful consideration to the arguments advanced in support of the preservation of the anonymity of the casual confidential informant. It is urged that, if the casual informant knows he may be called upon to testify under oath and be subject to cross-examination, he will refrain from imparting to the Government important information because of his reluctance to become involved in a controversy. It is further urged, and the Commission recognizes the validity of the claim, that the Government cannot in fairness accept information given to it in confidence and then be guilty of a breach of confidence.

Accordingly, the Commission has recommended that derogatory information supplied by the casual confidential informant may not be considered over the objection of the individual involved unless such casual informant is willing to disclose his identity and be subject to confrontation and cross-examination under oath either on the witness stand or by depositions or by written interrogatories.

This recommendation is subject to the qualification that if such casual confidential informant is dead, incompetent, or not subject of the jurisdiction, the derogatory information supplied by him may be considered subject to the cautionary note that the hearing examiner and the responsible agency head shall take into account and give due consideration to the fact that such informant has not been subjected to cross-examination.

Moreover, although the information supplied by such casual confidential informant is not admissible in the absence of the opportunity to confront

[30] P. 9, first annual report of the Industrial Personnel Security Review Program.
[31] Title 33, CFR, chap. 1, subchap. L, pt. 125, Apr. 27, 1956.

670

and to cross-examine him, the Commission has specifically recommended that the investigative agency may continue to receive such information and to embody it in its reports. This recommendation is based upon the view that while the information itself may not be admissible, it can and should in many instances supply leads which will facilitate the development of other information which *is* admissible under the recommendations made by the Commission.

Subpena Power

No department or agency in the executive branch of the Federal Government may issue subpenas to compel the attendance of witnesses unless such agency or department has been authorized to do so by Congress.

Although employees and other individuals subject to the current security programs are permitted under the appropriate regulations governing the respective programs to present witnesses in their own behalf and in refutation of the charges, the absence of statutory authority to issue subpoenas compelling their attendance makes it necessary to depend upon the willingness of the witness to appear.

Taking note of the situation, Attorney General Brownell, in a letter to President Eisenhower, said:

Even though the statute (Public Law 733) does not provide subpena power for witnesses, every effort should be made to produce witnesses at Security Board hearings to testify in behalf of the Government so that such witnesses may be confronted and cross-examined by the employee, so long as the production of such witnesses would not jeopardize the national security.

The Atomic Energy Commission is specifically authorized by statute [1] to issue subpenas in connection with such studies, investigations, and hearings as it deems necessary in exercising any authority provided in the law creating the Commission or in the administration and enforcement of the law.

Currently, the Atomic Energy Commission authorizes the issuance of subpenas by its General Manager in connection with hearings conducted by it involving employees, applicants for employment, and privately employed individuals requiring clearance for access to classified information and materials.

The Commission is of the opinion that the national security and the rights of individuals would be strengthened if both the Government and the individual, subject to certain restrictions and safeguards, were permitted to obtain the sworn testimony of witnesses through the use of the subpena power.

Accordingly, the Commission has recommended the following:

(1) Either the Government or the employee should be permitted to apply to the hearing examiner to issue subpenas, except as to confidential informants and identified informants who have given their information on the

---

[1] 42 U. S. C. 2201 (c).

condition that they will not be called as witnesses. Such application should state the name and address of such witness, as well as the substance of the testimony to be presented by the witness. If the hearing examiner deems the evidence relevant and not merely cumulative, he may issue the subpena.

(2) In the exercise of his discretion to issue subpenas, the hearing examiner should consider such factors as the time and expense involved by reason of the travel required.

(3) The witness should be compensated for travel expense and per diem, but where the cost is substantial, the hearing examiner may in his discretion require the parties to use deposition procedures.

(4) The Government should bear the cost of Government witnesses, but the hearing examiner should not subpena a witness for the employee until the employee deposits with the Government sufficient funds to pay the travel and per diem costs of such witness. In the event the employee is not cleared, the funds deposited by him shall be used to pay for his witness expenses. If, however, the employee is cleared, the funds deposited by him should be returned and the Government should bear the travel and per diem costs of his witnesses.

This grant of subpena power is not only desirable per se but is required to implement recommendations of the Commission as to confrontation set forth elsewhere in this report.

The subpena recommendations should apply to the proposed civilian employee and military personnel loyalty programs, and to the proposed industrial security, port security, and airport security programs.

In the military personnel program, the functions imposed upon the hearing examiners in connection with the issuance of subpenas should be exercised by the hearing boards of the respective military branches.

The requirement preventing the issuance of a subpena for confidential informants enables the Government to refrain from disclosing the identity of the confidential informant engaged in intelligence work and to honor its obligation to the casual informant whose information has been given subject to the condition that he will not be compelled to testify.[2]

Abuses of the use of the subpena are eliminated by the requirement that the testimony to be adduced must be relevant and not merely cumulative.

The costs involved in the payment of witness fees and travel expense are held to a minimum by the requirement which authorizes the use of oral depositions or written interrogatories when the actual appearance of the witness at the hearing would entail substantially greater expense.

---

[2] In this connection it is important to bear in mind that while such casual confidential informant is not subject to subpena, the information he supplies may not be used over the objection of the individual against whom charges have been preferred, unless such casual confidential informant is willing to subject himself to confrontation and cross-examination.

Privilege Against Self-Incrimination

NATURE OF THE PROBLEM

During the last few years the public has seen a succession of witnesses appear before congressional committees investigating Communist infiltration and subversion in the United States and refuse to answer questions concerning their past and present connections with the Communist conspiracy. In practically every case, the refusal to testify has been based upon the "privilege against self-incrimination," which is a shorthand expression of a basic constitutional right set forth in the fifth amendment to the United States Constitution: "No person . . . shall be compelled in any criminal case to be a witness against himself . . . ."

These numerous cases of "taking the fifth" have aroused the interest of the public in the subject of the privilege against self-incrimination, but they have failed to provide the public with more than a nodding acquaintance with the subject. The situation was well described by the then president of the American Bar Association when he said:

> At one extreme we hear references, made in good faith, I am sure, to "fifth amendment Communists," a phrase that conveys the idea, and is probably intended to, that the only persons who can properly claim the privilege [against self-incrimination] when asked about their Communist connections are conspiratorial Communists, and so it follows, it is thought, that anyone who seeks refuge behind the privilege supplies by the very act of making the claim conclusive proof that he is guilty of treason or espionage.
>
> At the other end of the spectrum there are those who, in equal good faith, would have us believe that nothing whatsoever can be inferred from the invocation of the privilege against self-incrimination, and that anyone who suggests that the exercise of this constitutional right raises any questions at all is somehow subverting the American way of life. Buffeted from all sides by such sharply differing views, the public is understandably confused.[1]

Pursuant to its mandate under Public Law 304 to develop a sound program that will protect the national security, and to implement such a program in a manner which will preserve basic American rights, the Commission on Government Security has examined the general problem of the use and abuse of the privilege against self-incrimination in those cases where an inquiry is being conducted with respect to communism or other subversive activities. The Commission has focused its principal attention, however, upon that

---

[1] Reprinted in full in U. S. News and World Report, Nov. 25, 1955, p. 86.

aspect of the general problem which is emphasized in the statement quoted above, namely, the extent to which inferences may properly be drawn from the fact that an individual has invoked the privilege in such a situation. In more precise terms, the Commission faced the problem of determining whether and to what extent the Federal Government, in the operation of its various loyalty-security programs, should use the fact of the invocation of the privilege as one of its criteria for the purpose of deciding whether an individual is suitable, on loyalty-security grounds, for employment in the Government or for clearance by it.

HISTORY AND PRESENT STATUS OF THE PRIVILEGE

In order that this particular problem might be placed in proper perspective, the Commission examined the history and present status of the privilege. The history began in the middle of the 17th century when the privilege against self-incrimination became a recognized part of the common law of England.[2] It represented an attempt to prevent the use of torture and similar inquisitional techniques as a part of the prosecutor's interrogatory procedure. This right not to be forced to be a witness against oneself was considered by the founders of our Government to be so fundamental a part of liberty under the law that it was preserved in the fifth amendment of our Federal Constitution and in all but two of the State constitutions. It is therefore, a firmly established principle of English and American jurisprudence that "no one shall be compelled to give testimony which may expose him to prosecution for crime."[3] This principle amounts to a constitutional command that prosecutors shall "search for independent evidence instead of relying upon proof extracted from individuals by force of law. The immediate and potential evils of compulsory self-disclosure transcend any difficulties that the exercise of the privilege may impose on society in the detection and prosecution of crime."[4]

In discussing the present status of the privilege, it should be kept in mind that the courts have until very recently been more concerned with defining the nature and delineating the scope of the privilege as it affects the basic rights of a defendant on trial or a witness appearing before courts and investigating bodies than with the question of the inferences which may be drawn from an invocation of the privilege by such individuals. It is in the former connection only that we may say that the present status of the privilege is clear and that the courts have enunciated specific legal rules concerning it. They may be summarized as follows: (1) a witness may properly invoke the privilege and decline to answer a question only

[2] VIII *Wigmore on Evidence* (3d Ed.), sec. 2250; note 101, p. 298.
[3] *Hale* v. *Henkel*, 201 U. S. 43, 66 (1906); *Counselmen* v. *Hitchcock*, 142 U. S. 547, 581 (1892).
[4] *U. S.* v. *White*, 322 U. S. 694, 698 (1944).

if he has reasonable cause to apprehend danger of criminal prosecution from a direct answer,[5] or that his answer may furnish a link in the chain of evidence needed to support such a prosecution.[6] The privilege does not relieve the witness of his duty to answer questions when his answers would merely tend to impair his reputation or cause him to suffer disgrace and humiliation.[7] (2) The privilege is applicable not only in ordinary civil and criminal proceedings but also to any proceeding where testimony is sought by legal process against the witness.[8] (3) The privilege may be deemed to have been waived unless it is explicitly invoked at the time the allegedly incriminatory question was first asked; i. e., if a partial answer is given, the witness must go on and make a full disclosure.[9] (4) The privilege does not justify a witness in his refusal to answer merely because he does not wish to incriminate others; i. e., the privilege is personal.[10] (5) The court has upheld the constitutionality of the so-called immunity bath statutes pursuant to which a witness may be compelled to answer a question if he is given immunity by statute from prosecution for the crimes revealed by his answer, so long as the immunity is in all respects commensurate with the protection guaranteed by the privilege itself.[11]

INFERENCES

These ground rules for the invocation of the privilege against self-incrimination do not, however, answer fully the particular question of central importance to the Commission, namely, in considering an individual's suitability for employment or clearance, what inferences, if any, may the Federal Government properly draw from the invocation of the privilege by the individual. This is a largely uncharted area, as the courts have only recently begun to consider this problem. In place of definitive legal rules, therefore, we have the sometimes exaggerated claims of the partisans of this issue. At one extreme there are those persons who assert that only a guilty person would resort to the privilege, and that therefor the mere fact of invocation of the privilege raises such a presumption of guilt (or perjury) as to make the individual ineligible for Government service. At

---

[5] *Hoffman* v. *U. S.*, 341 U. S. 479, 486 (1951).
[6] Ibid.
[7] *Smith* v. *U. S.*, 337 U. S. 137, 147 (1949).
[8] *U. S.* v. *White*, op. cit., p. 699.
[9] *Brown* v. *Walker*, 161 U. S. 591, 597 (1896).
[10] *Hale* v. *Henkle*, op. cit., p. 67.
[11] *Ullmann* v. *U. S.*, 350 U. S. 422 (1956), upholding the Immunity Act of 1954.

the other extreme, the claim is made that an exercise of the privilege does not dispel the presumption of innocence.

Attractive though it may be to some persons, the first position set forth above is no longer a tenable one, in view of the Supreme Court's recent decision in the *Slochower* case.[12] The Court therein had before it section 903 of the charter of the city of New York which provided that whenever an employee of the city utilized the privilege against self-incrimination to avoid answering a question relating to his official conduct, his tenure of office should terminate. The appellant, Slochower, was summarily dismissed (without hearing) from his position as associate professor at Brooklyn College because he had invoked the privilege before an investigative committee of the United States Senate. Slochower claimed that his rights under the 14th amendment were thereby violated. As interpreted and applied by the State courts, section 903 operated to discharge every city employee who invoked the fifth amendment.

In practical effect the questions asked are taken as confessed and made the basis of the discharge. No consideration is given to such factors as the subject matter of the questions, remoteness of the period to which they are directed, or justification for exercise of the privilege. The heavy hand of the statute falls alike on all who exercise their constitutional privilege, the full enjoyment of which every person is entitled to receive.

. . . .

At the outset we must condemn the practice of imputing a sinister meaning to the exercise of a person's constitutional right under the fifth amendment. The right of an accused person to refuse to testify, which had been in England merely a rule of evidence, was so important to our forefathers that they raised it to the dignity of a constitutional enactment, and it has been recognized as "one of the most valuable prerogatives of the citizen." *Brown* v. *Walker*, 161 U. S. 591, 610. We have reaffirmed our faith in this principle recently in *Quinn* v. *United States*, 349 U. S. 155. In *Ullmann* v. *United States*, decided last month, we scored the assumption that those who claim this privilege are either criminals or perjurers. The privilege against self-incrimination would be reduced to a hollow mockery if its exercise could be taken as equivalent either to a confession of guilt or a conclusive presumption of perjury. As we pointed out in *Ullmann*, a witness may have a reasonable fear of prosecution and yet be innocent of any wrongdoing. The privilege serves to protect the innocent who otherwise might be ensnared by ambiguous circumstances.

. . . .

. . . the Board seized upon his [Slochower's] claim of privilege before the Federal committee and converted it through the use of section 903 into a conclusive presumption of guilt. Since no inference of guilt was possible from the claim before the Federal committee, the discharge falls of its own weight as wholly without support.

We hold that the summary dismissal of appellant violates due process of law.

While this decision undoubtedly establishes as a matter of law that the Government may not adopt a policy of arbitrarily (without hearing) barring from employment or clearance any person who has invoked the privilege against self-incrimination, it also makes clear that the Constitution does not require the adoption of the contrary policy of prohibiting *any* inferences to

[12] *Slochower* v. *The Board of Higher Education of the City of New York*, 350 U. S. 551 (1956).

be drawn from an invocation of the privilege. Although the proponents of this position have argued that it would be improper for an employer to draw any inferences as to guilt from an invocation of the fifth amendment in view of the fact that the purpose of the privilege is the protection of an innocent person who might otherwise be ensnared by ambiguous circumstances,[13] the Court stated in the last paragraph of the *Slochower* decision:

> This is not to say that Slochower has a constitutional right to be an associate professor of German at Brooklyn College. The State has broad powers in the selection and discharge of its employees, and it may be that proper inquiry would show Slochower's continued employment to be inconsistent with a real interest in the State. But there has been no such inquiry here. . . .[14]

The legal boundaries within which a decision on the question of inferences must be made are therefore the following: The Government may not adopt an employment or clearance program based upon an arbitrary presumption of guilt, with resulting automatic ineligibility for employment or clearance, but it may adopt a program based upon reasonable inferences and proper inquiry.

In arriving at an answer, on policy grounds, to this basic question of inferences, sight must not be lost of the fact that employers and the public at large generally do, and will probably continue to, draw inferences of guilt from an invocation of the "privilege."[15] This practice appears to be well grounded empirically, for there is no reason to doubt that such inferences are probably correct in most of these cases. Further, this practice makes sense from a logical point of view as well. The Commission of Jurists has stated this point very clearly: [16]

> In our opinion a person who invokes this privilege can only lawfully do so in circumstances where the privilege exists. If in reliance upon this privilege a person refuses to answer a question, he is only justified in doing so if he believes or is advised that in answering he would become a witness against himself. In other words, there can be no justification for claiming this privilege unless the person claiming the privilege believes or is advised that his answer would be evidence against himself of the commission of some criminal offense. It follows from this, in our opinion, that a person claiming this privilege cannot thereafter be heard to say that his answer if it had been given would not have been self-incriminatory. He is in the dilemma that either his answer would have

---

[13] Griswold, The Fifth Amendment Today, Cambridge: Harvard University Press, 1955.

[14] *Slochower*, op. cit.

[15] See the statement of Mr. William J. Barron, labor relations counsel, General Electric Co.:

"I believe that an employee who uses the fifth amendment to avoid testifying concerning his Communist affiliations, raises serious doubts and questions in the minds of his associate, his community, and his employer. These questions may be sufficient to lead to his discharge from a plant of potential vital importance to national security, so long as the employee by his own conduct permits them to remain in existence. I think it clear beyond question, that an employer who discharges an employee because of the serious doubts and suspicions he has raised in pleading the fifth amendment has, in no sense, violated the employee's constitutional right. The employee's constitutional guarantee fully serves the purpose of protecting him from criminal prosecution, notwithstanding the fact that his employer and his community regard his silence in the face of accusaton or inquiry as raising grave doubts in their minds concerning him."

[16] Opinion of the Commission of Jurists (United Nations), Nov. 29, 1952.

been self-incriminatory or if not he has invoked his constitutional privilege without just cause. As, in our opinion, he cannot be heard to allege the latter, he must by claiming privilege be held to have admitted the former. Moreover, the exercise of this privilege creates so strong a suspicion of guilt that the fact of its exercise must be withheld from a jury in a criminal trial.

In addition to being supported by practice, the empiric facts, and logical analysis, a policy by the Government of drawing inferences of unsuitability for employment from the use of the privilege against self-incrimination is a necessary one for it in view of the fact that continued employment of such an individual is very likely to imperil the Government's relations with the public and with its other employees. In a sense, the Government as an employer must be granted the right to plead fear of Government incrimination as a reason for refusing to hire or for firing an individual who has pleaded the privilege.

Assuming as we must therefore that an inference of unsuitability for employment will continue to be drawn by the Government in these cases, that such inferences are natural, reasonable, and lawful, and that the Government will indulge in no arbitrary action based upon such inference, we face the question of how or in what manner the Government 'should or may act upon this inference. In actual practice, this question calls for a decision as to whether the employer or the employee must assume the burden of independently rebutting the inference.

In view of the fact that an individual has no absolute right to employment by the Government, and that there is no presumption of fitness for a particular position, it appears that the proper policy in these cases is for the Government to grant the individual an opportunity to explain his refusal to testify. The Government can, and should, after such proper inquiry,[17] determine whether the employment, continued employment, or granting of clearance of and to the individual is consistent with the loyalty-security interests of the Government. There would seem to be no reason why the Government must or should place upon itself any obligation to prove the guilt or unsuitability of the individual who has pleaded the privilege against self-incriminaton.

This principle has judicial support, for in a recent New Jersey case [18] dealing with the discharge of teachers from the public schools because of their refusal to testify before a congressional subcommittee, the Supreme Court of New Jersey stated that:

. . . In the instant matter the teachers' conduct before the congressional subcommittee reasonably calls for a fitness inquiry during which the teachers have a duty of cooperation and *an affirmative burden in the establishment of their fitness*. If they choose to remain silent under the protection of N. J. S. 2A: 81–5, they must do so with full realization that their administrative superiors may justifiably conclude that they are no longer fit to teach . . . [Emphasis added.]

---

[17] *Slochower*, ibid.
[18] *Laba et al.* v. *The Board of Education of Newark, Supreme Court of New Jersey*, A–58, Sept. term, 1956.

It is with these findings in mind that the Commission on Government Security has recommended that—

Refusal to testify upon the ground of self-incrimination, in any authorized inquiry relating to subversive activities conducted by a congressional committee, Federal court, Federal grand jury, or any other duly authorized Federal agency, as to questions relating to subversive activities of the individual involved or others, should be one of the criteria to be considered in the Government loyalty-security programs, unless the individual, after opportunity to do so, satisfactorily explains his refusal to testify.

It should be emphasized that while the privilege against self-incrimination is a basic constitutional right, the exercise of such right cannot and should not be free from inferences properly drawn by the Government in its loyalty-security programs aimed at the preservation of our national existence and way of life.

Separate Statements of Commissioners

General Reservation of Commissioners Cotton, McCulloch, Stennis, and Walter

Many of the recommendations of the Commission will require enactment of legislation by the Congress. We shall avail ourselves of any further information and exercise independent judgment when we again pass upon these recommendations as Members of the Congress of the United States.

COMMISSIONER.

COMMISSIONER.

COMMISSIONER.

COMMISSIONER.

685

Statement of Chairman Wright

As chairman of the Commission, I have been privileged to hold a position in the central flow of the materials considered and in constant contact with the processes of our work. Having enjoyed this unique opportunity for observation, I am constrained to offer a comment by way of supplementation in this closing chapter of the report. The opinions expressed, which could not have been included appropriately elsewhere, are my own, and not necessarily those of my associates of the Commission.

My first purpose is to commend my fellow Commissioners for their tireless and objective dedication to our task. There could be no more eloquent testimonial to the best of American traditions than their devoted service, given at great personal sacrifice, in the effort to protect both the national security and individual rights.

To observe the impressive accomplishments of the entire staff and to witness the unselfish response of the citizens called upon for aid in our endeavor has been heartening. The experience proves fully the wisdom of the Congress in making use of commissions of this kind for study of its legislative programs.

For the citizen from private life, an opportunity for objective study of the work of the legislative branch in the vital field of protecting national security is both instructive and reassuring. As an American who has reviewed the reports of various congressional committees and who has been privileged to examine the Government files, I am convinced that the investigative function of the Congress is both constructive and essential, and that on the whole the function has been discharged with fairness by sincere men seeking to meet a difficult responsibility. And I am grateful and proud that the Congress, despite the emotional stress of total war and uneasy peace, has proved able to enact legislation that in the main preserves without encroachment the principles of individual liberty and government by law.

The completion of the Commission's work does not bring to an end the need for continuing study of the demands of national security. The challenge which confronts the Nation is ever changing. In the short 18 months of the Commission's life, the 20th Congress of the Communist Party of the Soviet Union revealed a shift in conspiratorial strategy, raising new problems to be coped with. Recently, developments have made it clear that Mexico has become the unwilling center of Communist activity on this continent, imposing new burdens upon the American authorities who patrol the difficult terrain of this frontier, and suggesting the need for congressional consideration of additional safeguards.

Judicial decisions rendered during the past year have required modification of the security programs, and apparently similar changes can be anticipated for the future. Both the legal profession and an informed citizenry have found cause for concern in the judicial delays that have left in doubt many of the basic issues of the security system. Prosecutions under the Smith Act and the proceeding to declare the character of the Communist Party have been deferred. The logjam seems to be attributable to several causes. First, as recently noted by Justices Frankfurter and Harlan, the Supreme Court has appeared to direct its energies toward the disposition of "insignificant cases," thereby "doing injustice to the significant and important cases on the calendar. . . ." [1]

A second cause of uncertainty on these critical questions is the apparent tendency of certain lower courts, both district courts and courts of appeals, to allow cases involving the security laws to lie dormant on the calendar pending clarification by the Supreme Court. Under our judicial system, the proper concern of these lower courts is rather to assist the upper court by well-reasoned decision than to build a good record of affirmance and reversal. The maxim that "justice delayed is justice denied" is no less true in the field of security. When the Government is a litigant, the interests not only of the particular defendant but of all 170 million Americans are involved. Every defendant, even a Communist, is entitled to a fair and impartial trial. In these cases it is well to remember that often the defendant has by his own actions brought about his plight. He is certainly entitled to no more consideration than the 170 million parties litigant whom he seeks to subvert. Delays not premised upon necessity, appropriate extensions of time, or the principle that unnecessary constitutional questions should not be passed upon, inevitably impair the effective protection of the Nation. It is not easy for the Attorney General, charged with representing the interests of the people, to make his case after delays of 3 or 4 years. In the face of these obstacles, the Department of Justice's Internal Security Division has done a commendable job.

As this is written to meet a publication deadline, confusion has been compounded by the decision of *Jencks* v. *United States*.[2] When we are striving to survive the insidious attacks of the Kremlin seeking to destroy our government of law, it is disheartening that "blind justice" is unnecessarily blinded to realism. I respectfully urge the Congress that if we are to keep pace with our enemies who seek to infiltrate our Nation to subvert us, immediate legislation must be passed to negative the grave consequences that will flow from this confusing decision.

Such problems of security will command careful attention in the future. Continued study of the workings of the program will be imperative, and deserved criticism should be encouraged. But baseless, carping censure can

---

[1] *Ferguson* v. *Moore-McCormack Lines*, 352 U. S. 521, at 546 (1957).

[2] U. S. Supreme Court, June 3, 1957. The staff of the Commission, after hours of study, could not reach an accord either as to the legal consequences or probable effect of this decision.

serve only to discredit the responsible legislators and officials and to undermine the confidence in government that is essential to national security. In this respect the responsibilities of the public press assume a heightened significance. In a government built in a republican form superimposed upon the philosophies of a democracy, the operations of its officers cannot be cloaked in complete secrecy. An informed citizenry is a major premise of our governmental structure. But that same structure may be destroyed if a potential enemy is supplied with information critical to national self-preservation. The final responsibility for the difficult decisions of what shall be secret must be confided in those loyal and devoted public servants who are qualified to make the judgment. No citizen is entitled to take the law, and the safety of the Nation, into his own hands. With near unanimity, the American journalism profession has conscientiously observed these limits. But there are a few exceptional cases, which for some reason have escaped prosecution. The purveyor of information vital to national security, purloined by devious means, gives aid to our enemies as effectively as the foreign agent. I commend to the special consideration of the Congress the Commission's proposal for unequivocal prohibition of such irresponsible and unauthorized disclosure and for vigorous prosecution of every offender.

In closing, I am pleased to report that through the aid of the President in making available to us detailed studies conducted by other agencies and through the excellent management of our Executive Secretary, Mr. Douglas Price, the Commission has been able to complete its work with a saving of approximately $150,000 from the $882,500 appropriated for the work by the Congress.

Loyd Wright.

CHAIRMAN.

Proposed Legislation and Executive Orders

A BILL

To establish a Central Security Office to coordinate the administration of Federal personnel loyalty and security programs, to prescribe administrative procedure for the hearing and review of cases arising under such programs, and for other purposes.

Be it enacted by the Senate and House of Representatives of the United States of America in Congress assembled, That this Act may be cited as the "Federal Security Act".

TABLE OF CONTENTS

691

CHAPTER 5. INDUSTRIAL PERSONNEL SECURITY PROGRAMS

CHAPTER 6. DESIGNATION OF SUBVERSIVE ORGANIZATIONS

CHAPTER 7. STANDARDS AND CRITERIA FOR LOYALTY AND SECURITY DETERMINATIONS

CHAPTER 8. PROCEDURE IN LOYALTY AND SECURITY HEARINGS

CHAPTER 9. PROCEDURE FOR REVIEW AND FINAL DETERMINATION

CHAPTER 10. AMENDMENTS, REPEALS, AND OTHER PROVISIONS

Sec. 2. *Definitions.* As used in this Act—

(1) The term "Office" means the Central Security Office established by section 10 of this Act.

(2) The term "Director" means the Director of the Office appointed under section 11 (a) of this Act.

(3) The term "Board" means the Central Review Board established by section 11 (d) of this Act.

(4) The term "examiner" means a hearing examiner appointed under section 12 of this Act.

(5) The term "executive agency" means any department, agency, bureau, commission, office, or armed force in the executive branch of the Government, and any corporation whose share capital is wholly owned by the United States or any department or agency thereof.

(6) The term "head of the agency" or "agency head", when used in relation to any executive agency, means the head of such agency, or in the event of his incapacity or other absence, the officer of that agency who is authorized to act in his stead.

(7) The term "civilian employee" means any civilian officer or employee of any executive agency other than the Central Intelligence Agency or the National Security Agency.

(8) The term "applicant" means any individual who has made application for appointment or employment as a civilian employee.

(9) The term "sensitive position" means any office or employment in any executive agency which has been so designated by the head of that agency or his designee pursuant to authority conferred by law or Executive order.

(10) The term "loyalty program" means any program established by or pursuant to law or Executive order within any executive agency to prevent the appointment, employment, or retention as civilian employees of individuals of doubtful loyalty to the United States Government.

(11) The term "security program" means any program established by or pursuant to law or Executive order, and administered or supervised by any executive agency, to prevent untrustworthy individuals, in the interest of the national security, from gaining access to classified information or to any security facility.

(12) The term "security officer" means any officer or employee of any executive agency who is charged with the duty of carrying into effect in whole or in part the requirements of any loyalty or security program.

(13) The term "security clearance" means authorization duly given to any individual by the appropriate executive agency for access to classified information or to a security facility.

(14) The term "security facility" means the whole or any part of any—

    (a) installation or facility of any executive agency;

    (b) industrial plant or facility;

    (c) vessel, port, or port facility;

    (d) aircraft, airport, or airport facility; or

    (e) other area or facility,

which has been duly designated by the President or by any officer or employee of any executive agency, under any law or Executive order, in the interest of the national security, as a facility to which access may be granted only to those individuals who have received security clearance from the appropriate executive agency.

(15) The term "classified information" means any information or material which has been duly classified in the interest of the national security, by any officer or employee of any executive agency acting under authority conferred by law or Executive order, as "top secret" or "secret" or, in the case of the Atomic Energy Commission, as "atomic top secret" or "atomic secret".

(16) The term "government contractor" means any individual, partnership, corporation, association, institution or other legal entity obligated to furnish any goods or services to or for the use of any executive agency under the terms of any contract or subcontract containing any requirement for the safeguarding of classified information.

(17) The term "contractor representative" means any individual who is an officer, director, partner, member, employee, agent, or other representative of any government contractor.

(18) The term "national agency check", when used in relation to the investigation of any individual, means an investigation of that individual made upon the basis of written information supplied by him in response to official inquiry, and by reference to files of the Federal Bureau of Investigation and the Civil Service Commission, appropriate intelligence files of the Armed Forces, appropriate files of any other investigative or intelligence agency in the executive branch, and appropriate files of any committee or subcommittee of the Congress.

(19) The term "full field investigation", when used in relation to the investigation of any individual, means an investigation of that individual made by reference to all sources required for a national agency check, and in addition thereto:

> (a) law enforcement files of the municipality, county, and State within which that individual resides or is employed;
>
> (b) records of schools and colleges attended by him;
>
> (c) former employers of that individual;
>
> (d) references given by him; and
>
> (e) any other available source of information.

CHAPTER 1. CENTRAL SECURITY OFFICE

SEC. 10. *Central Security Office established.*

(a) There is hereby established in the executive branch of the Government a Central Security Office, which shall not be a part of or supervised by any other department or agency in the executive branch.

(b) The principal office of the Central Security Office shall be in the District of Columbia, but the Office or any duly authorized representative thereof may exercise any or all of its powers at any place.

(c) The Office shall have an official seal, which shall be judicially noticed.

SEC. 11. *Executive officers.*

(a) The Office shall be administered by a Director, who shall be appointed for a term of six years, and whose annual rate of basic compensation shall be $_____.

(b) There shall be in the Office an Assistant Director for Hearings and an Assistant Director for Administration, each of whom shall be appointed for a term of six years and shall receive compensation at the annual basic rate of $_____.

(c) There shall be in the Office a Central Review Board composed of three members. Each member of the Board shall be appointed for a term of six years, except that the three members first appointed under this subsection shall be appointed for terms of two, four, and six years, respectively. Any members of the Board appointed to fill a vacancy occurring before the expiration of the term for which his predecessor was appointed shall be appointed for the remainder of such term. Not more than two members of the Board may be members of the same political party. Each member of the Board shall receive compensation at the annual basic rate of $_____.

(d) The Director, each Assistant Director, and each member of the Board

694

shall be appointed by the President, by and with the advice and consent of the Senate. The President shall designate one member of the Board to serve as chairman. Any such officer may be removed by the President for inefficiency, neglect of duty, or malfeasance in office, but for no other cause.

(e) No such officer may engage in any business, vocation, or employment other than that of serving as such officer.

SEC. 12. *Hearing examiners.*

(a) Subject to the civil-service laws and the Classification Act of 1949, there shall be appointed in the Office by the Director hearing examiners in such number as he may determine from time to time to be required for the performance of the duties of the Office.

(b) All hearing examiners so appointed shall be selected from a special register which shall be established by the Civil Service Commission, and must possess such special qualifications as the Civil Service Commission shall prescribe after consultation with the Director.

(c) No individual appointed in the Office as a hearing examiner shall serve as such under this Act until he has satisfactorily completed a comprehensive course of instruction in the duties of his office which shall be established by the Director.

SEC. 13. *Other officers and employees.*

Subject to the civil-service laws and the Classification Act of 1949, there shall be appointed in the Office by the Director an Executive Secretary and such other officers and employees as the Director may determine from time to time to be necessary for the performance of the duties of the Office.

SEC. 14. *Investigation of personnel.*

No individual may be appointed to or employed in any position in the Office until the Civil Service Commission has conducted a full field investigation of that individual in conformity with the provisions of subsections (b) and (d) of section 40 of this Act.

CHAPTER 2. COORDINATION OF LOYALTY AND SECURITY PROGRAMS

SEC. 20. *Training and information programs.*

(a) The Director shall establish and maintain suitable initial and in-service training programs to provide for the instruction of officers and employees of the Office in their duties and responsibilities under this Act.

(b) The Director shall conduct periodic conferences of security officers of executive agencies to (1) furnish to such officers such information as may be required for the effective discharge of their duties and responsibilities, and (2) provide for the establishment to the greatest practicable extent of uniformity in the practices and procedures of executive agencies in carrying into effect loyalty and security programs.

SEC. 21. *Surveys and inspections.*

(a) The Director shall conduct continuing surveys and inspections of the regulations promulgated and the practices and procedures employed by executive agencies to carry into effect loyalty and security programs. Such surveys shall include studies with respect to:

(1) personnel security questionnaire forms used;

(2) facility clearance forms used;

(3) personnel screening practices and procedures used;

(4) training programs established by executive agencies for the instruction of security officers of such agencies;

(5) training programs established by executive agencies for the instruction of the personnel of contractor representatives as to the duties

of government contractors with respect to the safeguarding of classified information;

(6) manuals prescribing practices and procedures to be followed, within executive agencies and by government contractors, in safeguarding information affecting the national security; and

(7) programs of executive agencies for the classification and declassification of information affecting the national security.

(b) The inspection authority of the Central Security Office shall be limited to the examination and evaluation of procedures and practices of executive agencies in the administration of loyalty and security programs for the purpose of determining whether they are in accord with applicable acts of Congress, Executive orders, and rules and regulations promulgated by the Central Security Office. The Central Security Office shall not have authority to examine other documents or files of any executive agency.

(c) Upon the basis of surveys and inspections so conducted, the Director shall, after consultation with the executive agencies concerned, recommend to those executive agencies such changes in loyalty and security regulations, practices, and procedures as the Director may determine to be necessary or advisable in the interest of uniformity, simplicity, effectiveness, and economy.

(d) In the course of such surveys and inspections with respect to any executive agency, the Director shall determine whether (1) the information classification procedures of such agency result in the overclassification of information, and (2) such procedures provide effectively for the declassification of information when the need for its classification has ended.

SEC. 22. *Evaluation of contractor complaints.*

(a) The Director shall receive, investigate, and evaluate complaints made by government contractors with respect to the requirements imposed upon them under security programs of executive agencies.

(b) After consultation with interested government contractors and with the executive agencies concerned, the Director shall make his recommendations to such executive agencies for any changes in those requirements which may be determined by the Director to be necessary or desirable to establish greater uniformity, to eliminate inconsistencies in requirements, to eliminate unnecessary duplication of effort, to provide improved coordination of loyalty and security programs of executive agencies, or to improve the effectiveness of those programs.

SEC. 23. *Statistics.*

(a) The Director shall compile and maintain appropriate statistical records with respect to the results of each loyalty and security program administered or supervised by executive agenices.

(b) With regard to loyalty programs relating to civilian employees of executive agencies, such statistical records shall include:

(1) the number of individuals removed from Federal service on the ground that there was reasonable doubt as to their loyalty to the Government of the United States;

(2) the number of persons who resigned after receiving advice from the Government that there was derogatory information indicating reasonable doubt as to their loyalty;

(3) the number of applicants who have had hearings on loyalty grounds and the results thereof;

(4) the number of cases in which the advisory recommendations of examiners have been accepted by heads of executive agencies;

(5) the number of cases in which the advisory recommendations of examiners have been rejected by heads of executive agencies;

(6) the number of cases which have been reviewed by the Central Review Board and the results of such review;

(7) the number of cases in which the heads of executive agencies have accepted the recommendations of the Central Review Board;

(8) the number of cases in which the heads of executive agencies have rejected recommendations of the Central Review Board;

(9) the number of cases in which there has been readjudication of the loyalty issue; and

(10) the number of investigations resulting from national agency checks which disclose derogatory subversive information requiring the referral thereof to the Federal Bureau of Investigation for full field investigation.

SEC. 24. *Rules and regulations.*

(a) The Director shall promulgate regulations for the conduct of officers and employees of the Office in carrying out their duties under this Act.

(b) The Director shall prescribe rules of practice, consistent with the provisions of this Act, for the conduct of hearing and review proceedings under chapter 8 and chapter 9 of this Act.

(c) After consultation with the executive agencies concerned, the Director shall promulgate such regulations as he may determine to be necessary to provide for uniformity in the application and administration of loyalty and security programs of executive agencies. Such regulations shall include interpretative guides which shall be followed by screening officers of executive agencies in applying the loyalty and security standards prescribed by law or Executive order, and the criteria prescribed for the determination of loyalty and security questions, to particular fact situations.

SEC. 25. *Reports.*

(a) In January of each year, the Director shall transmit to the President and to the Congress a full and complete report concerning the operations of the Office during the preceding calendar year. Each such report shall contain a description of each loyalty and security program in effect during that year, and a detailed statistical analysis of the results of the operation of that program during such year. Each such report may contain the recommendations of the Director for such additional legislation, and for such additional executive or administrative action, as he may consider necessary or advisable for the improvement of any loyalty or security program.

(b) Upon request made by the President, the Congress or either House thereof, or any duly authorized committee or subcommittee of either House of the Congress, the Director shall make a special report concerning the operation of any loyalty or security program.

(c) Each executive agency charged with the administration or supervision of any loyalty or security program shall compile and transmit to the Director such information as he shall determine to be necessary to carry into effect the provisions of subsections (a) and (b) of this section.

SEC. 26. *Other duties.*

The Director shall perform such other duties as the President may direct with respect to the formulation, administration, supervision, study, and evaluation of loyalty and security programs.

CHAPTER 3. HEARING AND REVIEW OF LOYALTY AND SECURITY QUESTIONS

SEC. 30. *Hearings required.*

(a) Whenever any civilian employee of any executive agency, or any applicant for civilian employment in any such agency, is entitled by law or

Executive order under any loyalty program to a hearing under this Act upon any question concerning his loyalty to the United States Government, that hearing shall be conducted in accordance with the provisions of chapter 8 of this Act.

(b) Whenever any individual who is not an officer, employee, or member of any executive agency is entitled by law or Executive order under any security program to a hearing under this Act upon any question concerning his eligibility for security clearance, that hearing shall be conducted in accordance with the provisions of chapter 8 of this Act.

(c) Whenever any organization is entitled by section 64 of this Act to receive a hearing on the question whether that organization is of a category which may be designated for inclusion on the list described by section 60 of this Act, that hearing shall be conducted by the Office in accordance with the provisions of chapter 8 of this Act.

SEC. 31. *Review required.*

Whenever any individual or organization has received under section 30 a hearing upon any question, and the head of the executive agency concerned has determined that question, in conformity with or contrary to the recommendations of the examiner who conducted that hearing, in a manner unfavorable to the applicant for such hearing, that individual or organization shall be entitled upon timely application to a review of such determination by the Central Review Board in accordance with the provisions of chapter 9 of this Act.

CHAPTER 4. CIVILIAN EMPLOYEES LOYALTY PROGRAM

SEC. 40. *Investigation of civilian employees and applicants.*

(a) Whenever any individual is under consideration for appointment to or employment in any position in any executive agency, an investigation shall be conducted for the purpose of determining his loyalty to the United States Government and his suitability for service in that position. No individual may enter into service in any such position until that investigation has been completed, except that in any case in which the head of the executive agency concerned determines that an emergency condition requires the earlier entry of that individual into service, he may be tendered appointment or employment conditioned upon a favorable determination as to his loyalty and suitability upon the completion of the investigation.

(b) A national agency check shall be made with respect to each applicant considered for appointment to or employment in any nonsensitive position in any executive agency. A full field investigation shall be made with respect to (1) each applicant considered for appointment to or employment in a sensitive position in any executive agency, and (2) each civilian employee considered for transfer from a nonsensitive position to a sensitive position in any executive agency.

(c) In the case of an individual entering a position in the competitive service, the investigation shall be made by the Civil Service Commission unless there is in effect an agreement between the Commission and the executive agency concerned under which other provision is made for the conduct of that investigation. In the case of an individual entering a position not in the competitive service, the investigation shall be made by the executive agency concerned, except that if that agency has no investigative organization such investigation shall be made by the Civil Service Commission.

(d) If that investigation discloses derogatory subversive information, the matter shall be referred to the Federal Bureau of Investigation, which shall then conduct a full field investigation of that individual.

698

(e) Every report made by any investigative agency pursuant to this section shall include all information, favorable or unfavorable, obtained by that agency relative to the individual who is the subject of investigation.

SEC. 41. *Evaluation of personnel investigations.*

(a) The head of each executive agency shall designate, from personnel of that agency specially qualified for such service, one or more screening officers who shall be charged with the duty of—

(1) evaluating derogatory information relating to loyalty contained in reports of investigations of civilian employees of that agency and applicants for appointment or employment therein; and

(2) determining whether such reports disclose any substantial information justifying the issuance of a letter of charges as to the loyalty of any such individual to the United States Government.

(b) Whenever a screening officer determines that an investigative report contains any such information as to any such individual, that officer shall grant to the individual concerned an opportunity for an interview in which he may offer his explanation of that information. If that interview discloses the need for additional investigation, the screening officer may request, and the appropriate investigative agency shall conduct, that additional investigation.

(c) If, after such interview has been completed or declined by the individual concerned, the screening officer determines that the issuance of a letter of charges as to the loyalty of that individual is justified, such officer shall prepare and transmit to that individual such a letter of charges which shall be as specific and detailed as the interests of national security permit, and shall include such pertinent information as names, dates, and places in such detail as reasonably to permit answer to be made thereto. The letter of charges so transmitted must advise the individual concerned as to his right to a hearing in conformity with section 42.

(d) Before issuing any such letter of charges, a screening officer of any executive agency shall obtain the opinion of the appropriate legal officer of that agency on the questions whether:

(1) the proposed charges are based upon loyalty or upon suitability criteria;

(2) the proposed letter of charges is sufficiently specific and detailed; and

(3) all other procedural requirements for the issuance of such letter have been satisfied.

(e) Whenever any investigative report discloses information indicating that any civilian employee or applicant may be unsuitable, on any ground other than doubt as to his loyalty, for the position he holds or for which he is under consideration, action with respect to the question so raised shall be governed by the provisions of law and regulations applicable to the determination of the suitability of individuals for appointment to, or employment or retention in, that position, including the provisions of section 6 of the Act of August 24, 1912 (37 Stat. 555, as amended; 5 U. S. C. 652).

SEC. 42. *Loyalty hearings and determinations.*

(a) No civilian employee may be dismissed from his office or employment, and no applicant may be denied appointment or employment, in any executive agency on the ground that doubt may exist as to his loyalty unless that individual has been accorded an opportunity for a hearing in accordance with the provisions of chapter 8 of this Act, and (1) the head of that agency has determined, upon the basis of evidence received in that hearing, that there is reasonable doubt as to the loyalty of that individual to the United States

699

Government, or (2) the individual concerned has declined, or has failed to make timely application for, such hearing. Whenever the head of any executive agency makes any determination as to the loyalty of any individual, he shall transmit promptly to that individual written notice of such determination.

(b) Within the time prescribed by regulations which shall be promulgated by the Director, the recipient of any letter of charges issued under section 41—

(1) may file his sworn answer thereto, accompanied by any affidavits or other written statements he may care to submit; and

(2) upon the filing of such sworn answer, may request a hearing upon those charges in accordance with the provisions of chapter 8 of this Act.

(c) Whenever any civilian employee or applicant has availed himself of his right to receive a hearing upon a letter of charges issued by any executive agency under section 41—

(1) the screening officer shall forward that request, together with the letter of charges transmitted to that individual and all papers filed by him in reply thereto, to the Director for filing and hearing in accordance with the provisions of chapter 8 of this Act; and

(2) the head of that agency shall designate, from personnel of that agency, such counsel or other personnel as may be required to represent that agency at such hearing.

(d) Whenever an agency head determines, on the basis of all evidence contained in the record of any such hearing, that there is reasonable doubt as to the loyalty of any individual, that individual may, within such time as the Director shall prescribe by regulations, make written application to the agency head for a review of such determination. Upon receipt of timely application for such review, the agency head shall forward that request, together with all documents and records pertinent thereto, to the Director for review by the Central Review Board in accordance with the provisions of chapter 9 of this Act.

(e) If, after any such determination, the individual concerned declines, or fails to make timely application for, such review, such determination shall, upon the expiration of the period within which application for review may be made, become final and conclusive, and shall be binding upon the head of every other executive agency in the absence of a further determination by the head of such agency or his successor, made after consultation with the chief legal officer of that agency, to the effect that new information warrants a rehearing upon that question.

SEC. 43. *Transfer and suspension of civilian employees.*

(a) The head of each executive agency shall designate as a sensitive position each office and employment in that agency which is of such nature that its occupant could bring about a material adverse effect upon the national security.

(b) Whenever a screening officer in any executive agency receives information which is apparently reliable and which indicates that reasonable doubt may exist as to the loyalty of any civilian employee occupying a sensitive position in that agency, he shall transmit such information to the head of the agency or his designee, who shall not be lower in rank than Assistant Secretary, or its equivalent rank in that agency. If that officer determines that the character of that information and the weight to be given thereto are such as to require the immediate removal of that employee from such position for the protection of the national security, he shall—

(1) transfer that employee, without reduction in salary, to a nonsensitive position within that agency, if there is a vacancy in any such position in the agency for which that employee is qualified; or

700

(2) if no such position exists in the agency, suspend that employee from duty with compensation at the rate to which he was entitled at the time of his suspension.

(c) As soon as may be practicable after the transfer or suspension of any civilian employee, the screening officer shall (1) transmit to that employee written notice of the reasons for the transfer or suspension, and (2) request the appropriate investigative agency to conduct such additional investigation as may be required for determination of the question whether a letter of charges against that employee shall be prepared and transmitted to him in conformity with section 41. Such investigative agency shall give priority to the investigation of civilian employees who have been transferred or suspended under subsection (b).

(d) If it is thereafter determined that available information does not warrant the preparation of a letter of charges against a civilian employee transferred or suspended under subsection (b), he shall be restored to that position. If a letter of charges is prepared and transmitted to such employee, he shall continue in a transferred or suspended status in conformity with the provisions of subsection (b) until—

(1) he has declined an opportunity for hearing in conformity with section 42, or has failed to make timely application for such hearing; or

(2) if he makes timely application for such hearing, he has received that hearing and the head of the executive agency of which he is a member has made his determination on the question whether, upon all evidence contained in the record of hearing, there is reasonable doubt as to the loyalty of such employee.

(e) If the determination made by the head of an executive agency on that question is favorable to a transferred or suspended civilian employee, he shall be restored to duty in the position from which he was transferred or suspended. If the determination made by the head of the agency is unfavorable to such an employee, that employee may, within such time as the Director shall prescribe by regulations, make written application to the agency head for a review of such determination. Upon receipt of timely application for such review, the agency head shall forward such request, together with all documents and records pertinent thereto, to the Director for review by the Central Review Board in accordance with the provisions of chapter 9 of this Act.

(f) Whenever a transferred or suspended civilian employee of any executive agency makes timely application for such review, he shall be suspended from service in that agency without compensation pending final determination made by the agency head on the basis of such review. If the determination so made by the agency head is unfavorable to such a civilian employee, and he declines or fails to make timely application for such review, he shall be separated from the service of that agency upon the expiration of the period within which application for such review may be made.

(g) Whenever a civilian employee of any executive agency has been suspended without compensation from any position under subsection (f), and the head of that agency determines after review that reasonable doubt as to the loyalty of that employee does not exist, he shall be restored to that position, and shall be paid from funds appropriated to that agency a sum equal to (1) the amount of compensation which he would have received from that agency for the period of his suspension without compensation if he had been continued in active service in that position during that period, reduced by (2) the net amount of any compensation actually received by that employee for personal services rendered by him in any other employment or occupation during that period.

701

(h) Whenever a civilian employee of any executive agency has been suspended without compensation under subsection (f), and the head of that agency determines after review that reasonable doubt does exist as to the loyalty of that employee, he shall be separated from the service of that agency without reimbursement for any loss of compensation sustained by him during the period of such suspension.

(i) The restoration under this section of any transferred or suspended civilian employee to the position from which he was transferred or suspended shall not bar his removal from that position in conformity with the provisions of section 41 (e) of this Act.

SEC. 44. *Readjudications.*

The case of any civilian employee or applicant whose loyalty to the Government of the United States has been adjudicated or readjudicated before the effective date of this chapter under the provisions of Executive Order No. 10450, dated April 27, 1953, as amended, shall not be readjudicated under the provisions of this chapter in the absence of new evidence, acquired after the effective date of this chapter, which warrants the institution of proceedings under this chapter for the determination of the question whether there is reasonable doubt as to the loyalty of that individual.

CHAPTER 5. INDUSTRIAL PERSONNEL SECURITY PROGRAMS

SEC. 50. *Personnel security programs required.*

(a) Each executive agency engaged in the procurement of goods or services from government contractors shall, if such procurement involves access by contractor representatives to classified information or to any security facility, establish and administer, in such manner consistent with the provisions of this Act as the President shall prescribe, a security program to prevent access by untrustworthy individuals to such information or to any such facility.

(b) No contract shall be executed by any executive agency with any government contractor for the procurement of goods or services involving access by contractor representatives to classified information or to any security facility unless such contractor enters into an appropriate security agreement in writing under which that contractor is obligated—

(1) to withhold from any individual access to information and security facilities of any classification unless that individual holds a security clearance for access to information and security facilities of that classification; and

(2) to incorporate within any contract executed with any subcontractor, for the procurement of any goods or services required for the performance of the contract with that agency, such security provisions as may be prescribed in the security agreement executed with such executive agency.

SEC. 51. *Investigation of contractor representatives.*

(a) No executive agency shall grant to any contractor representative any security clearance for access to any information or security facility which has been classified as "secret" or "atomic secret" unless a national agency check has been made with respect to that individual by the appropriate investigative organization of such agency. If that check discloses as to that individual any derogatory subversive information requiring further investigation, the matter shall be referred to the Federal Bureau of Investigation, which shall then conduct a full field investigation of that individual. If the national agency check discloses as to that individual any other derogatory information requiring further investigation, such further investigation shall be conducted by the investigative organization of such agency.

(b) No executive agency shall grant to any contractor representative any security clearance for access to any information or security facility which has been classified as "top secret" or "atomic top secret" unless a full field investigation of that individual has been made by the appropriate investigative organization of that agency. If in the course of that investigation any derogatory subversive information is disclosed as to that individual, such investigation shall be transferred to the Federal Bureau of Investigation, which shall then conduct a full field investigation of that individual.

(c) If any executive agency has no investigative organization, the investigations required by this section to be made by that agency shall be made by the Civil Service Commission.

SEC. 52. *Evaluation of personnel investigations.*

(a) The head of each executive agency administering an industrial personnel security program shall designate, from personnel of that agency specially qualified for such service, such number of screening officers as may be required for the administration of that program. It shall be the duty of such officers to examine investigative reports made concerning contractor representatives, and to determine whether such reports disclose any substantial information raising doubt as to the eligibility of such individuals for any security clearance.

(b) Whenever a screening officer of any agency determines that an investigative report contains information raising doubt as to the eligibility of any individual to receive any security clearance, such officer shall grant to that individual an opportunity for an interview in which he may offer his explanation of the facts and circumstances upon which that information is based. Whenever such officer determines that such a report contains information raising doubt as to the eligibility of any individual to hold a security clearance previously granted, he shall accord to that individual an opportunity for such an interview unless that officer determines that immediate suspension of such clearance is necessary in the interest of the national security.

(c) If, after the conclusion of any such interview and any further investigation considered by the screening officer to be necessary, the derogatory information concerning that individual has not been explained to the satisfaction of the screening officer, he shall withhold or suspend the security clearance of that individual, and shall prepare and transmit to him a letter of charges which shall be as specific and detailed as the interests of national security permit, and shall include such pertinent information as names, dates, and places in such detail as reasonably to permit answer to be made thereto. The letter of charges so transmitted must advise the individual concerned as to his right to a hearing in conformity with section 53.

(d) Before issuing any such letter of charges, a screening officer of any executive agency shall obtain the opinion of the appropriate legal officer of that agency on the questions whether:

(1) the proposed letter of charges is sufficiently specific and detailed; and

(2) all other procedural requirements for the issuance of such letter have been satisfied.

SEC. 53. *Security hearings and determinations.*

(a) Within the time prescribed by regulations which shall be promulgated by the Director, the recipient of any such letter of charges—

(1) may file his sworn answer thereto, accompanied by any affidavits or other written statements he may care to submit; and

(2) upon the filing of such sworn answer, may request a hearing upon those charges in accordance with the provisions of chapter 8 of this Act.

(b) Whenever any individual has availed himself of his right to receive a hearing upon a letter of charges issued by any executive agency under section 52—

(1) the screening officer shall forward that request, together with the letter of charges transmitted to that individual and all papers filed by him in reply thereto, to the Director for filing and hearing in accordance with the provisions of chapter 8 of this Act; and

(2) the head of that agency shall designate, from personnel of that agency, such counsel or other personnel as may be required to represent that agency at such hearing.

(c) Upon the basis of all evidence contained in the record of such hearing, the head of the executive agency concerned shall make his determination on the question whether the individual concerned is eligible to receive or hold a security clearance. If the agency head determines that such individual is not eligible to receive or hold such security clearance, that individual may, within such time as the Director shall prescribe by regulations, make written application to the agency head for a review of that determination. Upon receipt of timely application for such review, the agency head shall forward that request, together with all documents and records pertinent thereto, to the Director for review by the Central Review Board in accordance with the provisions of chapter 9 of this Act.

(d) If, after any such determination, the individual concerned declines, or fails to make timely application for, such review, that determination shall, upon the expiration of the period within which application for review may be made, become final and conclusive, and shall be binding upon the head of every other executive agency.

CHAPTER 6. DESIGNATION OF SUBVERSIVE ORGANIZATIONS

SEC. 60. *Designation required.*

(a) The Attorney General shall compile, maintain, and publish, for the use of executive agencies in the administration of loyalty and security programs authorized by law or by Executive order, a list of the names of organizations heretofore or hereafter determined by him:

(1) to seek to alter the form of Government of the United States by force or violence, or other unconstitutional means; or

(2) to be organized or utilized for the purpose of advancing the aims and objectives of the Communist movement; or

(3) to be organized or utilized for the purpose of establishing any form of dictatorship in the United States or any form of international dictatorship; or

(4) to be organized or utilized by any foreign government, or by any foreign party, group or association acting in the interest of any foreign government for the purpose of (A) espionage, or (B) sabotage, or (C) obtaining information relating to the defense of the United States or the protection of the national security, or (D) hampering, hindering, or delaying the production of defense materials; or

(5) to have adopted a policy of advocating or approving the commission of acts of force and violence to deny others their rights under the Constitution of the United States; or

(6) to be affiliated with, or act in concert with, or be dominated or controlled by, any party, group, or association of the character described in paragraphs (1), (2), (3), or (4), above.

704

(b) No organization may be determined hereafter by the Attorney General to be of any category listed in subsection (a) unless that organization has been (1) investigated by the Federal Bureau of Investigation and (2) accorded an opportunity for hearing and review in conformity with the provisions of this chapter. No organization heretofore determined by the Attorney General to be of any of the categories listed in subsection (a) shall be entitled to hearing or review under this chapter.

(c) The designation of the name of any organization for placement on the list required by subsection (a) shall be accompanied by a statement which:

(1) describes the origin, history, aims, and purposes of that organization; and

(2) states the period of time during which that organization has belonged to one or more of the categories listed in subsection (a).

(d) Whenever the name of any organization is placed on that list, and such organization thereafter ceases to exist, its name shall be retained on the list, but shall be accompanied by a statement as to the date and circumstances of its dissolution.

(e) Upon a showing satisfactory to the Attorney General, he may in his sole discretion cancel the designation of any organization the name of which has been placed upon that list.

SEC. 61. *Notice of proposed designation.*

(a) Whenever the Attorney General, after appropriate investigation, proposes to designate the name of any organization for placement on the list required by section 60, he shall notify that organization of such proposal by registered mail directed to the last known address of the organization. If notice so transmitted cannot be delivered and is returned by the Post Office Department, the Attorney General shall cause such notice to be published in the *Federal Register,* and shall take any other available action to transmit actual notice thereof to that organization.

(b) Notice so given shall specify the charges made against that organization with such particularity as to permit it to answer and defend.

SEC. 62. *Notice of contest of designation.*

(a) Within such time after the giving of notice under section 61 as the Attorney General shall prescribe by regulations, that organization may file with the Attorney General written notice of its desire to contest the proposed designation. Such notice shall be signed by the executive officers (or persons performing the ordinary and usual duties of executive officers) of such organization.

(b) If no notice of contest is filed by that organization within the prescribed time, the Attorney General may, without further proceedings, make his final determination designating that organization for inclusion on the list required by section 60.

SEC. 63. *Discovery proceedings.*

(a) Whenever any organization files a notice of contest under section 62, the Attorney General shall, within such time thereafter as he shall prescribe by regulations, transmit to that organization a statement of the grounds for the proposed designation and such written interrogatories as he considers necessary to obtain facts pertinent to those grounds.

(b) Within such time thereafter as the Attorney General shall by regulation prescribe, that organization may file a verified reply to those interrogatories which shall be signed by the executive officers (or persons performing the ordinary and usual duties of executive officers) of that organization. The reply so made must answer each interrogatory completely and with particularity, and shall be limited to statements of fact. Such reply may be accompanied by affidavits duly executed by officers or members of the organization.

(c) If timely reply is made by that organization to such interrogatories, the failure of that organization to answer any interrogatory or any part thereof, or the submission by that organization of an evasive reply to any interrogatory or any part thereof, shall be deemed an admission of the facts to which such interrogatory or part refers. If that organization fails to make any timely reply to those interrogatories, such failure shall constitute an acquiescence by that organization in the proposed designation, and the Attorney General may, without further proceedings, make his final determination designating that organization for inclusion on the list required by section 60.

(d) If timely reply is made by any organization to interrogatories transmitted under subsection (a), such reply may be accompanied by a request for hearing before the Attorney General on the proposed designation, which request may be granted by the Attorney General in his discretion.

SEC. 64. *Hearing on proposed designation.*

(a) If, upon the basis of discovery proceedings under section 63, the Attorney General determines that the named organization should not be designated for inclusion upon the list required by section 60, he shall transmit to that organization written notice to that effect.

(b) If the Attorney General does not make such a determination, he shall notify that organization of (1) his continued proposal to so designate that organization, and (2) the right of that organization to obtain a hearing on that question before the Central Security Office.

(c) If an organization to which notice of right of hearing has been transmitted under subsection (b) files with the Attorney General its application for such hearing within the time prescribed by regulations of the Attorney General, the Attorney General shall—

(1) forward that application, together with all documents and records pertaining thereto, to the Director for filing and hearing in accordance with the applicable provisions of chapter 8 of this Act; and

(2) designate from personnel of the Department of Justice one or more individuals authorized to represent him at such hearing.

(d) Upon the basis of all evidence contained in the record of any such hearing, the Attorney General shall make his determination on the question whether the organization concerned is to be designated for inclusion on the list required by section 60.

(e) If any organization to which notice of right of hearing has been transmitted under subsection (b) fails to file with the Attorney General timely application for such hearing, the Attorney General may, upon the expiration of the time within which such application may be made, make his final determination designating that organization for inclusion on that list without further proceedings.

SEC. 65. *Review and final determination.*

(a) If a determination unfavorable to the organization concerned is made by the Attorney General, that organization may, within the time prescribed by regulations of the Attorney General file, with the Attorney General an application for review of that determination. Upon the filing of timely application for such review, the Attorney General shall forward that application, together with all documents and records pertaining thereto, to the Director for review by the Central Review Board in accordance with the provisions of chapter 9 of this Act. Upon the basis of the report of that review, the Attorney General shall make his final determination on the question whether that organization is to be designated for inclusion on the list required by section 60.

(b) If any organization which is entitled to such review of an adverse determination made by the Attorney General under section 64 (c) fails to file its application for review within the period prescribed, such determination of the Attorney General shall become final upon the expiration of that period.

SEC. 66. *Effect of final determination.*

Any final determination made by the Attorney General in conformity with the provisions of this chapter designating any organization for inclusion on the list required by section 60 (a) shall be final and conclusive, and may not be questioned or reviewed by any other officer, any executive agency, or any court.

CHAPTER 7. STANDARDS AND CRITERIA FOR LOYALTY AND SECURITY DETERMINATIONS

SEC. 70. *Loyalty of civilian employees.*

(a) No individual may be appointed, employed, or retained as a civilian employee if, upon all information, there is reasonable doubt as to his loyalty to the Government of the United States.

(b) In determining whether there is reasonable doubt as to the loyalty of any individual to the Government of the United States, activities and associations of that individual of one or more of the following categories may be considered:

(1) sabotage, espionage, or attempts or preparations therefor, or knowingly associating with spies or saboteurs;

(2) treason or sedition, or the advocacy thereof;

(3) advocacy of revolution, or force or violence, to alter the constitutional form of Government of the United States;

(4) intentional, unauthorized disclosure to any person, under circumstances which may indicate disloyalty to the United States, of documents or information of a confidential or nonpublic character;

(5) performing or attempting to perform his duties, or otherwise acting, so as to serve the interests of another government in preference to the interests of the United States;

(6) membership in, or affiliation or sympathetic association with, any party, group, or association which has been found by the Congress of the United States, or any agency or officer of the United States duly authorized by the Congress for that purpose:

(A) to seek to alter the form of Government of the United States by force or violence, or other unconstitutional means; or

(B) to have been organized or utilized for the purpose of advancing the aims or objectives of the Communist movement; or

(C) to have been organized or utilized for the purpose of establishing any form of dictatorship in the United States or any form of international dictatorship; or

(D) to have been organized or utilized by any foreign government, or by any foreign party, group, or association acting in the interest of any foreign government, for the purpose of (i) espionage, or (ii) sabotage, or (iii) obtaining information relating to the defense of the United States or the protection of the national security, or (iv) hampering, hindering, or delaying the production of defense materials; or

(E) to be affiliated with, or to act in concert with, or to be dominated or controlled by, any party, group, or association of the character described in (A), (B), (C), or (D), above;

(7) membership in or affiliation with any organization which has been found by the Congress of the United States, or any agency or officer of the United States duly authorized by the Congress for that purpose, to have adopted a policy of advocating or approving the commission of acts of force and violence to deny others their rights under the Constitution of the United States; and

(8) refusal to testify, upon the ground of self-incrimination, in any authorized inquiry relating to subversive activities conducted by any congressional committee, Federal court, Federal grand jury, or any other duly authorized Federal agency, as to any question relating to subversive activities of the individual involved or others, unless the individual, after opportunity, to do so, satisfactorily explains his refusal to testify.

(c) The enumeration contained in subsection (b) shall not be deemed to exclude consideration of any other factor tending to establish reasonable doubt as to loyalty.

(d) In determining the significance to be given for the purposes of this Act to membership of any individual in, or the association of any individual with, any organization, consideration must be given to:

(1) the character and history of that organization;

(2) the time during which such individual was a member of, or associated with, such organization;

(3) the actual knowledge of that individual, at the time of such membership or association, as to the nature and purposes of that organization;

(4) the extent to which the nature and purposes of that organization were publicly known at the time of such membership or association;

(5) the purpose for which that individual became a member of, or associated with, that organization;

(6) the degree to which that individual participated in the activities of that organization; and

(7) if that individual no longer is a member of, or associated with, that organization, the time at which his membership or association was terminated, the circumstances of such termination, and the degree to which he has separated himself from the activities of that organization.

(e) The normal relationships within the family shall not be deemed to create a reasonable doubt as to loyalty unless they fall within the class of close, continuing, or sympathetic association, and unless such association with members of the family is of such a nature as to indicate sympathetic association with an organization of the type described in paragraph (6) of subsection (b).

SEC. 71. *Security of contractor representatives.*

(a) No contractor representative may be granted or hold any security clearance if it is determined in accordance with the provisions of this Act, on the basis of all information, that his possession of such clearance will endanger the common defense and security.

(b) In determining for the purposes of this section whether the possession of any security clearance by any individual will endanger the common defense or security, activities and associations of that individual of one or more of the following categories may be considered:

(1) sabotage, espionage, or attempts or preparations therefor or knowingly associating with spies or saboteurs;

(2) treason or sedition or advocacy thereof;

(3) advocacy of revolution or force or violence to alter the constitutional form of Government of the United States;

(4) intentional, unauthorized disclosure to any person of classified information;

(5) performing or attempting to perform his duties, or otherwise acting, so as to serve the interests of another government in preference to the interests of the United States;

(6) membership in, or affiliation or sympathetic association with, any party, group, or association which has been found by the Congress of the United States, or any agency or officer of the United States duly authorized by the Congress for that purpose:

(A) to seek to alter the form of Government of the United States by force or violence, or other unconstitutional means; or

(B) to have been organized or utilized for the purpose of advancing the aims and objectives of the Communist movement; or

(C) to have been organized or utilized for the purpose of establishing any form of dictatorship in the United States or any form of international dictatorship; or

(D) to have been organized or utilized by any foreign government, or by any foreign party, group, or association acting in the interests of any foreign government, for the purpose of (i) espionage, or (ii) sabotage, or (iii) obtaining information relating to the defense of the United States or the protection of the national security, or (iv) hampering, hindering, or delaying the production of defense materials; or

(E) to be affiliated with, or to act in concert with, or to be dominated or controlled by, any party, group, or association of the character described in (A), or (B), or (C), or (D) above;

(7) membership in or affiliation with any organization which the Congress of the United States, or any agency or officer of the United States duly authorized by the Congress for that purpose, has found to have adopted a policy of advocating or approving the commission of acts of force and violence to deny others their rights under the Constitution of the United States;

(8) refusal to testify upon the ground of self-incrimination, in any authorized inquiry relating to subversive activities conducted by a congressional committee, Federal court, Federal grand jury, or any other duly authorized Federal agency, as to any question relating to subversive activities of the individual involved, or others, unless the individual, after opportunity to do so, satisfactorily explains his refusal to testify;

(9) refusal to testify upon the ground of self-incrimination, in any other authorized inquiry conducted by a congressional committee, Federal court, Federal grand jury, or any other duly authorized agency, unless the individual, after opportunity to do so, satisfactorily explains his refusal to testify;

(10) willful violations or disregard of security regulations, or recurrent and serious, although unintentional, violation of such regulations or unauthorized disclosure of classified information;

(11) any illness, including any mental condition, of a nature which in the opinion of competent medical authority may cause significant defect in the performance, judgment, or reliability of the individual, with due regard to the transient or continued effect of the illness and the medical findings in such case;

(12) any behavior, activities, or associations which tend to show that the individual is not reliable or trustworthy;

(13) any deliberate misrepresentations, falsifications, or omission of material facts from a Personnel Security Questionnaire, Personal History Statement, or similar document;

(14) any criminal, infamous, dishonest, immoral or notoriously disgraceful conduct, habitual use of intoxicants to excess, drug addiction, or sexual perversion;

(15) any facts which furnish reason to believe that the individual may be subjected to coercion, influence, or pressure which may cause him to act contrary to the best interests of the national security; or

(16) any other activity, association, or condition which tends to establish reasonable ground for belief that access by such individual to classified information or to any security facility will endanger the common defense and security.

(c) The provisions of subsections (d) and (e) of section 70 shall be applicable with respect to determinations made under this section.

CHAPTER 8. PROCEDURE IN LOYALTY AND SECURITY HEARINGS

SEC. 80. *Applicable law.*

(a) Determination whether any applicant is entitled to a hearing under this chapter shall be governed by the law or Executive order under which the action complained of was taken by the executive agency concerned.

(b) Determination of the questions presented by any letter of charges filed for hearing under this chapter shall be made in conformity with standards and criteria prescribed by the law or Executive order establishing the right of the applicant to that hearing.

SEC. 81. *Assignment of examiners.*

(a) Whenever any application is filed for hearing under this chapter, the Director shall place that application upon a hearing calendar, shall assign an examiner to conduct a hearing thereon, and shall notify each party to the proceeding as to the time and place of hearing.

(b) The Director shall take such action as may be required to insure to the greatest possible extent the prompt disposition of matters placed upon the hearing calendar. Priority of hearing shall be given to cases which involve the suspension from duty of civilian officers or employees of executive agencies because of the existence of doubt as to their loyalty to the United States Government.

SEC. 82. *Powers of examiners.*

(a) An examiner assigned to conduct any hearing under this chapter shall have the power to administer oaths for the purpose of taking evidence in that proceeding.

(b) Subject to the provisions of section 85, an examiner assigned to conduct any hearing under this chapter shall have the powers of a district court of the United States to issue process to compel witnesses to appear and testify in the hearing, and to compel the production of other evidence. Any process so issued may run to any part of the United States or its Territories, Commonwealths, and possessions.

(c) Any person who willfully neglects or refuses to appear, or refuses to qualify as a witness or to testify, or to produce any evidence in obedience to any subpena duly issued under authority of this section shall be fined not more than $500, or imprisoned for not more than six months, or both. Upon the certification by the examiner of the facts concerning any such willful disobedience by any person to the United States Attorney for any judicial district in which such person resides or is found, such attorney shall proceed by information for the prosecution of such person for such offense.

(d) Subject to the provisions of section 84, an examiner assigned to conduct any such hearing shall have the power to (1) authorize any party to such hearing to obtain the testimony of any person by deposition upon oral examination or by written interrogatories, and (2) appoint any person to take any such deposition or interrogatory. Any person so appointed shall have the power to administer oaths and to take such testimony.

SEC. 83. *Proceedings generally.*

(a) In any hearing conducted under this chapter the applicant for such hearing shall be allowed—

(1) a reasonable time to prepare for such hearing;

(2) to appear at his own expense at such hearing;

(3) to be represented, at his own expense, by counsel; and

(4) to present evidence and rebuttal evidence on his behalf.

(b) The rules of evidence applied by courts need not be applied in hearings under this chapter, but no evidence shall be received by the examiner in any such hearing unless it is relevant to one or more of the allegations contained in the letter of charges which provides the basis for such hearing.

(c) Any letter of charges issued by any executive agency may thereafter be amended by such agency, at any time before the conclusion of hearing thereon, to include additional or different charges. Whenever any such amendment occurs, the party who is the subject of inquiry shall be allowed such additional time as the Director shall by rule determine to be reasonable for the filing of the amended answer of such party to such additional or different charges.

(d) In any hearing upon any question concerning the loyalty of any civilian employee of any executive agency, or any applicant for appointment or employment in any such agency, that individual shall be permitted to offer evidence as to (1) his character and his reputation for veracity and integrity, and (2) his demonstrated appreciation of the need for the protection of the national security against foreign and domestic enemies.

(e) Each witness who appears before the examiner in any such hearing shall be examined under oath or affirmation. Subject to any right of confrontation conferred by section 84 upon the party who is the subject of inquiry, there may be received in evidence in any such hearing the affidavit of any witness offered by either party to such proceeding.

(f) All proceedings in any hearing under this chapter shall be made a part of the record, but only the examiner, personnel assigned for official duty at such hearing, the party who is the subject of inquiry, counsel for each party, and witnesses may be present at such hearing.

(g) The examiner shall cause to be prepared a verbatim stenographic transcript of all proceedings in each hearing, including all evidence received therein. At the conclusion of the hearing in each case the transcript of the record shall be authenticated by the certificate of the examiner.

(h) After the conclusion of the hearing in any case, the examiner shall prepare a written report thereon, which shall contain a recitation of the questions presented, a summary of the evidence received, his findings as to the facts as to each allegation made with respect to the party who is the subject of inquiry, and his conclusion on each question presented for hearing. Upon the completion of that report, it shall be forwarded to the Director, who shall transmit it to the head of the executive agency concerned for his action.

(i) If the determination made by the head of the executive agency is unfavorable to the party who is the subject of inquiry, a true and correct copy of the transcript of the record of proceedings in the hearing, and a true and correct copy of the report prepared by the examiner upon such hearing, shall be furnished without charge to that party as soon as may be practicable after timely application has been made by such party to the head of such agency for the review of that determination under chapter 9 of this Act.

SEC. 84. *Right of confrontation.*

(a) Except as otherwise specifically provided by this section, no derogatory information concerning the loyalty of any party who is the subject of inquiry in any hearing under this chapter may be received in evidence in such hearing, over the objection of that party, unless the supplier of such information is identified by name and——

(1) gives oral testimony under oath or affirmation before the examiner, subject to cross-examination by or on behalf of the party who is the subject of inquiry; or

(2) gives testimony under oath or affirmation by deposition or interrogatory in the taking of which opportunity has been accorded to that party to propound cross-questions or cross-interrogatories relevant to all allegations made by the supplier of such information with respect to that party; or

(3) gives testimony by affidavit executed under oath, and is available for the giving of further testimony on application by the party who is the subject of inquiry through the issuance of a subpena or by deposition or interrogatory.

(b) Confrontation of regularly established confidential informants engaged in obtaining intelligence and internal security information for the Government shall not be allowed where the head of the investigative agency determines that the disclosure of the identity of such informants will prejudice the national security. In such cases the report supplied by the investigative agency shall contain as much of the information supplied by the informant as may be disclosed without revealing the identity of the informant and without otherwise endangering the national security.

(c) If confrontation is not permitted under subsection (b), the hearing examiner shall furnish the party involved with the substance of the information obtained from such informant to the extent that such information is material to the consideration of the issues involved, and shall read into the record the substance of such information and the evaluation as to reliability placed upon such confidential informant in the investigative report.

(d) If the party who is the subject of inquiry questions the accuracy or completeness of the information furnished pursuant to subsection (c), that party may file with the examiner a written statement setting forth in detail so much of the information which is challenged as to accuracy or completeness. If the examiner is of the opinion that the additional investigation as to the specific matter challenged is required in the interest of ascertaining the facts, he shall request the investigative agency to make such additional investigation. Information obtained as a result of the additional investigation shall be treated in the same manner as provided for in the original investigation.

(e) Derogatory information supplied by confidential informants other than those described in subsection (b) shall not be considered, over the objection of the party involved, by any hearing examiner in arriving at his determination, or by any officer charged with the responsibility for making a final determination, unless such informants consent to the disclosure of their identity so as to enable the party involved to obtain their testimony through the issuance of subpenas or by depositions or written interrogatories.

(f) Derogatory information supplied by identified persons shall not be considered, over the objection of the party involved, by any hearing examiner in arriving at his determination, or by any officer charged with the responsibility for making a final determination, unless the party involved is given the opportunity to obtain the testimony of such identified persons through the issuance of a subpena, or by depositions or written interrogatories. If the party involved is given the opportunity to obtain the testimony of such identified persons through the issuance of a subpena, or by depositions, or written interrogatories, such derogatory information supplied by identified persons shall be considered. If the identified person supplying the derogatory information is unavailable for service of subpena or the taking of his testimony by deposition or written interrogatories because of death, incompetency, or other reason, such derogatory information may be considered by the examiner with due regard for the lack of opportunity for cross-examination.

(g) In any hearing under this chapter upon a letter of charges issued under chapter 5 of this Act, the right of confrontation granted by this section shall be limited to evidence received in support of charges of the kinds listed in paragraphs (1) through (8) of section 71 (b) of this Act. In any such hearing upon a letter of charges issued under any other security program, the right of confrontation granted by this section shall be limited in accordance with any express provisions of the statute or Executive order establishing or authorizing such program which restrict the right of confrontation in such hearing.

SEC. 85. *Issuance of subpenas.*

(a) Upon his own motion, or upon application made by any party to any hearing upon charges of the kinds listed in section 70 (b) or (c), or upon charges of the kinds listed in paragraphs (1) through (8) of section 71 (b) of this Act, the examiner may issue subpenas to compel the attendance of witnesses or the production of other evidence. Each such application for the issuance of a subpena to require the attendance of any witness must state the name and address of the witness desired and the substance of the testimony which such witness is believed to be qualified to give. Each such application for the issuance of a subpena to require the production of other evidence shall state the name and address of the person to whom it is to be directed and the nature of the evidence desired.

(b) The examiner shall deny any such application if he determines that the evidence sought (1) is not relevant to any issue presented for hearing, or (2) would be merely cumulative to other evidence received in the hearing. If, upon any such application, the examiner determines that a substantial sum would be required for the payment of per diem and mileage allowances incident to the issuance of a subpena, and that the evidence desired can be obtained by deposition or interrogatory, he may deny the application and require such evidence to be obtained by deposition or interrogatory.

(c) No subpena or other process may be issued by the examiner to compel the attendance, or otherwise to obtain the evidence, of—

(1) any individual certified by the head of any investigative agency of the executive branch of the Government to be a regularly established

713

confidential informant engaged in obtaining intelligence and internal security information for such agency; or

(2) any other individual, without the consent of such individual, if such individual is certified by the head of any such agency to have given information to such agency concerning the party who is the subject of inquiry upon the condition that the supplier of such information would not be called as a witness to testify with respect to information so given.

(d) The provisions of section 1821 of title 28, United States Code (relating to per diem and mileage allowances of witnesses), shall apply to witnesses summoned to appear at any hearing conducted under this chapter. The per diem and mileage allowances of witnesses summoned on behalf of the executive agency which is a party to the hearing shall be paid from funds appropriated to such agency. No witness shall be summoned by process issued on behalf of any party who is the subject of inquiry unless that party has deposited with the examiner such sum as he determines to be necessary to defray the per diem and mileage allowances payable to that witness. Such allowances of each witness so summoned shall be paid from the sum so deposited. If, after the conclusion of any hearing, the head of the executive agency concerned, upon the record of proceedings in that hearing, determines the question presented in a manner favorable to the party who deposited any such sum, there shall be paid to that party from funds appropriated to such executive agency a sum equal to the aggregate amount of all deposits so made by that party in that hearing.

SEC. 86. *Hearings on designation of organizations.*

(a) Whenever, in any hearing on the question whether any organization is of a category which may be designated for inclusion on the list required by section 60 of this Act, the examiner determines that such question can be decided fairly upon the basis of (1) the written statement of the grounds of the Attorney General for the proposed designation and the verified reply of that organization thereto and (2) answers to interrogatories, affidavits, or other written evidence supplied by that organization to the Attorney General and received in evidence at the hearing, the examiner may close the hearing without taking other evidence.

(b) If the organization concerned fails to make an appearance at any such hearing, the examiner shall prepare his report upon the basis of oral or written evidence offered and received in evidence.

(c) The rules of evidence applied by courts need not be applied in any such hearing, but the examiner shall maintain reasonable limitations as to the relevancy, competency, and materiality of the evidence received. The examiner in his discretion may receive in evidence the affidavit of any witness in lieu of his oral testimony.

(d) Whenever the examiner determines in any such hearing that the proposed testimony of any witness would be irrelevant, immaterial, cumulative, or repetitious, he may exclude that testimony.

(e) At any such hearing, objections to the admission or exclusion of evidence or other rulings of the examiner shall be limited to a concise statement of the reasons therefor. Argument in support of such objections may be limited in the discretion of the examiner.

(f) Notwithstanding the provisions of section 84, the examiner may receive in evidence, in any such hearing, information or documentary material offered in behalf of the Attorney General, in summary form or otherwise, without requiring the disclosure of classified information or the identity of any regularly established confidential informant engaged in obtaining intelligence and internal security information for any investigative agency.

714

CHAPTER 9. PROCEDURE FOR REVIEW AND FINAL DETERMINATION

Sec. 90. *Application for review.*

(a) Upon receipt of any application for review under this chapter, the Director shall—

    (1) transmit to the Board (A) the application for review, (B) a copy of the determination to be reviewed, (C) the examiner's report upon which that determination was based, and (D) the record of proceedings in the hearing upon which the examiner's report was based; and

    (2) notify each party to such review as to the time and place of any hearing which may be granted upon that review.

(b) Under rules prescribed by the Director, parties to any review under this chapter may be accorded an opportunity to submit to the Board briefs and oral argument upon any or all questions presented for consideration in that review. If such opportunity is accorded, the head of the executive agency concerned shall designate, from personnel of that agency, one or more individuals authorized to represent him before the Board.

(c) The Director shall take such action as may be required to insure to the greatest possible extent the prompt disposition of matters referred to the Board for review. Priority of review shall be given to cases involving the suspension from duty of civilian employees of executive agencies because of the existence of doubt as to their loyalty to the United States Government.

Sec. 91. *Applicable law.*

Determination of any question presented by any application transmitted to the Board for review under this chapter shall be made in conformity with standards and criteria prescribed by the law or executive order establishing the loyalty or security program under which such question arose.

Sec. 92. *Scope of review.*

(a) In the review of any case under this chapter, the Board shall—

    (1) review the proceedings taken in the hearing of such case by the examiner to determine whether they were taken in conformity with law and applicable regulations; and

    (2) prepare its written report of such review, and its recommendation as to the action to be taken by the head of the agency concerned with respect to each question presented for review.

(b) The review of any case shall be limited to an examination of the report of the examiner in that case and the record of proceedings in the hearing before the examiner. If in the opinion of the Board the report and record are insufficient to permit the preparation of its recommendation, the Board may return the report and record to the examiner who conducted the hearing, or to any other examiner, for such further proceedings as the Board may direct. Upon the completion of such proceedings, the record thereof shall be transmitted to the Board for its action thereon in conformity with subsection (a).

(c) If any member of the Board does not concur in any recommendation made by the Board in any case, he may prepare his separate report stating his reasons for his disagreement.

Sec. 93. *Final determination after review.*

(a) As soon as may be practicable after the completion of its review of any case, the Board shall transmit its report, and the separate report of any member of the Board, to the Director, who shall then forward each such report to the head of the executive agency concerned for his action thereon.

(b) The determination made by the head of that executive agency, upon the basis of the report or reports so transmitted to him, as to any question considered in that review, shall be final and conclusive, and may not be reviewed by any other officer, any executive agency, or any court.

CHAPTER 10. AMENDMENTS, 'REPEALS, AND OTHER PROVISIONS

SEC. 100. *Department of Defense Industrial Security Program.*

(a) Chapter 137 of part IV of subtitle A of title 10 of the United States Code is amended by adding at the end thereof the following new section:

"§ 2315. *Industrial security program.*

"(a) Notwithstanding the provisions of paragraph (4) of section 202 (a) of the National Security Act of 1947, as amended (5 U. S. C. 171a (c)), the Secretary of Defense shall establish and administer within the Office of the Secretary of Defense a single industrial security program relating to all aspects of military industrial security. Such program shall—

"(1) apply to all government contractors obligated to furnish goods or services to or on behalf of the Department of Defense and each department and agency thereof, including each armed force administered by any military department;

"(2) provide that no such military department or armed force shall adopt or enter into any industrial security agreement or provision with or applicable to government contractors until such agreement or provision has been approved by the Secretary of Defense; and

"(3) with respect to industrial personnel security, conform to the requirements of chapter 5 of the Federal Security Act except as otherwise specifically provided by this section.

"(b) As soon as may be practicable after the enactment of this section, all civilian officers and employees of each military department, and all civilian employees of the Army, Navy, Air Force, and Marine Corps, engaged in the administration of any industrial security program (except personnel engaged primarily in investigative or procurement duties) shall be transferred to the Office of the Secretary of Defense. Military personnel of such armed forces may be detailed for service in the Office of the Secretary of Defense in such numbers as the Secretary may determine from time to time to be necessary to carry into effect the provisions of this section.

"(c) Whenever chapter 5 of the Federal Security Act requires any investigation of any contractor representative to be made incident to any contract or agreement executed by the Department of Defense, any military department or agency thereof, or any armed force administered by any such military department, such investigation shall be conducted by the appropriate military investigative agency, as determined by the Secretary of Defense, unless such investigation is required by that chapter to be conducted by the Federal Bureau of Investigation.

"(d) The Secretary of Defense shall promulgate such regulations as he shall determine to be necessary to carry into effect the provisions of this section. To the greatest practicable extent, such regulations shall be uniform with respect to all military departments and all such armed forces."

(b) The analysis of such chapter is amended by adding at the end thereof the following:

"2315. Industrial security program."

Sec. 101. *Atomic Energy Act amendment.*

Section 143 of the Atomic Energy Act of 1954 (42 U. S. C. 2163) is amended by adding at the end thereof the following: "Whenever any contractor representative has received security clearance under the industrial personnel security program of any other executive agency, in conformity with the requirements of chapter 5 of the Federal Security Act, the Commission may grant to the holder of such clearance, without further investigation, access to Restricted Data if the Commission determines that (a) the standard of investigation required for the issuance of such clearance by such other executive agency is comparable to that required by the Commission for the granting of access to such Restricted Data, (b) the clearance granted by such other executive agency to that individual is currently in effect, and (c) no information possessed by the Commission indicates the need for further investigation of that individual before granting such access. Terms used in the preceding sentence which are defined by section 2 of the Federal Security Act shall in that sentence have the meanings given to them by such section."

Sec. 102. *National Labor Relations Act amendment.*

Section 9 (h) of the National Labor Relations Act, as amended (29 U. S. C. 159 (h)), is amended by adding at the end thereof the following: "The Board is authorized to determine, after notice and hearing, whether any affidavit filed under this subsection by or on behalf of any officer of any labor organization contains any false representation of fact. If the Board determines that any such affidavit does contain any such false representation executed under oath by any officer of any labor organization, the labor organization of which he is an officer shall have no right, while such individual continues to hold any office therein, to—

"(1) act as representative of any employee for the purposes of section 7 of this Act;

"(2) serve as an exclusive representative of employees of any bargaining unit under section 9 of this Act;

"(3) file any petition under section 9 (e) of this Act;

"(4) make, or obtain any hearing upon, any charge under section 10 of this Act; or

"(5) exercise any other right or privilege, or receive any other benefit, substantive or procedural, provided by this Act for labor organizations."

Sec. 103. *Issuance of process by International Organizations Employees Loyalty Board.*

(a) Under such regulations as the Civil Service Commission shall prescribe, the presiding member of the International Organizations Employees Loyalty Board established within the Commission by Executive Order No. 10422 of January 9, 1953, as now or hereafter amended, and the presiding member of any panel thereof, shall have the power, in the conduct of any hearing before such board or panel, to (1) administer oaths for the purpose of taking evidence in that hearing, (2) issue process to compel witnesses to appear and testify and to compel the production of pertinent documentary and other evidence, and (3) to appoint any person to take any deposition upon oral examination or any written interrogatories. Any process so issued may run to any place within any judicial district of the United States. Any person so appointed to take any deposition or interrogatories shall have the power to administer oaths incident to the taking of such evidence.

(b) The provisions of section 1821 of title 28, United States Code shall apply to witnesses summoned to appear at any such hearing. The per diem and mileage allowances of witnesses so summoned under authority conferred by this section shall be paid from funds appropriated to the Civil Service Commission.

(c) Any person who willfully neglects or refuses to appear, or refuses to qualify as a witness or to testify, or to produce any evidence in obedience to any subpena duly issued under authority of this section shall be fined not more than $500, or imprisoned for not more than six months, or both. Upon the certification, by the presiding member of such board or panel, of the facts concerning any such willful disobedience by any person to the United States Attorney for any judicial district in which such person resides or is found, such attorney shall proceed by information for the prosecution of such person for such offense.

SEC. 104. *Veterans' Preference Act amendments.*

(a) Section 14 of the Veterans' Preference Act of 1944 (5 U. S. C. 863) is amended to read as follows:

"SEC. 14. No employee of the Government of the District of Columbia shall be discharged, suspended for more than thirty days, furloughed without pay, reduced in rank or compensation, or debarred for future appointment except for such cause as will promote the efficiency of the service and for reasons given in writing, and the person whose discharge, suspension for more than thirty days, furlough without pay, or reduction in rank or compensation is sought shall have at least thirty-days' advance written notice (except where there is reasonable cause to believe the employee to be guilty of a crime for which a sentence of imprisonment can be imposed), stating any and all reasons, specifically and in detail, for any such proposed action; such employee shall be allowed a reasonable time for answering the same personally and in writing, and for furnishing affidavits in support of such answer, and shall have the right to appeal to the Civil Service Commission from an adverse decision of the administrative officer so acting, such appeal to be made in writing within a reasonable length of time after the date of receipt of notice of such adverse decision: *Provided,* That such employee shall have the right to make a personal appearance, and an appearance through a designated representative, in accordance with such reasonable rules and regulations as may be issued by the Civil Service Commission; after investigation and consideration of the evidence submitted, the Civil Service Commission shall submit its findings and recommendations to the proper administrative officer and shall send copies of same to the appellant or to his designated representative: *Provided, further,* That the Civil Service Commission may declare any such employee who may have been dismissed or furloughed without pay to be eligible for the provisions of section 15 hereof."

(b) Section 15 of that Act is amended by adding at the end thereof the following new sentence: "This section shall not apply to any preference eligible who has been furloughed or separated under chapter 4 of the Federal Security Act because of the existence of reasonable doubt as to his loyalty to the Government of the United States."

SEC. 105. *Repeal.*

The Act entitled "An Act to protect the national security of the United States by permitting the summary suspension of employment of civilian officers and employees of various departments and agencies of the Government, and for other purposes", approved August 26, 1950 (64 Stat. 476; 5 U. S. C. 22–1, 22–2, and 22–3), is repealed.

SEC. 106. *Effective date.*

Chapter 1 of this Act shall take effect on the date of its enactment. All other provisions of this Act shall take effect on the first day of the sixth month beginning after the date of its enactment.

A BILL

To prescribe a standard of loyalty to the United States Government for military personnel, to prescribe procedure for the determination of the loyalty of such personnel, and for other purposes.

Be it enacted by the Senate and House of Representatives of the United States of America in Congress assembled, That (a) part II of subtitle A of title 10 of the United States Code is amended by inserting therein, immediately after chapter 35 thereof, the following new chapter:

"Sec.   "CHAPTER 36. LOYALTY OF PERSONNEL

"621. Standard of loyalty for service in the Armed Forces.
"622. Hearings: when required.
"623. Boards of inquiry: composition; powers.
"624. Proceedings of boards of inquiry: generally.
"625. Proceedings: right of confrontation.
"626. Proceedings: issuance of subpenas.
"627. Evidence: criteria for determination of reasonable doubt as to loyalty.
"628. Review of board proceedings.
"629. Final determination: effect.
"630. Separation of personnel: conditions.
"631. Proceedings under the Uniform Code of Military Justice.
"632. Regulations promulgated by the Secretary of Defense and the Secretary of the Treasury.

"§ 621. *Standard of loyalty for service in the Armed Forces.*

"(a) Except as provided by section 630 of this chapter, no individual shall be appointed, enlisted, inducted, retained, called to active duty, or recalled to active duty as a member of any armed force if, upon all information, there is reasonable doubt as to his loyalty to the Government of the United States.

"(b) As used in this chapter, the term 'member of an armed force' means (1) an officer or enlisted member of any armed force or any component thereof, (2) a cadet or midshipman at any academy administered by any armed force, and (3) a member of any unit of the Reserve Officers' Training Corps supervised by any armed force.

"§ 622. *Hearings: when required.*

"(a) No member of an armed force may be separated from, or released from active duty, in that armed force, and no individual shall be denied appointment, enlistment, or induction in any armed force, on the ground that doubt may exist as to his loyalty to the United States Government, unless he has been accorded an opportunity for a hearing before a board of inquiry convened under section 623 of this chapter and (1) it has been determined pursuant to section 629 that there is reasonable doubt as to his loyalty, or (2) he has declined, or has failed within the time prescribed by subsection (b), to make application for such hearing.

"(b) Whenever it is believed that reasonable doubt may exist as to the loyalty to the United States Government of any member of any armed force, or any individual considered for appointment, enlistment, or induction in any armed force, there shall be transmitted to such individual a letter of charges

719

stating the ground for such belief and advising him of his right to receive a hearing under this chapter on the question whether there is reasonable doubt as to his loyalty. The letter of charges so given must be as specific and detailed as the interests of national security permit, and shall include such pertinent information as names, dates, and places in such detail as reasonably to permit answer to be made thereto. Such letter of charges must contain a full and complete statement of the rights and privileges of the individual concerned under this chapter. Within 30 days after receipt of such letter of charges, that individual—

"(1) may file his sworn answer thereto, accompanied by any affidavits or other written statements he may desire to submit; and

"(2) upon the filing of such sworn answer, may apply for a hearing upon those charges before a board convened under section 623.

"(c) Upon receipt of any such application, there shall be convened under section 623 a board of inquiry to conduct a hearing as to the loyalty of the applicant. The letter of charges issued to him, his sworn answer thereto, and all affidavits and other written statements filed by him in support of his answer shall then be transmitted to that board.

"(d) Whenever any board of inquiry is so convened, the Secretary concerned shall designate, from military personnel of the armed force administered by his department, counsel to represent such armed force in proceedings before the board, and shall designate for service with the board such other personnel as may be required to carry into effect the provisions of this chapter.

"§ 623. *Board of inquiry: composition; powers.*

"(a) A board of inquiry convened within any armed force under this section shall be composed of three commissioned officers of that armed force, each of whom must be senior in grade to the individual whose loyalty is the subject of inquiry. One member of the board, who must be a commissioned officer of that armed force qualified to serve as a law officer pursuant to section 826 (a) of this title, shall serve as presiding officer of the board. No officer may serve as a member of any such board if he has previously (1) taken part in any investigation as to the loyalty of the individual whose loyalty is the subject of inquiry by the board, or (2) represented the armed force of which he is a member in any capacity in the presentation of evidence concerning the loyalty of that individual in any case or proceeding.

"(b) The presiding officer of a board of inquiry convened under this chapter, and any commissioned officer designated by him to take any deposition on oral examination or written interrogatory, shall have the power to administer oaths for the purpose of taking evidence in any proceeding before the board.

"(c) Subject to the provisions of section 626 of this chapter, the presiding officer of a board of inquiry so convened shall have the powers of a district court of the United States to issue process to compel witnesses to appear and testify before the board and to compel the production of other evidence. Any process so issued may run to any part of the United States or its Territories, Commonwealths, and possessions. Section 847 of this title shall apply to the disobedience, by any person not subject to the Uniform Code of Military Justice, of any process so issued.

"§ 624. *Proceedings of boards of inquiry: generally.*

"(a) Each individual whose loyalty is the subject of inquiry by any board convened under this chapter shall—

"(1) be given written notice as to the time and place of hearing before the board;

"(2) be allowed a reasonable time to prepare for hearing before the board;

720

"(3) be allowed to appear at his own expense at proceedings before the board, except that the actual and necessary expenses of travel and subsistence incident to such appearance by any individual who has been denied induction or enlistment in an armed force because of doubt as to his loyalty shall be defrayed from funds appropriated to that armed force;

"(4) be furnished counsel selected by the Secretary concerned from military personnel of the armed force in which the board is convened;

"(5) be allowed to be represented before the board by counsel of his choice, at his own expense, if he so desires; and

"(6) be permitted to present evidence and rebuttal evidence on his behalf before the board.

"(b) The rules of evidence applied by courts need not be applied by any board of inquiry convened under this chapter in the case of any individual, but no evidence shall be received by the board unless such evidence is relevant to one or more of the allegations contained in the letter of charges furnished to such individual. The letter of charges issued by any armed force to any individual may be amended by such armed force, at any time before the conclusion of hearing thereon, to include additional or different charges. Whenever such an amendment occurs, the individual concerned shall have such additional time as the Secretary of Defense shall prescribe by regulations for the filing of his amended answer to such additional or different charges.

"(c) Each witness appearing before any such board shall be examined under oath or affirmation. Subject to the provisions of sections 625 and 626 of this chapter, any party to any proceeding before the board may take under oath or affirmation and offer in evidence before the board (1) depositions on oral examination taken in conformity with the requirements of subsections (b), (c), and (d), of section 849 of this title, and written interrogatories taken in conformity with regulations promulgated under section 631 of this chapter.

"(d) In any hearing upon any question concerning the loyalty of any individual, he shall be permitted to offer evidence as to (1) his character and his reputation for veracity and integrity, and (2) his demonstrated appreciation of the need for the protection of the national security against foreign and domestic enemies.

"(e) Either party to any such hearing may offer in evidence the affidavit of any witness if further evidence can be obtained from that witness by or on behalf of the other party through the issuance of a subpena requiring the attendance of that witness at the hearing, or through the taking of his testimony by deposition or interrogatory.

"(f) Only members of a board of inquiry may be present during its deliberation upon any case. All other proceedings of the board shall be made a part of the record, but only members of the board, personnel assigned for official duty with or before the board, the individual whose loyalty is the subject of inquiry, his counsel, and witnesses before the board may be present at such proceedings.

"(g) Each board of inquiry shall cause to be prepared a verbatim stenographic transcript of all proceedings in each case considered by the board. At the conclusion of the proceedings in each case the record shall be authenticated by the signature of the presiding officer of the board, or, in the event of his death, disability, or absence, by another member of the board.

"(h) Upon the conclusion of proceedings in any case, the board shall prepare a written report thereon, which shall contain a summary of the evidence received, the findings of the board as to the facts with respect to each allegation made with respect to the loyalty of the individual who is the subject of inquiry, and its conclusion on the question whether reasonable doubt exists as to the loyalty of that individual to the United States Government. If any member of the board does not concur in the conclusion stated by other members, he may prepare a separate report containing a statement of his reasons for nonconcurrence.

"(i) A true and correct copy of the record of the proceedings in the case of any individual, and a true and correct copy of each report prepared by the board or any member thereof in such case, shall be furnished to that individual without charge as soon as may be practicable after the completion of proceedings of the board in his case.

"§ 625. *Proceedings: right of confrontation.*

"(a) Except as otherwise specifically provided by this section, no derogatory information concerning the loyalty of any individual may be received in evidence by the board, over the objection of that individual, unless the supplier of such information is identified by name and—

"(1) gives oral testimony under oath or affirmation before the board, subject to cross-examination by or on behalf of the individual whose loyalty is the subject of inquiry; or

"(2) gives testimony under oath or affirmation by deposition or interrogatory in the taking of which opportunity has been accorded to that individual to propound cross-questions or cross-interrogatories relevant to all allegations made by the supplier of such information with respect to the loyalty of that individual; or

"(3) gives testimony by affidavit executed under oath, and is available for the giving of further testimony on application by the individual whose loyalty is the subject of inquiry through the issuance of a subpena or by deposition or interrogatory.

"(b) Confrontation of regularly established confidential informants engaged in obtaining intelligence and internal security information for the Government shall not be allowed where the head of the investigative agency determines that the disclosure of the identity of such informants will prejudice the national security. In such cases the report supplied by the investigative agency shall contain as much of the information supplied by the informant as may be disclosed without revealing the identity of the informant or otherwise endangering the national security.

"(c) If confrontation is not permitted under subsection (b), the board shall furnish the individual involved with the substance of the information obtained from such informant to the extent that such information is material to the consideration of the issues involved and shall read into the record the substance of such information and the evaluation as to reliability placed upon such confidential informant in the investigative report.

"(d) If the individual who is the subject of inquiry questions the accuracy or completeness of the information furnished pursuant to subsection (c), that individual may file with the board a written statement setting forth in detail so much of the information which is challenged as to accuracy or completeness. If the board is of the opinion that the additional investigation as to the specific matter challenged is required in the interest of ascertaining the facts, it shall request the investigative agency to make such additional investigation. Information obtained as a result of the additional investigation shall be treated in the same manner as provided for in the original investigation.

"(e) Derogatory information supplied by confidential informants other than those described in subsection (b) shall not be considered, over the objection

722

of the individual involved, by the board in arriving at its determination, or by any authority charged with the responsibility for making a final determination, unless such informants consent to the disclosure of their identity so as to enable the individual involved to obtain their testimony through the issuance of subpenas or by depositions or written interrogatories.

"(f) Derogatory information supplied by identified persons shall not be considered, over the objection of the individual involved, by the board in arriving at its determination, or by any authority charged with the responsibility for making a final determination, unless the individual involved is given the opportunity to obtain the testimony of such identified persons through the issuance of subpenas, or by depositions or written interrogatories. If the individual involved is given the opportunity to obtain the testimony of such identified persons through the issuance of subpenas, or by depositions or written interrogatories, such derogatory information supplied by identified persons shall be considered. If the identified person supplying the derogatory information is unavailable for service of subpena or the taking of his testimony by deposition or written interrogatories because of death, incompetency, or other reason, such derogatory information may be considered by the board with due regard for the lack of opportunity for cross-examination.

"§ 626. *Proceedings: issuance of subpenas.*

"(a) Upon application made by counsel for the armed force concerned or by or on behalf of the individual whose loyalty is the subject of inquiry before any board convened under this chapter, the presiding officer of the board may issue a subpena to compel the attendance of a witness or the production of other evidence. Each such application for the issuance of a subpena to require the attendance of any witness must state the name and address of the witness desired and the substance of the testimony which such witness is believed to be qualified to give. Each such application for the issuance of a subpena to require the production of other evidence shall state the name and address of the person to whom it is to be directed and the nature of the evidence desired.

"(b) The presiding officer of the board shall deny any such application if he determines that the evidence sought (1) is not relevant to any issue before the board, or (2) would be merely cumulative to other evidence received by the board in such proceeding. If, upon any such application, the presiding officer of the board determines that a substantial sum would be required for the payment of per diem and mileage allowances incident to the issuance of a subpena, and that the evidence desired can be obtained by deposition or interrogatory, he may deny the application and require such evidence to be obtained by deposition or interrogatory.

"(c) No subpena or other process of the board may be issued to compel the attendance, or otherwise to obtain the evidence, of—

"(1) any person certified by the head of any investigative agency of the executive branch of the government to be a regularly established confidential informant engaged in obtaining intelligence and internal security information for such agency; or

"(2) any other person, without the consent of such person, if such person is certified by the head of any such agency to have given information to such agency concerning the individual whose loyalty is the subject of inquiry by the board upon the condition that the supplier of such information would not be called as a witness to testify with respect to information so given.

"(d) The provisions of section 1821 of title 28, United States Code (relating to per diem and mileage allowances of witnesses), shall apply to witnesses summoned to appear before any board of inquiry convened under this chapter. The per diem and mileage allowances of witnesses summoned on behalf of the armed force in which the board is convened, or on behalf of any individual who has been denied induction or enlistment in an armed force because of doubt as to his loyalty, shall be paid from funds appropriated to such armed force. No witness shall be summoned in any case, by process issued by the board on behalf of any other individual whose loyalty is the subject of inquiry, unless that individual has deposited with the board such sum as the presiding officer determines to be necessary to defray the per diem and mileage allowances payable to that witness. The per diem and mileage allowances of each witness so summoned shall be paid from the sum so deposited. If, upon the record of proceedings before the board, the authority having power to make final determination under section 629 determines that reasonable doubt does not exist as to the loyalty of the individual who deposited any such sum, there shall be paid to that individual from appropriated funds a sum equal to the aggregate amount of all deposits so made by him in such proceedings.

"§ 627. *Evidence: criteria for determination of reasonable doubt as to loyalty.*

"(a) In determining for the purposes of this chapter whether there is reasonable doubt as to the loyalty of any individual, activities and associations of that individual of one or more of the following categories may be considered:

"(1) sabotage, espionage, or attempts or preparations therefor, or knowingly associating with spies or saboteurs;

"(2) treason or sedition, or advocacy thereof;

"(3) advocacy of revolution or force or violence to alter the constitutional form of government of the United States;

"(4) intentional, unauthorized disclosure to any person, under circumstances which may indicate disloyalty to the United States, of documents or information of a confidential or nonpublic character;

"(5) performing or attempting to perform his duties, or otherwise acting, so as to serve the interests of another government in preference to the interests of the United States;

"(6) membership in, or affiliation or sympathetic association with, any party, group, or association which has been found by the Congress of the United States, or any agency or officer of the United States duly authorized by the Congress for that purpose—

"(A) to seek to alter the form of government of the United States by force or violence, or other unconstitutional means; or

"(B) to have been organized or utilized for the purpose of advancing the aims or objectives of the Communist movement; or

"(C) to have been organized or utilized for the purpose of establishing any form of dictatorship in the United States or any form of international dictatorship; or

"(D) to have been organized or utilized by any foreign government, or by any foreign party, group or association acting in the interest of any foreign government, for the purpose of (i) espionage, or (ii) sabotage, or (iii) obtaining information relating to the defense of the United States or the protection of the national security, or (iv) hampering, hindering, or delaying the production of defense materials; or

"(E) to be affiliated with, or to act in concert with, or to be dominated or controlled by, any party, group, or association of the character described in (A), (B), (C), or (D), above; or

724

"(7) membership in or affiliation with any organization which has been found by the Congress of the United States, or any agency or officer of the United States duly authorized by the Congress for that purpose, to have adopted a policy of advocating or approving the commission of acts of force and violence to deny others their rights under the Constitution of the United States; and

"(8) refusal to testify, upon the ground of self-incrimination, in any authorized inquiry relating to subversive activities conducted by any congressional committee, Federal court, Federal grand jury, or any other duly authorized Federal agency, as to any question relating to subversive activities of the individual involved or others, unless the individual, after opportunity to do so, satisfactorily explains his refusal to testify.

"(b) The enumeration contained in subsection (a) shall not exclude from consideration any other factor tending to establish reasonable doubt as to loyalty.

"(c) In determining the significance to be given for the purposes of this chapter to the membership of any individual in, or the association of any individual with, any organization, consideration must be given to:

"(1) the character and history of that organization;

"(2) the time during which such individual was a member of, or associated with, such organization;

"(3) the actual knowledge of that individual, at the time of such membership or association, as to the nature and purposes of that organization;

"(4) the extent to which the nature and purposes of that organization were publicly known at the time of such membership or association;

"(5) the purpose for which that individual became a member of, or associated with, that organization;

"(6) the degree to which that individual participated in the activities of that organization; and

"(7) if that individual no longer is a member of, or associated with, that organization, the time at which his membership or association was terminated, the circumstancse of such termination, and the degree to which he has separated himself from the activities of that organization.

"(d) The normal relationships within the family shall not be deemed to create a reasonable doubt as to loyalty unless they fall within the class of close, continuing, or sympathetic association, and unless such association with members of the family is of such a nature as to indicate sympathetic association with an organization of the type described in paragraph (6) of subsection (a).

"§ 628. *Review of board proceedings.*

"(a) As soon as may be practicable after the completion of proceedings before any board convened under this chapter in the case of any individual, the board shall transmit a true and correct copy of the record of proceedings in such case and each report made thereon by the board or any member thereof to such reviewing authority as shall be prescribed by regulations promulgated by the Secretary concerned. Such reviewing authority shall—

"(1) review the proceedings of the board to determine whether they were taken in conformity with law and applicable regulations; and

"(2) prepare a written report of such review and its recommendation as to the action to be taken upon the report of the board.

"(b) Upon the completion of such report of review, it shall be transmitted, together with the record of proceedings before the board and each report made thereon by the board or any member thereof, to the authority having power to make final determination in that case.

"§ 629. *Final determination: effect.*

"(a) Final determination after review under section 628 shall be made—
  "(1) in any case arising in the Navy, Air Force, or Coast Guard, by the Secretary concerned;
  "(2) in any case arising in the Army which involves a commissioned officer of the Regular Army having more than three years of active service, by the Secretary of the Army; and
  "(3) in any other case arising in the Army, by the Army Security Review Board.
"(b) Upon the basis of the record and reports transmitted pursuant to section 628 with respect to the case of any individual whose loyalty has been made the subject of inquiry by a board convened under this chapter, the determining authority shall—
  "(1) determine whether there is reasonable doubt as to the loyalty of that individual to the Government of the United States; or
  "(2) if in the opinion of the determining authority the record and reports so transmitted are not sufficient to permit such determination to be made, return such record and report to the board for such further proceedings as such authority shall direct.
"(c) Whenever final determination is made under subsection (b) in the case of any individual, written notice as to the nature and effect of such action shall be transmitted to that individual.
"(d) Action taken under subsection (b) by the determining authority shall be final and conclusive, and may not be reviewed by any other officer or agency of the United States or by any court.

"§ 630. *Separation of personnel: conditions*

"(a) Whenever it is determined under section 629 that there is reasonable doubt as to the loyalty to the United States Government of a member of an armed force, that individual shall—
  "(1) if he is eligible upon his application to be retired or to receive retired pay under any provision of law, be retired or discharged and granted retired pay under that provision of law; or
  "(2) if he is not eligible to be retired or to receive retired pay in conformity with paragraph (1), but upon involuntary relief from active duty under honorable conditions for any reason other than the application of the provisions of this chapter would be eligible for retirement under any provision of law, be retired with the grade and retired pay to which he would be entitled if retired under that provision of law; or
  "(3) if he is not eligible for retirement or to receive retired pay in conformity with paragraph (1) or paragraph (2), but upon separation under honorable conditions for any reason other than the application of the provisions of this chapter would be entitled to receive severance or separation pay under any provision of law, be discharged with severance pay or separation pay computed as prescribed by that provision of law; or
  "(4) if he is not eligible for retirement or to receive retired pay, severance pay, or separation pay, be discharged.
"(b) Any member of an armed force discharged under this section shall be discharged under the conditions determined by the Secretary concerned to be warranted by the character of his previous service as a member of that armed force. In determining the character of such service, consideration may be given only to conduct of that individual while he was a member of that armed force, except to the extent that he has falsified official papers.
"(c) No individual discharged pursuant to this section under honorable

726

conditions who, at the time of his discharge, has performed at least 20 years of service computed under section 1332 of this title, may be barred because of such discharge from the receipt of retired pay under chapter 67 of this title upon his attainment of the age of 60 years.

"§ 631. *Proceedings under the Uniform Code of Military Justice.*

"(a) Whenever the Secretary concerned believes that (1) doubt may exist as to the loyalty of any member of an armed forced to the United States Government, and (2) such member is chargeable with any offense punishable under subchapter X of chapter 47 of this title, the Secretary may suspend proceedings under this chapter with respect to that member pending his trial under charges filed against him under chapter 47.

"(b) Nothing contained in this section precludes the institution of proceedings under this chapter with respect to any individual who has been so charged under chapter 47 of this title, but who has not been separated from the armed force of which he is a member pursuant to the approved sentence of a court-martial.

"§ 632. *Regulations promulgated by the Secretary of Defense and the Secretary of the Treasury.*

"(a) The Secretary of Defense shall promulgate appropriate regulations to carry into effect the provisions of this chapter with respect to the Army, Navy, Air Force, and Marine Corps. The Secretary of the Treasury shall promulgate such regulations with respect to the Coast Guard when it is not operating as a service in the Navy.

"(b) As nearly as may be practicable, all regulations so promulgated shall be uniform with respect to all armed forces. Subject to the provisions of this chapter, all such regulations shall conform to the greatest practicable extent to regulations promulgated by appropriate authority for the determination of the question whether there is reasonable doubt as to the loyalty of individuals who are civilian officers or employees of the United States."

(b) The analysis of part II of subtitle A of title 10 of the United States Code is amended by inserting therein, immediately after the item relating to chapter 35 thereof, the following new item:

"36. Loyalty of personnel . . . . 621".

SEC. 2. The amendments made by this Act shall take effect on the first day of the fourth month beginning after the date of enactment of this Act.

A BILL

To amend the Immigration and Nationality Act to provide more effectively for
immigration and passport security, and for other purposes

*Be it enacted by the Senate and House of Representatives of the
United States of America in Congress assembled,* That this Act may
be cited as the "Immigration and Passport Security Act."

TRANSFER OF FUNCTIONS INCIDENT TO ISSUANCE OF NONDIPLOMATIC VISAS

SEC. 2. (a) The Attorney General shall have all powers, duties, and functions heretofore exercised by the Secretary of State under the Immigration and
Nationality Act with respect to the issuance and revocation of visas, except that
the Secretary of State shall continue to exercise such powers, duties, and
functions with respect to diplomatic visas and visas issued to individuals who
are duly designated representatives of any foreign state in any international
organization as defined in subparagraphs (A), (B), and (C) of paragraph
(15) of section 101 (a) of such Act (8 U. S. C. 1101). The powers, duties,
and functions heretofore exercised by consular officers under that Act, including their authority to administer oaths incident to the issuance of visas,
hereafter shall be exercised by visa officers of the Immigration and Naturalization Service subject to the direction and supervision of the Attorney General.

(b) Paragraph (9) of section 101 (a) of the Immigration and Nationality
Act (8 U. S. C. 1101 (a)) is amended to read as follows:

"(9) The term 'visa officer' means any officer of the Immigration and
Naturalization Service designated by the Attorney General, under regulations prescribed by him under authority conferred by this Act and by
section 2 (a) of the Immigration and Passport Security Act, to serve in
any foreign state, the Canal Zone, or any outlying possession of the United
States, for the purpose of issuing immigrant or nonimmigrant visas."

(c) This section shall take effect on the first day of the sixth month beginning after the date of enactment of this Act.

DENIAL OF ADMISSION TO NATIONALS OF FOREIGN STATES REFUSING TO ACCEPT DEPORTEES

SEC. 3. Section 212 of such Act (8 U. S. C. 1182) is amended by adding at
the end thereof the following new subsection:

"(f) During any period in which any foreign state declines to accept
for admission any national of that state who is under final order of deportation from the United States, no immigrant or nonimmigrant visa (other
than a diplomatic visa or a visa issued to any duly designated representative of a foreign state as defined in subparagraphs (A), (B), and (C) of
paragraph (15) of section 101 (a)) may be issued to, and no bonded
transit may be authorized in conformity with section 238 for, any national
of that foreign state."

DETENTION AND SUPERVISION OF DEPORTEES

SEC. 4. (a) Section 242 (c) of such Act (8 U. S. C. 1252) is amended by inserting, immediately after the third sentence thereof, the following new sentence: "Whenever any such alien has violated any requirement or restraint imposed upon him under the third sentence of subsection (d), and the Attorney General determines that the national security requires the detention of that alien, such alien may be returned to custody under the warrant by which proceedings for deportation were initiated against him, and may be detained until his deportation can be effected."

(b) Section 242 (d) of such Act (8 U. S. C. 1252 (d)) is amended by inserting therein, immediately after the second sentence thereof, the following new sentence: "Any such alien shall, for the purpose of insuring that he will not engage in any subversive activity or maintain any subversive association pending eventual deportation, be subject to such requirements and such restraints upon his conduct and associations as the Attorney General shall prescribe in his case."

REPORTS ON CERTAIN WAIVERS

SEC. 5. Section 212 of such Act (8 U. S. C. 1182) is amended by adding at the end thereof the following new subsection:

"(g) In January of each year the Attorney General shall transmit to the Congress a report which shall (1) state the number of waivers which have been granted during the preceding calendar year under paragraph (4) of subsection (d), and (2) describe the circumstances under which each such waiver was granted. No such report shall include any intelligence or information the public disclosure of which would, in the opinion of the Attorney General, adversely affect the national security."

CENTRAL INDEX OF ALIENS

SEC. 6. Section 290 (a) of such Act (8 U. S. C. 1360) is amended by adding at the end thereof the following new sentence: "There shall not be included in such index the names of aliens lawfully entering, or who have lawfully entered, the United States pursuant to any provision of law permitting their entry without the issuance of visas or other travel documents."

REVOCATION OF NATURALIZATION

SEC. 7. Section 340 (a) of such Act (8 U. S. C. 1451) is amended by:

(1) striking out, in the first sentence thereof, the words "upon affidavit showing good cause therefor", and inserting in lieu thereof the words "upon their own initiative or upon the filing with them of an affidavit showing good cause therefor"; and

(2) adding at the end thereof the following new sentence: "The complaint in any proceeding instituted under this section shall be sworn to by the United States Attorney filing it."

PASSPORT SECURITY

SEC. 8. (a) Section 215 of the Immigration and Nationality Act (8 U. S. C. 1185) is amended by striking out—

(1) in subsection (a), the words "the United States is at war or during the existence of any national emergency proclaimed by the Presi-

dent, or, as to aliens, whenever there exists a state of war between or among two or more States, and"; and

(2) in the section caption, the words "IN TIME OF WAR OR NATIONAL EMERGENCY".

(b) Section 215 (b) of such Act is amended to read as follows:

"(b) After any proclamation has been made and published as provided for in subsection (a), and while such proclamation is in force, it shall, except as otherwise provided by the President, and subject to such limitations and exceptions as the President may authorize and prescribe, be unlawful for any citizen of the United States to—

"(1) depart from or enter, or attempt to depart from or enter, the United States unless he bears a valid passport;

"(2) travel to any country in which his passport is declared to be invalid; or

"(3) refuse to surrender upon demand any passport issued to him which has been lawfully revoked."

(c) Subsections (c), (d), (e), (f), and (g) of section 215 of such Act are hereby redesignated as subsections (f), (g), (h), (i), and (j) respectively.

(d) Section 215 of such Act is amended by inserting, immediately after subsection (b) thereof, the following new subsections:

"(c) If there is in effect any requirement, prescribed or authorized by law, for the procurement of a passport for any travel, no application made by any individual for the issuance of such passport may be granted, and each passport previously issued shall be revoked, unless the issuance or use of such passport is authorized under subsection (e), whenever there is reasonable ground to believe that the applicant, or holder of a previously issued passport, is going abroad or traveling abroad for the purpose of engaging in activities which will further the aims and objectives of any party, group, or association which has been found by the Congress of the United States, or any agency or officer of the United States duly authorized by the Congress for that purpose—

"(1) to seek to alter the form of Government of the United States by force or violence, or other unconstitutional means; or

"(2) to have been organized or utilized for the purpose of advancing the aims or objectives of the Communist movement; or

"(3) to have been organized or utilized for the purpose of establishing any form of dictatorship in the United States or any form of international dictatorship; or

"(4) to have been organized or utilized by any foreign government, or by any foreign party, group or association acting in the interest of any foreign government, for the purpose of (A) espionage, or (B) sabotage, or (C) obtaining information relating to the defense of the United States or the protection of the national security, or (D) hampering, hindering, or delaying the production of defense materials; or

"(5) to be affiliated with, or to act in concert with, or to be dominated or controlled by, any party, group, or association of the character described in paragraph (1), (2), (3), or (4), above.

Nothing in this subsection shall be construed to alter or limit the authority of the Secretary of State to deny any application for the issuance of a passport, or to revoke a previously issued passport, on any ground other than the ground described in this subsection.

731

"(d) In determining, for the purposes of subsection (c), whether there is reasonable ground for belief that any individual is going abroad or traveling abroad for any such purpose, consideration may be given to activities and associations of that individual of one or more of the following categories:

"(1) membership in any party, group, or association described in subsection (c); or

"(2) prior membership in any party, group, or association described in subsection (c), if the termination of such membership was under circumstances warranting the conclusion that the applicant continues to act in furtherance of the interests of such party, group, or association; or

"(3) present or past activities which further the aims and objectives of any such party, group, or association, under circumstances warranting the conclusion that he engages or has engaged in such activities as a result of direction, domination, or control exercised over him by such party, group, or association, or otherwise continues to act in furtherance of the interests of such party, group, or association; or

"(4) activities continued consistently over a prolonged period of time which indicate that he has adhered to the doctrine of any such party, group, or association, as such doctrine is expressed in the actions and writings of such party, group, or association on a variety of issues, including shifts and changes in the doctrinal line of such party, group, or association; or

"(5) any other conduct which tends to support the belief that the applicant is going abroad or traveling abroad for such purpose.

"(e) A passport may be issued to or held by any individual, notwithstanding the provisions of subsection (c), whenever personally directed by the Secretary of State for reasons deemed by him to be strictly in the public interest."

(e) Section 301 of such Act (8 U. S. C. 1401) is amended by adding at the end thereof the following new subsection:

"(d) Whenever any person is born outside of the United States and its outlying possessions, and under subsection (a) such person is a citizen of the United States at birth, the birth of that person shall be registered with a consular officer in the country in which that person was born within such time and under such regulations as shall be prescribed by the Secretary of State. If such registration is not made within the time so prescribed, it shall be presumed in the absence of proof to the contrary, for the purposes of any proceeding arising under or involving any right established by this Act, that such person is not a citizen of the United States by birth. This subsection shall take effect on the day six months after the date of its enactment."

(f) Nothing in any amendment made by this section shall be construed to alter or amend any provision of the Subversive Activities Control Act, as amended.

SUBVERSIVE ACTIVITIES CONTROL ACT AMENDMENT

SEC. 3. Section 6 of the Subversive Activities Control Act of 1950 (50 U. S. C. 785) is amended by adding at the end thereof the following new subsection:

"(c) Notwithstanding the provisions of subsection (a) and subsection (b)—

"(1) any member of any such organization may apply for the issuance or renewal of a passport or use a passport if such individual has obtained the consent of the Attorney General for such action; and

"(2) a passport may be issued to or renewed for any member of any such organization who has procured the consent required by paragraph (1) if such issuance or renewal has been determined by the Secretary of State personally to be in the public interest."

A BILL

To authorize certain investigative officers of the United States, with the approval of the Attorney General, to intercept and disclose under stated conditions wire and radio communications in the detection and prosecution of offenses against the security of the United States, and for other purposes.

Be it enacted by the Senate and House of Representatives of the United States of America in Congress assembled, That (a) chapter 93 of title 18 of the United States Code (relating to public officers and employees) is amended by adding at the end thereof the following new section:

"§ 1916. Disclosure of information obtained through the interception of certain communications.

"(a) In the conduct of any investigation to detect or prevent any offense against the security of the United States, any security investigative agency may, upon express written authorization given by the Attorney General to the head of such agency, intercept any wire or radio communication if that interception is specifically described as to place and time in the authorization so given. As soon as may be practicable after the end of each period of six calendar months, the Attorney General shall transmit to the National Security Council a report which shall state the number of interceptions authorized by him to be made under this subsection by each security investigative agency during that period, and the nature of the offense with respect to which each such authorization was given.

"(b) Information obtained by an officer or agent of a security investigative agency in any investigation through any interception so authorized may be disclosed (1) to the head of the security investigative agency making the investigation and to any officer, agency, or employee of such agency conducting or supervising the investigation, (2) by the head of such investigative agency to the President, the National Security Council, the head of any department or agency in the executive branch, or the head of any other security investigative agency when such disclosure is deemed by the head of such investigative agency to be advisable in the interest of the national security, (3) by any officer or agent of a security investigative agency in giving testimony in any criminal proceeding before any court, grand jury, or court-martial of the United States for the prosecution of an offense against the security of the United States, and (4) to any attorney for the United States who is duly authorized to engage in or supervise the prosecution of that offense. In any such proceeding, evidence obtained through any interception so authorized, if otherwise admissible, shall not be excluded because of the means by which it was obtained.

"(c) Whoever, having acquired as an officer, employee, or member of any department, agency, or armed force of the United States knowledge of any information obtained through any interception authorized pursuant

735

to subsection (a), willfully makes any disclosure of any part of that information which is not authorized by subsection (b) shall be fined not more than $5,000, or imprisoned not more than one year and one day, or both.

"(d) As used in this section—

"(1) the term 'security investigative agency' means the Federal Bureau of Investigation and the investigative agencies of the Armed Forces supervised by the Assistant Chief of Staff, G–2, Department of the Army; the Director of Intelligence, Department of the Navy; and the Director of Intelligence, Department of the Air Force;

"(2) the term 'offense against the security of the United States' means any offense punishable under chapter 37, 105, or 115 of this title; section 4 or section 15 of the Subversive Activities Control Act of 1950; or section 222, 224, 225, 226, or 227 of the Atomic Energy Act of 1954; and any attempt or conspiracy to commit any such offense; and

"(3) the terms 'wire communication' and 'radio communication' have the same meaning as when used in the Communications Act of 1934."

(b) The analysis of chapter 93 of title 18 of the United States Code is amended by adding at the end thereof the following new item:

"1916. Disclosure of information obtained through the interception of certain communications."

SEC. 2. The proviso contained in section 605 of the Communications Act of 1934 (48 Stat. 1103; 47 U. S. C. 605) is amended to read as follows:

"*Provided*, That this section shall not apply to the interception, receiving, divulging, publishing, or utilizing the contents of (a) any radio communication broadcast or transmitted by amateurs or others for the use of the general public, or relating to ships in distress, (b) any wire communication or radio communication intercepted by a security investigative agency pursuant to authorization granted in accordance with section 1916 (a) of title 18 of the United States Code, or (c) any assistance given by any common carrier in the interception of any wire communication or radio communication by any such agency pursuant to such authorization."

A BILL

To amend title 18, United States Code, to prohibit the unauthorized disclosure of certain information critically affecting national defense.

Be it enacted by the Senate and House of Representatives of the United States of America in Congress assembled, That (a) chapter 37 of title 18 of the United States Code (relating to espionage and censorship) is amended by inserting at the end thereof the following new section:

"§ 799. Unauthorized disclosure of certain information affecting national defense.

"(a) Whenever any information shall have been classified, in conformity with the provisions of any Executive order promulgated by the President, as 'top secret', 'atomic top secret', 'secret', or 'atomic secret', it is unlawful for any person who has obtained such information to communicate any part thereof to any person who is not authorized by law, Executive order, or regulations promulgated pursuant to law or any Executive order, to receive such information. No communication of any such information made by any officer, employee, or member of any department, agency, or armed force of the United States, or any officer or employee of any corporation the stock of which is owned in whole or in major part by the United States or any department or agency thereof, pursuant to authorization granted by the head of such department, agency, armed force, or corporation, to any member of the Congress, any joint committee of the Congress, any committee or subcommittee of the Senate or the House of Representatives, or any member of the staff of any such committee or subcommittee, shall be unlawful under this section.

"(b) Whoever, having obtained in any manner or by any means any information so classified, willfully communicates any part of such information in any manner or by any means to any person not authorized as prescribed by subsection (a) to receive such information, with knowledge or reason to believe that such information is so classified and that such person is not so authorized to receive such information, shall be fined not more than $10,000 or imprisoned not more than five years, or both.

"(c) For the purposes of this section—

"(1) the term 'top secret' or 'atomic top secret' means any information affecting the national defense of the United States in such degree that its unauthorized disclosure could result in exceptionally grave damage to the Nation; and

"(2) the term 'secret' or 'atomic secret' means any information affecting the national defense of the United States in such degree that its unauthorized disclosure could result in serious damage to the Nation."

(b) The analysis of such chapter is amended by inserting at the end thereof the following new item:

"799. Unauthorized disclosure of certain information affecting national defense."

EXECUTIVE ORDER NO. ———

Amendment of the Regulations Relating to the Safeguarding of Vessels, Harbors, Ports, and Waterfront Facilities of the United States.

By virtue of the authority vested in me by the Act of August 9, 1950, 64 Stat. 427, which amended section 1, Title II of the Act of June 15, 1917, 40 Stat. 220 (50 U. S. C. 191), and as President of the United States, I hereby prescribe the following amendments of the regulations prescribed by Executive Order No. 10173 of October 18, 1950, as amended by Executive Order No. 10277 of August 1, 1951, and Executive Order No. 10352 of May 19, 1952, which regulations constitute Part 6, Subchapter A, Chapter I, Title 33, of the Code of Federal Regulations:

1. Section 6.04–1 is amended to read as follows:

"§ 6.04–1. *Enforcement.* (a) The United States Coast Guard shall have primary responsibility for the enforcement of all rules and regulations in this part, except that final authority to determine the admission of persons to any restricted area in any port which constitutes an installation of the Army or the Navy shall be exercised by the armed service charged with the administration of that installation.

"(b) The rules and regulations in this part shall be enforced by the captain of the port under the supervision and general direction of the District Commander and the Commandant, and all authority and power vested in the captain of the port by the regulations in this part shall be deemed vested in and may be exercised by the District Commander and the Commandant.

"(c) The rules and regulations in this part may be enforced by any other officer of the Coast Guard designated by the Commandant or the District Commander."

2. Sections 6.10–1, 6.10–3, 6.10–5, and 6.10–7 of subpart 6.10 are amended to read as follows:

"6.10–1. *Issuance of documents and employment of persons aboard vessels.* No person shall be issued a document required for employment on a merchant vessel of the United States nor shall any person be employed on a merchant vessel of the United States unless the Commandant is satisfied that the presence of the individual on board will not endanger the common defense or security: *Provided,* That the Commandant may designate categories of merchant vessels to which the foregoing shall not apply.

"6.10–3. *Special validation of merchant marine documents.*—The Commandant may require that all licensed officers and certificated men who are employed on other than the exempted designated categories of merchant vessels of the United States be holders of specially validated documents. No such validation shall be granted to any person unless the Commandant is satisfied that such employment of that person will not endanger the common defense or security. The form of such documents, the conditions, and the manner of their issuance shall be as prescribed by the Commandant. The Commandant shall revoke and require the surrender of a specially validated document when he is no longer satisfied that the holder is entitled thereto.

739

"6.10–5. *Access to vessels and waterfront facilities.*—Any person on board any vessel or any person seeking access to any vessel or any waterfront facility within the jurisdiction of the United States may be required to carry identification credentials issued by or otherwise satisfactory to the Commandant. Except as otherwise provided by subparagraph 6.04–1 (a), the Commandant may define and designate those categories of vessels and areas of the waterfront wherein such credentials are required.

"6.10–7. *Identification credentials.* The identification credential to be issued by the Commandant shall be known as the Coast Guard Port Security Card, and the form of such credential, and the conditions and the manner of its issuance shall be as prescribed by the Commandant after consultation with the Secretary of Labor. The Commandant shall not issue a Coast Guard Port Security Card unless he is satisfied that the presence of such individual on board a vessel or within a waterfront facility would not endanger the common defense or security. The Commandant shall revoke and require the surrender of a Coast Guard Port Security Card when he is no longer satisfied that the holder is entitled thereto. The Commandant may recognize for the same purpose such other credentials as he may designate in lieu of the Coast Guard Port Security Card."

3. Subpart 6.10 is amended by striking out section 6.10–9 thereof, and inserting in lieu thereof the following:

"6.10–9. *Investigation.* (a) Before the Commandant determines, for the purposes of this subpart, that any person may have access to any vessel or waterfront facility at any port, the Commandant shall cause a national agency check to be made with respect to such person, which check shall include reference to files of the Federal Bureau of Investigation and the Civil Service Commission, appropriate military and naval intelligence files, appropriate files of any other Government investigative or intelligence agency, and the files of any appropriate committee of the Congress.

"(b) If the national agency check so conducted discloses with respect to such person any derogatory subversive information, the Commandant shall request the Federal Bureau of Investigation to conduct a full field investigation of such person and to transmit to the Commandant its report upon such investigation. If the national agency check discloses as to that person any other derogatory information which the Commandant believes requires further investigation, then such additional investigation shall be conducted by the Coast Guard.

"6.10–11. *Determinations.* Activities and associations of any person considered in connection with the determination, for purposes of this subpart, whether access by such person to any vessel or waterfront facility will endanger the common defense or security may include one or more of the following:

"(a) Sabotage, espionage, or attempts or preparations therefor or knowingly associating with spies or saboteurs;

"(b) Treason or sedition or advocacy thereof;

"(c) Advocacy of revolution or force or violence to alter the constitutional form of Government of the United States;

"(d) Intentional, unauthorized disclosure to any person of classified information or materials, or recurrent and serious, although unintentional, disclosure of such information and materials;

"(e) Performing or attempting to perform his duties, or otherwise acting, so as to serve the interests of another government in preference to the interests of the United States;

"(f) Membership in, affiliation or sympathetic association with any party, group, or association which has been found by the Congress of the United States, or any agency or officer of the United States duly authorized by the Congress for that purpose:

"(1) to seek to alter the form of Government of the United States by force or violence, or other unconstitutional means;' or

"(2) to have been organized or utilized for the purpose of advancing the aims and objectives of the Communist movement; or

"(3) to have been organized or utilized for the purpose of establishing any form of dictatorship in the United States or any form of international dictatorship; or

"(4) to have been organized or utilized by any foreign government, or by any foreign party, group or association acting in the interest of such foreign government for the purpose of (A) espionage, or (B) sabotage, or (C) obtaining information relating to the defense of the United States or the protection of the national security, or (D) hampering, hindering or delaying the production of defense materials; or

"(5) to have been affiliated with, or to act in concert with, or to be dominated or controlled by, any party, group, or association of the character described in (1) or (2) or (3) or (4) above;

"(g) Membership in or affiliation with any organization which has been found by the Congress of the United States, or any agency or officer of the United States duly authorized by the Congress for that purpose, to have adopted a policy of advocating or approving the commission of acts of force and violence to deny others their rights under the Constitution of the United States;

"(h) Refusal to testify, upon the grounds of self-incrimination, in any authorized inquiry conducted by a congressional committee, Federal court, Federal grand jury, or any other duly authorized agency unless the individual, after opportunity to do so, satisfactorily explains his refusal to testify;

"(i) Willful violations or disregard of security regulations, or recurrent and serious, although unintentional, violation of such regulations;

"(j) Any illness, including any mental condition, of a nature which in the opinion of competent medical authority may cause significant defect in the performance, judgment, or reliability of the employee, with due regard to the transient or continued effect of the illness and the medical findings in such case;

"(k) Any behavior, activities, or associations which tend to show that the individual is not reliable or trustworthy;

"(l) Any deliberate misrepresentations, falsifications, or omission of material facts from a Personnel Security Questionnaire, Personal History Statement, or similar document;

"(m) Any criminal, infamous, dishonest, immoral, or notoriously disgraceful conduct, habitual use of intoxicants to excess, drug addiction, or sexual perversion;

"(n) Any facts which furnish reason to believe that the person may be subjected to coercion, influence, or pressure which may cause him to act contrary to the best interests of the national security; or "(o) Any other activity or association which tends to establish ground for belief that the holding of security clearance by such individual will endanger the common defense and security.

"6.10–13. *Notice of determination.* Whenever the Commandant, acting under this subpart, and pending determination of his clearance, tentatively denies to any person access to any vessel or waterfront facility, or tentatively revokes any authorization previously granted to any person for access to any vessel or waterfront facility, upon the ground that such access might endanger the common defense or security, the Commandant shall transmit to such person written notice of such action which shall (a) state as fully as the interests of national security permit the reasons for such action, including such pertinent information as names, dates, and places in such detail as to permit reasonable answer thereto and (b) advise such person of his right to request a hearing in conformity with section 6.10–15 with respect to his eligibility for such access. Within the time prescribed by regulations promulgated by the Director of the Central Security Office, the recipient of any such letter of charges—

"(1) may file his sworn answer thereto, accompanied by any affidavits or other written statements he may care to submit; and

"(2) upon the filing of such sworn answer, may request a hearing upon those charges in conformity with section 6.10–15.

"6.10–15. *Hearings.* (a) If the person concerned makes timely written request for such hearing, the Commandant shall forward that request, together with a copy of the letter of charges transmitted to him and all papers filed by him in reply thereto, to the Director of the Central Security Office for filing and a hearing under the provisions of the Federal Security Act subject to the limitations contained in subsection (b).

"(b) Any person accorded a hearing pursuant to this section shall—

"(1) have the right of confrontation only with respect to evidence offered against him in support of any of the following charges:

"(a) sabotage, espionage, or attempts or preparations therefor, or knowingly associating with spies or saboteurs;

"(b) treason or sedition or advocacy thereof;

"(c) advocacy of revolution or force or violence to alter the constitutional form of government of the United States;

"(d) intentional, unauthorized disclosure to any person, under circumstances which may indicate disloyalty to the United States, of documents or information of a confidential or nonpublic character;

"(e) performing or attempting to perform his duties, or otherwise acting, so as to serve the interests of another government in preference to the interests of the United States;

"(f) membership in, affiliation or sympathetic association with any party, group or association which has been found by the Congress of the United States, or any agency or officer of the United States duly authorized by the Congress for that purpose;

"(1) to seek to alter the form of government of the United States by force or violence, or other unconstitutional means; or,

"(2) to have been organized or utilized for the purpose of advancing the aims and objectives of the Communist movement; or

"(3) to have been organized or utilized for the purpose of establishing any form of dictatorship in the United States or any form of international dictatorship; or,

"(4) to have been organized or utilized by any foreign government, or by any foreign party, group, or association acting in the interest of such foreign government, for the purpose of (a) espionage, or (b) sabotage, or (c) obtaining information relating to the defense of the United States or the protection of the national security, or (d) hampering, hindering, or delaying the production of defense materials; or,

"(5) to be affiliated with, or to act in concert with, or to be dominated or controlled by, any party, group, or association of the character described in (1) or (2) or (3) or (4) above;

"(g) membership in or affiliation with any organization which has been found by the Congress of the United States, or any agency or officer of the United States duly authorized by the Congress for that purpose, to have adopted a policy of advocating or approving the commission of acts of force and violence to deny others their rights under the Constitution of the United States;

"(h) refusal to testify upon the ground of self-incrimination, in any authorized inquiry relating to subversive activities conducted by a congressional committee, Federal court, Federal grand jury, or any other duly authorized Federal agency, as to questions relating to subversive activities of the individual involved or others, unless the individual, after opportunity to do so, satisfactorily explains his refusal to testify;

"(i) any other factor tending to establish reasonable doubt as to loyalty to the United States Government; and

"(2) be granted process to compel the attendance of witnesses or the production of other evidence only with respect to evidence as to which his right of confrontation extends under paragraph (1).

"(c) Upon the basis of the report of the hearing examiner of the Central Security Office, the Commandant shall make his determination on the question whether the person concerned is eligible to receive or hold a security clearance. The determination so made shall be final and conclusive unless that person makes timely application for review in conformity with section 6.10–17.

"(d) Any letter of charges issued under this section may thereafter be amended by the Commandant, at any time before the conclusion of hearing thereon, to include additional or different charges. Whenever such an amendment occurs, the person concerned shall have such additional time as the Director of the Central Security Office by regulation shall determine to be reasonable for the filing of his amended answer to such additional or different charges.

"6.10–17. *Review and final determination.* (a) Within the time prescribed by regulations promulgated by the Director of the Central Security Office, any person who has received an adverse determination under section 6.10–15 may file with the Commandant written application for the review of that determination by the Central Review Board in conformity with the provisions of the Federal Security Act. Upon the filing of timely application for such review, the Commandant shall forward that application, to-

743

gether with all documents and records pertinent thereto, to the Director of the Central Security Office for review in accordance with the provisions of chapter 9 of the Federal Security Act.

"(b) Upon the basis of the report of review by that Board, the Commandant shall make his determination upon the question presented, and his determination shall be final and conclusive."

EXECUTIVE ORDER NO. ———

By virtue of the provisions of the Civil Aeronautics Act of 1938 (49 Stat. 401 et seq., as amended), and as President of the United States, I hereby find that the security of the United States is endangered by reason of subversive activity, and I hereby prescribe the following regulations to safeguard civil aircraft, civil airports, and civil airport facilities affecting the national security from destructions, loss, or injury resulting from sabotage or other subversive acts, which regulations shall constitute Subpart D, Part 620, Subchapter E, Chapter II, Title 14 of the Code of Federal Regulations; and all agencies and authorities of the Government of the United States, shall, and all State and local authorities and all persons are urged to, support, conform to, and assist in the enforcement of these regulations and all supplemental regulations issued pursuant thereto.

"SUBPART D—AIRPORT SECURITY"

"§ 620.25. *Definitions.* As used in this subpart the words listed below shall mean:

"(a) *Secretary.* The Secretary of Commerce.

"(b) *Board.* The Civil Aeronautics Board.

"(c) *Administration.* The Civil Aeronautics Administration.

"(d) *Airport.* Any area of land or water subject to the jurisdiction of the Administration which is used, or intended for use for the landing and take-off of aircraft, and any appurtenant areas which are used, or intended for use, for airport buildings or other airport facilities or rights-of-way, together with all airport buildings and facilities located thereon.

"(e) *Restricted area.* The whole or any part of any airport which has been designated by the Board, in the interest of the national security, as an area to which access may be granted only to individuals who have been granted security clearance under this subpart.

"(f) *Airman.* Any citizen or national of the United States serving as an operator or as a dispatcher or a crew member of any aircraft.

"(g) *Security clearance.* Authorization duly given to any individual under regulations of the Board for (1) access to any Restricted Area, or (2) service as an airman on any flight subject to the jurisdiction of the Administration to or from any foreign country.

"(h) *National agency check.* An investigation of any individual made upon the basis of written information supplied by him in response to official inquiry, and by reference to files of the Federal Bureau of Investigation and the Civil Service Commission, appropriate intelligence files of the armed forces, appropriate files of any other investigative or intelligence agency in the executive branch, and appropriate files of any committee or subcommittee of the Congress.

"(i) *Full field investigation.* Any investigation of any individual made by reference to all sources required for a national agency check, and in addition thereto:

"(1) law enforcement files of the municipality, county, and State within which that individual resides or is employed;

"(2) records of schools and colleges attended by him;

745

"(3) former employers of that individual;

"(4) references given by him; and

"(5) any other available source of information.

"§ 620.26. *Airport security program.* (a) The Secretary and the Board shall establish and administer, in accordance with the provisions of this subpart, an airport security program in the interest of the national security. Such program shall include the designation of Restricted Areas, and the issuance of the security clearances required by this subpart.

"(b) No individual shall be granted access to any Restricted Area unless he holds a security clearance which is currently in effect.

"(c) No airman shall serve as such on any flight subject to the jurisdiction of the Administration to or from any foreign country unless he holds a security clearance which is currently in effect.

"§ 620.27 *Standard for security clearance.* No individual shall be granted or hold any security clearance required by this subpart if it is determined in accordance with the provisions of this subpart, on the basis of all available information, that his access to any Restricted Area, or his service as an airman on any flight subject to the jurisdiction of the Administration to or from any foreign country, will endanger the common defense or security.

"§ 620.28. *Criteria for Determinations.* In determining for the purposes of this subpart whether the granting of such security clearance to, or the holding of any such security clearance by, any individual will endanger the common defense or security, activities and associations of that individual of one or more of the following categories may be considered:

"(a) sabotage, espionage, or attempts or preparations therefor or knowingly associating with spies or saboteurs;

"(b) treason or sedition or advocacy thereof;

"(c) advocacy of revolution or force or violence to alter the constitutional form of government of the United States;

"(d) intentional, unauthorized disclosure to any person of classified information, or recurrent and serious, although unintentional, disclosure of such information;

"(e) performing or attempting to perform his duties, or otherwise acting, so as to serve the interests of another government in preference to the interests of the United States;

"(f) membership in, or affiliation or sympathetic association with, any party, group, or association which has been found by the Congress of the United States, or any agency or officer of the United States duly authorized by the Congress for that purpose:

"(1) to seek to alter the form of government of the United States by force or violence, or other unconstitutional means; or

"(2) to have been organized or utilized for the purpose of advancing the aims and objectives of the Communist movement; or

"(3) to have been organized or utilized for the purpose of establishing any form of dictatorship in the United States or any form of international dictatorship; or

"(4) to have been organized or utilized by any foreign government, or by any foreign party, group or association acting in the interests of any foreign government, for the purpose of (A) espionage, or (B) sabotage, or (C) obtaining information relating to the defense of the United States or the protection of the national security, or (D) hampering, hindering, or delaying the production of defense materials; or

746

"(5) to be affiliated with, or to act in concert with, or to be dominated or controlled by, any party, group, or association of the character described in (1), (2), (3), or (4), above;

"(g) membership in or affiliation with any organization which has been found by the Congress of the United States, or any agency or officer of the United States duly authorized by the Congress for that purpose, to have adopted a policy of advocating or approving the commission of acts of force and violence to deny others their rights under the Constitution of the United States;

"(h) refusal to testify upon the ground of self-incrimination in any authorized inquiry conducted by a congressional committee, Federal court, Federal grand jury, or any other duly authorized agency unless the individual, after opportunity to do so, satisfactorily explains his refusal to testify;

"(i) willful violations or disregard of security regulations, or recurrent and serious, although unintentional, violation of such regulations;

"(j) any illness, including any mental condition, of a nature which in the opinion of competent medical authority may cause significant defect in the performance, judgment, or reliability of the employee, with due regard to the transient or continued effect of the illness and the medical findings in such case;

"(k) any behavior, activities, or associations which tend to show that the individual is not reliable or trustworthy;

"(l) any deliberate misrepresentations, falsifications, or omission of material facts from a Personnel Security Questionnaire, Personal History Statement, or similar document;

"(m) any criminal, infamous, dishonest, immoral or notoriously disgraceful conduct, habitual use of intoxicants to excess, drug addiction, or sexual perversion;

"(n) any facts which furnish reason to believe that the individual may be subjected to coercion, influence, or pressure which may cause him to act contrary to the best interests of the national security; or

"(o) any other activity or association which tends to establish reasonable ground for belief that the holding of security clearance by such individual will endanger the common defense and security.

"§ 620.29. *Investigations.* No individual shall be granted security clearance under this subpart unless a national agency check has been made by the Board with respect to that individual. If in the course of that check there is disclosed as to the individual any derogatory subversive information, the investigation shall be transferred to the Federal Bureau of Investigation, which shall then conduct a full field investigation of that individual. If the national agency check discloses as to that individual any other derogatory information requiring further investigation, such further investigation shall be conducted by the Board.

"§ 620.30. *Evaluation of Investigations.* (a) The Board shall designate specially qualified personnel to act as screening officers in such numbers as may be required for the administration of the airport security program. It shall be the duty of such officers to examine investigative reports made concerning applicants for and holders of security clearance under this subpart, and to determine whether such reports disclose any substantial information raising doubt as to the eligibility of such individuals for any security clearance.

"(b) Whenever a screening officer determines that an investigative report contains information raising doubt as to the eligibility of any individual to receive any security clearance, such officer shall grant to that individual an

747

opportunity for an interview in which he may offer his explanation of the facts and circumstances upon which that information is based. Whenever such officer determines that such a report contains information raising doubt as to the eligibility of any individual to hold a security clearance previously granted, he shall accord to that individual an opportunity for such an interview unless that officer determines that immediate suspension of such clearance is necessary in the interest of the national security.

"(c) If, after the conclusion of any such interview and any further investigation considered by the screening officer to be necessary, the derogatory information concerning an individual has not been explained to the satisfaction of the screening officer, he shall withhold or suspend the security clearance of that individual, and shall prepare and transmit to him a letter of charges which shall recite, in a manner as specific and detailed as the interests of national security permit, each allegation which provides a basis for belief that his access to any restricted area, or his service as an airman on any flight subject to the jurisdiction of the Administration to or from any foreign country, will endanger the common defense and security. The letter of charges so transmitted shall include such pertinent information as names, dates, and places in such detail as reasonably to permit answer to be made thereto, and must advise the individual concerned fully as to his right to a hearing in conformity with section 620.31.

"(d) Within the time prescribed by regulations promulgated by the Director of the Central Security Office, the recipient of any such letter of charges—

"(1) may file his sworn answer thereto, accompanied by any affidavits or other written statements he may care to submit; and

"(2) upon the filing of such sworn answer, may request a hearing upon those charges in conformity with section 620.31.

"(e) Any letter of charges issued under this section may thereafter be amended by the Board, at any time before the conclusion of hearing thereon, to include additional or different charges. Whenever such an amendment occurs, the individual concerned shall have such additional time as the Director of the Central Security Office by regulation shall determine to be reasonable for the filing of his amended answer to such additional or different charges.

"§ 620.31. *Hearings.* (a) If the individual concerned makes timely written request for such hearing, the screening officer shall forward that request, together with a copy of the letter of charges transmitted to him and all papers filed by him in reply thereto, to the Director of the Central Security Office for filing and a hearing under the provisions of the Federal Security Act subject to the limitations contained in subsection (b).

"(b) An individual accorded a hearing pursuant to this section shall—

"(1) have the right of confrontation only with respect to evidence offered against him in support of any of the following charges:

"(a) sabotage, espionage, or attempts or preparations therefor, or knowingly associating with spies or saboteurs;

"(b) treason or sedition or advocacy thereof;

"(c) advocacy of revolution or force or violence to alter the constitutional form of government of the United States;

"(d) intentional, unauthorized disclosure to any person, under circumstances which may indicate disloyalty to the United States, of documents or information of a confidential or nonpublic character;

"(e) performing or attempting to perform his duties, or otherwise acting, so as to serve the interests of another government in preference to the interests of the United States;

"(f) membership in, affiliation or sympathetic association with, any party, group, or association which has been found by the Congress of the United States, or any agency or officer of the United States duly authorized by the Congress for that purpose:

"(1) to seek to alter the form of government of the United States by force or violence, or other unconstitutional means; or,

"(2) to have been organized or utilized for the purpose of advancing the aims and objectives of the Communist movement; or,

"(3) to have been organized or utilized for the purpóse of establishing any form of dictatorship in the United States or any form of international dictatorship; or,

"(4) to have been organized or utilized by any foreign government, or by any foreign party, group or association acting in the interest of such foreign government, for the purpose of (a) espionage, or (b) sabotage, or (c) obtaining information relating to the defense of the United States or the protection of the national security, or (d) hampering, hindering, or delaying the production of defense materials; or,

"(5) to be affiliated with, or to act in concert with, or to be dominated or controlled by, any party, group, or association of the character described in (1) or (2) or (3) or (4) above;

"(g) membership in or affiliation with any organization which has been found by the Congress of the United States, or any agency or officer of the United States duly authorized by the Congress for that purpose, to have adopted a policy of advocating or approving the commission of acts of force and violence to deny others their rights under the Constitution of the United States;

"(h) refusal to testify upon the ground of self-incrimination, in any authorized inquiry relating to subversive activities conducted by a congressional committee, Federal court, Federal grand jury, or any other duly authorized Federal agency, as to questions relating to subversive activities of the individual involved or others, unless the individual, after opportunity to do so, satisfactorily explains his refusal to testify;

"(i) any other factor tending to establish reasonable doubt as to loyalty to the United States Government; and

"(2) be granted process to compel the attendance of witnesses or the production of other evidence only with respect to evidence as to which his right of confrontation extends under paragraph (1).

"(c) Upon the basis of the report of the hearing examiner of the Central Security Office, the Chairman of the Board shall make his determination on the question whether the individual concerned is eligible to receive or hold a security clearance. The determination so made shall be final and conclusive unless that individual makes timely application for review in conformity with section 620.32.

"§ 620.32. *Review and final determination.* (a) Within the time prescribed by regulations promulgated by the Director of the Central Security Office, any individual who has received an adverse determination under section 620.31 may file with the Chairman of the Board a written application for the review of that determination by the Central Review Board in conformity with the provisions of the Federal Security Act. Upon receipt of timely application for such review, the Chairman of the Board shall forward that

749

application, together with all documents and records pertinent thereto, to the Director of the Central Security Office for review in accordance with the provisions of chapter 9 of the Federal Security Act.

"(b) Upon the basis of the report of review by that Board, the Chairman shall make his determination upon the question presented, and his determination shall be final and conclusive."

EXECUTIVE ORDER NO. ———

Amendment of Executive Order No. 10422 of January 9, 1953, as amended by Executive Order No. 10459 of June 2, 1953, Prescribing Procedures for Making Available to the Secretary General of the United Nations Certain Information Concerning United States Citizens Employed or Being Considered for Employment on the Secretariat of the United Nations.

WHEREAS Executive Order No. 10422 of January 9, 1953, as amended by Executive Order No. 10459 of June 2, 1953, prescribes procedures for making available to the Secretary General of the United Nations and the executive heads of other public international organizations certain information concerning United States Citizens employed or being considered for employment by the United Nations or other public international organizations of which the United States is a member; and

WHEREAS it has been determined that certain modifications of the procedures therein prescribed for the ascertainment of such information are desirable in the interest of effective administration:

NOW, THEREFORE, by virtue of the authority vested in me by the Constitution, statutes, and treaties of the United States, including the Charter of the United Nations, and as President of the United States, it is hereby ordered as follows:

1. Paragraphs 3 and 4 of Part I of Executive Order No. 10422, as amended, are amended to read as follows:

"3. (a) Upon receipt of such information concerning any citizen of the United States, the United States Civil Service Commission shall conduct a preliminary investigation with respect to that United States citizen, which shall include reference to the following:

"(1) Federal Bureau of Investigation files.

"(2) Civil Service Commission files.

"(3) Military and naval intelligence files as appropriate.

"(4) The files of any other appropriate Government investigative or intelligence agency.

"(5) The files of appropriate committees of the Congress.

"(b) If the preliminary investigation so conducted discloses that the named person previously has been granted security clearance upon the basis of a full field investigation incident to his employment by any department or agency of the United States Government, the investigative report or reports upon which such clearance was based shall be transmitted to the International Organizations Employees Loyalty Board established by part IV of this order, which shall consider such report or reports at the earliest practicable time. If the Board upon such consideration finds that such previous clearance was based upon a standard at least as exacting as that prescribed by part II of this order, and that the investigative report or reports upon which such clearance was based are sufficiently current, it shall thereupon transmit to the Secretary of State, for transmission to the Secretary-General of the United Nations, its determination that reasonable doubt as to the loyalty of that citizen to the government of the United States does not exist, and that there

751

is no reasonable ground for belief that he might engage in subversive activities against the United States. If the Board does not make such determination, it shall return such investigative report or reports to the Civil Service Commission with request for such further investigation pursuant to subparagraph (d) as may be required for a current determination whether such person fulfills the requirements of the standard prescribed by part II of this order.

"(c) If the preliminary investigation conducted under subparagraph (a) with respect to any citizen of the United States discloses no information which is derogatory within the standard prescribed by part II of this order, the Civil Service Commission shall so advise the Secretary of State promptly. Upon receipt of such advice, the Secretary of State may notify the Secretary-General of the United Nations that the United States has no objection to the temporary employment of that citizen of the United States by an international organization, for a period not exceeding three months, pending the completion and favorable evaluation of a full field investigation. If it is contemplated that the employment of that citizen of the United States by any international organization will continue for more than three months after the giving of such notification by the Secretary of State, the Civil Service Commission shall conduct the additional investigation required by subparagraph (d).

"(d) In the case of any citizen of the United States whose employment by any international organization for more than three months is contemplated, and who is not granted clearance for such employment under subsection 3 (b), the United States Civil Service Commission shall conduct a full field investigation with regard to said person, conforming to the investigative standards of the Civil Service Commission, which shall include reference to the following:

"(1) Local law-enforcement files at the place of residence and employment of the person, including municipal, county, and State law-enforcement files.

"(2) Schools and colleges attended by the person.

"(3) Former employers of the person.

"(4) References given by the person.

"(5) Any other appropriate source.

"4. Whenever in the course of any investigation conducted under paragraph 3 there is disclosed as to any person any derogatory subversive information, the matter shall be referred to the Federal Bureau of Investigation, which shall then conduct a full field investigation of that person."

2. Paragraphs 1 and 2 of Part II of Executive Order No. 10422, as amended, are amended to read as follows:

"1. The standard to be used by the Board in making an advisory determination as provided for in paragraph 5 of Part I of this order with respect to a United States citizen who is an employee of, or is being considered for employment by, the United Nations, shall be whether or not, on all the information available, there is reasonable doubt as to the loyalty of the person to the government of the United States, or whether or not, on all the information available, there is reasonable ground for believing that the person might engage in subversive activities against the United States.

"2. Activities and associations of such an applicant or employee which may be considered in connection with the determination of the existence of a reasonable doubt as to loyalty and of reasonable ground for believing that the person might engage in subversive activities may include one or more of the following:

"(a) Sabotage, espionage, or attempts or preparations therefor, or knowingly associating with spies or saboteurs;

752

"(b) Treason or sedition or advocacy thereof;

"(c) Advocacy of revolution or force or violence to alter the constitutional form of government of the United States;

"(d) Intentional, unauthorized disclosure to any person, under circumstances which may indicate disloyalty to the United States, of documents or information of a confidential or nonpublic character;

"(e) Performing or attempting to perform his duties, or otherwise acting while an employee of the United States Government during a previous period, so as to serve the interests of another government in preference to the interests of the United States;

"(f) Membership in, affiliation or sympathetic association with, any party, group, or association which has been found by the Congress of the United States, or any agency or officer of the United States duly authorized by the Congress for that purpose:

"(1) to seek to alter the form of government of the United States by force or violence, or other unconstitutional means; or

"(2) to have been organized or utilized for the purpose of advancing the aims and objectives of the Communist movement; or

"(3) to have been organized or utilized for the purpose of establishing any form of dictatorship in the United States or any form of international dictatorship; or

"(4) to have been organized or utilized by any foreign government, or by any foreign party, group, or association acting in the interests of such foreign government, for the purpose of (A) espionage, or (B) sabotage, or (C) obtaining information relating to the defense of the United States or the protection of the national security, or (D) hampering, hindering, or delaying the production of defense materials; or

"(5) to be affiliated with, or act in concert with, or to be dominated or controlled by, any party, group, or association of the character described in (1), (2), (3), or (4) above;

"(g) Membership in or affiliation with any organization which has been found by the Congress of the United States, or any agency or officer of the United States duly authorized by the Congress for that purpose, to have adopted a policy of advocating or approving the commission of acts of force or violence to deny others their rights under the Constitution of the United States;

"(h) Refusal to testify upon the ground of self-incrimination, in any authorized inquiry relating to subversive activities conducted by a congressional committee, Federal court, Federal grand jury, or any other duly authorized Federal agency, as to questions relating to subversive activities of the individual involved or others, unless the individual, after opportunity to do so, satisfactorily explains his refusal to testify;

"(i) Any other factor tending to establish reasonable doubt as to loyalty to the United States Government;

"(j) Any criminal, infamous, dishonest, immoral, or notoriously disgraceful conduct, habitual use of intoxicants to excess, drug addiction or sexual perversion;

"(k) Any facts which furnish reason to believe that the individual may be subjected to coercion, influence, or pressure which might cause him to engage in subversive activities against the United States;

"(l) Any other factors tending to establish reasonable ground for believing that the person might engage in subversive activities against the United States Government."

753

3. Paragraph 1 of Part IV of Executive Order No. 10422, as amended, is amended to read as follows:

"1. (a) There is hereby established in the United States Civil Service Commission an International Organizations Employees Loyalty Board composed of nine members designated by the President from officers and employees of departments and agencies of the United States Government. Of the members so designated, at least three shall be attorneys at law who are qualified to practice before the highest court of a State or of the District of Columbia, and at least three shall be officers or employees of a department or agency other than the Civil Service Commission.

"(b) Each officer or employee designated for service as a member of the Board shall so serve for a term of three years, except that three of the members first designated under this subparagraph shall serve for terms of two years, and three of the members first designated under this subparagraph shall serve for terms of one year. Upon the expiration of any term of any member of the Board he shall be eligible for redesignation for an additional term.

"(c) For the purpose of conducting hearings, and for the purpose of making determinations under subparagraph 3 (b) of Part I of this order, the Board shall be divided into three panels, each of which shall be composed of three members of the Board. The presiding member of each panel shall be a duly qualified attorney at law. At least one member of each panel shall be a member who is not an officer or employee of the Civil Service Commission."

4. Executive Order No. 10422, as amended, is amended by adding at the end thereof the following new parts:

"PART V—HEARINGS

"1. Each witness in any hearing conducted under this order before the Board or any panel thereof, shall be examined under oath or affirmation. Any member of such Board or panel may, subject to the provisions of this order, approve the taking of interrogatories under oath or affirmation to obtain the evidence of any witness.

"2. The right of any individual who is the subject of inquiry in any such hearing to confrontation by witnesses against him shall be limited to witnesses who give evidence against him in support of charges of the kinds listed in subparagraphs (a) through (i) of paragraph 2 of Part II of this order. Subject to that limitation, and to the qualifications prescribed hereinafter, no derogatory information concerning any individual who is the subject of inquiry in any hearing may be received in evidence, over the objection of that individual, unless the supplier of that information is identified by name and—

"(1) gives oral testimony under oath or affirmation before the Board or panel, subject to cross-examination by or on behalf of the individual who is the subject of inquiry; or

"(2) gives testimony under oath or affirmation by interrogatory in the taking of which opportunity has been accorded to that individual to propound cross-interrogatories relevant to all allegations made by the supplier of such information with respect to that individual; or

"(3) gives testimony by affidavit executed under oath, and is available for the giving of further testimony on application by the individual who is the subject of inquiry through the issuance of a subpena or by interrogatory.

"3. Confrontation of regularly established confidential informants engaged in obtaining intelligence and internal security information for the Government shall not be allowed where the head of the investigative agency determines that the disclosure of the identity of such informants will prejudice the

754

national security. In such cases the report supplied by the investigative agency shall contain as much of the information supplied by the informant as may be disclosed without revealing the identity of the informant and without otherwise endangering the national security.

"4. If confrontation is not permitted under paragraph 3, the Board shall furnish the individual involved with the substance of the information obtained from such informant to the extent that such information is material to the consideration of the issues involved; and shall read into the record the substance of such information and the evaluation as to reliability placed upon such confidential informant in the investigative report.

"5. If the individual who is the subject of inquiry questions the accuracy or completeness of the information furnished pursuant to paragraph 4, that individual may file with the Board a written statement setting forth in detail so much of the information which is challenged as to accuracy or completeness. If the Board is of the opinion that the additional investigation as to the specific matter challenged is required in the interest of ascertaining the facts, it shall request the investigative agency to make such additional investigation. Information obtained as a result of the additional investigation shall be treated in the same manner as provided for in the original investigation.

"6. Derogatory information supplied by confidential informants other than those described in paragraph 3 shall not be considered, over the objection of the individual involved, by the Board in arriving at its determination, or by any authority charged with the responsibility for making a final determination, unless such informants consent to the disclosure of their identity so as to enable the individual involved to obtain their testimony through the issuance of subpena or by depositions or written interrogatories.

"7. Derogatory information supplied by identified persons shall not be considered, over the objection of the individual involved, by the Board in arriving at its determination, or by any authority charged with the responsibility for making a final determination unless the individual involved is given the opportunity to obtain the testimony of such identified persons through the issuance of subpenas, or by depositions, or written interrogatories; if the individual involved is given the opportunity to obtain the testimony of such identified persons through the issuance of subpenas, or by depositions, or written interrogatories, such derogatory information supplied by identified persons shall be considered. If the identified person supplying the derogatory information is unavailable for service of subpena or the taking of his testimony by deposition or written interrogatories because of death, incompetency, or other reason, such derogatory information may be considered by the Board with due regard for the lack of opportunity for cross-examination.

"PART VI—SUBPENAS

"1. Whenever the Board or any panel is authorized by law to issue process to compel the attendance of witnesses or the production of evidence, the Board, or any panel thereof, on its own motion or upon application made by the individual concerned in a hearing upon charges of the kind listed in subparagraphs (a) through (i) of paragraph 2 of Part 2 of this Order, may issue subpenas to compel the attendance of witnesses or the production of other evidence. Each such application for the issuance of a subpena to require the attendance of any witness must state the name and address of the witness desired and the substance of the testimony which such witness is believed to be qualified to give. Each such application for the issuance of a subpena to require the production of other evidence shall state the name and address of the person to whom it is to be directed and the nature of the evidence desired. In determining whether any subpena shall be issued, the Board or panel shall consider such factors as the time and expense involved by reason of travel which would be required for compliance therewith.

"2. The Board or panel shall deny any such application if it determines that the evidence sought (1) is not relevant to any issue presented for hearing, or (2) would be merely cumulative to other evidence received in the hearing. If, upon any such application, the Board or panel determines that a substantial sum would be required for the payment of per diem allowance and mileage incident to the issuance of a subpena, and that the evidence desired can be obtained by interrogatory, it may deny the application and require such evidence to be obtained by interrogatory.

"3. No subpena or other process may be issued to compel the attendance, or otherwise to obtain the evidence, of—

"(1) any individual certified by the head of any investigative agency of the executive branch of the Government to be a regularly established confidential informant engaged in obtaining intelligence and internal security information for such agency; or

"(2) any other individual, without the consent of such individual, if such individual is certified by the head of any such agency to have given information to such agency concerning the individual who is the subject of inquiry upon the condition that the supplier of such information would not be called as a witness to testify with respect to information so given.

"4. No witness shall be summoned by process issued on behalf of any individual who is the subject of inquiry unless that individual has deposited with the Board or panel such sum as it determines to be necessary to defray the per diem allowance and mileage payable to that witness. If, after the conclusion of any hearing, the question presented is determined, upon the record of proceedings in that hearing, in a manner favorable to the individual who deposited any such sum, the aggregate amount of all deposits so made by that individual shall be returned to him. If, after the conclusion of any such hearing, such determination is adverse to that individual, the aggregate amount of such deposits, reduced by the aggregate amount of all sums actually paid from appropriated funds during such hearing for the per diem allowances and mileage of witnesses summoned upon the application of that individul, shall be returned to him.

"PART VII—DETERMINATIONS AFTER HEARING

"1. After the conclusion of the hearing in any case, the Board or panel shall prepare its written report thereon, which shall contain a recitation of the questions presented, a summary of the evidence received, its findings as to the facts as to each allegation made with respect to the individual who is the subject of inquiry, and its conclusion on each question presented for hearing. Upon the completion of that report, it shall be forwarded to the Chairman of the United States Civil Service Commission, who shall transmit it to the Secretary of State.

"2. A copy of such report shall be furnished to the individual who was the subject of inquiry as soon as may be practicable after the completion of the hearing."

This order shall become effective on _____.

756

Biographical Sketch of Commissioners and Staff

Commissioners

Chairman

Loyd Wright, Los Angeles, Calif., lawyer, LL. B., University of Southern California; LL. D., University of Ottawa; president, Los Angeles Bar Association, 1937–38; president, State Bar of California, 1940–41; president, American Bar Association, 1954–55; Chairman of the House of Delegates, International Bar Association; Commission on judicial and congressional salaries and other State and national commissions.

Vice Chairman

John Cornelius Stennis, DeKalb, Miss., United States Senator. B. S., Mississippi State College; LL. B., University of Virginia Law School; LL. D. Millsaps College; member of Phi Beta Kappa, Phi Alpha Delta fraternities; member of Farm Bureau; Mississippi and American Bar Association; president, State 4–H Club Advisory Council; elected to Mississippi House of Representatives; elected district prosecuting attorney, 16th Judicial District; appointed circuit judge, 16th Judicial District and three times elected; elected United States Senator in 1947 and currently serving in that office.

Members

Norris Cotton, Lebanon, N. H., United States Senator. Wesleyan University, George Washington University Law School; lawyer, firm of Cotton, Tesreau & Stebbins; prosecuting attorney for Grafton County, N. H.; justice, Municipal Court of Lebanon, Hagner & Co.; served during World War II as a member of the War Manpower Committee, majority leader, speaker, of the New Hampshire House of Representatives; elected to the 80th, 81st, 82d, and 83d Congresses; elected to the United States Senate in 1954 for 2 years; reelected to the United States Senate in 1956.

F. Moran McConihe, Cedarhurst, Long Island, N. Y., Pubic Buildings Commissioner. A. B., Princeton University; executive vice president of realty firm of Randall H. Hagner & Co.; served during World War II as a member of the War Manpower Commission and the United States Navy Manpower Survey Committee; named special consultant to the President on developing plans for eliminating temporary buildings in Washington, D. C.; member of National Association of Real Estate Boards, Washington Real Estate Board, and Citizens Zoning Advisory Committee of the District of Columbia.

William M. McCulloch, Piqua, Ohio. Member of the United States House of Representatives. Student College of Wooster, Ohio, L.L. B., Ohio State University; member Ohio State and American Bar Associations; member of Ohio House of Representatives 6 terms, serving 3 years as minority leader and 3 terms as speaker; elected to the 80th, 81st, 82d, 83d, 84th, and 85th Congresses; member of law firm of McCulloch, Felger & Fite; director, The Piqua National Bank and Trust Company; director, The Third Savings and Loan Company.

James P. McGranery, P. C., K. C. S. G., K. H. S.; Philadelphia, Pa., lawyer. LL. B.: Temple University Law School. LL. D.: Villanova University, National University, Manhattanville College. HH. D.: LaSalle College. Trustee: Immaculata College. Member of Advisory Boards: Temple University Law School, Villanova University, Mount Saint Joseph College, Maryland. Elected to: 75th, 76th, 77th, and 78th Congresses, U. S. House of Representatives. Resigned November 1943 to become the Assistant to the Attorney General of the United States. Resigned October 1946 to become Judge of the United States District Court. Resigned May 1952 to become the Atorney General of the United States. Awarded Medal of Merit by President Truman, 1946. Honorary member: Lawyers' Club of Philadelphia and Bar Association for the District of Columbia.

Edwin L. Mechem, Albuquerque, N. Mex., Governor of New Mexico. N. M. College of A & MA, State College, New Mexico, University of Arkansas, Fayetteville, Ark.; lawyer, practice of law with firms of Mechem & Mechem and Iden, Johnson & Mechem; 3 years special agent with the FBI; served as a member of the New Mexico Legislature; Governor of New Mexico 1951-54; elected Governor of New Mexico in 1956.

Franklin David Murphy, Lawrence, Kans., educator, Chancellor, University of Kansas, A. B., University of Kansas; M. D., University of Pennsylvania; LL. D. (hon.) Temple University; Sc. D. (hon.) University of Pennsylvania. Chairman, American Council on Education. President, State Universities Association.

James L. Noel, Jr., Houston, Tex., lawyer. Graduated from Southern Methodist University with civil engineering and law degrees; served as assistant attorney general of Texas; private practice of law; member of the Houston, American, and Texas Bar Associations; vice president of Houston Bar Association; chairman of State Bar of Texas Committee on Administration of Justice.

Susan B. Riley, Nashville, Tenn., educator, Professor of English. B. S., Blue Mountain College; A. M., Ph. D., George Peabody College for Teachers; graduate work at Vanderbilt and Columbia Universities; honorary degrees of LL. D., University of Chattanooga, and Litt. D., Blue Mountain College; national president, American Association of University Women; member of Advisory Committee of the Foreign Operations Administration; member of American Association of University Professors, American Council on Education.

Louis Samuel Rothschild, Kansas City, Mo., Under Secretary of Commerce. Ph. B., Yale University; Chairman of the Board, Inland Waterways Corporation; Chairman, Federal Maritime Board, Maritime Administration, United States Department of Commerce; United States Delegate, NATO Planning Board for Ocean Shipping; member, City Planning Commission, Kansas City, Mo.; chairman, Menorah Foundation for Medical Research; director, Midwest Research Institute, Kansas City, Mo.; member, National Advisory Committee for Aeronautics, Telecommunications Advisory Board; appointed to the Commission on Government Security by the President of the United States.

Francis Eugene Walter, Easton, Pa., Member of the United States House of Representatives. B. A., George Washington University; LL. B., Georgetown University; practice of law in Easton, Pa.; solicitor, Northampton County; director, Easton National Bank; vice president and director, Broad Street Trust Co., Philadelphia; elected to the 73d to 85th Congresses.

Staff

Administrative Director

D. Milton Ladd, Geneva, Fla., lawyer. LL. B., George Washington University Law School; LL. D., North Dakota Agricultural College; 33 years' Federal service in legislative and executive branches; 26 years with FBI as special agent in charge, Assistant Director and Assistant to the Director; member several interdepartmental intelligence committees; retired 1954 as assistant to the Director in charge of all FBI intelligence and criminal investigations; consultant on research, *A Report on World Population Migrations* (published 1956, George Washington University).

Chief Counsel

Samuel Halpern Liberman, St. Louis, Mo., lawyer. LL. B., University of Missouri; practiced law in the State of Missouri; president of the Bar Association of St. Louis; vice president, Missouri Bar Association; chairman of Missouri Bar Association committee to draft judicial articles for submission to the 1945 constitutional convention; served three terms in the house of delegates of the American Bar Association; city counselor of the city of St. Louis; Order of the Coif, Phi Alpha Delta.

Research Director

Richard A. Edwards, Easton, Pa., lawyer, educator. A. B., Indiana University; LL. B., Harvard Law School; Ph. D., Columbia University; associate professor of government and law, Lafayette College; consultant, Governor's Interdepartmental Committee on Migratory Labor, Commonwealth of Pennsylvania; coauthor, *American Constitutional Law,* the Foundation Press, Inc., 1954; member of the American Bar Association, United States Supreme Court Bar, American Political Science Association.

Project Surveys

Stanley J. Tracy, College Park, Md., lawyer. LL. B., George Washington University Law School; 35 years Federal service; author of articles and coauthor of book, *Labor Laws and Court Decisions,* annotated, 1925; retired 1954 as Assistant Director, FBI; two terms, president, General Alumni Association, George Washington University; research project director of book, *A Report on World Population Migrations,* published 1956 by George Washington University.

Chief Consultant

L. Dale Coffman, Los Angeles, Calif., lawyer, educator. B. A., State University of Iowa; J. D., State University of Iowa; LL. M., Harvard University; S. J. D., Harvard University; private practice of law; professor of law, University of Nebraska; dean of school of law, Vanderbilt University; dean of school of law, University of California; Phi Beta Kappa, Order of the Coif, Phi Delta Phi.

Executive Secretary

Douglas R. Price, Ruxton, Md. B. S., Wharton School, University of Pennsylvania; Assistant to Deputy Director, ICA; Republican National Committee, 1952–53; Eisenhower-for-President campaign staff, 1952–53.

CONSULTANTS

Richard E. Combs, Visalia, Calif., lawyer. A. B., LL. B., University of California; private practice of law; 18 years chief counsel, California Legislature's Committee on Un-American Activities; Phi Delta Phi.

J. Stewart Newlin, Wellington, Kans. University of Kansas; editor and publisher of the Wellington Daily News; executive secretary to the Governor of Kansas; public relations director, Kansas Highway Commission, and public relations director, Eisenhower-for-President headquarters.

Harry B. Reese, Chicago, Ill., lawyer, educator. B. A., Ohio State University; LL. B., Harvard University; assistant professor of law and associate director of legal research, Ohio State University College of Law; associate professor of law at Northwestern University Law School.

Lawrence G. Blochman, New York City, writer. B. A., University of California; 10 years newspaper experience; served as chief of Radio Program Bureau, OWI, during World War II; served as Deputy Director of OWI Operations in France; author of numerous books, both fiction and nonfiction.

Professional Staff

Research

Floyd D. Birdzell, Ph. B., B. S. L.-J. D., University of North Dakota; *J. Robert Brown,* A. B., M. A., Woodstock College; *Maurice D. Contor,* B A., Vanderbilt University, LL. B., Harvard Law School; *Morris M. Cramer,* A. B., Pennsylvania State University; *Jeanne F. Davies,* B. S., Madison College; *Phoebe H. Everett,* B. A., M. A., Syracuse University; *Leland G. Gardner,* A. M., LL. B., University of Michigan; *Edward W. Hassell,* B. S., American University; *Gilbert O. Hourtoule,* A. B., Montclair State Teachers College, M. A., Stanford University, Ph. D., Pennsylvania State University; *Irwin Langenbacher,* A. B., Central College of Missouri, A. B. B. A., University of Georgia, J. D. Emory University; *Samuel J. L'Hommedieu, Jr.,* B. S., University of Maryland, LL. B., LL. M., George Washington University; *Mary C. Martin,* LL. B., Lincoln College of Law; *William T. McDermott,* B. S., University of New Hampshire, Ed. M., Boston University, LL. B., George Washington University; *Frank J. McGee,* B. S., LL. B., Boston College, LL. M., Georgetown University; *Theodore C. Merlo,* A. B., Lafayette College, LL. B., Georgetown Law School; *Leroy S. Merrifield,* A. B., LL. B., University of Minnesota, S. J. D., Harvard University; *Francis G. Naughten,* B. S., LL. B., Georgetown University; *James C. Pressey,* A. B., Dartmouth College, LL. B., Harvard Law School; *Jack M. Reid,* B. Sc., University of Southern California, LL. B., Georgetown University; *Arthur A. Sharp,* United States Government Printing Office.

Legal

Elwyn J. Darden, B. A., LL. B., University of Mississippi; *Nelson Deckelbaum*, B. S., LL. B., Georgetown University; *Allan J. Farrar*, B. S., Indiana University, LL. B., Cornell University; *John Clifford Herberg*, B. A., LL. B., University of Minnesota, assistant counsel, Office of Senate Legislative Counsel; *Richard P. Hogan*, B. S., Xavier University; *Lucy Somerville Howorth*, A. B., Randolph-Macon Women's College, LL. B., University of Mississippi; *Robert J. McKinsey*, B. A., J. D., University of Chicago; *Joseph F. Salisbury*, B. A., University of Notre Dame, LL. B., Georgetown Law School; former attorney, Internal Security Section, Department of Justice; *Edward R. Taylor*, A. B., Lafayette College, LL. B., George Washington University.

Survey

Peter Barretta, Jr., B. S. foreign service, Georgetown University; *George Henry Becker, Jr.*, B. S., foreign service, Georgetown University, Ph. D., political science, Graduate Institute of International Relations, Geneva, Switzerland; *Col. William N. Egan, consultant*, Hoover Commission; former national vice president, American Institute of Industrial Engineers; *Paul C. Gerhart*, B. S., Southern Methodist University; *Edward C. Kennelly*, A. B., Holy Cross, LL. B., Harvard Law School, counsel for United States House of Representatives subcommittee on international operations; *Edwin B. Kugler*, B. S., Davidson College, 13 years with United States Navy, ONI; *George H. Martin*, newspaperman, Pulitzer Prize winner, staff consultant, Senate Crime Investigating Committee; *Edwin C. Maska*, B. S., Wharton School, University of Pennsylvania; *George Miller Norris*, Wharton School, University of Pennsylvania, former executive secretary, Loyalty Review Board; *Edward O. Poole*, LL. B., Columbus University Law School; *George E. Potter, Jr.*, A. B., Georgetown University; *Willis A. Potter*, LL. B., University of Washington, member Screening Board, Industrial Personnel Security Review Division, OSD; *Edgar F. Puryear*, LL. B., National University, special assistant to Administrator, Federal Security Agency; *Harold Ranstad*, A. B., LL. B., University of Minnesota; *Frank A. Stanton*, A. B., Boston College; *E. Newton Steely, Jr.*, A. B., University of Maryland; *Arthur P. Steuerwald*, B. S., Indiana State Teachers College, M. A., University of Chicago.

Index

Index

A

Abt, John, 102

Acheson, Dean, 373, 374, 377, 387, 388–389, 471

Act of March 3, 1871, 19, 22

Act of March 3, 1875, 530

Act of March 3, 1903, 527, 530, 570

Act of August 24, 1912, 699

Act of August 2, 1939, see Hatch Act

Act of July 26, 1947, see The National Security Act of 1947

Act of September 3, 1954, 534

Act of August 6, 1956, 618

Adler, Sol, 381, 383

Administration Handling of Violations and Related Matters, 212.

Advisory Committee on Uranium, 188

Advocacy of revolution or force or violence to alter the constitutional form of the Government, 46

    basis for determination of disloyalty, 46

Agriculture, Department of, 29, 161

Agricultural Adjustment Administration, 382

Air Force, Department of the, 25, 164, 165, 166

Air Force, U. S., 120, 127–128, 239, 259, 260, 289

Air Force Personnel Council, 130

Air transport security, see Civil air transport security program

Aircraft Industries Association, xv

Alien clearance, 271–273, 312

Alien crewmen, 520, 522, 538, 554–555, 603–604

Alien Registration Act of 1940, 526, 528, 530, 531

Aliens, foreign government officials, 520–522, 536–537, 553, 605–606

Aliens, international organization, 520, 523–525, 607

Aliens, nonimmigrant, 519–526

    categories of, 520–523, 535–538, 552

    Federal court decisions, 547-549

Aliens—Continued

    visa procedures for, 553–560

    refusal of visa for, 560–561

    revocation of visas, 561–562

    conditions of nonimmigrant status, 565–566

    waiver of visas, 566–567

    fingerprinting of, 604–605

Aliens, representatives of information media, 559, 612

Aliens, student, 523, 557, 610–611

Aliens, temporary visitors, 520, 522, 554

Aliens, temporary worker, 525–526, 558–559

Aliens, transit, 520, 522, 555–556, 592–602

Aliens, treaty, 523, 556–57

Allis-Chalmers Manufacturing Company, 277

Alverson, Joseph, 14

American Battle Monuments Commission, 160

American Communications Association, 328

American Communications Association v. *Douds*, 277

American Committee to Survey Trade Union Conditions in Europe, 475

American Council of Education, 319

American Federation of Labor, 327

American Jewish Congress, xv

The American Passport, 446

American Society for Industrial Security, xv, 273, 301

Arlington Memorial Amphitheater Commission, 160

American President Lines, Ltd., 572

Appeals:

    civilian personnel, 72–73, 74, 86

    atomic energy personnel, 224

    port security personnel, 351–352

    passport security cases, 488–491

Applicants for positions:

    recommendations of Commission concerning, 51–52

Armed Forces Industrial Security Regulations, 245–246, 249, 258, 296–297, 313

767

773

G

Galvan v. *Press*, 544
Gardner, Leland G., 762
Gardner, Trevor, 313
Garrett Corporation, 303
Garrison, Lloyd, 201
Gaston, Herbert A., 9
General Accounting Office, 105
General Advisory Committee, 190
General Agreement on Tariffs and Trade, 426
General Electric Company, 201
General Services Administration, 168, 177
General Tire and Rubber Company, 303
Gerhart, Paul C., 763
Gilman, Lawrence M., 419
Gladnick, Robert, 330 fn.
Glaser, Eda, 401
Glasser, Harold, 381 fn., 383
Glasser, McElrath, Oka and Symonds, In re, 626
Glassman, Sidney, 401
Gold, Ben, 44, 276, 277
Gold v. *United States*, 276–277
Goldman v. *United States*, 628
Goldsteen v. *United States*, 628
Goldwater, Barry, 277
Goodyear Aircraft Corporation, 303
Gordon, Joel, 401
Gore, H. Grady, 419
Gouzenko, Igor, 381, 605
Government Printing Office, 105
Greene v. *Wilson*, 250
Greenglass, David, 44
Griffin v. *U. S.*, 146
Groves, L. R., 188
Grumman Engineering Corporation, 303
Gwinn, W. P., 166–167, 300

H

H. R. 578, 82d Cong., 586
H. R. 5678, 82d Cong., 530
H. R. 722, 84th Cong., 439
H. R. 1570, 84th Cong., 604
H. R. 3588 (1947), 16
H. R. 3813 (1947), 16
H. R. 7439 (1950), 36, *see* Public Law 733
H. R. 8649 (1954), 628
H. R. 3882 (1956), 624
H. R. 10667 (1956), 37
H. R. 11721 (1956), 36, 37
H. R. 11841 (1956), 36
H. R. 3364 (1957), 529

H. R. 5239 (1957), 504
H. J. Res. 553 (1940), 628
H. Rept. 1365, 82d Cong., 2d Sess., 522, 530
H. Res. 262 (1954), 407
Hammarskjold, Dag, 403, 405, 409
Han-Lee Mao v. *Brownell*, 543
Hanson, George W., 14
Hardyman, Hugh, 473
Hargrove, Thomas A., 241 fn.
Hariseades v. *Shaughnessy*, 528
Hariseades v. *U. S.*, 540, 541
Harlan, John M., 35
Harmon v. *Brucker*, 117, 118, 146, 148
Harris, Jack Sargeant, 401
Harris, Oren, 504
Hassell, Edward W., 762
Hatch Act, 5, 17, 22
Hazeltine Corporation, 303
Headquarters Agreement Act of June 1947, 524
Headquarters Agreement Act of August 1947, 416
Health, Education, and Welfare, Department of, 161, 170, 318
Hearing boards, military
  continued maintenance in each of the services recommended, 140
Hearing examiners, civilian personnel:
  qualifications and functions of, 61–64
  report of, 70–72
  in Central Security office, 90, 515–516
Hearings, air transport personnel:
  confrontation, 512–513
  procedures similar to port security program recommended, 512–515
  right of subpena, 513–514
  appeals, 514–515
Hearings, atomic energy personnel:
  present procedure, 207–209
  confrontation, 208, 225–228
  right of subpena, 208, 228–229
  recommendations, 223–229
Hearings, Federal civilian personnel
  recommendations, 61–77
    hearing examiners, 61–64, 70–72
    role of agency at hearing, 64–65, 73–76
    employee counsel, 65
    attendance restricted, 66
    confrontation, 66–69
    witnesses, power to subpena, for the charged employee, 69–70
    witnesses, power to subpena for the Government, 69–70

Legislation, proposed—Continued
  to prescribe a standard of loyalty to the
    United States Government for military
    personnel (text of bill), 719–727
  to amend the Immigration and Nation-
    ality Act (text of bill), 729–733
  to authorize certain investigative officers
    of the United States, to intercept and
    disclose under stated conditions wire
    and radio communications (text of
    bill), 735–736
  to amend Title 18, United States Code, to
    prohibit the unauthorized disclosure of
    certain information critically affecting
    national defense (text of bill), 737
Legislative branch:
  necessity for employee screening program
    in, 101–105
Lehman, Herbert H., 382
L'Hommedieu, Samuel J., Jr., 762
Liberman, Samuel Halpern, biographical
  sketch, 761
Library of Congress, 105
Licensing system:
  responsibility of Atomic Energy Com-
    mission, 189, 210
Lichter v. *United States*, 253
Lie, Trygve, 371, 373, 375, 376, 379, 386,
  393, 394, 395, 398, 399–400, 403, 428
Linneman, Herbert F., 390
Lloyd-LaFollette Act (1912), 5, 20, 23, 38,
  81, 86, 87, 88
Lockheed Aircraft Corporation, 303
Lodge, Henry Cabot, 369, 391–392, 398–
  399, 402, 407
Los Alamos, New Mexico, 189
Loutfi, Omar, 400
Loyalty Rating Board, 6, 7
Loyalty Review Board, 10, 16, 31, 62, 396,
  397
Lundberg, Arne, 399

M

Mackenzie v. *Hare*, 545
Magnuson, Warren G., 323, 331
Magnuson Act, 500
Manager of Operations, 207–208, 210
Manhattan Engineering District, 188, 189,
  190–191, 193, 197, 199, 200–201, 221
Manpower, Personnel, and Reserve Forces,
  258, 259
Marine Vessel Personnel Division, 343, 346,
  348

Maritime credential endorsements:
  procedure for obtaining, 345–346
Marshall, George, 388
Marshall, John, 338, 546–547, 616–617
Martin, George H., 763
Martin, Mary C., 762
Maska, Edwin C., 763
Mastin, John, 580
Mauerman, Raymond J., 324 fn., 365
Mayock, Welburn, 572
Meat Cutters v. *The United States*, 278
Mechem, Edwin L.: biographical sketch,
  760
Meehan, M. Joseph, 309
Meloy, L. V., 14
Membership, affiliation or association with
    party or association inimical to United
    States interest
  basis for determination of disloyalty,
    46–47
Merchant Marine, 334, 343–344
Merlo, Theodore C., 762
Merrifield, Leroy S., 762
Merrow, Chester E., 411
Metallurgical Laboratory (Chicago), 188
Metallurgical Laboratory (Chicago), 188
Mexican Migratory Labor Acts, 531
Middleton, Mary A., 401
Military Liaison Committee, 190
Military personnel program:
  basis for, 111
  joint agreement initiating (text), 111–113
  uniform standards for enlisted and in-
    ducted personnel, 113–115
  legal basis, 115–118
  present program, 119–130
    security standard same as civilian per-
      sonnel security program, 119
    Army employs double standard, 119
    security criteria identical with civilian
      program, 119
    scope of security directive, 120
    court-martial and nonsecurity separa-
      tion action, 120–121
    security separations, 121–122
    types of discharge in security separa-
      tions, 121–122
    rejections from military service, 122–
      125
    security investigations, 125–126
    allegations, 126–128
    hearing board procedures, 129
    final review of security proceedings,
      129–130

Military personnel program—Continued
recommendations, 130–148
  loyalty standard recommended in lieu
    of security standard, 130–131
  same criteria for civilian and military
    loyalty programs recommended, 131–
    133
  continuation of use of security ques-
    tionnaire recommended, 133–135
  procedure in event of denial of enlist-
    ment, 135–136
  rights of enlistee or inductee rejected
    during preservice screening, 136–137
  use of inductees rejected for loyalty
    grounds in semimilitary status, 137
  continuation of present use of national
    agency check, 137–138
  continuation of investigations by all
    services, 138
  continuation of use of interview, 138
  continuation of triservice screening pro-
    cedures, 138–140
  continuation of hearing board proce-
    dures, 140
  closed hearings, 140
  confrontation and subpena privileges,
    140–144
  maintenance of separate boards of re-
    view, 144
  discharge dependent upon conduct
    during term of military service, 145–
    148
  text of proposed legislation to prescribe
    loyalty standard for, 719–727
Military Personnel Security Committee,
  127
Miller v. *Sinjan*, 453
Ming Mow et al. v. *Dulles*, 586
Mine, Mill and Smelter Workers, 277
Minton, Sherman, 36
Missouri Basin Survey Commission, 161
Mitsugi Nishikawa v. *Dulles*, 546
Monetary Research Division, 381, 383
Morgan, Gerald D., 171
Morse, David, 201
Moss, John E., 156
Mundt, Karl E., 373
Munitions Board, 240, 241, 242, 245
Munro, Leslie Knox, 399
Murphey, Charles, 580
Murphy, Franklin David, biographical
  sketch, 760
Murray, Tom, 36
Myers v. *United States*, 19

Mc

MacClain, George, 238 fn., 263
McConihe, F. Moran, biographical sketch,
  759
McCulloch, William M., biographical
  sketch, 759
  statement of reservation, 685
McDermott, William T., 762
McGee, Frank J., 762
McGranery, James, 387
  biographical sketch, 760
  dissent, 797
McKinley, William, 5, 527

N

Nardone v. *United States*, 628
National Advisory Committee for Aero-
  nautics, 25
National Board of Appeals, 333, 346, 351,
  352
National Capital Housing Authority, 161
National Capital Park and Planning Com-
  mission, 161
National Civil Liberties Clearing House,
  263
National Defense Research Committee, 188
National Forest Reservation Commission,
  161
National Guard, 125
National Labor Relations Act, 117, 274
National Labor Relations Act Amend-
  ment, 692
National Labor Relations Board, 161, 200–
  201, 202, 214, 231, 274–275, 277, 278, 625
National Labor Relations Board General
  Counsel Adminstrative Ruling Case No.
  410 (1952), 275
National Maritime Union, 327
National Mediation Board, 161
National Military Establishment, 199, 240
National Recovery Administration, 382
National Research Council, 188
National Science Foundation, 161, 290, 319
National security, defined, 48–49
National Security Act of 1947, 117, 159,
  240, 251, 716, 717
National Security Agency:
  exclusion from loyalty program, xviii, 50,
    51
National Security Council, 10, 31, 155, 156,
  157, 159, 171, 182, 466, 593
National Security Industrial Association, xv
National Security Resources Board, 25
National Security Training Commission, 161

782

National Union of Marine Cooks and Stewards, 328, 329
Nationality Act of 1952, 465, 482, 520, 521, 525
Nationality and naturalization. *See also* Immigration and Nationality:
  statutory provisions, 533–534, 567–568, 612
  Federal court decisions, 546–547
Naughton, Francis G., 762
Naval Personnel, Bureau of, 126, 127, 130
Navy, Department of the, 25, 135–136, 153, 154, 164, 166
Navy, U. S., 120, 126–127, 154, 236–237, 238, 239, 259, 260, 289, 324, 345
Navy Civilian Personnel Instructions, 33
"Need-to-know" policy, 302, 312–314
New York Bar Association, xv
New York Federal Grand Jury:
  investigation into disloyalty of American citizens employed at United Nations, 376–380
Newlin, J. Stewart, biographical sketch, 762
Niederlehner, Leonard, 116
Nixon, Richard M., 584
Noel, James L., Jr., biographical sketch, 760
Non-Defense Information, 212
"Nonimmigrant Visa," 560–561
Nonresident Alien Border-Crossing Identification Cards, 566–567
Norris, George Miller, 763
Norris v. *The City of Boston*, 526
North Atlantic Treaty Organization, 310, 311
Nowak v. *U. S.*, 549, 591

O

Oak Ridge, Tenn., 191, 197, 198, 200, 201, 211
Oak Ridge Institute of Nuclear Studies, Oak Ridge, Tenn., 563
O'Conor, Herbert R., 415
Office for Emergency Management, 154
Office for Government Reports, 154
Office of Censorship, 154
Office of Defense Mobilization, 235
Office of Education, 523
Office of Facts and Figures, 154
Office of Industrial Personnel Security Review, 262, 263, 284, 295–296
Office of Industrial Security, 244
Office of International Administration and Conferences, 391, 421

Office of Naval Intelligence, 564, 575
Office of Personnel Security Policy, 247, 258
Office of Scientific Research and Development, 188
Office of Security (Department of Defense), xx, 280, 289, 291, 292–293, 302
Office of Security (Department of State), 564, 609
Office of Security and Intelligence, 189
Office of Security Review, 165
Office of Special Investigations, 127
Office of Special Political Affairs, 373, 381
Office of Strategic Information, 157, 306
Office of Strategic Services, 383
Office of the Coordinator of Information, 154
Office of War Information, 154, 155
Offshore Procurement Program, 309, 310–311
Older, Julia, 401
Olmstead v. *United States*, 628
Orloff v. *Willoughby*, 118
Osborn v. *The Bank of the United States*, 547
Oppenheimer, J. R., 188

P

Palmer, Clive W., 14
Pan-American Airways, 594–595, 596, 597
Pan American Institute of Geography and History, 426
Pan American Sanitary Bureau, 426
Pan American Union, 426
Panama Canal, 25
Panama Canal Company, 161
Panama Railroad Company, 25
Panuch, J. Anthony, 381
Parker v. *Lester*, 253, 500
Passport Office, 445, 462, 463–465, 467, 468, 474–475, 482, 484–485, 487, 488–490, 493–494
Passport security program:
  summary of recommendations, xxii
  evolution of passport program, 446–450
  legal basis, 450–462
    court decisions, 453–460
    criminal sanctions relating to passports, 460–461
  present program, 462–470
    statistics on refusals of passports, 1952–1956, 463

Presidential proclamation 3004, 452
Presidential proclamation of August 8, 1918, 527
Pressey, James C., 762
Pressman, Lee, 102
Price, Byron, 374
Price, Douglas R., biographical sketch, 762
Probationary employees:
  recommendations of the Commission for protection of, 52–53
Procedures for Safeguarding Classified Documents and Other Classified Information, 212
Public Health Service, 551
Public Law 291, 79th Cong., 416
Public Law 357, 80th Cong., 416
Public Law 402, 80th Cong., 563
Public Law 831, 81st Cong., 500
Public Law 428, 83d Cong., 417
Public law 637, 83d Cong., 440
Public Law 112, 84th Cong., 417
Public Law 623, 84th Cong., 417
Public law 733 (1950), 22, 23, 24, 27, 30, 32, 39, 40, 41, 53, 54, 58, 60, 71, 72, 78, 79, 203, 204
  effect of *Cole* v. *Young* decision, 35
  extension of statutory authority, 26, 35–36
  intent of applicability, 36
  original applicability, 25
Public Law 298 (1952), 29
Public Law 304 (1955), xiii, xiv, xvi, 4, 17, 41, 615
Public Law 330 (1955), 17, 24
Public Law 893 (1956), 624
Public Law 786 (1956), 615
Puryear, Edgar F., 763

Q

"Q" clearance 192, 205
  defined, 192, 205
  abolishment recommended, 222

R

Radiation Laboratory, University of California, 563
Radio Act of 1927, 627
Railroad Retirement Board, 161
Ramspeck, Robert, 13
Ranstad, Harold, 763
Reactor Handbook, 195
Reconstruction Finance Corporation, 161

Reed, Jane M., 401
Reed, Stanley F., 36, 276, 461
Rees, Edward H., 8, 9, 16, 36
Reese, Harry B., biographical sketch, 762
Refugee Relief Act of 1953, 582, 583, 587, 588
Refugees:
  recommendations on admission of, 583–590
  admission of Hungarian refugees, 583–590
  report of Vice President on, 584
  President's message on, 584–585
  Opinion on statutory provision for admission of, 586–587
  inadequate screening of, 588–590
Registration statutes, Criminal statutes, primary, 623–624
Reid, Jack M., 762
Reinstatements, statistics on, 38
Remington, William W., 44
Renegotiation Board, 161
Republic Aviation Corporation, 303
Research, unclassified, 318–319
Review boards, military:
  continued use of separate boards recommended, 144
Rheem Manufacturing Company, 303
Richmond, Alfred C., 349
Rieger, John, 588
Riley, Russell L., 611
Riley, Susan B., biographical sketch, 760
Robeson, Paul, 458
Robeson v. *Dulles*, 458
Rogers, Byron G., 391
Roosevelt, Franklin D., 6, 7, 188
Rosenberg, Allan, 102
Rosenberg, Ethel, 617–618
Rosenberg, Julius, 44, 617–618
Rosenhan v. *U. S.*, 503
Ross, John C., 373
Rosser, Don, 329 fn.
Roth v. *Brownell*, 18
Rothschild, Louis Samuel, biographical sketch, 760
Royal Commission on Espionage of the Commonwealth of Australia, 45
Royal Dutch Airlines, 595–596
Rubin, Martin H., 401
Rusk, Dean, 374
Russell, Donald, 373, 381

785

DISSENT

OF

JAMES P. McGRANERY

Member of the Commission on Government Security

as to

Certain Recommendations in the Foregoing Report Concerning

Central Security Office

Repeal of Veterans Preference Act

Federal Judiciary

Wiretapping

Dissent of Commissioner McGranery to Certain Recommendations of the Report

It is interesting to recall that the late Mr. Justice Brandeis voiced his belief that a dissent was an exercise—not in hostility—but in clarification. And in his famous letter to Robert W. Bruere (1922) Mr. Justice Brandeis counseled: "Refuse to tolerate any immoral practice (e. g., espionage). But do not believe that you can find a universal remedy for evil conditions or immoral practices in effecting a fundamental change in society (as by state socialism). . . . Remedial institutions are apt to fall under the control of the enemy and to become instruments of oppression."

With a bow to the memory of that distinguished jurist, this member of the Commission on Government Security records his dissent as to certain of the recommendations presented in the foregoing report. He desires to exercise his right to differ in the same atmosphere of amicable frankness which—he is happy to state—characterized the deliberations of the Commission conferences. And, parenthetically, he considers it fair to add that during these conferences he presented suggestions as to security criteria and procedures (many of which were adopted and are incorporated in the foregoing report), and in addition, he offered frank, constructive criticisms of proposed procedures (some of which were accepted).

Now, pursuant to the obligations of his oath of office as a member of the Commission, he considers it his duty to submit in writing to the President of the United States, and to the Congress of the United States, the reasons for his reluctance to join in those certain recommendations which appear to him to be repugnant to the spirit of our democratic Republic and which would add an unjustified burden upon the taxpayers of this Nation, or which are irrelevant to the question of Government security.

The security of the Nation is the obligation of every citizen, but its first line of defense is the security of the Government. The problem of Government security in the United States—a Republic based on democratic principles—presents a paradox, since many procedures which might contribute, in the abstract, to an efficient security system, could well—by concrete innovation to our present government—cause either the loss of the whole Bill of Rights heritage—which has been termed "liberalism 'by negation' at its classic best"—or more directly result in the destruction of our constitutional

Government, with its "barriers to the untrammeled exercise of power by any group."

Our forefathers saw no contradiction between constitutional checks or the separation of powers and effective government. James Madison, the philosopher of the Constitution, in *The Federalist*, revealed his personal knowledge of men and of the practical business of government when he said:

But the great security against a gradual concentration of the several powers in the same department, consists in giving to those who administer each department the necessary constitutional means and personal motives to resist encroachments of the others. * * * It may be a reflection on human nature that such devices should be necessary to control the abuses of government. But what is government itself, but the greatest of all reflections on human nature? If men were angels, no government would be necessary. If angels were to govern men, neither external nor internal controls on government would be necessary. In framing a government which is to be administered by men over men, the great difficulty lies in this: *you must first enable the government to control the governed; and in the next place oblige it to control itself.* A dependence on the people is, no doubt, the primary control on the government; but experience has taught mankind the necessity of auxiliary precautions.

If this Nation, as originally and presently constituted, is to survive, it must adopt security procedures that are in harmony with its essential constitutional framework. To use other means in the name of efficiency or expediency would be to weaken the foundations of our freedom by the building of an extravagant and false facade: a topheavy superstructure masquerading as efficient, expedient security. The words of Mr. Justice Brandeis remind us sharply that: "The doctrine of the separation of powers was adopted, not to promote efficiency but to preclude the exercise of arbitrary power. The purpose was not to avoid friction, but by means of the inevitable friction to save the people from autocracy."

For, in this changing yet changeless human world, the expedient is often self-defeating, the pseudo-efficient is finally and forever ineffective. The navigator has learned that the arc route across the ocean is the most direct. The skillful and knowledgeable surgeon uses a blade adapted to the contours of the vascular system. The architect knows that, while it is more difficult to improve the security and efficiency of a house while keeping intact its original design, this is in reality the only way to achieve the desired result without putting unsafe stress on the foundations, without erasing the original simplicity of concept. It is always easier to add another wing, another floor; but another problem is added, too; and soon the original structure has vanished from view.

Central Security Office

Hence it is that I must express a vigorous dissent from the recommendation in the preceding report for: *"the creation of a Central Security Office in the executive branch independent of any existing department or agency."* (P. 89 et seq.)

It is perhaps unnecessary at this time to dwell upon the inherent evil of the pyramiding of administrative devices, the superimposing of agency upon agency and the empire-building proclivities which frequently go hand in hand with the creation of overseers. Yet it should be pointed out that no problem is solved by shifting primary executive responsibility from agencies and officials having that primary responsibility to superimposed administrative creations, even where the latter are described as advisory. The power to suggest too easily becomes the power to demand.

There is no substitute for sound administrative procedures and the exercise of commonsense. The time has come for emphasis to be placed on the spirit of the law.

It would have been refreshing, indeed, if the Commission had seen fit to submit a final report correcting existing procedures and practices without finding it necessary to enlarge and complicate the Government structure while adding no guarantee of increased effectiveness. What is needed is a correction in those existing procedures which fail to achieve Government security with minimum delay and maximum protection of the civil rights of the loyal employee. What is needed is the will to make corrected procedures work. There is no assurance that a new agency would be perfect. It is necessary to hold mistakes of judgment to a minimum and, once having occurred, then fix responsibility and seek to avoid their recurrence. This can best be done by holding accountable those officials and agencies having the primary responsibility.

There can be no doubt that there is a need for uniformity in security procedures but there is also a need to preserve the responsibility of the departments and agencies for the proper administration of the security program.

It has been well stated that our Government is a government of laws, not of men. At the present time the various departments and agencies of our Government function in accordance with the laws enacted by the Congress. The head of each department and each agency has the duty of conducting the department or agency in accordance with the laws enacted by the Congress, in accordance with the Constitution which he has sworn to protect and defend; and the President of the United States as the Chief Executive under the Constitution is ultimately responsible for the conduct of the executive branch of the Government.

This member of the Commission believes that the Congress in its wisdom and in the exercise of its constitutional power can legislate effectively and uniformly concerning the security of the Government and the methods of procedure to be followed by the departments and agencies. He further submits that the departments and agencies will act in accordance with this legislation without the policing supervision of a Central Security Office as described in the foregoing report to *"provide the necessary catalyst to immeasurably strengthen the potential good to flow from"* . . . *"other recommendations for improvements and to eliminate many of the general serious deficiencies of the present programs."* (P. 95—report.)

This member of the Commission suggests that the proposed legislation may well provide regulations which cover the various areas involved in security; define the investigative responsibility; make crystal clear the criteria in establishing reasonable doubt of loyalty; provide that questionable reliability for reasons other than disloyalty be treated according to existing administrative procedures (e. g., Civil Service Commission, etc.) and not in the content of security against disloyalty; outline the adjudicatory steps with right of appeal; spell out the right to counsel, to subpena, and to confrontation consistent with the national security (i. e., FBI and CIA, confidential sources, and investigative techniques to be protected); provide that the Government employee may be placed on leave with pay until such time as the head of a department or agency may determine that there is reasonable doubt of his loyalty; provide further that reasonable doubt of the loyalty of *any* Government employee be the basis for his separation from the Government by action of the head of the department or agency; provide for coordination with the National Security Council, the Civil Service Commission, the Attorney General, and other agencies. And this member of the Commission respectfully submits that the procedures and policies thus legislated will be an effective means of insuring the security of the Government without the creation of a complicated superstructure (whether called "Central Security Office" or by any other name) which would be economically unsound and administratively unwise.

This member firmly recommends that the Congress enact a law to exclude from any and all Government positions anyone concerning whose loyalty there exists a reasonable doubt. It is essential to recognize that no individual has an absolute right to be employed by the Government and it is equally essential to recognize that the people of these United States have an absolute right to a constitutional government secure from infiltration by even one disloyal employee. Any reasonable doubt as to the loyalty of an individual employee must be resolved in favor of the Government. The procedure by which the head of an agency or a department determines that such a reasonable doubt exists should be provided by uniform laws and regulations consistent with the spirit of the Constitution and its amendments.

The recommended procedure must be possible within the present constitutional and legislated framework of our Government without such an alteration as would result from the establishment of a superagency.

The recommended procedure should be sufficiently definite to fix responsibility in each department and/or agency, while providing uniform practice and centralized action, and should be capable of execution in each department or agency by the application of the respective principles or criteria for the said department or agency as prepared by this Commission and as subsequently to be enacted into law by the Congress.

The appeal or review provided under the security procedure should be to a Board of Security Advisors appointed by the President with the advice

800

and consent of the Senate; and this review should be advisory to the head of the department or agency.

Provision should be made for copies of (1) Preliminary decisions, with findings, of department or agency heads; (2) final advisory recommendations, with findings of fact of Security Advisors' Board; (3) final decisions, with findings, of department or agency heads: to dismiss—to be transmitted to the Secretary of the National Security Council and to the Attorney General (copies for the attention of the Attorney General to be accompanied by additional copies for investigation by the FBI and for FBI files).

Nothing in the procedure hereinbefore and hereinafter recommended by this member will preclude continuance of existing procedure for certain checks on all civilians entering employment in the executive branch (as provided in Executive Order 10450) embracing national agency check and certain inquiries conducted by the Civil Service Commission and/or the employing agency.

It should be noted that the procedure hereinafter recommended does not apply to the area of Government employees who are unsuitable and hence not adapted to positions of trust solely because of character defects or habits of unreliability (e. g., alcoholics or perverts) ; since these employees should be dealt with according to the normal disciplinary procedure of the department or agency (if civil service status or if excepted employee).

The following skeleton outline of procedures recommended by this member of the Commission are submitted for consideration by the Congress:

SUGGESTED OUTLINE OF SECURITY PROCEDURES

PROCEDURE TO BE FOLLOWED WHEN THE LOYALTY OF A GOVERNMENT
EMPLOYEE IS FOUND TO BE IN REASONABLE DOUBT

1. The head of a department or agency [1] will have before him information on which to decide whether the loyalty of the Government employee is prima facie to be regarded as in doubt. A Government employee will be so regarded if—

(a) He is employed in the Government of the United States; and simultaneously:

(b) He is or has been a member of the Communist [2] Party, or in such a way as to raise reasonable doubts about his reliability as to loyalty, is or has been sympathetic to communism, associated with Communists or Communist sympathizers, or is susceptible to Communist pressure.

Each case will be assessed in the light of the particular facts and by application of the respective principles or criteria for the said depart-

---

[1] That is, the person responsible for the department or agency to which the Government employee belongs.
[2] The term "Communist" is used to cover Communist, Fascist, any foreign ideological group or conspiracy having as its purpose the overthrowing of the Government by force and violence.

ment or agency prepared by the Commission on Government Security and subsequently enacted into law by the Congress.

2. If the responsible head of the department or agency rules that there is evidence sufficient to raise reasonable doubt of loyalty, the Government employee is at once to be so informed and to be placed on leave with pay and copies of the decision by and findings of the head of the department or agency concerning the said employee are to be promptly transmitted to the Secretary of the National Security Council and to the Attorney General (copies for the attention of the Attorney General to be accompanied by additional copies for the investigative purposes of the FBI).

3. The Government employee will at the same time be given any particulars, such as the date of his alleged membership, or the nature of the alleged sympathies or associations, that might enable him to clear himself. There will however have to be limits to the information given for he cannot be given such particulars as might risk the national security by disclosure of certain sources of evidence (i. e., confidential sources and investigative techniques of FBI and CIA).

4. At the same time the Government employee will be asked to say whether he admits or denies the allegation. If he admits the allegation he will be dealt with as described in paragraphs 9 and 10 below. If he does not admit the allegation he shall have 14 days in which to make written representations to the head of the department or agency if he so wishes, which time may be extended for good cause shown.

5. The head of the department or agency will reconsider his prima facie ruling in the light of any representations the Government employee may make in writing and at a hearing before a committee of three employees of the same department or agency—with right of counsel assured. If the head of the department or agency decides that there is no reason for varying it, the Government employee shall be so informed and shall then have 7 days in which to decide whether to ask for a reference to the Security Advisors' Board. If he does not ask for such a reference he will be dealt with as in paragraph 8 below. If he does ask for a reference to the Security Advisors' Board the latter will be asked to consider the case as soon as possible.

6. The function of the Security Advisors' Board is set out in its terms of reference. Where there is no suggestion of Communist or Fascist, etc., associations or sympathies, cases of character defects will not be referred to the tribunal, and appeals will be dealt with under the normal disciplinary procedure of the department or agency.

7. In discharging its functions the Security Advisors' Board will take into account the representations made by the Government employee. It will hear him in person, if he so wishes; and it will afford him the opportunity to be represented by counsel. He may also ask third parties to testify to the Board as to his record, reliability, and character. In the special circumstances of these cases the proceedings must be governed by the requirement that neither sources of evidence nor evidence which might en-

danger the national security by the disclosure of sources (e. g., confidential sources and investigative techniques of FBI) can be given to the person concerned. The Security Advisors' Board will therefore count it as an important part of its functions to see that anyone appearing before it can make his points effectively and will adapt its procedure in such a way as to give him and/or his counsel the best possible opportunity of bringing out the points which he wishes to bring to its notice. Confrontation of persons who have supplied derogatory information shall be allowed to the maximum extent consistent with the national security. The Board will be assisted by counsel appointed by the Attorney General to act as amicus curiae.

8. On receiving the report of the Security Advisors' Board, the head of the department or agency will reconsider his prima facie ruling, and if he decides to uphold it, he will give the Government employee an opportunity of making representations to himself or his representative. Similar opportunity will be given when the Government employee does not wish his case to go to the Security Advisors' Board.

9. If the prima facie ruling is finally upheld, copies of the decision of and findings by the head of the department or agency concerning the Government employee will be promptly transmitted to the Secretary of the National Security Council and to the Attorney General (copies for the attention of the Attorney General to be accompanied by additional copies for the files of the FBI).

10. If a Government employee is dismissed because of a reasonable doubt of his reliability in regard to security, his rights under the civil service retirement system or the agency retirement system shall be nullified.

11. The President shall, with the advice and consent of the Senate, nominate and appoint three persons to serve for a term of 6 years as members of the Board of Security Advisors, one of whom the President shall designate as Chairman of the Board of Security Advisors; two shall be learned in the law and any two shall constitute a quorum.

12. The Board of Security Advisors shall, following a hearing of a referral, submit its findings and recommendations to the head of the department or agency from which the reference originated and shall simultaneously submit exact copies of the aforesaid findings and recommendations (1) to the Secretary of the National Security Council, and (2) to the Attorney General (copies for the attention of the Attorney General to be accompanied by additional copies for the investigative purposes and/or files of the FBI). The Board of Security Advisors shall in all cases be assisted by counsel appointed by the Attorney General to act in the capacity of amicus curiae, to advise as to the law in its application to the facts and to assist in bringing to the attention of the Board all evidence which may be relevant to the inquiry and helpful in arriving at a proper determination of the question of reasonable doubt of the employee's loyalty. The said counsel shall in no instance act as prosecutor.

13. It is submitted that the hearing committee of employees of the same department or agency shall be impaneled from a list prepared by the head of the agency or department together with the Civil Service Commission; that such employee members be chosen with emphasis on qualifications of experience in government, personal integrity, and sound judgment. This board shall act as members of a jury in determining facts. Therefore, no special training qualifications are required. Services of counsel appointed by the Attorney General shall be available to them to instruct them as to the application of the law to the facts which they find; and said counsel shall act as amicus curiae, not as prosecutor, to assist the board in arriving at a proper determination of the facts. These proceedings should be as informal as possible and the technical rules of evidence shall not be controlling. The rights of the employee to counsel and to subpena shall, however, be observed in this proceeding as in the proceeding of appeal to the above-described Board of Security Advisors.

Insofar as possible, there should be no public disclosure of the inquiry prior to the finding of the head of the department or agency that reasonable doubt exists of the employee's loyalty.

This member of the Commission believes that the inquiry may be conducted within the present framework of Government with minimum delay and maximum protection of the rights of the loyal employee and of the security of the Government.

The weaknesses of delay, uncertainty, and lack of uniformity in the existing system would be corrected by impaneling the board of inquiry from the same department or agency as the employee and defining its function to be that of a jury in the Anglo-Saxon tradition; while specialized training in the law and information as to the techniques of an alien ideological conspiracy could be made available where needed through the counsel appointed by the Attorney General and acting as amicus curiae.

The opportunity for appeal and an objective, detached, judicial review would be made available through the transmittal of the case to the Board of Security Advisors, appointed by the President, with the advice and consent of the Senate. This member of the Commission recommends that 2 of the 3 members of the review board should be learned in the law; and that a quorum should be any 2 of the 3 members. The Congress in its wisdom and the lawful exercise of its power should provide further qualifications to insure a fair and impartial decision in each case—so reasoned and analyzed as to be of the greatest assistance to the head of the department or agency whose ultimate responsibility it is to determine whether such a reasonable doubt of loyalty exists as to justify severance from Government employ in the interest of Government security.

This member of the Commission further submits that security officers in the various departments or agencies should be appointed from lists prepared by the Civil Service Commission—which lists should include prior qualifications of education, training, and experience necessary for the valid discharge of security duties.

If in addition to such education, training, and experience, it is considered proper by the Congress to provide specialized briefing in the legislation and security regulations, and specialized study in recent foreign ideological techniques, such briefing and study courses may be provided by the Civil Service Commission with special instructors and lecturers being made available by the FBI, the CIA, and other existing investigative divisions of Government departments or agencies.

It is respectfully contended that such briefing and training courses for employees with previous high educational and experience qualifications are normally carried on by many departments and agencies (e. g., FBI, State Department, Treasury, etc.).

Certainly a new agency is not required in order to provide such a training course—provided, of course, that proper qualifications for positions are required de novo.

It would be unwise and, this member of the Commission believes unnecessary, to refer to each section in the Commission report where reference is made to the Central Security Office.

And so it would appear to be sufficient to indicate that wherever such reference is made, he believes that the desired objective of Government security can be and must be achieved within the existing framework of the executive branch of the Government with the aid of appropriate legislation.

Repeal of Veterans Preference Act

This member of the Commission wishes to dissent from the Commission recommendation (p. 86) that: *"Veterans and nonveterans should be afforded equality of treatment. Section 14 of the Veterans Preference Act should be repealed,"* and questions whether the act of the Congress which created the Commission contemplated its inquiry into the operation of an act not directly related to the subject of Government security—and essentially concerned with the welfare of those citizens of this Nation who served as members of her Armed Forces.

This member of the Commission on Government Security, not a member of the Hoover Commission and not presently a Member of the Congress of the United States, is reluctant to join in a recommendation concerning legislation which extends beyond the scope of Government security that he is properly authorized to examine.

Federal Judiciary

This member wishes to express a vigorous dissent from the Commission recommendation (p. 106) that: *"The judicial branch of the Government should take effective steps to insure that its employees are loyal and otherwise suitable from the standpoint of national security"*; and he submits that this recommendation is irrelevant to the scope of the Commission inquiry, not based on any need that has been demonstrated by facts ascertained or ascertainable, a gratuitous conclusion drawn from premises that are purely conjectural.

The independence of the Federal judiciary has throughout America's history been the warranty of constitutional government in this Republic. A Federal judge is mindful of the sacred responsibility that is his whether presiding over a trial, hearing an argument, instructing a grand jury or a petit jury, sentencing a defendant, or preparing an opinion. The Founding Fathers provided for continuation of judicial service during good behavior of the judge and, it is submitted, would have found it as difficult as does this member of the Commission—to envisage the possibility that any conscientious judge—or as the Commission report expresses it (p. 106) : *". . . Federal judges, busy with ever-crowded court calendars, must rely upon assistants to prepare briefing papers for them."*

It is submitted that such a Federal judge is not "busy"—he is either lazy or confused. In either instance, the remedy is to proceed to impeach the individual judge—not merely to decontaminate the crutch upon which he leans. The Commission report continues to explain, excuse, accuse, and conjecture (p. 106)—

"False or biased information inadvertently reflected in court opinions in crucial security, constitutional, governmental or social issues of national importance could cause severe effects to the Nation's security and to our Federal loyalty-security system generally."

This journey into a fanciful world has summoned up a hypothetical judge who is not only lazy and confused but almost unconscious—certainly unaware that his opinion is "inadvertently" reflecting false or biased information.

This member of the Commission is happy to report that no evidence was presented at Commission conferences tending to indicate that such a judge is now a member of the Federal judiciary, by appointment of the President of the United States with the advice and consent of the Senate.

Neither was any evidence presented that at any time in our history such a judge menaced national security by being "busy with the ever-crowded court calendars" or by inadvertent acceptance of "false or biased information."

This member of the Commission regrets the unwarranted intrusion into the judicial branch of our Government by the recommendation in the foregoing report.

Wiretapping

This member of the Commission wishes to record agreement with the recommendation of the Commission (pp. 627–629) that the Congress enact a statute permitting Federal law-enforcement officials and/or selected military intelligence agencies to employ the wiretapping technique in the investigation of security violations but only upon the specific authorization of the Attorney General; and that the said law should eliminate the evidentiary disability now applicable to information procured by wiretapping in criminal prosecutions for violations of our security laws.

This member submits that it is his belief that such a law should include similar authorization for wiretapping if the said officials are engaged in the investigation of a case where an individual's life is in jeopardy by kidnaping.

This member of the Commission submits that such authorization should be limited to cases "wherein the life of an individual citizen or the life of our Nation is at stake"—to quote the words of J. Edgar Hoover, the universally esteemed Director of the Federal Bureau of Investigation.

It is further submitted by this member of the Commission that the Congress, in its wisdom, should provide affirmatively in the same statute that all other wiretapping—not falling within the scope of these two types of investigation—shall be prohibited and the violation of such prohibition shall be punishable by imprisonment *and* fines.

For, as Mr. Justice Holmes has said, wiretapping is "dirty business." The rights of our citizens to freedom from invasion of their privacy of communication should be protected. And only those who menace the life and liberty of an individual by kidnaping or the security of our country are the proper subjects of wiretapping.

Our vigilance must be twofold—we must ever guard the rights of an individual citizen as zealously as we guard our Nation's security.

There can be no security if we sacrifice liberty; there can be no liberty without security.

With this final word, I have the honor to express profound appreciation to the President of the United States for the opportunity of service granted me by his appointment.

COMMISSIONER.